The REXX Handbook

The REXX Handbook

Gabriel Goldberg

Philip H. Smith III

McGraw Hill, Inc.

New York   St. Louis   San Francisco   Auckland   Bogotá
Caracas   Lisbon   London   Madrid   Mexico   Milan
Montreal   New Delhi   Paris   San Juan   São Paulo
Singapore   Sydney   Toronto

01584960 - 3/1/93

Library of Congress Cataloging-in-Publication Data

Goldberg, Gabriel.
   The REXX Handbook / Gabriel Goldberg, Philip H. Smith III.
     p. cm.—(J. Ranade IBM series)
   Includes bibliographic references and index.
   ISBN 0-07-023682-8
   1. REXX (Computer program language) 2. IBM microcomputers—
programming. I. Smith, Philip H., III. II. Title. III. Series.
QA76.73.R24G65 ~~1191~~ 1992
005.13'3—dc20

9129979
CIP

1 2 3 4 5 6 7 8 9 0 DOC/DOC 9 7 6 5 4 3 2

ISBN   0-07-023682-8

The sponsoring editor for this book was Jerry Papke, the editing
supervisor was Kimberly A. Goff, and the production supervisor was
Suzanne W. Babeuf.

Printed and bound by R. R. Donnelly & Sons Company.

To my parents, Hyman and Naomi Goldberg,
who started me on the path which led to this book;
to Donna Walker, who endured and supported this
project from concept to final editing, with love.
Gabriel Goldberg

To my wife and best friend Anita Hillyer Smith
for her love and support throughout this project and
always; and to my parents for teaching me to love
both words and knowledge, and for giving me
the tools to create both.
Philip H. Smith III

Contents

Preface

In the short history of computing, significant and fundamental shifts of direction are rare. In recent years, the challenge of making computing systems easier to use has generated a number of generic ideas that have become pervasive, and which span systems and ideology. REXX is one of those ideas. REXX was conceived and developed by a single individual. Mike Cowlishaw has a deep and overriding commitment to the process of simplification through elegant and consistent design.

It was my good fortune to be in charge of the IBM Hursley Laboratory during the period when Mike Cowlishaw, who at the time was a member of IBM's System Assurance Laboratory, created REXX. I should hasten to say that I claim no credit whatsoever; REXX is the product of a dedicated individual problem committed to the solution of a problem. He did so not because he was asked to; not because he was expected to; not even because there was any job-related requirement for him to do so, because he was supposed to be wholly dedicated to the evaluation of products developed by others; but he did so because Mike Cowlishaw saw the need and the solution, and got on with it, almost *despite* his management rather than *because* of them.

Since then, many others have contributed to make refinements and extensions to the broad architecture that Mike laid down and to implement REXX for a wide variety of systems. REXX is good because so much of it is obvious; it is elegant and straightforward to use and easy to learn. Initially, REXX was used internally in IBM, and only later launched as a product. The decision to offer it as a product came as a result of the growing reputation and enthusiasm for REXX by the professionals inside IBM. It was not the result of some grand product strategy. The positive acclaim with which REXX has been received stems from its excellence rather than any commercial promotion; it is a product that has been promoted largely by word of mouth within the internal IBM professional community. It is a computer language with natural characteristics that will run and run. I am proud that I was in charge of the laboratory that provided the working environment where REXX could blossom.

The proof of the pudding is in the eating, and so I have tried to determine the opinion of REXX users. The easiest way to do so is to consult the various conference disks that exist on IBM's world-wide network and are used by IBM people, round the world, to share tools and knowledge. I should add that this system of sharing tools and knowledge within the internal IBM VM community was first developed by Mike Cowlishaw. He developed the first TOOLS EXEC, and this has now been extended to cover all of IBM's interests and embrace every professional activity. There are now literally thousands of these conference disks, or forums, as they generally known. Any individual can create a forum to share knowledge about a particular issue, professional activity, product, or even just to gossip. Mike created several forums to get feedback from REXX users so he might provide support and fix bugs as well as get suggestions for enhancements. One of these forums was aimed at gaining an insight into where REXX had contributed to an improvement in productivity. The entries are overwhelmingly positive. I quote a small number of people all over the world to highlight that REXX is judged by amateur and professional alike to be a natural tool. What more need be said?

EXTRACTS FROM REXXBEN FORUM

As a user of REXX for the last three-plus years, I can attest to the ease of learning REXX as opposed to other languages. I first laid hands on a VM terminal in March of that year, and six months later took over the programming tasks of my Information Centre. I was so naive, I didn't know that there was a *REXX User's Guide*: I taught myself from the *Language Reference*. My background? High School graduate. No college or IBM programming courses. Was my stuff good at the beginning? Maybe, maybe not—but it was functional.

Since that time, my programs have grown in complexity and function. I have written several applications that have proven beneficial for the National Service Division. My programs have saved my staff thousands of man-hours a year due to task automation. Could the programs have been done in another language? Yes, but they would not have been as supportable or portable. REXX was chosen as the language to write one application for NSD called COMIT (Consolidated On-line Management Information Tool). COMIT utilizes IOS3270, RXSQL, QMF, and GDDM to provide our end-users an easy-to-use interface to relational databases, complete with graphics. If it were not for REXX, this application would most likely still be in the design phase in some I/S shop somewhere.

A couple of years ago, NSD took a request to an I/S shop, and was informed it would take two years and some outrageous sum of money to write the code. A group from around the country was assembled to write the code. Nine months later, we had the code up and on-line. This saved the Division hundreds of thousands of dollars. Why? Because it was written in REXX.

   — *Dave Lohmoeller, Sr. Analyst, Atlanta*

I wrote my first line of code in 1962; since then I have written code in every generation of language. Over the past few years, I have been occupied with maintaining and rewriting code produced by other people in various languages including FORTRAN, EXEC 2, and PL/S3. Of all the code, that written in REXX has been least difficult to understand. I use REXX in new or replacement code whenever possible. I have not seen any recent figures for the cost of software maintenance, but it used to be rather greater than that of initial development.

   — *Allan Jones, Customer Engineering, London*

I was introduced to VM, and REXX, in January of 1983. At the time, I had prototyped a hotline support system on a S/34, and was seriously considering using RPG for development. Then I met REXX. In less than four months, a co-worker and I learned enough about REXX to code, test, and make available almost 11,000 lines of code, which had once been the RPG prototype. That code has been in use now for almost seven years, and has been extended several times by several people as the business has changed. I doubt that it would have survived, or even gotten off the ground, if it hadn't been for REXX. It's hard to quantify exactly what savings REXX brought us, but one thing is for sure: without it, all our jobs would be just a little bit tougher. Even a person who hasn't been exposed to programming can pick up REXX in a matter of days, if not hours. Their code may be rough around the edges, but to the person who wrote it, it does the job *they* want it to do. Perhaps it's the quick sense of satisfaction that using REXX brings that makes it so popular and attractive.

   — *David J. Martin, Systems Programmer, Boca Raton*

I keep saying that REXX is the only "real" fourth-generation language!

   Try to imagine what the (computer) world would look like now, if REXX had been available on the PC from the beginning (instead of BASIC and BAT files. . .) and on MVS/TSO ten years ago!

   Last year I had to present REXX to MVS customers, and I got the following question/remark: "Why is IBM now (1988) making so much publicity about a programming language that is 10 years old?"

   What would have been *your* answer to that?

   — *De Ceulaer Guy, FSC VM, Belgium*

I was first introduced to REX(X) when it still was an unofficial tool offered by Mike to speed up EXEC procedures. I started using it just to be able to produce faster code. Later, when EXEC 2 was offered, I tried to use that for a while, but was turned off by its clumsy syntax. Only then did I learn to appreciate the syntactical beauty of the REXX language.

I also use REXX to build small prototyping models, and then use the running REXX code as a basis (like pseudocode) for actual full application code with PL/I or whatever (mostly for MVS). There are several other languages which could get a specific job done on several machines, but REXX is available for them all (MVS, VM, and PS/2). Anybody who has to write applications on more than one operating system knows how valuable such a common tool as REXX really is.

— Juhani Lausas, ECMVS Development, Uithoorn Holland

I've been writing programs since 1962, and have used FORTRAN, PL/I, LISP, C, EXEC(0), EXEC 2, an occasional assembler, and finally, REXX. There is simply no contest when working code must be delivered in a hurry. A few examples:

- I did an EXEC/GDDM prototype in under an hour. Conversion to FORTRAN took twice that long—even though I use a preprocessor (written in REXX, of course) that makes FORTRAN look as much like REXX as I can manage, and even though the REXX code had solved the algorithmic issues.

- The FORTRAN preprocessor itself was done in about three hours after work. Its predecessor, written in FORTRAN and with less function, took me two days to do.

- A virtue that hasn't been mentioned for engineering/scientific people is that the variable-precision numerics can get you out of a bind. One algorithm, implemented in REXX, generated numbers that would have overflowed IBM's floating-point representation. We were able to avoid some ghastly errors in the middle of a long FORTRAN number-cruncher. Other languages have the same feature, of course—for example, LISP (but I hate to do numerics in LISP).

- College-level students working in the Caracas Centre learn REXX in a couple of days. This cuts down training-time overhead to near zero. In fact, much more time is spent learning VM than in learning REXX.

- Another feature of REXX is simply that people like it. It does not attempt to be repressive—one feels that the language is trying to help you. It is like having a nice working environment: going to work there is a pleasure.

Measuring "productivity increases" due to one programming language versus another is very difficult. It is very expensive to implement experiments of "project X with language A" vs. "project X with language B". I would submit instead that if customers—and IBM internal users count as customers too—accept it, then it's productive.

— Juan Rivero, Caracas Scientific Centre

I am an SE in the field. In my 23-plus years in IBM, I have written incidental code in almost every language commonly used: I've coded CLIST, EXECs—you name it. I am *not* a developer; so richness, speed, and numerous other metrics are less meaningful to me. What is important is to have a language that I can easily remember (I may not code in it for months), and easy to understand and debug.

I had an assignment last year to assist an emerging MVS customer (VSE) in their conversion. One assignment was to inventory their rather large and undocumented COBOL source base, and try to make sense of which files were used by which program, and how. I decided to try to learn REXX while solving this little scan/parse problem. I sat at my terminal with a REXX reference handy, on-line HELP, and the invaluable library of working EXECs on the TOOLS disks. I had a working, straight-through (no error handling) REXX program that would process COBOL source and find **ASSIGN** statements and begin the required relation file in *less than one day*.

The use of **TRACE** can cut through the toughest debugging problems. The real beauty for me was as I got to handle all those little special cases and needed some powerful string handling functions—by God, they were there. There was usually more than one built-in function to solve the problem. In one week, I was merrily coding **SELECT/WHEN** structures and all sorts of functions, and processed all file calls (including CICS files) to the point where we inventoried their 500 COBOL programs completely.

I know it sounds like I'm bragging about me. I'm not. I'm bragging about REXX. I can't imagine anyone who has ever truly coded a problem in a variety of languages, and then used REXX, ever questioning its benefits.

— *WMORGAN at SFOVMIC1*

From a purely syntactical point of view, given enough time, I can do almost anything with almost any language. However, I can usually do it faster with REXX. REXX shares the best features of many languages. The features that I find help the most are:

Interpretation   The time it takes to code and test software is directly related to the time it takes for one iteration of code-compile-link-run-debug. Since we all make mistakes, we go through this sequence of steps many many times. An interpreted language shortens this sequence. Usually, it takes a matter of seconds to code and test a change to a REXX program, as compared to hours or even overnight for changes to compiled languages. Here is a savings of (on the average) about one person/hour per change. Assuming we introduce about one bug in every 20 lines of code, that's a savings of one person/hour per 20 lines of code. Multiply that by the number of lines of code we've developed in the last ten years!

Debugability   REXX offers an extremely powerful **TRACE** capability... one that can reduce the time to debug significantly. Again, assuming we can save half a person-hour per bug in debugging time because of REXX's debug tools, and assuming a bug every 20 lines of code—do the multiplication!

Simplicity   The simplicity of the REXX language is self-evident. There are only a few basic instructions and they behave in a consistent manner...not only consistent with each other, but also consistent with what we expect. There are really two benefits to simplicity. The first is that

REXX is easy to learn. I learned it from the on-line 3270 HELP panels available in the early 1980s. I still haven't read a formal REXX manual—I haven't had to. The second benefit of simplicity is that it makes it easier to code a correct REXX program. We need to study bugs/KLOC (bugs/thousand lines of code) of REXX compared to other languages.) Intuitively, I would guess that bugs/KLOC of REXX would be significantly lower than bugs/KLOC of any other language. (This is not the standard bugs/KLOC-after-test, but bugs/KLOC-before-test—something we've never tried to measure as far as I know.) This reduces the number of iterations of code-test-debug required to provide function. The third benefit of simplicity is ease of maintenance. It is simple to add new function or adapt to a new environment with a simple language.

Ease of linkage   One of the biggest problems I have had with traditional IBM languages is that they almost force me to introduce strong dependencies between two modules in the same system. REXX forces me to remove these dependencies. I find that it's much safer to re-use a REXX function than a PL/I function, because the side-effects of the function don't come back to haunt me. Besides, to use a REXX function, I just have to know its name, its arguments, and what it does. I don't have to know how to link it in, or what side effects it might have. This makes it much easier to re-use REXX code than code in most other languages.

Other languages provide subsets of these advantages. For instance, APL is interpretive, but not simple. PL/AS is fairly simple (even though declarations make it more complex than REXX), but not interpretive; nor is it easy to debug. C is neither simple (too many ways to shoot yourself in the foot), nor easy to debug, nor interpreted.

All these things add up to provide one more unquantifiable benefit: satisfaction. REXX allows me to provide high-function, high-quality tools quickly. That makes this job worth doing.

— *Tom Bartenstein*

Mike, I suspect that most of the true beneficiaries of REXX will never hear of this forum, since they are not programmers and are unlikely to browse IBMVM. Frankly, I do it myself only out of a twisted streak of voyeurism, but that's another story—so let me start on this story.

The bottom line on the business today is: "so much to do, so little time", which applies to just about everyone's job. The only help they've got is a workstation, with PROFS. In this environment, the ability to create your own custom productivity tools is not "nice to have", it is an absolute survival issue. The traditional application development process, while important, is essentially powerless to assist the average Joe get his daily job done: either his justification is several orders of magnitude below the rounding threshold, or he can't wait 18 months to get the application (by which time the need will have changed to something else). This is where REXX comes in: even the most inexperienced user can, with a bit of help, create fairly sophisticated one-off personal productivity tools. Sure, they may be pretty basic—travel expense calculators, PROFS mods, PF key setters, XEDIT macros, etc.—but it all adds up; and if only one in a hundred is a keeper that can be made available to all, that is still big stuff. A quick scan of our location team disk shows nearly 200 user-written REXX programs, with another 200 or so utility-type programs that were created by our system support people. Then there are the internal IBM tools disks, if you're experienced enough to "go shopping". When we hire co-op students here in Canada, it is virtually a mandatory requirement that they know REXX. Their work terms will be spent writing productivity tools for their departments. As a result, almost every internal business process I know of has a REXX program or two somewhere in the path.

Finally, the capability to prototype a significant application, batch or on-line, right at the user's desk, should not be overlooked. Interactive spec-ing and application design may make old hands nervous, but it's fast and it gets the right job done right the first time. Compiled REXX code completes the job.

So, on top of programmer productivity, let's add a factor for the average office worker. I think there may be about 100,000 of them world-wide (in IBM). If all these little tools and aids have added a mere 0.1% to their productivity, that's still 100 headcount saved. That's ten million dollars per year, folks (Canadian dollars, anyway)—And I suspect the real number is *significantly* greater.

— *Perry Bowker, Announcements Manager, Toronto, Canada*

I analyzed executable files on the VM tools disks. Here's what I found:

Language	EXEC	XEDIT	GDDM	Module	LEXX	Total
REXX	2343	1058	23	15	162	3601
EXEC 2	48	96	1	0	0	145
EXEC 1	37	1	0	0	0	38
Other	0	0	0	562	0	562
Total	2428	1155	24	577	162	4346

83% of all executable files are coded in REXX
92% of the XEDIT macros are coded in REXX
96% of the EXECs are coded in REXX

On a personal note, many of the previous appends express my sentiments. REXX is easy to learn, use, and maintain. It is rich in function.

I've coded in:

- REXX, EXEC1, EXEC 2
- CLIST on TSO, DOS batch "language"
- Assembler, FORTRAN, PL/S, PL/I, PASCAL, C

- BASIC, APL
- etc.

and REXX is definitely my favorite. I pretty much use it exclusively now.
— *John Paleveda, Fishkill*

I joined A/PTO (Asia/Pacific Technical Operations) of IBM Japan in 1985.
They gave each new employee a bunch of programming lectures that
included many programming languages—COBOL, PL/I, Pascal, 370
Assembler, Prolog, C, and JCL—but not REXX. What a mess! I never use
the languages I was taught, except Assembler in my job as a programmer.
I have written hundreds of programs on VM—and I always used REXX,
which I studied myself with the *REXX User's Guide*, and sometimes
Assembler when I needed significant performance. I've even tried to write
programs using PL/I; but I found it is a waste of time especially for small
programs. I've been captured by REXX because of its simplicity; declara-
tion-free, powerful string operation; and so on. I wonder why there is no
REXX lecture for new engineering employees!
— *Takanori SEKI, Tokyo System Evaluation Laboratory*

IBM recently paid Mike Cowlishaw the highest tribute by making
him an IBM Fellow. This is awarded to a very small group of key professionals who, through their innovation, have earned complete freedom to pursue whatever research interests them. The last entry from
the REXX BENEFITS forum tells it all:

I believe the greatest benefit to IBM as a company was the selection of
Mike as an IBM Fellow. Letting him run loose for five years could result
in *anything*!
— *Joe Davis, End-user Support, Southern Area 8 AIC*

By Sir John Fairclough

Editors' Notes

In editing a work of this scope, with chapters by many different authors, a dilemma arises: whether to attempt to ensure similarity in voice and tone among authors. We have attempted to preserve each chapter's flavor, while editing for consistency.

Another challenge arose in the form of overlap between chapter topics, resulting in duplicated information. Again, the solution was to leave most things alone.

Contributors' biographies appear at the end of the book.

Readers are invited to provide feedback on and updates to the book by completing the form provided at the back.

TERMINOLOGY

VM versions

While this is not a VM book, REXX's origin dictates that VM topics predominate. VM has evolved steadily over the past ten years, through different versions and releases, with different names. Many chapters refer to the most current VM releases, without naming them; others mention features added at various points.

The same is true of IBM documentation: some chapters cite manuals by name. The same information may appear in different manuals in different VM releases.

We have attempted to adopt a consistent nomenclature for different VM releases, allowing precise determination of what features are available in what release. Fortunately, REXX facilities in every release were a superset of those in the previous release, allowing a simple hierarchy:

Release	Full name and description
VM / 370	Virtual Machine Facility/370; the no-charge precursor to VM/SP. Did not include REXX, EXEC 2, or XEDIT.
VM / SP 1-5	Virtual Machine/System Product Release 1 through Release 5; introduced in 1981. Included **CMS 1** through **CMS 5.**
VM / XA SP	Virtual Machine/Extended Architecture System Product; VM for System/370-Extended Architecture (370/XA) hardware, introduced in 1988. VM/XA SP had two releases and a sub-release (VM/XA SP Releases 1 and 2, plus VM/XA SP Release 2.1); these included **CMS 5.5** for Releases 1 and 2, and **CMS 5.6** for VM/XA SP Release 2.1.
VM / SP 6	Virtual Machine/System Product Release 6; introduced in late 1988, but not installed by many installations. Included **CMS 6**.
VM / ESA	Virtual Machine/Enterprise Systems Architecture; announced in 1990, with two options, the **370 feature** (essentially VM/SP Release 7) and the **ESA feature** (essentially VM/XA SP Release 3). Converged functional differences between VM/SP and VM/XA SP, providing a single CMS Level 7 or simply **CMS 7**.

User groups

Some chapters refer to **SHARE, GUIDE,** or **VMSHARE**.

SHARE and GUIDE are IBM user groups, meeting four and three times a year respectively, in major cities in the United States. Meetings consist of presentations by IBM, customers, and vendors on a wide variety of topics, including IBM and vendor hardware and software. User groups also produce **requirements**, which provide formal input to the IBM planning and development process.

SHARE and GUIDE memberships are free, but require certain IBM hardware and software. SHARE's telephone number is (312) 822-0932; GUIDE's is (312) 644-6610.

VMSHARE is a VM-specific electronic conference, available to SHARE and GUIDE members for a nominal fee of US$1200/year. Residing at McGill University in Montreal, Canada, VMSHARE is considered a "must" by many VM system programmers, for its timely and correct information on VM problems, and the access to VM experts it provides.

DOCUMENT REFERENCES

Many chapters refer to publications issued by IBM and other vendors. Products such as VM and SQL/DS (among many others) evolve rapidly, and are described by similarly evolving documentation. Chapter authors cite specific titles and order numbers of publications used at their installations or for reference when writing their chapters. Consider these references to be somewhat generic; determine the document editions which are applicable to your environment or requirements.

THE FUTURE

REXX is evolving rapidly, is the subject of initial standards activities, is appearing on more and more IBM computing platforms, and is becoming available on diverse non-IBM platforms. Future editions of this book will likely have even greater non-VM and non-IBM participation.

Acknowledgments

Linda Suskind Green of IBM Endicott made numerous important contributions to this book. As SAA Procedures Language Interface owner, she coordinates the multitude of REXX activities throughout IBM. We benefited from her extensive network of IBMers, her knowledge of REXX activities within and outside IBM, and her commitment to REXX exploitation throughout the computer industry.

Fifteen IBM authors wrote twenty chapters. This significant contribution from IBMers world-wide presents *definitive* information on REXX implementations, usage, history, and products which exploit or enhance it.

Stanford Linear Accelerator Center (SLAC) authors contributed several chapters, including a brief but informative description of how REXX quickly became a key part of VM service at SLAC.

VM Systems Group provided "time and furniture" for the many tasks required during the year in which this book was created.

Mike Cowlishaw played several roles: he originated and implemented REXX, and made it available first to IBMers and then to the VM community; he supported efforts to recruit chapter authors; he committed early to participation, long before the book was a well-structured project; and he contributed a valuable historical perspective.

Thomas J. Piwowar & Associates, Incorporated converted chapter source files into the camera-ready pages from which McGraw-Hill printed this book. Tom and Pete Dodge helped navigate exquisitely precise specifications for formatting, allowing us to focus on the people and chapters of the book.

The REXX community was immensely supportive of this book. Many people provided suggestions and guidance which helped shape the book. The VMSHARE conference provided electronic communication with authors around the world, facilitated by several human gateways, especially Chip Coy of IBM Endicott.

Reviewers provided a final quality and consistency check: Bob Flores of CIA, Linda Suskind Green of IBM, Rich Greenberg of Locus Computing Corporation, Barry Leiba of IBM, Ray Parker of Software Ag, Jeff Savit of Merrill Lynch, Elisabeth P. Smith, Philip H. Smith Jr., Jay Tunkel of IBM, and Saba Zamir of Merrill Lynch Teleport Communications. Errors and omissions are, of course, our responsibility.

Figures in Bebo White's chapters originally appeared in his chapter on REXX in *The VM Applications Handbook*, edited by Gary McClain, ISBN 0-07-044948-1, Intertext Publications, McGraw-Hill Book Company.

Finally, we thank Gary McClain, who in addition to contributing the chapter in this book on REXX Education, demonstrated the technique of assembling a book written chapter-by-chapter by assorted expert authors. Gary and his book were catalysts in our starting this project.

TRADEMARKS

The following are trademarks of International Business Machines: AD/Cycle, Application System/400, AS/400, CICS/ESA, GDDM, GDDM-REXX, ImagePlus, MVS/ESA, MVS/SP, NetView, OfficeVision, Operating System/2, OS/2, Operating System/400, OS/400, Personal System/2, Presentation Manager, PS/2, Presentation Manager, SAA, Systems Application Architecture, S/390, System/370, System/390, SQL/Data System, SQL/DS, VM/ESA, VM/Enterprise Systems Architecture, and VM/XA.

BlueLine Software, Inc. and SOURCEBANK/VM are trademarks of BueLine Software, Inc.

MS-DOS is a trademark of MicroSoft.

Portable/REXX and T-REXX are trademarks of Kilowatt Software.

DECwindows is a trademark of Digital Equipment Corporation.

KEDIT and Personal REXX are trademarks of Mansfield Software Group. The Personal REXX product has recently transferred from Mansfield Software Group to Quercus Systems.

PostScript is a trademark of Adobe.

Unix is a trademark of AT&T.

The REXX Handbook

General Information

This section introduces REXX history and fundamental concepts, and presents topics applicable to all present and future REXX users. Tutorials on topics such as programming style, idioms, debugging, and maintenance teach "REXXthink" to all levels of programmers, whether REXX is fhe first or tenth programming language learned.

1

REXX Origins

By Michael F. Cowlishaw

In this chapter you'll find a little of the history of the REXX programming language, how and why it was written, and its main advantages (and disadvantages).

SOME HISTORY

During the 1970s and 1980s, the VM/370 (Virtual Machine/370) operating system and its derivatives were the interactive development environment of choice for most of IBM and many of its customers. This operating system borrowed many features from earlier systems, including the concept of controlling the system by commands (character strings, typed by the user, which control and direct the operating system and its applications). VM's command language, especially in the CMS (Conversational Monitor System) component, is one of the simplest and most readable ever devised.

Like other command-driven operating systems, CMS provided the ability to "wrap up" commands with a little programming logic; these simple programs were written in a language called EXEC. This allowed enhancements and new commands to be written rapidly and much more easily than in the native assembler language used for writing low-level commands.

In the 1970s, C. J. Stephenson and others at the IBM T. J. Watson Research Center realized that, if applied consistently, this concept of a command programming language was extraordinarily powerful: a single language could provide the extension language—or **macro** language—for a wide variety of applications. They took the EXEC language and generalized and improved it for this enhanced role; the new language was called EXEC 2.

EXEC 2 proved the concept of a general macro language. It was used mostly for writing system commands and macros for a wide variety of editors. Its interpreter was, and probably still is, the finest example of efficient and robust System/370 assembler code.

However, EXEC 2 (like its predecessor and most other macro languages of the 1970s and even early 1980s) assumed that macro programs would be mostly commands, with relatively little "glue" of logic and variables. Accordingly, it was designed to allow commands (literal strings, usually in uppercase) to be written plainly, whereas language keywords and variables were identified by a prefix of an ampersand. A command, followed by a test of its result, might look like this:

```
COPYFILE &FNAME &FTYPE &FMODE = BACKUP =
&IF &RC GT 0 &TYPE Copy failed with return code &RC
```

This style, while adequate for simple commands, proved cumbersome for the large and complex programs and macros that were soon being written in EXEC 2. It became clear to me that a new language was needed, one based on the more classical syntax and semantics used by languages in the tradition of ALGOL, PASCAL, and PL/I, yet including the command and string programming facilities that EXEC 2 had proven to be so effective and powerful.

This new language, initially called **REX** (because the name sounded nice), was very much driven by the desire to make programming easy. It borrows most of its features from other languages, especially PL/I and EXEC 2, but these features are modified or expressed in ways that make them easy to use (and not necessarily easy to implement!). The code fragment shown above would look quite different; literal strings are quoted, but language keywords and variable names are not obfuscated by special characters:

```
'COPYFILE' fname ftype fmode '= BACKUP ='
if rc>0 then say 'Copy failed with return code' rc
```

This difference between the two languages becomes more striking as the complexity of the program increases.

The first specification for the language is dated 29 March 1979. This was written before any implementation was even designed, and it was circulated to a number of people for comment; this began the tradition of documentation before implementation that characterized the development of REXX. This first specification included three sample programs written in REXX to show how the language would look; those programs would seem familiar to today's REXX programmers, although some details have changed.

My first implementation of REXX was made freely available over IBM's internal network in late 1979 and rapidly became popular. The electronic mail network made it easy for people to exchange ideas and make suggestions for improvements. Also, because the language was limited to one (large) organization, it was possible to make some rather large changes in response to these suggestions.

As a result of this direct feedback, the language quickly evolved to meet the needs of its users through a number of releases over the next few years. By 1982 it had become essentially the language known today; its name gained an **X** to avoid any confusion with other products, with a rarely-used expansion to match: **REstructured eXtended eXecutor**. REXX was included in the third release of IBM's VM/System Product, shipped in 1983.

It was soon discovered that IBM's customers liked the language just as much as did the "internal" users. Only two years later, the first non-IBM implementation (by the Mansfield Software Group, for PC-DOS) became available, and in 1987 IBM announced that REXX was to be the Procedures Language for its Systems Application Architecture (SAA). This was followed by implementations for a number of operating systems. The first REXX compiler was developed at IBM's Vienna Laboratory, following research by the IBM Haifa Scientific Center, and was delivered to customers in 1989. By 1990 there was sufficient interest in the language to justify the first international "REXX Symposium for Developers and Users", organized by the Stanford Linear Accelerator Center in California.

1991 sees the beginning of a new phase in REXX's history, as work starts on preparing an ANSI standard for the language.

ADVANTAGES

REXX is a programming language which was developed for its users rather than for the convenience of its implementers—those who implement its compilers and interpreters. For example, it hides the underlying mechanisms of hardware from the programmer, except where it is absolutely necessary and appropriate to expose them.

Further, in the first five years of its life the core of the language was defined and implemented by a single person (based on feedback from hundreds of early users) and was constrained by an explicit design philosophy. This has led to a language which is coherent and does what its users want it to do, and which has a sound base for future evolution.

This design approach gives REXX several advantages over older languages:

- REXX programs can be made very readable, since there is a minimum of required punctuation or special characters.

- REXX has only one data type, the character string, so no declarations are needed. This makes writing programs in the language both attractive and productive, as the programmer doesn't have to worry about underlying hardware representations. REXX operators are optimized for common string operations such as concatenation, and are supported by powerful parsing and word instructions and functions.

- REXX arithmetic is defined as decimal arithmetic, with precision selected by the programmer rather than by the underlying hardware. Exponential notation is supported both in scientific form and in the multiple-of-three form usual in engineering or financial applications. Results of arithmetic operations therefore match users' expectations far better than results from the binary arithmetic used by most other languages.

- REXX puts no inherent limits on the size of strings (including those that represent numbers). Again, this removes many of the headaches that often plague programmers.

- REXX is a small language. This makes it approachable and easy to learn.

- REXX was specifically designed to be a general-purpose extension (**macro** or **"glue"**) language. That is, it lets users easily tailor and enhance advanced software systems. Like most human written languages, REXX is based on simple character strings. It also has special mechanisms for rapid environment switching and simple error handling that are especially suited to this use.

- REXX has no reserved words. This allows robust programs to be written that will not be invalidated by future additions to the set of language instructions. Not only does this mean that programmers need not learn keywords they do not use, but this is also extraordinarily important when using the language for application extension.

- Software vendors can distribute macros written in REXX which, even though they are processed in source form, can remain almost immune to changes in the REXX language itself. This benefits users, since installing a new level of REXX (which is usually part of the underlying operating system) is unlikely to break macros provided with an application or written by the user. It also benefits software vendors, since much less maintenance and fewer updates will be needed.

- REXX is very system-independent. This gives it the advantages of portability and wide application. This means that people need to learn fewer programming languages; there is no longer the need for a new command programming language for every application and operating system.

- Finally, REXX has several unusual features, such as associative arrays and dynamic variable scoping, that make many algorithms much easier to design and implement.

These advantages have led to rapid acceptance of REXX as a language for procedure automation, application extension, and scripting. Its users cover the spectrum of programmers, from secretaries or workstation users who just wish to customize their environment in a flexible way, to professional programmers writing or prototyping whole subsystems of software in REXX.

DISADVANTAGES

Designs that provide for human variability and preferences inevitably are more costly to implement than those that ignore human nature. The most obvious cost is in performance; for example, REXX's decimal arithmetic will be slower than binary arithmetic until manufacturers provide hardware support for user-friendly arithmetic. REXX's dynamic nature means that, even with advanced compilers, programs in REXX are usually slower than those written in languages that move most of the burden of data conversion and typing onto the programmer.

Even so, as hardware speeds increase exponentially, REXX becomes useful for more and more applications; for example, it has already been used successfully for prototyping image processing algorithms and for extensive mathematical research.

The second disadvantage of REXX is that it is relatively hard to implement. This, however, is a task that is done infrequently; the investment rapidly pays off in improved user programs and productivity.

Finally, REXX's data type, the string, is not well supported by many other languages, so there can be extra cost involved in data conversions when REXX invokes or uses programs written in these lower-level languages. This cost can be important when small programs with little function are called, but if significant processing is to be done, then data conversion on entry and return is relatively inexpensive.

THE FUTURE

Programming languages are among the most enduring features of computer science and the computer industry; they take a decade or more to become established, and can then survive for generations of programmers and operating systems. REXX is now widely recognized as the leading extension and macro language. It has broken new ground, and, I hope, will continue to break new ground while holding to its original principles. One can expect it to change to meet the changing needs of its users, and that is the most important feature of any tool.

Procedures Language in SAA

By Chip Coy and Linda Suskind Green

INTRODUCTION TO SAA

Systems Application Architecture, typically abbreviated **SAA**, is IBM's structure to provide cross-system consistency among hardware and software platforms for application programmers and application users. The SAA definition contains hardware and software platforms, a common programming interface, a common user interface, common communications support, and a set of common applications. The SAA definition is controlled and supported by an IBM management process.

The SAA definition—or, more accurately, the systems and products that implement the SAA definition—allows applications to be moved between systems, allows applications to span systems, and provides applications with an end-user interface that has a style in common with those of other applications implemented using SAA standards. Beyond the application, use of SAA facilities also allows portability of programmers and end-users. Programmers find the SAA programming interface on each of the SAA environments, and end-users find applications with a familiar end-user interface.

Hardware platforms

Hardware platforms for SAA are System/390 (and its predecessor, System/370), Personal System/2, and Application System/400. SAA operating systems are MVS/ESA (with one or more of MVS/APPC, TSO, IMS/DC, and CICS/ESA providing the SAA environment), VM/ESA (with CMS providing the SAA environment), OS/2, and OS/400.

Common Programming Interface

The SAA Common Programming Interface (CPI) comes in two parts: **languages** and **services**. CPI languages are the programming languages needed by application programmers and users. CPI services are the set of callable services needed by application programs written in CPI languages.

CPI languages are a bit different from SAA operating systems; languages are specifications that do not call out a specific IBM product (the SAA operating systems are directly specified in SAA publications). For information on which IBM products provide implementations of CPI languages, refer to *SAA CPI Summary* (GC26-4675).

The CPI languages are C, COBOL, PL/I, RPG, Procedures Language, and Application Generator.

The Procedures Language consists of the REXX language with extensions such as support for Double-Byte Character Sets (DBCS) and environmental interfaces. These interfaces have the same semantics on each system, but the syntax may be different. Environmental interfaces currently defined are the variable pool and the system exits.

Services in SAA are much like the languages—a set of specifications that do not call out specific IBM products. Refer to *SAA CPI Summary* for specifics of the current services set and which IBM products implement the specification. The current set of services is:

Communications	Interface for program-to-program communication based on IBM's SNA logical unit type 6.2 (LU 6.2). Facilities include starting and ending conversations, sending and receiving data, and synchronization primitives.
Database	Interface to databases through Structured Query Language (SQL).
Query	Provides access to relational data and control over data appearance in formatted reports.
Repository	Provides access to an organized, shared, integrated collection of information supporting both business and data processing activities.

Presentation   Provides a comprehensive set of services for
                                   information display in both character-
                                   oriented and graphical window-oriented
                                   formats.

Dialog   Provides display and control of user interac-
                                   tion via panels on a screen.

Common Communications Support

The SAA **Common Communications Support** (CCS) provides protocols needed to allow SAA systems to communicate with one another. This includes both base-level line protocols, such as SNA and OSI,
and higher-level protocols, such as APPC, network management, and
object content architectures.

The current set of protocols and the names of the implementing
IBM products can be found in *SAA CCS Summary* (GC31-6810).

Common User Access

The SAA **Common User Access** (CUA) defines rules for the dialog
between humans and computers in three different areas:

Physical consistency   The actual hardware used for human/com-
                                   puter interaction. This covers areas such as
                                   keyboard layout (to ensure that the **ESC** key
                                   is where the user expects it to be) and use of
                                   the mouse.

Syntactical consistency   The sequence of display elements and order
                                   of keystrokes to request actions. For exam-
                                   ple, the title is always in the same place on
                                   an application screen, and double-click on
                                   the mouse always selects an item.

Semantic consistency   The meaning of the CUA elements. For
                                   example, **QUIT** and **CANCEL** are clearly
                                   differentiated and always perform the same
                                   action, no matter which system or applica-
                                   tion is involved.

CUA is important for all applications, to eliminate frustration
resulting from syntax and semantics changes when moving from one
application to another, or when moving from one system to another
and losing one's way on the keyboard itself!

Common Applications

SAA **Common Applications** are the set of applications provided by
IBM and identified as common across the SAA environments.

Current examples are OfficeVision (IBM's office automation system), AD/Cycle (IBM's SAA development platform), and ImagePlus (IBM's image-processing platform).

SAA management process

To ensure consistency in SAA, IBM put together a management team to keep order and encourage progress in the SAA arena. The management team includes the SAA Executive, Earl Wheeler, who created SAA and has been at its helm since the first SAA announcement in March 1987. In addition, for each SAA interface, an SAA Interface Owner has responsibilities for:

- Definition, maintenance, and publication of the SAA interface specification (for REXX, this is the *CPI Procedures Language Reference*)
- Use of a change management process to ensure release-to-release compatibility in all SAA environments
- Specification and assignment of levels to authorized versions of the specification
- Definition of a compliance tool or process to be used by each implementing IBM product when certifying the product for compliance with the SAA interface specification

REXX'S HISTORY IN SAA

How did REXX come to be part of SAA? Before SAA, in early 1986, the Cross System Consistency (CSC) task force was chartered by Earl Wheeler, IBM senior vice president and general manager of its Programming Systems line of business. The CSC task force debated many topics, but REXX was not one of the debated issues. According to Rick McGuire, one of the main technical figures in SAA REXX development and the VM representative to the CSC task force, only a small amount of time was required for the task force to decide on REXX's inclusion. Most of the time involved was spent convincing the task force that a procedures language was a key part of the CSC structure, and a much smaller amount in debating between REXX and the only other contender—CMS's EXEC 2. This IBM task force of key technical personnel saw two points that in retrospect look obvious:

1. Not everything can be done by traditional languages; an EXEC language (later called a Procedures Language) is needed to **glue** various parts of an application system together.
2. REXX was the only logical choice for this language.

CURRENT STATE OF PROCEDURES LANGUAGE

Supported SAA environments

All IBM SAA implementations are interpreters available as part of the base operating systems. They are not separate products. This is a requirement for Procedures Language to fulfill its roles in SAA, which will be described later. Procedures Language is now available in all four SAA environments. The support at different language levels is described below.

CMS (SP, XA, ESA)

REXX has been available in the VM environment since 1983 (REXX language level 3.2) in VM/SP Release 3. It was originally called **System Product Interpreter**. This predated the IBM SAA announcement in March of 1987. The initial definition of Procedures Language was based on what was then available in VM. This definition was the initial SAA Procedures Language Level 1 definition. It included all elements in REXX language level 3.40, plus OPTIONS ETMODE and the variable pool interface. The Level 1 definition was updated in late 1988 to include additional REXX instructions such as CALL ON and SIGNAL ON. This is equivalent to REXX language level 3.46. The Double Byte Character Set (DBCS) extensions to the REXX language were also added at this time. VM implemented this in an SPE to VM/SP available in June 1989.

Level 1 extensions became available to all VM customers when VM/SP and VM/XA were combined to become VM/ESA, announced in September 1990.

TSO/E

REXX was first available in TSO/E version 2 release 1 in December 1988. This was the SAA Procedures Language Level 1 definition without extensions (REXX language level 3.4). In June 1989, TSO/E added the Procedures Language Level 1 extensions described above via an APAR, making the REXX language level 3.46.

OS/2 Extended Edition

REXX was initially delivered in release 1.2 of OS/2 Extended Edition (EE) in March 1990. This version includes both Level 1 (the original definition plus the extensions described above) and Level 2, implemented simultaneously. The Level 2 definition of SAA Procedures Language was announced by IBM in June 1990. It is equivalent to REXX language level 4.0 plus new REXX system exits. Also premiering with this version is the new consistent title for all IBM REXX manuals. It is a combination of Procedures Language, REXX, and the system that implements it; for example, the title for OS/2 is *Procedures Language 2 / REXX*.

OS/400

In August 1990, IBM fulfilled its 1987 promise of making Procedures Language available on all SAA environments, with the announcement of OS/400 release 3. This implementation contains all elements of Level 1 (original definition plus extensions) and all of Level 2 except for stream I/O support. This is language level 3.48. It is called Procedures Language 400/REXX.

Additional IBM implementations

VM compiler

In June 1989, IBM delivered a REXX compiler for the VM environment. This implements the full SAA Level 1 definition (including extensions), except for the **INTERPRET** and **TRACE** instructions. Since IBM has not indicated that the compiler will be available on other environments, this is not an SAA compiler. This compiler was delivered to meet a stated customer need on VM.

The compiler offers an added feature called SAA flagging. When this option is in effect, a warning message is issued for non-SAA items found. This includes VM extensions to the SAA Procedures Language definition, as well as VM system-specific or application-specific commands.

OS/2 Standard Edition

In November 1990, IBM recognized that for REXX to be more widely used, it must be more widely available. Therefore, it included REXX in OS/2 Standard Edition (SE) release 1.3. Although SE is not the official SAA environment, the same version of REXX is now available in both SE and EE.

Using CPI services from Procedures Language

As part of the SAA promise, all CPI languages work with all CPI services, provided that the language and the service exist on a given operating system. This connection is often referred to as a **CPI binding**.

For Procedures Language, the Communication Interface binding exists on VM. The Repository binding exists on TSO. The Dialog Manager and Database bindings exist on OS/2. These are official SAA bindings, which means that when they are implemented on other systems, they will look exactly the same, and therefore code written on one system will be portable to other systems.

SQL has an excellent interface on VM between **REXX** and the VM implementation of the CPI Database Interface service. It is not the official SAA link or binding between Database and Procedures Language; the binding is still undergoing refinement, so that what is seen on one system will be portable to the other three SAA systems.

OS/2 has a binding between Procedures Language and the Query Callable Interface. Again, this is not the official SAA binding.

PROCEDURES LANGUAGE PLACE IN SAA

REXX was put into SAA to be used in two ways: as a system procedures language and as a macro language. In addition, REXX is often used as a simple application development language, as a prototyping language, and in personal computing. Note that these were not the original reasons REXX was added to SAA, but are valid uses for REXX on SAA systems.

Procedures Language

As you can see by the SAA name for REXX, the procedures language role is the primary reason REXX was added to the SAA languages. This role has been called by many different names, all meaning approximately the same thing. Some of these names include **glue language**, **system extension language**, **EXEC language**, and **shell language**. These all mean that what is written in REXX is used to control the running environment, by providing outer structure for what needs to be done or controlled. This role is characterized by the specification of the operating system's command line interface as the environment to which Procedures Language residual text is sent for further interpretation. This includes system-specific commands, as well as commands to invoke whole applications. This role allows REXX programmers to write new system commands, which can personalize their environments. It also allows access to other programs or data. This could be viewed as **gluing together** those other programs and/or data. Alternatively, it could be viewed as a navigational dialog. It can even selectively invoke applications if certain conditions are met (as coded REXX instructions) because users have entered certain information passed to the REXX control program. It also allows users to store operations knowledge in an organized fashion. The key phrase here is **stored knowledge**; the REXX programmer, regardless of previous coding ability/training, is able to capture a set of operations (a **procedure**) for reuse at a later time. A trivial CMS example of storing knowledge for later reuse is shown below. Here the sequence of commands to view the last page of a console log file is captured in a procedure for later use:

```
/* Show the last page of a VM console file */
'EXECIO 1 CP (STEM R. STRING SPOOL CONSOLE CLOSE TO * CLASS A NOHOLD'
parse upper var r.1 . . num .
queue 'BOTTOM'
queue 'BACKWARD'
'EXEC PEEK' num '(FOR *'
```

Another example of **stored knowledge** is the set of instructions to be executed when an environment is started. For example, in the CMS and OS/2 environments, a single procedure can be used in either environment to do personal customization of the environment:

```
/* PROFILE EXEC for CMS and STARTUP.CMD for OS/2 */
parse source environment .
select
  when (environment = 'CMS') then do
    'CP SET ACNT OFF'              /* Shut off annoying message */
    'ACCESS .CORRESPONDENCE B'  /* Access notebooks SFS directory */
    'ACCESS 399 O/A'                    /* Access the PROFS disk */
  end
  when (environment = 'OS/2') then do
    'start C:\cmlib\startcm.cmd coy'     /* Start 3270 emulator */
    'detach d:\login.cmd'                /* Get to local system */
    'start d:\pctools\pmdiary'            /* Start diary/clock */
    'cls'                                 /* Clear screen */
  end
  otherwise say "I don't know about environment" environment
end
```

Macro language

An equally important SAA role for REXX is that of macro language. This role is very similar to the Procedures Language role. In this case, the selected environment is the command line interface presented by the application to the application user. An example of this would be a text editor, such as XEDIT on VM or KEDIT on the PC. This role allows the application user to personalize the application by grouping together application commands with REXX logic and sometimes including system commands. This is often used to perform repetitive tasks, and can extend the application user interface.

Several different groups of people could use REXX to write application macros. The application writer could ship macros with the application. A second potential macro writer is the local support group for the application. This could be a full-fledged IS shop or a local administrator. The last REXX macro writer is often the application user. These people all run within the application environment, writing programming logic potentially mixed with application commands.

Auxiliary roles

Although many people use REXX for the following roles, these are not the original reasons REXX was added to SAA.

Simple application language

Historically in CMS, REXX has proven to be a popular application development language as well as being used for its SAA roles. Interpretive execution for debugging, the convenience of an untyped language, and powerful string-handling facilities make Procedures Language a "natural" for many character-oriented applications where the need for programmer productivity strongly outweighs requirements for execution performance. The CMS compiler was introduced to enhance REXX's use in this role.

Prototyping

Programmers must often verify algorithms or test ideas. REXX is well suited to this type of activity, because of its ease of use and built-in debugging capabilities. It is also ideal because of its interactive mode of operation. In this role, when an algorithm is satisfactory, it can be rewritten in another compiled language to obtain better performance when the program is put into production. Often programs start as prototypes (and therefore were intended to be rewritten in another language) but, because the code works well, are never rewritten.

Personal computing

REXX is very good for personal computing—programs written for one's own use (stored knowledge). The program may be used once or many times, but usually only by the writer or a small set of friends. These are generally small programs, but can (and sometimes do) become quite large. Because REXX is so easy to learn and write, it is often used in this role.

PROCEDURES LANGUAGE FUTURE IN SAA

Many good things are coming for Procedures Language in the future. The top priority from an SAA standpoint is upgrading all IBM implementations to the full SAA Procedures Language Level 2 definition. The OS/2 implementations have achieved this. In addition, IBM will make all available CPI services work with REXX; this is another key element to the SAA promise.

By definition, SAA's reason for being is to provide compatibility across different implementations. This compatibility is achieved in part by sharing some interpreter code, as well as by a rigorous review process to detect differences that need to be fixed. Another element of achieving this compatibility is having reference manuals prepared as much as possible from a common source. This compatibility is important, not only between IBM interpreters, but for the VM compiler as well.

IBM plans to have future SAA Procedures Language level extensions and/or new level definitions. Diverse requests for new language features are received from a variety of sources, including user groups such as SHARE (which has a very active REXX language project), REXX implementers inside and outside IBM, and individual REXX users. Language is being added to the SAA definition prudently. This is in part due to REXX's history of adding features with a high ratio of usefulness to language complexity. Also, when features are added to the SAA definition, they are meaningful and able to be implemented on all systems. See the chapter "Language Evolution and Standards Activities" for more information on this process. For this reason, each Procedures Language/REXX implementation will have system-specific extensions that will never be part of the SAA definition. Within IBM, these extensions are carefully controlled by the SAA Procedures Language Interface Owner (PLIO). The chapter on "SAA Portability" provides details on the IBM system extensions.

The announcement of Procedures Language Level 2 achieved a key goal of having Procedures Language be a superset of REXX. All language features in Cowlishaw's *The REXX Language* are included in the SAA Procedures Language definition, along with elements beyond the REXX definition. This is a key element of the SAA Procedures Language strategy. Another goal is having the American National Standards Organization (ANSI) and the International Standards Organization (ISO) adopt a REXX standard. At that time, the relevant part of the IBM SAA Procedures Language definition would probably converge with the standards body definition.

Other specific goals are to continue enabling non-English use of REXX and to make it easier to migrate from Procedures Language/REXX to non-REXX—i.e., from a non-typed to a typed world. As stated above, there are many IBM customer requests for additional function, primarily from SHARE. These include requests for global variables, traversing stem variables, and allowing expressions in compound variables. These are currently being investigated by the IBM REXX Procedures Language Architecture Review Board

(ARB), described in the chapter "Language Evolution and Standards Activities". Once the ARB approves and specifies them, REXX language additions become very strong candidates for inclusion in future SAA Procedures Language extensions. These extensions are packaged together by the PLIO, who is responsible for ensuring that anything declared to be part of the SAA Procedures Language definition is delivered by all IBM implementations. Therefore, Procedures Language will probably be extended based on traditional REXX ideas, which include customer requirements.

3

Fundamental Concepts

By Bebo White

This chapter provides an overview of fundamental REXX concepts. The most critical of these concepts are covered in more extensive detail in later chapters. The concepts are described in terms of REXX's application both as a high-level, multi-purpose programming language and as a procedure/macro definition language. Examples shown for CMS should translate easily to other operating systems which support REXX.

REXX, as a programming language, has a unique and distinctive "look and feel". Users often describe the language as **comfortable**. On first exposure to a REXX program, users are often struck by an important fundamental characteristic—**readability**.

REXX was designed in the belief that programs should be highly readable, both for the benefit of the author/programmer and for that of a reader/user/maintainer. Human factors research in language design indicates that readability is improved by use of:

1. Mixed case

2. Free formatting

3. Punctuation only to avoid ambiguity

Programming languages which support long (and therefore descriptive) variable and module/subprogram names also contribute to program readability. Simple programs consisting of sequential module calls are readable as such with addition of minimal language syntax or semantics, in order to provide logical programming structures.

The role of program variables in a readable program environment is further supported by REXX's use of **natural data typing**. While strong data typing is a desirable feature in high-level programming languages supporting specific types of data manipulation, it places upon a reader/programmer the additional burden of knowing relevant data types and operations defined for them. An ideal macro language should be weakly typed, or should place maximum emphasis on symbolic manipulation where data types are defined within the context of the data usage. No data type or variable definitions or declarations should be necessary.

Structured Design is a paradigm which has become an accepted standard for programming languages developed in the past twenty years. Definitions of the goals of structured design are as varied as the systems designed to implement those goals. However, it is generally agreed that one goal is **logical readability**. Use of a small set of well-defined logical programming constructs eliminates the digressions which can occur in unstructured "spaghetti" program code. It can be demonstrated that the resulting programs are more bug-free, readable, maintainable, and transportable. While such features are quite desirable for most programs, they are especially desirable for command procedures and macros.

An ideal macro language should operate independently of the hardware and the operating system within which it functions. This concept allows programmers maximum independence and permits the greater functionality allowed by macro portability. For vendors such as IBM which support multiple operating systems, this independence has allowed the potential for a common interface. The variety of computing platforms to which REXX has been successfully ported demonstrates its adherence to this concept.

In summary, REXX is a language which can be used:

- As a high-level programming language for applications which can best use its characteristics
- As a macro language with unprecedented simplicity or complexity
- As a **prototyping** or **pseudocode** language, given its emphasis on readability and natural data typing

A quote from the Mansfield Software Group's *REXX Language Overview* says it best:

> If REXX were just another language, it would be interesting because of its conscious design to emphasize ease of use. But since REXX also encompasses a set of standard interfaces, it represents something more—a tool for fully exploiting the facilities of an operating system; a portable, standard macro language for multiple applications; and a facility for constructing applications out of available building blocks.

GENERAL PROPERTIES OF THE REXX LANGUAGE

Above all, REXX is a complete high-level programming language with powerful facilities for handling text strings. It has logical constructs and many other properties of a structured language.

The original REXX implementation was an **interpreter**. This meant that REXX programs could only be parsed, translated, and executed word for word and line by line. Interpretation also generally implies that when a program error occurs, the program immediately halts, and the position of the error is known exactly. Another language which is often interpreted is BASIC. Such languages are quite unlike FOR-TRAN, where programs are first translated into machine code by a **compiler** and subsequently loaded into memory and executed. When an error occurs in compiled programs, special facilities (and talents) are often required to isolate the cause and remedy it. The primary disadvantage of interpreted programs is that they use far more system resources, and execute more slowly, than compiled programs.

Recently, REXX compilers have been introduced. These compilers offer the advantages of REXX with the performance associated with compiled languages. However, since the REXX definition allows for dynamic procedure execution or recursive interpretation (the INTER-PRET instruction), not all REXX programs can be interpreted and compiled with comparable results.

COMPONENTS OF THE REXX LANGUAGE

REXX programs are constructed from the following basic components:

Clauses or statements	Each program line usually contains at least one statement. REXX deals with one clause at a time.
Tokens	Each clause can be divided into tokens separated by blanks.
Expressions	Tokens may form expressions in a clause.
Instructions	One or more clauses containing REXX keywords which perform a task.
Assignments	Clauses defining variables to contain given values.
Separators	Semicolons (";") separate clauses on a line; a comma continues a clause on the following line.

The SPCON program shows examples of these elements:

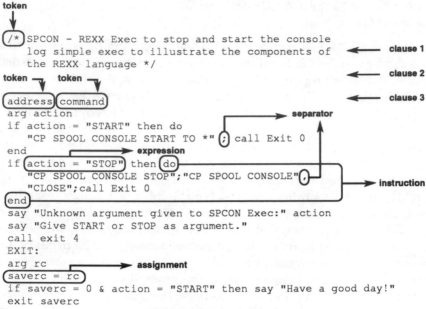

Figure 1. The elements of REXX are illustrated.

The following is a more detailed description of each element.

Clauses

Five varieties of clauses can be distinguished in a REXX program, as illustrated in the next figure:

1. Null clauses—blank lines, ignored by the REXX interpreter. They are generally used to improve program readability.

2. Labels—defined by a token (such as **EXIT** in the next figure) and followed by a colon (": "); they indicate the start of a subprogram or a branch point (reachable by the REXX **CALL** or **SIGNAL** instructions).

3. Assignments—have the general form:

   variable = *value*

   for example:

   saverc = 42

4. Instructions—of the general form:

   keyword *action* [keyword]

   for example:

```
if xyz then do
   :
end
```

5. Commands—clauses possibly containing an expression that is
   evaluated and passed to an external environment such as CP,
   CMS, or XEDIT for execution; for example:

```
'CP SPOOL CONSOLE START TO *'
```

Tokens

A clause consists of tokens, which may be described as "islands of data
in a sea of spaces". Every item delimited by blanks inside a clause is
defined as a token. The special characters comma (", "), semicolon
(";") and colon (":") are also used as token delimiters. For example,
EXIT in the figure is a token since it is preceded by a blank and followed
by a ":". The five most common varieties of tokens are:

1. Comments—*Any* text between an opening /* and a closing */ is a
   comment and is ignored by the REXX interpreter. CMS REXX
   programs *must* start with a comment (this is the mechanism by
   which CMS determines that a file of filetype **EXEC** is written in
   REXX and not EXEC or EXEC 2). The two characters composing
   the comment delimiters *must* not be separated; if they are, they
   become two different tokens.

2. Strings—Any text delimited by single or double quotes (for example, "**START**") is a string. An empty string ("") is called the **null
   string**. In order to include quotes inside a string which uses them
   as a delimiter, simply repeat them:

```
the_quote_dog_quote_ran = 'The ''dog'' ran'
```

   In CMS REXX, strings are limited to 250 characters.

3. Symbols—These have the following properties:

   - They are composed of any combination of non-operator characters (**A**
     through **Z**, **0** through **9**, "**@**", "**#**", "**$**", etc.); for example, @?**freD** is a
     valid symbol.

     REXX language level 4.00 removes the characters "**$**", "**£**", "**#**", and
     "**@**" from the list of valid symbol characters, although existing imple-
     mentations need not disable them. This change was made because
     those characters are not represented by the same hexadecimal values
     in all countries, causing portability problems.

   - Lowercase letters in symbols are translated to uppercase (unless placed
     inside quotes), so @?**freD** is translated to @?**FRED**.

- If a symbol does not start with a period (" . ") or a digit (0 through 9), it may be used as a variable and assigned a value:

  ```
  saverc = rc
  ```

- A symbol may also be a label (**EXIT :**) or a REXX keyword (**ARG, IF, DO,** etc.).

4. Numbers—Valid numbers consist of one or more digits optionally preceded by the "+" or "-" sign, optionally including a decimal point. Symbols may be defined to be numbers, but a number cannot be the name of a variable (otherwise it would be possible to redefine numbers—for example, 0 = -1). REXX is a typeless language, which means there are no integer or real variables; all numbers are considered as character strings.

5. Operators—The characters +, -, /, %, *, |, &, =, ¬, >, and < are operator tokens.

Clauses (after removal of redundant blanks and comments) may consist of a combination of tokens no longer than 500 characters.

Expressions

An expression is composed of terms and operators. There are three varieties of terms:

1. Strings—These are identified by a pair of delimiting quotes or double quotes, for example, **'START'**. Such strings are also known as **literal constants**.

2. Symbols—These may be variables, in which case they are replaced by their values; if a symbol does not have a value, it is translated to uppercase, that is, the default value of a symbol is its name in uppercase.

3. Function calls—These may be added anywhere in an expression and have the general form:

   ```
   function-name([expression][,[expression]] . . )
   ```

where *function-name* is a string or a symbol. The expressions are separated by commas and compose the function argument list. The use of functions and function names in expressions is analogous to that in other high-level programming languages. For example, the **ABS** function returns the absolute value of a numeric value:

```
x = abs('-0.414')
```

assigns value 0.414 to variable X.

Each operator acts on two terms (except for prefix operators, which act on the term following). There are four varieties of operators/operations:

1. String concatenation—Concatenation takes place between any two strings, combining them to form a single string. Strings may be concatenated with a blank or without a blank (using abuttal or the symbol | |). For example, if variable **ACTION** contains value **START**, then **ACTION** '1' (**ACTION** concatenated with literal '1' with an intervening blank) resolves to value **START 1**; **ACTION**'1' (**ACTION** concatenated with literal constant '1' with no intervening blank) resolves to value **START1**; and **ACTION**| |1 (**ACTION**, '1', and the | | operator) also resolves to value **START1**.

2. Arithmetic operators—REXX has seven arithmetic operators that may be used between numeric strings. The majority of these operators are similar to those of other programming languages:

   ```
   +     Add
   -     Subtract
   *     Multiply
   /     Divide
   %     Integer division
   //    Modulo division
   **    Exponentiation
   ```

3. Comparative operators—Comparisons may be made between any two strings. If the result of the comparison is true, 1 is returned; otherwise 0 is returned. The results of comparative operations are quite sensitive to the string characteristics of REXX and can lead to erroneous results. There are eight comparative operators/operations in REXX. For example, given the variable **ACTION** containing **START**, the following comparisons can be defined:

   ==   True if the terms are exactly equal, including blanks and leading zeros; for example:

   ```
   action == " START "
   ```

   is false.

   =   True if the terms are equal after removing leading and trailing blanks and leading zeros, e.g.:

   ```
   action = " START "
   ```

   is true.

   ¬==   True if the terms are not exactly equal (the inverse of ==);
   or /==   for example:

   ```
   action /== " START "
   ```

   is true.

¬=, /=,   Not equal (the inverse of =); for example:
<>, *or* ><

```
action /= " START "
```

is false.

>   Greater than; for example:

```
5 > 3
```

is true.

<   Less than; for example:

```
5 < 3
```

is false.

>= *or*   Greater than or equal to, but not less than; for example:
/<

```
5 >= 3
```

is true.

<= *or*   Less than or equal to, but not greater than; for example:
/>

```
5 <= 3
```

is false.

4. Logical (boolean) operators—These act on logical terms (variables or strings) which contain **1** (true) or **0** (false). The result of a logical operation is always **1** or **0**. There are four logical operators in REXX:

&   (AND) The result is **1** if both terms are true; for example:

```
saverc = 0 & action = "START"
```

is true.

| (Inclusive OR) The result is **1** if either term is true; for example:

```
saverc = 0 | action = "START"
```

is true.

&&   (Exclusive OR) The result is **1** if either (but not both) of the terms is true; for example:

```
action = "START" && saverc = 0
```

is false.

¬   (NOT) The result is **1** if the input term is **0**, and **0** if the input term is **1**.
Expression evaluation is from left to right, evaluating expressions in parentheses first and following the usual algebraic precedence rules for operators:

¬, /, -, +	Unary prefix operators
**	Exponentiation
*, /, %, / /	Multiplication and division
"", | |	Concatenation, with or without an intervening blank
=, <, >, *etc.*	Comparison operators
&	AND
|, &&	OR and exclusive OR

Instructions

Instructions are identified by a REXX keyword or a group of REXX keywords specifying a particular task. For example:

```
if a = b then do
    call subroutine
    xx = function(y)
end
```

In this example, **IF**, **THEN**, **DO**, **CALL** and **END** are REXX keywords.

Assignments

A variable is a symbol that may change value during execution of a REXX program. For example, it may be useful to make a variable assignment at the beginning of a macro, and then allow the value to be changed a number of times during processing. If another execution is required using a different value, the variable need be changed in only one place (where it was initialized). This process is called **assigning a value to a variable**. An assignment has the following general form:

```
symbol = expression
```

This statement is interpreted by replacing the current value of the symbol with the value resulting from the evaluation of the expression.

An expression may be any operation which results in a value that can be associated with a symbol. Occurrence of an assignment operator ("=") indicates to REXX that the clause which follows is an expression. There are four types of symbols which occur in expressions:

1. Constant symbols—A constant symbol is a symbol that starts with a digit (0 through 9) or a period. For example, 165&$7 is a valid constant symbol. Constant symbols may not be used as variables.

2. Simple symbols—A simple symbol does not start with a period or a digit. For example, in the preceding examples, **ACTION** is a valid simple symbol. Simple symbols may be used as variables.

3. Compound symbols—A compound symbol does not start with a period or digit, and has at least one period in it, with characters on either side. Before the symbol is used in an expression, values of the simple symbols on the right side of the period are substituted. For example, if I contains 2 and ACTION.2 contains RESTART, then ACTION.I will be interpreted as the value RESTART. Compound symbols may be used as variables.

4. Stems—A stem contains one period, the last character. It may not start with a digit or period. For example, ACTION. is a valid stem; ACTION. = ' ' sets all variables that start with stem ACTION. to the null string. Stems may be used as variables.

Assignments are very common and flexible clauses. The assigned value is substituted for any symbols when REXX interprets a clause.

A symbol without an assigned value is unchanged and is translated to uppercase.

Separators

Separators are defined as special characters which indicate the ending or continuation of a clause. Some rules to note:

- Normally each clause occupies one physical program line.
- Multiple clauses on one line are separated by a semicolon (";").
- A clause spanning more than one line is continued with a comma (",") at the end of each line to be continued. The continuation character is not interpreted as a meaningful part of the clause.

INTERPRETATION OF A REXX PROGRAM

When a REXX program is interpreted, each clause is subjected to two processes.

1. Translation—In general, all components except strings are automatically translated to uppercase. Subsequently:

   a. Comments are ignored.
   b. Substitution occurs: each token is checked to see if it is a variable, in which case it is replaced by its value; variables not previously referenced are dynamically defined.

2. Execution—There remain only three types of clauses that require some action:

a. Instructions recognizable as REXX keywords are executed.

b. Assignments are made; these are identified by the equals operator (=) as in many other programming languages. All variables occurring in assignments change their value.

c. System commands are executed; strings not recognized as any of the other clause types are passed to the calling environment for execution (for example, CMS or XEDIT).

Very few programming languages include the concept of recursive interpretation. In REXX, this is accomplished by the INTERPRET instruction. This instruction can be used to initiate additional scanning of a clause, thereby treating what had been perfectly innocent data as a program fragment. Consider:

```
data = 'NewValue'
interpret data '= 5'
```

This will:

1. Build the string NewValue = 5

2. Execute NewValue = 5

The result is that variable NEWVALUE is assigned the value 5.

THE REXX ENVIRONMENT MODEL

REXX is usable as a command or macro language for applications which have internal commands. It is also an extremely effective programming language, because it can utilize separately compiled program packages as REXX subprograms. These capabilities are facilitated by the **REXX environment model**.

Recognition and understanding of this model can be of great use to REXX programmers and to anyone who wishes to understand REXX programs.

Elements of the environment model are:

- There are essentially no illegal commands or statement forms in REXX (there may, however, be expressions which are illegal syntactically).
- Commands and statement forms can be categorized into those which are meaningful to the REXX interpreter and those which are not.
- Commands or statement forms which REXX does not understand are passed to the underlying environment in which REXX is executing, using the command interface defined for the environment.

When a REXX program is invoked, the calling environment, for example, CMS or XEDIT, is the default environment in which commands will be executed. An EXEC file invoked from XEDIT is passed on to CMS by XEDIT, thus making CMS the calling environment.

This is called the **addressed** environment. Executing commands inside REXX programs may be achieved via a clause of the form:

```
expression;
```

expression is evaluated, resulting in a character string which does not represent a legitimate REXX operation and is therefore submitted to the addressed environment for execution. For example:

```
'CP SPOOL CONSOLE START TO *'
```

After execution of the command, control is returned to the interpreter after setting a return code appropriate for the addressed environment. This return code is assigned to a special REXX variable, RC. CMS EXECs and XEDIT macros should check the value of this variable in the event alternative action is required. For example, the following EXEC issues the **ESTATE** command, and displays a message when return code **28** (file not found) is returned. In this example, the calling environment is CMS; for XEDIT macros, the procedure is similar.

```
/* RCTEST EXEC to show the use of the RC variable */
   arg fn ft fm
   'ESTATE' fn ft fm
   if rc = 0 then do
      say 'File' fn ft fm 'exists.'
      call exit 0
   end
   if rc = 28 then do
      say 'File' fn ft fm 'not found.'
      call exit 28
   end
   say 'Return code' rc 'from ESTATE command.'
   call exit rc
EXIT:
   arg rc
   exit rc
```

The previous explanation of CMS processing is actually oversimplified. For example, the clause:

```
'ESTATE' fn ft fm
```

requires additional processing by CMS. After substitution of variables **FN**, **FT**, and **FM**, the complete string is passed to CMS for execution. At this time CMS analyzes **ESTATE** using normal CMS command resolution:

1. If a file called **ESTATE EXEC** is found, it is executed.

2. If **ESTATE** is defined as a synonym for an EXEC file, that EXEC is executed.

3. If **ESTATE** is a resident CMS command, it is executed.

4. If **ESTATE** is a module (compiled program), it is executed.

5. If none of the above actions occur, **ESTATE** is passed to CP for resolution and possible execution.

Thus, if a file called **ESTATE EXEC** is found on any minidisk accessed by the virtual machine in which CMS is running, this EXEC is executed. In order to avoid this, the **COMMAND** environment should be used. This environment may be defined by adding the clause:

```
address command
```

at the beginning of the program. In this way, the entire program is placed in the **COMMAND** environment. The **COMMAND** environment is strongly recommended for all EXEC files, to make them more efficient and more predictable. It implies that all strings go directly to CMS for execution and are processed according to the CMS command form:

```
Processor CommandName ArgumentList ( OptionList

EXEC      FILELIST    * * B        ( APPEND
```

Therefore:

- EXEC invocations must be prefaced by the processor name EXEC:

```
'EXEC ESTATE' fn ft fm
```

- CP commands must be prefaced by the processor name CP:

```
'CP SPOOL CONSOLE START TO *'
```

If **CP** were omitted from the above **SPOOL** command, it would fail if **ADDRESS COMMAND** were in effect.

The environment model indicates why REXX is potentially system- and hardware-independent. It is, in this way, capable of passing commands to any system which supports its execution.

Critical to the success of this model is REXX's emphasis on symbolic processing. Analysis of clauses, statements, and commands within this model depends on the ability to **PARSE**, **INTERPRET**, and make substitutions symbolically.

REXX data typing and data structures

As mentioned previously, data values are typeless symbols, and if a symbol looks like a number it can be used in calculations (with rules about maximum integer size, fuzz, and rounding set by the user or defaulted). However, the language's designer, Mike Cowlishaw, has made it clear that data typing is not excluded from future implementations:

> . . .though at present there seems to be little call for this. . . Strong typing, in which the values a variable may take are tightly constrained, has become a fashionable attribute for languages over the last ten years. In this author's opinion, the greatest advantage of strong typing is for the interfaces between program modules. Errors within modules that would be detected by strong typing (and would not be detected from context) are much rarer and in most cases do not justify the added program complexity.

Cowlishaw's concept of how type checking would be implemented is interesting. He envisions "ASSERT-like instructions that assign data type checking to variables during execution flow". This implies that checking could be controlled, and only that which was desired would be used. It also implies that types could still change dynamically, and that the checking facilities could be made to anticipate that change.

Considering their "typelessness", REXX variables are fundamentally scalar (one name, one value). It would therefore appear impossible to define any type of data structure using such variables.

In lieu of well-defined data structures, REXX allows users to define "families" of variables using compound symbols and stems. Defining such families (data structures) is quite simple, but can be extremely effective.

REXX compound symbols are symbols containing a period (". ") or periods. The portion of the symbol to the left of the period defines a stem. The portion to the right of the period identifies a value specifying an element within the family of symbols identified by the stem (like a subscript, but actually far more powerful). For example, LINE.CURRENT is a member of the family of variables defined by LINE.. The stem variable is basically dimensionless in that no declaration of its size, shape, or permissible element values is required. LINE.CURRENT would seem to imply that LINE. is a one-dimensional data structure. This is incorrect, in that LINE. could also have a member named LINE.OLD.1. Given a conventional interpretation of data structures in programming languages, such a definition would be ambiguous in that it implies that one element of LINE., namely LINE.CURRENT, is scalar (one-dimensional) and another element, LINE.OLD, is structured. In REXX, however, this is possible, due primarily to the fact that REXX variables are dynamically allocated upon their first reference. Therefore, LINE.OLD.1 has no logical relationship to LINE.CURRENT other than reference via their common stem.

In analysis of compound symbols, value substitutions occur as with scalar variables except that the periods operate as symbol delimiters.

Therefore, the single symbol `LINE.OLD` is analyzed in terms of the two symbols `LINE.` and `OLD`.

Despite possible convoluted data structures, REXX compound variables are generally used in a way consistent with that of simple array data structures in other languages (`LINE.1`, `LINE.2`, `LINE.3`, etc.).

REXX CONTROL ABSTRACTIONS AND KEYWORD INSTRUCTIONS

The REXX programming language is oriented to a "single-entry, single-exit" programming methodology. The language control structures represent carefully designed structured programming concepts embodied in a syntax which completely forbids the unconditional transfer (`GOTO` statement)—and makes the user like it. The need for a `GOTO` instruction has been completely eliminated by providing unique instructions for accomplishing particular "acceptable" operations which would otherwise justify its inclusion. Certain keyword strings provide the syntactical basis as a programming language. These keywords provide the capability for compound statement construction, selection (conditional) processes, and repetition processes. These operations are similar in form and function to those of other programming languages which emphasize a structured program approach (e.g., Pascal, FORTRAN 77, etc.).

Conditional processing is accomplished in REXX by use of the `IF` instruction, optionally accompanied by `ELSE`:

```
if expression [;] then instruction
[else [;] instruction]
```

where the following rules apply:

- *expression* must have value 1 (true) or 0 (false).
- The `THEN` is obligatory, followed by the instruction to be carried out if the expression is true.
- `ELSE` may optionally be specified, followed by the instruction to be carried out if the expression is false.

The `NOP` instruction (no-operation) is useful when no operation should occur when a certain condition is met:

```
if action ¬= "START" then nop
```

This instruction is necessary because null clauses following `THEN` are not allowed. Comparative operators can be used in the expressions governing an `IF` condition.

Loops group instructions and optionally execute them repetitively via the DO/END construct. Loops may appear in different forms depending upon function. For example, there are **simple DO** groups:

```
do
    instruction1
    instruction2
    :
end
```

The instructions in the loop are executed once only.

There are simple repetitive DO groups:

```
do n|forever [until expru | while exprw]
    instruction1
    instruction2
    :
end
```

where *n* is any non-negative integer (or an expression resulting in one). Instructions in the loop will be executed *n* times or **FOREVER**. If **WHILE** or **UNTIL** was specified, the keyword must be followed by a logical expression resolving to 0 or 1. The loop is then executed **UNTIL** the condition is true or **WHILE** the condition is true.

There are controlled repetitive DO loops:

```
do name = expri [to exprt] [for exprf] [by exprb] [until expru |
while exprw]
    instruction1
    instruction2
    :
end [name]
```

The controlled repetitive loop at least contains a control variable (**NAME**), which is assigned an initial value by *expri*.

If no other keywords are given, the control variable is incremented by 1 and the loop is executed forever.

Execution may be halted by specifying a value following the **TO**, **FOR**, **UNTIL**, or **WHILE** keywords. Values following **TO** and **FOR** are numbers indicating the value of the control variable when the loop is to terminate (**TO**) and the number of times the loop should be executed (**FOR**), respectively.

If the control variable name is specified on the **END** statement, REXX verifies that there is a matching **DO** statement. This can be useful inside nested loops.

The **LEAVE** instruction ends a (repetitive) loop regardless of any condition controlling the loop being met. Control passes to the next clause after the corresponding **END**. **LEAVE** is the acceptable manner for exiting a **DO FOREVER** loop.

The **ITERATE** instruction interrupts the current iteration through a loop, returning control to the top of the loop.

There is no **GOTO** instruction, since leaving a loop in that manner would mean that the loop would never terminate. This is due to the fact that scoping is entirely dynamic and not lexical. Likewise, once a loop has been exited, it cannot be reentered.

The **SIGNAL** instruction can also be used to exit from active loop constructs. This instruction is designed to be used with REXX subprograms or error handlers.

The **EXIT** instruction terminates a REXX program immediately when encountered. The format is:

```
exit [expression]
```

The string in *expression* is returned to the calling environment. This allows a return code to be set; for example, **EXIT 4** sets variable **RC** to **4** in the calling REXX program.

EXIT instructions are necessary to allow termination before the last line of a program. Otherwise execution would continue to the last line of the program.

CONCLUSION

REXX is a programming language designed "by programmers for programmers who understand the job to be done and want it done quickly and efficiently". Its designer was not afraid to emphasize such virtues as readability and natural data-typing, when other new languages pride themselves on terse and arcane syntax and strong data-typing. The REXX language does not attempt to provide overly extensive functionality, but rather offers an unembellished structure which allows a well-defined interface to system-dependent operations. At the same time, it provides the ability to perform fundamental yet critical operations, such as parsing.

The REXX I/O Model

By Bebo White

The REXX input/output model incorporates simple, device-independent input and output data streams in a manner very similar to those of programming languages such as C and Pascal. These data streams are associated with terminal input/output, providing the interaction typical of interpretive program and/or macro operation.

Device-dependent input and output is also possible within this model. These operations are allowed through REXX's operating system interface. Thereby, REXX users in a particular system environment can use the device I/O operations within that environment with which they are presumably familiar. This model also defines a REXX interface to independently developed user-interface systems such as the RiceMail mail system discussed in the chapter "A Sample REXX Application".

Application of this model presents a system-independent view of how REXX programs acquire input data and output program values.

Figure 2 is a graphical representation of the elements of the REXX input model.

The program argument list

The first element of the REXX input model is the **argument list**. The argument list is a special form of input consistent with the expected form of many REXX applications. Macros written in REXX should operate

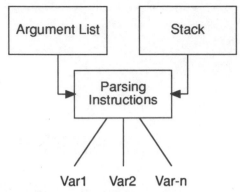

Figure 2. The elements of the REXX input model.

like system commands, which generally have arguments and options.

Values in the argument list are provided to the REXX program or subprogram when it is executed (invoked). Program statements are used to capture and parse values included in the argument list.

The REXX **ARG** and **PARSE ARG** instructions take an argument list (the string following the macro name on the command line) and parse that list according to a specified template. This template is usually defined to be consistent with the syntactical form of the commands in the environment where the macro is to be operative. These instructions are nondestructive, in that the original argument list is retained. The specified template can be as simple as a list of program variable names for which a one-to-one mapping between argument values and template variables is accomplished. More sophisticated parsing may be accomplished using pattern matching, absolute and relative column matching, and parsing after the evaluation of an expression. Provisions are also made for "capturing" extraneous argument list elements and "skipping" elements. These REXX parsing operations emphasize the fundamental reliance on string and character manipulation procedures, in that the argument string is treated as a single string entity and no data type checking occurs during the process.

Using the stack for input

The second element of the REXX input model is the **stack**.

This element results from REXX's evolutionary development with IBM's VM/CMS operating system. A fundamental CMS processing component is a two-part storage area called the **console stack** (or simply the **stack**). Many CMS operations rely upon the stack as a processing area. Numerous CMS commands and operations offer the option of writing output to the console stack. The console stack itself is subdivided into two buffers:

1. The terminal input buffer

2. The program stack

The function of the terminal input buffer is to retain lines keyed in from the virtual console (the user's terminal) until CMS has the opportunity to process them. Line processing operates in a **FIFO** (first-in, first-out) fashion.

The program stack serves as temporary storage for lines (or files) being exchanged by programs executing in CMS. CMS commands and EXEC control statements are used to manage the program stack and data flow through it.

The order or sequence in which CMS normally reads and processes input lines within the stack is sequential and well defined:

1. Lines in buffers within the program stack

2. Lines from the terminal input buffer

3. Lines keyed directly from the terminal.

Figure 3 illustrates from the "top down" how the processing of lines within the stack occurs. Arrows represent REXX instructions which perform operations on the stack.

CMS also allows partitioning of the program stack into dedicated working buffers. In this manner, stack operations may be directed at only a particular portion (buffer) of the stack. This capability may be

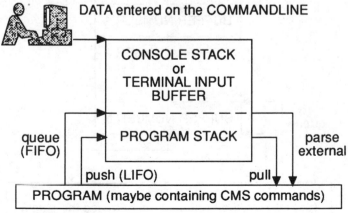

Figure 3. The console stack

used to affect the processing sequence of lines within the program stack.

Such partitioning is accomplished using the CMS **MAKEBUF** and **DROPBUF** commands. **MAKEBUF** creates a new buffer within the program stack; subsequent stack operations are localized to that buffer, independent of the status of the remainder of the program stack. **DROPBUF** discards a particular buffer or range of buffers from the program stack. It is important to emphasize that **MAKEBUF** and **DROPBUF** are CMS commands and not REXX instructions. Their use clearly illustrates how REXX can exploit operations native to the environment within which it operates.

Figure 4 illustrates the effect of partitioning the program stack using **MAKEBUF**:.

Using the program stack permits REXX programs to receive input from the terminal or from any other facility (CMS, other macros, etc.) which has access to the program stack and is capable of inserting values on it.

REXX **PULL** and **PARSE PULL** instructions read a line of data from the program stack. If the program stack is empty, then according to the stack processing sequence, a terminal read will be invoked. The line of

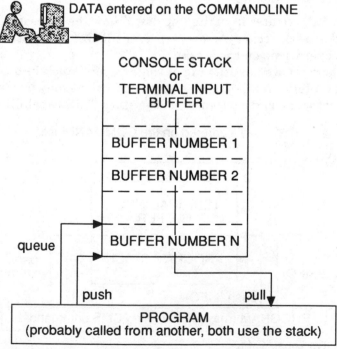

Figure 4. The effect of partitioning of the program stack.

data acquired by either **PULL** instruction is processed with respect to a specified template in the same manner as the **ARG** and **PARSE ARG** instructions.

In the following example, values of variables **file_mode** and **file_type** are read from the terminal when the program stack is empty. The apparent effect of this operation is simple terminal input, or input via a standard input data stream.

```
/* */
pull file_mode file_type
'ACCESS 194' file_mode
'LISTFILE *' file_type file_mode
exit
```

Because of the program stack's importance in the REXX input model, REXX versions on other platforms simulate its function, as discussed in subsequent chapters dealing with non-CMS REXX implementations.

Device-dependent operations using the program stack

Consistent with the REXX environment model, the stack allows REXX programs to use alternative operating system facilities for device-dependent input. **EXECIO** is an example of such a facility available to CMS users. Use of **EXECIO** in CMS EXECs and XEDIT macros has become so widespread that many REXX users think of **EXECIO** as a REXX language facility. Some REXX implementations for other platforms have, for this reason, incorporated **EXECIO** as an equivalent operation.

A similar operation gaining popularity among CMS users is IBM's **CMS Pipelines** product (see the chapter "CMS Pipelines"). This facility allows REXX users to interact with the stack and with other programs in a manner similar to that of the Unix pipeline model.

Virtual console/terminal output

The first element of the REXX output model involves interactive output to the virtual console/terminal. In CMS REXX, this operation is provided by the **SAY** instruction. This instruction writes data to a standard terminal output stream.

The **SAY** instruction, when followed by an expression, writes to the virtual console a scanned version of that expression. All value substitutions are made in the expression according to the rules of scanning and analysis of statements and clauses.

Using the stack for output

The second element of the REXX output model is the **stack**. Output operations to the program stack are analogous to the input operations previously described.

REXX PUSH and QUEUE instructions write data strings to the program stack. Each instruction implements a conceptual model in the mind of the programmer of the stack as a **FIFO** (first-in, first-out) device or a **LIFO** (last-in, first-out) device.

The QUEUE instruction adds a line of data to the end of a currently active buffer within the program stack. This is FIFO queueing. Comparably, the PUSH instruction adds a line of data to the beginning of a currently active buffer within the program stack. This is LIFO queueing.

Since no provisions are made via the REXX SAY instruction for output to files or any devices other than the virtual console, the stack supports REXX's ability for device-dependent output. This is consistent with the REXX environment model. An example of this capability is the EXECIO command discussed previously. EXECIO provides CMS users the capability to write REXX output to a wide variety of output devices.

Stack status

While the program stack is an important part of the REXX input/output model, it must again be emphasized that it is a CMS component, and not peculiar to REXX. Therefore, operations in REXX programs using the stack can have effects external to those programs. A simple example involves data which remains in the stack upon completion of a REXX program. Since CMS examines the stack contents prior to input from the terminal, these contents will be interpreted by CMS. In most cases, these stacked lines are not legitimate CMS or CP commands, leading to CMS error messages such as UNKNOWN CP/CMSCOMMAND.

It is therefore often of interest during the execution of a REXX program to know the status of (the current number of lines in) the program and/or console stacks. One reason is that the number represents the maximum number of PULL instructions which can be executed without terminal input.

Several facilities for obtaining such information are available to REXX programmers:

- SENTRIES (CMS command)
- QUEUED (REXX function)

- **EXTERNALS** (REXX function)
- **DMSSEQ** (CMS function in Release 6 and later)

SENTRIES is a CMS command which determines the number of lines currently in the program stack. When **SENTRIES** is issued, CMS returns the number of lines in the program stack (but not the terminal input buffer) as a return code. The **QUEUED** and **EXTERNALS** functions return the number of lines in the console and program stack, respectively. The CMS **DMSSEQ** function (in VM/SP Release 6 and later releases) is equivalent to the REXX **EXTERNALS** function; like **SENTRIES**, **DMSSEQ** returns the number of lines as a return code.

Broader applications of the PARSE instruction

The **PARSE** instruction assigns data from various sources to one or more variables:

```
parse [upper] operand [template]
```

ARG and **PULL** operands of **PARSE** have already been described as elements of the REXX input model. Other useful **PARSE** operands are:

PARSE EXTERNAL	The next string from the terminal input buffer is parsed while the program stack is left unaltered. If the console stack is empty, a terminal read results. This operation is useful for forcing input to come from the terminal.
PARSE SOURCE	The data parsed contains information about the program being executed: the environment (**CMS**), the function (**EXEC, COMMAND, SUBROUTINE, FUNCTION**), the complete file identifier, the command name or synonym used to invoke the REXX program, and the default address environment.
PARSE VALUE expression WITH template	The expression is evaluated and the result is parsed according to the template following the **WITH**:

```
parse value '' with a b c
```

initializes variables **A, B,** and **C** to null strings.

PARSE VAR name	The value of variable **NAME** is parsed; it may also occur in the template, providing a very useful trick to remove words from a string one by one:

```
options = 'first second third'
parse var options option options
/* Now OPTION contains "first"; OPTIONS
contains "second third" */
```

This parses the value of **OPTIONS** with the template **OPTION OPTIONS**, i.e., removes the first word of **OPTIONS** and places it in **OPTION**.

Other input/output models

The input/output model described in *The REXX Language—A Practical Approach to Programming* is not completely implemented in CMS REXX, but is available in OS/2 REXX. The model includes facilities for:

- Character input streams (**CHARIN**)
- Character output streams (**CHAROUT**)
- Line input streams (**LINEIN**)
- Line output streams (**LINEOUT**)
- Counting characters remaining in a character input stream (**CHARS**)
- Counting lines remaining in a character input stream (**LINES**)

CONCLUSION

This overview of the REXX I/O model illustrates the simple yet powerful mechanism the language provides for device-independent input and output. The versatility of this model has allowed REXX to be used for a wide variety of applications on diverse hardware and software platforms.

Other chapters in this book provide more precise descriptions of the model elements and examples of their use in meaningful REXX programs and macros.

Chapter 5

REXX Programming Style

By Jeffrey B. Savit

INTRODUCTION

Programming style is a personal and controversial subject, but an important one, since it can dramatically affect the quality of a program. This chapter discusses REXX programming style, and suggests and illustrates REXX programming techniques to improve program quality.

REXX is a rich programming language that makes it possible for a task to be programmed in various ways. In addition to modern programming methods applicable to most languages, such as structured programming and modularity, REXX's unique properties and problem domain add extra criteria for "good" REXX programming style.

OBJECTIVES FOR A PROGRAMMING STYLE

Before describing "good" REXX style, it is useful to specify what it should help accomplish:

Correctness and robustness   Few other attributes of a program are
                                  interesting if it crashes or produces incorrect
                                  outputs! This is critical for REXX programs,
                                  which are frequently used to implement
                                  system facilities and often are unshielded
                                  from direct user inputs.

Fast development	REXX is excellent as a fast prototyping language. REXX eliminates the compile/link/test cycle of traditional languages and provides excellent interactive debugging facilities. REXX's "natural" type system also allows construction of programs with less effort than other languages.
Readability and maintainability	Most programs are read far more frequently than they are written, and have long lifetimes of maintenance and change. Attention to good programming style can make a REXX program more easily understood and modified by later readers, including the original author.
Performance	Most REXX implementations are interpreted, and lack the speed possible with assembler language or compiled languages. Nonetheless, small investments of effort can pay off in performance good enough to allow REXX's advantages to be applied in a surprisingly large number of problem domains.
Portability	The advent of REXX implementations beyond its VM origins, and its adoption by IBM as the Systems Application Architecture Procedures Language (SAA PL), makes portability increasingly important. Although REXX shields programs from machine-dependent details (such as word length) to a degree rarely found in older languages, care must be taken to make REXX applications truly portable. See the chapter "SAA Portability" for details on writing portable REXX programs.

FLOW OF CONTROL

The traditional focus for pronouncements on program style is program flow of control. Like all respectable modern programming languages, REXX encourages a GOTO-less style of programming. REXX does have a GOTO-like instruction, SIGNAL, but its use should be restricted to error exits from main-line code. Normal flow of control should be implemented with built-in REXX facilities for selection and iteration.

Selection—IF and SELECT

IF and SELECT conditionally execute statements. The THEN action of an IF statement is executed if the boolean expression evaluates to a true value; optionally, an **ELSE** action can be specified for execution if the boolean expression is false:

```
if utilization > threshold then call OVERLOAD

if . . . then do
    :
end
else do
    :
end
```

THEN and **ELSE** clauses can themselves be compound statements, including **IF**, as shown below. Since **ELSE** clauses match the nearest **THEN**, an **ELSE NOP** may be needed, as shown below, to properly associate an **ELSE** with an outer **IF**. This can also be done by including the inner **IF** in a **DO** group. The following **ELSE** is then automatically associated with the outer **IF**:

```
/* Use NOP to associate ELSE with outer IF */
if attempts > maximumattempts
then if ¬alreadywarned then call ISSUEWARNING
                 else nop
else attempts = attempts + 1

/* Use DO group to associate ELSE with outer IF */
if attempts > maximumattempts then do
    if ¬alreadywarned then call ISSUEWARNING
end
else attempts = attempts + 1
```

The **SELECT** instruction is better than a cascade of **IF/THEN/ELSE** sequences when a single action is selected from a number of alternatives. The two statement groups below cause equivalent effects, but the **SELECT** group is a better choice than the **IF/THEN/ELSE**:

```
/* Cascaded ELSEs */
if      event = 'READER'  then call READERFILE
else if event = 'TIMER'   then call TIMERELAPSED
else if event = 'MESSAGE' then call USERMESSAGE
else if event = 'CONSOLE' then call OPERATORCOMMAND
else say 'Unknown event type' event

/* SELECT statement */
select
    when event = 'READER'  then call READERFILE
    when event = 'TIMER'   then call TIMERELAPSED
    when event = 'MESSAGE' then call USERMESSAGE
    when event = 'CONSOLE' then call OPERATORCOMMAND
    otherwise say 'Unknown event type' event
end
```

In both cases each alternative is tested and the corresponding action taken, but SELECT more clearly expresses selection of a single alternative from many and makes it harder to incorrectly code the logic or mismatch an ELSE statement.

With either method, the most frequent case should be specified first for efficiency. Also, the situation in which none of the tests is true should be considered. SELECT will fail with an error if none of the conditions is satisfied and no OTHERWISE has been coded.

Iterative programming

REXX provides varied methods for specifying loops via the DO statement:

```
do while condition                /* Pre-test loop while true */
   :
end

do until condition                /* Post-test loop until true */
   :
end

do forever                  /* Endless loop terminated within body */
   :
   if condition then leave
   :
   :
end

do loop variable = start to end by increment
                            /* Counting loop with loop index */
   :
end

do n                        /* Loop a fixed number of times, */
                            /* without an index variable */
   :
end
```

DO WHILE and DO UNTIL

DO WHILE tests the loop condition before executing the body of the loop, and repeats the loop as long as the condition remains true. DO UNTIL tests the loop condition after the loop is traversed and ends when the condition becomes false. Consequently, a DO UNTIL loop always executes at least once, but a DO WHILE loop can have null cases, since the loop body is not executed if the condition is initially false.

This property is used to represent different logical situations. Examples of loops that fall naturally into either the WHILE or UNTIL type are shown below. The loop that does disk cleanups is a WHILE loop, since it isn't needed at all if the specified disk utilization is below the threshold value. The second loop is also a **WHILE** because its body operates on data that is present only if the guarding boolean is true. In this case, which is representative of all **WHILE** loops that read a file from start to end, a "priming" statement is used to initialize the boolean condition.

```
/* Perform disk cleanup -- only if needed */
do while UTILIZATION(diskid) > threshold
   fileid = OLDESTFILE(diskid)
   say 'Erasing old file 'fileid 'to free up disk space.'
   'ERASE' fileid
end

/* Add the first column in 'MY DATA A'. Return 0 if no such file */
/* Loop body is never executed if the file doesn't exist */
sum = 0
'EXECIO 1 DISKR MY DATA A (VAR X' /* Read line 1 from file, set RC */
do while rc = 0                        /* RC = 0 if read worked */
   parse var x t .
   sum = sum + t
   'EXECIO 1 DISKR MY DATA A (VAR X'    /* Read next line from file */
end
```

UNTIL loops should only be used when there is never a null loop of zero iterations. For example, when using **DO UNTIL**, the prompt question is always issued at least once:

```
/* Prompt for a YES or NO-the loop body is executed at least once */
do until answer = 'YES' | answer = 'NO'
   say 'OK to proceed?  Enter YES or NO:'
   pull answer
end
```

DO FOREVER

DO FOREVER loops run until the loop body terminates the loop with **SIGNAL, RETURN, EXIT**, or (typically) **LEAVE. DO FOREVER** is useful to execute what is sometimes called an "N-and-a-half" loop, in which you need to perform some of the loop's body before exiting it. It is often used when multiple exits from a loop are needed.

```
/* Loop with multiple exit points */
do forever
   say 'Enter employee id, or Q to quit'
   pull key
   if key = 'Q' then leave
   say 'Add, Delete, Browse, or Quit? (Enter A, D, B, or Q)'
   pull action
   select
      when action = 'A' then call ADD
      when action = 'D' then call DELETE
      when action = 'B' then call BROWSE
      when action = 'Q' then leave
```

```
          otherwise say 'Please enter one of the actions available.'
       end
   end
```

DO FOREVER is powerful and general, and can even be used to simulate all the other loop types. Nonetheless, it is generally not the best technique, since the reader has to scan the loop's body to determine all possible reasons for loop termination. This is true for all loops that can terminate via LEAVE, EXIT, SIGNAL, or RETURN. In general, it is best to adhere to the principle of "single entry, single exit" for each loop.

Multiple exit points are best used to implement escape situations, as illustrated above. The other usual method is to shield the remainder of the loop with an IF statement, and check for all of the exit reasons on the DO. This leads to unnecessarily deeply nested code and duplicated tests (with the possibility of forgetting to duplicate them).

```
/* Alternative coding with DO UNTIL */
do until key = 'Q' | action = 'Q'
   say 'Enter employee id, or Q to quit'
   pull key
   if key <> 'Q' then do /* Reversed logic skips rest of loop body */
      say 'Add, Delete, Browse, or Quit? (Enter A, D, B, or Q)'
      pull action
      select
         when action = 'A' then call ADD
         when action = 'D' then call DELETE
         when action = 'B' then call BROWSE
         when action = 'Q' then nop
         otherwise say 'Please enter one of the actions available.'
      end
   end
end                        /* The DO FOREVER was clearer, wasn't it? */
```

Repetitive DO instruction
Repetitive DO formats are useful when a fixed number of loop iterations are needed—for example, to traverse a table or to process a known number of items.

```
/* Repetitive DO instructions */

/* Set X to the smallest value in array A., which */
/* has N values labeled A.1, A.2, ..., A.N */
x = a.1
do i = 1 to n
   if a.i < x then x = a.i  /* x = min(x, a.i) ok if a. is numeric */
end
```

```
/* Add up how many lines of SCRIPT input are on CMS A-disk */
lines = 0
'LISTFILE * SCRIPT (STACK DATE'    /* Stack info about SCRIPT files */
do queued()                        /* Iteration for each stacked line */
   parse pull filename filetype filemode lrecl recs blocks .
   lines = lines + recs
end
say 'You have a total of' lines 'lines in SCRIPT files.'
```

It is possible to join WHILE, UNTIL, and iterative formats of DO loops into a single statement. This can add expressive power and clearly show the reason for the loop; quite often it can actually eliminate the entire loop body! If overused, it can also obscure the reason for the loop's termination, so it should be applied judiciously.

Many varieties of logic errors are possible when coding a loop in *any* programming language, especially if loop terminating conditions are not properly understood and coded. For example, in the common task of serially searching a table for a value, the search may terminate either when the value is found or when the end of the table is reached.

```
/* Search stemmed array A for value matching X */
do i = 1 to n while a.i <> x
end
if a.i = x then say 'Found it!'                /* Was X in the table? */
```

The above code looks correct and compact, but can produce incorrect output if the table size, N, can expand and contract. This code will erroneously type Found it! if N has just been decreased by 1 and the N+1th value in the table (now outside the range being searched) contains X. This code would also be dangerous in a traditional language, where I would be an out-of-range array bound if the array didn't contain the searched-for value.

A loop that explicitly increments the array index avoids the first problem:

```
/* Alternative search with WHILE loop */
i = 1
do while i <= n & a.i <> x
   i = i + 1
end
if i <= n then say 'Found it!'

/* Alternative search with DO FOREVER */
/* Never refers to A.I when I > N */
i = 1
do forever
   if i > n then leave
   if a.i = x then leave
   i = i + 1
end
if i <= n then say 'Found it!'
```

When the terminating predicate is well understood, you can apply knowledge about it to improve the program. For example, the serial search can be made about 50 percent faster (in all languages!) by using a sentinel value to mark the end of the table. This reduces the number of tests per loop traversal from 2 to 1: a subsequent test determines whether X was found inside the table or outside it.

```
/* Canonical serial search with sentinel value */
sentinel = n + 1
a.sentinel = x
i = 1
do while a.i <> x
   i = i + 1
end
if i <= n then say 'Found it!'
```

The SIGNAL statement

SIGNAL causes transfer of control to a named label, and a syntax error and program halt if the named statement is not present in the program. SIGNAL is useful for implementing error exits or other types of "out-of-line" code that should not obscure the main processing region of a program. SIGNAL should not be used to implemement normal program looping and branching logic.

SIGNAL ON *condition* is also useful for setting up predefined error exits that REXX takes on abnormal conditions. Conditions supported are:

ERROR	Branch to label ERROR if a host command ends with a non-zero return code.
	This must be used with caution, since many commands yield non-zero return codes in non-error situations. For example, EXECIO yields return code 2 when end-of-file is reached, and XEDIT commands that move to the top or bottom of a file yield return codes of 1.
FAILURE	New in CMS 6; branch to label FAILURE if a host command ends with a negative return code.
NOVALUE	Branch to label NOVALUE if a REXX variable is used in an expression without having had a value assigned to it.
	This is extremely valuable for detecting uninitialized variables. In the absence of this statement, REXX returns the name of the variable as its value, treating it like literal character data.

HALT   Branch to label **HALT** if the user issues an **HI** command from the terminal, telling REXX to **Halt Interpretation**. This gives the REXX program a chance to intercept the halt request and terminate gracefully.

SYNTAX   Branch to label **SYNTAX** if a REXX language error occurs. This is important for handling all types of run-time errors in a REXX program, including invalid calls to functions, improper data types in expressions, and many other situations.

When an error routine is invoked, special variable **SIGL** contains the line number of the REXX statement that raised the condition. The actual statement can be displayed by using the **SOURCELINE** function. For the **SYNTAX** condition, special variable **RC** contains the REXX error number; the text associated with that error is available using the **ERRORTEXT** function.

```
/* TYPEOUT:  Read and type a file, using SIGNAL for error exits */
address command                      /* Select CMS command environment */
arg fname ftype fmode .                        /* Get fileid */
signal on SYNTAX
if fname = '' | ftype = '' then signal NOFILE    /* Missing fileid */
if fname = '?' then signal HELP
if fmode = '' then fmode = '*'                  /* Default filemode */
'EXECIO * DISKR' fname ftype fmode '(FINIS STEM LINES.'
if rc <> 0 then signal BADREAD
do i = 1 to lines.0
   say lines.i
end
exit 0

NOFILE:
say 'You must specify a filename!'
exit 24
HELP:
say 'The format of this command is:'
say '     TYPEOUT filename filetype <filemode>'
exit 0
BADREAD:
say 'Error return code' rc 'trying to read' fname ftype fmode
exit rc
SYNTAX:
say 'REXX program error' rc':' errortext(rc)
say 'Error occurred in line' sigl':' sourceline(sigl)
exit 9999
```

PROGRAM FORMATTING

REXX program statements should be formatted to visibly show which statements are logically related and which execute under the control of surrounding **DO**, **SELECT**, or **IF/THEN/ELSE** constructs. This illustrates program flow of control and makes it easier to read and understand REXX programs.

Indentation rules are extremely personal choices, with different people preferring different degrees of indentation and placement of subordinate statements. Many styles can help create readable and aesthetically pleasing programs, as illustrated below. It is important that whichever style is selected be used consistently, and that it graphically illustrate the dynamic structure of the program.

```
/* REXX indentation styles */

/* Different ways of formatting IF statements */
/* END aligned under matching DO, THEN, or IF */

do while . . .
   if . . . then
      do
         select
            when . . .
            when . . .
            when . . .
            otherwise . . .
         end
      end
   else do
   :
   end
end


/* END aligned with controlled code segment */
do while . . .
   if . . . then
      do
         select
            when . . .
            when . . .
            when . . .
            otherwise . . .
            end                           /* Matches SELECT */
         end                              /* Matches DO */
   else do
   :
     end
   end                                    /* matches DO WHILE */


/* Different ways of formatting IF statements */
if . . .
then . . .
else . . .
```

```
if . . .
   then . . .
   else . . .

if . . . then do
   :
   end
```

It's all too easy, when programming in block-structured languages that use keywords like END to terminate a statement group, to create mismatched or missing END statements. One way to avoid this is to code the END statement when you enter the DO or SELECT, then insert statements between them. This makes it easy to properly indent the enclosed code and eliminates errors caused by missing or misplaced END statements.

It is good practice and good manners, when updating a program written by other people, to use the original author's indentation scheme, unless it is truly unreadable. This gives the program a consistent appearance, instead of containing the indentation methods of every programmer that worked on it.

REXX EXPRESSIONS AND VALUES

Many of the preceding suggestions apply equally to other languages. REXX, in addition to its predominant use as a system procedures language, has features that dramatically affect programming style.

Type System

Unlike in traditional languages, the **type** of a REXX expression is determined at run-time. The current REXX language deliberately provides no method of predeclaring a variable to be a scalar or array, or to contain particular types of values (strings, integers, or floating-point numbers).

Instead, REXX variables and expressions are interpreted "naturally", according to the REXX design philosophy of "no surprises". If a string operator, such as concatenation, is applied to a variable, the variable is treated as a string, even if it was previously used for arithmetic. Notably, if a value is used with an arithmetic operator, REXX will attempt to treat its character representation as a number and perform the operation, and will cause a run-time error if the string is not a syntactically proper numeric value.

Strongly typed languages, such as Pascal, prevent run-time errors by checking all expressions for type compatibility at compile time. This adds safety, but at the cost of requiring that each variable be explicitly declared and only capable of taking on one type of value. REXX gives programmers the freedom to let any variable take on any value, but requires judicious use of this freedom.

For example, nothing in REXX prevents using the same identifier for completely different types of value, as shown below:

```
pay = (payrate * hours) - taxes                    /* 'Pay' is a number */
if pay > 0
then pay = 'Today is payday: you are receiving $'pay
else pay = 'Your withholding exceeds your pay, please pay us $'pay
say pay                                            /* 'Pay' is a string */
```

While this is legal REXX, it would certainly confuse most readers in all but trivial REXX programs.

REXX shifts responsibility for type checking to the programmer. For example, the **DATATYPE** function should be used to ensure that otherwise-unverified numeric inputs are numeric. This can be used in two forms:

```
/* Using the DATATYPE function */

say 'Pick a number:'
parse pull x
if ¬datatype(x, 'NUM')              /* Returns TRUE if X's type matches */
then say 'Not a number!'                            /* second argument */
    :
if datatype(x) <> 'NUM'                     /* Returns X's data type */
then . . .
```

Both forms are useful and can be used to implement code that validates user inputs, as shown below:

```
do until datatype(age, 'NUM')
    say 'Please enter your age:'
    parse pull age
end
```

The boolean form of **DATATYPE** also allows checking for properly formed hexadecimal or whole numbers easily:

```
If datatype(inputarg, 'X')
then say '"'inputarg'"' is a hex value with decimal value'
x2d(inputarg)
else say '"'inputarg'"' is not a valid hexadecimal string'

say 'Enter number of cookies:'
parse pull cookies
if ¬datatype(cookies, 'W')                 /* Is it a whole number? */
then say 'We only sell complete cookies!'
```

Boolean values and arithmetic *

REXX boolean expressions are 0 or 1 values, allowing programmers to use boolean values in arithmetic expressions. This leads to compact but confusing code, and should usually be avoided. The next example shows a boolean variable used as a word index into a string to generate one of two CMS commands.

```
/* Boolean values in expressions */

/* Under CMS, the CMSFLAG function returns 0 or 1 to indicate if */
/* a CMS flag setting is turned on */
htflag = CMSFLAG('CMSTYPE')           /* Save CMS terminal output flag */
'SET CMSTYPE HT'          /* Issue 'Halt Typing' to suppress messages */
:
/* Set the HT flag back to its original value: */
/* either Resume Typing or keep Halt Typing status */
'SET CMSTYPE' word('RT HT', htflag+1)     /* htflag+1 yields 1 or 2 */

/* Less clever, but clearer method of doing the same */
if ¬htflag then 'SET CMSTYPE RT'
```

Character orientation of data

REXX represents values as character strings and then applies them according to a program's operators. This can occasionally cause surprises:

```
x = '10';   y = '4';   b = x > y                    /* True! */
x = '10MB'; y = '4MB'; b = x > y          /* False! 10MB < 4MB */
```

In the first case, X and Y are treated as numeric values—whether with or without quotes. The "natural" comparison to use for > is an arithmetic comparison, and 10 is greater than 4.

In the second case, REXX "knows" that X and Y are not numeric and therefore uses a string comparison. Since the first character of X, 1, is less than the first character of Y, 4, X is less than Y. Technically speaking, the relational operator > is **overloaded** with different semantics based on the data to which it applies.

The problem can be avoided by ensuring that numeric comparisons are made against completely numeric strings to avoid character comparisons. This also includes leading and trailing blanks, which can be removed by using the STRIP function or by adding zero to the variable in question (if the value is numeric).

Literal data values and quoted strings

REXX strings are normally enclosed within apostrophes or quotes. REXX also permits strings to be built from unquoted text by converting the text's literal values to uppercase:

```
say hello everybody                        */* Types:  HELLO EVERYBODY */
```

In the above example, REXX looks for variables named **HELLO** and **EVERYBODY**. If it finds them, it substitutes their values; otherwise it converts the symbols to uppercase and uses the result.

Unquoted strings should be avoided, even though they seem convenient. REXX looks up each word in its symbol table, to see if it is a REXX variable, and then concatenates the words, causing minor performance overhead. The real danger, however, is that unexpected results and errors can result if variable names or REXX operators are present:

```
/* Errors with unquoted literal strings */

/* Sometimes fails (if any of the words is a variable) */
erase my file a                     /* Becomes 'ERASE MY FILE A' */
a = 200
erase my file a                /* Becomes 'ERASE MY FILE 200'  Error! */

/* Always fails (since it includes REXX operators) */
copyfile * data a = = b        /* "*" interpreted as multiplication */
```

REXX literal data should be in quoted strings to avoid this type of error. This is especially true in large programs, where innocent words could easily become the names of variables.

Short-circuit expressions

REXX does not "short-circuit" boolean expressions; it executes each clause in an expression even if a preceding clause guarantees the final true or false result. This means that care must be taken to avoid error conditions:

```
/* This results in an error if INTERVAL is zero */
if (interval <> 0) & (events/interval>threshold)
then say 'Slow down!'

/* This correctly guards against division by zero */
if (interval <> 0) then
   if (events/interval>threshold) then say 'Slow down!'
                                  else say 'Pour it on!'
```

Compound variables

REXX compound variables are a powerful method of storing and retrieving aggregates of information. Compound variables are specified with a **stem** followed by one or more tokens; these tokens are used like array subscripts in traditional languages. Unlike traditional arrays, the subscript need not be numeric, nor need the same stem always be used with the same number of subscripts. A powerful advantage of REXX is that compound variables can be accessed as "content address-able storage". This is illustrated below, where CMS filenames and file-types are used as indexes for a stemmed variable:

```
/* Use compound variables to answer questions about files */
fdate. = ''                                /* Set default value */
'EXECIO * DISKR FILES LIST A (FINIS STEM LIST.' /* Get list of files */
do i = 1 to list.0          /* Look at each (LIST.0 set by EXECIO) */
   parse var list.i file
   'LISTFILE' file '(LIFO DATE'
   parse pull fname ftype fmode lrecl recs blocks yymmdd hhmmss .
   fdate.fname.ftype = yymmdd hhmmss
end

do forever
   say 'Enter a filename and filetype or Quit'
   pull fname ftype
   if fname = 'QUIT' then leave
   created = fdate.fname.ftype
   if created = ''
   then say 'This file is not in the list of files'
   else say fname ftype 'was created' created
end
```

When numeric indices are used with compound variables, such as when **EXECIO** is used with the **STEM** option, it is customary for the "zeroth" variable element to contain the number of elements, as illus-trated below. This is useful but not always adhered to, so use caution when determining the number of elements to process. Two programs commonly used to create stemmed variables, **EXECIO** and CMS Pipelines, set the zeroth element.

To keep track of indices in a compound variable, maintain the list of suffixes in a string variable. You can then traverse the words in this variable if you need to process each compound variable:

```
/* Create a list of names */
namestem. = ''
name = GETNEXTNAME()
do while name <> ''
   if namestem.name = ''                      /* Name not seen yet? */
   then namelist = namelist name              /* Then remember it! */
   namestem.name = NAMEINFO(name)     /* Data associated with name */
   name = GETNEXTNAME()
end

/* Process each name in the list */
do while namelist <> ''
   parse var namelist name namelist      /* Take 1st name from list */
   say name namestem.name                /* Use saved data */
end
```

REXX SUBPROGRAMS

Modern programming style encourages building programs from subprograms, each of which implements a part of the overall task. Subprograms should implement logical abstractions, such as "get next input record" or "compute cosine of an angle".

Modularity in program design

Structuring programs along these lines yields important advantages. Programs are more compact, since common code sequences exist in only one place and are called from program parts that need them. Code can be placed in program libraries and reused in new applications to cut development time and cost.

Program maintainability is improved, since a change or correction to a task performed by a subroutine need only be made in one place. This also aids program portability. In the next example, subroutine GETNEXTRECORD detects whether it is running under CMS or Mansfield Software Group's Personal REXX on a PC, and uses appropriate I/O commands for each environment. If this code had to be corrected or changed to support new systems, changes could be made in the one subroutine, instead of in all program locations that read the input file.

```
/* Example using a subprogram for portable I/O */
x = GETNEXTRECORD(inputfilename)
do while x <> ''
   :
   x = GETNEXTRECORD(inputfilename)
end
   :
GETNEXTRECORD:            /* Do file I/O in either Personal REXX or VM */
   arg fileid
   parse source pcdos .
   if pcdos = 'DOS' then do            /* Use REXX I/O model on PC */
      if lines(fileid) = 0 then        /* Test for end-of-file */
         return ''
         else return linein(fileid)
   end
   else do                         /* Use CMS EXECIO command under VM */
      'EXECIO 1 DISKR' fileid '(VAR TEMP'
      if rc <> 0 then                  /* Was the read successful? */
         return ''
         else return temp
   end
```

In top-down design, programmers iteratively refine tasks by breaking them into smaller and smaller pieces until they can be expressed directly in programming language statements. In bottom-up design, programmers construct programs from low-level facilities by building larger subprograms from smaller ones. Most programmers combine both styles: a top-down viewpoint frames the overall program and the tasks needed to accomplish it; the bottom-up approach builds from a toolkit of routines.

Subprograms should also be used when a group of statements is longer than can be viewed at one time or has too many levels of control to be easily read. Statements can be moved to an internal REXX subprogram and a CALL statement inserted in their place. This is especially appropriate if the statements are taken at the boundary of an inner loop, IF, or SELECT that represents a single task or abstraction.

There is a slight performance penalty for calling a procedure instead of executing its contents in-line, but keeping code readable and maintainable makes it worthwhile. In-line code should not grow so long that it cannot be easily viewed and understood as a whole. If you program from printed listings, divide code when it spans a page of printout. Otherwise, divide code when it exceeds the number of lines of code easily viewed on your text editor's screen.

Scope of REXX identifiers

By default, REXX subprograms within a program file (internal subprograms) share identifiers visible to the calling program. This is useful, since calling and called programs can operate on the same data. This can also cause unexpected side effects and errors. In the example below, the subroutine's DO loop changes I and interferes with the calling program's loop.

```
/* Example of side effect caused by a shared variable */
do i = 1 to n
   call SUB
end
:
SUB:
do i = j to k              /* Will interfere with calling program */
   :
end
return
```

The PROCEDURE instruction isolates a subprogram from its calling environment. Identifiers it uses are private to it and separate from the rest of the program. Visibility of variables can be controlled by adding an EXPOSE list of shared variables. Subprograms should use PROCEDURE (which may also be used with **function** subprograms) to prevent side effects, especially in large programs, and use EXPOSE to deliberately make variables visible in both scopes. PROCEDURE and EXPOSE are illustrated below.

REXX uses **dynamic** scope instead of the **lexical** or **static** scope of most languages. In lexically scoped languages, variables known to a subprogram are specified by the subprogram's position in the program text and do not change from call to call. REXX scopes are dynamic, and a subprogram inherits the scope from which it is called.

When procedure S1 is first called, there is no variable C, so S1 types the literal value C. When S2 calls S1, S1 has access to S2's private variables B and C and types their values. It also no longer has access to the variable A. When S1 is called from S3, variables C and B are no longer known, but the original A variable is visible again.

```
/* Example of REXX dynamic scope */

/* Try this one out on your system! */
a = 1; b = 2;
call S1; call S2; call S3
  :
S1:                               /* A and B are visible */
say a b c              /* '1 2 C' -- unless called from S2 or S3 */
return
S2: procedure                 /* No calling variable visible */
b = 4                  /* Private variables known to this scope */
c = 3
say a b c                 /* 'A 4 3' -- literal values for 'A' */
call S1                   /* S1 will only see S2's variables */
return
S3: procedure expose a                    /* Only A is visible */
say a b c              /* '1 B C'  -- inherits 'A' variable */
call S1                   /* S1 called from S3 sees only 'a' */
return
```

Dynamic scope can add flexibility in programming, but can also add confusion! Observe caution when a procedure calls a subprogram that operates on shared variables, to ensure that it operates on the expected variables. Consistently use EXPOSE lists to identify global variables used in a procedure or function.

INTERACTION WITH THE EXTERNAL ENVIRONMENT

REXX is frequently used to interact with external environments: as a command processor for CMS, MVS, MS-DOS/PC-DOS, or Unix, or as a macro language processor for editors such as XEDIT, KEDIT, and ISPF and for other applications such as KPROBE, NETVIEW, and so on. This is a unique area of strength for REXX, but care must be taken to interact with the external environment properly and to execute without undesired side effects.

PARSE ARG

REXX programs receive command line arguments and function parameter list values through the REXX **ARG** and **PARSE ARG** instructions. When parsing inputs, the programmer must ensure that all required arguments have been provided and are valid.

For example, a program that processes a file under CMS will need at least the file's **filename** and **filetype**, but may provide a default **filemode** indicating which disk the file is on. The next example checks for a filename and filetype, and assumes filemode * (indicating that CMS should search for the file on all accessed disks) if no mode is given.

```
/* Program to process a file, with default filemode */

/* DOIT command:  Front-end DOIT module with REXX program */
arg fn ft fm
if fn = '' | ft = '' then signal MISSING  /* Name or type omitted! */
if fm = '' then fm = '*'        /* Default the mode if not given */
'ESTATE' fn ft fm                       /* See if the file exists */
if rc <> 0 then exit rc       /* Give up if the file's not there */
'DOIT' fn ft fm                     /* Otherwise process the file */
exit rc
```

Almost as important as checking for required inputs is ensuring that erroneous extra parameters are not provided. For example, the previous example could be changed to check for additional, unwanted parameters by using the changed **PARSE** statement and following **IF**:

```
/* Logic to test for extra argument */

/* DOIT command:  Front-end DOIT module with REXX program */
arg fn ft fm extraarg
if extraarg <> '' then       /* See if too many args were provided */
signal EXTRAARGGIVEN
   :
```

You may wish to eliminate this test if you prefer to be "forgiving" in your syntax checking. If so, you probably should insert an extra argument variable name or a . placeholder to prevent a typing mistake from causing an error in the REXX program. For example, if a user types **DOIT myfile data a extrajunk** in the first version of this command, REXX will assign the values **A EXTRAJUNK** to the variable **FM**. This will almost certainly cause a logic error further on, since the filemode should be a single letter specifying a CMS disk mode.

Preserving external option settings

Many REXX programs are used as part of a command environment, such as CMS or XEDIT. These systems have option settings that may be queried and set. When a REXX program changes one of these variables, it should return it to the prior value, in order to not disturb the operation of programs that may be calling it.

For example, in macros written for XEDIT, it is good practice to issue the command **SET LINEND OFF** to ensure that logical line-end characters (#) present in data are treated as data instead of as the end of command lines. The XEDIT command **EXTRACT** obtains the current setting of options like **LINEND**:

```
'COMMAND EXTRACT /LINEND'      /* Get current option LINEND setting */
'COMMAND SET LINEND OFF'    /* Ensure that any LINEND in NEWTEXT is */
'COMMAND REPLACE' newtext          /* not treated as one by XEDIT */
'COMMAND SET LINEND' linend.1           /* Reset LINEND setting */
```

Similar considerations apply equally to other XEDIT, CP, and CMS options, as well as to option settings available in other environments. In MS-DOS/PC-DOS and Unix, for example, the **PATH** and current directory should be preserved by applications. In CMS, the **CMSTYPE** option, used to allow or suppress CMS terminal output, is often abused. EXECs should be careful to save and restore the existing setting:

```
/* Saving and restoring CMSTYPE */
ht = CMSFLAG('CMSTYPE')                          /* Get current flag */
'SET CMSTYPE HT'                    /* Halt Typing to suppress noise */
:
if ht then 'SET CMSTYPE RT'           /* Resume typing if appropriate */

/* Saving and restoring CP's IMSG (informational message) */
parse value diag(8,'QUERY SET') with . 'IMSG' imsgvalue .
'CP SET IMSG OFF'            /* Don't want informational message */
'CP PURGE RDR' spoolid                /* from this PURGE command */
'CP SET IMSG' imsgvalue                 /* Restore IMSG setting */
```

Preserving stack contents

CMS programs frequently communicate via the **CMS program stack**, a logical buffer of lines to pass from program to program, or act as simulated keyboard input. REXX programs that use the stack should not disturb the stack's current contents; a common error is to accidentally read lines already on the stack, disrupting both the program's logic and that of a possible calling program.

In the next example, the REXX program **OUTER EXEC** stacks a line for each disk accessed by CMS. On the first call to **INNER EXEC**, **INNER** stacks one line for each file on the first accessed disk, but after processing them, consumes the remaining lines stacked by **OUTER**:

```
/* INNER EXEC reads lines that belong to OUTER EXEC */

/* OUTER EXEC */
'QUERY DISK (STACK'          /* Stack info about each CMS minidisk */
do i = 1 to queued()                /* Loop over the stacked lines */
```

```
   parse pull . . mode .        /* Look at information for each disk */
   'EXEC INNER' mode            /* Process each accessed mode */
end

/* INNER EXEC */
arg mode .
'LISTFILE * *' mode '(STACK'  /* Stack a line for each file on disk */
do i = 1 to queued()            /* Loop over all stacked lines */
   parse pull fn ft fm .        /* Look at information for each file */
     :
end
```

The most general method to prevent this in CMS is to create and
destroy a new stack level for the program's exclusive use, as shown
below. CMS allows multiple levels of program stack to be created and
destroyed; each program can create its own level and process it without
disturbing the current stack contents, by remembering the number of
lines to process:

```
/* Using MAKEBUF to create a stack level */

/* INNER EXEC */
arg mode .
q = queued()                   /* Get number stacked before we start */
'MAKEBUF'                                      /* Make a buffer */
bufno = rc                                     /* Save its number */
'LISTFILE * *' mode '(STACK' /* Stack a line for each file on disk */
do i = 1 to queued()-q       /* Process all lines in current buffer */
   parse pull fn ft fm .       /* Look at information for each file */
     :
end
'DROPBUF' bufno            /* Remove the buffer, restore prior state */
```

An additional method is to add a sentinel value that cannot possibly
appear in the true stacked lines (be careful here!) and use that in place
of counting lines:

```
/* Using a sentinel value to detect end-of-stack */
push '/**/'                               /* LIFO stack sentinel */
'LISTFILE * *' mode '(LIFO'               /* Stack lines LIFO order */
do forever
   parse pull fn ft fm .
   if fn = '/**/' then leave              /* Found sentinel:  quit */
     :
end
```

CONCLUSION

Good programming style can make REXX programs more reliable, efficient, and readable. While there is no single "correct" style, attention to
matters of style can improve the quality of REXX programs.

6

REXX Idioms

By Philip H. Smith III

Like users of any programming language, REXX programmers are familiar with its idioms—constructs and techniques unique to REXX, powerful but unintuitive uses of its facilities, and tricks which exploit REXX-operating system interface features.

Because of REXX's VM origins, most of the last category depend on VM-specific features, or on emulation of VM operating system-level features in other environments (for example, the Mansfield Personal REXX emulation of the CMS program/console stack, or EXECIO in MVS/TSO).

Idioms are used in REXX for the same reasons they are used in other computing and natural languages:

Performance	An idiom may be more efficient than other coding choices.
Functionality	There is sometimes no other reasonable alternative.
Elegance	An idiom may appear obscure, while in fact offering a powerful and concise means to an end.

These reasons equate to the same thing: a better way to perform necessary work.

A danger in exploiting idioms is a tendency towards overly clever code—which, while clear to the author when created, is difficult or impossible for another programmer (or, sometimes, the author) to understand months or years later. Examples of this include elaborate schemes to avoid generating multiple short-term variables (loop counters, for example), or assembler-style constructs based on modulo return codes.

However, careful use of idioms improves REXX performance, readability, and productivity.

Idioms discussed in this chapter are all clever to varying degrees; it is up to individual programmers to decide whether a particular technique is too obscure for inclusion in a personal REXX toolbox.

LOGICAL VARIABLES AND LOGICAL VALUES

REXX logical variables have values of 0 or 1. Logical variables can be tested implicitly:

```
initialized = 0
:
initialized = 1
:
if initialized then . . .
```

rather than:

```
initialized = 0
:
initialized = 1
:
if initialized = 1 then . . .
```

or:

```
initialized = 'NO'
:
initialized = 'YES'
:
if initialized = 'YES' then . . .
```

While the differences may seem slight, the first example is more readable and efficient.

Some programmers may wish to use symbolic values rather than 0 and 1:

```
true = 1; false = 0
:
initialized = false
:
initialized = true
:
if initialized then . . .
```

This adds minimal overhead for handling variables TRUE and FALSE, but can improve readability.

Any REXX comparison yields a logical value; output from TRACE Intermediates shows this, in >O> entries. This is why logical variables can be tested implicitly: the test is actually a simplified "normal" REXX comparison!

Many built-in REXX functions which return values of 0 or 1 may appear in comparisons instead of using an intermediate variable:

```
if datatype(count, 'W') then . . .
```

not:

```
count_type = datatype(count, 'W')
if count_type then &ellip
```

Advantages are obvious: code is more compact, and creation of a single-use variable is avoided.

User-written functions which return logical values can aid in creating compact, readable code. In complex applications, such functions may be advisable even if they will be called only once: a single function call whose purpose is obvious—for example, a CHECKFILE which verifies that a fileid is valid and exists—is more readable and, because of localization of function, often easier to maintain or port to another system than the same code embedded in the mainline.

Logical values can be used when creating functions which return logical values or when setting logical variables. For example, CHECKFILE might be as simple as:

```
CHECKFILE:
procedure
arg fn ft fm
'ESTATE' fn ft fm
return (rc = 0)
```

(The parentheses in the last line are optional, but aid readability.) The RETURN evaluates the expression RC = 0 and returns the result: if the RC variable is indeed equal to zero, a 1 is returned; if it is non-zero, a 0 is returned. CHECKFILE thus might be used:

```
do until CHECKFILE(fn ft fm)
   say 'Enter fileid:'
   pull fn ft fm
end
```

Similarly, mainline code can use logical values to set a logical variable to be tested later:

```
'SUBCOM XEDIT'
xedit = (rc = 0) & ¬cmsflag('SUBSET')     /* 1 if non-subset XEDIT */
:
if xedit then address xedit 'MSG' text
else say text
```

Logical variable **XEDIT** is set to 1 if XEDIT is active and CMS SUB-SET is not; this variable is tested later to determine where output should be routed.

Logical variables can also be used in arithmetic. For example, to determine the number of days in a particular year:

```
year = substr(date('S'), 1, 4)
days = 365 + (year//100 <> 0) * (year//4 = 0)
```

While obscure at first glance, this sets **DAYS** to **365** in all cases except leap years (years divisible by four which are not also centuries) and to **366** in leap years.

Another complex example handles the case where two values are allowable—for example, where a version of **CHECKFILE** should accept a return code of **28** (indicating file not found):

```
do until CHECKFILE(fn ft fm) = 0
   say 'Enter fileid:'
   pull fn ft fm
end
:
CHECKFILE:
procedure
arg fn ft fm
'ESTATE' fn ft fm
return rc * (rc <> 28)
```

This example is perhaps overly clever, but experienced REXX programmers will recognize its elegance and power and will probably find it worthwhile. It returns **0** if the **ESTATE** return code is **0** or **28**, and the return code otherwise (for example, if a part of the specified fileid is invalid).

A simple **IF** would also suffice:

```
if rc = 28 then return 0
else return rc
```

but requires an additional line and is less efficient.

If one of several conditions should return the same result, logical values can also be used, in conjunction with **FIND** or **WORDPOS** (**WORD-POS** is part of SAA REXX, unlike **FIND**). For example, if **CHECKFILE** should return **1** for return codes **0**, **28**, and **36**, and **0** otherwise:

```
CHECKFILE:
procedure
arg fn ft fm
'ESTATE' fn ft fm
return find('0 28 36', rc) > 0 /* Or return wordpos(rc, '0 28 36') > 0 */
```

This is easier to maintain than:

```
:
select
   when rc = 0 then return 1
   when rc = 28 then return 1
   when rc = 36 then return 1
   otherwise return 0
end
```

Finally, logical variables themselves can be used in boolean operations:

```
initialized = 0
fileidfound = 0
:
initialized = (rc = 0)
:
fileidfound = CHECKFILE(fn ft fm)
:
if initialized & fileidfound then . . .
```

Logical variables and values can simplify and improve the efficiency of complex programs, while maintaining readability.

NESTED IF STATEMENTS

REXX allows logical (boolean) expressions in **IF** statements:

```
if a = b & (c = d | e = f) then . . .
```

Unlike some languages, REXX evaluates the entire logical expression when the **IF** executes. In cases such as the above, this causes no problem. However, consider the following, where COSTLY is a function requiring significant resources to execute:

```
if a = b & COSTLY(d, e, f) then . . .
```

If **A** is not equal to **B**, the function call is (probably) wasted.

In these cases, the following might be preferable:

```
if a = b then if COSTLY(d, e, f) then . . .
```

If **A** and **B** are unequal, the first **IF** fails, so COSTLY is not invoked.

In some cases, one might *want* the entire expression evaluated (perhaps because each function may have desirable side effects); recognize how REXX handles such cases, and use nested **IF**s when appropriate.

PARSE

The PARSE instruction is one of the most powerful yet underutilized REXX facilities, and is unique to the language. As such, "normal" uses of PARSE qualify as REXX idioms.

PARSE can process variables, data from the CMS console and program stacks, function responses, and REXX internal information (PARSE SOURCE, PARSE VERSION).

Data can be parsed based on blank-delimited tokens, literal strings, variable strings, absolute column positions, relative column positions, and (in IBM OS/2 and AS/400 REXX, or other REXX language level 4.00 implementations) variable column positions.

EXEC 2 programmers will remember writing complex EXEC 2 code to decompose a standard CMS parameter list:

```
somecommand fn ft fm(someoption)
```

In REXX, PARSE makes it easy:

```
line = 'somecommand fn ft fm(someoptions)'
 :
parse var line cmd fn ft fm '(' options ')' .
```

PARSE is usually faster than multiple SUBSTR calls, and is easier to read and maintain.

For example, parse a date into month, day, and year:

```
parse var date mm '/' dd '/' yy .
```

not:

```
mm = substr(date, 1, 2)
dd = substr(date, 4, 2)
yy = substr(date, 7, 2)
```

PARSE is complex enough that an entire chapter in the *REXX User's Guide* is devoted to it, as well as an eight-page entry in the *REXX Language Reference*. REXX programmers should exploit PARSE.

Unintuitive PARSE uses include:

```
do until key <> ''
   say 'Enter key:'
   pull key
end
parse var somevar first 2 second 20 rest 1 . ':' +2 data 1 (key)
value .
```

The single **PARSE** does the work of three separate **PARSE** instructions:

```
   :
parse var somevar first 2 second 20 rest
parse var somevar . ':' +2 data
parse var somevar (key) value .
```

Special values returned by **PARSE SOURCE** can allow a single REXX program to be invoked via multiple synonyms, and to act differently based on the synonym used:

```
   :
parse source . . fname ftype . callname .
select
   when abbrev('APPLE', callname, 2) then . . .
   when abbrev('BANANA', callname, 2) then . . .
   when abbrev('CARROT', callname, 2) then . . .
   when abbrev('DAMSON', callname, 2) then . . .
   otherwise
   say 'Program "'fname ftype'" invoked as unknown fruit type.'
end
```

This example handles invocation via any of four different synonyms, with different results for each. This is especially useful for XEDIT macros which perform similar functions depending on invocation name or environment, as it simplifies maintenance and improves performance (since only one copy need be loaded into virtual storage).

PARSE SOURCE can also handle different invocation *types*—command, subroutine, or function:

```
   :
parse source . calltype .
   :
select
   when calltype = 'SUBROUTINE' then return
   when calltype = 'FUNCTION' then return answer
   otherwise
   say answer
   exit
end
```

If invoked as a subroutine, no result is returned (one could be, of course, and would set the special variable **RESULT**); if invoked as a function, a function result is returned; and if invoked as a command, the answer is simply typed.

Another use would be to verify the invocation type and, if not appropriate, issue an error message.

SUBROUTINE CALLS VS. FUNCTIONS

REXX functions may be called as subroutines using the **CALL** instruction. Usually this is not advantageous, since few functions do anything except return a result. However, the DIAG function—and some user-written functions—is sometimes useful without processing the result:

```
call diag 8, 'CLOSE 00D'
```

The result of the CLOSE is not of interest to the program, and using CALL makes this clear.

Little is actually saved: the function will return a value whether it is invoked as a function or as a subroutine, and REXX will place it in variable RESULT. The example is thus exactly equivalent to:

```
result = diag(8, 'CLOSE 00D')
```

However, using the CALL format makes it clear that the response is not used.

LIST PROCESSING

REXX is well suited to text processing, thanks to its lack of data typing and extensive string-related functions.

Programs often process lists of blank-delimited (or other-character-delimited) tokens, each of which must be processed separately. For example, to process options on a CMS command invocation:

```
  :
arg fn ft fm '(' options ')' .
do while options <> ''
   parse var options option options
   select
      when option = 'TYPE' then . . .
      when option = 'NOTYPE' then . . .
        :
      otherwise
      say 'Invalid option "'option'".'
      exit 24
   end
end
```

Initially the OPTIONS variable contains the entire options string. Each time the loop executes, the first token—the next option keyword—is parsed into OPTION; the SELECT then tests and handles each option specified. If an option keyword implies additional parameters following the keyword, the object of the WHEN clause can further parse OPTIONS, removing and validating those parameters.

STEMMED OR COMPOUND VARIABLES

REXX supports simple (scalar) and compound (vector and array) variables. REXX compound variables are also called **stemmed** variables, since each consists of a **stem** (a portion ending in a period) and a **tail** (the portion after the period, which in most other languages is a vector or array subscript). For example, the compound variable NAME.1 consists of the stem NAME. and the tail 1. Unlike most programming languages, however, REXX compound variables have few restrictions on vector and array subscripts. Moreover, the stem variable itself can be assigned a value in REXX:

```
name. = 'nothing'
```

This causes subsequent references to any variable with a stem of NAME. to return the same value as the stem, unless that particular compound variable has been explicitly assigned another value after the initial assignment. Of course, since the possible set of variables starting with that stem is infinite, setting the stem simply creates a single special-case variable, and any existing variables with that stem are deleted.

REXX compound variables are not usually referred to as vectors or arrays, since they are not truly either. In most languages, existence of a variable with a subscript of 3 implies the existence of similar variables with subscripts of 1 and 2 (and, in some languages, 0). In REXX such existence is neither required nor implied.

Languages with true arrays also may allow references to array members using a different array geometry than was defined. For example, in most FORTRAN implementations, member 11 of an array called ITEMS which was defined as a 10 by 10 array may be referred to as either ITEMS(2,1) or ITEMS(1,11). This works because when the array is defined, all the members occupy contiguous storage; thus ITEMS(2,1) immediately follows ITEMS(1,10), as would ITEMS(1,11) had the array been defined in that manner.

Since any two REXX compound variables sharing the same stem are extremely unlikely to occupy contiguous storage—and the tails need not be numeric—such tricks cannot be used.

However, lack of restriction on variable tails allows "associative memory", relating variable structures by tail value. This means that REXX can often do work which the program would otherwise need to:

```
   :
'EXECIO * DISKR' fn ft fm '(FINIS STEM L.'
data. = ''
do i = 1 to l.0
   parse var l.i user data
   data.user = data
end
do forever
   say 'Enter user name:'
   pull user
   if user = '' then leave
```

```
      if data.user = '' then say 'No value for' user'.'
      else say 'Value for' user 'is' data.user
end
```

Each time a user name is entered at the prompt, the program need not search a list of known users to see if that user is known or to find the value for that user. REXX does the work, and by setting a default value at the start, unknown names are handled easily. An alternative technique in this case is to eliminate setting the stem and to use the **SYMBOL** function to test whether each value exists:

```
:
'EXECIO * DISKR' fn ft fm '(FINIS STEM L.'
do i = 1 to l.0
   parse var l.i user data
   data.user = data
end
do forever
   say 'Enter user name:'
   pull user
   if user = '' then leave
   if symbol(data.user) = 'LIT' then  say 'No value for' user'.'
   else say 'Value for' user 'is' data.user
end
```

This method is one line shorter; however, it is vulnerable to previously defined values for **DATA.** variables and is less elegant in cases such as the following:

```
'EXECIO * DISKR' fn ft fm '(FINIS STEM L.'
count. = 0
users = ''
do i = 1 to l.0
   parse var l.i user .
   count.user = count.user + 1
   if find(users, user) = 0 then users = users user
end
do while users <> ''
   parse var users user users
   say 'User' user 'appeared' count.user 'times.'
end
```

By setting the stem, the program can increment **COUNT.** variables as each user occurs in the input file; again, REXX performs most of the work.

Without setting the stem, the first loop would need an additional test:

```
users = ''
do i = 1 to l.0
   parse var l.i user .
   if symbol(count.user) = 'LIT' then count.user = 1
```

```
      else count.user = count.user + 1
      if find(users, user) = 0 then users = users user
   end
```

This example also illustrates using a string to contain a set of blank-delimited compound variable tails. Since those tails are arbitrary tokens, there is no simple way to determine which variables are defined for a particular stem. When defined tails are recorded in a string, the program can parse the list of tails and reference each compound variable in turn.

Another example:

```
sets = translate(diag(8, 'QUERY SET'), ',', '15'x)
settings = ''
do while sets <> ''
   parse var sets set set '=' setting.set . ',' sets
   settings = settings set
end
:                                       /* Main processing */
do while settings <> ''
   parse var settings set settings
   'CP SET' set setting.set
end
```

The **TRANSLATE** normalizes the string returned by CP: it
changes the hexadecimal 15 which separates each logical line into a
comma, like those which separate the other values.

CP settings are preserved by the first loop and restored by the second, presumably after processing which may have changed them.

A caveat about using compound variables: tails may contain embedded blanks or mixed-case characters; numeric tails may also have leading zeros. Because of the unintuitive nature of such tails, most programmers rarely deliberately create such variables, but they can easily occur when reading data from a file.

For example, suppose **AGES FILE A2** contains the following:

```
*Age Name (First/last)   Number
   27 Sharon Sudol        000001
   29 Phil Smith          000002
   29 Mike Johnson        000003
   42 Gabe Goldberg       000004
   :
```

The following program would have problems:

```
arg n .           /* Only argument is first name or employee number */
:
'EXECIO * DISKR AGES FILE A2 (FINIS STEM L.'
age. = ''
do i = 2 to 1.0
   if substr(1.i, 1, 1) = '*' then iterate    /* Ignore comments */
```

```
    parse var l.i age.i first.i last.i number.i
    name = first.i              /* Get first name for AGE. reference */
    age.name = age.i            /* In case lookup by first name */
 end
 say age.n                 /* Look up by first name or employee number */
```

Aside from not checking for values other than the expected set, this fails because it sets variables **AGE.000001** and **AGE.Sharon** for Ms. Sudol, rather than **AGE.1** and **AGE.SHARON** as anticipated. Using **PARSE UPPER VAR** would avoid the latter problem.

A similar problem arises with leading and trailing blanks; assume a similar program which reads the retrieval key from the terminal:

```
 :
 pull n
 say age.n                 /* Look up by first name or employee number */
```

If the user enters ƀsharon (where "ƀ" is a leading blank), the lookup fails because variable **AGE.ƀSHARON** is not defined.

EXPLOITING THE RIGHT FUNCTION

The **RIGHT** built-in function right-aligns text (pads it with blanks or a fill character on the left). It can also retrieve the last n bytes of a string:

```
 :
 a = 'some string or other'
 b = right(a, 4)
```

This sets **B** to **ther**, not to **some** as might be expected. Rather than a problem, this is a feature to exploit: there are at least three other ways to get the **first** n bytes of a string (**SUBSTR**, **LEFT**, and **PARSE**), but **RIGHT** is the only simple way to get the **last** n bytes.

SPACE TO COMPRESS OUT UNWANTED CHARACTERS

The **SPACE** function places a specified number of blanks between words (blank-delimited tokens) in a string; however, it can also compress blanks or (in combination with **TRANSLATE**) any unwanted character from a string.

For example, to remove blanks from user input, slashes from a date, or commas from a number:

```
 :
 pull userinput
 /* Concatenate all words in whatever the user enters */
 userinput = space(userinput, 0)
 /* If the user entered A B C, USERINPUT is now = ABC */
```

```
⋮
/* Get USA format date with slashes removed */
date = space(translate(date('U'), ' ', '/'), 0)
/* If today is 01/31/90, this sets DATE to 013190 */
⋮
/* Remove commas from human-style large number */
n = '199,467,221'
n = space(translate(n, ' ', ','), 0)
/* Now N = 199467221 */
```

TRANSLATE TO REARRANGE A STRING

As its name implies, the **TRANSLATE** function performs character translations, using PL/I-style input and output translate tables. **TRANSLATE** has two idiomatic uses: to uppercase a string, and to rearrange a string column by column.

If no translation tables are specified, **TRANSLATE** uppercases the input string:

```
uvariable = translate(mvariable)
```

This is preferable to use of the **UPPER** instruction, which is not part of the formal REXX language specification and is thus not necessarily portable.

By specifying the input string (the first argument) and the input translate table (the third argument) as column positions, and the string to be operated on as the output translate table, **TRANSLATE** rearranges the string. For example, given a date in U.S. format (*mm/dd/yy*) which must be arranged in *yy/mm/dd/* order for sorting, one could use multiple **SUBSTR** calls:

```
⋮
date = '01/31/90'
⋮
date = substr(date, 7, 2)substr(date, 4, 3)substr(date, 1, 3)
/* Now DATE = 90/01/31 */
```

Using **TRANSLATE**, only one function call is required:

```
⋮
date = '01/31/90'
⋮
date = translate('78612345', date, '12345678')
/* Now DATE = 90/01/31 */
```

The "column positions" need not be numeric; the following works:

```
date = translate('abcdefgh', date, 'hgfedcba')
```

All that is required is that the first and third arguments relate to each other—that is, contain the same characters in different orders.

This last idiom is quite obscure, and warrants comments in code using it! In utility programs executed thousands of times per day, significant resources can be saved; in CMS REXX, the SUBSTR example above uses almost three times the resources of the TRANSLATE method.

SUMMARY

Like any tool, language idioms can be abused. Used carefully and correctly, they are a valuable and powerful tool which simplifies programs and makes them more efficient.

Tuning REXX Programs

By David Gomberg

WHY IS TUNING REQUIRED?

REXX, like other languages frequently implemented by interpreters, is sometimes accused of being a "slow" language. If this means that programs written in REXX are for some reason *inherently* slow, the charge is wrong. A language that permits clear and concise expression of the desired result will admit of fast implementations. Even if the language processor must analyze a program to determine that it is one for which a fast implementation is possible, this can be done. Such a feature is common in **optimizing compilers**.

Of course, a particular REXX implementation may have long program preparation times (typically interpreters require almost no preparation time, compilers somewhat longer) or may produce executable programs that are slow to execute. In this case, you must try to make your REXX program run faster, or **tune** it.

This chapter discusses ways to tune REXX code. Some suggestions apply to all REXX processors; other ideas will be more fruitful with one processor than with another. Finally, a summary of tuning ideas is presented.

OPPORTUNITIES FOR PERFORMANCE IMPROVEMENT

Boundary crossings

Many REXX programs issue host commands. These commands may be operating system commands, such as a program to modify the user's view of an existing system command, or they may be subcommands for a specific environment, such as editor macros.

Whenever a program issues many system commands, it must cross the interface or **boundary** between the REXX environment (which supports such activities as creating variables and modifying their values) and the host (system or editor) environment. Since these two environments are often quite isolated from one another, crossing the boundary may be costly.

To save on the cost of boundary crossing, try to minimize the number of times you cross. Reducing crossings can save up to 40 percent or more of the resources used by a program. One way to do this that is allowed by many hosts is to combine many operating system or editor commands into one super-command by stringing them together with separator characters in between. For example:

```
/* Issue three commands the slow way */
'SET BLIP ON'
'SET BLAP OFF'
'SET BLOP AUTO'
```

Might be improved:

```
/* Issue the same three commands a faster way */
'SET BLIP ON  #',
'SET BLAP OFF #',
'SET BLOP AUTO'
```

Note the # added between commands: this is the separator character in this example. By giving each command its own line, and using line continuation (with the comma), most of the clarity of the original is retained.

Sometimes it is difficult to see where two commands are issued consecutively because there is a lot of intervening REXX code. It is often worthwhile to analyze a program for host commands to see where they can be packed together.

Reduce work required

Another idea for reducing program execution cost involves reducing the amount of work required. Often one way of expressing a desired result involves much more computation than another way of expressing the same result. For example, here are two ways to set variable **A** to **0123456789**:

```
/* Set A = '0123456789' the slow way */
a = ''
do i = 0 to 9
   a = a||i
end
```

```
/* Set A = '0123456789' a faster way */
a = '0123456789'
```

Clearly the first example is easier to generalize if you want to expand the setting to **0001020304. . .99**, but often that generality is not needed—and you usually pay for it. If a numeric function that is needed in your program is called repeatedly with only a few known values, it may be faster to save them when they are computed and reuse them when they are needed again:

```
/* Generate factorials */
FACT:
arg n
i = 1
do j = 1 to n
   i = i*j
end
return i

/* Generate factorials; save and reuse values */
FACT:
arg n
if datatype(f.n) = 'NUM' then return f.n
i = 1
do j = 1 to n
   i = i*j
end
f.n = i
return i
```

Note that the second example is faster only if there are repeated calls to **FACT**: otherwise storing the result is just extra processing, and costs resources instead of saving them.

IDENTIFYING TUNING OPPORTUNITIES

Avoid "myths"

The most important idea in program tuning is to avoid generating "myths"—rules about how to make programs faster that may or may not be true in another program or another release of the software.

It is easy to be trapped by myths. For example, CMS REXX programmers "know" that using **PARSE** is "always" faster than assignment, but this may not be true in some programs or in other REXX implementations. **PARSE** is a much more general facility than assignment, and can sometimes be quite a bit slower, depending on the function requested. Even if a particular myth is successful a dozen times, remember that it is a myth. Be prepared to discard it as circumstances change and it becomes false.

Be realistic

Not every program has critical performance requirements. A program run once a month to print mailing labels may take ten minutes and still be quite acceptable; the same ten minutes would not do for an editor macro invoked several times per hour!

You cannot afford to tune every program, so expend your tuning resources on those which are most critical.

Use the right measurement tools

Measure *any* program whose resource use is so great as to be a concern. When you measure, use a metric that corresponds to the environment and users affected by your code.

Use **elapsed time** in single-task situations where the work of others does not interfere with your work. Use **processor time** (or expansion of parallel background work) when multitasking.

In the latter case, some follow-up work may be needed to determine whether processor use or input/output is causing time consumption. I/O interference can cause serious problems in some complex situations.

Plan to tune, but do it last

Write clearly; you cannot change a program to make it faster if it is so complex that you cannot easily understand how it works. Don't be obsessed by resource consumption from the beginning: first make the program as simple as possible; then ensure that it is correct; and finally, look at performance.

TUNING TECHNIQUES

Isolate the problem

The first critical step is isolating the problem. This means identifying the program part responsible for the unacceptable performance.

Often, but not always, this part of the program will involve a loop. Small test programs using loops to execute a code fragment repeatedly can be used to verify the performance problem and to evaluate alternative code to do the same job. For example, to process each word in a variable:

```
/* Use WORD() to get each word of a string */
do i = 1 to words(a)
   x = word(a, i)
   :
end
```

```
/* Use PARSE to get each word of a string */
do while a <> ''
   parse var a x a
   ⋮
end
```

These fragments successively assign each word of **A** to **X**. Which one is faster depends on the REXX implementation. Using code fragments is a good way to verify and measure which parts of your code are taking so much time.

A test program such as the **REXXTRY** example in the "Debugging" chapter can be invaluable in such experimentation.

Examine the cause

Now that you understand which part of the program is slow, examine the cause:

- Is the language implementation unacceptably slow?
- Is the program poorly implemented?
- Is REXX an inappropriate choice for the application?
- Is the application an inappropriate choice for the platform?

TUNING SOLUTIONS

Fix the language implementation

If you can demonstrate that the performance characteristics of a program are beyond reason, seek cooperation from the vendor of your implementation. For example, one REXX program took longer to terminate than to execute: the time required to execute the program statements was **less** than the time required to return to the operating system thereafter. In this case, the vendor fixed the problem in the next release.

If you cannot get adequate cooperation from the vendor, you must address the problem yourself. Some REXX implementations are distributed with source code. If you can adequately identify the performance problem and its source, you may be able to compose a remedy yourself and install it. If this corrects the trouble you are having you are done. Unfortunately, not all REXX implementations include source and sometimes fixes are difficult to develop.

Use REXX more effectively

Sometimes you can find another way to express the same ideas without using a slow construct. For example, to look up a word in a list, you might use:

```
/* Look up a word in a list */
list = linein('ONELINE.DAT')
:
in = index(list, ' 'word' ')
```

Or you could use a variable array:

```
/* Look up a word in a list */
l. = 0
list = linein('ONELINE.DAT')
do i = 1 to words(list)
   w = word(list, i)
   l.w = 1
end
:
in = l.word
```

INDEXing a long list is often slow, so the second method using variables may be significantly faster if the variable management scheme is sophisticated and fast.

Rewrite some or all of the program

REXX may not be the best choice of programming language for your application; in this case, the best fix may be to rewrite the offending code section in another language. This strategy is especially effective if your REXX processor is an interpreter and you have a compiler for REXX or another language available. You need not move all the code to the other environment—just the slow part.

   If you have only a clumsy language available that is fast (such as an assembler) and don't have the familiarity you would like with it, consider using a consultant for that part of the work. If you make that kind of investment, be sure that what you build is as general as possible without sacrificing efficiency.

Live with the situation

Lastly, you may decide that the cost of trying to address the problem you are suffering from is greater than the value of finding a solution. In this case, you may decide to live with the problem. When you are forced to adopt this alternative, it pays to continue to complain to the vendor, and in public forums such as user groups.

SUMMARY

When tuning REXX programs, look for the following possibilities:

1. Reduce crossing the interface to the host system.
2. Think of ways to do less, giving optimization a chance.

3. Defer tuning until the function is complete.

4. Validate the measurement method.

5. Isolate the problem.

6. Complain to the vendor.

7. Fix it / Avoid it / Live with it!

Most tuning efforts are more successful than you would initially think, so jump in to performance improvement in your most important programs!

User Interface Design and REXX

By Richard Schafer

BASIC PRINCIPLES

There are many good sources for basic principles of user interface design, and many lists of basic principles that should be followed. Sometimes the area is called **human-computer interaction**, sometimes **human factors**, but the invariant is a concern for user-centered software design, based on research into how humans behave when faced with computer tasks. Although different studies list different principles in different ways, a short list of important principles will usually include:

Consistency	What users see and do should be consistent, and how the program reacts to similar user actions should be consistent.
Simplicity	Users should not need to understand the complexity of the tools being used.
Naturalness	Sometimes known as **intuitiveness**, or the principle of the least surprise. Users should not be surprised at how the program acts, and should feel that the interface matches their intuitive predictions.
Feedback	Programs should let users know the result of an action, good *or* bad.

Visibility   Users should not have to remember previous
                                actions in order to proceed further, but
                                should be given visual clues.

Software developers writing user interfaces in REXX should
remember these principles (or an equivalent set) when designing the
interface. There is little reason today to design a program whose
interface only works in a line-at-a-time, question/answer mode.
Screens and dialog panels provide a much richer environment. At the
same time, developers should recognize that the program being
designed does not exist in a vacuum; it is not the only program the
user will ever see, but will probably be one of a collection of programs
that the user interacts with, so that consistency is a concern not just
inside the program, but between programs as well. Users may have
varying amounts of training, and what may seem natural or intuitive
to one may seem foreign or counterintuitive to another. In cases like
that, user interfaces must allow users to gain help about how to
interact with them.

Judicious use of color (when available) can aid and direct the user.
Bad use of color, however, can equally confuse users. (Probably everyone has seen programs where color was used so extensively that
almost everything was a different color, and the effect was blinding.)

SYSTEMS APPLICATION ARCHITECTURE—
COMMON USER ACCESS

In 1987, IBM announced Systems Application Architecture (SAA), a
scheme for building applications which can be developed and used
consistently across the major IBM architecture lines: the PS/2, the
AS/400, and System/370 platforms. Part of that architecture is
Common User Access (CUA), which defines rules and guidelines for
how user interfaces should be designed and implemented. CUA covers eight areas of the user interface:

1. Key usage
2. Scrolling
3. Selection
4. HELP
5. Mouse usage
6. Color and emphasis
7. Data entry
8. Messages

Each of these areas has specific rules and guidelines based on human factors research. (For a bibliography listing some recent references in the field, see the Recommended Readings appendix of the IBM *CUA Design Guide*.)

CUA is built around a recognition that the three IBM platforms for applications support users of a range of devices—from non-programmable terminals like 3270s to programmable workstations like PS/2s running OS/2 Extended Edition, which have a wide range of capabilities. For example, the typical user of a host-attached 3270 terminal does not have a mouse or other pointing device, and probably cannot display graphics. On the other hand, the user of a personal computer running OS/2 has both abilities. Different conceptual models are defined to allow software developers to maximize portability of their code and user knowledge. CUA defines two user interface models: the **Entry Model** for non-programmable terminals and the **Graphical Model** for the OS/2 environment. The Graphical Model has a **Text Subset**, defined for the non-programmable terminal environment which offers a limited collection of graphical interfaces.

ENTRY MODEL

The Entry Model is aimed at the many applications that are essentially data entry applications. These typically have panels with menus and prompts on 3270-type terminals. Many of these applications may be revisions of old applications, adapted to fit CUA screen layout guidelines. Screen elements like pop-up windows for dialogs or messages are optional in the Entry Model. Users can be asked to work with an action-object sequence, where the action to be performed is chosen first, then the object on which the action is to be performed is selected. An example of this kind of program is ISPF, where users work through a hierarchy of menus, selecting actions to be performed such as editing a file, and finally are presented with a panel where the file to be acted on can be selected. While Entry Model applications may be appreciated in situations where the user has no prior knowledge of the program (e.g., an automatic teller machine, which can assume no previous use), such a hierarchy of menus will frequently annoy experienced users.

The Entry Model screen typically is composed of the following elements, from top to bottom of the panel:

1. Panel title

2. Instructions

3. Selection or data entry fields

4. Message area

5. Command area

6. Function key area

All but the command and instruction areas are fundamental and must be present in a CUA-compliant application.

GRAPHICAL MODEL

In contrast to the Entry Model, the Graphical Model assumes that users have the capability of the OS/2 Presentation Manager to work with, including a mouse, pop-up windows, graphics, etc., and makes extensive use of the underlying windowing capabilities of OS/2. An application conforming to the Graphical Model has panels with action bars with pull-down menus, for example.

One other major difference between the Graphical Model and the Entry Model is the requirement for an object-action sequence, which means that the user first selects an object to be acted upon (perhaps by pointing at it and clicking a mouse button), then chooses an action to be performed, usually by making a choice from a pull-down menu off the action bar. In addition to the Entry Model panel features, action bars, scroll bars, and other features such as pop-up windows are now required, but the basic window arrangement stays the same, to allow the carryover of user knowledge.

THE TEXT SUBSET OF THE GRAPHICAL MODEL

The Text Subset of the Graphical Model is intended for users of non-programmable terminals, but follows the Graphical Model guidelines (such as the object-action sequence) wherever reasonable. Action bars, for example, are supported, although with some differences in how they are activated because of the half-duplex nature of 3270-type terminals. Of course, some features such as scroll bars and proportional fonts are no longer available because of the same hardware constraints.

DETAIL AND COMPLEXITY

Details about the exact rules defining the two models are found in a pair of IBM manuals, the *CUA Basic Interface Design Guide* and the *CUA Advanced Interface Design Guide*. The former contains the description of the Entry Model and the Text Subset, the latter the full Graphical Model. The number of detailed rules for CUA applications is little short of staggering, ranging from general screen layout (e.g., the command area must always be at the bottom of the screen, above the function key area) to explicit requirements for colors (e.g., unavailable choices in a pull-down menu on a color 3270 should be blue and low intensity with an * over the first character on a monochrome 3270) to what characters should be used for pop-up window borders. The table for color usage in the Entry Model and Text Subset fills approximately one and a half pages; the matrix of features fundamental though optional fills six pages.

REXX AS A LANGUAGE FOR CUA DEVELOPMENT

CUA is not a product. Recognizing this is fundamental to understanding the place that REXX has for CUA applications. Each software developer or company must develop (or buy) its own collection of tools to support the development of CUA-compliant applications. REXX is the official SAA Procedures Language, and as such is guaranteed to exist on every SAA system capable of supporting CUA, unlike the other SAA languages, which are supplementary billable products. Thus REXX is the only language that a developer can be sure of finding in every SAA environment. If only for prototyping an application into several platforms, REXX offers a handy "first step" to building structures of a CUA-compliant application.

However, REXX by itself is probably insufficient for building robust CUA applications without major effort. In OS/2, for example, the current implementation does not have good enough interfaces to the Presentation Manager to efficiently allow construction of windowed applications without building function packages (in some other language) to handle the system calls. In CMS, a REXX program using CMS Session Services cannot follow the recommendation for window borders, since Session Services enforces a different character for window border corners than is recommended by the *Basic Interface Design Guide*. In many cases, merely the minutiae of dealing with all the CUA requirements—building tools to support pop-up windows, action bars, etc.—are enough to deter someone from attempting to design a CUA application; tools are necessary to aid the REXX programmer in CUA development.

TOOLS TO AID DEVELOPMENT OF CUA REXX

A basic tool for development of CUA programs is a dialog manager, which can be given screen definitions and asked to present the screen, accept user input, then return data to the program. The SAA Dialog Tag Language (DTL), a markup language based on the International Standards Organization Standard General Markup Language, is used to define panels for use in CUA applications. The ISPF Dialog Manager is one of the tools available to transform DTL into displayable panels. REXX programs can call ISPF services for panel display and manipulation. In OS/2, the OS/2 Dialog Manager performs similar functions, although the interface between REXX and the Dialog Manager will need to be written in another language. CMS Session Services does not support DTL, but can build similar panels for programs that must not depend on anything but the native operating system for underlying support programs. The XMENU product from VM Systems Group has an XMENU/DTL component to allow the developer to generate panels in a powerful screen-painting environment, then automatically create the DTL for transportation to other environments.

Still, none of these tools provides the REXX developer with the ability to automatically ensure that his or her application follows the CUA guidelines. Merely using Dialog Tag Language does not guarantee that all six pages of CUA stylistic guidelines are followed, nor the one and a half pages of color guidelines. An interesting product from VM Systems Group, XMENU/SAA, offers a CUA Guide Mode, which aids in this process, developing CUA-compliant screens automatically. CUA Guide Mode prompts developers through the whole process, automatically positioning screen elements and assigning colors to match CUA requirements. Action bars, the command area, etc., are generated by XMENU CUA Guide Mode without the developer constantly having to check the panel against rules in the IBM Design Guides. In addition, since XMENU's REXX interface provides a convenient way of manipulating the resulting panels, passing data back and forth, dealing with PF keys, etc., the development time for a CUA-compliant REXX application may be considerably shortened.

CONCLUSION

There is nothing stopping the REXX programmer from building an easy-to-use human interface. With the assistance of any of several tools, the REXX programmer can quickly build everything, from a prototype of an application to test the human interface, to a complete application.

9

Debugging

By Peter Hunsberger

With REXX, as with most programming languages, there are really two forms of debugging:

1. Fixing coding errors generated while writing a program
2. Finding logic errors in the design of a program

Most of this chapter will concentrate on the first form of debugging, for which REXX offers a good set of tools.

For the second form of debugging, REXX offers about the same capabilities as any other third-generation language: the syntax of the language promotes good structure, but cannot help if the program design itself is incorrect. This does not prevent the writing and debugging of large REXX programs; it simply means that you must follow the same techniques for generating structured code as with any other language of its type. This includes top-down design, perhaps with CASE tools, or at a minimum sketching out the data and logic flows.

Pay attention to the variables and data flows you will use in a large REXX program. By default, REXX shares all variables between subroutines or functions that are part of the same file. However, there is currently no easy way to share large amounts of data between subroutines and functions coded in separate files. The default sharing of variables between routines in the same file can be the cause of difficult-to-find problems in REXX programs. It can be controlled by using EXPOSE with the PROCEDURE instruction. The fact that variables cannot easily be shared between routines in separate files may restrict freedom in implementing a design.

Other chapters in this book describe coding conventions to help create programs that can be debugged. They also point out how to avoid some common REXX programming errors, so that you will have less debugging to do in the first place. It is worth spending time evolving a coding style that can be read easily and that follows a standard. Even if no one else will ever see the program, it can be quite a shock returning to a poorly coded program after several years and trying to figure out what it does.

Guidelines to prevent the need for debugging

In general, you can make REXX debugging easier by following two guidelines:

1. Use the PROCEDURE instruction in subroutines and functions to ensure that only those variables you intend to share are common between routines. Occasionally, when large amounts of data are to be shared between routines, this may be cumbersome. This is only a guideline; don't get carried away.

2. Limit use of the INTERPRET instruction. It can have unexpected side effects, so ensure that you understand completely what it is doing. Some people suggest that it not be used unless absolutely necessary. It can, however, create very powerful programs with minimal work.

For CMS REXX programmers there is an additional guideline:

▪ Use MAKEBUF and DROPBUF commands in conjunction with the REXX QUEUED function to manipulate the CMS program stack. This helps ensure that only items you expect to be on the stack are seen by your program.

VM DEBUGGING CONSIDERATIONS

If you are maintaining someone else's program, determine if it was written to be maintained with EXECUPDT. If it was, there will be a version of it with a currency 1 character ("$" in the U.S.) as the first letter of the filetype—for example, $EXEC. The "Maintenance" chapter discusses how programs are maintained using EXECUPDT.

Beware of programs that have been loaded into memory with EXE-CLOAD. If you change such a program, you must either EXECDROP the copy in memory or **EXECLOAD** the new version using the **PUSH** option, so that you will execute the updated copy.

TOOLS AND TECHNIQUES

The most general debugging tool is the REXX **TRACE** instruction. It is discussed below; there are several other useful tools and techniques.

REXXTRY

Sooner or later you will encounter a REXX instruction or function that just does not seem to be producing the expected results. Perhaps the easiest way to find the true behavior of such an instruction is with a small test EXEC, often called **REXXTRY**:

```
/* REXXTRY -- Interpret REXX statements */
address command
trace o
say 'ADDRESS COMMAND and TRACE 0 in effect.'
say 'Enter EXIT to terminate.'
RESTART:
signal on SYNTAX
signal on ERROR
do forever
   parse pull string
   interpret string
end
exit
SYNTAX:
ERROR:
say 'Error' rc 'running' string': ' errortext(rc)'.'
signal RESTART
```

This program lets you type in REXX statements and see the results. You can enter multiple statements by separating them with semicolons ("`;`"); you can thus even test loops:

```
rexxtry
ADDRESS COMMAND and TRACE 0 in effect.
Enter EXIT to terminate.

do i = 1 to 10;say 'I is equal to' i;end
I is equal to 1
I is equal to 2
⋮
```

REXXTRY gracefully handles most errors so that you can correct them and try again.

OS/2 Standard Edition 1.3 and OS/2 Extended Edition 1.2 and higher provide a program called **PMREXX** which can be used to call this program and give it a nice OS/2 Presentation Manager interface.

You can sometimes use interactive tracing to get much the same results, but remember that errors may terminate the program, and variables you create may affect the program. **REXXTRY** is particularly useful while editing programs, as you can invoke it to see how an instruction works and exit back to editing.

TRACE instruction

The REXX **TRACE** instruction is probably the most common way to debug REXX programs. It has several operands that determine the type of tracing:

A   (All) Displays all instructions before execution. Somewhat useful for debugging.

C   (Commands) Displays commands sent to the operating system before execution and non-zero return codes after execution. Not particularly useful for most debugging.

E   (Errors) Traces commands sent to the operating system that result in errors. This is perhaps most useful for programs running in a service machine where activities are logged. It can be used to note unusual events. It is rarely used directly in debugging.

I   (Intermediates) Traces intermediate results during instruction evaluation. Particularly useful for understanding the **INTER-PRET** instruction, but can result in very lengthy displays when used in regular debugging.

L   (Labels) Traces labels passed during execution. Useful for determining if program flow is correct.

N   (Negative or Normal) Traces commands sent to the operating system that result in negative return codes. This is the default setting, and as such it can cause some problems. In particular, testing for an addressing environment that does not exist will return a negative return code. The solution is to use **TRACE O** instead.

O   (Off) Turns off all tracing.

R   (Results) Traces all final results of evaluation before execution. Perhaps the most useful trace for general debugging, particularly in combination with interactive tracing as explained below.

S   (Scan) Traces all remaining instructions without executing them. Useful for checking program syntax, but not much else. Some REXX implementations do not provide **TRACE Scan**.

Two modifiers can be used with the above operands:

!   Toggles **host command execution inhibit**. When host command execution inhibit is enabled, host commands—statements normally sent to the current **ADDRESS** environment for execution—are traced but not executed. This is useful for debugging programs where commands might have side effects you wish to avoid. For example, consider the case of debugging a program that will generate a VM saved segment: program testing should not destroy the current segment contents! Some REXX implementations do not provide **TRACE !**.

?   Toggles interactive tracing. With interactive tracing, the interpreter pauses after each instruction displayed by the current trace instruction. The next section discusses interactive tracing in detail.

Interactive tracing

The most powerful way to debug a REXX program is with **interactive tracing**. When interactive tracing is enabled, the interpreter stops after each statement traced. You can then enter any REXX instruction to further display the current state of the program or to alter the program state. For example, if you suspect that a subroutine is misbehaving, you might add **TRACE ?R** to the top of the subroutine. When execution reaches the first instruction of the subroutine, it will be executed and the interpreter will pause. You can then type in a command such as:

```
say x y
```

to display the contents of variables **X** and **Y**. If you press the **ENTER** key without entering anything, the interpreter executes the next instruction. To skip pausing for several instructions, you can enter the **TRACE** command with the number of pauses you want to skip. For example:

```
trace 10
```

executes the next 10 instructions without pausing. A negative number causes instructions to be skipped without displaying them. This can be useful for skipping large amounts of displayed data. For example, given the following code fragment:

```
trace ?i
do i = 1 to 100
   interpret x.i
end
```

a lot of data will be displayed during debugging. If you are not interested in the first 50 iterations through the loop, you might enter:

```
trace -150
```

at the first interactive prompt. Note that three instructions are evaluated for each pass through the loop.

You can enter an equals sign ("=") from the interactive tracing prompt to reexecute a statement or host command. This is useful when, for example, you correct the problem that caused the command to fail, and wish to test it without restarting the program.

When using interactive tracing, be careful of the **ADDRESS** environment in effect, and make sure to use proper strings to execute commands. For example, when tracing an XEDIT macro on CMS, you might want to list all files of a certain type on your A-disk. Do this with a command similar to the following:

```
address command 'LISTFILE TEST* DATA'
```

The **ADDRESS COMMAND** ensures that the command goes to CMS rather than to XEDIT. The quotes around the **LISTFILE** command ensure that it is not treated as a set of REXX variables. Without the quotes, REXX would try to multiply the contents of variable **TEST** by the contents of variable **DATA**, which would probably result in an error—and certainly in unexpected results!

When you are finished with interactive tracing, you can use either the **TRACE O** instruction to end all tracing, or the **EXIT** instruction to terminate the program. The latter is particularly useful if ending the program won't have any side effects, since it lets you quickly resume editing the program to correct any problems found.

SIGNAL ON

The REXX **SIGNAL** instruction can also be useful for debugging some programs. In particular, **SIGNAL ON NOVALUE** can find commands not enclosed in quotes or that use uninitialized variables.

Programs that use **INTERPRET** may also include **SIGNAL ON SYNTAX** and **SIGNAL ON ERROR** to catch errors caused by bad data passed to **INTERPRET**.

CALL ON

REXX language levels 3.46 and 4.0 add the **CALL ON** instruction. This works essentially like the **SIGNAL ON** instruction except that it allows returning from the error handler with continued program execution. This in itself is useful for programs that can have multiple points of failure, but must provide error recovery and continue execution. In addition, this feature can be exploited to create debugging capabilities allowing examination and possibly modification of commands before they are sent to the operating system. For example, a REXX EXEC that only sends commands to CMS could use:

```
trace o
call on ERROR
address test
```

If the **TEST** subcommand environment does not exist (the normal case), an error will be generated whenever a command is executed. **TRACE O** suppresses the trace resulting from the negative return code caused when attempting to address a nonexistent addressing environment that would result if the default trace mode was in effect. This causes the REXX interpreter to call subroutine **ERROR** for each command that would normally be executed. This subroutine can determine the instruction causing the error using function call **SOURCELINE (SIGL)**. Such a routine might resemble the following:

```
ERROR:
e_data = sourceline(sigl)
say 'Command to be executed:'
say e_data
say 'Execute, Skip, or set Return code? (E/S/R rc)'
pull e_answer +1 1 . ret
select
   when e_answer = 'E' then address command e_data
   when e_answer = 'R' then rc = ret
   otherwise rc = 0
end
return
```

This allows conditional command execution. More sophisticated handlers might also allow modifying the command or changing variables to be passed to the command. The capability to set the return code is useful for injecting errors to test program error handling.

In this example, a **PROCEDURE** instruction is not used with the error handler, so that any variables can be used as part of the command to be executed.

The EXECCOMM interface

With some REXX implementations (including any which comply with the SAA definition), it is possible for external programs to access variables created by REXX.

For CMS this interface is called **EXECCOMM**. It is an assembler language-level interface, called via SVC 202 with the fourth word of the extended parameter list pointing to an SHVBLOCK (mapped by **SHVBLOCK MACRO**).

Non-REXX programs that use REXX programs as macros will often use the **EXECCOMM** interface to pass information back and forth between themselves and the macro. For example, this is how the XEDIT **EXTRACT** subcommand sets REXX variables. A consideration when using this interface is that multiple REXX variables can be created or accessed using a single **EXECCOMM** call; make sure to chain through all of the SHVBLOCKs when debugging such a program, to be sure you know all variables affected.

REXXDUMP
One **EXECCOMM** function allows chaining through all variables that currently exist in the program. This allows writing a short program to display all variables currently active in the program. Alternatively, you might create a version of the program to display only variables matching parameters passed as program arguments. Note that this interface does not return the initialized value of a variable stem; that is, given:

```
a. = ''
a.1 = 'hi'
a.9 = 'there'
```

the interface will return *only* the values of variables **A.1** and **A.9**, not the **A.** variable stem.

This type of program is particularly useful in conjunction with programs that use the **INTERPRET** instruction to create new variables. For large numbers of variables it can be faster than using interactive trace to look at each variable. It can also tell you if unexpected variables were created. For example, you may find that you initialized a variable using a misspelled variable name.

The REXX compiler
Installations that have the REXX compiler may want to exploit it for the additional debugging it can provide. In particular, a REXX program may execute without errors, yet still contain syntax errors in some (unexecuted) parts of the program. Using the interpreter, these errors will be found only if all code paths are tested. Since the REXX compiler examines and reconciles all code in a program, it finds and reports these types of errors.

10

Maintenance

By Peter Hunsberger

There are two reasons for modifying a program:

1. The program function needs to be modified.

2. A program problem needs correction.

In both cases, the first requirement for maintenance is a well-written program with good structure. If you cannot follow program flow, it will be difficult to modify and maintain.

The second requirement for maintenance is good documentation. Even if you have written the program yourself, sooner or later you will find yourself wondering what a particular piece of code does. If you have not documented the program, it may take hours to figure out. Even worse, you may figure out (or remember) only part of the program function, and make modifications that ignore other functions that the program performs.

Part of program maintenance is also updating the associated documentation.

Minor and major enhancements

For planning purposes you may want to divide maintenance into two types:

Minor   Enhancements that can be done in a few days or less

Major   Enhancements that require more than a few days work

Depending on your installation and how you work, "a few days" will vary; the reason for making this distinction is to allow you to better plan work loads. Minor enhancements are considered part of routine maintenance and are done by regular support staff. Major enhancements are scheduled work items to be started and completed on predetermined dates. Such enhancements may be done by support staff or a different development group.

This division of labor helps ensure that support staff does not bog down in making major enhancements, and instead can provide quick turnaround on minor enhancements. Also, since major enhancements will probably involve more changes to the program, this process helps ensure that enough time is allocated to do such changes, and that they will not be rushed.

Sometimes many minor enhancements are grouped together and scheduled as one major enhancement. This is particularly true if support staff only fixes bugs, but this can at best be a judgment call, as discussed below.

Bugs versus new function

Whenever you make functional changes to a program, also update the end-user documentation. This may also be true for bug fixes: one person's bug is another person's feature. Sometimes this results in a requirement for a functional enhancement, such as a new option that allows both old buggy behavior and new corrected behavior. At some point you may find that this type of bug fix becomes a major enhancement. When this happens, it may be best to leave it and schedule it as part of a major enhancement process.

Another chapter discusses **debugging**: tracking down and fixing bugs.

CHANGE HISTORY

When changing a program, it is a good idea to record the changes. In VM, some of this can be done for you by using **EXECUPDT** and the CMS update scheme to maintain your program, as explained below. By physically tracking program changes, a maintenance history benefits you and other programmers. This is particularly true where more than one person may work on a given program. Such a history should track who made a change, when, and why. This history can often be kept as comments in the program.

VM-SPECIFIC MAINTENANCE

Shared minidisks

If you change a program on a disk that many users also access in Read/Only mode, ensure that you do not destroy the version currently in use. To do this, rename the existing version and then copy over the new version. Many installations use an EXEC to do this to minimize the time during which no usable file is on the disk. For example:

```
/* EXEC to copy files to the B-disk */
arg fn ft fm .
if ft = '' then exit 24              /* Need at least 2 arguments */
if fm = '' then fm = 'A'       /* Default to copying from A-disk */
tempfile = 'COPYB CMSUT1 B0'
address command
'ESTATE' fn ft fm                        /* Make sure file exists */
if rc <> 0 then exit rc
oldft = strip(left(ft, 5))'OLD'
'ERASE' fn oldft 'B'                /* Get rid of any old version */
'ERASE' tempfile
'COPYFILE' fn ft fm tempfile '( OLDDATE'      /* Copy new version */
if rc <> 0 then exit rc
'RENAME' fn ft 'B =' oldft 'B0'   /* Rename current version to old */
if rc <> 0 then exit rc
'RENAME' tempfile fn ft 'B2'      /* Rename new version to current */
exit rc
```

This EXEC retains only one old version of the file. If you copy the same file twice in a row, some people that have accessed the disk may experience errors. You might add more robust error handling, or allow mixed-case fileids.

EXECUPDT

Components of the VM operating system have long been maintained with programs using the CMS update scheme. The process for creating such update files is documented in the *CMS User's Guide*. The basics are as follows:

1. The input file must be fixed format (RECFM F). Prior to CMS 6, it must also have a logical record length (LRECL) of 80; in later releases, the LRECL may be between 80 and 255 inclusive. The input file must also contain sequence numbers in the last eight columns of each line (columns 73 to 80, if the file is RECFM F, LRECL 80). To separate such files from the final executable form of the program, they are given a filetype that starts with a currency 1 character ("$" in the U.S.); for example, $EXEC or $XEDIT.

2. **Control** files, with filetype CNTRL, describe the update hierarchy; the actual updates are listed in **auxiliary control** or **AUX**
files, with filetype AUXxxxxx. Control filenames can be anything
significant to you or your installation. As an example, file PSS
CNTRL might contain:

```
TEXT MACS DMSSP CMSLIB OSMACRO
TEXT AUXUSR
TEXT AUXLCL
TEXT AUXBEL
TEXT AUXPSS
```

This file specifies four different levels of auxiliary control file, from
AUXPSS through AUXUSR (notice that the control file is processed
from the bottom up). The MACS statement is optional for REXX programs, but is necessary for most other languages.
3. Auxiliary control files list updates to be applied to a specific
program. The filename corresponds to the program being maintained, and the filetype to the level of update from the CNTRL
file above. As an example, a file named MENU AUXPSS might
contain:

```
PSS065 Allow MENUOLD and REXX MENU command to work together
PSS055 Fix to MENU system for VM/SP 5
PSS042 Level set, updates folded into source - 88-08-03
```

Updates are specified by the first token on each line and are followed by an optional description. Updates are applied from the
bottom up, that is, PSS042 would be applied first in the example.
4. Actual update files contain code changes. They have the same
filename as the program to be updated and the filetype specified
in the first token of the auxiliary update file. For example, using
the above auxiliary control file, the first update would be named
MENU PSS042.

The most common way to create these update files is using XEDIT
with the UPDATE or CTL options. To create a fix for program MENU
EXEC, you would edit MENU AUXPSS auxiliary control file and add the
line:

```
PSS066 Fixes to MENU system for VM/ESA 1
```

The command:

```
XEDIT MENU $EXEC (CTL PSS
```

would apply the updates in MENU AUXPSS to the MENU $EXEC source
file. Changes made using XEDIT will create update control records

in **MENU PSS066**, using a specific CMS update format. The XEDIT **UNTIL** option can be used to stop applying updates at a particular update. For example:

```
XEDIT MENU EXEC (CTL PSS UNTIL PSS042
```

This simplifies changing a specific update without changing CNTRL and AUX files. If an update that follows such a changed update depends on it, you may have to manually change the later update to reflect new sequence numbers. If you attempt to apply updates and receive an error message, you can XEDIT the update files involved (the one you changed and the later one which would not apply) and resolve the line numbering conflict manually, changing the control records to reflect the new sequence numbers.

After creating the update, you create a new version of the program using the **EXECUPDT** command:

```
EXECUPDT MENU EXEC (CTL PSS
```

This applies updates implied by **PSS CNTRL** to **MENU $EXEC** (**MENU PSS042**, **MENU PSS055**, **MENU PSS065**, and **MENU PSS066**) and creates a new **MENU EXEC**. If you specify the filetype with the **EXECUPDT** command (it defaults to **EXEC**), you do not include the leading currency symbol.

Restrictions and alternatives

Although the above process is an extremely powerful way to track changes to a program, it can be somewhat cumbersome. In particular, if a fix or enhancement requires significant changes and testing, you may spend more time in generating the updated file than in testing. There is nothing to stop you from modifying the real program directly. That is, you can change the **EXEC** file from the above examples—but don't change the **$EXEC** file, lest you make a mistake! In particular, if you wish to add a **TRACE** instruction for debugging, go ahead and edit the program directly. You may even make an initial test version of the fix by editing the file directly. Once you have determined that it works, you can generate the update and apply it. Since a new final version of the end program will be created using **EXECUPDT**, you need not worry about changes made to the previously generated version. Thus, for an **EXEC**, a typical sequence of maintenance events might be:

1. Edit the **EXEC** to add **TRACE** to find the problem.

2. Edit the **EXEC** to create a test version of the fix.

3. Test the changed version of the **EXEC**.

4. Edit the $EXEC using the CTL option to create an update-format version of the fix.

5. Use EXECUPDT to create the new EXEC.

6. Test the new EXEC.

7. Update the documentation.

Some installations enhance the CMS update program and XEDIT to allow variable format (RECFM V) files to be updated by placing sequence numbers in columns 1 to 8 of the file instead of the last eight columns. This simplifies coding programs which allow source lines longer than 72, and allows more natural coding styles for REXX. The CMS 6 enhancement allowing input files of up to 255 characters reduces the need for such a modification.

Another problem with EXECUPDT is that you must manage the source file for the program. If only a few people are responsible for changing the program, this should be minor, but if responsibility is spread across many people, you may find people making conflicting changes. In such cases, you may need some form of source management. This may be as simple as a file that records who is working on a given program at any point, or as complicated as a commercial source management system.

REXX compiler considerations

The CMS REXX compiler can introduce source management considerations similar to those discussed above. You may also wish to use EXECUPDT with the compiler. This is possible—you must just name source files appropriately.

When modifying a program to be compiled, remember that INTER-PRET is not supported, and work around this restriction. Similarly, special compiler options must be used for the SOURCELINE function, and it is probably best not to use it.

11

Documentation

By Peter Hunsberger

There are basically three forms of documentation to accompany a
REXX program:

1. The program itself

2. End-user documentation

3. Documentation for support staff

The chapter on coding style explains how to create readable, self-
documenting code, so not much more on that topic will be said here.

End-user documentation depends on the application itself, and
should not normally depend on the language used to create the program. However, when the REXX **INTERPRET** instruction is used to
execute user-supplied text, it is important to note its limitations. In
particular, you should mention that all structures (**IF**s, **DO** loops, etc.)
must be completed on a single line. For example, the following could
not be executed by **INTERPRET**:

```
if option = '' then option = '(TEST'
else option = '('option
```

This would have to be entered as:

```
if option = '' then option = '(TEST'; else option = '('option
```

To facilitate later maintenance, REXX program documentation should cover several areas:

- Purpose (including what it was *not* designed to do)
- Structure
- Expected inputs and outputs, including return codes produced
- External routines called, not including common operating system commands (such as **EXECIO** and **MAKEBUF** in CMS)

Documentation of what each statement does should be part of the program comments, and not maintained separately. Again, **INTER-PRET** may be an exception, particularly if it is used to execute user-supplied input.

IN-LINE COMMENTS

There are several schools of thoughts about commenting REXX programs. To some extent this is caused by the fact that comments can slow down REXX processing. In particular, do *not* separate comments from instructions with semicolons ("*;*"), as this creates two clauses that the interpreter maintains separately. For example, the semicolon should be removed from:

```
do i = 1 to 100;            /* Process the input */
```

This is not necessary if the program will be compiled.

Some commenting styles put comments in front of the instructions:

```
/* Process the input */        do i = 1 to 100
```

This is a matter of personal taste, or might be specified in installation coding standards.

Most programs should contain a header block of comments that explains the program's purpose, any special considerations, and information such as the author and the maintenance history. Some programmers prefer to put such blocks at the end of the program, so that the interpreter need not parse them when starting the program. This does not save much, since the first external subroutine referenced will cause the comments to be parsed anyway. However, if you prefer this coding style, it is useful to include a comment at the beginning of the file indicating that the rest of the comments are at the end (most people read programs from the beginning, not the end).

INTERNAL DOCUMENTATION

Non-trivial programs should include at least a short explanation that is displayed if incorrect parameters are provided. In addition, many people like to allow for such HELP to be invoked explicitly, usually by entering a question mark ("?") as the first argument. For example:

```
/* Example of internal HELP documentation */
parse arg fn ft fm extra '(' options
if fn = '?' | extra <> '' then signal HELP
  :
HELP:
say 'Format is:
say '          fn ft fm ( options'
say 'Where:'
say '          fn - is the filename of the file to processed.'
  :
exit 24
```

Some programmers maintain this explanation as comments, which are displayed using the SOURCELINE function. However, this may not provide any advantages, and it requires that the program know (and maintain) line numbers of the HELP information. It also complicates using the REXX compiler.

EXTERNAL DOCUMENTATION

The techniques shown above are adequate for small programs. For large programs with large amounts of documentation, such techniques may slow execution. In addition, changing documentation requires modifying the program itself. In such cases, it is wise to use external documentation. Doing so also allows end-user documentation to be accessed independently of the program or to be included as part of a HELP system.

External documentation can be displayed using the CMS HELP command:

```
if fn = '?' | extra <> '' then address command 'HELP MYPROG'
```

For OS/2 you can use the VIEW command:

```
if fn = '?' | extra <> '' then 'VIEW MYPROG.INF'
```

In both cases, files must be appropriately formatted. For OS/2, the raw input file must also be compiled; this is worthwhile, since the the OS/2 VIEW command provides powerful hyper-text capabilities and allows images to be included in the documentation.

Other operating systems provide other means of displaying HELP files. Some VM installations have alternatives to the CMS HELP command. Again, installation standards may determine what is appropriate for your programs.

12

Object-Oriented REXX

By Simon Nash

INTRODUCTION

Object-oriented programming is not a new idea; it was introduced in the Simula language in the 1960s, refined by successive generations of Smalltalk through the 1970s, and exposed to a wide audience by the Smalltalk-80 system in the early 1980s. Smalltalk-80 created considerable interest in object-oriented programming, with many people seeing the object-oriented paradigm as an opportunity for a significant advance in software technology; this interest has grown steadily. Object-oriented techniques have started to take a place within mainstream programming, with the introduction of object-oriented variants of established languages such as C and Pascal. Smalltalk is becoming increasingly popular, and new object-oriented languages such as Actor and Eiffel have appeared.

Growing interest in object-oriented programming has created an environment in which software vendors see an **object-oriented** label for their products as highly desirable. Language designers are creating object-oriented variants of almost every existing programming language. In this climate, it would be only too easy to produce a "me-too" object-oriented REXX that simply follows this trend. Such a language might well compromise traditional strengths of REXX, while offering no significant benefits over other object-oriented languages. Alternatively, REXX could ignore the development of object-oriented programming technology as irrelevant to its purposes. This could eventually result in a decline in REXX's popularity in an increasingly object-oriented world.

It is against this background that IBM is researching object-oriented extensions for REXX. The objectives are to evaluate the need for such extensions and to produce a design for them that emphasizes the essential REXX objective of simplicity for the programmer. It is intended that the resulting language follow the spirit of REXX, maintain the usability of REXX, extend the usefulness of REXX, and have some particular advantages as an object-oriented programming language.

In the tradition of REXX, this design has been implemented as a running prototype, available to the internal IBM user community. The practical experience that is being gained from using object-oriented REXX is being put to good use as the design is refined. Though this work has successfully demonstrated the usefulness of object-oriented REXX, there is no commitment that it will be available in any IBM product.

MOTIVATION AND BENEFITS

REXX is typically used as a procedures language, in which it invokes various externally supplied services, together with control logic and some degree of user interaction. External services are usually invoked by means of string commands, but procedure and function calls can also be used. Control logic is provided by REXX language facilities. User interaction may include command options to the REXX program, simple REXX stream-based input/output, or externally provided menu, panel, or dialog services. In all these cases, user interaction is under the control of the REXX program, which has a single sequential thread of control, and user input (and other) events can be received only when specifically requested by the REXX programmer.

This model of user interaction is well suited to single-tasking operating systems such as CMS and DOS, which support only a single thread of control per user. REXX programs for such systems can provide user interfaces that compare favorably with what could be achieved by programming in another language. Indeed, REXX often allows such interfaces to be created more productively than in other languages, and REXX is therefore often used specifically to support user interaction.

The last few years have seen the emergence of graphical user interfaces that present a very different model of user interaction. The user-program interaction is no longer controlled by the program, with the user providing input when requested by the program; instead, the user controls program operation by providing any input event at any time, to which the program must respond. The natural platform for this user interaction model is an operating system that integrates support for graphics, multitasking, and windowing. This combination of features allows users to work with multiple applications concurrently, enabling substantially greater personal productivity than is possible with a single-tasking system.

Programming this new style of application in REXX presents problems. The single-threaded nature of a REXX program makes it difficult for it to be driven by arbitrary user interaction events occuring at arbitrary times. In addition, the complexity and cost of dealing with the APIs (Application Programming Interfaces) provided by typical full-featured windowing systems go far beyond reasonable bounds for a language with the simplicity and usability goals of REXX. Any attempt to solve these problems by providing necessary services in a form suitable for use by REXX encounters the problem that REXX deals only with character strings, an abstraction that is not a good match for the user interface objects that are being manipulated. These difficulties mean that REXX cannot easily be used when a state-of-the-art graphical user interface is required. Instead, these user interfaces are implemented either by programming in a less productive lower-level language, or by means of a specialized interface builder.

It is the desire to provide REXX support for such programming that has provided the primary motivation for research into design of object-oriented extensions to REXX. With object-oriented extensions, REXX can create applications that fully support graphical user interfaces, event-driven programming, and concurrent programming. In the REXX tradition, the extended language provides excellent usability, flexibility, and productivity for the creation of these new-style applications. Full compatibility with current REXX provides an easy migration path for existing REXX programs (and programmers).

Although the ability to manipulate user interface objects is very important, REXX object support has much wider applicability. Objects are a natural abstraction for many real-world entities as diverse as books, bank accounts, orders, and mailboxes. In the domain of software, they can function as abstract data types for either general-purpose or special-purpose use. Integration of concurrency allows REXX to control and synchronize a number of concurrent activities. These features enhance the applicability of REXX for such uses as cooperative and distributed processing, multimedia scripting, and discrete event simulation, as well as all current uses of REXX. REXX programs can also exploit the well-known benefits of object-oriented programming, which include better program structuring using data abstraction and encapsulation, and easier code reuse through class inheritance and object composition.

LANGUAGE DESIGN CONSIDERATIONS

The addition of object-oriented capabilities to an existing programming language presents interesting challenges. Of particular interest is the relationship between the base language and the new object-oriented features. A common approach is to create a **hybrid** object-oriented language which combines use of the base language to manipulate existing data types with new language constructs to create and manipulate a new **object** data type. With this approach, there are varying degrees of integration of the new object-oriented programming model into the base language. A well-integrated model, typified by C++ and Object Pascal, ensures a coherent language in which object extensions blend well with the existing language framework, though perhaps at the cost of some flexibility in the object-oriented mechanisms provided. The alternative approach, taken for example by Objective-C, incorporates object mechanisms designed to support a particular programming model into a base language that has a very different programming model, leading almost to a language within a language.

There are many ways in which object support could be added to REXX. The chosen design was the result of a desire to produce a language that retains REXX's strengths of simplicity and usability while adding power in the form of object-oriented programming and concurrency. These goals led to the development of a unified conceptual framework for the extended language, rather than a sharp distinction between the base language and the extensions. The result is that, unlike most other object-oriented extensions of existing languages, the extended language does not adopt the hybrid approach described above. Instead, object-oriented REXX is a **pure** object-oriented language in the sense that every data item is an object, including REXX strings.

OBJECTS AND MESSAGES

All data in a REXX program takes the form of character strings, with numbers being a special case of strings. The addition of object support means that this is no longer the case. The fundamental unit of data is now an **object**, not a string, and the value of a variable is an

object reference, which can be thought of as a pointer to an object. Objects can be strings and numbers, as before, but they can also be other things, such as windows, icons, vectors, or databases. They provide a powerful new abstraction facility for REXX programmers and bring the benefits of object-oriented programming to REXX. These powerful new facilities are integrated into the language as upward-compatible extensions, ensuring that current (string-based) REXX programs run unchanged.

In object-oriented REXX, an object is the basic unit of data. The data it contains is **encapsulated**, i.e., cannot be directly accessed or manipulated from outside the object. Instead, a request must be made to the object for the information or action desired. These requests are known as **messages** and are the only means by which objects communicate. A message contains a **message name** (e.g., PRINT or +), which specifies the kind of request being made, and may contain argument values. When a **sender** object sends a message to a **receiver** object, the receiver runs a **method** (determined by the message name) that performs the requested action and sends a **reply message** (which may carry a **result object**) back to the sender. In summary, an object is a combination of some encapsulated data (its **state**) and methods which act on that data (its **behavior**).

Messages can be sent in various ways. The most common way involves a new syntax for general message sending. This uses the tilde (~) character, which is currently unused in REXX. New kinds of terms and clauses are introduced for messaging. For example, the expression assigned in:

```
new_rect = myrectangle~rotate(angle)
```

is a messaging term that sends the message ROTATE to the rectangle object MYRECTANGLE. The message has one argument: the number object ANGLE. Examples of messaging clauses are:

```
myfile~open('R')
myfile~close
```

which open and close the file object MYFILE.

Messaging terms and clauses have the same syntax; the difference is the context in which they appear. They consist of an optional receiver, followed by the messaging tilde, followed by a message name, followed by an optional argument list enclosed in parentheses, with arguments separated by commas.

Messaging terms and clauses differ only in their treatment of the result object. A messaging term evaluates to its result object (like a REXX function call), whereas a messaging clause sets the variable

RESULT to its result object if there is one (like a REXX **CALL** instruction).

REXX operators (e.g., "+") are also treated as messages to objects. This is shown in the following REXX program:

```
/* This illustrates the use of objects */
jack = 3
jill = jack + 4
```

The first instruction creates a new number object that has the value 3 and makes variable **JACK** refer to this object. The next instruction sends a message with a name of + and an argument of the number object **4** to the object referred to by variable **JACK** (the number **3**). This object runs its method for +, which performs the addition and creates a result object of the number **7**, and variable **JILL** is set to refer to this object.

This simple example shows how REXX arithmetic is handled with objects. String handling is similar: the objects are strings, and the methods correspond to the REXX string operators (e.g., | |) and built-in functions (e.g., **SUBSTR**).

USES OF MESSAGES

Messages can obtain information about objects. For example:

```
myrect_origin = myrectangle~origin
```

causes the rectangle object referred to by variable **MYRECTANGLE** to return its origin point, which is assigned to variable **MYRECT_ORIGIN**. This use of messaging generally involves a messaging term, as in the above example.

Another use of messages is as commands that cause objects to perform a desired action. For example:

```
myrectangle~setwidth(100)
```

sends a **SETWIDTH** message to the rectangle object, setting its width to 100 space units. This use of messaging often involves a messaging clause, as in the above example.

The above examples show the sending of a single message. Messaging terms can also be combined to send a series of messages. For example:

```
left_side = myrectangle~origin~x
```

sends an **ORIGIN** message to a rectangle object, and then an **X** message to the point object that is the result of the **ORIGIN** method.

If the message receiver is omitted from a messaging term or clause, the message is sent to the current environment object. This gives a convenient way to refer to **public objects**, which are named objects provided for use in any method. For example:

```
time_now = ~clock~time
```

obtains the current time from the public CLOCK object. Since the CLOCK message specifies no receiver, it is sent to the environment object, which looks for the object it knows by the name CLOCK (the clock) and returns it. The second message TIME is then sent to the clock object.

CLASSES, SUBCLASSES, AND INHERITANCE

An object consists of state and behavior. Objects that have the same behavior can be categorized as a **class**. A class is represented by a **class object** that provides methods for the **instances** (i.e., members) of the class and is capable of creating a new instance of the class when sent a **new** message. For example, in a graphics system, all rectangle objects may have the same methods ORIGIN, WIDTH, HEIGHT, MOVE, SETSIZE, and DRAW, even though different rectangle objects have different positions and sizes (state data). A rectangle class object can therefore be defined, with all rectangles being instances of the rectangle class.

A class need not define all the methods it provides to its instances. It can be a **subclass** of some other class (its **superclass**), which means that it **inherits** (has access to) all the methods that its superclass provides. The subclass can override or supplement these inherited methods as required. A subclass is typically a specialization of its superclass; for example, the class of rectangles could be a subclass of the class of polygons. Support is also provided for **multiple inheritance**, which allows a class to inherit from more than one superclass.

Class objects can be sent messages just as any other object can. For example, a new AREA method can be defined for the public rectangle class by executing:

```
~rectangle~define('AREA', 'return self~width*self~height')
```

which creates a **method object** containing the code for the method and adds it to the rectangle class's collection of methods, giving it the name AREA. (The special variable SELF used in this method refers to the receiver of the AREA message.) The next time a rectangle object is created, it will have an AREA method that calculates its area. For example:

```
new_rect = ~rectangle~new(50, 50, 100, 100)
rect_area = new_rect~area
```

will assign 2500 to **RECT_AREA**.

It is important to understand the differences between the **DEFINE** and **AREA** methods in the above example. The **DEFINE** method is executed by the rectangle class object when it receives a **DEFINE** message; however, the **AREA** method is provided by the rectangle class to the rectangle objects that are instances of the class. This means that the rectangle class object cannot handle an **AREA** message; only rectangle objects (instances of the class) can. Conversely, rectangle objects cannot handle **DEFINE** messages; only the rectangle class object can. The **DEFINE** and **AREA** methods are not different in nature; they just play a different role with respect to the rectangle class. These roles are distinguished when necessary by referring to a class's **own methods** (executed by the class object, like **DEFINE**) and its **instance methods** (executed by the class's instance objects, like **AREA**).

Some objects are **primitive**, i.e., they are defined by the language and their behavior cannot be changed by reprogramming. Examples of such objects include numbers and character strings. In contrast, **programmable** objects are defined by a programmer, with behavior that is programmed in REXX (or a lower-level compiled language such as C). Examples of such objects include rectangles and classes.

OBJECT AND METHOD VARIABLES

A programmed object's encapsulated data consists of variables and their values. Just as in REXX, variables are created when they are assigned to, and are not declared. There are two kinds of variables: **object variables** are associated with an object and persist for the lifetime of that object, whereas **method variables** are associated with a method activation and cease to exist when the method returns. There are no global variables, but public objects can be used to hold systemwide information.

Each method must distinguish between the object and method variables to which it refers. It does so by exposing its object variables on a METHOD instruction, just as REXX allows variables from a caller to be exposed on a PROCEDURE instruction. For example, the instruction:

```
method expose a b. c
```

at the start of a method exposes the variables **A** and **C**, as well as any variable starting with the **B.** stem. This means that references to these variables are taken as referrring to object variables with these names, and all other variable references are taken as referring to method variables.

OBJECT-BASED CONCURRENCY

REXX does not provide concurrency, so REXX programs have a single sequential thread of control. A multitasking system allows more than one REXX program to be running at a time, but REXX provides no built-in means for coordinating the activities of such programs.

Object-oriented REXX supports concurrency by allowing any number of objects to be active (executing) at a time, exchanging messages to communicate and synchronize with each other. This is **object-based concurrency**, so called because the basic unit of concurrency is an object rather than a separate concept such as a process or thread. It is as if each object were a separate tiny computer, with its own processor to run its methods, some local memory for its object and method variables, and communication links to other objects for sending and receiving messages. This is a programmer's model that must be simulated to a greater or lesser extent according to the hardware and system execution environment being used.

The inherently concurrent nature of REXX objects carries with its advantages the potential for problems that would not arise with a sequential language. These include the following:

Synchronization problems	These are the result of events in different objects happening in an unexpected order. This is easily prevented by ensuring that the objects exchange appropriate synchronizing messages. In practice, it is rare that the normal message interchange between cooperating objects fails to provide the required synchronization.
Inconsistency problems	These can occur when data within an object is accessed by more than one method at a time. For example, a method may read data that is in an inconsistent state because of partial execution of another method that updates the same data. To prevent such problems, an object runs only a single method at a time unless the programmer explicitly specifies otherwise.
Deadlock	This results when a programming error results in two (or more) methods entering a blocked state that cannot be cleared until the other proceeds. Unfortunately, solutions to problems of synchronization and inconsistency can result in deadlock. There is no simple solution, but automatic deadlock detection and good debugging tools ease the problem considerably.

Concurrent execution of objects is initiated by means of **early reply**. This provides a reply (with optional result) to the sender before the end of the executing method, so that the sender can continue execution in parallel with the receiver from the point of reply. For example, a write method for a write-back cache could be written as:

```
parse arg data              /* Save data to be written */
reply 0                     /* Tell the sender all was OK */
self~disk_write(data)          /* Now write the data */
```

Concurrent execution can also be initiated by a message sender by means of a **START** message. For example, suppose:

```
nextline = infile~readline
```

performs a synchronous line read into variable **NEXTLINE**. The line read can be performed asynchronously by writing:

```
proxy = infile~start~readline
/* do other work */
nextline = proxy~result
```

which creates a proxy object that waits for the line read to complete while allowing the sender to proceed with other work. The proxy holds the result when it becomes available, and the sender obtains it from the proxy when required.

SUMMARY

REXX is a programming language designed for usability, with particular emphasis on string handling and decimal arithmetic. Adding object-oriented extensions and support for concurrency enhances its uses, particularly in the area of graphical user interfaces. The chosen design for object support integrates REXX facilities for dealing with character strings and numbers, combining the strengths and simplicity of REXX with the benefits of object-oriented programming. Concurrency is provided by means of simple high-level abstractions that exploit the object-based programming paradigm. The resulting extended language is a REXX that is equipped to play a leading role in the rapidly evolving world of computing in the 1990s.

ACKNOWLEDGMENTS

Many people have contributed to the design of object-oriented REXX. Brian Payton developed techniques for object-oriented programming in REXX and used these to produce a prototyping system. Bruce Lucas designed and prototyped an object-oriented REXX and demonstrated its use in building graphical user interfaces. John Bennett, Aran Lunzer, and Dave Mitchell worked with me on development of the current language and its prototype implementation, contributing many important ideas for the language. The members of IBM's REXX Architecture Board, particularly Mike Cowlishaw and Brian Marks, have helped improve the language in various ways. Alan Prescott has provided essential management support. Finally, Ian Brackenbury initiated this project and maintained a clear vision for it. The contributions of these and all who provided encouragement, ideas, and comments are much appreciated.

Usage

This section presents real-world REXX issues, describing how REXX is used to implement large applications, the value of REXX as a macro language, and the use of CMS function packages to extend the REXX language.

13

A Sample REXX Application— RiceMail

By Richard Schafer

OVERVIEW

RiceMail is a CMS electronic mail system, allowing CMS users an easy-to-use way of sending and receiving electronic mail, saving mail messages, and working with collections of saved mail called **notebooks**. Making heavy use of native CMS functions such as XEDIT, RiceMail consists of two user commands:

MAIL   for sending and receiving electronic mail

MAILBOOK   for working with saved electronic mail notebooks

  MAILBOOK, the oldest part of the current program, was originally developed in 1984 to complement an EXEC 2-based mail command written at MIT by Dave Burleigh. In 1986, the MIT program was replaced by the current **MAIL** program as a totally new REXX application, and merged with **MAILBOOK**. **MAIL** and **MAILBOOK** function essentially identically, with the major difference being the source of the electronic correspondence: the user's reader or a notebook on disk. (Actually, even that distinction is not exact, since one of **MAIL**'s functions is to move incoming mail from the user's reader to an "inbox" on disk.)

As this is an XEDIT-based application, both linemode and 3270 users are supported, although most users at the over 500 sites using the code are 3270 users, using full-screen displays. Users are presented with a menu of mail items which may be selected for reading, deleting, replying to, forwarding, or printing. The full power of XEDIT is available to the user.

GENERAL STRUCTURE

RiceMail consists of two entry programs, **MAIL EXEC** and **MAIL-BOOK EXEC**, which set up the environment and call XEDIT, passing control to **MAILBOOK XEDIT**, where all the work is done (note the zeros in **MAILBO0K**—this allows invocation of **MAILBOOK EXEC** from within XEDIT without accidentally invoking the XEDIT macro). There are three small assembler language routines and some small subsidiary REXX pieces:

MAILLOAD	loads a mail file from the reader directly into XEDIT storage (assembler).
IUCVTRAP	is a message-trapping routine written by Arty Ecock of the City University of New York.
RXSETVAR	replaces some **INTERPRET** statements (assembler).
MAILIDPR	is an RFC822 address parser (REXX).
MAILOPTS	is a standard option defaults setting routine.
MAILPROF	converts PROFS messages into RFC822 messages.

MAILBO0K XEDIT is approximately 8000 lines of REXX, with many subroutines, kept in a single REXX program to avoid the problem of sharing REXX variables between external routines. Two filetypes contain the record of electronic correspondence:

NOTEBOOK	is the actual collection of mail, in standard CMS NOTE-BOOK format.
NOTEINDX	is an index file for the notebook, for performance improvement; also contains cross-session information.

PROFILES

One of the most praised features of RiceMail is the amount of user tailorability it provides. Two levels of profiles are supported, called **MAIL-SYS XEDIT** and **MAILUSER XEDIT**, for site-wide option settings and individual user settings, respectively. Options are passed back and forth from the mainline code via **GLOBALV** variables. A pair of simple REXX programs named **GETMAIL** and **SETMAIL** allow the programs to query and set any of the long list of options, using a simpler syntax than the CMS **GLOBALV** command. **SETMAIL**, for example, is essentially:

```
parse arg option value
address command 'GLOBALV SELECT MAIL SETLP' option value
```

Since the profiles are REXX programs themselves, some users make full use of REXX's abilities to set options:

```
arg screenmode
cmd = GETMAIL('COMMAND')   /* Determine if this is MAIL or MAILBOOK */
if cmd = 'MAIL' then do
   select
      when screenmode = 'READ' then 'SET PF5 REPLY'
      when screenmode = 'SEND' then 'SET PF5 SEND'
      otherwise nop
   end
   'SETMAIL MENU.FIELDS FROM DATE SUBJECT SIZE'
end
else 'SETMAIL MENU.FIELDS FROM TO DATE SUBJECT'
```

Because the options are stored in GLOBALV variables, the entry programs take special care to save and restore these values when the command is called recursively. (Without that, calling **MAILBOOK** from inside **MAIL** would destroy the value of the **MENU.FIELDS** option in the above example.) One of the options is the name of who to contact should an error cause termination of the program, so that many sites insert a line in their **MAILSYS XEDIT** file of the form:

```
'SETMAIL CONTACT.PERSON the Operator at 555-1212'
```

so the error message will say **Contact the Operator at 555-1212 immediately**. There is tremendous synergy between REXX and XEDIT in the profiles. Some users have developed highly complex processing in their **MAILUSER** profile, setting everything from PF keys to **MAIL** options to XEDIT reserved lines.

RFC822 PARSER

Since the entire RiceMail system is to fit into the Internet and BITNET RFC822-format mail handling network, a key part of RiceMail is the **MAILIDPR** routine, which parses RFC822 addresses.

RFC822 describes a form of mail addressing in use at thousands of sites around the world connected via the Internet and BITNET. The basic form of an address is:

```
user@domain
```

where **domain** can be quickly described as a series of words separated by periods, and **user** can be anything acceptable to the administrative domain **domain**. In most environments, **user** is the userid of the person sending the mail. In CMS environments, **domain** can be as simple as an RSCS nodename. Thus a simple form of an RFC822 address would be:

```
MAILMNT@RICEVM1
```

If this were the extent of RFC822 addresses, parsing them would be as simple as:

```
parse var address user '@'domain
```

However, there are numerous complications. Comments (for example, a person's real name) can be included on either side (and even theoretically in the middle) of the **userid@domain** string by enclosing them in parentheses—and these comments may contain the @ character! The two most common forms of address currently in use are the following:

```
My Full Name <myuserid@mydomain>

myuserid@mydomain (My Full Name)
```

Multiple addresses can be present, separated by commas. The following example, taken from RFC822, shows a valid, but **very** complicated set of addresses:

```
Important folk:
Tom Softwood <Balsa@Tree.Root>,
"Sam Irving"@Other-Host;,
Standard Distribution:
   /main/davis/people/standard@Other-Host,
   "<Jones>standard.dist.3"@Tops-20-Host;
```

The REXX **PARSE** statement is not nearly capable of parsing this kind of syntax by itself. The traditional language means of parsing this would be a finite-state machine, examining the address character by character. REXX, however, allows taking chunks of the address string, as shown in the following extract:

```
/*******************************************************************/
QSTRINGS: procedure expose qstring. errors
/* Extract quoted strings from the address, replacing them with a */
/* placeholder, saving the extracted strings for possible later use.*/
parse arg string
q = 0
errors = 0
do forever
   parse var string leading '"' +0 bq +1 quoted '"' +0 eq +1 trailing
   if bq <> '"' then return leading
```

```
      if eq <> '"' then do
         queue 'EMSG Missing closing quote after string starting:',
          left(quoted, 10)
         errors = 8
         q = q + 1
         q5 = right(q, 5, '0')
         qstring.q5 = quoted
         return leading || 'AA'x || q5
      end
      q = q + 1
      q5 = right(q, 5, '0')
      qstring.q5 = quoted
      string = leading || 'AA'x || q5 || trailing
   end
```

Using routines like QSTRINGS allows the parser to reformat the address into chunks so that eventually it can be parsed with something like:

```
parse var addr leftcomment '<'user'@'domain'>' rightcomment
```

and finally pass back the **user**, **domain**, and perhaps a personal name to the mainline code.

USER INPUT PROCESSING

The main processing loop of **MAILBOOK XEDIT** is a loop surrounding an XEDIT **READ** subcommand, which puts its results on the stack. Because each of the three display modes of RiceMail (**read**, **send**, and **menu**) has different requirements for how the screen should be read, the read method is stored in a variable whenever a mode is created or reentered. Two basic stems of global variables are kept, named **global** and **mail_option**. Switching between the modes is then done by code like the following:

```
/* Perform the actual mode change, assuming ACTIVE_MODES */
/* has already been rotated. */
screen_mode = word(global.active_modes,1)
if screen_mode = 'NOMENU' then s_m = 'MENU'
else s_m = screen_mode
select
   when s_m = 'MENU' then do
      global.tty_prompt = 'MailMenu: Enter command or !'
      global.screen_read = 'NOCHANGE NUMBER TAG'
   end
   when s_m = 'SEND' then do
      global.tty_prompt = 'SendMail: Enter command or !'
      global.screen_read = 'ALL NUMBER TAG'
   end
   when s_m = 'READ' then do
      global.tty_prompt = 'ReadMail: Enter command or !'
      global.screen_read = 'CMDLINE TAG'
```

```
      end
      otherwise
      global.error_condition = 'Invalid screen mode in SwitchMode:',
                               screen_mode
      signal ERROR
   end
   'XEDIT' global.stamp '$$'s_m'$$ ='
```

Once the user is settled in a mode, however, RiceMail must interpret the input it is given. Although XEDIT allows users to define PF keys that take effect before, after, or instead of anything done to the screen, the REXX macro writer is not given enough information by the READ command to use that flexibility. Since most standard PF keys take effect afterwards, the code essentially requeues any PF or PA key to the end of the stacked input, as follows:

```
/* Functions defined for the PA keys are made to appear last on the */
/* stack:  the first time encountered, we push them to the back. */
   when type = 'PAK' then if cmdi <= onstk then do
      nstk = nstk + 1
      str.nstk = str.cmdi
   end
   else do
      if words(str.cmdi) = 3 & word(str.cmdi,3) = "=" then
      cmd = global.last_xedit_cmd.screen_mode
      else do
         parse var str.cmdi .  .  cmd
         cmd = 'PAK' cmd
      end
      call COMMAND
   end
```

As each input line is processed, if it is a command issued via PF key or the command line, RiceMail decides whether it is a **MAIL** command or not by a call to the **ABBREV** internal subroutine (discussed below), and attempts to execute the command, passing anything not known as a Mail command directly to XEDIT.

SOME INTERESTING TRICKS

ABBREV

The REXX **ABBREV** function allows a program to determine if one string is an abbreviation of another. In the situation where the program needs to determine whether a word is an abbreviation of one of a number of words, an extension to **ABBREV** must be devised. The following routine is how RiceMail handles this situation:

```
SHORT: procedure expose mail_option. global. me.
/* A function that checks whether its first argument is potentially */
/* an abbreviation of one of its additional arguments. */
arg needle, haystack
needle = ' 'needle
parse value ' 'haystack with (needle) +0 fullword minlength .
if ¬ datatype(minlength, 'W') then return 0
if fullword = ' ' | length(needle)-1 < minlength then return 0
else return find(haystack, fullword)
```

The **haystack** is a variable containing a series of words followed by the minimum abbreviation of the word. For example:

```
'QQUIT 2 SEND 2 PRINT 2 SWITCH 2'
```

Duplicate name handling

Like any reasonable electronic mail program, RiceMail allows the user the option of having multiple recipients for a message being composed. However, there being little point in sending the same message twice to the same person, a means of detecting duplicate recipients was needed. There are numerous approaches to this problem, but RiceMail chose a feature of REXX to handle the situation without complicated coding: using compound variables as a form of associative memory, essentially passing the search down to the level of REXX internals. REXX variable name substitution allows *any* character to be used in a variable name past the stem part, so that a variable name of:

```
global. johndoe@somewhere.earth.edu
```

is a valid variable name. The routine below returns a 1 or a 0, depending on whether or not the userid and domain pair has previously been used:

```
DUPLICATE:
/* Make sure not to add duplicate people to send lists. */
parse arg dup_user, dup_node, list
address = dup_user'@'translate(dup_node)
if mail_option.send.mixed.ignore then address = translate(address)
if symbol('SEND.LIST.ADDRESS') == 'VAR' then return 1
else do
    send.list.address = 1    .
    return 0
end
```

Compilation

Early versions of RiceMail used the REXX **INTERPRET** statement in a number of places, usually in order to set the value of a variable whose name would be known only at run-time. With the advent of the CMS

REXX compiler, however, with its significant performance advantages for a program like RiceMail, but no support for **INTERPRET**, some recoding was necessary. Most cases were solved by using a routine provided in an appendix to the compiler manual, **RXSETVAR**. This routine, written in assembler language, uses **EXECCOMM** to handle setting variables that would previously have required **INTERPRET** to accomplish, allowing changing (for example):

```
interpret array'.i = 'array'.j'
```

to:

```
call RXSETVAR array'.i', value(array'.j')
```

IBM graciously and explicitly chose *not* to copyright this routine, allowing software developers to use it freely.

DYNAMIC CALL

One use of **INTERPRET** in RiceMail remained, however, that could not be replaced by **RXSETVAR**. For ease of maintenance, the list of valid commands and their minimum abbreviations is stored in a global variable (actually, three: one for each display mode). After the command name being called is determined, the interpreted version of RiceMail would execute:

```
interpret 'call' cmd 'options'
```

where **cmd** was the name of the command expanded to full length to match the subroutine name, and **options** were any command line operands. The **CALL** statement, unlike most other REXX statements, does not allow variable substitutions to determine the name of the routine being called. How could this use of **INTERPRET** be replaced? After a number of attempts, a new routine, **XCALL**, was written which used **SIGNAL** to pass control to the correct routine. The original **CALL** statement was changed to:

```
global.command_word = cmd
call XCALL options
```

and the **XCALL** routine appears as follows:

```
XCALL:
signal value(global.command_word)
```

The dynamically determined subroutine is called, receiving the same argument that **XCALL** received, and returns directly to the point of the call to **XCALL**, so the **XCALL** routine does not need a **RETURN** statement itself.

This technique would not be sufficient if more than one argument needed to be passed to the eventual routine, but RiceMail never does that.

CONCLUSION

RiceMail has proved to be an extremely useful tool for many users, and a good example of the way in which REXX programs can build upon native CMS services to provide a much richer environment.

14

Complex Application Issues

By Graeme Hewson

INTRODUCTION

This chapter discusses writing and maintaining a complex REXX application. What is a complex application? Typically, it is a complete package with many users. It may be available commercially, or developed and used internally by an installation. The users will mostly be remote from the developers, which suggests that the package should enable them to become largely self-reliant in its use. The users should feel comfortable and confident in using the package.

Consider the following:

- Users need complete documentation about how to install the package, how to use it, and what to do if things go wrong. On-line help should be provided.

- The package may be used in ways not anticipated by the developer, perhaps in a host environment with an unusual configuration. Therefore, the package must be very flexible. This flexibility can be provided by the package automatically adapting to its environment, by a configuration file which the user can tailor, by a rich set of command options, or by a combination of these.

- A complex application is large in terms of the number of lines of code: it will inevitably contain bugs. It will also encounter situations outside its control, such as a required resource being unavailable. It must react gracefully to these internal and external errors and attempt to minimize disruption to users' work. Clear error messages help users quickly identify problem causes.

The needs of the developers must also be considered. A complex application is prone to change and enhancement; it should be written for change. Meaningful symbol names and useful comments aid familiarization (or refamiliarization!) with the program before changes are attempted. Changes should be well documented. A good development system will automatically track changes and allow them to be removed if necessary.

A complex application, then, is qualitatively as well as quantitatively different from a simpler application. A greater percentage of code is devoted to **cushioning** users—to detecting and reporting errors. Complexity arises not only in code but also in the supporting structure: documentation, packaging and distribution, and maintenance facilities.

Inevitably, in discussing ways in which REXX uses and interacts with an operating system, reference must be made to a particular operating system; this chapter is biased towards VM.

THE USER'S PERSPECTIVE

Consider how an application interacts with users and adapts to their working environments.

Configuring the application

An application comes to users with a default configuration. For instance, XEDIT, the CMS editor, puts the command line at the bottom of the screen, puts a scale line in the middle, and highlights the current line.

Once users are familiar with an application, they often want to customize it and automate the customization, so that each time the application is initialized, the customization is in effect.

Perhaps a supervisor wants the application to have a standard configuration for a group. The application can be customized to the group's standard settings and still allow individual users' settings, or possibly the supervisor could specify that users cannot change some settings. Further, a system administrator might provide a group of users with a standard configuration to ensure consistency of use.

Configuring interactive applications

If the application has a command line interface (that is, allows the user to issue commands as well as enter data in predefined screen areas), it may be convenient to store the configuration as a series of application subcommands in a **profile** macro. This macro may be just a special instance of a more general application macro facility which uses the CMS subcommand environment facility.

XEDIT, for instance, executes the **PROFILE XEDIT** macro on initialization; this macro is typically written in REXX. As the profile executes, it may issue subcommands to the **XEDIT** subcommand environment (application subcommand environment names are usually the same as the name of the application, as are macro filetypes). One such command is **EXTRACT**, by which the macro can request information about the file, the terminal, and so on. The information is returned from XEDIT in one or more REXX variables.

REXX programs cannot themselves create subcommand environments. A profile macro might pass commands to the REXX application through the external data queue (in CMS terminology, the program stack) by **QUEUE**ing or **PUSH**ing them. This is convenient for the application if it normally reads commands from the external data queue. A limitation of this technique is that a macro cannot check the results of commands it issues—it must issue them "blind". Another limitation is that macros cannot ask the application for a piece of information—all information the macro needs must be passed to it in advance by the calling program. Nevertheless, these may not always be serious limitations.

As a convenience to users, the application might have a **learn mode**. Rather than having to write a profile as a separate step, the user might be able to issue subcommands to the application, for automatic profile creation. XEDIT, for instance, has a subcommand (actually a macro) called **STATUS** which "remembers" over 50 settings in a macro it writes to disk. This macro can be executed later to restore the settings.

CMS global variables

Developers may choose to use a configuration file instead of, or as well as, a profile. There may be a standard operating system facility to read a configuration file on behalf of the application. An example of this in CMS is the use of **global variables**.

Several CMS commands take their default settings from global variables. Global variables are maintained by CMS, and may be set or read by all programs. When a program sets a global variable, it may tell CMS to maintain the variable permanently; CMS writes such variables' names and values to a disk file called **LASTING GLOBALV** and maintains them in storage. The CMS **GLOBALV** command manipulates global variables.

Users may set default options for some CMS commands using the
DEFAULTS command. For example:

```
defaults set help detail
```

sets defaults for HELP. DEFAULTS internally saves default settings
using GLOBALV commands.

The application may include a configuration program to provide a
similar function to DEFAULTS. This program might issue the following
command to CMS:

```
'GLOBALV SELECT group PUTP name1 name2 . . . namen'
```

GLOBALV keeps global variables in groups; the same variable name
may exist in different groups. Here *group* is the group name. The name
of the application might be a suitable group name. Global variables to
be set have the same names as REXX variables in the program—the
names of the REXX variables are passed to the GLOBALV command in
this example. GLOBALV does not uppercase the names (as the interpreter or compiler does), so they must be specified in uppercase. The
PUTP parameter causes global variables to be set permanently.

When the application initializes, it issues a GLOBALV command to
retrieve REXX variables:

```
'GLOBALV SELECT group GET name1 name2 . . . namen'
```

If the global variables are not already in storage, GLOBALV reads them
into storage from the user's LASTING GLOBALV file.

Although not required, it is a good idea for users to include the command GLOBALV INIT in their PROFILE EXEC. This does the following:

- Loads permanent global variables into storage.

- Compresses the LASTING GLOBALV file, if necessary, by removing
  redundant entries. When a permanent global variable is set, its entry
  is simply added at the end of the file. If the file is not compressed periodically, it grows indefinitely.

Adapting to the user's configuration

Just as users may configure an application, they may configure the
operating system in various ways, or system programmers may modify a vendor's default configuration. The application must allow for this
and make as few assumptions as possible. If the application makes
assumptions, it should, if possible, ensure that the required conditions
are met; assumptions should, of course, be documented.

Users should not be required to pass information to the application
if it can obtain the information by other means at run time. However,

users may wish to enter the information anyway (perhaps to override a default); it is possible for an application to be too "helpful", acting against the wishes of experienced users.

Obtaining information from CMS

Much information about CMS is available from the CMS QUERY command. This command normally displays output on the terminal, but may be told to return information in the program stack (external data queue). For example, if the program wished to write a work file on a minidisk, it could use the following code to find the read/write minidisk with the most room:

```
 :
'MAKEBUF'
queued = queued()
'QUERY DISK MAX (LIFO'
if queued()-queued < 2 then max_mode = ''
else parse pull . . max_mode .
'DROPBUF'
 :
```

The MAKEBUF command creates a new buffer in the CMS program stack in which the output of the QUERY command is stacked LIFO (last in, first out). The DROPBUF command drops the buffer, including the header line normally displayed on the terminal. If no read/write disk is accessed, the stack contains a message to this effect; there is no header line.

Obtaining information from CP

Normally, CP commands are issued from REXX programs by the CP command. The DIAG function, subcode 8, may be used instead, and returns command output to the program. For example, the following code fragment uses DIAG to determine if the virtual machine is logged on or disconnected (running without a terminal) and reacts accordingly:

```
parse value diag(8, 'QUERY VIRTUAL CONSOLE') with . . where .
if where == 'DISCONNECTED' then . . .
else . . .
```

Planning for large numbers

Sometimes numbers used in interacting with the operating system will exceed the default DIGITS setting of 9, and NUMERIC DIGITS 10 should be used instead. Newer VM versions support 31-bit storage addressing. CMS record numbers are 31-bit numbers; in some cases, a record number exceeding 9 decimal digits may be encountered.

The **ESTATE** and **ESTATEW** commands verify the existence of a disk file (the latter also verifies that the file is on a read/write disk). They should be used in preference to the older **STATE** and **STATEW** commands, which support only files of 65,535 records or less (that is, files whose size is a 16-bit number or less).

Parsing arguments

In CMS, the parsing facility can simplify parsing command arguments. The programmer defines the command syntax using the **Definition Language for Command Syntax** (DLCS); the definition is compiled and kept separately from the program in a syntax table. When the program executes, it calls the parser to validate arguments and expand any abbreviations. The parser can translate arguments from one national language (such as French or German) to the language the application expects; this facility is beyond the scope of this chapter.

Consider REXX program **MYPROG** with syntax:

```
MYPROG fn [{MYFILE|*} [fm]] [([options] [)]]
```

The command requires a filename to be specified. The filetype, if specified, must be **MYFILE** or * (which means the default, i.e., **MYFILE**). The filetype serves as a marker for the filemode, which, if specified, must be the third argument token. If required, options follow a left parenthesis. Assume valid options are:

```
FRom label
REPlace
MERGE
```

FROM may be abbreviated to two or three letters, and requires specification of a value (*label*). **REPLACE** and **MERGE** are keywords and do not take values. Options may be terminated with a right parenthesis, although this is not required.

The entire argument string is available to the program in **ARG(1)**. A REXX instruction to parse the string is:

```
arg fname ftype fmode extra '(' options ')'
```

with additional code to parse variable **OPTIONS**. The program must determine that if **FTYPE** was specified, it was specified correctly; that **EXTRA** was not specified; and so on. All this is done for it by the parser, which issues appropriate error messages if necessary.

In DLCS, the command syntax might be:

```
:DLCS APP USER AMENG :;
   :CMD 01/MYPROG MYPROG :;            :* The entry for MYPROG
```

```
:OPR FCN(FN) :;
:OPR FCN(FT(MYFILE),CHAR(*)) STOP :;
:OPR FCN(FM) :;
:OPT KWL(<FROM 2>) FCN(ALPHANUM) :;
:OPT KWL(<REPLACE 3>
          <MERGE 5>) :;
```

DLCS statements terminate with :; and may be continued on as many lines as necessary. Comments start with :* and continue to the end of the line.

The DLCS statement is the first statement in the source file (although comments may precede it).

APP is the application identifier for the command or commands following. The application identifier must be three alphanumeric characters; the first character must be alphabetic. For example, DMS is the application identifier for CMS itself.

USER specifies that the source file contains user syntax definition statements. When called by the program, the parser searches first for the user syntax definition. If the parser cannot find the user syntax definition, it uses a system syntax definition, if available. The system syntax table is saved in shared virtual storage to improve performance, but must be installed by the system programmer or administrator.

AMENG identifies the national language: American English.

Together, DLCS statement operands uniquely determine the filename of the compiled syntax table.

Commands are defined with CMD statements. 01/MYPROG is the **unique identifier** for the MYPROG command. The parser uses the unique identifier specified to it by the program to locate the correct entry in the syntax table. This allows having different commands with the same name; the program determines by context which definition to use. The unique identifier is a string of one to sixteen characters. The first character is used as an index key to speed access to definitions by using its EBCDIC value. If, though, the first two characters are hexadecimal digits (as in the example), their byte value is used as the key. For efficiency, keys in the table should be unique if possible; if there are more than 256 entries in the table, the keys should be evenly distributed by index key (that is, they should not all start with the same character).

The FNAME operand is defined with the first OPR statement. The parser uses the FN system function to validate the filename. There are about 20 system functions available. User functions can be coded in assembler language if necessary.

The second OPR statement defines the FTYPE operand. Here two functions are used. The FT function inspects the filetype, if specified, to see if it is MYFILE. If it is not MYFILE, the CHAR function is called, which checks to see if it is *. **STOP** means that the operand need not be specified and that if it is not, no more operands may follow; if the argument continues, it must contain a left parenthesis to mark the start of the options.

Similarly, if the third operand is specified, the third **OPR** statement inspects it to verify that it is a valid filemode.

CMS command options may be specified at execution time in any order; the order in which **OPT** statements are specified in the DLCS source file is immaterial. The first **OPT** statement defines a keyword-value pair. The **FROM** option may be abbreviated to a minimum of two letters, and its value must be alphanumeric. The second **OPT** statement defines the two keyword options. The statement has been written on two lines in the example to improve readability.

When the DLCS statements have been coded, they are compiled with the **CONVERT COMMANDS** command. If issued from within XEDIT, this command uses the current file if the filename is not specified.

The **MYPROG** program might start as follows:

```
/* Sample program to demonstrate the CMS command parser */
   address command
   false   = 0
   true    = 1
   applid  = 'APP'
   uniqueid = '01/MYPROG'
/* Set the defaults */
   ft      = 'MYFILE'
   fm      = 'A1'
   label   = ''
   replace = false
   merge   = false
   'SET LANGUAGE (ADD' applid 'USER'
   if rc <> 0 then exit rc
   'PARSECMD' uniqueid '(APPLID' applid
   if rc <> 0 then exit rc
/* Get operands; the parser has ensured that a filename is present */
   parse upper var token.2 fn 9
   optstart = false              /* Left parenthesis not seen */
   do i = 3 to token.0 while ¬ optstart
      select
         when code.i == 'OPTSTART' then optstart = true
         when i = 3 then nop     /* Filetype cannot be altered */
         when i = 4 then parse upper var token.i fm
         otherwise . . .
      end
   end
/* Get the options */
   do i = i to token.0 while optstart
      select
         when code.i == 'OPTEND' then optstart = false
         when token.i == 'FROM' then do
            i = i + 1
```

```
        label = token.i
      end
      when token.i == 'REPLACE' then replace = true
      when token.i == 'MERGE'   then merge   = true
      otherwise . . .
    end
  end
  :
```

SET LANGUAGE identifies the application to the parser and specifies that a user syntax table will be used.

PARSECMD gets the program's argument string directly; the program need not pass the string to the command. If **PARSECMD** detects a syntax error, it issues an error message and exits with return code **24**. If the argument string is syntactically correct, **PARSECMD** returns a number of variables to the program. The number of tokens in the program's command line—including the command name and any parentheses—is returned in variable **TOKEN.0**. The command name (as specified in the DLCS **CMD** statement) is returned in **TOKEN.1**, the filename is returned in **TOKEN.2**, and so on.

Corresponding to each **TOKEN.i** variable is a **validation code**, which describes the token and is returned in variable **CODE.i**. If the token is a left parenthesis (to mark the start of the options), the validation code is **OPTSTART**. If the token is a right parenthesis, the validation code is **OPTEND**. Anything following a right parenthesis in the argument string is considered a comment, and is returned in a single variable with validation code **COMMENT**. Keywords have validation code **KEYWORD**. If a token has been validated by a function, the validation code is the function name. For instance, **CODE.3** in the example could have value **FT** or **CHAR**. Finally, the command name has a validation code of **COMMAND**.

The parser returns keywords uppercased and expanded to their full lengths. This allows a simple test for the **FROM** keyword, for instance.

The parser does not translate values specified in the argument string; the program uppercases the filename and (if specified) the filemode. CMS expects a filemode to be in uppercase, but supports mixed-case filenames and filetypes (and is case-sensitive). By convention, though, user commands translate filenames and filetypes. It is suggested that this translation be done *only* in the routine which parses the user's argument string; subroutines should use the **PARSE ARG** instruction. This maintains generality and ensures that the program may easily be amended to support mixed-case filenames and filetypes if necessary. In addition, **PARSE ARG** is slightly faster than ARG when the CMS interpreter is used.

The program also truncates the filename to eight characters: this is the maximum length of a filename or filetype in CMS. CMS commands issued by the program would typically not object to a longer string (CMS would itself truncate the string). By receiving a "clean" parameter, though, the program protects itself against a potential (and rather subtle) bug.

SET LANGUAGE causes the user syntax table to be loaded from disk each time the program is run. It may in practice be preferable to issue the command only when necessary, to improve performance. The program could issue the QUERY LANGUAGE ALL command, returning the information in the CMS program stack, to see if the syntax definition is already loaded. This command returns the current language identifier (for instance, AMENG) followed by one or more pairs of lines. The first line of a pair is an active application identifier. The second indicates whether the system files, user files, or both are active; it may contain SYSTEM, USER, or ALL, respectively. For example, the command might return the following information:

```
AMENG
DMS
SYSTEM
```

The following fragment shows how the program might use the QUERY LANGUAGE ALL command:

```
   :
'MAKEBUF'
queued = queued()
'QUERY LANGUAGE ALL (FIFO' /* Stack the application identifiers */
parse pull                             /* Remove langid */
found_appl = false
do (queued()-queued)/2 while ¬ found_appl
   parse pull q_applid         /* Get application identifier */
   parse pull                        /* Remove filetype */
   if q_applid = applid then found_appl = true
end
'DROPBUF'
if ¬ found_appl then do
   'SET LANGUAGE (ADD' applid ' (USER'
   if rc <> 0 then exit rc
end
   :
```

Issuing error messages

Clear and unambiguous error messages help users diagnose—and, if possible, correct—problems more quickly. If a user cannot correct a problem, good error messages help the developer provide assistance. Messages should be numbered so that they may be easily located in a reference manual or on-line HELP system if a more detailed explanation is needed.

The text of CMS messages is held in a **message repository**. In many common situations, a standard CMS message can be displayed by the **XMITMSG** command. Displaying standard messages, using CMS facilities, has advantages for the user:

- The application acts in a way consistent with CMS commands.
- If the meaning is not entirely clear (for instance, the message may include a subroutine return code), the CMS **HELP** facility or a manual may provide a detailed explanation.
- CMS formats messages according to the user's **CP SET EMSG** setting. Users may choose to have both the message header and the message text displayed, either alone, or neither. CMS provides the REXX **DIAG** function, subcode **5C**, to format a message according to the user's EMSG setting. Users should be encouraged to use the **ON** setting to display both parts.

For example, if the user has set **EMSG ON**, the following code:

```
disk = 'B'
'XMITMSG 37 DISK (ERRMSG CALLER MYP'
```

displays the message:

```
DMSMYP037E Disk B is accessed as read/only
```

The **XMITMSG** command reads the message text from the CMS repository and substitutes variable **DISK** into it. The message header structure is: **DMS** is the application identifier for CMS; **MYP** is the calling program name, which was passed to the command. It identifies to the user which program issued the message. The default caller name is the first three characters of the program name. If these are the same as the application name, though, the default is the next three characters; this follows the CMS method of naming modules **DMSxxx**. Message numbers of **99** or less are formatted with leading zeros to display three digits; the maximum message number is **9999**. **E** is the message severity. Message severities which are conventionally used are:

R	Response required from the user
I	Information
W	Warning
E	Error
S	Severe error
T	Terminal (fatal) error

Severity s is generally used by CMS to indicate a programming error; T indicates an error that causes CMS to ABEND. The message header and text for R, S, and T messages are always displayed; in these cases, the EMSG setting is ignored.

Finally, the ERRMSG option in the example causes the message to be displayed according to the EMSG setting. Alternatively, DISPLAY may be specified to display the message without regard for the EMSG setting.

If the message should not be displayed directly by CMS (for instance, if the application writes full-screen menus), XMITMSG may return the message into REXX variables. The command:

```
'XMITMSG 37 DISK (ERRMSG CALLER MYP VAR'
```

sets variables MESSAGE.0 and MESSAGE.1. MESSAGE.0 contains the number of message lines (1, in this case), and MESSAGE.1 contains the message. If a message is contained in more than one line, it is continued in MESSAGE.2, MESSAGE.3, and so on.

The source of the CMS system messages is file DMSMES REPOS. Programmers may look in this file for suitable messages to use. If a suitable message is not found, an application repository may be created; this may be especially useful if a message is issued from more than one place in the application. The source of an application repository might look like:

```
& 3
02340101E Count value &1 exceeds the maximum of &2
```

The first line of the example is the control line. The ampersand (&) is the substitution character for messages; any single special character may be used. 3 specifies that message numbers of 999 or less are displayed with three digits, as are those in the CMS system repository. 4 may be specified to cause all message numbers to be displayed with four digits.

The second line defines a message. It breaks down as follows:

Columns 1-4	Message number (0234).
Columns 5-6	Message format (01). There may be several messages with similar text and the same message number; the FORMAT option of the XMITMSG command specifies which message format to display. The format number is between 01 and 99 inclusive. 01 is the default; these columns could be blank.
Columns 7-8	Line number (01). The line number field allows developers to force a message to be displayed on more than one screen line. Also, if the message text is too long to fit on one line of the source file, the text may be continued by

specifying the same line number. Again, **01** is the default and these columns could be blank.

Column 9   Severity code (**E**).

Columns 11-72   Message text. Within the message text, **&1** and **&2** are parameters which are substituted by the **XMITMSG** command.

Once the source file has been created, the message repository must be compiled with the **GENMSG** command. The repository is then activated with the **SET LANGUAGE** command, which, as seen above, also activates syntax definitions.

The **SET LANGUAGE** command expects the compiled repository to have the name *applid*UME. If the application identifier is **APP** and the source is in file **APPUME REPOS A**, the command **GENMSG APPUME REPOS A APP** compiles the repository. The following program displays the message:

```
/* Sample program to display message 234 */
/* in the user message repository */
address COMMAND
applid = 'APP'
max_count = 100
'SET LANGUAGE (ADD' applid 'USER'
count = 123
'XMITMSG 234 COUNT MAX_COUNT (ERRMSG APPLID' app
```

If the program is called **MYPROG**, it displays:

```
APPMYP234E Count value 123 exceeds the maximum of 100
```

Suppressing unwanted error messages

It may be almost as important to suppress unwanted messages (possibly distracting or confusing to the user) as to issue clear error messages. Unwanted messages are generally issued by the operating system in response to a command issued by the application on behalf of the user; they may be:

- Informational messages confirming that a command has successfully completed.

- Error messages indicating command failure, when the failure is unimportant. Attempting to erase a non-existent work file before writing a new one is an example.

- Significant error messages the application should "translate" into its own terms.

Several CMS commands can be called either from the terminal or from a program. They may issue certain messages if called from the terminal, but not if called from a program. **ERASE** and **STATE/ESTATE** are prime examples. In CMS REXX, the **CMS** subcommand environment simulates issuing commands from the terminal. This is the default environment for EXECs. If the **COMMAND** subcommand environment is used, **ERASE** and **STATE/ESTATE** do not issue the **File not found** error message. It is desirable to use the **COMMAND** environment anyway, as it is more efficient: the search for EXECs (performed by the **CMS** environment) is bypassed.

The user may issue the **HT** (halt typing) Immediate command during program execution to suppress CMS terminal output. The **RT** Immediate command causes output to resume. A program may control this flag with the **SET CMSTYPE RT** and **SET CMSTYPE HT** commands (Immediate commands are recognized only when entered at the terminal). A program may in this way suppress unwanted messages from CMS commands. **ACCESS** is an example of a command which issues an informational message when it completes successfully. The following code fragment illustrates the use of **SET CMSTYPE**:

```
cmstype = CMSFLAG('CMSTYPE')
if cmstype then 'SET CMSTYPE HT'
'ACCESS 194 C'
retc = rc
if cmstype then 'SET CMSTYPE RT'
if retc <> 0 then do
   'ACCESS 194 C'
   :
end
:
```

The example also shows use of the **CMSFLAG** function, which allows inspection and thus preservation of several CMS flags. If **HT** is already in effect, the **SET CMSTYPE** commands are not issued. If the **ACCESS** command fails, it is reissued to cause it to display an error message.

Several CP commands issue informational messages. The following code fragment suppresses such a message from the **LINK** command:

```
parse value DIAGRC(8, 'LINK FRED 191 291 RR') with rc 10 17 msg '15'x
if rc <> 0 then do
   say msg
   :
end
:
```

The **DIAGRC** function differs from the **DIAG** function in that it prefixes the result with the CP return code and condition code; the example obtains the return code in variable **RC**. If **RC** is greater than zero, it corresponds to the numeric portion of the message header. CP appends a new-line character (hexadecimal 15) to a message; this is

removed in the example. If the message were not required, the code
could be:

```
parse value DIAGRC(8, 'LINK FRED 191 291 RR', 1) with rc .
```

Here the third argument specifies the length of the buffer into which
CP places data (the default buffer size is 4096).
Since the data is not required, a short buffer may be used; this can
improve performance.

Finally, a source of unwanted messages may be the REXX language
processor itself. The default trace setting of a program is N (Normal):
failing commands are traced. (In CMS, a failure is indicated with a negative return code.) All trace messages may be suppressed by using
TRACE O (Off).

Returning from the application

In general, a user's working environment should be restored to the
state it had on entry to the application. If any settings were altered,
they should be restored. The potential difficulty of doing this (if the
application ABENDs, for instance) implies that the user's settings
should not be changed if at all possible.

The application should close disk files it opens, and not rely on CMS
to do so. It might return to a front-end program written by the user;
CMS would automatically close disk files only when this program
ended.

Application return codes should be documented, for the convenience
of users who will be calling the application from a front-end program.
Programmers should consider using standard CMS return codes, documented in the *System Messages and Codes* manual. For example, 24
generally means an invalid command line was used, 28 means a
required file was not found, and so on. Another scheme (used by CP) is
to set the return code to the error message number. This may allow a
more exact analysis of the error by a calling program.

SUPPORT TOOLS

This section discusses tools for supporting the development process.

The CMS UPDATE facility

When an application is changed (perhaps to add a new feature), the
change should be well documented—preferably automatically. It
should be possible to identify the program or programs affected by the
change and the source lines added, replaced, or deleted by the change.

The CMS UPDATE facility fulfills these requirements. The fundamental idea is that a base source file is never changed; instead, **update**

files are applied to the base source to generate a new file. Several CMS utility programs call the **UPDATE** command to generate a version of the source file with changes applied. Programmers need not normally be directly concerned with the contents of update files, since XEDIT creates them automatically, when used in **update mode**.

Update files may be applied cumulatively, with each file corresponding to a particular change. For each changed program, a file called an **auxiliary control file** or **AUX** file is created, containing the filetypes of the update files to be applied. The AUX file may (and should) contain comments giving the reason for each change.

Update files may be grouped; for example, each group may correspond to an application version or release level. This is done by having a separate AUX file for each group of updates, for each program. Each AUX file contains the filetypes of the update files in the group. Each application has a single control file specifying the filetypes of the auxiliary control files.

The application control file might look like this:

```
TEXT MACS
* Auxiliary control files follow
TEXT AUXREL2 Release 2
TEXT AUXREL1 Release 1
```

The filetype of the control file is **CNTRL**; the filename might, for convenience, be the name of the application—for example, **APP**. The **TEXT** and **MACS** fields are used for assembling and compiling application source. They are not used for REXX applications, and are not discussed in this chapter.

A programmer might enter:

```
xedit prog1 $exec (ctl app
```

to code a new change to release 2 of **PROG1**. XEDIT processes file **APP CNTRL** from the bottom up. It finds filetype **AUXREL1**, disregarding the preceding and following fields on the line, and looks for file **PROG1 AUXREL1**. If there have been no changes in release 1 of **PROG1**, the file will not exist; this is not an error, so XEDIT continues processing the **CNTRL** file. The next filetype is **AUXREL2**; **PROG1 AUXREL2** exists, so XEDIT reads it. Because the first three characters are **AUX**, XEDIT treats it as an auxiliary control file. Assume that the AUX file contains:

```
FLAPJACK Update for the FLAPJACK feature in release 2
FONDUE   Update for the FONDUE feature in release 2
```

Again processing from the bottom up, XEDIT applies the updates in file **PROG1 FONDUE**. The programmer has not yet coded the **FLAPJACK** feature, so file **PROG1 FLAPJACK** does not yet exist. Since this is the highest-level update file in the highest-level AUX file, XEDIT writes changes the programmer now makes to **PROG1** into this file.

Sequence numbers and SIDCODEs

Base source files (**PROG1 $EXEC** in the example) have fixed-length records. In VM releases prior to VM/SP Release 6, files maintained with the CMS update facility had to have fixed-length 80-byte records; in later releases, the source files must be fixed-length, but records may be between 80 and 255 bytes in length. Records are numbered sequentially, usually in increments of 1000 or 10000; the sequence numbers are in the last eight columns (columns 73 to 80 if the source file contains 80-byte records). Control statements in the update files refer to these sequence numbers. XEDIT may be used to sequence the base source file. If the XEDIT command **SET SERial ALL 10000** is issued, the file will be sequenced in increments of 10,000 when the file is written to disk (the default increment is 1000).

If requested, XEDIT will write a **Support Identification Code** (SIDCODE) for each update in the eight columns before the sequence numbers (columns 64 to 71 if the file contains 80-byte records). The SIDCODE may be specified when XEDIT is invoked, or via the **SET SIDCODE** XEDIT subcommand. The SIDCODE is typically the name of the update, for easily determining which update added or changed a particular line.

For example, the programmer might issue:

```
xedit prog1 $exec (ctl app sid flapjack
```

When the update file is written to disk, XEDIT adds the SIDCODE to changed and added records. Text must not be placed in columns which will be overwritten by sequence numbers or SIDCODEs. The truncation column should be set accordingly; when the screen is updated by pressing the ENTER key or a PF key, text placed after the truncation column is not displayed or added to the file. Although this is some help in flagging misplaced text, it would be better if the screen physically prevented the programmer from entering code past the truncation column. This may be done by using a narrow virtual screen. The following EXEC sets up a narrow virtual screen and window and calls XEDIT:

```
/* EXEC to XEDIT a file in a narrow virtual screen. */
/* The file area has 63 columns for editing with a SIDCODE. */
   address command
   arg fileid '(' xopts
   'QUERY DISPLAY (LIFO'
   parse pull . plines ./* Number of lines on physical screen */
   'DEFINE VSCREEN REXX' plines '70 0 0'
```

```
'DEFINE WINDOW  REXX' plines '71 1 2 (NOBORDER'
queue 'SET VERIFY 1 63'
queue 'SET TRUNC 63'
'XEDIT' fileid '(WINDOW REXX' xopts
'DELETE WINDOW REXX'
'DELETE VSCREEN REXX'
```

The EXECUPDT command

When an update has been coded, the EXECUPDT command applies updates to the base source file and creates an executable version of the REXX program. EXECUPDT is an EXEC; it calls the UPDATE command internally. For example, the command to create an executable version of PROG1 is:

```
execupdt prog1 (ctl app sid
```

The default filetype is EXEC; this is the filetype of the **output** file. EXECUPDT puts a dollar sign ($) at the start of the specified or default output filetype to determine the filetype of the input file. The output file has variable-length records. If SIDCODEs are used, the maximum length of the output records is 16 less than the source file record length; if not, the maximum length is eight less than the source file record length.

Application development system

A large development team may benefit from using an application development system. Such systems provide at least the following basic facilities:

- Source and other files are held in a central library. A developer may "lock" or "check out" a file to perform maintenance on it. While a file is in this state, no other developer may simultaneously work on it. When required changes have been made, the file (or updates) may be replaced in the library and the file unlocked.

- A hierarchy of libraries exists. When a change or set of changes has been made to a file, the file is effectively "frozen" by promoting it to the next level of the hierarchy. Staff responsible for testing the application may work with this frozen version. They in turn may promote changed files to the next level of the hierarchy, which may contain the application "release" version.

- A comprehensive set of reports is available to developers, supervisors, and managers.

Application development systems commercially available include the Library Management Facility (LMF) component of ISPF/PDF from

IBM and SOURCEBANK/VM from BlueLine Software.

Custom tools

If they are otherwise unavailable, developers may wish to write two tools which can be implemented easily (perhaps using XEDIT macros). They could perhaps be extended and become powerful tools in their own right.

Preprocessor

Using variables rather than "hard coding" constants in programs has great advantages in terms of making them flexible and readable. A variable such as **MAXIMUM_COUNT** is more readily understood than a constant value of, say, 100. If the value must be changed, it needs to be changed in only one place.

There are disadvantages, though, to using variables in this way:

- Variables must be initialized at execution time. If there are many variables, there may be significant overhead involved.

- There is overhead in fetching the value of a variable.

- A compiler may be unable to maximally optimize a clause which uses the value of a variable.

- If the language processor does not support REXX language level 4.00, positional parsing patterns cannot be used.

By using a preprocessor the developer may use symbolic (or **manifest**) constants, with the attendant advantages outlined above. Symbolic constants are then translated into constants (numbers or literal strings) within the program. For example, the developer may write %MAXIMUM_COUNT; the preprocessor might translate this to 100.

Program linker

There are advantages in writing an application as a number of separate programs instead of as one large program. Each small program may be more readily comprehended; a single large program may be difficult to understand and manage. Work may be divided between more than one developer.

There are disadvantages to this when using an interpreter:

- External disk-resident routines must each be loaded separately, incurring additional I/O and CPU overhead. They may need to be loaded each time they are called.

- There is CPU overhead in calling an external routine. The interpreter must first search for a built-in routine and possibly an internal routine before that (if the name of the routine is not specified in quotes). The CMS interpreter normally searches for an assembled or compiled external routine before searching for an external REXX program.

- When an external routine returns to its caller, the interpreter discards lookaside buffers it may have used to save the internal form of the program. If the external routine is called again, the interpreter must retranslate each executed clause.

In CMS, a REXX program may be made resident in storage by the **EXECLOAD** command. The following subroutine checks to see if a program is already storage-resident and, if not, loads the program:

```
EXECLOAD: procedure
   parse arg name
   'EXECSTAT' name 'EXEC'
   if rc = 4 then do
      'EXECLOAD' name 'EXEC'
      if rc <> 0 then exit rc
   end
   else if rc > 4 then do
         'XMITMSG 2 NAME "EXEC" (FORMAT 8'
         exit 28
   end
   return
```

The **EXECSTAT** command gives return code 0 if the program is in storage (perhaps in shared storage if it has been installed by the system programmer), 4 if the program is not in storage but is on disk, or 8 if the program does not exist.

CPU overhead of calling external REXX routines may be minimized in CMS by bypassing the search for an assembled or compiled routine. This may be done by issuing the **EXEC** command to the operating system; however, only a single argument string may be passed to the routine, and only a numeric result (return code) may be returned. Alternatively, the following undocumented feature may be used:

```
CALL 'EXEC name' . . .
```

or

```
'EXEC functionname'(. . .)
```

That is, the name of the routine is prefixed with EXEC and both enclosed in quotes; the routine is called in the normal way with a **CALL** instruction or by a function call. Because the feature is undocumented, its use should be carefully controlled. Perhaps names of external REXX routines could be declared to a preprocessor, which would generate the required code.

The advantages of writing an application as several separate programs may be combined with the advantages (in terms of efficiency) of having a single program. A utility program could be written to combine the separate programs into a single large program. To ensure compatibility between development and release versions of the application, it might automatically generate at the top of each program a label containing the program name, date, creating (merging) userid, and a PROCEDURE instruction.

REXX TECHNIQUES

Earlier sections of this chapter have discussed ways to use CMS in building REXX applications. This section concentrates on the use of REXX.

Routine linkage

It is generally considered to be good practice when calling an internal routine to formally pass all values the routine needs through its arguments, and for the routine to formally RETURN its result. This has the great advantage of minimizing program complexity; developers need be concerned only with variables local to a routine, and need not consider effects outside the routine of changing a variable value. In other words, routines should have a "barrier" between themselves and their callers, in the form of PROCEDURE instructions.

If a subroutine is called from only one routine and is logically close to its caller, it may be expedient not to use the PROCEDURE instruction in it. For example, the subroutine may logically be part of a nested DO group, taken out of the calling routine to reduce the apparent complexity of the caller.

Between these two extremes of having a rigid barrier and no barrier, it is possible to have a permeable barrier by using the EXPOSE option of the PROCEDURE instruction. EXPOSE works symmetrically: the subroutine has access to exposed variables of its caller, and the caller has access to exposed subroutine variables. In this way, the subroutine may informally receive its arguments and return its result.

Global variables

Although using the formal PARSE ARG mechanism is generally beneficial, in certain cases it may be inconvenient or may even **increase** the chances of introducing program bugs.

Consider a program structured like this, where all the subroutines include a PROCEDURE instruction (without EXPOSE):

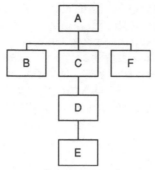

Routine **A**, the main routine, calls subroutine **B**, which initializes a variable containing a file identifier. Subroutine **E** writes the file. The file identifier is passed formally, and so must be known to routines **A**, **C**, and **D**, even though they do not use it.

If an error occurs in the program for which there is an enabled condition trap, the error routine must close the file. Since the subroutines all contain a **PROCEDURE** instruction, the error routine sees only variables belonging to the subroutine in which the error occurred. For the error routine to know the file identifier, the **name** of the variable containing the file identifier must be the same in all subroutines. Programmers cannot, for example, name the variable **FILEID** in subroutine **C** and **FILE_ID** in subroutine **D** (though this would be undesirable in any case, as it would hinder program readability). Further, if the error occurs in subroutine **F**, the file identifier will be unavailable to the error routine, and the error routine will be unable to close the file. It is far more practical here to use only one variable, known globally in the program (including subroutine **F**) by using **EXPOSE** on the **PROCEDURE** instructions.

If a program has many global variables (describing the layout of file records, say), the **EXPOSE** list may become unmanageably long. REXX language level 4.00 allows a variable list to be specified indirectly by using a variable reference. If the language processor does not support this feature, the programmer may instead use a collection of compound variables and specify their stem in the **EXPOSE** list. To avoid unwanted substitution, compound symbols (starting with a digit) should be used in the tail. In REXX, a constant symbol is not restricted to containing only digits; by definition, it starts with a digit or a period, but otherwise it may contain any characters that are valid in a symbol. Digits alone may be used in the tail, but other characters may be used as well to improve readability. For example, subroutine **E** might start:

```
E: procedure expose global.
parse arg output_record
```

```
file_id = global.6file_id
type = substr(output_record, global.6output_record.6type, 1)
:
```

The 6s here may perhaps be considered large inverted commas, each prefacing a constant. If they were not used (if simple symbols were used in the tails of the compound symbols), variables used in the subroutine could be inadvertently substituted into the compound symbol. Since the **OUTPUT_RECORD** variable is assigned by the **PARSE** instruction in the example, the derived name of the compound symbol in the following clause would be incorrect:

```
type = substr(output_record, global.output_record.type, 1)
```

A side benefit of using a collection of compound variables this way is that it reveals whether a variable is global, thus contributing to program readability. Programmers may extend this scheme and use two stems (for example, **GLOBALV**. and **GLOBALC**., or perhaps ?. and !.) to distinguish between global variables whose value may change through the program and global variables (or "constants") whose value, once assigned, does not change.

Returning information to the caller

The result of a subroutine or function is a single string; this is generally all that is required. If a routine (subroutine or function) interacts with the operating system or the user, the situation is usually more complicated. At the very least, the success or failure of the routine must be communicated to its caller.

In general, **control information** must be separated from the **data** returned. If the routine is internal to the program, this is easily arranged by exposing the required variable or variables. If the routine is external to the program, the result string must be broken down somehow by the caller into component control and data parts. This may be done by separating components with a special character or by using particular result string positions for the components. (The **DIAGRC** function supplied with the CMS REXX interpreter takes the latter approach.)

The control part of the result may correspond to a completion code indicating success or failure of the called routine, or it may be subdivided into (for instance) a completion code, an action code, and a message. Consider an application which presents a series of full-screen menus to the user. Messages must be displayed in reserved fields within the menus, so the **SAY** instruction cannot be used. A routine, on returning to its caller, might wish to return:

- A completion code indicating success

- An action code indicating that the user wishes to "escape" to another branch of the menu hierarchy
- An informational or warning message
- Data retrieved from a file

Using a special character (such as X'00') to separate the parts of the result, the caller might then have the following:

```
call EXTERNAL_ROUTINE
parse var result comp_code '00'x action '00'x message '00'x data
  ⋮
```

Having the parts in this order does not preclude use of the special character in the data.

Condition traps

Enabling condition traps makes a program more robust. With conditions (SYNTAX and HALT) whose default action is ending program execution, the program may tidy up before returning to its caller, or an interactive application may allow the user to continue with another subfunction. Additionally, the program may detect other error conditions which otherwise could have gone unnoticed, but have pernicious effects.

SYNTAX trap

Syntax errors in REXX are very broadly defined. Along with true syntax errors, they include many other errors.

In common with the other condition traps, the initial setting of the SYNTAX trap on entry to a REXX program is OFF. If the program does not enable the trap—if it has no SYNTAX trap routine—then if the SYNTAX condition is raised, the program returns to its caller with error 40 (Incorrect call to routine). Note that this is *not* the same as returning a result; if the calling REXX program traps the SYNTAX condition, the error is available to it in the special variable RC. If the program's caller is a REXX program which has not enabled the SYNTAX trap either, the caller will return to *its* caller with error 40.

In this way, the error may be transmitted upward through the calling sequence until it encounters an enabled SYNTAX trap. This allows programmers to code a general SYNTAX trap routine in the top-level program alone, rather than one in each external routine, which perhaps would overly complicate the application. Alternatively, while having an overall error routine, an interactive application could have one for each subfunction.

Error routines, like any code, are themselves liable to errors. The SYNTAX trap routine is no exception.

If a syntactically invalid clause (such as a **SELECT** instruction with a missing **END** clause) is encountered, an interpreter may be unable to parse the source beyond the clause. This means that if the **SYNTAX** trap routine is defined after the invalid clause, the interpreter may be unable to invoke it.

Similarly, if the **SYNTAX** trap routine attempts to invoke an internal routine which is beyond the invalid clause, the interpreter may fail. If the **SYNTAX** trap routine calls a built-in or external routine, the interpreter will normally attempt to first search the entire program for an internal routine. This search may be overridden by specifying the name of the routine in quotes. So when coding a **SYNTAX** trap routine:

- Place it as close as possible to the top of the program.

- Place internal routines it calls as close as possible to the top of the program.

- Specify names of built-in or external routines it calls in quotes.

The program might look like:

```
      call INIT
      signal on SYNTAX
      call MAIN
      call TIDYUP
exit answer
SYNTAX:
      say 'Syntax error at line' sigl':' 'ERRORTEXT'(rc)
      say 'Source line is:'
      say 'SOURCELINE'(sigl)
      call TIDYUP
exit ''
TIDYUP:
   :
```

TIDYUP uses variables established by the **INIT** routine, so the **SYNTAX** trap is not enabled until after **INIT** has been called.

HALT Trap

A **HALT** trap routine can detect a user attempt to terminate execution of the program. In CMS, the **HI** Immediate command does this; the **HX** Immediate command terminates execution of all programs, and cannot be trapped. If the program executing when the user enters the **HI** command has enabled the **HALT** trap, the situation is straightforward: the **HALT** trap routine is entered immediately.

If the trap is not enabled, then, as with the **SYNTAX** trap, the default action is to end program execution and return to the caller. REXX displays error number **4** (**Program interrupted**) for the called program; the caller receives error **40**. Again, the condition may be transmitted upward though the calling sequence as a **SYNTAX** error. If a calling REXX program has the SYNTAX trap enabled, its SYNTAX trap routine will be entered. Under these circumstances, though, the HALT is still active. The first instruction of the routine may be executed, but then the HALT condition is raised. If the program has no HALT trap routine, the language processor ends execution with error 4.

For this reason, if a calling program has enabled the HALT trap but not the SYNTAX trap, the HALT trap routine will not be entered; the language processor looks for an enabled SYNTAX trap on being passed error 40.

So to trap the HALT condition, a program which calls other programs must enable **both** the HALT and SYNTAX traps. The first instruction of the SYNTAX trap routine should be a dummy instruction, such as NOP. If a HALT is not active, control will fall through to the rest of the SYNTAX trap routine; if a HALT is active, control will pass to the HALT trap routine after the dummy instruction has been executed.

NOVALUE trap

REXX defines the default value of a simple or compound symbol to be the characters of the symbol, translated to uppercase. For example, the default value (if not already defined as a variable) of the simple symbol fred is FRED. This feature is most valuable for end-users writing simple macros; they may, for instance, issue commands to the environment without needing to use literal strings. In a complex application, though, the feature may produce very subtle bugs. For example, a programmer may mistype a variable name on the right-hand side of an assignment instruction. This may not be noticed in execution until much later (when it may be difficult to determine the cause of the error)—or may be noticed only by the program writing bad data to a file.

Each REXX program should enable the NOVALUE trap. It may be considered sufficient to enable the NOVALUE trap without coding a trap routine. The language processor will then end program execution with error 16 (Label not found) if the NOVALUE condition is raised. This could be reflected as a syntax error in a calling REXX program, to be handled in the way outlined above. This approach would be particularly appropriate for straightforward external routines which do not interact with the operating system—that is, routines which return only data and not a completion code as well. As previously discussed, this sort of routine may not have a SYNTAX trap routine either, in the interest of minimizing program complexity.

Acknowledgments

The author wishes to thank Dave Richards and Steve Derbyshire of VM Solutions for their help and support in the writing of this chapter.

Extending CMS REXX with Function Packages

By Larry Oppenheim

INTRODUCTION

One of REXX's outstanding features is its extensibility. VM installations commonly supplement the rich set of built-in functions with external functions written in interpreted REXX. These external functions appear to users as integral with REXX; the only drawback is relatively poor performance. CMS REXX function packages take this extensibility one step further, offering performance approaching that of built-in functions.

This chapter's main purpose is to show how to write an actual function package, including a complete example. The first part of the chapter defines function packages and how they interface with CMS. The second part examines reasons for using function packages, and the third part is a "cookbook" for writing function packages. The final section ties everything together by analyzing a sample function package.

Most REXX implementations offer similar methods of extending the language; this chapter deals only with CMS REXX.

WHAT IS A FUNCTION PACKAGE?

A function package is a library of external functions written in System/370 assembler language. Therefore, external functions written in REXX do not qualify for membership in a function package. An external assembler function may be one of the following:

1. A module created with the GENMOD command. The module may have the same name as the function itself or be prefixed by RX. (Use of RX is explained in a later section.)

2. A member of one of the three supported function packages, each one also a CMS MODULE:

RXUSERFN   User level; searched first.

RXLOCFN   Local level; searched second.

RXSYSFN   System level; searched last.

Therefore, an external assembler function is the fundamental building block of a function package.

The idea behind the three levels is to differentiate between packages that might be written by general users (RXUSERFN), system support staff (RXLOCFN), and IBM (RXSYSFN). In fact, the "standard" functions CMSFLAG, DIAG, DIAGRC, and STORAGE are not built-in functions; they are implemented in VM REXX as external functions, grouped in RXSYSFN.

Functions in function packages often share common code and subroutines. Also, each function is a candidate for loading as a CMS nucleus extension. (Nucleus extensions are commands which can be invoked the same way as resident nucleus commands, avoiding disk access.) The first time a member function is invoked, the entire function package is loaded into storage as a nucleus extension, and the entry point to the specific function is declared as a nucleus extension. A significant performance benefit results from the fact that it is not necessary to reload the function or the package from disk on subsequent calls.

WHY USE FUNCTION PACKAGES?

There are three main reasons for using function packages: improved performance, ease of maintenance, and the need to customize REXX.

Improving performance

1. In the function search order, function packages are located before files of filetype XEDIT or EXEC. (The search order for REXX functions is described in detail in the section "How function packages are written".)

2. As discussed above, function packages remain resident in storage after loading. Nucleus extensions play an important role in the

improved performance. To better understand why requires a closer look at this CMS facility.

Nucleus extensions

Nucleus extensions allow the user to extend the CMS nucleus without having to directly modify it. A user first loads a nucleus extension into virtual storage with the **NUCXLOAD** command. The CMS **NUCEXT** function establishes an entry point callable via SVC 202 or SVC 204, the standard CMS command interfaces.

Nucleus extensions must be relocatable, because they are loaded at different locations each time. Relocatability is accomplished through careful coding, or by specifying **RLDSAVE** on the **LOAD** command.

CMS manages nucleus extensions with a chain of control blocks called **SCBLOCKs**. Each loaded nucleus extension is represented by a single SCBLOCK, which includes its name and entry point address. Each time a nucleus extension is used, it is moved to the head of the chain. The most frequently used commands thus cluster at the start of the chain.

Ease of maintenance

Grouping functions into a single module means that common code and subroutines may be shared, reducing duplicate code and thus maintenance effort. For example, the function package provided at the end of this chapter contains routines that convert decimal strings to binary and binary values to decimal. These routines may be reused by any string function added to the package.

Tailoring VM REXX to individual needs

Even though VM REXX provides an extensive set of built-in functions, many installations need to add their own. For example, the standard **DATE** built-in function provides ten ways to format the current date, but no way to convert a date between formats. The **DIAG** built-in function, while very powerful, only supports a subset of CP diagnose codes. REXX can be extended by placing "improved" versions of those functions in a function package.

HOW FUNCTION PACKAGES ARE WRITTEN

This section provides a "cookbook" approach to writing function packages. Since an assembler external function is the primary building block of a function package, the process can be divided into two steps:

1. Writing an external function

2. Placing an external function into a function package

The discussion below uses the **POSBM** function, which is presented in its entirety at the end of the chapter.

Writing an external function

How external function searches are done
It is very helpful to understand how the REXX interpreter resolves calls to external functions:

1. Prefix the name with **RX**.

> If the REXX program includes a call to **POSBM**, the name is thus changed to **RXPOSBM**. This allows functions to be written with little risk of conflict with CP or CMS commands.

2. Execute via a normal CMS command call, SVC 202 (SVC 204 in later CMS releases).

> With the correct parameter list for an external function call, the SVC processor attempts to execute **RXPOSBM**. If a module or nucleus extension is found, the search terminates.

3. Check the three standard function packages.

> ▪ The first package is queried by issuing:
>
> ```
> RXUSERFN LOAD RXPOSBM
> ```
>
> ▪ If **RXPOSBM** resides in **RXUSERFN**:
>
> The loader portion of **RXUSERFN** makes **RXPOSBM** available as a nucleus extension.
>
> The SVC originally issued in step 2 is reissued. Now it succeeds, because **RXPOSBM** has been identified to the system.
>
> ▪ If the command **RXUSERFN LOAD RXPOSBM** fails, the remaining two packages are queried in the same manner:
>
> ```
> RXLOCFN LOAD RXPOSBM
> RXSYSFN LOAD RXPOSBM
> ```
>
> ▪ If **RXPOSBM** is found in one of the function packages, the search terminates.

4. Remove the RX prefix.

> REXX next searches for a file named **POSBM** *filetype*, where *filetype* is the filetype of the currently executing program (for example, **POSBM XEDIT** if the currently executing program is an XEDIT macro). If found, this file is executed as an interpreted external function.
>
> If the search fails, and the filetype sought was not **EXEC**, an additional search is made for **POSBM EXEC**.

5. Execute directly via SVC 202/204.

An SVC 202 or SVC 204 is issued against the original name, **POSBM**.

The basic parameter list structure

A six-word parameter list called an **extended plist** or **EPLIST** is created when an external function is invoked from a REXX program. When the external function gains control, register 0 points to the six fullword pointers as follows:

```
EPLIST     DS   0F
           DC   A(COMVERB)   #1:  => 'EXEC '
           DC   A(BEGARGS)   #2:  => Start of argstring
           DC   A(ENDARGS)   #3:  => 1 past end of argstring
           DC   A(FBLOCK)    #4:  => 0 when assembler function invoked
EPARGLST   DC   A(ARGLIST)   #5:  => Argument list
EPFUNRET   DC   A(SYSFUNRT)  #6:  => Two-level pointer to returned result
```

The first three fullwords (**COMVERB**, **BEGARGS**, and **ENDARGS**) can be ignored because they are not used by the called function. The fourth fullword (**FBLOCK**) can also be ignored because it is zero when an assembler function is invoked. The fifth and sixth fullwords contain information relevant to an assembler function:

EPARGLST	Pointer to argument list passed.
EPFUNRET	Two-level pointer to storage used to return result to caller.

Ensuring proper call type

An assembler external function first determines if it was properly called as a function. If not, **ARGLIST** and **SYSFUNRT** will be invalid. This is determined by checking the high-order byte of register 1 for a value of **X'05'**:

```
         CLI   24(R13),X'05'  (R1 was saved at displacement 24 from R13)
         BNE   ERROR
```

To determine whether the function was invoked by the **CALL** instruction, test the high-order bit of register 0 for **1**. If the function was invoked by **CALL**, it is legal but not necessary to return a result. The example in this chapter does not test for this distinction.

Receiving passed arguments (getting data in)

The argument list pointed to by **EPARGLST** (the fifth fullword of the extended plist) is a series of address-length fullword pairs terminated by a doubleword containing **X'FF'**. Each address-length pair describes a single argument. There are three possibilities:

Normal argument string	Address and length both non-zero.
Null argument specified	Address non-zero, length zero.
Argument omitted	Address zero.

Consider a function which uses the same arguments as the standard POS built-in function:

```
POS(needle, haystack<, startpos>)
```

POS returns the position of string *needle* within string *haystack*. The optional *startpos* specifies the column within *haystack* at which to begin searching; if it is not specified, searching begins at column 1.

The following DSECT might describe the argument list:

```
ARGS      DSECT
NEEDLE    DS    F    Address of argument 1
NEEDLEL   DS    F    Length  of argument 1
HAYSTAK   DS    F    Address of argument 2
HAYSTAKL  DS    F    Length  of argument 2
START     DS    F    Address of argument 3
STARTL    DS    F    Length  of argument 3
FENCE     DS    D    Doubleword of X'FF'
```

The next example shows how the function accesses passed arguments, using register 11 to address the ARGS DSECT:

```
        L     R11,EPARGLIST    Load pointer to passed arguments
        USING ARGS,R11         Establish addressability
        LM    R8,R9,NEEDLE     Get argument 1
        LTR   R8,R8            Is it there?
        BNP   ERROR            No, return with error
* Apply the same check for argument 2
        LM    R2,R3,HAYSTAK    Get argument 2
        LTR   R2,R2            Is it there?
        BNP   ERROR            No, return with error
* Check for the optional third argument
        LM    R0,R1,START      Get argument 3
        BNP   ...              Branch to main processing
*    R8/R9 = addr/length of NEEDLE
*    R2/R3 = addr/length of HAYSTAK
*    R0/R1 = addr/length of START
```

Returning a result

The assembler external function obtains storage for data returned to the calling program. This storage is an EVALBLOK, and might be described by the following DSECT:

```
EVALBLOK DSECT
EVPAD1   DS    F    Reserved (should be set to 0)
EVSIZE   DS    F    Size of EVALBLOK in doublewords
```

```
EVLEN    DS    F     Length of data portion in bytes
EVPAD2   DS    F     Reserved (should be set to 0)
EVDATA   DS    C     The start of the returned character string
```

The address of the acquired **EVALBLOK** must be placed in **SYSFUNRT** (pointed to by **EPFUNRET** in the extended plist). Therefore, one of the first steps is saving the value stored in **EPFUNRET**:

```
L     R10,EPFUNRET
ST    R10,FUNRETSV
```

Subroutine **GETBLOK** illustrates **EVALBLOK** creation.

```
* R1 contains the byte length of the data to be returned
GETBLOK DS    0H
        LA    R0,EVDLEN+7(,R1) Add workarea length and round up
        SRL   R0,3             /8 = doublewords
* This is the number of doublewords in the entire EVALBLOK
        DMSFREE DWORDS=(0),TYPE=USER,TYPECALL=SVC,ERR=ERROR
        LR    R2,R1            Save address of EVALBLOK in R2
* Next fill in some EVALBLOK fields
        USING EVALBLOK,R2      Addressability
        XC    EVPAD1,EVPAD1    Zero out both of the
        XC    EVPAD2,EVPAD2     pad fields
        ST    R0,EVSIZE        Store total block length (doublewords)
        ST    R1,EVLEN         Length of DATA (in bytes)
* Return data buffer pointer to caller in R1
        LA    R1,EVDATA        Point to the result buffer
        BR    R14              And return
```

The function will place data being returned into the buffer pointed to by R1.

Just before the function returns, a pointer to the **EVALBLOK** must be stored in **SYSFUNRT**, the word *pointed to* by **EPFUNRET** (word 6 of the extended plist). This is why it was necessary to save **EPFUNRT** at the beginning:

```
L     R10,FUNRETSV   Restore saved value of EPFUNRET
ST    R2,0(,R10)     Store EVALBLOK address (R2) in SYSFUNRT
```

Finally, registers are restored and a zero return code is set, indicating that the function completed successfully:

```
LM    R14,R12,12(R13) Restore the registers
SR    R15,R15         Set a zero return code
BR    R14             Return
```

Summary
POSBM, a faster version of the REXX **POS** built-in function, is based on the Boyer-Moore string search algorithm. The basic idea is to move the

pattern (*needle*) more than one character at a time when attempting to find a match within the larger string (*haystack*). A 256-character table (**SKIPTAB**) is built to define the pattern, with each position representing the corresponding character in the character set.

First, the 256-byte **SKIPTAB** is filled with the length of *needle*. Then, starting from the right of *needle*, each character is read, and its offset is placed in that character's index within **SKIPTAB**. Here is an example, using the string **FUNC** as the *needle*:

	A	.	C	.	.	F	.	.	N	.	U	.	Z
SKIPTAB position (hex)	C1		C3			C6			D5		E4		E9
Original values	4	4	4	4	4	4	4	4	4	4	4	4	4
Values with 'FUNC'	4	4	0	4	4	3	4	4	1	4	2	4	4

The **Original values** row shows that each byte in **SKIPTAB** is first filled with value **4**, the length of **FUNC**. The next step is to examine the rightmost character of **FUNC**. Since it is zero positions from the end, **0** is placed in position **X'C3'** of **SKIPTAB**, the position representing the code for **C**. Next, **1** is placed in position **X'D5'**, since **N** is an offset of one from the rightmost character; **2** is placed in position **X'E4'**, and **3** in position **X'C6'**.

Now that the table has been "compiled", here is how it is used in a string search:

```
"Needle"   = FUNC
"Haystack" = THIS IS A FUNCTION PACKAGE
   1)        FUNC
   2)            FUNC
   3)                FUNC
   4)              FUNC
```

Step 1   **FUNC** is lined up under **THIS**. **C** is not equal to **S**, so the **SKIPTAB** value for **S** is fetched. This is **4**, so move **FUNC** four positions to the right. (Remember that all **SKIPTAB** entries which represent characters *not* in **FUNC** will contain **4**.)

Step 2   The **C** in **FUNC** is compared to a blank, **X'40'**. They are not equal, so once again **FUNC** is moved four positions to the right.

Step 3   The **C** in **FUNC** is compared to **U**; they are not equal. Looking up the position for **U** in **SKIPTAB** gives **2**. Thus **FUNC** is moved only two positions to the right.

Step 4   The **C** in **FUNC** is compared to **C**. For the first time, this is a match. Because the position for **C** in **SKIPTAB** contains **0**, this is a possible match. A reverse compare is performed on the remaining characters of the string, and finds that all characters do indeed match. The offset within *haystack* is returned by the function. (If the characters did not all match, then *needle* would slide over just one position, and the process would continue.)

It should be clear that the advantage of this technique is the ability to move the pattern to the right more than one character at a time. This saving of search steps results in faster performance. The cost is the need to compile a new **SKIPTAB** for every pattern searched.

The complete code for the **POSBM** external function follows.

POSBM function code

```
        TITLE 'RXPOSBM: Faster string search to replace POS()'
RXPOSBM  CSECT
* Faster version of the REXX Pos() built-in function. It is based
* upon the Boyer-Moore string search algorithm, invented in 1976
* by Robert S. Boyer and J. Strother Moore, now with the University
* of Texas at Austin.
*
* The format of the POSBM function is the same as that of the
* standard built-in function POS:
*
*       POSBM(needle,haystack<,startpos>)
*
* Input: Arguments 1 and 2 required, argument 3 optional
*
* Output: Returns the location of 'needle' within 'haystack'
*
*    If argument 3 is omitted, the search begins at the first
*  character of 'haystack'. Otherwise the search begins at
*  'startpos', which must be a positive whole number.
*
        USING RXPOSBM,R12
        STM   R14,R12,12(R13) Save registers.
        LR    R11,R0          Obtain pointer to extended plist
* Ensure proper call type (function or subroutine). This means
* that the high-order byte of Register 1 MUST BE X'05'.
* (R1 was saved at displacement 24 from R13.)
        CLI   24(R13),X'05'   Called with proper plist?
*       CLI   24(R13),EPFUNSUB
*
        BNE   ERROR           No, don't continue.
* Now that it has been established that we have been invoked as
* either a subroutine or a function, we can proceed with the
* processing of the six-word extended plist.
*    - The plist is pointed to by R0 (which we saved in R11)
*    - The words in the plist which are relevant to functions are:
*      Word 5 (EPARGLST), the list of arguments passed to the function
*      Word 6 (EPFUNRET), pointer to the result returned to the caller
```

```
          USING EPLIST,R11      Addressability to the plist
          L     R10,EPFUNRET    Pointer to the fullword which will
*               be used to return a pointer to the result string
          ST    R10,FUNRETSV    Save pointer to free up R10
          L     R11,EPARGLST    Pointer to the argument list
***********************************************************************
* End of code common to all functions/subroutines                    *
***********************************************************************
* Validate the arguments. Arguments 1 and 2 (the 'needle' and the
* 'haystack' are required. Argument 3 (the starting column position
* to search) is optional.
          DROP  R11
          USING ARGS,R11        We want to use our own names
*
*   1. If argument 1 is specified, the pointer to that argument will
*      be a positive address.
*   2. If NO ARGUMENTS were specified, then the pointer will contain
*      the value of -1 (X'FFFFFFFF').
*   3. If argument 1 is omitted but following arguments were specified,
*      then the pointer will contain the address zero.
*   A check for a positive address is all that is needed.
*
          LM    R8,R9,NEEDLE    Get Argument 1
          LTR   R8,R8           Is it there?
          BNP   ERROR           No, return with error
* Apply the same check for argument 2
          LM    R2,R3,HAYSTAK   Get Argument 2
          LTR   R2,R2           Is it there?
          BNP   ERROR           No, return with error
* Check for the optional third argument
          LM    R0,R1,START     Get Argument 3
          BNP   POSBM01         OK if it is omitted
* Argument 3 was specified, convert from decimal to binary
          BAL   R14,D2B         Convert to a binary number
          LTR   R15,R15         Zero return code?
          BNZ   ERROR           No, return with error
*   R8/R9 = addr/length of NEEDLE
*   R2/R3 = addr/length of HAYSTAK
*   R0/R1 = addr/length of START
* Now that we have a non-default starting position, we must
* add it to the start address of 'haystack' and reduce the
* total length left.
          BCTR  R1,0            Subtract 1 from the offset
          AR    R2,R1           Add increment to start of 'haystack'
          SR    R3,R1           Update the new 'reduced' length
POSBM01   DS    0H
          LTR   R9,R9           Test the length of 'needle'
          BZ    RETURN0         Return 0 if it is null
          CR    R9,R3           Is 'needle' longer than 'haystack'??
          BH    RETURN0         Yes - return 0 ('needle' not found)
          C     R9,CONST1       Is 'needle' 1 byte long??
          BNE   BOYERMOR        No - go ahead with Boyer-Moore algorithm
* Do a straight search, since we are looking for a single character.
          IC    R4,0(,R8)       Place the single 'needle' char in R4
          LR    R6,R2           'Haystack' pointer is in R6
```

```
POSBM02   DS    0H
          CLM   R4,B'0001',0(R6)  Compare current characters
          BE    MATCHONE          We found a match on a single character
          LA    R6,1(,R6)         Bump 'haystack' pointer to next byte
          BCT   R3,POSBM02        Try again
          B     RETURN0           We didn't find the char, so result is 0
* Since our 'needle' is more than one char, use Boyer-Moore
BOYERMOR  DS    0H
* Precompile the 'needle' into a table where each element
* represents one of the 256 EBCDIC characters. Each table element
* which corresponds to a character in 'needle' is assigned THE
* OFFSET OF THAT CHARACTER FROM THE END (rightmost position) of
* 'needle'.
*
*   Step 1: Fill every element in the table with the length of 'needle'
*
          LA    R10,SKIPTAB       R10 will be the index register
          L     R11,F'256'        R11 will be the loop counter
INITTAB   DS    0H
          STC   R9,0(,R10)        R9 contains the length of 'needle'
          LA    R10,1(,R10)       Bump R10 to next byte in table
          BCT   R11,INITTAB       ...until we have filled all 256 bytes
*
*   Step 2: In each SKIPTAB element corresponding to a character
*           in the 'needle', store the offset of the character from
*           the end MINUS 1.
*
          LR    R5,R8             R5 will be index register to 'needle'
          LR    R11,R9            Length of 'needle' in R11
          BCTR  R11,0             Get length of 'needle' minus 1
          SR    R4,R4             Clear R4 in preparation for add
FILLTAB   DS    0H
          LA    R10,SKIPTAB       Restore the SKIPTAB address
          IC    R4,0(,R5)         Place a character from 'needle' in R4
          AR    R10,R4            Use contents of R4 as index into
SKIPTAB
          STC   R11,0(,R10)       Store offset of byte into SKIPTAB
*    (the offset happens to be the current value of the loop counter)
          LA    R5,1(,R5)         Index to next position in 'needle'
          BCT   FILLTAB
* After falling through the loop, there is still 1 skip value to store:
          LA    R10,SKIPTAB       Restore the SKIPTAB address
          IC    R4,0(,R5)         Place a character from 'needle' in R4
          AR    R10,R4            Use contents of R4 as index into SKIPTAB
          STC   R11,0(,R10)       Store offset of byte into SKIPTAB
* Now we can start to search.
* First, initialize starting pointers to 'needle' and 'haystack';
* then compute 'haystack' length - 1 and starting skip value:
          LR    R5,R8             R5 is index register for 'needle'
          LR    R6,R2             R6 is index register for 'haystack'
          LR    R11,R3            Length of 'haystack' in R11
          BCTR  R11,0             Decrement length for end of string test
          LR    R7,R9             Length of 'needle' in R7
          BCTR  R7,0              Decrement R7, for starting skip value
* Now, we scan 'needle' from RIGHT to LEFT, to determine how far
```

```
* to move 'needle' for each character in 'haystack'
SRCHLAST DS     0H
         LA     R10,SKIPTAB      Restore SKIPTAB address
         CR     R11,R7           Check if 'haystack' is exhausted
         BNL    RETURN0          It is, so we return 0
         AR     R6,R7            Add skip value to address of
* 'haystack' (this effectively slides the 'needle' to the right)
         IC     R4,0(,R6)        Place a byte from 'haystack' in R4
         AR     R10,R4           Use R4 contents as index into SKIPTAB
         IC     R7,0(,R10)       Place character from SKIPTAB into R7,
*                                establishing the new skip value
         LTR    R7,R7            If skip value 0, a match is possible
         BNZ    SRCHLAST         Try again by sliding to the right
* Now we have a possible match. We will do a REVERSE brute-force
* compare:
         LR     R12,R6           Save current pointer to 'haystack'
         LR     R5,R8            Get 'needle' address
         BCTR   R5,0             Decrement 'needle' address
         AR     R5,R9            Add length to point to LAST character
         LR     R7,R9            Length of 'needle' in R7
*** R5  => rightmost character in 'needle'
*** R6  => current position in 'haystack'
*** R7  = loop counter
REVLOOP  DS     0H
         CLC    0(1,R5),0(R6)    Compare a single byte
         BNE    NOMATCH          Compare failed, drop out
         BCTR   R6,0             Decrement 'haystack' pointer
         BCTR   R5,0             Decrement 'needle' pointer
         BCT    R7,REVLOOP       Ok so far - try next character
         B      GOTMATCH         If we get this far, we succeeded
NOMATCH  DS     0H
         LA     R7,1             Match not found, set skip value to 1
*        LA     R10,SKIPTAB      Restore SKIPTAB address
         LR     R6,R12           Restore current pointer to 'haystack'
         B      SRCHLAST
GOTMATCH DS     0H
         LR     R6,R12           Restore current position in 'haystack'
         BCTR   R9,0             Reduce start of 'haystack' by 1
         SR     R6,R9            R6 now contains ordinal position
* We come here if 'needle' was one character, and we found a match
MATCHONE DS     0H
     ** Here we must convert R6 to an EBCDIC number **
         L      R0,R6            B2D expects binary number in R0
         BAL    R14,B2D          Convert from binary to EBCDIC
         B      FINISH
*
RETURN0  DS     0H
     ** This is the common exit point for a '0' result
         LA     R0,0
         BAL    R14,B2D
FINISH   DS     0H
* Now R1 points to the first byte of the decimal number placed in
* the EVALBLOK, and R2 points to the header of the EVALBLOK.
* Our last task is to return the pointer to the EVALBLOK, which
* was stored in a fullword POINTED TO by field EPFUNRET (word
```

```
* number 6 in the extended plist).
          L      R10,FUNRETSV    Restore saved value of EPFUNRET
*    (Note the 2 levels of pointers in returning the data)
          ST     R2,0(,R10) Store EVALBLOK address (R2) in second pointer
          LM     R14,R12,12(R13) Restore the registers
          SR     R15,R15         Set zero return code
          BR     R14             Return
ERROR     DS     0H
* Setting any non-zero return code will cause the REXX exec
* to terminate with the message "Invalid call to routine".
          LM     R14,R12,12(R13) Restore the registers
          LA     R15,36          Set non-zero return code
          BR     R14             Return
**************************************************************
* B2D: Convert a fullword binary number to its decimal
*      equivalent in EBCDIC.
* Input:
*    R0: The binary number to be converted
*
* Output:
*    R0: Undefined
*    R1: Address of first byte of decimal number placed in EVALBLOK
*    R2: Address of the EVALBLOK (set during call to GETBLOK)
*
B2D       DS     0H
* First, check to see if we have a simple one-digit answer
          CL     R0,=F'10'       Does the number qualify?
          BNL    LONGWAY         No, the result is > 1 digit
* We are in luck! We can take the fast path
          L      R1,CONST1       Set length equal to 1, so GETBLOK
          BAL    R14,GETBLOK        will acquire a 1-byte data area
* After call to GETBLOK, R1 => data portion of just acquired storage
          LA     R0,240(,R0)     Construct the one-byte answer
          STC    R0,0(,R1)
          BR     R14             return
* We have to do it the hard way
LONGWAY   DS     0H
          CVD    R0,DWORD        Convert from binary to decimal
          OI     DWORD+7,X'0F'   Change sign from X'0C' to X'0F'
          SR     R15,R15         Clear R15
POWLOOP   DS     0H
* First time through the loop, we compare to the value 10
          CL     R0,POWER+4(R15) Longer than this power?
          LA     R15,4(,R15)     Point to next table entry
          BNL    POWLOOP         number is larger or equal
          SRL    R15,2           Calculate length (R15/4)
          LR     R1,R15          R1 = size of data to acquire
          LR     R4,R1           Save size of data in R4
          BAL    R14,GETBLOK
* Now R1 => data portion of the just acquired storage
          BCTR   R4,0            Subtract 1 for EX
          SLL    R4,4            Shift for Length 1 of UNPK
          EX     R4,UNPACKIT     Final conversion step
          BR     R14             Return
*
```

```
UNPACKIT DS    0F
         UNPK  0(0,R1),DWORD(8) Unpack into the return area (EVDATA)
*
******************************************************************
* D2B: Convert an EBCDIC string of decimal characters to
*      the binary equivalent.
* Input:
*    R0: Address of the first byte of the field
*    R1: Length of the field
*
* Output:
*.   R0: Undefined
*    R1: Fullword containing converted value
*    R15: 0 if conversion successful, otherwise 1
*
D2B      DS    0H
         STM   R15,R1,SAVEAREA Save registers 15, 0, and 1
         LR    R15,R0          Address of decimal string in R15
* Each digit must be a decimal value (between 0 and 9):
D2BLOOP  DS    0H
         CLI   0(R15),C'0'     Digit less than 0?
         BL    D2BERROR        If yes, this is an error
         CLI   0(R15),C'9'     Digit more than 9?
         BH    D2BERROR        If yes, this is an error
         LA    R15,1(,R15)     Point to the next digit
         BCT   R1,D2BLOOP      Continue in loop
* Do the conversion to binary
         L     R15,SAVEAREA    Restore address of input
         L     R1,SAVEAREA+8   Restore length of input
         BCTR  R1,0            Decrement length for EX
         EX    R1,PACKIT       Pack the value
         CVB   R1,DWORD        Convert packed value to binary
         LTR   R1,R1           Was the third argument zero?
         BZ    D2BERROR        A start position of zero is illegal
         SR    R15,R15         Return code = 0
         BR    R14             Return
PACKIT   PACK  DWORD,0(0,R15)  Object of EX instruction
* An error of some kind has occurred, so send back a non-zero
* return code.
D2BERROR DS    0H
         LA    R15,1           Set non-zero return code
         BR    R14             Return
******************************************************************
* GETBLOK: Subroutine to obtain an EVALBLOK
*
* Input:
*    R1: Length of EVDATA (length of data to be returned)
*
* Output:
*    R0: Number of doublewords in the entire EVALBLOK
*    R1: Address of EVDATA (our result buffer)
*    R2: Address of the EVALBLOK
*
GETBLOK  DS    0H
         LA    R0,EVDLEN+7(,R1) Add workarea len plus rounding (7)
```

```
                 SRL    R0,3                Convert to doublewords (divide by 8).
       * This is the number of doublewords in the entire EVALBLOK
                 DMSFREE DWORDS=(0),TYPE=USER,TYPECALL=SVC,ERR=*
                 LTR    R15.R15             Storage successfully acquired?
                 BNZ    ERROR               No, error return
                 LR     R2,R1               Save address of EVALBLOK in R2
       * Fill in some of the EVALBLOK fields
                 USING  EVALBLOK,R2         Addressability
                 XC     EVPAD1,EVPAD1       Zero out both of the
                 XC     EVPAD2,EVPAD2         pad fields
                 ST     R0,EVSIZE           Store total block length (doublewords)
                 ST     R1,EVLEN            Length of DATA (in bytes)
                 LA     R1,EVDATA           Point to the result buffer
                 BR     R14                 And return
       ****************************************************************
                 TITLE  'Constants, workareas, and DSECTs'
       SKIPTAB   DS     256C
       CONST1    DC     F'1'
       SAVEAREA  DS     16F                 Temporary save area for registers
       FUNRETSV  DS     F                   Save area for return string pointer
       *                                    (pointer placed in EPFUNRET)
       DWORD     DS     D                   workarea for packed to binary convert
       POWER     DS     0F                  Powers of 10 Table
                 DC     A(1,10,100,1000,10000,100000,1000000)
                 DC     A(10000000,100000000,1000000000)
       POWEREND  DC     A(-1)     end of powers list
                 REGEQU ,
                 EPLIST ,
       EVALBLOK  DSECT  ,
       EVPAD1    DS     F                   Reserved
       EVSIZE    DS     F                   Total block size in doublewords
       EVLEN     DS     F                   Length of data in bytes
       EVPAD2    DS     F                   Reserved
       EVDLEN    EQU    *-EVALBLOK          Length of workarea
       EVDATA    DS     C                   The returned character string
       * DSECT to describe our argument list
       ARGS      DSECT  ,
       NEEDLE    DS     F                   The pattern we are searching for
       NEEDLEL   DS     F                   The length of the pattern
       HAYSTAK   DS     F                   The string which contains the pattern
       HAYSTAKL  DS     F                   The length of the string
       START     DS     F                   The starting column for the search
       STARTL    DS     F                   The length of the starting column
       FENCE     DS     F                   The last possible end position
                 REGEQU ,
                 NUCON  ,
                 END    ,
```

Placing external functions in function packages

The previous example is a complete assembler external function; the remaining task is placing it in a REXX function package.

This requires obtaining storage and moving the program into that storage as a nucleus extension. The code which has been loaded may then be called by **RXUSERFN** to invoke any of the member functions. An entry for each user function must be added to the **FUNLIST** table in **RXUSERFN**.

The next section shows basic code which implements a function package. All that needs to be done is to insert the code for the prior example, **RXPOSBM**, just after the label of that name.

The function package skeleton

```
USERFN    CSECT *
          USING *,R12
          USING NUCON,0
          LR    R10,R14        Save return address
          SLR   R2,R2          Assume it's NUCEXT "RXUSERFN" only.
*                              (On entry to an established
*                              nucleus extension, R2 contains
*                              the address of the SCBLOCK.)
*********************************************************************
*  1. Check for arguments. Assume RXPOSBM() was issued by a REXX
*     program. This causes 'RXUSERFN LOAD RXPOSBM' to be issued.
*     We must search the FUNLIST table for the entry RXPOSBM.
*********************************************************************
          CLI   ARG1(R1),X'FF'  Any arguments?
          BE    GOLOAD          Branch if not - go install
          CLC   ARG1(8,R1),=CL8'LOAD'  This an explicit load?
          BNE   BADPL           Branch if not - complain
*         Note: We do not have to handle RESET because the
*               package has not yet been loaded
*
*=> LOAD request, so check function name against FUNLIST
*    example: (RXUSERFN LOAD RXPOSBM)
          LA    R4,LENTRY       Length of FUNLIST entry (8)
          LA    R2,FUNLIST      Start of function table
          LA    R5,EFUNLIST     End of function table
CHECK     DS    0H
          CLC   ARG2(,R1),FUNLNAME(R2)  Names match?
          BE    GOLOAD          Br if yes - go do
*                               appropriate NUCEXTing
          BXLE  R2,R4,CHECK     Continue testing if more
* R2 => start of FUNLIST, R4 contains increment value (8),
* R5 => end of FUNLIST
          LA    R15,1           Indicate function not found
          BR    R10             Not in list - return
*********************************************************************
*  2. Assume we found 'RXUSERFN' in the FUNLIST table. We will use
*     the CMS NUCEXT function to establish both 'RXUSERFN' and
*     'RXPOSBM' as nucleus extensions. This involves moving all
*     the code between the label 'FREEGO' and the end of the
*     program into free storage.
*********************************************************************
*=> NUCEXT "RXUSERFN" as well as specific function (e.g. if
```

```
*    LOAD was specified on invocation).
GOLOAD   DS    0H
         LA    R0,FREELEND     Length of code in doublewords
*                              Get the storage
         DMSFREE DWORDS=(0),TYPE=NUCLEUS,ERR=NOSTORE
         LA    R8,FREEGO       Start of free storage code
         L     R9,=A(FREELEN)  Get length of code in bytes
         LR    R7,R9           Copy length for MVCL
         LR    R4,R9           Save for later use
         LR    R3,R1
         LR    R6,R1           Free storage area start
         SPKA  0               Set nucleus key
         MVCL  R6,R8           Move code to free storage
*****************************************************************
*  3. Fill in the NUCEXT plist for the entire function package.
*     Note the use of the SYSTEM and SERVICE attributes.
*     A nucleus extension with the 'SYSTEM' attribute
*     will remain active after an abnormal end. The
*     'SERVICE' attribute means that during abend processing, the
*     nucleus extension is called with the following special
*     parameter list:
*         DS    0F
*         DS    CL8'nucleus extension name'
*         DS    CL8'PURGE'
*         DC    8X'FF'
*****************************************************************
         ST    R3,NLADDR       Entry point address
         ST    R3,NLSTART      Start address
         MVI   NLFLAG,SYSTEM+SERVICE Request service call
         ST    R4,NLLEN        Length
         LA    R1,NLIST        -> PLIST
         SVC   CMS202
         DC    AL4(1)          Fall through error
         LTR   R15,R15         Did everything go smoothly?
         BNZR  R10             No, return directly
*-> See if we have a function....
         LTR   R2,R2           Install "RXUSERFN" only?
*                              (We didn't load a function.)
         BZR   R10             Br if yes - return to caller
*        R15 already 0 from above....Use to clear fields
*****************************************************************
*  4. Fill in the NUCEXT plist for the individual function.
*     Note that here we use the SYSTEM attribute and omit
*     the SERVICE attribute. The entry point of the function
*     is obtained from the FUNLIST table.
*****************************************************************
         ST    R15,NLSTART     ..start address
         ST    R15,NLLEN       ..length
         MVI   NLFLAG,SYSTEM   ..no service calls!
* R2 points to FUNLIST entry to be installed.
* R3 points to start of NUCXLOADed area.
         A     R3,FUNOFFS(,R2) Calculate true start address
         ST    R3,NLADDR       Add to startup PSW
         MVC   NLNAME,FUNLNAME(R2) Copy startup name
*    Issue SVC...
```

```
          SVC    CMS202
          DC     AL4(1)           Immediate exit on error
          BR     R10
          DROP   R12
          LTORG
*******************************************************************
*  5. Here is the beginning of the code which will remain in
*     free storage.  It is responsible for processing any LOAD
*     or RESET request:
*     a. A LOAD call (such as 'RXUSERFN LOAD RXUSER2') identifies
*        the passed function as an entry point in RXUSERFN.
*        This is known as 'AUTOLOAD' because the code is already
*        in storage.
*     b. A RESET request is the result of the NUCXDROP program
*        being used to explicitly unload the nucleus extension.
*        The code here "turns off" the function by issuing the
*        NUCEXT 'CANCEL' plist. This is identified by passing an
*        address of 0 in the 'DNLADDR' (entry point) field.
*     c. A PURGE service call is ignored (see item #4 above).
*******************************************************************
          SPACE 2
FREEGO    DS     0D               Force doubleword alignment
*                                 of DMSFREE loaded code.
          USING  *,R12
          B      STARTCOD
          DC     CL8'>USERFN<'    Eye catcher for storage dump
STARTCOD  DS     0H
          LR     R10,R14          Save return address
          CLC    ARG1(8,R1),=CL8'LOAD'    Is this a load?
          BE     CHK4ARGS         Yes, check for any args
          CLC    ARG1(8,R1),=CL8'RESET'   Reset?
          BE     DOOFF            Yes, turn off functions
          SLR    R15,R15          In case of service call
          CLM    R1,B'1000',=X'FF' Is it an ABEND call??
          BER    R14              Branch if yes - quick quit
          LA     R15,4            No, set error RC
          BR     R14              and return
          SPACE 1
CHK4ARGS  DS     0H
          LA     R15,1            Set possible return code
          CLI    ARG2(R1),X'FF'   Any arguments passed?
          BER    R14              No, error (already loaded)
*-----------------------------------------------------------------*
* AUTOLOAD: switch on selected function                           *
*-----------------------------------------------------------------*
*                                                                 *
* 'LOAD' request.  Check function name against FUNLIST.           *
*                                                                 *
* Only turn on the requested (autoload) function.                 *
*-----------------------------------------------------------------*
          SPACE 1
          PUSH   USING            Save USING status
          USING,DNUCX,R13         Use save area for PLIST
AUTOLOAD  DS     0H
          MVC    DNLIST(LNLIST),NLIST Move skeleton to workarea
```

```
          LR      R3,R1            Save old plist pointer
          LA      R4,LENTRY        Length of FUNLIST entry
          LA      R5,EFUNLIST      End of function table
          LA      R2,FUNLIST       Start of function table
          LA      R15,1            Set error return code
CHECK1    DS      0H
          CLC     ARG2(,R3),FUNLNAME(R2) Check against name
          BE      TURNON           Found - turn function on
          BXLE    R2,R4,CHECK1     Loop for another check
          BR      R10              Return with RC = 1
TURNON    DS      0H
          MVC     DNLNAME,FUNLNAME(R2) Copy startup name
          LA      R1,DNLIST        -> PLIST
* See if the function is ALREADY a nucleus extension.
*    (Note that the QUERY form of NUCEXT requires a -1 in the
*    address.)
          LNR     R15,R15          -1
          ST      R15,DNLADDR      Query form of NUCEXT plist
          SVC     CMS202
          DC      AL4(1)           Fall through if error
          LTR     R15,R15          Exists?
          BZR     R10              Yes, immediate return
          L       R6,FUNOFFS(,R2)  Load address offset
          ALR     R6,R12           True start address
          ST      R6,DNLADDR       Add to startup PSW
* Issue SVC...
          SVC     CMS202
          DC      AL4(1)           Ignore errors
          BR      R10              Return
          POP     USING            Restore USING status
*---------------------------------------------------------------*
* RESET call: switch off functions                              *
*---------------------------------------------------------------*
DOOFF     DS      0H
          LA      R5,FUNLIST       -> to function list
          LA      R1,NLIST         -> to NUCEXT plist
FUNLOOP   DS      0H
          LT      R15,FUNOFFS(R5)  Any more to cancel?
          BZR     R10              0 = all done ... Get out
          MVC     NLNAME(8),FUNLNAME(R5) Copy startup name
*     Issue SVC
          SVC     CMS202
          DC      AL4(1)           Ignore errors
*     (we ignore errors e.g.: function already cancelled)
          LA      R5,LENTRY(,R5)   -> next item in FUNLIST
          B       FUNLOOP
* Skeleton PLIST for invoking 'NUCEXT'
NLIST     DS      0D               NUCEXT plist
          DC      CL8'NUCEXT'      Name
NLNAME    DC      CL8'RXUSERFN'    Function package name
          DC      X'FF'            System mask enabled
NLKEY     DC      X'04'            System key
NLFLAG    DC      AL1(SYSTEM)      NUCEXT flag
          DC      X'00'            Spare flags
NLADDR    DC      A(0)             Entry point address
```

```
          DC     AL4(*-*)            private
NLSTART   DC     A(0)               Start address
NLLEN     DC     F'0'               Length
LNLIST    EQU    *-NLIST            Length of list
*****************************************************************
*  6. Create the FUNLIST table itself:
*****************************************************************
* List of functions included in this package, with their offsets
FUNLNAME  EQU    4,8                Offset and length of name
FUNOFFS   EQU    0,4                Offset to the routine
FUNLIST   DC     A(RXPOSBM-FREEGO),CL8'RXPOSBM'
LENTRY    EQU    *-FUNLIST          Length of a single entry
          DC     A(RXUSER2-FREEGO),CL8'RXUSER2'
          DC     A(RXUSER3-FREEGO),CL8'RXUSER3'
EFUNLIST  DS     0H                 End of the FUNLIST proper
          DC     A(*-*)             End fence
*****************************************************************
*  7. Insert the code for RXPOSBM here:
*****************************************************************
RXPOSBM   DS     0H
          TITLE 'RXPOSBM: Faster string search to replace POS()'
*---------------------------------------------------------------
*  Code for assembler function RXPOSBM is inserted here
*---------------------------------------------------------------
RXUSER2   DS     0H
*---------------------------------------------------------------
*  Code for assembler function RXUSER2 would go here
*---------------------------------------------------------------
RXUSER3   DS     0H
*---------------------------------------------------------------
*  Code for assembler function RXUSER3 would go here
*---------------------------------------------------------------
*****************************************************************
*  8. Define common symbolic assignments
*****************************************************************
          TITLE 'USERFN:  Common symbolic assignments'
CMS202    EQU    202                CMS SVC 202
ARG1      EQU    8,8                First argument
ARG2      EQU    16,8               Second argument
          REGEQU
          DS     0D                 Get to doubleword boundary
FREELEN   EQU    *-FREEGO           Bytes of free storage code
FREELEND  EQU    (*-FREEGO+7)/8  Doublewords of free storage code
*****************************************************************
*  9. END OF FREE STORAGE CODE.  DSECT for NUCEXT plist follows:
*****************************************************************
* NUCEXT PLIST flags:
SERVICE   EQU    X'40'
SYSTEM    EQU    X'80'
*   DSECT for NUCEXT plist
DNUCX     DSECT
DNLIST    DS     CL8    'NUCEXT' Name
DNLNAME   DS     CL8    'RXUSERFN' Function name
DNLMASK   DS     X'00'           Mask
DNLKEY    DS     X'04'  SYSTEM for RXUSERFN
```

```
*                        (04 - system, E4 - user)
DNLFLAG  DS    AL1 (SYSTEM)    NUCEXT flag
         DS    X'00'           Spare flags
DNLADDR  DS    A               Entry point address
         DS    AL4 (*-*)
DLSTART  DS    A               Start address
DLNLLEN  DS    AL4 (FREELEN)   Length
```

XEDIT Macros

By Philip H. Smith III

When VM/System Product was released in 1981, two major CMS innovations were the second-generation EXEC language, **EXEC 2**, and the System Product Editor, **XEDIT**. Besides being used for system procedures, EXEC 2 could be used for something called **XEDIT macros**.

WHAT IS AN XEDIT MACRO?

XEDIT macros are (typically, although by no means always) small programs which automate, customize, or simplify some aspect of XEDIT. Macros have filetype **XEDIT** and are invoked just like built-in XEDIT subcommands—that is, the user simply types the macro name as if it were a built-in subcommand, and, after failing to recognize it as a built-in subcommand, XEDIT attempts to execute a macro by that name. In fact, several "built-in subcommands" are implemented as macros (**ALL**, **HEXTYPE**, **CAPPEND**, and others).

The CMS community quickly embraced XEDIT and the concept of XEDIT macros, and today macros are used for a myriad of functions:

- Issue a sequence of **SET** subcommands to tailor the XEDIT environment
- Add a "subcommand"
- Improve the interface to a built-in subcommand

- Automate a tedious series of subcommands for a common (or specific) task
- Use XEDIT as a full-screen display manager, perhaps prompting for input, processing it, and invoking another application
- Drive XEDIT as a text processor, performing work under program control

XEDIT macros were a great innovation: no such interface had existed for the previous CMS editor, EDIT. When REXX was introduced in VM/SP Release 3, it was supported for XEDIT macros, much to everyone's relief. For all the reasons that REXX is preferred to EXEC 2 for EXECs, it is also preferred for XEDIT macros. Soon all new XEDIT macros from IBM were written in REXX, and many existing macros were converted from EXEC 2 to REXX.

XEDIT MACRO FACILITIES

Most important to development of XEDIT macro popularity was the fact that several XEDIT subcommands were specifically designed to be used from macros, i.e., to make XEDIT programmable:

CMSG/EMSG/MSG	Displays text on the screen: on the command line (**CMSG**), as an error message (**EMSG**), or as a "plain" message (**MSG**).
CURSOR	Places the cursor on the physical or logical screen.
PRESERVE	Saves most current settings, to be restored using **RESTORE**.
REFRESH	Displays the screen immediately, while continuing macro execution (normally XEDIT writes the screen only at subcommand end).
RESTORE	Restores settings saved with **PRESERVE**.
SOS	("Screen Operation Simulation") Simulates terminal actions (keystrokes): hardware TAB keys, CLEAR, etc.
STACK	Places file lines in the program stack; a macro can read these and process them.
TRANSFER	Stacks the result of a **QUERY**, so that a macro can read and process it.

VM/SP Release 3 added the **EXTRACT** subcommand. **EXTRACT** offers a superset of the information available via **QUERY** or **TRANSFER**, and—best of all—places the information directly in REXX variables. For example:

EXTRACT /CURSOR/

sets ten REXX variables, CURSOR.0 through CURSOR.9. CURSOR.0 receives the number of CURSOR.*n* variables set (that is, 9). This convention—variable *stem*.0 containing a count of *stem*.*n* variables—is now used by CMS EXECIO and many IBM and other vendor products to indicate the scope of an action.

Besides being cleaner—freeing macro programmers from dealing with the stack—EXTRACT is preferred to TRANSFER because it returns more information. For example, TRANSFER CURSOR returns only four values, representing the cursor position on the screen and in the file the last time the screen was displayed, whereas EXTRACT /CURSOR/ also returns the cursor position if the screen were displayed at that instant (which may have been changed by prefix subcommands or subcommands in the macro) and the current cursor priority (the weighting given to the operations which changed the cursor position).

After EXTRACT was introduced, TRANSFER enhancements ceased, demonstrating the XEDIT developers' choice of EXTRACT as the best technology for processing XEDIT information in macros. As a result, many very useful EXTRACT operands have no corresponding QUERY or TRANSFER operand, such as NBSCOPE, LASTLORC, and BASEFT.

THE PROFILE XEDIT

Users were encouraged to learn to exploit XEDIT macros by the PROFILE XEDIT. This macro, invoked by default whenever a file is XEDITed, typically consists of several SET subcommands which customize the XEDIT environment.

Since XEDIT is highly tailorable, with over 80 SET subcommands—and has some poor defaults (for example, STAY OFF and SCALE ON)—even novice users often wish to customize it; sophisticated users' PROFILEs often change XEDIT so much that it is unrecognizable to and unusable by others!

Many installations install a PROFILE on a common disk to perform installation default processing. Installation defaults also provide novice users with a starting point when they experiment with creating their own PROFILEs.

PROFILE arguments

The PROFILE macro receives an argument string consisting of the XEDIT fileid and options specified, and can thus determine the file to be edited, perhaps setting filetype-specific options. For example, the PROFILE might force WIDTH 255 when EXECs are edited:

```
/* PROFILE XEDIT fragment which defaults to WIDTH 255 for EXECs */
arg fn ft fm '(' options ')' rest
if ft = 'EXEC' then do
   if find('W WI WID WIDT WIDTH', options) = 0 then
 · options = options 'WIDTH 255'
end
'COMMAND LOAD' fn ft fm '(' options ')' rest
```

The LOAD subcommand

The power of the PROFILE is increased by the LOAD subcommand, which is valid *only* in the PROFILE and must be the first XEDIT subcommand executed: subsequent LOADs fail, and any other XEDIT subcommand executed first causes an implicit LOAD.

LOAD reads the file to be edited from disk into storage. LOAD arguments are the same as XEDIT command arguments, including options. Since the file read has not yet taken place when the PROFILE starts execution, a clever PROFILE can process the arguments—particularly any fileid specified—and then issue the LOAD, perhaps with different arguments.

For example, the PROFILE can allow the filetype to default to one commonly edited, allowing the user to specify only a filename:

```
/* PROFILE XEDIT fragment which defaults filetype to 'EXEC' */
arg fn ft fm '(' rest
if ft = '' then ft = 'EXEC'
'COMMAND LOAD' fn ft fm '(' rest
```

The PROFILE can also use the CMS GLOBALV facility to note the fileid specified each time XEDIT is used; then if invoked with no fileid, it can LOAD the last file edited, by default:

```
/* PROFILE XEDIT fragment which defaults to last file edited */
arg fn ft fm '(' rest
if fn = '' then          /* No file specified, get previous */
address command 'GLOBALV SELECT XEDIT GET FN FT FM'
'COMMAND LOAD' fn ft fm '(' rest
address command 'GLOBALV SELECT XEDIT SET FN FT FM'/* Save */
```

LOAD is another illustration of how XEDIT was designed for macro programmability.

The PROFILE option

The XEDIT command PROFILE option specifies the macro to execute as the PROFILE. This allows application-specific PROFILEs, and is used heavily by XEDIT applications such as FILELIST and NAMES (see the section "XEDIT applications from IBM").

Arguments specific to the PROFILE being used can be passed after a closing parenthesis in the parameter list, enabling further programmability:

```
/* PROFILE which uses non-standard arguments */
arg fn ft fm '(' options ')' moptions
do while moptions <> ''
   parse var moptions moption moptions
   select
      when moption = . . .
         :
   end
end
```

"ONE-SHOT" MACROS

XEDIT is an extremely powerful editor, with many flexible subcommands. Certain editing tasks, however, require repetition of a unique series of subcommands.

"One-shot"—single-use—XEDIT macros are ideal for this purpose. Such macros solve specific problems and are not intended to be saved and used again—but avoid endless repetition and thus aid productivity.

"One-shot" macros used as PROFILEs are also useful for performing the same set of changes on a set of files.

USING MACROS

The macro interface

XEDIT macros are XEDIT-oriented procedures, in the same way that EXECs are CMS-oriented procedures. When invoked, macros have a default environment (**ADDRESS** setting) of **XEDIT**. This means that when an XEDIT macro is executed, lines not recognized as REXX instructions or assignments are passed to XEDIT for execution, just as in an EXEC they are passed to CMS.

When XEDIT is initialized, it creates a CMS subcommand environment called **XEDIT**. When a subcommand is not recognized by XEDIT, XEDIT looks for a macro. If one is found, it is loaded into storage (if not already present) and executed.

SET MACRO ON

By default, XEDIT searches for built-in subcommands before looking for a macro, as described above. However, if the subcommand:

```
SET MACRO ON
```

is issued, XEDIT searches for macros *before* looking for built-in subcommands.

While imposing obvious (and significant) performance overhead, this allows XEDIT macros to override built-in subcommands easily. A better way to override specific subcommands, however, is using synonyms, as described below.

Synonyms

Unlike CMS synonym processing, XEDIT searches for synonyms *before* built-in subcommands or macros. This allows users to override—or front-end—a built-in subcommand by defining a synonym for it which executes a macro:

```
SET SYNONYM CHANGE 1 MACRO MYCHANGE
```

When a **CHANGE** subcommand is entered, the **MYCHANGE** macro gets control instead. This macro might do various things, such as log the change for auditing/recovery purposes, or detect errors and offer a full-screen menu so the user can correct the syntax before issuing a "real" **CHANGE** subcommand.

For novice users, or in XEDIT-based applications, such macros can aid productivity and control while maintaining standard XEDIT syntax.

COMMAND and MACRO

The **COMMAND** and **MACRO** subcommands force execution of named subcommands or macros:

```
COMMAND TOP
MACRO MYCHANGE /DOG/CAT/
```

bypasses synonym and macro processing and executes the **TOP** subcommand, then bypasses synonym and subcommand lookup and invokes the **MYCHANGE** macro.

Since **TOP** is a built-in subcommand and **MYCHANGE** is not, these results are hardly surprising. However, if the user has used **SET MACRO ON** or has set a synonym for **TOP** or **MYCHANGE**, use of **COMMAND** or **MACRO** forces the expected result.

In addition, for **MYCHANGE** to execute a generated or corrected **CHANGE** subcommand as described above, it needs a way to avoid synonym processing—otherwise it will just reinvoke itself!

To avoid problems with synonyms or **SET MACRO ON**, especially in shared or distributed macros, it is advisable to prefix *all* XEDIT subcommands in macros with **COMMAND** or **MACRO** as appropriate.

Implicit SET subcommands

XEDIT allows issuing **SET** subcommands implicitly—that is, without specifying the keyword **SET**. For example, the following are equivalent:

```
SET FNAME PROFILE
FNAME PROFILE
FN PROFILE
```

(**FN** is a built-in abbreviation for **FNAME**.)

The latter two commands are **implicit** **SET** subcommands—after XEDIT determines that there is no built-in **FNAME** or **FN** subcommand, it attempts to execute the command string as a **SET** subcommand.

This feature, originally implemented to simplify conversion from the original CMS EDIT editor (which had no explicit **SET** subcommand), saves typing and is very handy. However, macro writers should understand when they are issuing a **SET** subcommand, and specify it explicitly:

```
COMMAND SET FNAME PROFILE
```

Besides being "pure", this again ensures the expected result.

Macro naming

XEDIT defines subcommand names as containing only alphabetic characters. Thus when XEDIT parses subcommand names from command strings, special characters which are valid in CMS filenames—such as numerics and some punctuation—signify the end of the subcommand name. So if a macro called **THING2** exists, typing **THING2** results in:

```
DMSXDC542E No such subcommand: THING
```

Or, if a macro called **THING** exists, it will be invoked with a parameter of 2.

Forcing execution of **THING2** requires the **MACRO** keyword:

```
macro thing2
```

While this is confusing to the novice, it allows macros to function as built-in subcommands, which allow operands to abut the command verb—for example:

```
c/dog/cat
```

which invokes the **CHANGE** subcommand (or a synonym) with an operand string of /dog/cat.

Besides enabling natural use of macros as subcommands, this feature can be used to avoid accidental execution of a macro. For example, accidental execution of the macro used as a PROFILE by the CMS **FILELIST** utility is likely to result in an error message—and an empty file! (The macro deletes any existing lines in the file, preparatory to adding a new set.) Fortunately, this macro is named **X$FLST$X**, and thus cannot be executed without being prefixed with **MACRO**.

THE PARSE MACRO

IBM provides **PARSE XEDIT**, a tool for parsing XEDIT macro argument strings.

A macro can stack the argument string it was passed, and call **PARSE** with a column at which to start parsing and the desired operand format(s) to parse. In response, **PARSE** stacks column numbers indicating the starting and ending positions of objects parsed.

PARSE handles trivial operands like numbers and words, and also complex XEDIT objects like line targets and delimited strings. Objects are parsed according to normal XEDIT subcommand parsing rules— that is, non-alphabetic characters delimit certain types of operands.

While **PARSE** is somewhat slow, consisting of 200+ lines of REXX, it allows easy creation of XEDIT macros which accept operands like built-in subcommands.

PREFIX MACROS

By default, file lines displayed on the XEDIT screen have a five-character **prefix area** preceding them. **Prefix subcommands** entered in the prefix area affect the lines they are entered on. Built-in prefix subcommands add, delete, move, copy, and duplicate lines, define SCALE or TAB line locations, and perform other functions.

VM/SP Release 3 introduced **prefix macros**. Prefix macros extend prefix subcommands the same way "regular" XEDIT macros extend subcommands. In fact, several "built-in" prefix subcommands are macros (**S/SS, X/XX, SI, </<<, and >/>>**).

An unrecognized prefix subcommand—that is, anything entered in a prefix area which is not a built-in prefix subcommand—invokes a prefix macro, just as unrecognized command line subcommands invoke macros.

Prefix macros also have filetype **XEDIT** and resemble ordinary macros. The same macro can be used for command line and prefix invocation: a special parameter list is passed, so the macro can determine that it was invoked as a prefix macro.

Prefix macro arguments

The first word of a prefix macro parameter list is **PREFIX**.

The second is the function: one of **SET**, **SHADOW**, or **CLEAR**.

SET and **SHADOW** are similar, and mean that the macro was invoked from a file line or a shadow line—a line displayed to represent one or more lines hidden by Selective Line Editing (usually by using the **ALL** macro).

CLEAR means that a **pending** prefix subcommand—one redisplayed in a prefix area as a result of a **SET PENDING** subcommand, presumably issued by an earlier invocation of the prefix macro—was cleared by being overtyped or blanked. This notification is required so that the macro can reset any special handling, such as clearing a marked block (see the section "Block prefix subcommands" for an explanation of marked blocks).

The third operand is the file line number on which the prefix subcommand was specified. For shadow lines, this is the line number of the first undisplayed line.

Any additional operands are those specified in the prefix area when the macro was invoked—typically a count or number of lines. Since the prefix area is five characters, up to two arguments, totalling up to 4 bytes, are possible.

Dual-purpose macros

As mentioned earlier, the same macro can support command line and prefix invocation. While a command line macro invocation can specify operands which appear like the special prefix macro arguments, this is unlikely.

Dual-purpose macros typically operate like the following:

```
/* Some comment */
'COMMAND EXTRACT /LINE/'
arg prefix function line operands
if prefix = 'PREFIX' then 'COMMAND LOCATE :'line
else arg operands
```

The few lines of code at the beginning detect prefix invocation and make the invoking line the current line, so that the body of the macro operates on the correct lines. The body then operates as if the macro was invoked from the command line.

After a prefix macro completes, XEDIT restores the current line to its location when the macro was invoked; prefix macros thus need not restore the current line.

SET PENDING

The **SET PENDING** subcommand allows prefix macros to place text in the prefix area after execution. Four operands exist: **ON**, **BLOCK**, **ERROR**, and **OFF**.

ON sets a "simple" pending prefix subcommand:

```
SET PENDING ON K
```

to be executed next time a key is pressed.

BLOCK tells XEDIT to set a pending subcommand, but to remember that it is part of a marked block:

```
SET PENDING BLOCK KK
```

SET PREFIX SYNONYM

Since the prefix area is only 5 bytes long, most prefix macros have one-or two-character names. Such short names, however, are unintuitive to maintain and distribute, are easy to accidentally invoke from the command line, and frequently conflict with macros on other accessed disks.

XEDIT provides the SET PREFIX SYNONYM subcommand to map macro names to prefix subcommands. For example:

```
SET PREFIX SYNONYM K PREFIXK
```

requests that a K prefix subcommand invoke macro PREFIXK.

Many XEDIT users use a naming convention such as PREFIX*xx* or PRF*xxxxx* to distinguish prefix macros, and put SET PREFIX SYNONYM subcommands in their PROFILEs to enable their use.

By combining multiple SET PREFIX SYNONYM subcommands with REXX PARSE SOURCE, a single prefix macro can provide several similar prefix functions. For example, U and L prefix macros to uppercase and lowercase lines of text could be combined into one PREFIXUL macro, which would choose the appropriate function via PARSE SOURCE:

```
/* PREFIXUL XEDIT -- L and U prefix subcommands */
    arg p f l rest
    if f = 'CLEAR' | p <> 'PREFIX' then exit
    parse source . . . . . pcmd .
    select
        when pcmd = 'U' then cmd = 'UPPERCAS'
        when pcmd = 'L' then cmd = 'LOWERCAS'
        otherwise
        signal ERROR
    end
    'COMMAND LOCATE :'l 'COMMAND' cmd rest
    if rc = 0 | rc = 1 then exit
ERROR:
    'COMMAND SET PENDING ERROR' pcmd rest
    exit
```

Block prefix subcommands

Some prefix subcommands have a **block** form. Used to mark a block of lines to perform an action on, these are typically the prefix subcommand specified twice—for example, D to delete a line and DD to mark the start and end of a block of lines to delete.

Prefix macros can use EXTRACT /PENDING KK and EXTRACT /PENDING BLOCK KK to detect the extent of pending prefix subcommands.

Block prefix subcommands are commonly invoked using SET PREFIX SYNONYM to call the same macro as the non-block format. For example, the PRFSHIFT macro implements the >, <, >>, and << prefix subcommands to shift data left and right on one or more lines.

Four synonyms are automatically set:

```
SET PREFIX SYNONYM > PRFSHIFT
SET PREFIX SYNONYM < PRFSHIFT
SET PREFIX SYNONYM >> PRFSHIFT
SET PREFIX SYNONYM << PRFSHIFT
```

PRFSHIFT checks for a block format and whether the block's other end is already pending. If so, it shifts all lines in the block; if not, it uses **SET PENDING BLOCK** to leave the partial block pending.

Since prefix macros tend to affect only the line they are entered on, most lend themselves to block forms which affect multiple lines. The additional programming complexity is not great, and is justified by the increased functionality.

XEDIT FROM FILETYPE EXEC

Although the default EXEC **ADDRESS** environment is **CMS**, it can be redefined. This means that even EXECs can act as XEDIT macros—issuing XEDIT subcommands, **EXTRACT**ing information, etc.

Such EXECs can use the CMS **SUBCOM** function to determine if XEDIT is already active, and reset the **ADDRESS** environment as appropriate:

```
   :
address command 'SUBCOM XEDIT'
if rc = 0 then address 'XEDIT'
```

A typical example of this would be an EXEC which invokes XEDIT in UPDATE mode:

```
/* XUP EXEC */
address command
arg fn ft '(' options
'SUBCOM XEDIT'
if rc = 0 then address 'XEDIT'
'XEDIT' fn ft '* (CTL LOCAL' options
exit rc
```

If **XUP** does not check to see if XEDIT is already active, it will create a second XEDITor—that is, the second file being edited will not be in the same XEDIT ring as the previous file; the status area at the bottom right will say **1 File**, and the user will have to **QUIT** or **FILE** the second file to get back to the first file.

With the check, the second file is added to the ring, and the user can easily move between files in the ring.

The caveat when using this technique is that if another environment is entered from the first XEDITor—for example, **FLIST**—and the **XUP** is issued from that environment, the results may not be what the user expects: the user will not be shown the second file until returning to XEDIT.

XEDIT AS A FULL-SCREEN DISPLAY MANAGER

XEDIT can be used as a display manager, using subcommands such as SET RESERVED, SET CTLCHAR, and READ, which were designed to be used from macros.

These facilities are not full-featured and are somewhat cumbersome to use; they are thus best suited to small, simple applications, although large, complex XEDIT-based display management systems have been written.

SET RESERVED and SET CTLCHAR

SET RESERVED defines static lines on the XEDIT screen. These are often used to display a PF key legend or other information about the environment.

SET CTLCHAR defines control character strings to be interpreted in RESERVED lines. These allow definition of highlighted and input (unprotected) fields in RESERVED lines, which can be used with READ (see below) for user input.

For example, to define a reserved line on the last line of the screen, with the word **bright** highlighted:

```
'SET CTLCHAR ? ESCAPE'
'SET CTLCHAR + PROTECT HIGH'
'SET CTLCHAR - PROTECT NOHIGH'
'SET RESERVED -1 NOHIGH This word is?+bright?-and this one is not.'
```

READ

The READ subcommand traps user input and returns it to the macro in the CMS stack. Operands control whether READ traps all screen changes or only the command entered, and whether changes to file lines are trapped without being applied to the file being edited.

Changes to RESERVED lines—using SET CTLCHAR to define input fields—are also trapped:

```
'SET CTLCHAR ? ESCAPE'
'SET CTLCHAR = NOPROTECT NOHIGH'
'SET CTLCHAR | PROTECT NOHIGH'
'SET RESERVED 3 NOHIGH Enter your
name:?=_____?|'
'READ ALL TAG'
```

```
do queued()
   parse pull tag text
   select
      when tag = 'ETK' then . . . /* ENTER key */
      when tag = 'PFK' then . . . /* PF key */
      when tag = 'RES' then . . . /* RESERVED line field */
         .
         .
      end
end
```

An undocumented feature, exploited by several IBM applications such as HELP, honors **CTLCHAR** sequences in file lines when the **READ** subcommand is used with the **NOCHANGE** option. This allows definition of "template" files containing **CTLCHAR** sequences; an XEDIT application can alter and display these files as full-screen panels.

Thus if the file being edited contained the line:

```
Enter your name:?=_____?|
```

The macro could avoid the **SET RESERVED**:

```
'SET CTLCHAR ? ESCAPE'
'SET CTLCHAR = NOPROTECT NOHIGH'
'SET CTLCHAR | PROTECT NOHIGH'
'READ NOCHANGE TAG'
do queued()
   parse pull tag text
   select
      when tag = 'ETK' then . . . /* ENTER key */
      when tag = 'PFK' then . . . /* PF key */
      when tag = 'RES' then . . . /* RESERVED line field */
         .
         .
      end
end
```

For this trivial example, little is saved, but for true display management applications involving many screen fields, separating screen format from macros provides greater flexibility and simplifies maintenance. In addition, the screen can be scrolled by normal XEDIT subcommands; many full-screen display management systems have poor support for scrollable panels.

XEDIT applications from IBM

Several IBM CMS utilities are XEDIT display management applications, including **HELP**, **FILELIST**, **MACLIST**, **RDRLIST**, **SENDFILE**, **NAMES**, **NOTE**, and **PEEK**. Some of these environments resemble XEDIT and allow some XEDIT subcommands; in others, XEDIT is totally hidden from the user.

These utilities use (relatively) small front-end EXECs which do setup and then invoke XEDIT with a specific PROFILE. The PROFILE names mostly follow a pattern: X$*xxxx*$X, where *xxxx* relates to the utility name—for example, X$FLST$X for FILELIST and X$NAME$X for NAMES. Some of these PROFILEs are still EXEC 2 (in older VM releases), but all illustrate XEDIT display management techniques.

XEDIT AS A TEXT PROCESSOR

Besides general editing tasks, XEDIT is ideal for general text processing. With an application-specific PROFILE, diverse file manipulation which might otherwise be performed using EXECIO and REXX can be performed equally simply using XEDIT. In addition, such macros can easily improve control and usability, perhaps prompting for a PF key press to verify changes.

XEDIT's SORT function (actually another macro, which calls a CMS module) is also sometimes the easiest way to sort a small file, since it avoids the need for manipulation of work files and is available on all systems.

SUMMARY

XEDIT is a rich and powerful editor. Its integrated REXX macro capabilities increase its power, enabling unlimited extensions. VM users can and should benefit from exploiting REXX and XEDIT macros.

Chapter 7

Application Macros

By Philip H. Smith III

DESCRIPTION AND MOTIVATION

Many application environments include a **script language**, a means of writing programs to execute application subcommands. These scripts—commonly called **macros**—were originally used to automate a process. For example, a user might issue the same subcommands whenever the application is invoked; by grouping those subcommands in a macro, time and effort spent typing (and mistyping!) the same sequence is avoided.

Besides simple encapsulation of commonly used subcommands, macros extend an environment essentially without limit by adding new "subcommands". In many environments, macros are invoked just like subcommand primitives, and are thus indistinguishable.

It is often easier to implement relatively simple application primitives for use from macros, rather than imagining—and binding—the precise syntax and function users will want. XEDIT illustrates this. A text editor must split and join lines of text; the XEDIT SPLIT and JOIN "subcommands" are actually macros. Most users are unaware of this, and are surprised to find these "simple" functions implemented as REXX programs.

Macros also **capture intelligence**: by solving a problem once and writing a macro to automate the process, effort is saved if the user needs to solve the same problem again. In addition, the macro may be exploited by less-skilled users, increasing their productivity and that of the more-skilled macro writer.

Recognition of these benefits led to development of diverse script languages. Some superficially resembled the CMS EXEC language, but no two were alike. For each new environment, users had to learn a new language—if they bothered. Many users muddled along typing the same sequence of application subcommands simply because it was too much trouble to learn yet another language.

CMS EXECS

The CMS EXEC language was an appealing choice for an application macro language, since it was available on all VM systems, but IBM provided no documented method for communicating between EXECs and applications.

Clever programmers found ways to interface to EXEC—IBM's Display Management System (DMS) and Kolinar Corporation's XMENU (now a VM Systems Group product) are examples—but these were exceptions. Installations like the University of Waterloo used a modified EXEC processor as part of a heavily modified CMS EDIT to allow EDIT macros, but, again, this was the exception.

A common technique was using an EXEC to stack a series of application subcommands and then invoke the application. This had shortcomings:

- The CMS EXEC language operates only on one- to eight-character tokens, limiting application subcommand operand lengths.

- Stacked commands lack programmability: once they are stacked, their execution cannot be controlled.

- Some full-screen applications do not use the CMS stack, so stacked commands are not executed.

REXX and EXEC 2 macros

VM/SP Release 1 brought EXEC 2, XEDIT, and XEDIT macros. As the "XEDIT Macros" chapter discussed, XEDIT macros were a great innovation and helped secure the success of XEDIT and VM/SP, and later of REXX itself.

Several CMS facilities were added with EXEC 2 to enable XEDIT macros. Besides adding the ability to execute EXECs with filetypes other than EXEC, CMS was enhanced to support untokenized parameter lists, and the CMS subcommand environment facility was added to allow communication between EXECs and applications.

Perhaps the best news was that these enhancements were flexible and general enough that they could be exploited by other applications. Subsequent CMS releases extended these facilities, which are now important application enabling tools.

Many IBM and vendor applications, including offerings from VM Systems Group, Systems Center, TRAX Softworks, Quercus Systems, Mansfield Software Group, and others, now allow extensions via REXX or EXEC 2 macros; indeed, most experienced VMers *expect* new environments to support them. With the addition of REXX to SAA, guaranteeing its availability on all SAA platforms, this expectation is reasonable.

PARAMETER LISTS

VM/370 offered one EXEC processor. An EXEC was passed a CMS parameter list consisting of eight-character tokens, with parentheses also tokenized. Commands entered from the terminal were translated to uppercase.

Thus a standard CMS command invocation:

```
exec mything somename sometype somemode (thisisalongoption
```

resulted in a seven-token standard parameter list consisting of eight-character tokens. The MYTHING EXEC would receive five arguments: SOMENAME, SOMETYPE, SOMEMODE, (, and THISISAL; note truncation of the final, long token.

While simple to create and parse, this format was extremely limiting. Command tokens longer than eight characters are often useful, and tokenized parentheses caused problems when they were not option markers.

EXEC 2 introduced the **extended parameter list**, which includes pointers to the command verb and the untokenized, untranslated command string. The extended plist allowed EXEC 2 command arguments and variables that were not limited to eight characters—vital to exploitation in XEDIT macros. REXX uses the extended parameter list, and can thus manipulate the entire untokenized command string. The extended plist is mapped by EPLIST MACRO.

CMS SUBCOMMAND ENVIRONMENTS

A **CMS subcommand environment** is a formal interface permitting one program to pass subcommands to another program for execution. An application defines a subcommand environment using CMS services. An application macro (a REXX or EXEC 2 program)—or any other program called from the application—can then execute application subcommands.

Subcommand environments enable two-way interprogram communication: programs which use subcommand environments to pass subcommands to an application can also use subcommand environments to allow the application to communicate with the program.

REXX and EXEC 2 use this feature to allow subcommand environments such as XEDIT to access REXX variables directly, using the **EXECCOMM** subcommand environment. Thus an XEDIT macro can execute XEDIT subcommands such as **EXTRACT**, which can set EXEC variables in the macro.

A REXX or EXEC 2 program creates its own generation of the **EXECCOMM** subcommand environment, so macros called from within macros do not interfere with each other.

This important addition (developed for XEDIT's **EXTRACT** subcommand) allowed macros to be fully integrated with applications—invoking application subcommands, which could then access and even set variables within the calling macro.

Examples of CMS subcommand environments

XEDIT
The best-known usage of a subcommand environment is XEDIT, which defines a subcommand environment called **XEDIT**, through which REXX or EXEC 2 macros (or other called programs) execute XEDIT subcommands. XEDIT uses the **EXECCOMM** subcommand environment defined by REXX or EXEC 2 to transmit information back to the macro directly, in EXEC variables.

DMSXFLxx
XEDIT also creates subcommand environments called **DMSXFLST**, **DMSXFLPT**, **DMSXFLRD**, and **DMSXFLWR**. These provide a faster application interface to files being edited than XEDIT subcommands passed via the **XEDIT** subcommand environment.

Using **DMSXFLxx**, programs can verify that a file is in XEDIT storage (**DMSXFLST**); set the current line pointer (**DMSXFLPT**); "read" lines from a file (**DMSXFLRD**); and "write" (insert) lines (**DMSXFLWR**), using an interface similar to normal CMS file I/O.

This interface was provided to improve the performance of CMS utilities such as **FILELIST** and **NAMES**, but is documented (in current VM releases, in *CMS Application Development Guide for Assembler*) and available for exploitation.

CMS and COMMAND

CMS creates a subcommand environment called CMS, which performs CMS command resolution. This searches for command abbreviations and synonyms, EXECs, nucleus extensions, MODULEs, and CP commands, according to various CMS settings.

This code was embedded in the CMS nucleus, and required REXX to perform special processing when ADDRESS CMS (the default) was in effect to mirror normal CMS command resolution.

Since addition of the CMS subcommand environment in VM/SP Release 4, *any* application can execute CMS commands using normal command resolution. While this sounds trivial, it was an important addition, obviating complex application-specific code for CMS command resolution.

The normal CMS command interface is known to REXX as if it were a subcommand environment called COMMAND, although there is not actually any such subcommand environment.

And more . . .

As CMS grows and develops, subcommand environments are being added and exploited:

Name	**Function and Release Added**
SRPI	Server-Requester Programming Interface (VM/SP 5); supports communication with service virtual machines or workstations.
CPICOMM	Common Programming Interface Communications (VM/SP 6); provides Systems Application Architecture (SAA) Common User Access program-to-program communication facilities.
CPIRR	Common Programming Interface Resource Recovery (VM/ESA Release 1.0); provides Systems Application Architecture (SAA) Common User Access interprocess error handling facilities (CMS CRR—Coordinated Resource Recovery).

REXX and subcommand environments

The ADDRESS instruction

The REXX ADDRESS instruction specifies the subcommand environment to which non-REXX statements are passed for execution. The default subcommand environment is CMS in a REXX program with filetype EXEC, or *filetype* in a REXX program with any other filetype. However, a field in a control block (FBLOCK; see the section "In-storage programs") specified when the EXEC is invoked can specify another default subcommand environment name (or even a PSW, for use in special cases).

Once executing, the REXX program can invoke any subcommand environment via the ADDRESS instruction.

An XEDIT macro can thus issue CMS commands or subcommands to any subcommand environment:

```
/* Some random XEDIT macro */
address command 'SUBCOM BANANA'        /* Is BANANA active? */
if rc <> 0 then                /* No, we must initialize it */
address cms 'BANANA INITIALIZE' /* Tell BANANA to initialize */
if rc <> 0 then exit rc               /* That failed, exit */
'TOP'            /* Go to the top of the file being XEDITed */
address banana 'READ INPUT FILE A' /* Tell BANANA to read it */
exit rc
```

This example illustrates invocation of the CMS command environment and three different subcommand environments:

COMMAND   To execute the CMS SUBCOM function without looking for an EXEC with the same name.

CMS   To execute the CMS BANANA command with full CMS command resolution, so that an EXEC will be executed if found, or a MODULE if no EXEC exists.

XEDIT   The XEDIT TOP subcommand is passed to XEDIT by default when no ADDRESS instruction precedes it, since the default subcommand environment in an XEDIT macro is XEDIT.

BANANA   The READ subcommand is passed to the BANANA subcommand environment for execution.

If the macro needed to issue several BANANA subcommands, it might be more effective to use ADDRESS to change the subcommand environment for the duration:

```
  ⋮
address banana                 /* Change the ADDRESS setting */
'READ INPUT FILE A'        /* Tell BANANA to read the file */
'READ ANOTHER FILE A'          /* And this other file too */
  ⋮
address            /* Restore the original ADDRESS setting */
```

ADDRESS with no operands restores the ADDRESS setting to its previous value.

Exploiting subcommand environments

A minor benefit of subcommand environments is that they cannot be invoked casually or accidentally, so parameter list validation can sometimes be bypassed. This also allows them to have the same name as the invoking application—that is, the XEDIT subcommand environment is called XEDIT, not XEDITSUB or another derivative; this aids understanding and debugging.

REXX programs can easily detect whether a particular subcommand environment is active by using the SUBCOM function directly. Given the environment name, SUBCOM exits with a return code of 0 if the environment exists, 1 if not:

```
:
address command 'SUBCOM XEDIT'       /* Is XEDIT active? */
if rc = 0 then address 'XEDIT'   /* Yes, let's talk to it */
:
```

This adds intelligence to EXECs which may be invoked from various environments, without requiring special parameters to identify the caller.

Developing subcommand environments

While REXX exploits subcommand environments for its own purposes and can invoke those created by other applications, it offers no facilities for creating them.

Subcommand environments were designed to be used from assembler language programs. In early releases of VM/SP, the SUBCOM facility was poorly documented; as its use and capabilities grew, documentation improved. In VM/XA SP, a new SUBCOM assembler language macro was provided. This macro formalized the calling interface and simplified its use.

Creating and managing subcommand environments

Subcommand environments are created and managed using the CMS SUBCOM function. This manages chained control blocks called SCBLOCKs, each representing a named subcommand environment. SUBCOM macro invocations generate SUBCOM calls to create, delete, or query a particular environment or (in later releases) a list of environments, or to return the linked list anchor.

The SCBLOCK representing a defined subcommand environment contains a chain forward pointer, the environment name, the Program Status Word (PSW) of the environment, flags indicating options (persistence, etc.), and a user word. The user word typically points to an application-specific control block and enables continuity across invocations.

Invoking subcommand environments

A subcommand environment is invoked via a SVC 202 or CMSCALL macro with a special call type flag (byte 0 of R1 for SVC 202, or the CALLTYP= operand on a CMSCALL macro).

The old-style tokenized parameter list points to an 8-byte subcommand environment name, while parameters for the subcommand environment are in the extended (untokenized) parameter list.

When the subcommand environment gains control, it receives pointers to both parameter lists and its SCBLOCK. The user word is thus always available to the called environment.

The SUBCOM and CMSCALL macros are documented in *CMS Application Development Guide for Assembler*; the SCBLOCK is mapped by SCBLOCK MACRO.

IN-STORAGE PROGRAMS

Another CMS facility which adds both function and performance is the ability to execute in-storage REXX or EXEC 2 programs.

The original EXEC processor read the entire program from disk every time it was invoked. For a program invoked repeatedly, this caused significant I/O overhead.

Editing macros are often invoked repeatedly—especially in XEDIT, whose design philosophy encourages subcommands which act on a single line to be reinvoked using the REPEAT subcommand for multiline effects.

Since XEDIT implements subcommands such as SPLIT and JOIN as macros, IBM realized that avoiding the overhead of reading the macro file for each invocation promised a significant performance improvement. The solution was extending the extended plist to support in-storage programs. Since the extended plist is a list of fullword addresses, rather than the actual command text, this was easy; an optional additional fullword field points to a **file execution block** (FBLOCK).

When an XEDIT macro is invoked, it is read into storage if it is not already present. A list of **adlen** pairs—fullwords containing a line address and length—is created, and an FBLOCK is filled in with the program fileid, pointers to the start and end of the list of adlen pairs, and the initial subcommand name (XEDIT). The FBLOCK is mapped by FBLOCK MACRO.

Before CMS 5, XEDIT managed in-storage macros itself. In CMS 5, the in-storage EXEC concept was enhanced and generalized with the addition of the EXECLOAD facility (and related commands EXECDROP, EXECMAP, and EXECSTAT) and the "installation segment" (INSTSEG) DCSS, and XEDIT was changed to use this mechanism. The XEDIT PURGE subcommand drops files from storage and from the in-storage list; in CMS 5 and later it uses EXECDROP. The EXECLOAD mechanism is well suited to exploitation by other applications which use REXX macros, although few do so yet.

CMS 6 extended in-storage EXECs further, adding the SEGGEN command to save programs and data in DCSSs; applications which use REXX macros can also benefit from the performance benefits of this facility.

EVOLUTION

The subcommand environment concept is being increasingly exploited by applications. The CMS REXX support for arbitrarily named subcommand environments, and for EXECs with filetypes other than EXEC, enables REXX to be used for application macros. The SUBCOM concept is evolving gradually.

Nucleus extensions

The CMS subcommand environment implementation and the SUBCOM function spawned CMS nucleus extensions and the NUCEXT function; both use the same parameter list and control block formats, managed in separate lists. CMS REXX uses nucleus extensions for add-on function packages.

Like subcommand environments, nucleus extensions can persist beyond CMS end-of-command processing. This makes them ideally suited for mutual exploitation: a nucleus extension can define a subcommand environment and exit to CMS, and a REXX program invoked later can execute subcommands through the subcommand environment.

System exits

A recent addition to the SAA REXX specification and the CMS implementation is application exits for system functions used by REXX. These include storage management, console I/O, stack manipulation, host commands, external function calls, tracing, and initialization/termination.

These exits allow macros to be bound even more tightly to the application. For example, a full-screen application could trap all REXX console I/O and display it in its own window.

The exits are designed for use from assembler language, and are documented in *CMS Application Development Guide for Assembler*.

NON-CMS REXX

Implementations of REXX on non-CMS platforms are including facilities which enable its use for application macros.

This is important, since it allows users to move between platforms with minimal retraining.

The EXECCOMM interface for application/macro communication is also part of the SAA REXX language definition, although the name need not be EXECCOMM for the interface to be SAA-compliant.

SUMMARY

Many application environments are sophisticated enough to warrant a scripting or macro capability. Much development effort has been expended on designing and implementing this for various environments.

In conjunction with products such as **CMS Pipelines**, **RXSQL**, **SQL/EXEC**, **GDDM-REXX**, and **REXXIUCV**, described in other chapters, REXX macros offer power never dreamed of by the original application authors.

CMS applications should exploit REXX and the CMS facilities which enable its use for application macros.

Platforms

REXX is available on a growing variety of computers and software environments. This section describes the use of REXX in computing platform-specific terms.

Interlude

By T.Y. Johnston

I attended the semi-annual SHARE meeting in Houston in early March 1981. One of the sessions there was on something called **REX** by a Mike Cowlishaw. There wasn't anything else interesting, so I went to it. This was my first exposure to REX (REXX).

It was a revelation. The Stanford Linear Accelerator Center (where I worked) had run Wylbur for about a decade. Wylbur was a text editor with a useful EXEC language, but it was coming to the end of its road. When I saw REX my first reaction was, "This is where Wylbur should have gone, but never will." Like nearly everyone in Mike's audience that day, I wanted REX, but I knew of no way to obtain it.

We had just installed a 3081 (the first one external to IBM running VM). Over the next several months we worked with IBM to help make the early support program for the 3081 very successful. A few months later John Akers, then an IBM vice president, now chairman and CEO, visited our site. My boss (the computer center director) and he had a very pleasant conversation, and Akers said that IBM wanted to do something to thank us for our help. What should they do?

When we discussed this offer, I remembered Mike's talk and REX, and suggested that they give us REX. IBM agreed, and around March of 1982, we had REXX at SLAC. It was an immediate success. Within weeks physicists who had resisted EXEC 2 were merrily writing REX EXECs. Our first record of number of EXECs on the system is for July 1982. A small table shows the growth of REX over the other languages:

TABLE 1. Numbers of EXECs.

Date	EXEC	EXEC 2	REXX
July 82	6385	9302	1187
July 83	6850	11,667	7912
July 84	7501	13,158	14,814
July 86	7030	13,878	31,209
July 88	6338	12,460	41,854
July 90	6174	11,525	51,301

As can be seen, REX took off and has only slowed down a little.

During 1982 we worked with IBM development trying to convince them that REX should be part of the product. One never knows with IBM what effect one has had, but when VM/SP Release 3 was announced in 1983, REXX was a part of it.

By 1984 a few hundred happy physicists and programmers had been joined by thousands of other VMers, who enjoyed the richer and friendlier world provided by REXX.

REXX for CMS

By Gary K. Brodock

INTRODUCTION

The **Conversational Monitor System**, usually referred to as **CMS**, is an operating system that runs under control of the Control Program (CP). CMS and CP are the two base pieces of the VM product offered by IBM. CMS provides a user-friendly interface to various parts of the system through a large set of user commands and functions. It was recognized in the beginning that CMS needed a method for grouping frequently used instructions together. At times, users wanted to add simple logic statements around commands to provide conditional execution based on certain other system parameters. The CMS EXEC language was developed to meet this need and was used for many years. Desire for a more comprehensive language led to the creation of EXEC 2, similar in function to CMS EXEC but with more features. However, neither CMS EXEC nor EXEC 2 was as user-friendly as desired, or provided a total functional package.

In the late 1970s, REXX was developed on CMS to meet these needs, providing a very friendly environment with a rich set of functions. Since that time, it has undergone quite a bit of fine tuning. However, the basic structure of this implementation has not changed much; this chapter describes features as implemented in VM/ESA Release 1. Because of various updates to the VM implementation in past releases, users running on older implementations may not have all the functions described here. Likewise, future VM releases may contain additional enhancements.

The first topic in this chapter is the mechanisms for invoking a REXX program, whether from the CMS command line, from a module, from an application program, or from an XEDIT session. The next section describes subcommand handlers. It presents the standard address environments, CMS and COMMAND, and also explains how to create your own address environment. Information on processing subcommands and handling return codes, including successful calls, errors, and failures, is presented. The widely used technique of calling internal, built-in, or external routines is presented next. It describes the search order for finding called routines, and provides hints on their use. Next, the mechanism for accessing the variable pool (the EXECCOMM interface) is described. Included are the various operations that can be performed using the SHVBLOCK request blocks and the Callable Services Library routines. The final section describes the differences between the CMS implementation and the REXX language definition. The CMS implementation includes system-specific additions, and also minor discrepancies. Trouble spots are described, so that users can understand where problems may arise in transporting programs to and from CMS.

INVOKING THE INTERPRETER

This section describes how a program is invoked as a command from CMS, as a routine called from a module or application program, as a command from XEDIT, and as a file in main storage.

The CMS environment

Some CMS indicators affect the way commands are resolved and must be understood to know how the actual resolution takes place. Assume that the command GETDATE is entered on the CMS command line. CMS looks at the **IMPEX** indicator and makes its first decision based on that. IMPEX, or implicit EXEC, being set ON (the default) means that CMS will automatically look for an EXEC while it is trying to resolve the command. If IMPEX is set OFF, CMS will look only for a command (nucleus routine, nucleus extension, or MODULE) with that name and will bypass any EXECs. Therefore, with IMPEX set ON, the GET-DATE EXEC will be executed. Since there are three EXEC processors on CMS, an indicator in the source file must direct CMS to the REXX interpreter. This is done by having a REXX comment as the first line in the program. In addition, if the program being called from another program and the parameter list shows that the user calltype is X'05', the called program is assumed to be in REXX. If the first line of the program starts with **&TRACE**, it is assumed that the program is written in EXEC 2. If the character ***** or characters **/*** do not appear in the first four characters and the string **EXECPROC** appears in positions 5 through 12, then the program is assumed to be in an "alternate" format. The name of the alternate format EXEC processor is in positions 13 through 20 (see the chapter "Exploiting Compiled REXX and the REXX Compiler" for other details of the alternate format). Otherwise, the program is assumed to be a CMS EXEC.

The EXEC can either be in virtual storage (in a DCSS or as a result of an **EXECLOAD** command) or reside on any accessed disk. If IMPEX is **OFF**, it is still possible to execute the **GETDATE EXEC**, but you must explicitly tell CMS to do this. In this case, you must prefix the name of the EXEC with **EXEC**—that is, the command would be **EXEC GETDATE**.

Another consideration in CMS command resolution is synonyms and abbreviations. These features are interrelated, in that one file specifies both synonyms and abbreviations. CMS allows synonyms and abbreviations to be independently activated or deactivated; i.e., abbreviations with the **SET ABBREV ON/OFF** command and synonyms with the **SYNONYM** command. The default setting for **ABBREV** is **ON**; the default for synonyms is to have only the system synonyms available. A synonym file consists of one-line entries that contain the system command, the user synonym, and the minimum abbreviation length. Assume that file **MYSYN SYNONYM** (which must be fixed format, with a logical record length of 80) contains the following records:

```
GETDATE GETDATE    4
GETDATE GDATE      2
MANAGER TIMECARD   4
MANAGER SICKDAY    4
MANAGER VACATION   3
MANAGER PERSONAL   4
```

Additionally, assume that the user has entered the command **SYNONYM MYSYN** and the command **SET ABBREV ON**, which activates the noted synonyms and allows abbreviations. Note how the synonym file is used. If the first search for an EXEC in storage or on any accessed disk fails, CMS attempts to resolve the name using synonyms and abbreviations (if they are activated). This might be the case had the user entered **GD** on the command line instead of **GETDATE**. The second line of the file shows that **GD**, **GDA**, **GDAT**, and **GDATE** are all valid synonyms for **GETDATE**. So the next step after not finding an EXEC called **GD** would be to resolve this to **GETDATE** and repeat the search. The first line shows that **GETD**, **GETDA**, and **GETDAT** are also valid abbreviations for **GETDATE**. The user could type any of the above on the command line and, assuming no EXECs with that name existed, CMS would invoke the GETDATE EXEC. An exception to these rules is when the user precedes the EXEC name with EXEC, such as EXEC GETDATE; in this case, no synonym or abbreviation resolution is done on the EXEC name.

Users should be aware that if no EXEC is found after the above searches, CMS will attempt to find a CMS command or module to satisfy the request. This search also involves synonym and abbreviation resolution, but since it is not directly related to EXECs, it is not discussed here.

An interesting use of synonyms is to have one EXEC process several different requests based on what the user types in. The last four lines in the above synonym file create the necessary synonyms for this example. They tell CMS to invoke the MANAGER EXEC whenever the user types in TIMECARD, SICKDAY, VACATION, or PERSONAL (or any valid abbreviation of these). The user knew that the processing for all four functions would be quite similar, so the synonym file was set up to call the MANAGER EXEC in these four cases. Note that if the user types in an abbreviation (such as VAC) and an EXEC with that name exists on an accessed disk, the MANAGER EXEC will not be invoked. The MANAGER EXEC might do the following to determine how it was called and how to proceed:

```
/* MANAGER EXEC -- Keep track of employee hours and */
/*                 submit the on-line timecard */

/* Common code could be here... */
  :
parse upper source . . . . . howcalled .
select
   when abbrev('TIMECARD', howcalled, 4) then call TIMECARD
   when abbrev('SICKDAY' , howcalled, 4) then call SICKDAY
   when abbrev('VACATION', howcalled, 3) then call VACATION
   when abbrev('PERSONAL', howcalled, 4) then call PERSONAL
   otherwise . . .
end
/* Common code could be here also... */
  :
```

TIMECARD, SICKDAY, VACATION, and PERSONAL could be internal or external routines.

Invocation from a module

A REXX program may be called from a CMS module using any of the following standard forms of parameter list (**plist**):

- Tokenized plist only—The user calltype is X'00' and R0 is not used.

- Extended plist—The user calltype is X'01' or X'0B'; R1 points to a doubleword-aligned 16-byte field containing the following:

```
CL8'EXEC'
CL8'execname'
```

The remainder of the tokenized plist is not used. The extended plist must be pointed to by R0, and a file descriptor block (an **FBLOCK**) may be provided if desired.

- The six-word extended plist—The user calltype is **X'05'** with the other conditions the same as for the extended plist. This form is necessary if more than one argument string is to be passed or if the EXEC is being called as a function. Storage used to contain returned data (in an **EVALBLOK**) must be freed by the caller.

The CMSCALL macro is the preferred way to make the calls because the parameters allow the user to set up the plists and calltype information. It also allows the user to pass a plist that resides above the 16MB line. For more information on this macro, see the *CMS Application Development Guide for Assembler.*

Using the extended parameter list offers the following additional features over the tokenized plist only:

- One or more parameter strings, mixed-case and untokenized, may be passed to the program, and one string may be returned from it when it completes execution.

- A program other than the one defined by the tokenized plist may be used, allowing files with a filetype other than **EXEC.**

- The default target for subcommands (other than that derived from the filetype) can be specified.

- Programs may be executed from storage, thereby improving performance for programs being executed repeatedly.

Invocation from an application program

Application programs written in languages such as VS FORTRAN or VS COBOL can call REXX using a Callable Services Library (CSL) routine. This is very useful when the program has to issue CMS or CP commands.

The general format is to call **DMSCSL** and tell it to invoke the **DMSCCE** routine (the interface to a REXX program) as follows:

```
CALL DMSCSL DMSCCE, retcode, execname, number_of_args,
            arg1, arg1_length, . . ., argn, argn_length,
            return_area, return_area_length
```

The specific call format depends on the language issuing the call. For more information on these calls and their return codes, refer to the

CMS Application Development Reference or the *Procedures Language VM / REXX Reference.*

The XEDIT environment

REXX programs can be invoked from the XEDIT environment as XEDIT macros or CMS commands. The method that XEDIT uses to resolve the command entered on the XEDIT command line depends on the setting of **MACRO** (how XEDIT determines what to look for first) and **IMPCMSCP** (how XEDIT is to handle unknown commands). Refer to the "XEDIT Macros" chapter for a detailed discussion of this topic.

Direct in-storage invocation

If the user wants to invoke a REXX program residing in main storage directly, invoke a program whose filetype is not **EXEC**, or invoke a program whose default environment is not the same as the filetype, then the following method must be used. The program must first be loaded into main storage and then a file block (FBLOCK) created that describes the program. A descriptor list must be built that points to each line in the in-storage program. This is simply a list of address/length pairs for the lines. The actual format of the file block and descriptor list are as follows:

```
*** FBLOCK -- EXEC file execution control block
          DS    0F
FBLNAME   DS    CL8          Filename
FBLTYPE   DS    CL8          Filetype
FBLMODE   DS    CL2          Filemode
FBLLFI    EQU   *-FBLNAME    Length of fileid
FBLEXTL   DS    AL2(0)       Extension block length (words)
FBLDLS    DS    AL4          Descriptor list start
FBLDLE    DS    AL4          Descriptor list end
FBLPREF   DS    CL8          Explicit initial prefix
FBLENAME  DS    CL8          Explicit environment name
FBLSEXIT  DS    AL4          System Exit vector address
FBLEUSER  DS    AL4          System Exit User Word
FBLLENL   EQU   *-FBLNAME    Length of FBLOCK (bytes)
FBLLEND   EQU   (FBLLENL+7)/8 Length of FBLOCK (dwords)

*** Descriptor list for in-storage program
PROG      DS    0F
          DC    A(line1),F'len1'  Address, length of line 1
          DC    A(line2),F'len2'  Address, length of line 2
   :
          DC    A(lineN),F'lenN'  Address, length of line N
PROGEND   EQU   *
```

General ideas about file blocks are:

- The in-storage program lines do not have to be contiguous, because each is defined separately in the list.

- The filename is still required for an in-storage program, since it determines the program name. Similarly, the filetype sets the default host command environment, unless the name in the extension block (**FBL-PREF**) explicitly overrides it.

- If the extension length (**FBLEXTL**) is four or greater, the third and fourth fullwords (**FBLPREF**) form the eight-character environment address that overrides the filetype, and thus form the initial **ADDRESS** environment to which commands are issued. This address may be all characters (blank, CMS, etc.), or it may be a PSW for non-SVC subcommand execution. This field may be set to **8X'00'** if not required. If this field is a PSW, it must be in a valid format for the mode of the virtual machine (370-XA mode or System/370 mode).

- If the extension length is six or greater, the fifth and sixth fullwords form an eight-character environment name that is used for the default address unless this is a non-SVC command execution. In this case, the fourth and fifth fullwords are used as a PSW for non-SVC subcommand execution. The **PARSE SOURCE** instruction and the **ADDRESS** function return this environment name, and the PSW in the fourth and fifth fullwords is used to invoke subcommands.

- Exits are defined at the invocation of the language processor by specifying a pointer to the exit vector (**FBLSEXIT**). The next fullword, the eighth, is used to pass a user word value that is returned to the parameter list when an exit is entered. In addition to creating the file block and associated information, a tokenized plist and an extended plist have to be created. The fourth word of the extended plist must point to the file block describing the in-storage program.

SUBCOMMAND HANDLERS

This section describes how subcommands are handled in the CMS environment (**ADDRESS CMS**), the command environment (**ADDRESS COM-MAND**), and user-defined environments. It also points out conventions for handling **ERROR**s and **FAILURE**s in subcommands.

The CMS environment

Under CMS the default environment for subcommands (also called host commands) for a REXX program is CMS. Subcommands issued under the CMS environment are treated as if the command was entered on the CMS command line (the language processor uses CMSCALL with a calltype of **X'0B'**). The tokenized plist and the extended plist are both created and normal command resolution is done. The IMPEX and IMPCP flags, which control implicit EXEC and implicit CP command resolution, are checked as normal. Synonym and abbreviation resolution are done according to the SET ABBREV and SYNONYM settings. EXECs have priority over modules with the same name. EXECs can be explicitly invoked by prefixing the name with EXEC, and similarly, CP commands can be explicitly invoked by prefixing with CP. No cleanup is performed after the command finishes, and interrupts are not canceled.

The COMMAND environment

Execution of subcommands in the COMMAND environment is faster because the system does not do as much. There is no search that starts with EXECs and continues with modules and CP commands, there is no synonym resolution, and there is no uppercasing of the tokenized plist. The language processor passes the command to CMS using CMSCALL with a calltype of X'01'. In order to run an EXEC, the command has to be prefixed with EXEC; and in order to run a CP command, it must be prefixed with CP. Otherwise, CMS will assume that the command is the name of a module. No cleanup is performed after the command finishes, and interrupts are not canceled.

The COMMAND environment offers interesting advantages because of the way subcommands are processed. For example, a trick that can be done in the COMMAND environment, but not normally in CMS, is to manipulate files with mixed-case names. Since the plist is not uppercased, mixed-case names can be passed to and used by CMS. The mixed-case portion of the command should be enclosed in quotes or be formed from data values to prevent any potential uppercasing of the value as a result of REXX variable resolution. An example of a general routine to pass mixed-case commands to CMS would be:

```
/* MIXED EXEC -- Pass mixed-case commands to CMS */
parse arg command parameters /* Read in the command and parameters */
                             /* with the case preserved */
command = translate(command)    /* Uppercase just the command name */
address command command parameters    /* Send the command to CMS */
exit rc                        /* Pass return code back to caller */
```

This program could be invoked with the following command:

```
mixed erase PRINTER OFSLOGfl
```

Declaring user subcommand environments

Users may create and use their own subcommand environments from within a REXX program. This is accomplished by first setting up the environment (creating the program to handle the commands) and then telling REXX where to direct the subcommands. Setting up the environment is accomplished with the CMS SUBCOM macro. Because of the complexity of the macro, it is not presented here. Users who want to fully understand the SUBCOM macro should look in the *Application Development Reference for CMS*.

The basic structure of this is to load a command processing routine (using, for example, **NUCXLOAD**), give it a name such as **MYENVR**, and then invoke the SUBCOM macro to pass this information to CMS. Then the user's EXEC can use the REXX statement, **ADDRESS MYENVR**, to direct subcommands to this processing routine. In fact, this is the method that XEDIT uses during its initialization to allow XEDIT subcommands from REXX macros.

For user-defined environments, subcommands are passed using the SUBCOM plist with a calltype of **X'02'**. R1 points to the tokenized plist that contains the subcommand entry point, and R0 points to the extended plist.

Non-SVC subcommand invocation

An alternative non-SVC fast path is available for issuing subcommands. This may be used where a minimum-overhead subcommand call is needed. This fast path is used if the eight-character environment address (**FBLEPREF** field in the FBLOCK pointed to by the extended plist on entry) is a PSW, signified by the fourth byte being **X'00'**. Alternatively, if the PSW is made available to the EXEC, the **ADDRESS** instruction can be used. When a PSW is used for the default address, the **PARSE SOURCE** string contains a ? for the environment name, unless an explicit name was also provided. This PSW must also be in the correct format for the addressing mode the program is using (System/370 or 370-XA).

This interface is defined as follows:

1. Control is passed to the routine by executing an LPSW instruction to load the environment address. On entry to the processing routine, the following registers are defined:

    R0   Extended plist, as per normal subcommand call—the first word contains a pointer to the PSW used, the second and third words define the beginning and end of the command string, and the fourth word is 0.

    R1   Tokenized plist—the first doubleword contains the PSW used; the second doubleword is **2F'-1'**. The top byte of R1 does not contain a flag.

R2   The original R2, as encountered on the initial entry to the language processor's external interface. It is intended to allow for the passing of private information to the subcommand entry point, typically the address of a control block or data area. This register is safe only if the EXEC is invoked with a BALR to the entry point contained at the label **AEXEC** in the CMS nucleus; otherwise, the SVC processor alters this register.

R13   Points to an 18-fullword savearea.

R14   Contains the return address.

All other registers are undefined.

2. The called program must save R9 through R12 and restore them before returning to the language processor. All other registers may be used as work registers.

3. On return to the language processor, R9 through R12 must be unchanged, and R15 should contain the return code (which will be placed in the variable RC as usual). Contents of other registers are undefined. The language processor sets the storage key and mask that it requires.

Return codes from subcommands

A general convention is to separate subcommands into three categories: those that complete successfully, those that complete with errors, and those that cause failures. The return code from the subcommand should be placed in R15, and indicates the completion status. Zero means successful completion of the subcommand, a positive number means an error occurred (perhaps due to an invalid option or a file not found), and a negative number means a failure (usually due to a severe problem during processing).

CALLING FUNCTIONS AND ROUTINES

The normal search order for functions and called routines is used in the CMS implementation of REXX. This includes internal labels first, built-in functions second, and external routines last. The external routine may be a module, a nucleus extension, or a REXX program. All use the same plist, but the language processor provides an FBLOCK only when the routine is called through the EXEC interface. The search for external routines has the following order:

1. Look in the DBCS function package. (Double-Byte Character Sets, DBCS, are used to support languages that have more characters than can be represented by 8 bits; e.g., Korean Hanguel and Japanese Kanji.)

2. Prefix the name with **RX** and attempt to execute a program with that name using CMSCALL.

3. Interrogate and load if necessary the function packages **RXUSERFN**, **RXLOCFN**, and **RXSYSFN**, in that order. The name is still prefixed with **RX**.

4. Remove the **RX** prefix from the name, and check all directories and accessed minidisks for a file with that name and a filetype the same as that of the program being executed (such as **XEDIT** if an XEDIT macro is running). Next, check for a file with a filetype of **EXEC**. The IMPEX CMS setting does not influence this search.

5. Lastly, attempt to execute the function with its original name using CMSCALL.

When calling a module, the module can reside above the 16MB line (in a 370-XA virtual machine). The module can pass data residing above the 16MB line back to the calling program because, in 370-XA virtual machines, REXX programs can reside above the 16MB line. AMODE 31 and AMODE ANY programs are invoked in 31-bit mode if called from the language processor in a 370-XA virtual machine. In a 370-XA virtual machine, the following applies:

- REXX modules run in a 31-bit addressing mode.
- REXX allocates REXX control blocks above the 16MB line except for the REXX work area.
- REXX handles interfaces between REXX programs and applications, regardless of their addressing mode.

If the module the language processor is calling has AMODE 24, the language processor calls the module in 24-bit mode and the following are copied below the 16MB line, if necessary:

- The six-word extended plist
- The argument list pointed to by the fifth word in the six-word extended plist
- The strings the argument list points to

The language processor always calls a module in 24-bit mode when running in a System/370 virtual machine, regardless of the module's AMODE.

The user calltype is **X'05'** in these cases, indicating that the six-word extended plist is used. The fifth word of this plist points to the argument list, and the sixth word points to a fullword location in USER storage (which is zero on entry) that is used to store the address of an EVALBLOK if a result is returned. If the called routine does not return a result, this field must remain unchanged.

Since a function must return a result but a subroutine does not need to, a routine must know how it was called. R0, bit 0, is set to 0 if the routine is called as a function and set to 1 if it is called as a subroutine. If the called routine is a REXX program, **PARSE SOURCE** can be used to determine how it was called.

ACCESSING THE VARIABLE POOL

EXECCOMM

When the interpreter is initializing processing for a new program, it creates a subcommand entry point called **EXECCOMM**. Routines called from a REXX program (commands, subcommands, or external routines) can then use the current **EXECCOMM** entry point to set, fetch, and drop individual REXX variables. Routines can also fetch all variables in sequence or fetch the private information about the program. This manipulation of the internal variables is all done with the REXX processor's internal mechanisms; therefore, user routines do not have to know anything about this process.

EXECCOMM is invoked using both the tokenized and the extended plists with the CMSCALL mechanism. The user calltype should be set to **X'02'** to signify a subcommand call. R1 must point to a plist containing the 8-byte string **EXECCOMM**. R0 points to the extended plist containing the following information:

- Word 1 contains the value in R1, minus the calltype.

- Words 2 and 3 must be identical (zero, for example) because no arguments are allowed.

- Word 4 points to the first of a chain of one or more SHVBLOCK request blocks.

On return from CMSCALL, R15 contains the return code from the entire set of requests. The possible return code values are:

0 or positive	The entire plist was processed, and the composite (logical OR) of bits 0-5 of the **SHVRET** bytes is in R15.
-1	The entry conditions were invalid (words 2 and 3 of the extended plist are not equal, for example).

-2

Insufficient storage was available for a set request. Some request blocks may have been processed and some may remain unprocessed.

-3 *(from SUBCOM)*

No **EXECCOMM** entry point was found, perhaps because it was not called while a REXX program was active.

The SHVBLOCK request block

The format of the request block is as follows:

```
SHVBLOCK DSECT ,
SHVNEXT  DS    AL4   Pointer to next request block
SHVUSER  DS    F     For user use except during "Fetch Next"
SHVCODE  DS    CL1   One character function code
SHVRET   DS    XL1   One byte of return codes
*        DS    H'0'  Unused halfword, should be 0
SHVBUFL  DS    F     Length of "Fetch" value buffer
SHVNAMA  DS    A     Address of variable name
SHVNAML  DS    F     Length of variable name
SHVVALA  DS    A     Address of value buffer
SHVVALL  DS    F     Length of value
SHVBLEN  EQU   *-SHVBLOCK  Length of the block
```

The following return code flags can be set for each individual operation requested:

```
SHVCLEAN X'00'   Execution OK
SHVNEWV  X'01'   Variable did not exist
SHVLVAR  X'02'   Last variable transferred (for "N")
SHVTRUNC X'04'   Truncation occurred during "Fetch"
SHVBADN  X'08'   Invalid variable name
SHVBADV  X'10'   Value too long (EXEC 2 only)
SHBBADF  X'80'   Invalid function code
```

The EXECCOMM functions

Through the **EXECCOMM** interface, users can set, fetch, or drop variables, fetch all variables, or fetch private information. For the set, fetch, or drop, users may choose direct or symbolic names. For the direct name interface, the variable name is used exactly as passed. For the symbolic name interface, normal variable name uppercasing is performed, and also substitution in compound variables is done. Specifying an uppercase function code (**S**, **F**, or **D**) signifies that the direct interface is being used, and specifying a lowercase function code (**s**, **f**, or **d**) signifies that the symbolic interface is being used. The following table describes the specific actions for each function code:

S and s (Set variable) **SHVNAMA/SHVNAML** describe the name of the variable to be set, and **SHVVALA/SHVVALL** describe the value to be assigned to it. The name is validated to ensure that it does not contain invalid characters, and the variable is then set from the value given. The name can be a stem, in which case all variables with that stem are set, just as in an assignment statement. If the variable set did not exist before the operation, **SHVNEWV** is set.

F and f (Fetch variable) **SHVNAMA/SHVNAML** describe the name of the variable to be fetched. **SHVVALA** specifies the address of the buffer for the data, and **SHVBUFL** contains the length of the buffer. The name is validated to ensure that it does not contain invalid characters, and the variable is then located and its value copied to the buffer. The total length of the variable is put into **SHVVALL**; if the value was truncated because the buffer was too small, **SHVTRUNC** is set. No padding is done if the length of the value is less than the buffer length. If the variable is a stem, the initial value (if any) is returned. If the variable did not exist before this operation, **SHVNEWV** is set, and the value returned is the derived name (uppercase of the name, substitution performed for compound variables).

D and d (Drop variable) **SHVNAMA/SHVNAML** describe the name of the variable to be dropped. **SHVVALA/SHVVALL** are not used in this case. The name is validated to ensure that it does not contain invalid characters; and the variable is then dropped, if it exists. If the name given is a stem, all variables starting with that stem are dropped.

N (Fetch next variable) The next (or first) defined variable name and value are returned. This function may be used to search through all the variables known to the language processor. The order in which the variables are returned is not specified. The language processor maintains a pointer to its list of variables; this is reset to point to the first variable whenever either a host command is issued or any function other than **N** is executed through the **EXECCOMM** interface.

Whenever an **N** (Next) function is executed, the name and value of the next variable available are copied to two buffers supplied by the caller.

SHVNAMA specifies the address of the buffer into which the name is to be copied, and **SHVBUFL** contains the length of that buffer. The total length of the name is put into **SHVNAML**, and if the name was truncated, **SHVTRUNC** is set. This bit is also set if the value was truncated. No padding takes place if the name is shorter than the length of the buffer. When **SHVLVAR** is set, the end of the list has been found, the internal pointers have been reset, and no valid data has been returned. Repeated execution of the **N** function (until **SHVLVAR** is set) will therefore locate all REXX variables in the current generation.

P   (Fetch private information) Fixed information about the program being executed is returned. The following sub-functions are available (only the first letter is needed for **ARG**, **SOURCE**, and **VERSION**; **PARM** must be supplied in total):

ARG   (Fetch primary argument string) The first argument string that would be parsed by the **ARG** instruction is copied to the user's buffer.

PARM   (Fetch the number of argument strings) This number is placed in the caller's buffer, formatted as a character string.

PARM.n   (Fetch the *n*th argument string) Argument string *n* is placed in the caller's buffer. Returns a null string if argument string *n* cannot be supplied (whether because it was omitted or null, or fewer than *n* argument strings were specified). **PARM.1** returns the same result as **ARG**.

SOURCE   (Fetch source string) The source string, as described for **PARSE SOURCE**, is copied to the user's buffer.

VERSION   (Fetch version string) The version string, as described for **PARSE VERSION**, is copied to the user's buffer.

Interface to REXX variables using the
Callable Services Library

Programs written in Assembler, OS/VS COBOL, VS FORTRAN, VS Pascal, PL/I, C, or REXX can be invoked from a REXX program and through the CSL interface can access the variable pool of the caller. The following routines are available:

DMSCDR   Drop a variable or variables

DMSCGR   Get the value of a variable

DMSCGS   Get special REXX values

DMSCGX   Retrieve names and values for all variables one at a time

DMSCSR   Set the value of a variable

More information about these routines is found in the *VM/ESA CMS Application Development Guide for Assembler*.

DEBUGGING HINTS FOR REXX PROGRAMS
UNDER CMS

The following sections cover starting interactive debug of REXX programs and actions available while in debug.

Invoking interactive debug

The ? prefix on the REXX TRACE statement option is one way in which interactive debug can be started in a REXX program. This means that the source program must be modified in order to initiate debug with this method. However, there are CMS Immediate commands that are very useful while debugging and do not require any source file changes. These CMS commands are HI, TS, and TE. These are called Immediate commands because they are executed as soon as they are entered from the command line, even if some other program is currently running.

The HI—Halt Interpretation—command is very useful when a REXX program is looping or when the user wants to stop its execution. This command is preferred over the HX—Halt eXecution— Immediate command because it does not cause CMS to ABEND (HX does). The language interpreter checks a flag (set when HI is entered) after each clause is processed. If the flag is on, the program is ended and an error message given. The remaining parts of the environment are not affected. If there are several EXECs active because of nested calls, each EXEC in turn will be halted. One warning is necessary here: the program stack is cleared when an HI causes a REXX program to terminate.

In cases where a program might be looping and the user does not want to halt the program, the TS—Trace Start—Immediate command can be used. This causes the language interpreter to enter interactive debug, as if a TRACE ?R statement had been executed. The language interpreter displays the clause being executed and pauses for user input. At this point, the user has the full capability of interactive debug. The TE—Trace End—command resets the trace flag and turns off tracing. The main problem with using the TE command while in interactive debug is that most of the time the interpreter is at a pause point. This means that the interpreter is waiting for input from the user, and CMS Immediate commands are not recognized. If your program executes a longer-running module, you may have time to enter the TE Immediate command before the language interpreter reaches another pause point. Otherwise, you may enter the REXX TRACE O instruction or the CMS command SET EXECTRAC OFF (set EXEC tracing off), and that will turn off the tracing flag.

The TS Immediate command or the SET EXECTRAC ON command can both be entered on the command line before starting execution of a REXX program. This causes interactive debug to be entered at the start of the program. No changes (such as adding a TRACE statement) are required in the source program. The tracing flag is automatically turned off at end of command, and only then, so the presetting of the flag will work.

Interactive debugging of programs

Adding a **?** to the trace option on any **TRACE** statement will invoke interactive debug when that statement gets executed. Alternatively, as was mentioned above, there are a couple of methods that are external to the program—**SET EXECTRAC ON** and **TS**. While in interactive debug, the interpreter pauses after executing most clauses in the program. The actual pause points depend on the current trace setting—**A, C, E,** etc. If **TRACE A** is in effect, the pause points are after each clause is executed; for **TRACE C**, the pause points are after the display of any host command, etc. At these pause points (indicated by a **VM READ**), there are three actions that can be taken by the user:

1. **Enter a null line (no characters, not even blanks)**: the language processor resumes execution until the next pause point is reached. In this manner, a user can step through the program from pause point to pause point. If **TRACE A** or **TRACE R** is active, the pause points will be each clause.

2. **Enter an equal sign (=)**: the language processor reexecutes the last clause and then pauses again. This is very useful when an **IF** clause is about to take an undesired branch. The user is able to change the value of any variable (see the next item in this list for instructions on how to do this) and then execute the **IF** clause again, this time taking the desired branch.

3. **Anything else entered**: the language processor treats the line entered as one or more clauses to be executed immediately. This is very similar to an **INTERPRET** statement in that all clauses in the line entered must be complete—**DO/END, IF/THEN/ELSE**, etc. Clauses not recognized by the language processor are passed to the host system to be processed. The **!** trace prefix has no effect on host commands entered from the debug prompt, and the special variable **RC** is not changed. After the line has been executed, the language processor pauses again, unless the line entered was a **TRACE** instruction. In this case, the tracing action is altered and execution continues to the next pause point (if any). If the user wants to change the **TRACE** setting but not continue execution, this can be done by entering **CALL TRACE** *trace_action*.

4. One other tracing option is available while at a debug pause point, entering **TRACE** *n*. If *n* is a positive number, then execution continues but the next *n* pause points are skipped. If *n* is a negative number, then execution continues and tracing is suspended for the next *n* clauses that would have been traced. All pause points for those *n* clauses are also skipped.

Trace settings are saved and restored across subroutine calls; therefore, users can selectively alter tracing while in subroutines without affecting the other parts of the program.

There are a few exceptions to rules of tracing because of certain clauses that cannot be safely reexecuted. For this reason, the language processor does not pause after processing them, even if they are traced. These exceptions are:

- Repetitive DO clauses on the second or following times around the loop
- END clauses (these are not very useful places to pause anyway)
- THEN, ELSE, OTHERWISE, or null clauses
- RETURN and EXIT clauses
- SIGNAL and CALL clauses (the language processor pauses after the target label is traced)
- Any clause that raises a condition being trapped by a CALL ON or SIGNAL ON statement (the language processor pauses after the target label for the CALL or SIGNAL is traced)
- Any clause that causes a syntax error; these can be trapped by a SIGNAL ON SYNTAX but cannot be reexecuted

LANGUAGE DEFINITION AND VM/ESA
RELEASE 1 DIFFERENCES

The CMS implementation of REXX under VM/ESA Release 1 differs from the language definition in two ways. First, some additional enhancements are available on CMS that are not defined by the language, and second, there are some minor deviations in the CMS implementation.

CMS specific enhancements

Two additional options are available for the PARSE statement, EXTERNAL and NUMERIC. PARSE EXTERNAL obtains the next string from the terminal input buffer (system external event queue). If this buffer is empty, a console read results. PARSE NUMERIC obtains the current numeric controls in the order DIGITS FORM FUZZ.

An UPPER instruction is available that uppercases the contents of variables that are passed to the instruction. The variables follow the keyword UPPER and are delimited by blanks.

Several built-in functions and function enhancements are also available. These include:

DATATYPE(option)   Additional options **C** and **D**. If **C** is specified, the function returns **1** if the passed string is a mixed SBCS/DBCS string (SBCS—Single Byte Character Set, DBCS—Double Byte Character Set). If **D** is specified, the function returns **1** if the passed string is a pure DBCS string enclosed by SO and SI bytes.

DATE(option)   Additional options **C** and **J**. If **C** is specified, the function returns the number of days, including the current day, since January 1 of the last year which is a multiple of 100. If **J** is specified, the function returns the date in the format *yyddd.*

EXTERNALS()   Returns the number of elements in the terminal input buffer (system external event queue).

FIND(string, phrase)   Searches **string** looking for the first occurrence of the sequence of blank-delimited words **phrase**, and returns the word number of the first word of **phrase** in **string**. Multiple blanks between words are treated as a single blank for the comparison.

INDEX(haystack, needle, start)   Returns the character position of **needle** in **haystack** or **0** if not found. If the starting position of the search, **start**, is not specified, the search starts at the first character.

JUSTIFY(string, length, pad)   Returns the blank-delimited words in **string** justified to both margins (to a length **length**) by inserting **pad** characters between the words. The default pad character is a blank.

LINESIZE()   Returns the current terminal line width (the point at which the language processor will break lines displayed using the **SAY** instruction). **0** is returned in the following cases:

- The language processor cannot determine the terminal line size.
- The virtual machine is disconnected.
- The command **CP TERMINAL LINESIZE OFF** is in effect.

In full-screen CMS, **LINESIZE** returns **999999999**, since the terminal line width concept does not apply.

USERID()   Returns the system-defined user identifier.

Several external functions are available:

CMSFLAG(flag)   Returns the status of the following CMS flags:

ABBREV   Returns **1** if ABBREV is set **ON**, **0** if set **OFF**.

AUTOREAD	Returns **1** if AUTOREAD is set **ON**, **0** if set **OFF**.
CMSTYPE	Returns **1** if console output will be displayed (**SET CMSTYPE RT**), **0** if not displayed (**SET CMSTYPE HT**).
DOS	Returns **1** if the virtual machine is in the DOS environment (**SET DOS ON**), **0** if not (**SET DOS OFF**).
EXECTRAC	Returns **1** if EXEC tracing is turned on (**SET EXECTRAC ON**), **0** if tracing is off (**SET EXECTRAC OFF**).
IMPCP	Returns **1** if unrecognized commands are sent to CP (**SET IMPCP ON**), **0** if not (**SET IMPCP OFF**).
IMPEX	Returns **1** if EXECs may be invoked by filename (**SET IMPEX ON**), **0** if not (**SET IMPEX OFF**).
PROTECT	Returns **1** if the CMS nucleus is storage-protected (**SET PROTECT ON**), otherwise returns **0** (**SET PROTECT OFF**).
RELPAGE	Returns **1** if pages are to be released on return to CMS command level (**SET RELPAGE ON**), **0** otherwise (**SET RELPAGE OFF**).
SUBSET	Returns **1** if you are in CMS subset, otherwise returns **0**.
CSL('routine_name retcode parms. . .')	Allows a REXX program to call a routine that resides in the Callable Services Library. Blanks separate the parameters passed, not commas as in the built-in functions.
DIAG / DIAGRC (code, passed_data)	Communicates with CP via a dummy DIAGNOSE instruction and returns data as a character string. **DIAGRC** returns the same string as **DIAG** with the return code and condition code from CP prefixed to it. *code* is the DIAGNOSE code being sent to CP, and *passed_data* is optional input data for the DIAGNOSE. The supported diagnose codes are **00**, **08**, **0C**, **14**, **24**, **5C**, **60**, **64**, **8C**, **C8**, **CC**, **F8**, and **210**.
DBCJUSTIFY(string, length, pad, option)	Double-byte justify: formats a string by adding *pad* characters between non-blank characters to justify to both margins and length of *length* bytes. Rules for adjustment are the same as for the JUSTIFY function. The default *pad* character is a blank. *option* is used to control the counting rule. *Y* counts

	SO and SI within mixed strings as one; *N* does not count the SO and SI; *N* is the default.
STORAGE(address, length, data)	Returns the current virtual machine size if no arguments are supplied. Otherwise, returns **length** bytes from user memory starting at address **address**. If not specified, the default **length** is 1. If **data** is specified, after the old value is retrieved, storage starting at **address** is overwritten with **data**.

Miscellaneous differences

There are several places where the VM/ESA Release 1 implementation differs from the REXX language definition. Although these are minor differences, they can cause confusion and inconsistent results in programs run on multiple systems. These differences are:

- Literal strings may span lines.

- Semicolons are not implied at linend if in the middle of a literal string.

- A comma at linend does not mean continuation if in the middle of a literal string.

- Labels are permitted in an interpreted string, but are ignored.

- No indicator is returned if an **EXECCOMM** delete does not drop any variables.

- An assignment of the form *symbol=;* is not an error and sets *symbol* to null.

- The new features in Level 2 of the SAA Procedures Language definition have not been implemented yet. These are:

    - Input/output functions—**CHARIN, CHAROUT, CHARS, LINEIN, LINE-OUT, LINES, STREAM**
    - Enhancements to the **VALUE** function to set variable values and to access external variable pools
    - Binary strings and the related **B2X** and **X2B** functions
    - **PARSE LINEIN** to parse the next line from the default character input stream
    - Subsidary lists on the **PROCEDURE EXPOSE** and **DROP** statements
    - **CALL ON NOVALUE, NOTREADY**, and **SYNTAX**
    - **SIGNAL ON NOTREADY**
    - **PARSE** templates containing variable numeric patterns

LIMITS OF THE LANGUAGE PROCESSOR

The following chart shows the maximum limits for REXX running under CMS on VM/ESA Release 1:

Clause length	500 bytes
Literal strings	250 bytes
Symbol (variable name) length	250 bytes
Variables	16MB
Nesting control structures	250
CALL, MAX *and* **MIN** *arguments*	20
Queue entries	Memory
Queue entry length	255
NUMERIC DIGITS *value*	Memory
Notational exponent value	999 999 999
Hexadecimal strings	250 bytes
C2D *input string*	250 bytes
D2C *output string*	250 bytes
D2X *output string*	500 bytes
X2D *input string*	500 bytes

20

System Product Interpreter Performance Tips

By Perry Ruiter and Carl Forde

INTRODUCTION

REXX was designed as an interpreted language without data typing. These design decisions made it very powerful, yet easy to learn and manipulate. This user-friendly nature can mislead programmers into believing that they have written a well-performing program when in fact there are coding techniques available to improve its performance.

This chapter provides examples of good and bad programming using CMS REXX. Many of the tips offered are specific to that implementation, although some may be universally applicable. However, one hopes for performance improvements, so something that is bad today may be good tomorrow. Therefore, this chapter also provides tools and abilities to *determine* performance in an environment.

Understanding how to determine the performance of a code segment enables evaluation of both REXX program efficiency and whether recommendations in this chapter hold true in a specific environment. At the very least, applying the recommendations outlined will increase code robustness.

PROGRAM TIMING

When work is begun on a slow program, it is quite likely that the troublesome section(s) are already known. If not, well-placed statements like:

```
say time('E')
```

and

```
'CP QUERY TIME'
```

or

```
'CP INDICATE USER'
```

can help determine them. Be careful about placing too much value on the elapsed time indication, as that can vary significantly depending on other system activity. More important are the virtual and total times (VIRTCPU/TOTCPU in QUERY TIME output; VTIME/TTIME in INDICATE USER output). These will remain fairly repeatable.

Another technique that may be unfamiliar is extracting the troublesome portion into its own little program, putting a DO 1000 loop around it, executing it to determine resources used, and making changes and re-running it to see differences. The reason for running it a thousand or so times is to minimize the impact of REXX start-up and termination on the results. Clearly it is not necessary to run something a thousand times if it takes a minute to run, since start-up and termination are only a small portion of this. However, suppose that what is wanted is to determine the most efficient looping construct. There will not be much difference between do 1; end and do i=1 to 1; end, since the resource consumption will be skewed by start-up and termination overheads. There will, however, be a substantial difference between do 1000; end and do i=1 to 1000; end. Here again, pay more attention to VTIME and TTIME than elapsed time, since other system activity can affect elapsed time. It is often a good idea to run a test or measurement two or three times in quick succession to remove skewing due to facilities like minidisk caching. You may also want to EXECLOAD a program before running it. Usually the best time for taking measurements is when the system is lightly loaded, perhaps evenings or weekends.

In order to establish whether changes have a positive effect on performance, in the sense of reduced resource consumption, it is necessary to reliably determine the resources consumed. Simple CP QUERY TIMEs are awkward, since they require some arithmetic for interpretation, and the results are somewhat coarse. Fortunately, these problems can be overcome with a REXX program such as the following, which extracts information via **DIAG(C)**:

```
/* TIME:  Time a process in the UNIX style

   Invocation:  as a CMS command

   Parameters:  the command to be timed with its arguments

   Result:      Elapsed real time (sec.micro)
                Virtual time      (sec.micro)
                System time       (sec.micro)
                Total time        (sec.micro)
*/
real_time = time('E')                   /* Set elapsed time to zero */
numeric digits 20             /* Make sure we can handle big numbers */
start_time = diag('C')                /* Get current resources used */
(arg(1))                                  /* Execute the argument */
stop_time = diag('C')                 /* The current resources used */
real_time = time('E')                 /* how long in real seconds */
start_v_time = c2d(substr(start_time, 17, 8))
start_t_time = c2d(substr(start_time, 25, 8))
stop_v_time  = c2d(substr(stop_time, 17, 8))
stop_t_time  = c2d(substr(stop_time, 25, 8))
digits = length(trunc(real_time))      /* # places ahead of period */
v_time = (stop_v_time - start_v_time)/1000000/* Convert to seconds */
t_time = (stop_t_time - start_t_time)/1000000/* Convert to seconds */
s_time = t_time - v_time
say 'Elapsed real time (sec.micro) =' format(real_time, digits, 5)
say 'Virtual time      (sec.micro) =' format(v_time, digits, 5)
say 'System time       (sec.micro) =' format(s_time, digits, 5)
say 'Total time        (sec.micro) =' format(t_time, digits, 5)
exit rc
```

ADDRESS

ADDRESS tends to be poorly understood, and therefore underutilized. It indicates to REXX the target environment for execution of non-REXX statements. In REXX programs with filetype **EXEC**, by default, this environment is **CMS**. This was chosen so that new REXX programmers could enter CMS commands in REXX programs and have them executed as they would be from the CMS command line. **ADDRESS COMMAND** causes the normal search order to be bypassed and the command to be executed directly via an SVC (supervisor call). Bypassing the normal search order like this provides a significant performance benefit. This performance benefit is even greater for commands issued from XEDIT macros or environments other than **EXECs**. Most important is to **ADDRESS** the correct environment for each command.

ADDRESS COMMAND is usually the first line (after the opening comments) at the top of a program. This changes the default execution environment for the entire program, or until another **ADDRESS** statement is executed. To execute a single command using a different environment, perhaps COMMAND rather than CMS, use:

```
address command cms_command
```

For example, the following determines whether a file exists and displays an error message if not:

```
address command
 ⋮
address cms 'ESTATE SOME FILE *'
 ⋮
```

Putting ADDRESS CMS in front of ESTATE causes the DMSSTT-002E File SOME FILE * not found error message to be displayed, whereas ADDRESS COMMAND suppresses the message.

The current environment can be determined with the ADDRESS function:

```
environment = address()
```

Then it can be changed, and commands will pass directly to the new environment. The original environment can be restored with:

```
address
```

or

```
address value environment
```

(The latter might be preferable when multiple environments are being used, as ADDRESS with no operands restores only the *previous* environment.)

Using ADDRESS COMMAND isn't as easy as simply adding a line to the top of each program; other changes will (probably) be required. For example, all CMS commands executed must be in uppercase when using ADDRESS COMMAND. If a REXX program calls STUFF EXEC from the COMMAND environment, it isn't enough to specify 'STUFF'; it must become 'EXEC STUFF'.

COMMENTS

If a comment spans multiple lines, the entire comment should be enclosed by a single pair of delimiters (/* and */) rather than by a pair of delimiters on each line. That is, use as few comment delimiters as possible. This reduces processing time to interpret the comments.

DROPPING VARIABLES

Something that surprises many people is that in CMS and TSO/E
REXX, except in one specific case, DROP is little more than a NOP. Most
people, after reading the description of DROP, think of it as a way of
releasing the storage that a variable occupies, so that it can be reused
by other variables. Nothing could be further from the truth. All DROP
does is flag variables as unused. This flagging causes future references
to the variable to return its name, as all unused REXX variables do,
rather than its contents. Storage assigned to it remains assigned. The
only way to reuse the storage is to reuse the variable.

The exception, which does release storage for reuse, is the DROP of an
entire stem:

```
drop a.                              /* Frees storage */
drop a.1 a                    /* Does not free storage */
```

LOOPS

To iterate through a loop a specific number of times when it is not necessary to know which iteration is currently being processed, it is much
faster to omit the counter; that is, use:

```
do 17
 .
 .
end
```

instead of:

```
do j = 1 to 17
 .
 .
end
```

For example, a loop to process stack items would look like:

```
do queued()
 .
 .
end
```

This works because functions encountered in a DO statement are executed only once, when the statement is first encountered. There is thus
no need to create a temporary variable for use in a DO statement; it only
wastes time and memory.

If a loop counter is required, there are several ways to implement it.
From slowest to fastest, they are:

```
do j = 1 while j <= 17
 .
 .
end
```

```
do j = 1 until j >= 17
  :
end

do j = 1 to 17
  :
end
```

and

```
do j = 1 for 17
  :
end
```

One caveat:

```
do j = 5 for 10
```

is not the same as

```
do j = 5 to 10.
```

The first loop counts from 5 up to and including 14, while the second loop counts from 5 up to and including 10. In general, provided that B is greater than or equal to A:

```
do j = a for b-a+1
```

is the same as:

```
do j = a to b
```

REXX allows specifying the name of a counter after the END statement of a loop. This looks like:

```
do j = 1 for 7
  :
end j
```

This causes automatic checking to ensure that loops are correctly nested. However, there is extra overhead involved in doing this. While it is helpful, a good indentation style renders it unnecessary.

ITERATE

Frequently a program must loop through a group of items and, depending upon a particular characteristic that an item may or may not possess, do something to the current item or merely go on to the next one. Here is the natural way to write it:

```
do until no_more
   call GET_NEXT
   if characteristic then do
      :
   end
end
```

Unfortunately, this is also an expensive way to write it. The same thing can be achieved more efficiently using **ITERATE**:

```
do until no_more
   call GET_NEXT
   if ¬ characteristic then
      iterate
   else do
      :
   end
end
```

By using **ITERATE** we have saved REXX having to work its way to the bottom of the loop each time through. Even though the statements are not being executed, REXX must still parse them to determine where the loop ends.

PARSE VERSUS SUBSTR

Is **PARSE** always faster? One frequently sees the recommendation to use **PARSE** rather than **SUBSTR**. Before putting blinders on and vowing to always use **PARSE**, time it using the **TIME** program shown above. **PARSE** can perform well when the conditions favor it. Generally, this means short strings. As string length grows, **PARSE** performance deteriorates. Here's how to break apart the output of a CP **QUERY FILES** with **PARSE**:

```
parse value diag(8, 'QUERY FILES', 80) with . 'FILES:' files 'RDR,' .
parse value diag(8, 'QUERY READER ALL', (81+files*81)) with,
 . '15'x files
do while length(files) > 0
   parse var files this_file '15'x files
   :
end
```

Now the same code using **SUBSTR**:

```
parse value diag(8, 'QUERY FILES', 80) with . 'FILES:' files 'RDR,' .
files = diag(8, 'QUERY READER ALL', (81+files*81))
start = index(files, '15'x)
do while length(files) > start+1
   last = index(files, '15'x, start+1)
   this_file = substr(files, start+1, last-start-1)
   start = last
   :
end
```

The **PARSE** example is straightforward and easy to understand. The **SUBSTR/INDEX** example requires a bit of thought to fully comprehend. Even on a VM/XA system with 14,000 reader files, the **SUBSTR** example takes just over four seconds to complete, while **PARSE** requires more than four minutes! To be fair, **PARSE** is actually faster if there are 100 or fewer reader files, and it can hold its own up to about 200 files. After that, it rapidly loses ground to **SUBSTR**.

PARSE would be faster if an enhancement was made to the REXX variable structure to keep a pointer to the starting position within a string. Then parsing a variable into itself, a frequent occurrence, would simply require an update of this pointer.

EXTERNAL ROUTINES

In REXX, an **internal** routine is one that is defined somewhere within the file currently being interpreted. An **external** routine is one that is contained in a separate file.

If the external routine is written in REXX, it can be invoked using its filename. There are several ways this can be done. As a function or subroutine, **SWILL EXEC** would be invoked:

```
x = swill()                                 /* Function call */
call swill                                  /* Subroutine call */
```

This method of invoking external REXX programs is quite expensive, and should be used only if the benefits of this type of call are required. The fastest way to invoke **SWILL EXEC** is as a host command:

```
address command 'EXEC SWILL'
```

If the routine is written in assembler or a compiled language, then the routine may be invoked by its filename, but will probably be invoked by one of several other methods. This is discussed in detail in the chapter "Extending CMS REXX with Function Packages". Briefly, REXX first prefixes the subroutine name, as it appears in the program, with **RX**. If the routine is not found with this name, REXX tries several variants on the name; if still unsuccessful, it uses the name as originally coded. The point is to use the proper name for best performance. To invoke **RXLDEV MODULE** most efficiently, use:

```
x = ldev(. . .)
```

The following call will work:

```
x = rxldev(. . .)
```

However, there will be a substantial performance impact on each call as REXX struggles to resolve the name. More than one program has been improved simply by reworking such calls.

Preloading

Performance of frequently referenced external routines can be improved by preloading them. The benefit gained from doing this ranges from mild to amazing.

REXX programs are preloaded by the CMS EXECLOAD command. Since duplicates are permitted, care must be taken to avoid loading multiple copies of the same program. The duplicate program is just hidden until the newly loaded one is dropped. It is quite easy to mistakenly load a REXX program several times, thereby losing some of the benefits this provides. Some benefit is also lost by not removing comments. There is no advantage to wasting memory by loading them.

Modules must be relocatable to be preloaded by the CMS NUCXLOAD command. If the object files that make up the module are available, it is quite easy to make the module relocatable by using the RLDSAVE option on the LOAD command. This technique has proved beneficial with IND$FILE, IBM's PC file transfer module. A relocatable version of this module was generated and NUCXLOADed, improving an application significantly.

Somewhat surprising is that benefit can even be realized on VM/XA and VM/ESA systems which offer minidisk caching using expanded storage.

Shared REXX programs

Newer VM releases permit REXX programs to be placed into shared discontiguous saved segments (DCSS). This is similar to having a REXX program EXECLOADed, except that all users run the same program copy. Placing a REXX program into shared storage is not something the average VM user is permitted to do; a system programmer is required. Probably only widely and heavily used REXX programs should be placed in shared storage; the TIME program given earlier is a poor candidate. If, for example, a heavily used PROFS exit has been developed—perhaps one executed whenever a note is sent—some benefit will be gained by doing this. Again, compress out comments before loading the program.

BUILT-IN FUNCTIONS

REXX provides an extensive collection of built-in functions. These functions should be neither underutilized nor overutilized. For example, something like the following is often encountered in REXX programs:

```
'SENTRIES'
queued = rc
```

The same thing can be achieved using a standard REXX function:

```
queued = queued()
```

Not only is this significantly faster, it is also portable across REXX implementations.

However, the fastest function call is one not performed; for example:

```
if c2x(type) = '11' then . . .
```

can be written:

```
if type = '11'x then . . .
```

This is at least as readable and is faster, since the function call has been eliminated.

THE RXSYSFN FUNCTION PACKAGE

The CMS system function package (**RXSYSFN**) provides three routines:

CMSFLAG   Determine CMS flag settings.
DIAG   Issue DIAGNOSE codes.
STORAGE   Query and update virtual machine storage.

This collection of routines is a standard part of REXX under CMS, yet seems to be frequently overlooked. Using functions provided, rather than equivalent native CMS or CP commands, can significantly improve performance. For example, a code fragment might look like:

```
'QUERY CMSTYPE (STACK'
pull . '=' cms_type .
'SET CMSTYPE HT'
:
'SET CMSTYPE' cms_type
```

The equivalent, using **CMSFLAG**:

```
rt = cmsflag('CMSTYPE')
'SET CMSTYPE HT'
:
if rt then 'SET CMSTYPE RT'
```

The **CMSFLAG** function not only is substantially faster, but also returns a logical value, which simplifies and clarifies restoring the value.

The **DIAG** function is available in two flavors, **DIAG** and **DIAGRC**. The difference is that **DIAGRC** provides the return code and condition code along with the other results. Not all DIAGNOSE codes are supported, so a review of the *System Product Interpreter Reference* is in order. A quick overview of some popular uses of **DIAG**:

DIAG(8)	is the best method of issuing CP commands and capturing the results.
	Some programmers prefer **EXECIO CP** because it returns distinct lines in the stack; however, **PARSE** using the '15'x (linend) character as a delimiter works equally well, and **DIAG(8)** is much faster.
DIAG(14)	is a powerful tool for handling reader files; a simple routine to read blocks onto disk is often useful for debugging purposes, for example, when **RECEIVE** cannot read a file.
DIAG(64)	loads and purges discontiguous saved segments.

STORAGE is much faster and easier to use than dealing with the output of a **CP DISPLAY** command captured via **DIAG(8)**.

One caution: **STORAGE** is restricted to addresses in the virtual machine in which it is used, and so cannot examine storage in a DCSS.

DIAG(8) BUFFER SIZES

Just as the **DIAG(8)** default buffer size of 4096 bytes can be overridden with a larger size (as in the example in the section "PARSE versus SUBSTR"), it can also be overridden with a smaller size. Often the required result is quite a bit less than 4096 bytes. If this is the case, it is beneficial to save storage by overriding the **DIAG** default buffer size with a smaller one.

In fact, if the command being issued returns multiple lines, and the information needed is within the first few lines, then a buffer only large enough for those lines may be used. For example, **QUERY SET** is a command that is frequently issued to determine and save the current setting of an option before changing it. Two frequently changed settings, **MSG** and **EMSG**, are on the first line. If they are the only settings of interest, the buffer size need not be large enough to contain the rest of the query output.

Remember that **DIAG(8)** returns only complete lines. This means that a buffer size of 16 bytes is not adequate to determine the current **MSG** setting: the buffer must be at least large enough for the whole line. It is possible, however, to deliberately set a buffer too small when the output is not needed. For example, a buffer length of 1 might be used for a **LINK** whose output is not required.

It is not necessary to specify a buffer size that is a multiple of eight; **DIAG(8)** rounds it up.

RECURSION

The classic example of using recursion to compute factorials also illustrates where it should not be used in interpreted REXX. Just because a function or routine can be expressed recursively does not mean it is best implemented that way. Before choosing a recursive implementation of an algorithm over a non-recursive version, **TIME** them both.

For example, the recursive factorial implementation:

```
FACTORIAL: procedure
parse arg n .
if n <= 0
then return 1
return FACTORIAL(n-1) * n
```

is much slower and uses more memory than the non-recursive version:

```
FACTORIAL: procedure
parse arg n .
factorial = 1
do j = 1 for n
   factorial = factorial * j
end
return factorial
```

Used properly, recursion is a powerful coding technique; used carelessly, it wastes cycles and memory.

INTERMEDIATE RESULTS

Unless required for clarity, avoid storing intermediate results in variables. Whenever a variable is created or set, it must be inserted in the variable tree, and the tree must be rebalanced. The cost of doing this repeatedly quickly adds up. A function can be used in most places a variable can be used. For example:

```
b = bitand(a, '3f'x)
c = c2d(b)
```

can be written:

```
c = c2d(bitand(a, '3f'x))
```

Learn to exploit **PARSE VALUE**. For example:

```
settings = diag(8, 'QUERY SET)
parse var settings . 'TIMER' timer ',' .
```

can be written:

```
parse value diag(8, 'QUERY SET') with . 'TIMER' timer ',' .
```

if **SETTINGS** is not needed later in the program.

EXECIO

EXECIO is awkward to use, and most things **EXECIO** does can be done better some other way. **EXECIO** is used most often to execute CP commands and for file I/O.

For CP commands, use **DIAG(8)** instead. Recall the '**QUERY READER ALL**' example; using **SUBSTR/INDEX** required about four seconds to process 14,000 reader files. **EXECIO** with the **STEM** option completes in just under three seconds. However, **EXECIO** uses more than twice as much memory as **DIAG**. **EXECIO** receives the CP output into a buffer, sets all the variables, and finally frees the buffer. So while the variables are being built, and until the buffer is freed, there are two copies of the output. There is also the storage and management overhead of the 14,000 variables introduced into the REXX variable tree. The **DIAG** function avoids double buffering and the variable tree work. So although **EXECIO** completes faster in this example, it requires an extra 1.5MB of virtual storage for overhead.

EXECIO's second problem is that it returns CP output as distinct lines. Viewing output of a **QUERY SET**, for example, as a long string (the way it is returned by **DIAG**) rather than as separate lines makes extracting desired settings much easier. It can be done with a single **PARSE** statement. As separate lines it is necessary to loop through, searching them for setting(s) of interest.

The REXX language definition includes functions to perform file I/O. Most REXX implementations include these functions; unfortunately, IBM did not include them in CMS REXX. Fortunately, three of the standard I/O functions (**LINES**, **LINEIN**, and **LINEOUT**) are available for CMS. They were included as part of the 1990 VM Workshop Tools Tape. Many REXX programmers use these routines exclusively and find them superior to **EXECIO** in every way.

EXECIO permits returning items via the stack or via REXX variables. Timings do not show much of a difference between the two; however, stack string lengths are limited to 255 bytes. This can be a severe limitation.

COMPRESSING REXX PROGRAMS

A common technique for reducing program execution time is to **compress** or **squeeze** it. REXX compressors remove comments and unnecessary blanks from programs, and place as many statements as possible on one line. This works by reducing the overhead as the interpreter repeatedly scans programs during execution. With no blank lines or comments to process, the interpreter spends its time executing code.

In most cases, however, there is not much benefit to doing this. The interpreter's overhead in filtering out comments and blank lines is already fairly low. The most significant improvement is in REXX programs that have large loops containing many blank lines or comments. The typical improvement in such REXX programs is about 1 or 2 percent. For REXX programs executed often, this performance increase may be worthwhile.

CMS Pipelines is shipped with a filter called **CMPRREXX** that compresses REXX code (for information on CMS Pipelines, see the chapter "CMS Pipelines"). Other compressors can be found in various user groups and on some bulletin boards. Always test a new compressor before trusting it with production REXX programs. Some do not handle constructs like nested comments, quotes in comments, or comment delimiters within strings.

SORTING

As in any other language, the speed of a REXX sort is highly dependent upon the algorithm used. One of the most efficient algorithms is the Order n(log n) **Shell** sort. It works by sorting words that are large distances apart first and reducing the sort distance by half as each pass is sorted.

The version presented here is intended to be called as an external routine which receives two parameters: a string of blank-delimited items to be sorted, and optionally an **A** or **D** to specify whether the items are to be sorted in ascending or descending order.

There are a few points to be made about this routine. The first is that special consideration has been given to handling the fact that the REXX operators > and < do **not** impose an ordering on the set of all strings, which is the domain of all REXX variables. To illustrate this, consider the following examples:

```
103 > 1F3   and   1F3 > 1E3   but   103 < 1E3           /* EBCDIC */
2E1 > 2D1   and   2D1 > 201   but   2E1 < 201           /* ASCII */
```

The first two expressions are evaluated lexicographically, since at least one operand can only be a string, while the third expression is evaluated arithmetically, since the E is taken to be an exponent.

REXX has no numeric data type, so it assumes that something that *can* be interpreted as a number *is* a number. Usually this is what is desired. When REXX compares two strings that look like numbers, the result is a numerical comparison. When at least one of the two strings does not look like a number, the result is a lexicographical comparison. The trouble arises when a string can be interpreted both ways. Then REXX depends on the context of the variable in the statement to determine how it should be compared. In the above example, `1E3` can be interpreted in two different ways, depending on the other operand.

To avoid complications like this, the sort routine determines whether it is sorting numbers or words. If it is sorting words, it assigns a non-numeric value to a variable. If it is sorting numbers, it assigns a zero-length string to the variable. This variable is then appended to both operands on the `IF` statement where the comparisons are done. Appending a non-numeric value forces comparisons to be done lexicographically, while appending a zero-length string has no effect on the result of the comparison. In this way, lists of numbers are always sorted arithmetically, and lists of words are always sorted lexicographically. That is, sorting is done consistently and in the manner expected.

The second point worth mentioning is that the direction construct:

```
if direction = 'A' | direction = '' then
   :
   if word.m append > word.n append
   :
else
   :
   if word.m append < word.n append
   :
```

could be more compactly written as:

```
ascending = (direction = 'A' | direction = '')
   :
if ((ascending & (word.m append > word.n append) ,
 | (¬ (ascending & (word.m append < word.n append)) then do
   :
end
```

The expanded version is better because REXX evaluates all the predicates in conditional statements. Splitting the `IF` statement and repeating the sort statements reduces the number of predicates that must be evaluated through each loop iteration, and so provides significantly improved performance.

Another interesting aspect is the way items to be sorted are passed to the routine. Since the stack might have other data on it, which could cause the sort routine to sort data that should remain untouched, items are passed as a list of blank-delimited words. This list is parsed into a stem variable for the sort. Using a stem considerably reduces the number of calls to the WORD function. It also reduces the number of concatenations that must be done, since the list is not broken apart and put back together again many times as the sort proceeds. The downside is the additional memory requirement.

```
/* SHLLSORT - sort a string of words or numbers using the Shell sort
              algorithm order n*Log(n)

    Invocation:  as an external function

    Parameters:  a list of words or numbers to be sorted

    Returns:     the sorted list

    NOTE:        The REXX comparison operators, "<" and ">", do *NOT*
                 impose an ordering on the domain of all character
                 strings, the only data type REXX has.
                 The reason for this is that some strings "look like"
                 numbers,. If both operands look like numbers then the
                 comparison is done arithmetically; otherwise it is done
                 lexicographically.  For example:
                     103 > 1F3 & 1F3 > 1E3  but 103 < 1E3   /* EBCDIC */
                     2E1 > 2D1 & 2D1 > 201  but 2E1 < 201   /* ASCII  */
                 What happens here is the first two expressions are
                 evaluated lexicographically, since at least one operand
                 can only be a string, while the third expression is
                 evaluated arithmetically, since the 'E' is taken to be
                 an exponent.

                 This routine handles this situation by checking to see
                 if the list to be sorted contains only characters used
                 in numbers. In the case where numbers are being sorted,
                 a variable is set to a zero-length string, and in the
                 case where words are being sorted, the variable is
                 assigned to a non-numeric.  Then in the IF statement
                 where the comparisons are done, the variable is appended
                 to each word, and so when numbers are being sorted, the
                 comparisons are done arithmetically, and in the case
                 where words are being sorted, the comparisons are done
                 lexicographically. The important thing is that either
                 way, the comparisons are done consistently.
*/
address command                         /* Non-REXX commands go to SVC */
parse source . mode .
parse value space(arg(1)) with list
parse upper value arg(2) with direction .
if find('SUBROUTINE FUNCTION', mode) = 0 ,
    | ¬ ( direction = 'A' ,                          /* Ascending */
      | direction = '' ,                             /* Default */
      | direction = 'D')                             /* Descending */
then do
    'XMITMSG 475'
```

```
      exit 40
end
if verify(list, '0123456789- Ee') = 0/* Sorting a list of numbers? */
then append = ''                         /* Arithmetic string compares */
else append = 'z'              /* Lexicographic string compares */
true    = (1==1)
false   = (0==1)
word.0 = words(list)
jump   = word.0
do j = 1 for word.0
   word.j = word(list, j)
end
if direction = 'A' | direction = ''   /* Default order is ascending */
then do while jump > 1
   jump = jump % 2            /* Words move half as far each time */
   do until (noswap)                         /* Sort each section */
      noswap = true
      do m = 1 for (word.0 - jump)           /* Don't go off end */
         n = m + jump
         if word.m append > word.n append then do
            temp   = word.m            /* Sort two words ascending */
            word.m = word.n
            word.n = temp
            noswap = false
         end
      end
   end
end
else do while jump > 1
   jump = jump % 2            /* Words move half as far each time */
   do until (noswap)                         /* Sort each section */
      noswap = true
      do m = 1 for (word.0 - jump)           /* Don't go off end */
         n = m + jump
         if word.m append < word.n append then do
            temp   = word.m            /* Sort two words ascending */
            word.m = word.n
            word.n = temp
            noswap = false
         end
      end
   end
end
list = word.1
do j = 2 for word.0 - 1
   list = list word.j
end
return list
```

CONCLUSION

Improving REXX performance usually means reducing the work the
REXX interpreter must do: shorter code path length; fewer variable

assignments, creations, and deletions; and minimal host environment interaction. This means learning the language and exploiting its features. It also means trying to anticipate the work the interpreter will have to do to fulfill each request, and coding to minimize that work.

21

REXX Compiler for CMS

By Willi Ploechl

OVERVIEW

The unique qualities of the REXX language make it extremely popular for application programs. Some of these programs have become very large (several of them 10,000 lines or more!). Their execution consumed a considerable fraction of the CPU time on the system. Each time they were run, they had to be **interpreted** by the (unquestionably excellent!) CMS REXX interpreter. Consequently, REXX users asked for a better-performing alternative in order to reduce the required CPU time. One way to achieve this is using a compiler.

Consider the basic **differences** between a REXX **interpreter** and a REXX **compiler**. (The following description is necessarily rudimentary and incomplete.)

Interpreter   Uses a **single-step** method. On every invocation of a REXX program, the interpreter:

- Checks the program for correctness.
- Determines whether each symbol is a variable, constant, label, keyword, etc.
- Allocates storage for variables and constants.
- Computes addresses for variables, constants, labels, etc.
- Frees storage.
- etc.

Compiler   Uses a **two-step** method.

1. At **compile time**, the "compiler proper" checks/allocates/computes everything that can be checked/allocated/computed (note that, because of their dynamic nature, compound variables cannot be allocated or assigned addresses at compile time). Code is generated.

2. At **run time**, i.e., at the invocation of a compiled program, the generated code is executed using the library routines of the **run-time system** (see the section "In-line code versus run-time system routines)".

The fact that the first step is not performed at run-time is an obvious reason that a compiled program executes faster than an interpreted one.

Another reason for requiring a REXX compiler was enhanced code security; REXX source programs are prone to undesired changes, which often lead to unexpected problems.

Studies and investigations

The **IBM Scientific Center Haifa** analyzed performance problems of interpreted REXX programs and studied ways to improve performance. Conclusions were:

1. The following items are **performance-critical**:
   - Name derivation of and access to compound variables
   - Arithmetic
   - Memory allocation
   - Conversions
   - Fetching and allocating values

2. It is **feasible to build a REXX compiler**. The potential performance improvement (CPU time) might range from a factor of 2 to 10, heavily dependent on the instruction mix of the program.

3. It is **hard to compile a REXX program**—as opposed to a PL/I or COBOL or C program—because:
   - Program structure is dynamic (e.g., there exists no block concept as in other languages—**PROCEDURE** is an instruction whose execution indicates the start of a procedure; the execution of a **RETURN** indicates its end).
   - **SIGNAL** can transfer control to practically any instruction in a program.
   - Variables
     - are not **declared** (i.e., have no explicit data type, scope, size, or lifetime).
     - can be shared with external programs (in CMS via **EXECCOMM**).
     - can be created dynamically.

- The precision of arithmetic operations and comparisons can be set dynamically (via **NUMERIC DIGITS** and **NUMERIC FUZZ**, respectively).
- Program text can be created dynamically (either by evaluating an expression or by reading a string) and executed using **INTERPRET**.

4. Instead of machine code, so-called **threaded code** should be generated by a REXX compiler (threaded code means a string of instructions for a virtual REXX machine).

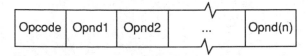

| Opcode | Opnd1 | Opnd2 | ... | Opnd(n) |

Figure 5. Threaded code instruction with n operands

Implementation

The **IBM Vienna Software Development Laboratory** carefully studied the Haifa reports, performed investigations of its own, and then accepted the challenge of building a CMS REXX compiler.

Principal design goals were:

- **Improved run-time performance**
  It was interesting to determine, during the design, implementation, and testing phases, whether Haifa's findings were correct. As one can see, they generally were.

  1. The items listed were indeed performance-critical, and special care was taken to enhance their performance.

  2. Performance was improved by a factor of more than 10. This factor depends heavily on the instruction mix of the program: pure command procedures show almost no improvement, while programs doing substantial arithmetic or accessing compound variables heavily fare much better.

  3. It turned out that compiling a REXX program was not so difficult, but that optimizing was very difficult indeed! The task of compiling was simplified by delegating many functions to library routines of the run-time system, and by not supporting the **INTERPRET** and **TRACE** instructions.

  4. It was discovered that generating System/370 machine code instead of threaded code resulted in slightly better run-time performance (a finding also supported later by Haifa).

- **Cooperation of compiled and interpreted REXX programs**
  Compiled and interpreted REXX programs should be able to call

and be called by each other, without restrictions on the interpreted programs. Furthermore, the user should not need to be aware whether a compiled or interpreted REXX program is executing.

- **Language and functional equivalence**
  REXX programs should give the same results regardless of whether they are being executed in compiled form or being interpreted. All language constructs supported by the REXX interpreter should also be supported by the REXX compiler (except TRACE and INTERPRET).

- **Better code security**
  It is much more difficult to modify an object program than a source program, so compiling REXX could provide this.

- **Improved diagnostics and documentation**
  A compiler can issue better diagnostic messages, and produces listings which can contribute to better documentation.

In-line code versus run-time system routines

It is possible to generate only in-line code for all instructions of a program. However, this would lead to tremendously large compiler output for each program. It was clear that the best approach was to provide a set of library or **run-time system** routines (**RTS** routines). The compiler had to balance the need to be fast (in-line code) with the need to conserve space (invocations of RTS routines). This was achieved by generating in-line code for addressing simple variables, stems, constants, and compiler-generated labels; for performing logical operations; for addition and subtraction; for IF, SELECT, DO, LEAVE, ITERATE, and some other things. Addressing compound variables, performing arithmetic functions other than addition and subtraction, string handling, built-in functions, etc., are performed in RTS routines. Other REXX instructions cause a mixture of in-line code and RTS routine invocations to be generated.

Dual representation of numeric values

It turned out that the vast majority of numbers used in REXX programs are integers with an absolute value of far less than $2**31$. They are usually used as indices for loops and substrings, or as counters. Without going into details or reasons, it was decided to keep numbers in the range from $-2**29$ to $2**29-1$ in binary format, thus allowing the compiler to generate in-line code for fast integer arithmetic.

COMPILER

Overview

In order to achieve a quality product with acceptable compile-time performance, it was decided to build a conventional state-of-the-art compiler with no high-risk advanced technology features. Because compilation performance is not critical, the compiler was implemented in C.

User-friendliness was one of the main goals, and this is reflected in:

- The way the compiler is installed
- The way the compiler can be invoked (via command, EXEC, or dialog)
- The extensive error checking provided
- Listings generated (compiler options, source, and cross reference)

Compiler structure

The REXX compiler is divided into a **kernel** and a **shell**.

The **kernel** (which is the compiler proper, in the classical sense) consists of the following modules:

- Tokenizer
- Parser
- Global analyzer/optimizer
- Flattener
- Code generator
- Postoptimizer
- Final makeup

The **shell** provides different services for the compiler proper, and consists of the following modules:

- Controller
- Environment interface
- Symbol table
- List generator
- Debugging aids

Information flow inside the compiler

Unlike many existing compilers, the REXX compiler does not require any work files; all intermediate information [symbol table, abstract

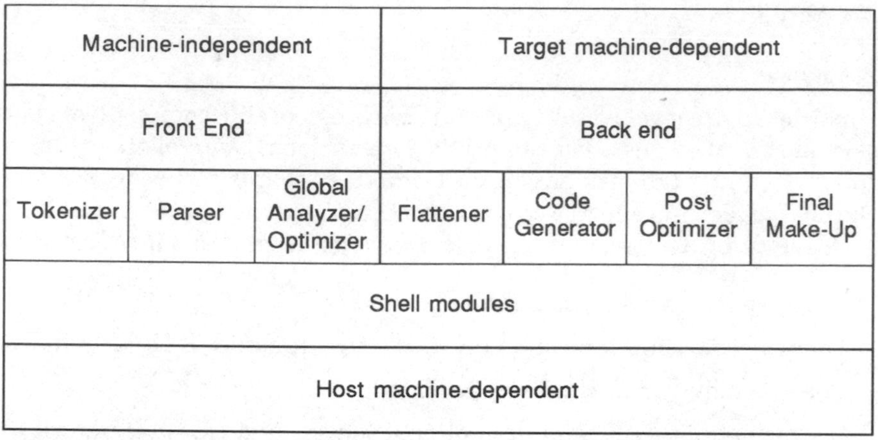

Machine-independent			Target machine-dependent				
Front End			Back end				
Tokenizer	Parser	Global Analyzer/ Optimizer	Flattener	Code Generator	Post Optimizer	Final Make-Up
Shell modules							
Host machine-dependent							

Figure 6. CMS REXX compiler structure

syntax tree (AST), preliminary machine code, etc.] is kept in virtual storage. This makes handling simple for the average user, but it also requires a large amount of virtual storage when compiling large programs (5,000 or more instructions)! However, it was felt that this approach was the right one—especially in an era where storage is becoming cheaper.

Figure 7 shows in conceptual form the main input and output of the modules.

The kernel modules

These modules constitute the compiler proper.

Tokenizer

The Tokenizer performs the lexical analysis of the REXX source. Tokens are recognized using a finite-state machine.

None of the detected errors will stop tokenization.

Parser

The Parser's main task is checking the REXX source against its high-level syntax while generating its internal representation, the abstract syntax tree (AST1).

The tokens are further classified as keywords, variables, labels, or constants. Variables, labels, and constants are then entered into the symbol table. The keywords are used to identify which type of AST node must be generated.

Most of the REXX user errors are found by the analyzing part of the Parser. The same error-handling strategy is used as in the Tokenizer: none of the errors stops compilation.

Global Analysis and Global

Global Analysis checks the program for consistency and completeness.

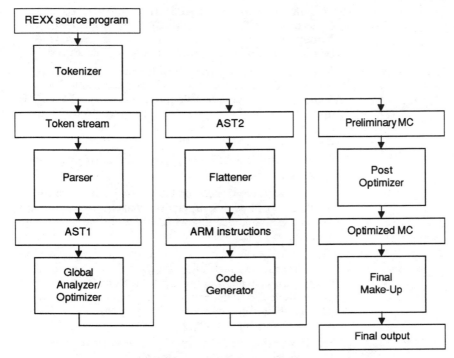

Figure 7. Conceptual flow diagram of the CMS REXX compiler

Optimization

Global Optimization is performed on the AST1; its output is AST2.

The following optimizations are performed:

- Constant folding.
- Common subexpression elimination.
- Value propagation.
- Keeping addresses of compound variables in internal pointers.
- Reducing search time for compound variables in **DO** loops: the search starts not at the top of the tree (as is the case with the REXX interpreter, variables are stored in a **balanced binary tree**), but at the first compound variable found (**next**-search, **same**-search).

Flattener

Flattening of the AST2 is done by traversing the tree while generating code for an Abstract REXX Machine (ARM).

The Flattener breaks down the high-level language elements like control structures, data structures, and expressions to assembly-level elements. Expressions are broken down to sequences of ARM instructions, and temporaries are introduced. In the same way, control structures like **IF**, **DO**, and **SELECT** are translated into sequences of simple logical compares and branches. At this point compiler-generated labels are introduced.

Code Generator   The Code Generator is the first module of the compiler which is completely target machine-dependent. The major decision made by this module is which of the ARM instructions can be implemented as in-line code for the target machine. For those which cannot, invocations of RTS routines are generated.

Addresses for the different types of data are also generated at this point.

Low-level type optimizations are done in this module. Based on bookkeeping of register contents, unnecessary register exchanges and storing into temporaries can be avoided.

The output of the Code Generator (preliminary machine code) consists of machine instructions, address tags for the operands used, and branch tags. Code for branching and data access is generated assuming the **worst case**, which means that the code for loading the base register is always generated.

Postoptimizer   The Postoptimizer eliminates unnecessary addressing code for branches and data access.

Final Makeup   In the last step, main tasks are resolution of branch tags and relative data addresses, and producing the final format output.

The shell modules

These modules provide services to all other compiler modules in order to hide operating system details from the rest of the compiler.

One module, the Controller, controls the entire compilation process. Global tables are maintained, and each compiler phase is initiated depending on compiler options and the result of the preceding compiler phase.

These modules form a shell around the kernel modules. The Controller module sits above and the rest of the shell modules beneath the kernel modules of the compiler.

Environment Interface

- Read source into virtual storage
- Parse compiler options
- Storage management
- Other operating system interfaces (date, I/O, etc.)

Symbol Table

▪ Maintain constants, variables, and labels

List Generator

▪ Maintain error messages
▪ Produce requested listings (source, cross reference)

Debugging Aids

▪ Dump global tables (symbol table, AST1, AST2, machine code, final output)
▪ Trace internal interfaces (token stream, ARM instructions)
▪ Produce an object program listing (similar to an assembler listing) of the generated code

Controller

▪ Initiate compiler phases and their dumps
▪ Keep global tables (AST1, AST2, preliminary compiler output, final compiler output)

RUN-TIME SYSTEM

This section is not nearly as large as that on the compiler, but its size is not related to the importance of its subject. **The efficiency of the run-time system is primarily responsible for the performance improvement** of compiled REXX programs.

Why is a run-time system needed?

The section "In-line code versus run-time system routines" mentioned that the size of the compiler's output is the main reason for having a set of library routines comprising the run-time system. Another reason was to allow these routines to be installed in one place in storage to be shared by all compiled REXX programs (in VM, such a saved entity is called a **discontiguous saved segment** or **DCSS**), thus saving considerable virtual storage. An additional reason is the fact that it is simpler to change a small RTS routine than a large, complicated compiler module; such changes might become necessary for reasons of maintenance or improvement.

Contents of the run-time system

▪ Routines invoked from the compiled REXX program, like routines for:

  ▪ addressing compound variables

- string handling
- certain kinds of arithmetics
- performing the PARSE instruction
- etc.

- Routines invoked from other RTS routines, namely for:
  - conversions between various data representations
  - invoking system services
  - storage management
  - etc.

Highlights of the run-time system

In order to achieve the highest possible speed, it was decided to:

- use a fast linkage to run-time routines, without saving all registers on each call.
- use special **pool storage management**, which minimizes the need to call system storage services, which can be expensive.
- write the RTS routines in assembler language, in order to choose the most efficient instructions.

CONCLUSION

The CMS REXX compiler has been in use for more than a year, and its users are happy with its performance and quality. The fact that it supports the same level of language as the CMS REXX interpreter (except for INTERPRET and TRACE) makes it especially attractive: the user can debug a REXX program with the interpreter—which is very convenient—and then compile and run it—which gives excellent performance. It seems that a fully compatible pair—interpreter and compiler—could be the ideal team for *every* programming language!

22

Amiga REXX

By Marvin Weinstein

INTRODUCTION

The Amiga name applies to a family of desktop computers based on the Motorola 680xx family of processors. All members of the Amiga family run AmigaDOS, a proprietary multitasking operating system. From the 68000-based Amiga-500 to the top-of-the-line 68030-based Amiga-3000, all Amigas are capable of running the same software (subject, of course, to memory limitations).

Recently, Amiga computers have received a great deal of attention as remarkably costeffective multi-media platforms. Not enough attention, however, is paid to the unique opportunities these machines offer as low-cost technical workstations. One of the most attractive features of the newest version of the Amiga's operating system, AmigaDOS-2.0, is that it includes a marvelous realization of the REXX language.

Amiga REXX, or ARexx, is an implementation of the REXX language which takes advantage of powerful features of the Amiga operating system. By exploiting the Amiga's multitasking operating capabilities and easy interprocess communications, William Hawes has created a version of REXX which is far more than a replacement for the limited scripting language originally provided with AmigaDOS. Since the use of ARexx to customize the Amiga's command line interface (which resembles the interface found on mainframes or older PCs) is similar to the way in which REXX is used on other platforms, this chapter does not focus on this aspect. Instead, it focuses on those aspects of ARexx, and their relation to the general Amiga environment, which are unique to this realization of REXX.

WHAT IS SPECIAL ABOUT AREXX?

On most platforms only one REXX program can execute at a time. Since the Amiga multitasks, multiple ARexx programs can run simultaneously. Furthermore, ARexx fully exploits the Amiga's message passing ability, allowing asynchronously running REXX programs to communicate with one another and exchange information as if they were part of a single larger application. To do this, a process simply opens a **message port** and sleeps, waiting for a message to arrive. When a message arrives, the process wakes, reads the message, notifies the sender that the message was received, and acts upon its contents. This sort of message passing between ARexx programs and/or other applications opens up an entire world of possibilities for creating large ARexx applications out of small, independently running processes, each of which can run either synchronously or asynchronously. Each process can own its own data, carry out operations upon this data when instructed to do so, and report results of such operations to the master program. Thought of in this manner, ARexx programming on the Amiga offers many features and capabilities advertised for object-oriented programming languages such as Smalltalk, C++, Objective-C, and Eiffel. Thus, although ARexx does not provide inheritance, nor does it run as fast as a compiled language, ARexx programs can be written so as to mimic key elements of object-oriented languages. More significantly, ARexx programs can be used to create **modular** or **plug-compatible** software, which can be easily configured by the end-user—which, after all, is the goal of object-oriented design.

Customizing applications using ARexx

Including an ARexx message port in a program lets the user add custom features to commercial applications. For example, special routines can be written for drawing mathematically defined shapes in a mouse-oriented structured drawing program, thus customizing the application for local users. A later example shows how to customize the ProVector drawing program to simplify the task of drawing various elements of Feynman diagrams. Feynmam diagrams are a powerful graphical shorthand for describing the terms in a mathematical expansion, and have structural elements which are called **photons** (sinusoidal lines) and **gluons** (objects which resemble springs). Anyone who has attempted to create these shapes in a standard drawing program knows how difficult this chore is. With ARexx, however, the task is rendered as simple as clicking on an icon or making a menu selection, and then using a mouse to define the length of the desired line or diameter of the desired loop. This information is returned to the ARexx program, which computes the desired shape using mouse-generated information and instructs the application to plot the result. One can also add a CAD-like interface to what is, fundamentally, a drawing program by writing ARexx programs. In most true CAD programs, lines, circles, arcs, etc., are created by typing commands which specify both the object and its precise location and properties. Very few CAD programs use a mouse-driven user interface. Most ARexx-capable applications allow the user to create new menus and/or menu entries. For this reason, creating an effective CAD facility is as simple as adding new menu selections. Given this flexibility, users now have the option of buying a drawing program and, with some work, using it as a special-purpose CAD program. The gain is that for general use, the drawing program has a much friendlier user interface than the average CAD program.

Combining commercial applications using ARexx

Since any program can open a message port and send and receive ARexx messages, an important way to use ARexx is as user-defined "glue" which ties together pre-existing, independent programs into a single unit. In this way, custom applications can be created to perform tasks which could not be accomplished by any of these software modules alone. A way to exploit this flexibility is to create a comfortable front end for TeX, Donald Knuth's computerized typesetting system. This system is extremely powerful, and has no peer when it comes to typesetting technical documents which contain mathematical formulas. However, since TeX is designed to run on a multiplicity of platforms and to produce device-independent output, the user interface is usually fairly primitive. Creating a TeX document involves using an editor to create an ASCII file, using a version of the TeX program to process this ASCII file, and finally, using another program to print the final copy. While this way of doing things makes TeX very portable, on a given platform such as the Amiga it would be much nicer if interacting with TeX had more of the flavor of dealing with an integrated, WYSIWYG, scientific desktop-publishing application. Given an ARexx-capable editor such as TxEd Plus or Cygnus Ed, an ARexx-capable implementation of TeX such as AmigaTeX, and an ARexx-capable TeX previewer, this can be done by writing a few simple ARexx programs, rather than by creating a large, customized piece of software. One advantage of the ARexx approach is that it is easy to customize an application for a small market segment, something which would ordinarily be prohibitively expensive. Another is that when a better editor appears, it is not difficult to remove the old one and plug the new one in its place. In general, modifications of this sort only involve altering a few lines of code in each of a few ARexx programs. One of the programming examples in this chapter shows how to do this. This application can be expanded in scope by adding menu items to the editor to provide on-line HELP for TeX commands and to provide shortcuts for certain frequently used TeX commands. This is an example which exploits both ARexx's ability to customize a single application and its ability to coordinate the functioning of three independent programs, to create what appears to be a single application run entirely from within the editor environment. Another enhancement of this scientific desktop-publishing system is integration of a database facility into the package. This sort of integration is useful in a university or laboratory setting, when it is desirable to keep information on applicants for post-doctoral positions. A list of applicants can be accumulated as a text file on a mainframe. An ARexx program can read this file and use it to create a database file on the Amiga. Later, as the applications are read, the user can use the Amiga's GUI to record the names of people who sent letters of recommendation and memorable comments as part of the records. Finally, a beautifully formatted document can be produced containing important information by simply selecting the desired subset of records and invoking another ARexx program which extracts the necessary information from selected records and writes a TeX file. Generally, this program is designed to load the final text into a local editor, cause AmigaTeX to process the file, and finally close down the database. In this way, the database and TeX facilities appear to be part of one application. A database can also be used in conjunction with TeX and the editor to provide a facility for storing and retrieving often-used references. A package of TeX macros, PHYZZX, is widely used at various laboratories and universities to prepare papers and other documents. A feature of this package is that it allows assigning dummy names of the form \asampleref to references to articles or books. This macro automatically assigns a number to each name, based on the order of appearance of the reference in the document. In this way, the dummy name can be used to indicate the actual reference; thus, if references are removed or moved to other parts of the paper, the page numbers will still be correct. As it turns out, people often have standard lists of references, and they would like to be able to keep a list of dummy names for use in multiple papers. Of course, simply importing a document containing all often-used references will not do the correct thing, as numbers will be assigned to each of them, regardless of their use in the text and their order of appearance. To circumvent the problems caused by simply importing a general list of often-used references, these references can be kept in an ARexx-capable database instead. It is then straightforward to create a TeX macro to invoke an ARexx program, which in turn invokes the database and retrieves the record. The same program can take the selected record and write necessary information to a file which will eventually contain only those references used in the paper. In general, ARexx's ability to serve as a central coordinator for multiple applications creates many opportunities for creatively customizing the working environment. Experience has shown that the possibilities are limited only by one's imagination.

ARexx libraries

The previous discussion talked about customizing a drawing program to plot mathematical functions. Obviously, in order to do this, the ARexx program must have access to special functions such as SIN and COS, which are not standard parts of REXX's repertoire. Fortunately, the Amiga supports the concept of shared libraries, a special type of which can be accessed by ARexx. The virtue of shared libraries is that many REXX programs can use the same functions without taxing system resources. ARexx supports libraries written to access the system's math functions and graphical user interface. These libraries must be installed in the usual way, and the resident ARexx process must be notified of their existence. For example, in the case of the math library, this is accomplished by adding:

```
call addlib('REXXMATHLIB.LIBRARY', 0, -30, 0)
```

to the program. Clearly, one area of opportunity for the developer is to provide libraries to enhance ARexx's capabilities.

A QUESTION OF ACCEPTANCE

This chapter has so far focused on how a full multitasking REXX implementation creates possibilities for customizing the environment. Of course, these opportunities will only be realized if commercial developers accept ARexx as their universal scripting language and provide consistent, extensive support for language features. Early on it became clear that this sort of organized growth could occur only if Commodore formally supported ARexx. Fortunately, with the advent of AmigaDOS 2.0, ARexx is now an integral part of the operating system. Moreover, Commodore is heavily involved in the process of suggesting standards for incorporating ARexx in applications. Now that ARexx is an established feature of all future Amigas, and developers will be able to count on its presence, one can only begin to imagine the new and creative uses to which ARexx will be put.

SAMPLE PROGRAMS

Customizing a drawing program

This section discusses two ARexx programs. The first was written for ProVector, the structured drawing program discussed earlier. This program allows the user to draw **gluon lines**. It works in a similar manner to the built-in drawing tools. When run, the program takes over the mouse. If the user holds down the left mouse button and moves the mouse, a **rubber band** line appears, indicating the beginning and length of the desired gluon line. When the user clicks a second time, the program reads initial and final mouse coordinates, and uses this information to calculate the desired cycloid. When the array of xy coordinates for points on the gluon has been computed, this array is passed back to the host application, ProVector, for display. Passing the REXX array to the application by simply specifying the stem variable illustrates the ARexx **REXX Variable Interface** (RVI).

Program operation is fairly easily understood. After parsing arguments into variable COMMAND, it executes the statement:

```
options result
```

This ARexx instruction is an extension of the REXX language. It instructs ARexx to expect the host application to return a string, which it is to assign to variable RESULT. This is one of the two ways in which the host application communicates with an ARexx program; the second is through RVI variables. Following the OPTIONS instruction is a line which is also not a standard REXX feature. The ADDLIB instruction tells ARexx to add library REXXMATHLIB.LIBRARY to the list to search when attempting to resolve a function call. The first argument is the library name; remaining arguments specify things such as library entry point, version number, etc. These are usually as shown in the example. The main part of the program is controlled by a SELECT/WHEN/OTHERWISE construct, which branches depending upon the value of variable COMMAND. The program is invoked with an argument because of the way the ProVector GetUserData command operates. Its syntax is:

```
GetUserData rubber band-type min max OK-Macro Cancel-Macro
```

This call terminates execution of the ARexx program and tells ProVector to receive at least *min* and at most *max* points through manipulation of the mouse. The *rubber band-type* argument is either 1 or 2. 1 indicates that a simple line should be displayed joining the last user-defined point to the present mouse position; 2 indicates that a rectangle should be displayed. As with other drawing tools, double-clicking the left mouse button indicates to ProVector that the user has finished entering data. At this point, ProVector executes one of the ARexx macros specified as the *OK-Macro* and the *Cancel-Macro*. If the user terminates data input in the normal manner, the *OK-Macro* is executed; if the user terminates by hitting the ESC key, ProVector's normal way of aborting a tool's action, the *Cancel-Macro* is executed. As will be apparent from reading the program, both the *OK-Macro* and the *Cancel-Macro* call the same program with different arguments. This method of interaction with the host application is quite flexible and allows the application to handle all mouse moves, etc., at high speed, with control returning to ARexx only after all mousing around has finished. When a user selects the Gluon option from the ProVector menu, the program is executed without arguments, and so the first WHEN clause is executed. The Prompt and EndPrompt commands post messages for the user, or remove such messages if they exist. This code fragment begins with EndPrompt to close any open message windows and to post a new message to indicate the current drawing option in effect. Next ARexx executes the GetUserData option, which waits for the user to provide mouse input. If the user hits ESC, the macro is called with argument QUIT, which causes ProVector to close its message window. On the other hand, if the user inputs two points, the macro is called with argument CONTINUE, and the main loop is executed. Other interesting commands are GetInputPoints *endpts*, GetPage-Size *pgsz*, and PolyLine *numpts points*, all of which interact with ProVector through the REXX Variable Interface. For example:

```
'GetInputPoints endpts'
numpts = result
```

causes coordinates, which the user enters by clicking on the left mouse button, to be sent back to the REXX array associated with the ENDPTS. stem variable. At the same time, variable RESULT is set to the number of points returned. Similarly:

```
'GetPageSize pgsz'
```

sets variables PGSZ.X1, PGSZ.Y1, PGSZ.X2, and PGSZ.Y2, to the x and y coordinates of the points which the user entered in response to the call to GetUserData. Except for these commands, which belong to the host application, and the obvious calls to the REXXMATHLIB SIN and COS functions, etc., the program is pure REXX.

```
/** REXX: GLUON.PVRX */
/* Use the mouse to input coordinates of a gluon line, provide */
/* straight-line rubber banding, and plot the calculated cycloid. */
   arg command
   result = ''
   options result
/* Make sure REXXMATHLIB.LIBRARY has been added to the function list */
   call addlib('REXXMATHLIB.LIBRARY', 0, -30, 0)
/* Check the argument */
   select
       when command = '' then do
          'EndPrompt'
          'Prompt "Gluon: ESC to cancel"'
          'GetUserData 1 2 2 "gluon continue" "gluon quit"'
       end
       when command = 'CONTINUE' then do
          'GetInputPoints endpts'
          numpts = result
          'GetPageSize pgsz'
          rlen = min(abs(pgsz.x1-pgsz.x2), abs(pgsz.y1-pgsz.y2))/16
          pi = 2 * acos(0)
          'EndPrompt'
          'Prompt "Working"'
          length = sqrt((endpts.0.x-endpts.1.x)**2,
            + (endpts.0.y-endpts.1.y)**2)
          cth = (endpts.1.x-endpts.0.x)/length
          sth = (endpts.1.y-endpts.0.y)/length
/* Calculate how many full loops fit in this distance */
          numloops = (length/rlen)%1
          if numloops = 0 then numloops = 1
          rlen = length/numloops
          oneloop = 8
          r = rlen/2.6
          v = length/(oneloop*numloops + oneloop/2)
          delth = 2*pi/oneloop
          do i = 0 to oneloop*numloops-oneloop/2
             th = delth*i
             vi = v*i
             costh = cos(th)
             sinth = sin(th)
             points.i.x = endpts.0.x + cth*(vi-r*(costh-1))-sth*r*sinth
             points.i.y = endpts.0.y+cth*r*sinth + sth*(vi-r*(costh-1))
          end
          numpts = numloops*oneloop-oneloop/2+1
          'PolyLine numpts points'
          object = result
          'ChangeEdgeType object 1'
          'EndPrompt'
          'GetUserData 1 2 2 "gluon continue" "gluon quit"'
          'Prompt "Gluon: ESC to cancel"'
       end
       otherwise 'EndPrompt'
   end
   exit
```

Tying together AmigaTeX, Preview, and TxEd Plus

This section examines a program used to join three commercial applications into a scientific desktop-publishing program. The goal is to use ARexx to reconfigure an ARexx-capable editor to make it appear as a dedicated—almost WYSIWYG—scientific word processor. This is accomplished by adding menu options to launch ARexx programs which do the real work. A menu option is added for TeXing and Previewing the current file. Selecting this option launches an ARexx program to start AmigaTeX and Preview, if they are not already running, and to handle all subsequent TeX error messages as they occur. In the case of TxEd Plus, configuring menu options to perform this task is done by means of an ARexx program launched when the editor starts. This very simple program is discussed here. This section deals with the program which coordinates interactions between the editor, AmigaTeX, and Preview. Since TeX and Preview run as separate tasks, the program must first save the current file to disk or memory, so that TeX can access it. Next, AmigaTeX must be told to load the file and create a device-independent (DVI) file. If Preview is running and has defaulted to the **Track File** option, AmigaTeX automatically forwards the processed file to Preview for display; hence the program does not have to handle this part of the interaction. However, the ARexx program will tell Preview where to write the DVI file when it is finished displaying it. As the program is launched under the auspices of the editor, the editor will be the default ARexx host. This means that calls to the **ADDRESS** function will obtain the name of the editor's ARexx message port. Communication with AmigaTeX and Preview is accomplished by simply changing this default host. Thus, to send an command to AmigaTeX, merely preface the command with `address AmigaTeX`. For example:

```
address TeXPreview 'CD ram:'
```

tells the Preview program to write the DVI file to the `ram:` disk. Essentially, this line sends an ARexx message containing the string `CD ram:` to Preview's ARexx message port. When the Preview program is notified that a message has arrived, it reads it, performs the indicated command, and replies to the message, indicating either success or failure. After the previewer responds, the ARexx program which sent the message can continue. This illustrates synchronous message passing; however, it is also possible to send the message without forcing the program to wait for a response. Such asynchronous messaging is very useful for launching REXX programs which need not complete their task before the calling program finishes what it is doing. Although the principal aim in presenting this example is to exhibit the way in which message passing allows separately running programs to communicate, the example provides instances of the use of the OPTIONS RESULT instruction, REXXARPLIB.LIBRARY, and the ADDRESS COMMAND instruction, which sends a command to AmigaDOS for execution. A typical ADDRESS COMMAND is:

```
address command 'RUN PREVIEW'
```

which launches Preview as an asynchronous process. Because the AmigaDOS RUN command replies immediately after launching the program, the ARexx program can issue the command and continue. Thus the program must check to be sure that all processes launched with this trick are actually functioning.

With the preceding discussion and a general idea of the goals, most REXX users should be able to easily follow the sample code. Once the user has launched the program by selecting the TeX this file option from the user menu, the first step is obtaining the current filename and directory path from the editor. TxEd commands used for this purpose are STATUS D and STATUS F. Again, these commands must be preceded by an OPTIONS RESULT statement. Thus, as a result of the fragment:

```
options result
. . .
'STATUS D'
directory = result
```

the file's path is assigned to variable DIRECTORY. If the edited file has no name, the program prompts the user to supply one; or, failing that, the program supplies a name of its own. The program next checks that both AmigaTeX and Preview are running; if not, it launches them. This is done with the showlist('P', portname) command, which returns a string containing a list of all open message ports. Once both programs are active, the program tells AmigaTeX to process the current version of the file, and waits to handle any errors which may occur. Among the small set of ARexx commands recognized by AmigaTeX are TeXify, Abort, CD directory name, NextPrompt, and Prompt. Some useful commands that the previewer knows: CD directory, ToBack, ToFront. CD directory name tells both programs where to write files they produce; ToBack and ToFront tell the previewer to move its window behind all other open windows. All these commands cause immediate consequences, and return immediately. The NextPrompt command, however, does not return until TeX either completes processing the file or encounters an error. Since this may not happen for some time, AmigaTeX does not immediately reply to the NextPrompt command, thus suspending execution of the ARexx program which sent the

command. Once the **NextPrompt** command returns, it is possible to
determine the state AmigaTeX is in with the **Prompt** command. This
instructs AmigaTeX to write the requisite information to the Amiga's
clipboard. This information can be retrieved using ARexx's **GETCLIP**
function. The meaning of the TeX prompts and the actions taken in
response to each is noted in comments in the sample program.

```
/* TXEDTEXIFY.TXE--Macro to send the current edited file to TeX. */
/* Checks if TeX and the Previewer are running, starts them if not. */
   options result
   directory = ''
   dev = ''
   subdir = ''
/* Make sure REXXARPLIB.LIBRARY has been added to the list. */
   call addlib('REXXARPLIB.LIBRARY', 0, -30, 0)
/* Now get current filename and directory for later use. */
/* Note that there is always a current directory even if it is blank. */
   'STATUS D'
   directory = result
   :
   (code for getting the file's directory)
   :
/* Get a filename. If the editor loaded a file, one exists; however, */
/* if the editor is creating a new file, there may be no filename. */
/* Extract the filename; if blank, prompt for a name. */
   'STATUS F'
   if result <> '' then filename = result
   else do
      :
      (code for handling the missing filename)
      :
   end
/* Use the REXXARPLIB FILELIST function to expand the name, to handle */
/* directory paths with embedded spaces. */
   call filelist(directory||filename, fullfilename,, expand)
   if fullfilename.0 = 0 then fullfilename.1 = directory||filename
   if index(fullfilename.1, 'Ram Disk') <> 0 then
   fullfilename.1 = delstr(fullfilename.1, 4, 5)
   'SAVEAS' fullfilename.1
/* Check to see if TeX and TeXPreview's message ports are open. */
/* If not, run the programs; when everything is available, tell */
/* AmigaTeX to begin processing this file. */
   call CHECKFORTEX()
   call CHECKFORPREVIEW()
   call STOPTEX()
   address AmigaTeX 'TeXify' fullfilename.1
/* Now wait around to see what happens in the TeXing process. */
/* Handle no \bye command in the TeX file, other TeX errors, etc. */
MISSINGFILE:
/* Tell TeX to let you know when it has reached a prompt. */
   address AmigaTeX 'NextPrompt'
/* TeX has either finished or needs help.  Tell it to */
/* write the current prompt to the ARexx clipboard. */
   address AmigaTeX 'Prompt'
```

```
/* Extract the prompt from the clipboard. */
   promptstring = strip(getclip('AmigaTeX.Prompt'))
/* Handle any problems and/or exit. */
/*   **      Completed successfully, exit. */
/*   *       Send TeX the \bye command and wait for **. */
/*    ?      Error occurred; open another TxEd session to display */
/*           the log file containing the TeX messages. */
/*   file    Missing file, post a requester asking for input. */
   select
      when promptstring = '**' then nop
      when promptstring = '*' then do
         address AmigaTeX 'TeXify \bye'
         SIGNAL MISSINGFILE
      end
      when promptstring = '?' then do
         'txed_tex/toerror'
         parse var filename name'.'tex
         name = 'dvifiles:'name'.log'
         address AmigaTeX 'NextPrompt'
         address TeXpreview 'ToBack'
         call delay 100
         address command 'e 'name' sticky txed_tex/editerror'
      end
      when promptstring = 'file' then do
         problem = "TeX can't find a file you told it to input"
         problem = problem||"a file\I can continue by input-ing "
         problem = problem||"the file whose\name appears below "
         problem = problem||"(e.g. nul) , or abort and\"
         problem = problem||"display the TeX log file to show "
         problem = problem||"you your error.\What should I do?"
         answer =  request(10, 10, problem, 'nul',,
            ' Continue TeX ', '  Abort  ')
         if answer <> '' then address AmigaTeX 'TeXify 'answer
         else do
            address AmigaTeX 'TeXify nul '
            address AmigaTeX 'Abort'
            parse var filename name'.'tex
            name = 'dvifiles:'name'.log'
            address AmigaTeX 'NextPrompt'
            address TeXpreview 'ToBack'
            call delay 100
            address command 'e 'name' sticky txed_tex/editerror'
         end
         signal MISSINGFILE
      end
      otherwise nop
   end
   exit
/* Subroutine to check to see if TeX is up */
CHECKFORTEX:
   if ¬ showlist('P', 'AmigaTeX') then do
/* Tell the host application to resize its window to almost fill */
/* the screen. */
      WINDOW 0 0 screencols()-10 screenrows()
/* Open a console window for AmigaTeX to run in by issuing the run */
```

```
/* command to AmigaDOS. Startup_TeX is the name of an ARexx program */
/* which arranges for this window to close automatically when */
/* AmigaTeX closes itself down. */
      constring = "newwsh con:"screencols()-10"/"screenrows()-10
      constring = constring||"/10/10/'TeXWindow'/c CMD Startup_TeX"
      address command constring
/* Give things time to get up and running.*/
      do i = 1 to 50
         if ¬ showlist('p', "AmigaTeX") |¬showlist('p', "TeXpreview") ,
            then call delay 20
         else leave i
      end
   end
/* Wait for the double-splat prompt which indicatest that AmigaTeX */
/* is ready and then tell it where to write its files. */
   address AmigaTeX 'NextPrompt'
   address AmigaTeX 'CD work:dvifiles'
   return 0
/*  Subroutine to check for previewer if TeX is up */
CHECKFORPREVIEW:
   if ¬showlist('P', 'TeXpreview') then do
      address command run preview
      call postmsg(50, 50, "Waiting for the previewer to start up")
      do i = 1 to 350
         if ¬showlist('P', 'TeXpreview') then call delay 40
         else leave i
      end
      call postmsg()
   end
   pmessage = "The previewer is open but it is not set up so "
   pmessage = pmessage||"that TeX can send the file to \it as "
   pmessage = pmessage||"each page finishes. To make that happen "
   pmessage = pmessage||"choose the Track File \or Track Page "
   pmessage = pmessage||"option from the tracking menu \To "
   pmessage = pmessage||"close this window click on the close "
   pmessage = pmessage||"gadget in the upper left hand corner"
   if ¬showlist('P', 'TeX:dvistream') then ,
      call request(10, 10, pmessage,,)
   address TeXpreview 'CD work:dvifiles'
   return 0
/* If TeX is doing something, stop it and bring it back to ** prompt */
STOPTEX:
   do istop=1 to 50
      address AmigaTeX 'Abort'
      if rc=0 then leave istop
   end
   return 0
```

23

REXX in GCS

By Ken Holt

INTRODUCTION

GCS? What's that?

Unlike other programming environments discussed in this book, GCS is not an environment that the typical user is likely to know of or have access to. GCS (**Group Control System**) is included as part of VM (whether the installation installs GCS is another matter). GCS was introduced by IBM in VM/SP Release 4, and has been included in every VM release since then (with the exception of VM/XA SP Release 1).

A special-purpose environment

GCS is a special-purpose environment which supports native VM/VTAM and its friends. The people most likely to use it are:

- VM systems programmers supporting networks
- VM applications programmers writing VTAM applications, or applications requiring true multitasking

GCS is a curious hybrid with a number of similarities to MVS and CMS. On the CMS side, it uses the CMS file system, and the feel of the console handling and command structure is very "CMS-ish". On the other hand, it offers no native CMS applications programming interfaces; for instance, data management services are provided through simulation of MVS-type system calls.

GCS provides a full multitasking environment. This contrasts with CMS, which is basically a single-threaded system, although you can sort of make it multitask if you're willing to hijack system interfaces and do some fancy programming. GCS's multitasking support closely parallels the MVS model, going so far as to use the same task-management system calls as MVS.

GCS also provides a full VTAM API (Application Programming Interface), virtually identical to the MVS VTAM API. If you migrate a pure VTAM application (using only VTAM APIs) from MVS to VM, there is an excellent chance that it will run without modification. On the other hand, if the application fiddles with control blocks or uses less-common features of MVS task or data management (or sometimes even common ones), the application may need significant work to make it run in GCS.

Narrow focus

If you look closely at GCS, you may be puzzled when you discover what IBM left out, seemingly without any pattern. The reason is that GCS is a **tactical** component, designed to fill a short-term need. Therefore, very little was put into GCS which is not needed by VM/VTAM and company. IBM appears to be heading toward a time when GCS is no longer needed, with its functions delivered by a CMS version providing true multitasking and VTAM API support.

SAME LANGUAGE AS REXX IN CMS (ALMOST)

A fairly common misperception is that REXX in GCS is somehow a less capable implementation than the REXX found in CMS. The truth is that the REXX *language* itself is essentially the same in GCS as in CMS, with a few exceptions.

External function libraries

External function libraries (**RXSYSFN**, **RXLOCFN**, and **RXUSERFN**) are not supported in GCS. This makes it virtually impossible to extend the language. It can also cause nasty surprises if one does not realize that some commonly used construct is actually implemented as an external function. **DIAG** and **DIAGRC**, for instance, are not available in REXX under GCS.

ADDRESS environments

REXX in GCS recognizes only two **ADDRESS** environments: **GCS** and

COMMAND, with GCS the default. ADDRESS GCS resolves commands in the following way:

1. Look for an EXEC (filetype GCS).
2. Try invoking as a GCS command (native GCS command or LOADCMDed module).
3. Try as a CP command.
4. Give up.

ADDRESS COMMAND, on the other hand, does the following:

1. Try invoking as a GCS command (native GCS command or LOADCMDed module).
2. Give up.

SIGNAL ON HALT

The SIGNAL ON HALT instruction is accepted but meaningless in GCS, since there is no HI Immediate command to raise the HALT condition.

OTHER IMPLEMENTATION ISSUES

There are a few other notable differences, which are not strictly language issues.

Program stack

REXX programs in a given task can use the program stack to pass data back and forth. However, GCS maintains a separate program stack for each task, so you cannot pass data between tasks in this way.

Console stack

There is no console input stack. Console input is routed to the proper task by the GCS REPLY command; you cannot reply to an input request that is not already pending. As ugly as this is, it makes pretty good sense. If GCS were to just accept console input, should it treat the input as a command and send it to the COMMAND task, or should it stack it for another task? If so, which one?

Immediate commands

GCS does not support the following Immediate commands:

HI   Halt Interpreter: terminate execution of REXX and EXEC 2 programs.

HO   Halt Override: suppress SVC tracing.

HT	Halt Typing: suppress console output.
RO	Resume Override: resume SVC tracing.
RT	Resume Typing: resume console output.
TE	Trace End: terminate REXX or EXEC 2 tracing.
TS	Trace Start: start (or resume) REXX or EXEC 2 tracing.

If these are entered in GCS, they are processed as normal commands (if they even exist).

If a program has the same name as a GCS Immediate command, it will never be executed: the system-defined Immediate command always takes precedence. GCS Immediate commands are:

- GDUMP
- HX
- ETRACE
- ITRACE
- SDUMP
- QUERY
- REPLY

REXX programs in GCS

GCS REXX programs have filetype GCS rather than EXEC. While this might be viewed as creating confusion, it's really a nice idea: it allows the flexibility of having separate REXX programs for both CMS and GCS on the same disk. For example, if you run both GCS and CMS on your userid, you probably would not want the same PROFILE EXEC for both environments.

REXX: the only game in town

REXX is the only procedures language supported on GCS; EXEC and EXEC 2 are finally gone. This means that the opening /*...*/ is not required in GCS. However, it's advisable to continue the practice; some other procedures language might run on GCS some day. This may not be very likely, but it's cheap insurance—and makes one less nit to worry about if you ever have to migrate REXX code to another environment.

THE GCS COMMAND ENVIRONMENT

This is the area that offers the greatest challenge. This is because GCS lacks the robustness which gives REXX so much of its usefulness in other environments.

Stacking command responses

This is the most troublesome area; commands do not offer options to stack GCS command responses. In addition, since external function packages are not supported, **DIAG** and **DIAGRC** are not available to capture CP command responses. This, of course, severely limits how much you can manage your environment.

Manipulating files

This is another big problem. GCS does not offer even elementary file-manipulation commands like **ERASE**, **STATE**, **RENAME**, or **TYPE**. Nor does it provide the bizarre but useful **EXECIO** command. So there are no provisions for REXX programs in GCS to manage, manipulate, or even read or write files.

The alternatives

What if you desperately need to do some of these things? In most cases you can write an assembler program to do these things, but it's probably not going to be as pretty as it would have been in CMS. Also, the author has placed several utility programs in the public domain, some of which address a few of the problems noted above (**ERASE**, **STATE**, and **TYPE**). A section at the end of this chapter provides information on how to obtain these public domain materials.

It is probably possible to build some sort of command front-end utility to capture GCS command output to the program stack. Likewise, it is possible to write a functional replacement for **DIAG/DIAGRC**, although at the time of this writing there is no evidence that anyone has succeeded at either task. It might even be possible to port **EXECIO** from CMS to GCS, but again, there is no evidence of success in this area.

The future

IBM has participated in dialogs with the GCS committee of SHARE for several years. Numerous suggestions for GCS improvements have been submitted to IBM through a formal requirements process.

Beginning late in 1989, IBM's attitude towards GCS has undergone a dramatic change. IBM is now acutely aware of the issues discussed above, and has responded very favorably to a number of the committee's requirements. It appears that IBM intends to address these deficiencies in future releases of GCS.

SPECIAL CAPABILITIES IN GCS

Life is not all bad in GCS. Its multitasking lets you do something that you cannot do in CMS: run several REXX programs concurrently.

One of the public domain utilities written by the author is called SLEEPER; this can launch up to eight separate tasks, each waking periodically to run its own command, which could easily be a REXX program. The tasks can run different programs, or they can all invoke the same REXX program (perhaps with different arguments). These, in turn, can invoke other REXX programs or other applications. You can set up a few background tasks to awaken and monitor things from time to time, or perhaps give something else in the system a nudge if it seems to have hung up.

Another public domain program, SEARCH, scans for specified data patterns in memory (up to eight concurrent searches are supported, each in its own subtask). Suppose you're seeking a particular data pattern in memory. In GCS, you need not kill the application or take a dump; you can SEARCH for the pattern while the application is still running.

SUMMARY

REXX under GCS is often frustrating because of the mixed message one receives. REXX runs in GCS, and is given several nice interfaces (like the shared variable interface), but then one discovers rather quickly that many important facilities are missing. This results in the same kind of bewilderment and frustration one might feel if confronted by a well-marked path leading to a welcome mat in front of a locked door. The good news is that IBM is earnestly trying to locate a key.

PUBLIC DOMAIN SOFTWARE

The author's public domain GCS utilities package is available from several sources:

- Waterloo VM Modifications tape. Available from the University of Waterloo, Waterloo, Ontario, Canada. You are permitted to copy someone else's tape.

- VM Workshop Tools Tape (1988 and 1990). Distributed to each installation represented at the annual VM Workshop, an annual event held at various universities in the United States. You are permitted to copy someone else's tape.

- VMSHARE. The latest version of the package is always on-line.

24

REXX for PC-DOS and MS-DOS

By Charles Daney

INTRODUCTION

When the DOS operating system (called **PC-DOS** or **MS-DOS**) for the IBM PC came out in the early 1980s, it had a very crude language for writing system command procedures, called the **batch language**. This amounted to little more than a way to gather several commands into a disk file for submission to the operating system—a **batch** of commands, hence the name. Other operating systems of that era already had much better languages and facilities for the same purpose, such as the Unix shell language or EXEC 2 in CMS.

Of course, for the first few years, other system facilities and applications available in DOS were also very limited. However, because of the relatively low price of PCs compared to minicomputers and mainframes, millions of users created a very attractive market for software developers, so applications gradually became much more powerful and sophisticated. With the advent of such things as hard disks, communications, and laser printers, personal computer systems became much more complex as well. DOS kept up with some of these developments—for instance, by providing a hierarchical file system which made management of files on hard disks much easier—but improvements in its batch language were never commensurate with the general advances in hardware and software.

"Power users" began making up for batch language deficiencies in diverse and ingenious ways. By exploiting various tricks allowed by the operating system and writing a variety of utilities in other languages, impressive results were accomplished. Unfortunately, the level of expertise required to accomplish these feats was fairly high—well beyond reach of most regular PC users.

In the meantime, REXX made its first appearance in CMS (1983), widening the gap between procedures language capabilities on mainframes and PCs, despite a narrowing gap in other areas. Finally, in 1985, Personal REXX from the Mansfield Software Group appeared. The approach that Personal REXX took in implementing the REXX language on PCs went beyond simply offering the REXX language in an environment which badly needed something of the kind but which was otherwise foreign and inhospitable in comparison to the environment in which REXX originally evolved.

Personal REXX was, and remains, a complete implementation of the REXX language, without unreasonable compromises. However, instead of simply transplanting mainframe concepts and culture into a very different milieu, the developers of Personal REXX attempted to give PC users something of substantial value within their own environment. This was done by translating the best and most powerful aspects of VM and CMS that were relevant to REXX into a form that fit well into DOS, at the same time adding capabilities that exploited the best attributes of DOS and PCs.

Personal REXX was also the first implementation of REXX outside of IBM and the first implementation on an operating system other than VM. Personal REXX is a portable implementation of the language, and has been ported to several very dissimilar environments. Presently only the DOS and OS/2 versions are commercially available. The versions on these two platforms are very similar in features and functionality. Although this chapter deals primarily with the DOS version, nearly everything here applies to the OS/2 version as well.

TYPICAL REXX APPLICATIONS ON PCS

In general, REXX is used on a PC in most of the same ways as in other computing environments: quickie procedures, prototyping, application macros, and building new applications out of general-purpose tools. This section looks at PC-specific examples, and at things in Personal REXX that help in writing PC applications. Examples range from simple to sophisticated.

If there is one category which best describes how the REXX language is most fruitfully used, it is **personal programming**. This refers to the kind of programming an individual PC user is most likely to do on his or her own initiative for any of a large number of purposes. It stands in contrast to the kind of programming done by (possibly large) groups of programmers who develop commercial software or "mission-critical" applications. Although personal programming is usually done by single individuals (or sometimes informal collaborations of two or three), its end result may well be useful to—and used by—many. "Personal" computers have succeeded by empowering individuals to use computer technology for their own ends, and accordingly, personal programming is the kind of programming best suited for such purposes.

Other tools besides REXX which are used for personal programming include the BASIC language, application macros, and the system batch language. REXX, of course, is at least the equal of any of these. By contrast, languages such as C or assembler are much more rarely used for personal programming, because of the much higher level of skill and discipline required for their proper use. Even professional programmers will generally choose to employ personal programming tools for "pet" projects of their own, if possible, because results can be achieved much more quickly and easily.

System customization and tailoring is the simplest form of personal programming. This is the function that system batch and procedure languages have always performed. It may involve nothing more than wrapping a procedure around a system command in order to add new options, change defaults, provide more help or error messages, or add new functions to an existing command. The purpose of this is to make the system easier for a specific individual to use by making it react more like he or she expects it to act, and to facilitate the most common operations. It is also a way of recording and encoding experience one has gained with the system, in order to relieve the burden of remembering trivial details.

A good example of this might be a front-end for the COPY command that adds the following features:

1. If no options are used on the command, or the single option ? is used, display HELP information such as the syntax of the command and the meaning of the available switches.

2. If a single file is being copied to another, check whether the target file exists, and give the user an opportunity to reconsider before overwriting it.

3. A completely new option to append a file to an existing target file rather than overwriting it.

Although these can be done with a DOS batch file, it is awkward. And anything that involves a dialog with the user cannot even be done in the batch language unless special-purpose utilities are available. For instance, COPY could be made interactive by a front end that prompts for the source and target filenames and any special handling required. REXX's normal SAY and PULL instructions can be used for simple dialogs of this sort. Personal REXX adds various other functions for making more elaborate dialogs. In particular, it is possible to read a character at a time from the keyboard, and to write anywhere on the screen. (ANSI.SYS provides a DOS way of writing anywhere on the screen, but requires the use of highly non-intuitive escape sequences.)

For really elaborate dialogs, many users prefer to interact using menus and windows. This is especially desirable in preparing canned procedures to be used by anyone other than regular computer users. This shades into the kind of personal programming that typically involves window systems. It is really a kind of application-building by means of a front end that provides a number of menus to guide a user through available functions. While there are many add-ons to DOS that support menu building, it's also easy to do in Personal REXX by means of the RXWINDOW function package. This has the advantage over other menu systems that it has the power of REXX behind it. Simple REXX logic makes it possible for menu systems to select choices to present on the basis of many factors, such as existence of files, date and time, or identity of the user.

The next step up from menu systems, but still in the category of personal programming, involves use of substantial amounts of logic in REXX to implement application functions either directly or by selectively invoking building-block tools and utilities written in other languages. Building blocks used may be simple system commands like COPY and RENAME, or sophisticated applications like a communication program or database system.

When used in this mode, REXX operates as a full programming language: capabilities are there to implement almost any function. Usually, however, building blocks written in other languages are used whenever possible for convenience, as well as for better performance. In this mode, REXX acts as the "glue" or cement between the building blocks. Personal REXX, as implemented in DOS, provides a number of different kinds of glue for interfacing between applications. The list includes an enhanced form of the CMS console stack, global variables (as provided by the GLOBALV command), and the REXX application programming interface (API). Each of these is examined in a little more detail later.

Almost any nontrivial application (except, perhaps, a calculator or the like) needs to work with data files. For a long time, the EXECIO command was the only way of using files in CMS REXX, but Personal REXX has always had the CHARIN/CHAROUT and LINEIN/LINEOUT functions for file I/O, as originally specified by Cowlishaw, which have now appeared in most REXX implementations. In addition, Personal REXX has system-specific built-in file system functions for utility tasks like erasing or renaming files or adding and deleting directories.

The kind of personal programming that is possible with such means is very substantial. A typical application of this sort might be a personal electronic mail handling system. One part of the application uses a communication program (such as REXXTERM, discussed in a later chapter) to periodically poll various external services where one might receive mail (e.g., MCI Mail, CompuServe, the corporate mail system) and download new mail. Another part of the application allows the user to browse the incoming mail and generate replies or forward items to others. Yet another part uses a database system to store important messages in a filing cabinet for future reference.

Even with REXX, such an application could be developed only by a fairly skilled user. However, REXX does at least place such development within the range of the time available to this type of user—it can be done possibly an order of magnitude more easily than in C or assembler language—and such an application could be used by a much larger group of individuals who could not have developed it themselves.

This kind of application development is very similar to prototyping, in which a fully functioning application (not just the user interface) is put together as quickly as possible in order to experiment with functionality, user interface, file structures, and algorithms. Prototyping is the practice of "building the first one to throw away". It may be done within the context of a project which aims to deliver commercial-quality products. Yet it requires the same sort of tools as personal programming in order to get results as quickly as possible and to permit rapid change to try out different approaches.

One major aspect of REXX is not present in most other general-purpose programming languages. This is the fact that it can be used as a macro or script language for applications such as editors and communication programs. This reflects the CMS heritage of REXX. The EXEC language which preceded REXX can be thought of as the macro language of the operating system. Its original function was just to invoke a series of commands, with perhaps a little conditional logic based on the results of each command. CMS enabled the EXEC language (at the time of EXEC 2) to act as the macro language for any application by defining simple interfaces for executing commands from macros and sharing variables with the application. This capability is as much a matter of properly defined interfaces as it is of the language. In any case, REXX continued the tradition.

In the case of Personal REXX on PCs, the two best-known examples of REXX used as a macro language are the KEDIT text editor (also from the Mansfield Software Group) and the REXXTERM communication program. In these cases, too, REXX has uses ranging from customization of the underlying application to full fledged systems in which the underlying application plays only a part.

KEDIT adds an interesting wrinkle in that it contains a built-in subset of REXX called **KEXX**. Macros can be written in KEXX that change the behavior of any key, allowing users to customize the interface to a major extent. Macros can also be written in KEXX or REXX that are interpreted as KEDIT subcommands. This permits adding entirely new subcommands to the editor, or allowing it to work seamlessly as part of a larger application.

In REXXTERM, macros (by convention called **scripts** in this context) can be written in REXX and used to customize the program and automate many aspects of its operation. Because REXXTERM is a terminal emulator, it is almost always used to connect to some other interactive computer environment, and hence it can automate operation of the remote system as well. Thus REXX can be used in macros for systems which have no native REXX processor. The simplest and most usual example of macro usage is the **autologon** procedure, which contains all the boring details of connecting through a network and entering user names and passwords. In REXXTERM such procedures can be identified in a dialing directory and invoked automatically whenever a particular system is called; from that point, REXX scripts can be written with any level of complexity, in the same way as is possible in any other context.

INVOKING REXX PROGRAMS

The DOS operating system has only very basic native facilities compared with other operating systems like CMS and Unix. It lacks, in particular, a keyboard stack, the concept of a subcommand environment, and "hooks" for a command language interpreter like REXX. A reasonable implementation of REXX requires these facilities, and more. Since REXX originated in CMS, it is not surprising that they were already available there—REXX reflects its CMS heritage in many ways. In all other environments, most of these facilities have had to be added.

Although its facilities are rudimentary in many respects, DOS has the one fortunate characteristic of being a very "open" system that allows relatively straightforward extension. This is because code can be loaded in a **terminate and stay resident** (TSR) mode; this is analogous to CMS nucleus extensions. Once loaded, code can be invoked by **software interrupts**, which are analogous to System/370 SVC instructions (for instance). All system extensions of this sort are requested by the user in one of several ways: by placing commands in a configuration file called `CONFIG.SYS`, by placing commands in an initializing batch file called `AUTOEXEC.BAT`, or by running commands at other times during a session as required.

This sort of procedure differs from a "system generation" process which is typical of more complex operating systems, and it has various advantages in terms of allowing users to change system characteristics easily, as needed. Various components of Personal REXX may be loaded as TSRs to enable corresponding system facilities. The only one of these which must be present to run REXX is the **interrupt manager**. This small TSR controls a software interrupt used for communication among other components of Personal REXX, such as the language processor and the stack.

The REXX interrupt manager is necessary because there is no system-defined interprocess communication facility in DOS. Its function is to support various application programming interface (API) services such as REXX macro invocation, subcommand handlers, function packages, and the keyboard stack. There are only eight software interrupt numbers specifically reserved for applications, and there are no standards as to how these are to be allocated. REXX arbitrarily picks one number for its own use, but a user may override this by specifying any other available number in an environment variable. This variable is accessible to any program which uses REXX services, so that a proper software interrupt call to the interrupt manager can be generated. The default interrupt number used is satisfactory for most situations, so that most users never need to worry about this detail.

The REXX language processor itself may be either permanently resident or transient at the user's discretion. Making it resident avoids the overhead of loading it every time it is needed. Having it resident also simplifies use by applications such as KEDIT and REXXTERM which run REXX macros. The disadvantage of having it resident is that it occupies memory, whether actively in use or not. If it has been made resident, it can, however, be unloaded when the memory is required for other uses.

If the interpreter is resident, it is invoked by a small command (**RX**) which locates the resident interpreter through the interrupt manager. So, in this mode, to run a REXX program the user enters the **RX** command, followed by the name of the program, followed by parameters to the program:

```
RX <option switches> program name <program parameters>
```

If the interpreter is not resident, it is simply invoked by its own name (**REXX**) instead of **RX**. Both the **REXX** and **RX** commands also allow various option switches, which control things like compilation and tracing options. These options, and others, can also be specified in environment variables so that they need not be included on each command. The program name can include a three-character extension, but the default is REX, which need not be explicitly specified.

One convenient option switch is /TR, which is followed by a tracing option such as might be used as the operand of a TRACE instruction. This provides a convenient way to enable tracing without having to modify a program. Another way to invoke certain tracing options without changing a program is with the RXTRACE environment variable. This is especially helpful for enabling tracing in REXX programs called from another REXX program or in application macros.

Applications can allow users to invoke REXX macros in many different ways. For instance, REXXTERM can run a REXX macro whenever the user issues a command that is not one of the built-in commands. It also can issue a macro named in the dialing directory whenever a connection is established to a particular number in the directory. Regardless of how they originate, requests to start a REXX macro all go through the interrupt manager, unless the REXX command is used explicitly.

Simple as it is, use of RX or REXX commands can be irritating to users who want to start a program from the system command line just by giving the name of the program and its parameters. This is, of course, all that is needed in CMS to run a REXX program, or to run batch files in DOS. However, the system command processor COMMAND.COM provides no hooks to allow for such processing of REXX commands. Personal REXX circumvents this problem by offering another small TSR utility called the **batch manager** which inserts itself into the system interrupt handler chain in order to invoke the interpreter whenever a file whose name matches the command name, and whose extension is REX, is found. After this TSR is installed, REXX programs can be run as easily as EXE, COM, or BAT programs.

Other utilities available from third parties provide various enhancements to the DOS command line interface. One such is PCED from the Cove Software Group. It does several useful things, like allowing the command line to be edited with normal editing keys, providing for creation of short aliases for longer commands or strings of commands, and keeping a history of commands entered. PCED has an option that lets a user run REXX programs without needing to use the REXX or RX command. It also provides a utility that allows use of its command alias facility from inside REXX programs.

Personal REXX is not a pure interpreter. It "compiles" all programs to an internal form before execution begins. This form is more compact than simple tokenization, which is used in many other implementations. This internal form is also very efficient to execute. Many redundancies in addition to tokenization are eliminated for processing code involving loops and conditional statements. The result is that Personal REXX is one of the most efficient implementations of the language. However, there are certain minor effects on the practical usage of REXX programs as a result of this strategy.

The principal one is that there may be a noticeable delay when starting a program while it is being compiled. This is not apparent for small programs (or for average-size programs on reasonably fast hardware like 80386-based machines), but the compilation process itself is redundant if the program is used again. It can be avoided, for a further savings in execution time, by retaining the compiled "object code". This is controlled by option switches. If one chooses to save the compiled code, it is appended at the end of the source code, after an "end-of-file" character. In this way, the code is invisible to utilities like editors that should not interfere with it, and it is automatically stripped off when the file is changed. The interpreter looks for it when running a program, and will bypass the compilation process if the object code is already present.

REXX LANGUAGE AND IMPLEMENTATION COMPATIBILITY

Version 2.0 of Personal REXX implements virtually all of the 3.50 version of the REXX language definition as described in the first edition of Cowlishaw's *The REXX Language*. This is roughly the same as the initial SAA Procedures Language specification. It also implements all language features which were in VM/SP Release 6 CMS but not in the 3.50 specification, except for the double-byte character set (DBCS) features. This includes the EXTERNALS, FIND (superseded by WORDPOS), INDEX (superseded by POS), JUSTIFY, and USERID built-in functions, the EXTERNAL operand of PARSE, and the UPPER instruction.

There are minor variances of Personal REXX from the 3.50 specification in the areas of the LINEIN/LINEOUT functions (relative line numbers are not supported) and the CHARS and LINES functions (which return only the value 1 if more input remains). Also, the DATE and TIME functions are reevaluated whenever they are called, rather than once in each expression.

Mansfield has announced that version 3.0 of Personal REXX will include all the language changes implemented in REXX 4.0, as described in the second edition of Cowlishaw's book. REXX 4.0 corresponds to the version implemented by IBM in OS/2 version 1.2. Version 3.0 of Personal REXX should be available by the time this appears in print. In order to retain upward compatibility, Personal REXX 3.0 preserves certain earlier language features, such as allowing $, @, and # in symbol names.

Personal REXX has a couple of small extensions which are not in any version of the language specification. First, the tilde (~) and caret (^) are allowed as alternative forms of the negation symbol (usually ¬). Second, the TRACE instruction allows a prefix of $ on the trace setting. This toggles output to a printer instead of the display.

The fact that Personal REXX is not a pure interpreter and processes a source file completely before execution begins entails differences in the way tracing and error handling behave during execution. (There should be no differences for syntactically correct programs that do not use tracing.) In particular, as with a compiler, syntax errors that go undetected in other implementations may be detected by Personal REXX, because the statements are processed even though they are not reached during execution. Likewise, many conditions that would normally be handled by SIGNAL ON SYNTAX are instead caught during initial compilation. Finally, certain instructions which do not generate object code, such as THEN and SELECT, cannot be traced.

Additional compilation process options cause the compiled internal format to be saved. Subsequent program invocation may use this compiled code rather than reprocessing the source code. In this case, other minor deviations from standard language behavior may result. In particular, the SOURCELINE function is not available, and trace output is limited. Even when the program is executed from object code, tables are usually kept which permit references to the source code line numbers. These tables can optionally be omitted, in which case the SIGL variable will not be maintained, and line numbers will not be reported in case of run-time errors.

Certain arbitrary limitations present in CMS REXX have been relaxed in Personal REXX. For instance, there is no particular upper limit on the number of arguments that can be passed to a built-in, internal, or external function. (The limit on the processed length of a clause tends to be the limiting factor.) There is a limit of 1000 characters on the processed internal length of a clause, as compared with 500 in CMS.

APPLICATION PROGRAMMING INTERFACES

Function packages and external functions

In addition to built-in functions and internal functions of a procedure, Personal REXX supports external functions written in REXX as separate files, and functions written in any language which are gathered together in a **function package**. A function package must be **declared** by means of a call to the interrupt manager. Up to 10 packages can be declared (made active) at any one time. If a function call in a program is neither internal nor a known built-in function, the interpreter passes the name and a pointer to the function arguments to each active function package. The package can either handle the function or indicate that it does not recognize it. If no function package elects to handle the function, the interpreter looks for a disk file to process the function.

The function package registration process does not require up-front declaration of the names of functions handled in the package, which is why each must be called when there is a function to perform. This has the advantage of flexibility, in that a package might elect to handle a given function at one time but not another. On the other hand, code for a function package must be resident when a program is running, since the interpreter cannot afford the overhead of loading packages every time a name must be resolved. Typically, function packages are implemented either as TSRs or as part of application programs. In the case of TSRs, functions provided by the package will be available in any REXX program as long as the TSR is loaded. The RXWINDOW package provided with Personal REXX to facilitate creation of text-mode windows and menus is an example of this sort of package. The functions which are included in a package implemented as part of an application are available only while the application is active. KEDIT and REXXTERM, for instance, both provide functions in this manner.

If the interpreter does not find an external function in any active function package, it searches for a disk file with the same name as the function and an "appropriate" extension. This search process is very much like the initial search for the program file, or, indeed, like the search for any program in DOS, in that the interpreter looks first in the current directory and then in other directories named in the PATH environment variable. The appropriate extension for the name of an external function is usually the same as the extension of the file from which it is called. (In fact, the extension is determined by the application which initially invoked the REXX program or macro.) This has the effect, which is sometimes useful and sometimes not, that different files may be invoked for the same function depending on whether it is called from a REX, KEX (KEDIT macro), or RXT (REXXTERM script) program. (A similar "feature" is present in other environments, like CMS.) If this is a problem, a program can force the use of a particular extension by naming it explicitly in the function call. That is, if a KEX macro must invoke the LOOKUP.RXT file, it could use:

```
answer = lookup.rex('phonbook.dat', name)
```

or even:

```
answer = 'c:\funclib\lookup.rex'('phonbook.dat', name)
```

Subcommand handlers

The Personal REXX API deals with subcommand handlers in much the same way as it deals with function packages. Each subcommand handler corresponds to an **environment**, in the sense of something that can be named in an ADDRESS instruction as a destination for commands. Every such environment is described by a control block called an **environment block**. This control block contains, among other things, the name of the environment and the address of the entry point the interpreter should call in order to pass a command. (Environment blocks are also used to describe function packages, as many fields serve analogous purposes.)

Most applications that are capable of running REXX macros naturally have their own subcommand environment for processing commands. This is defined by an environment block passed by the application at the time the interpreter is called to handle the macro. It becomes the default command environment for the macro. Environments with the names DOS and COMMAND are special cases. They are automatically defined for every macro. The DOS environment processes commands in much the same way as they would be processed from the command line when the "batch manager" is active. That is, files with an extension of REX are assumed to be REXX programs and have priority over EXE, COM, or BAT files. The COMMAND environment works the same way, except that it does not consider files with an extension of REX for execution.

In addition to these default environments, the API allows declaration of additional **resident environments** in the same way as function packages are declared, that is, by a call to the interrupt manager. Unlike an application program, a resident environment generally remains loaded as a TSR and so is available for use in REXX programs at any time during a session. A resident environment can be used to add new commands to the operating system, though the commands can be used only from REXX programs and not from DOS.

The default environment specified when a REXX macro is invoked by an application has a somewhat special status, in that its environment block may call for certain kinds of special processing by the interpreter. For one thing, the environment block may specify that a list of directories which is different from the list in the DOS PATH variable should be searched for external commands and functions. In this way, applications can avoid requiring certain directories in the PATH used globally. The environment block also specifies what is used as the the default file extension for REXX macros or functions.

Another feature which can be enabled through the environment block is service exit routines. These exit routines are called by the interpreter during processing of the program for several functions which would normally be done by calls to the operating system. There are three types of services currently supported. These are for keyboard input, screen output, and reading of the program source file. The first two are useful in applications that want to control how keyboard input and screen output are done by REXX. Without these, REXX I/O would not be well integrated with the application's own handling of the screen and keyboard. The source file input service provides a way for an application to pass a program to REXX for execution without reading from disk. This might involve code kept in memory and managed by the application, such as macros assigned to keys.

Other programming interfaces

Personal REXX supports the REXX shared variable interface almost exactly the way CMS does. The control block format is the same, and all subfunctions are the same, including the "fetch next variable" function which can access all active REXX variables.

Personal REXX also supports an interface for a subcommand or function (in a function package) to generate a REXX signal. Such an interface, surprisingly, is missing from all other known implementations of REXX, yet it could be of great use in an application where asynchronous events are possible. For instance, REXXTERM uses this interface to generate a signal when a line drop occurs on the communication port. REXXTERM macros can include a handler for this signal to provide for orderly cleanup, without continually having to check that the connection exists.

THE KEYBOARD STACK

There are several ways in which REXX can enable communication among building blocks used in a REXX program. The shared variable API is one such method. It allows the application which invokes a REXX macro and processes commands and function calls to read and write REXX variables directly. It also permits external programs invoked from a REXX procedure and written in other languages to access the REXX variables of the calling program.

Another mechanism involves the **keyboard stack**, also known as the **program stack** or the **console stack**. (The latter refers to the old days of computing when a keyboard was called a "console".) As originally implemented in CMS, the stack was essentially a surrogate user. A line of data on the stack was supposed to represent a line entered by a user, and it could be read by a program as if it had come from a user at a terminal. This represents one application for the stack: providing typed-ahead input to external programs. However, the stack has also come to be used for storage of (possibly substantial amounts of) data, or for communication between separate REXX procedures or between a REXX procedure and an external program. In this mode, the stack serves as a kind of in-memory temporary file or an unnamed scratch data area.

The stack is a native system service only in CMS. Personal REXX supplies an equivalent as an add-on to DOS, enhanced in several ways. In particular, instead of being line-oriented, PC applications often interact with users a character at a time. Accordingly, Personal REXX allows reading or writing individual characters from or to the stack. There is even a **PRESS** utility for communicating non-ASCII characters (like function keys) to applications through the stack. This is very useful for applications which require user interaction for successful launch (as opposed to command line arguments). An arbitrary delay can also be inserted between characters of the stack to accommodate timing-dependent programs, or simply to leave enough time between inputs so that screen displays can be viewed.

The Personal REXX stack is implemented as yet another TSR called the **stack manager**, which is independent of the interpreter. This allows the stack to function even when the interpreter is not active, just as it would in CMS. One application for this is preparing a sequence of commands to be executed by DOS after a REXX program has terminated.

Several Personal REXX utilities facilitate use of the stack. Some of these are directly analogous to CMS commands of the same name— **MAKEBUF** and **DROPBUF** in particular, which allow use of independent "buffers" within the stack. Other utilities offer capabilities not present in CMS. **DISABLE** and **ENABLE** temporarily suspend (and reenable) the stack as a source of program input. This allows data to be kept in the stack even across calls to programs that would try to read keyboard input.

A utility of another kind which is often useful is the stack device driver. This is a standard DOS device driver, and as such is loaded based on a command in the **CONFIG.SYS** file when DOS is booted. The device driver's name is **STK**, and it is used as a recipient of data passed as standard output of another program. Received data is placed on the stack for another program to read. For instance, the command:

```
dir *.* >stk
```

places all output of **DIR *.*** on the stack (in first-in, first-out order). **STK** is a write-only device, since programs that read from the standard input stream automatically receive data from the stack if any is present, so an assist from STK is unnecessary. The device can also be used like a DOS file, as in:

```
copy somefile.dat stk
```

which places the contents of SOMEFILE.DAT on the stack.

In other environments, such as OS/2, an alternative means of getting program output onto the stack is to use piping to a command (RXQUEUE), which then places the data on the stack. In DOS, this is roughly like redirection to a device, but has the overhead of loading a command (and the fact that DOS implements piping with intermediate disk files) as a drawback. Also, use of a command instead of a device driver for this precludes using the stack as an output file as in the copy example.

ADDITIONAL BUILT-IN FUNCTIONS

The REXX language has an impressive collection of built-in functions for character-string handling. However, it is very weak in the area of file system and operating system services. There are two reasons for this. One is that such things are harder to standardize across diverse systems (although it has been done to some extent in C, for example). The other reason is that REXX, being a command language, has tended to rely on system commands to access such services. For instance, in CMS, one uses ACCESS, RENAME, ERASE, LISTFILE, EXECIO, QUERY, and so forth.

In some ways, however, it would be better to utilize such services with a function-call syntax. Certainly, in an environment like DOS where there is a relatively high overhead to finding and loading commands, it is much more efficient to have these services implemented as built-in functions or function packages. Function syntax also tends to be somewhat more convenient for passing multiple parameters and returning result strings. (Even when command output can be redirected to the stack, parsing it to extract the information wanted can be error-prone.)

Personal REXX has addressed the need for ready access to system services without relying on additional commands by providing a number of additional functions which are on an equal footing with the standard built-in functions (in that there is no extra effort involved in using them). There are several general categories of such functions.

The first category is **hardware information**. This involves various functions to return information on the number and type of disks installed, the number of serial and parallel ports, and the size and type of display. It is helpful to have information of this sort in order to make generalized programs that can be adapted to run on different computers with different configurations.

A second category is **hardware access**. This is a much more important group which allows direct access to hardware, primarily the keyboard and screen. There are functions to write, in character mode, anywhere on the screen and have control over screen attributes. There is also a function to read from the screen (good for saving/restoring parts of the screen or reading what another program has written there). The cursor shape and position can be controlled, and individual keystrokes can be read from the keyboard (including scan codes, if needed). Arbitrary timed delays can be included in a program, and the speaker can be controlled; and at a very low level, any memory or I/O port address in the machine can be read or written.

The third category, perhaps the most important, consists of **DOS and file system functions**. There are functions for manipulating and navigating the hierarchical file directory system. There are functions for creating, renaming, deleting, and changing attributes of files (and directories). One of the most used functions of all is DOSDIR, for scanning through all or selected files in a directory. Another important function allows REXX to read DOS environment variables. Although some (though not all) of these capabilities can be used through system commands (as they must be in BAT files), it is almost always easier and quicker to use a REXX built-in function.

Three functions in this category are of special use in building robust file-oriented utilities with a minimum of effort. They handle operations which are often neglected when writing something "quick and dirty", at the expense of making the result less general and harder to use. The first of these functions is PARSEFN, which parses a DOS file identifier, possibly a fairly complicated object, into the drive letter, directory path, filename, and file extension. The second is DOSFNAME, which takes a simple file identifier that may consist of just name and extension, and expands it into a form with an explicit drive letter and directory path. The third is DOSPATHFIND, which searches a list of directories (a **path list**) for a specified file and returns its fully qualified name (if found).

The fourth and last category is **miscellaneous**. It includes very general functions that REXX "forgot", such as UPPER and LOWER for case translation of strings (TRANSLATE with a single argument does UPPER, though one might easily not know this, and there's no easy way to do the more useful translation to lowercase). The other important one is DATECONV, for date conversion between any of the formats supported by the DATE function. This is a difficult operation (in some cases) which is very handy for normalizing date formats or for converting to a "base" date format useful for date arithmetic.

Since REXX is so often used for prototyping and personal applications, there is a real need for facilities to build "nice" user interfaces. It has been many years since the line-at-a-time **SAY/PULL** model of user interaction has been adequate for anything but the quickest and dirtiest of throw-away utilities. (Except, perhaps, for "filter" utilities, which are best used for program rather than human input and output.) Windows and menus are now generally accepted as the minimum standard for a decent user interface. (Of course, their use does not guarantee good results.)

For this reason, Personal REXX includes a function package of basic functions called **RXWINDOW** for handling windows, menus, and input fields. It includes functions for opening, closing, hiding, moving, and adding borders to windows. Another series of functions reads and writes data within windows. These are basically analogous to functions for reading and writing on the screen, except that coordinates are relative to the window. Finally, there are functions for defining and reading from input fields within a window.

CMS-LIKE UTILITIES

When Personal REXX was introduced in 1985, the only other REXX implementation available was in CMS. Since all extant REXX code was CMS-oriented, most significant programs made liberal use of certain CMS utilities. These had, in fact, evolved along with REXX and were designed to work with and supplement features of the language. Consequently, Personal REXX included DOS implementations of some of these utilities, specifically **LISTFILE**, **EXECIO**, and **GLOBALV**. Although REXX is no longer in any way a CMS-specific language, and the original rationale for including CMS utilities in the package has diminished, a few of the capabilities of each of these utilities are not easily available in any other form. If one were designing from scratch, these capabilities should probably be provided in a function package.

In CMS, **LISTFILE** is the primary file-directory listing command, analogous to **DIR** in DOS. When used in REXX, it is primarily used with the **STACK** or **ENVVAR** options to put the results of a directory either on a stack or directly into REXX variables. Because the Personal REXX **DOSDIR** built-in function returns the same information, the usefulness of **LISTFILE** is diminished. However, it still has options that give it more functionality in certain situations. These options, curiously, have never been implemented in the IBM CMS **LISTFILE**, although users have added them as local modifications or otherwise implemented them independently.

The first useful option added in the Personal REXX **LISTFILE** allows sorting directory entries, in ascending or descending order, based on several criteria, such as name, extension, date, and size. (This would be less important if REXX had a native facility for sorting values of a stem variable.) Another useful option is the ability to limit files selected to only those before or since a given date. DOS file system features which are not available in CMS are explicitly supported. For instance, files can be selected on the basis of attributes such as "system" and "read-only", and in order to support hierarchical directories, there is an option to search subdirectories recursively for files.

The GLOBALV command was added to CMS because there never was, and still is not, any other way to share data between separate REXX programs, since REXX has no notion of variable scope outside of a single program. In a DOS environment, many normal GLOBALV uses could in principle be handled with environment variables. However, GLOBALV does provide richer functionality, and DOS environment variables usually do not easily allow for handling any great amount of data. The GLOBALV version in Personal REXX is almost identical in capability and usage to the CMS version. Like the latter, its primary advantage is the ability to separate variables into named groups, to reduce the likelihood of name collisions between variables used by independent applications.

The third CMS utility that Personal REXX supports is EXECIO. The LINEIN/LINEOUT built-in functions, which provide file I/O directly in the language, make EXECIO largely superfluous. It does, however, provide limited capabilities for searching files for specific strings. If these are needed, they may be performed more efficiently by EXECIO than by equivalent programming in REXX. Otherwise, use of EXECIO is better replaced by REXX code, especially for line-by-line file processing. The primary overhead of using EXECIO is loading the program itself. Not only is program loading in DOS fairly slow, but memory constraints make it impractical for EXECIO to use the TSR mechanism to avoid reloading in a manner analogous to the CMS nucleus extension capability.

CONCLUSION

Personal REXX was developed jointly by Quercus Systems and Mansfield Software. Released in 1985, it was the first commercially available implementation of REXX following the initial one in CMS. In 1989 it became the first commercially available implementation in OS/2. The same code has been ported to other environments (see the chapter "REXX for the VAX"). Personal REXX has been tuned to the point where it is one of the most efficient implementations in any environment.

The developers feel that the primary strengths of REXX are as an application prototyping language and a "universal macro language".

The platforms on which Personal REXX is established—MS-DOS/PC-DOS and OS/2—are evolving very rapidly, and clearly need the capabilities REXX provides. Personal REXX will continue to evolve along with them. In particular, a version of Personal REXX for Microsoft Windows will be available in 1991.

REXX for Tandem

By Keith Watts

INTRODUCTION

This chapter describes **T-REXX**, a REXX implementation for Tandem
systems. T-REXX is compatible with Cowlishaw's formal REXX language specification. All statements, built-in functions, and expression
operators perform as specified. Furthermore, the complete Cowlishaw
I/O model is provided. This enables reading and writing files with relative and absolute line and character positioning. The product also
includes language extensions to exploit the Tandem environment.

THE TANDEM SYSTEM PLATFORM

Tandem's GUARDIAN operating system is markedly different from
other REXX environments. System components are high-quality and
resist user tampering. There are few concepts to learn, so users gain
competence quickly.

The most remarkable feature of Tandem systems is how process
communication is performed. Interprocess communications (IPCs) are
indistinguishable from file and device accesses. For example, a program which can communicate interactively with a terminal can use
the same protocol to communicate with a process. Network destinations are identified by a leading filename qualifier. This allows pro-

grams to communicate with terminals, files, and processes throughout the network.

USER ENVIRONMENT

Tandem provides a command interpreter environment called **TACL** which includes an embedded macro language (confusingly also called TACL). This is similar to integration of REXX in CMS, or CLIST in MVS/TSO.

The command interpreter is similar to a UNIX shell (a process which interfaces with terminals, accepts commands entered, and starts processes or tasks in response to user requests), but differs syntactically. Standard program file destinations can be redirected on the command line, and programs can be scheduled for completion as background, rather than foreground, processes.

T-REXX is initiated as a standard TACL command. Default input and output streams are connected to any redirected input and output files. Thus, **PULL** and **LINEIN** read data from any redirected input file, and **SAY** and **LINEOUT** write to any redirected output file. T-REXX procedures can easily transform file contents using powerful REXX language parsing and symbol substitution capabilities. TACL commands are passed to the current external command environment (**ADDRESS** setting). The T-REXX **TACLIO** extension allows REXX procedures to provide input and receive output directly from other commands operating as separate processes. This feature is described later.

Full-screen editors are available in the TACL environment, but there are few other full-screen interactions. There are no equivalents to the full-screen utilities commonly available on VM and MVS systems.

SYSTEM PROGRAMMABILITY

GUARDIAN is a closed system. It has a call interface for system service requests, but no published interfaces for system extensions. TACL is also a closed, proprietary environment. Tandem provides excellent implementations of common programming languages, including a sophisticated NonStop SQL implementation as an optional operating system extension. Other system components and utilities are completely different from those of other systems.

There is no true equivalent to assembler language; there is instead a low-level language called TAL. This language is higher level than assembler, but lower than C. TAL can produce native object code, but this operates in an application rather than a system context. There are no documented operating system exits.

The absence of an assembler and operating system exits should not be construed as shortcomings; their effect is that GUARDIAN interactions are well defined and well behaved. There are no low-level calling conventions, for example, system routines which require specific machine register values.

WHY REXX IS NEEDED BY TANDEM USERS

When users of other systems confront the Tandem environment, they are initially shocked. The file naming convention is simple, but different from those of other systems. When a file is being edited, it cannot be browsed by other users. When a file is changed, any older copy is lost. The embedded TACL macro language is capable, but difficult to learn.

An experienced operating system user may feel completely unproductive when first encountering the Tandem system, and it can take months of adjustment to achieve proficiency.

T-REXX allows REXX users to be productive immediately. Procedure source prepared on other systems can be transferred to Tandem and executed with minimal changes.

T-REXX is derived from a product (available from the author) called Portable/REXX, for MS-DOS and PC-DOS on the IBM PC. As a consequence, procedures developed with the PC product are likely to execute on Tandem unchanged.

For veteran Tandem users who are unfamiliar with REXX, T-REXX complements TACL capabilities. A few lines of REXX can often accomplish feats which TACL procedure developers can achieve only with great difficulty, if at all. The ease of developing REXX procedures, their readability, and the naturalness of interactive tracing yield significant human productivity gains.

INVOKING REXX PROGRAMS

T-REXX procedures are invoked by a standard TACL RUN command, which has the following syntax (< and > characters indicate optional parameters):

```
RUN EX </<in infile> <, out outfile> <,. . .>/> procedure-name <arguments>
```

where:

/in infile	A redirected input file to use as the default input stream. When this is omitted, default input arrives from the terminal.
/out outfile	A redirected output file to create or replace as the default output stream. When this is omitted, default output is sent to the terminal.

<,...>	Other **RUN** command options. For example, **NOWAIT** indicates to execute the procedure in the background.
procedure-name	The procedure to perform (i.e., **cat**, in the example below). The procedure name can be any standard Tandem filename.
arguments	One or more optional arguments to pass to the procedure. These are accessed by standard **ARG**, **PARSE ARG**, and **ARG()** requests.

Examples

These examples show uses of the **RUN EX** command. They use **EX** rather than the full **RUN EX** syntax; this shorthand style can be established during TACL initialization.

The examples invoke a REXX procedure called **CAT** which transmits the file(s) specified to standard output. If an argument of ! is specified, lines are read from the console and sent to standard output; if an argument of - is specified, the standard input file is sent to standard output.

The two commands shown for each example have the same result.

Example 1

```
EX /out file1/ CAT !
EX /out file1/ CAT -
```

Lines typed at the keyboard are sent to file **file1**. If **file1** previously existed, new lines are added to the end; if it did not exist, it is created. This is a simple way to create a new file. Keyboard input is terminated by the standard mechanism for terminating console input streams, **<Cntrl>-Y**. This terminating character is not added to the file.

Example 2

```
EX /in file1/ CAT -
EX CAT file1
```

file1 is read and sent to default output (the console). This displays **file1** on the terminal.

Example 3

```
EX /in file1, out $S/ CAT -
EX /out $S/ CAT file1
```

This is almost identical to the above, but output is directed to destination **$S** (the print spooler). This prints **file1**.

The CAT procedure

The REXX procedure used above follows:

```
/* CAT REXX procedure */
CAT:
arg file files
if file = '' | file = '?' then signal HELP
do while COPYOUT(file) = 0
    parse var files file files
end
exit 0
/* COPYOUT -- Copy an input file to stdout */
COPYOUT: procedure
arg infile
if infile = '-' | infile = '!' then
call lineout "!", "Please enter input below (Ctrl-Y to quit)"
if infile = '-' then infile = ''           /* => Standard input */
if lines(infile) = 0 then return 1      /* Empty/undefined file */
do while lines(infile) > 0
    say linein(infile)                 /* Whatever comes in, goes out */
end
if infile <> '' then
call charout infile                            /* Close input file */
return 0
HELP:
call lineout "!",,
  "Usage: EX </in infile, out outfile/> CAT input-files"
exit 1
```

LANGUAGE EXTENSIONS

T-REXX extends REXX for the Tandem environment, allowing access to file system objects and internal system information.

File/path access functions

The Tandem file system has a naming hierarchy:

- System
- Volume
- Subvolume
- Filename

T-REXX functions provide information describing volumes, subvolumes, and files. Additional functions enable alteration of default name components, which are used when partially qualified filenames are subsequently referenced.

System information functions

Other functions describe systems, processes, devices, and disks.

DELAY function

A **DELAY** function was added to suspend execution for a specified duration. This is particularly useful in procedures which operate as background system monitors.

TACLIO IPC path

TREXX provides a **TACLIO** inter-process communication (IPC) path for dynamic control of TACL command operation. This allows T-REXX programs to trap command output lines, conditionally perform subcommand sequences, or define edit macros.

TACLIO is a bidirectional IPC path between T-REXX and TACL commands and subcommands. The design is based on Cowlishaw's stream I/O model, but is a half-duplex protocol governed by the T-REXX procedure. For each **TACLIO** output request, corresponding replies are retained in a private memory queue and retrieved by **TACLIO** input requests. Use of a private queue avoids conflicts with the standard external data queue, which can store results filtered from **TACLIO** output.

Requests are sent from a T-REXX procedure to TACL via the **LINE-OUT** function, writing to file **TACLIO**. Output from TACL commands and subcommands is similar, using the **LINEIN** function and reading from file **TACLIO**. The number of lines to be read cannot be determined, but the **LINES** function (again, using file **TACLIO**) determines whether more exist. **TACLIO** mode is concluded by closing the **TACLIO** input stream with **LINEOUT**.

For example, **TACLIO** could control a conversational editor, using editor facilities to extract lines with line numbers and display them on the terminal (note that **LA** and **END** are editor subcommands):

```
EDLIST:
arg fname                          /* Get name of file to display */
call lineout 'TACLIO', 'EDIT' fname            /* Edit the file */
do while lines( 'TACLIO' ) > 0
   call linein 'TACLIO'                /* Absorb edit startup lines */
end
call lineout 'TACLIO', 'LA'        /* List lines with line numbers */
do while lines( 'TACLIO' ) > 0                  /* Process the lines */
   parse value linein( 'TACLIO' ) with lno text       /* Get data */
   say fname "("lno")" text   /* Display file, line number, text */
end
call lineout 'TACLIO', 'END'                  /* End editor session */
do while lines( 'TACLIO' ) > 0
```

```
      call linein 'TACLIO'          /* Absorb edit conclusion lines */
end
call lineout 'TACLIO'          /* Close: conclude TACLIO processing */
exit
```

TACLIO is a major T-REXX feature. It connects the output of numerous pre-existing system applications and utilities, and can dynamically compose SQL queries and parse returned row information, using Tandem's SQLCI utility.

IMPLEMENTATION CHARACTERISTICS

Portability emphasis

Portability was a major design goal during T-REXX development; most important was being able to transport REXX procedures to Tandem and execute them with little or no change. To achieve this, T-REXX conforms to the formal REXX language specification, and includes every feature exactly as specified. However, Cowlishaw's specifications and those of other REXX implementations, such as IBM's SAA Procedures Language, are not always congruent. These other sources have been carefully monitored, so that standard language definitions will be provided in T-REXX.

ANSI C development

As mentioned earlier, T-REXX was derived from an IBM PC product called Portable/REXX. It was developed using standard ANSI C language concepts wherever possible, using Tandem C and Microsoft C compilers. These compilers have a common antecedent, Lattice C. By following ANSI C specifications, REXX was migrated from the PC to the Tandem with few surprises. A paper documenting this experience is available from this chapter's author.

PLANS

User-written functions

Other REXX environments allow user-written functions to dynamically augment the standard set of built-in functions. When T-REXX was initially developed, there was no consensus on how this extensibility should be accomplished. Several implementors have since agreed to follow methods initially introduced in the MVS/TSO REXX implementation; however, function extensibility is not yet part of the formal REXX language specification.

T-REXX can achieve cooperative processing with programs written in other languages in numerous ways; Tandem's IPC mechanisms are clearly one approach. User-written built-in functions offer advantages and disadvantages. For example, extensions provide significant efficiency gains over interprocess communications. However, extensions expose REXX processing to logic catastrophes; there is no similar exposure with IPCs. Extending built-in functions with user-developed logic is under consideration.

Cross-environment development

Tandem provides a reliable production system environment. It is an expensive use of resources to develop REXX procedures in this system when these could be developed in the more economical PC-DOS/MS-DOS environment. Hence, cross-environment development is a key objective. Procedures which perform parsing, symbol substitution, and standard file access are portable now; a future objective is development of portable full-screen interactive procedures in the PC environment which can be transferred to Tandem.

REXX in TSO/E and Other MVS/ESA Address Spaces

By Gerhard E. Hoernes

INTRODUCTION

Other chapters of this book demonstrate that REXX is a very general language and is largely system-independent. Because of this generality, REXX is well suited for applications which must execute on different platforms, because only system commands are platform-specific.

What is REXX in TSO/E?

This question may appear trivial, but is the source of much confusion. **REXX the language** is defined elsewhere in this book and is the same; it adheres to the formal language definition. Features were added to make REXX more useful in TSO/E: for instance, to enable sharing of internal CLIST services/routines, REXX had to be packaged with CLIST, which in turn is part of TSO/E. Thus the REXX implementation for MVS/ESA is part of TSO/E. However, the REXX design is such that REXX programs can execute in any MVS/ESA address space, although without the benefits of the CLIST services/routines.

What is REXX in TSO/E? It is the implementation of the REXX language, packaged with TSO/E but capable of executing within or outside TSO/E, including a REXX execution environment. This chapter does not describe the REXX language. It describes the environment within which REXX programs execute, how REXX programs interact with this environment, and how this environment fits into and reacts with TSO/E and the rest of the MVS/ESA system.

The TSO/E implementation is based on the CMS implementation. Portability was part of the original design of the language and of the CMS implementation; thus the CMS code was written without intermingling system-dependent and system-independent code. System-dependent code was placed in subroutines and macros. This allowed porting code between the two systems, and assured complete compatibility of the two platforms.

RELATIONSHIP BETWEEN TSO/E REXX AND OTHER REXX IMPLEMENTATIONS

Partly because of the origin of REXX and partly because of the thrust of openness and compatibility in the data processing field, compatibility with other platforms was considered very important in the design of TSO/E REXX.

TSO/E REXX was intended to support all REXX features, including extensibility, and to provide as much compatibility as possible:

1. TSO/E REXX must be compatible with CLIST, the command procedure language from previous TSO/E releases, allowing easy translation of existing CLISTs to REXX.

2. It should be possible to port REXX programs from CMS to MVS/ESA with minimal changes, and to write REXX programs which can be run on either system.

3. Nothing should preclude compatibility with PS/2- and PC-based implementations.

Therefore, TSO/E REXX supports two forms of some functions—one for CMS and another for CLIST compatibility. At first glance, this appears to introduce inconsistency or redundancy, but it was necessary for maximal compatibility. As an example, consider searching for a REXX program or command in the two systems. In CMS, the command processor searches for a REXX program with the name specified, and then, if none is found, for a command. In TSO/E without REXX, the search order is the opposite: first the system searches for a command; if none is found, it searches for a CLIST. For CLIST compatibility, the search order for REXX programs would need to be that of TSO/E; for CMS compatibility, the opposite would be required. In this case there cannot be a general compromise. For some users and some applications, one order is absolutely required; for others, the other is appropriate. This is particularly important when REXX programs and commands have the same name, potentially allowing the wrong one to execute. It also affects performance, because one DD is always searched first. (**DD** stands for **data definition**, the MVS/ESA term for a program-defined name for a dataset or group of datasets; a DD is associated with datasets by an **allocate** command or service.) If the DD searched first consists of several concatenated datasets, the effect is even more severe, because of the many implied disk I/O operations. In this case of search order, there is no "correct" answer, so REXX supports a flag which defines the search order. The default is the search order of CLIST; this can be reversed by changing the flag.

In some cases compatibility with both environments is achieved by providing equivalent but different functions. An example is the two variable interfaces. The CLIST variable interface was extended to accommodate REXX variables, and the CMS variable interface was also implemented. This interface allows porting of code between CMS and TSO/E.

The REXX language is system-independent except for the data queue or stack, which shows its CMS origins. There is no MVS/ESA concept equivalent to the CMS stack, so one was incorporated into the TSO/E implementation. This feature is discussed later in this chapter.

REXX does not rigidly define system functions used by the language; the stack is an example of this. Implementing REXX interfaces to system functions in TSO/E has interesting side effects. One major difference between CMS and MVS/ESA is **tasking**. CMS is a single-task, non-multiprocessing system with a clearly defined environment which cannot be changed. The intent of the TSO/E design is to allow REXX program execution in *any* MVS/ESA address space. This requirement forces the design to cope with the multitasking environment, including issues such as locking and sharing of stacks, files, and memory. Unlike CMS, MVS/ESA enforces ownership of memory by a task rather than by the system in general, further adding to the complexity.

Along with the other compatibility concerns, it was also necessary to consider REXX operation in the Interactive System Productivity Facility (ISPF) environment and to support the TSO command on the ISPF command line. The ISPF environment is not present in native MVS/ESA, but is common and pervasive in TSO/E installations, and therefore had to be considered carefully.

To summarize, the design intent was to implement the full REXX language, make REXX TSO/E as compatible with both CLIST and other REXX implementations as possible in both function and interfaces, and *not* limit the function to the least common denominator, but provide as much flexibility, extensibility, and tailorability as possible.

TSO/E REXX BASICS

MVS/ESA address spaces

As mentioned earlier, TSO/E REXX execution is not limited to TSO/E, but may occur in *any* MVS/ESA address space. It is thus important to understand aspects of MVS/ESA before discussing TSO/E REXX in detail. The MVS/ESA operating system supports simultaneous execution of multiple independent applications. The means of achieving separation between these activities is called **address spaces**.

A program executing in an address space can address private virtual storage in its own address space and virtual storage common to it and other address spaces, but cannot address the private virtual storage of other address spaces.

Some program products, such as TSO/E, operate in their own address spaces, providing specialized services required by their own applications. When an application (or user program) operates in an address space, the services available depend on the type of host address space.

Figure 8 illustrates multiple address spaces, some sharing address ranges with others:

In this figure, TSO/E and VTAM provide a platform of functions above that of basic MVS/ESA services. Programs executing in such an address space may call on services either in the base or provided specif-

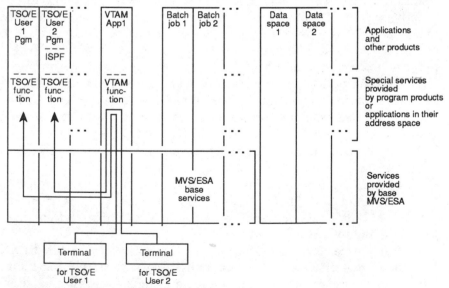

Figure 8. MVS/ESA address spaces

ically within that one address space. The figure also shows batch jobs executing in their own address spaces. Programs in these batch address spaces do not have access to special services beyond those of the base MVS/ESA system. Two data spaces are shown on the right side of the figure; they are included to show that they have no address-ability in common with any address space.

In the TSO/E address space, services associated with interactive pro-cessing are provided. Once the creation of the address space by MVS/ESA is completed, the TSO/E address space is controlled by the **TMP** (Terminal Monitor Program), which receives control and remains active and in control until **LOGOFF**, at which time the address space is destroyed. The TMP remains in a two-step loop, reading and executing commands from the input (normally the user terminal). After each command completes execution, the TMP issues a **READY** message to indicate command completion, and starts the loop again by waiting for another command. When the TMP starts, it initializes an environment within the address space. This environment allows execution of an extensive set of commands—the TSO/E command set—which can be augmented by users, installations, or other program products. Examples of base TSO/E commands are **LISTA** (list allocated files) and **LISTDS** (list information about datasets). ISPF is a program product which is invoked as a TSO/E command and adds commands or services. The **ISPF** command starts the ISPF program product, which builds its own TSO/E subenvironment on top of the standard TSO/E environ-ment, thereby creating an additional set of services for REXX programs and programs executing in that subenvironment.

TSO/E and its predecessor, TSO, have a command language called **CLIST**. The word **CLIST** is a short form of **Command list**. When first introduced, CLISTs were simply lists of commands. Later linguistic constructs were added similar to those in most application languages. This development continued over many years, until today CLIST has evolved into a full-fledged application language. Today many products written by both users and vendors use CLIST as an application lan-guage. Because of its history, CLIST is not as consistent as newer lan-guages. This is because in adding new statements, downward compat-ibility had to be assured; thus enhancements did not permit the consistency common in modern languages.

REXX as a system-wide language

REXX, on the other hand, is a very consistent language, although in many ways it is not unlike CLIST. It is a command language, but in addition, it can be used to write prototypes and applications. If a REXX program is executing in the TSO/E address space, the REXX program and commands called from within it can use TSO/E services, as shown in the previous figure. If ISPF is active for TSO/E user 2 as shown in the figure, REXX programs called from within ISPF can use ISPF services, in addition to TSO/E services and MVS/ESA services. If the editor is active within ISPF, REXX programs can also use editor services. This is a hierarchical structure in which each environment adds to the available services of the previous one. REXX programs can use any commands available on any level of that hierarchy.

Programs which use only MVS/ESA services can execute in any MVS/ESA address space. The REXX interpreter is such a program. REXX programs are thus not limited to the TSO/E address space: they may be used in any MVS/ESA address space. (Data spaces do not support executable code; thus they do not support REXX.) For example, the NetView environment is totally different from the TSO/E environment; NetView uses REXX extensively. (In NetView, REXX programs are called CLISTs, because NetView functions may be implemented using the NetView CLIST language or REXX. The NetView CLIST language has its origins in the the TSO/E CLIST language, but has evolved independently and is now different.)

However, if the REXX program executes outside the TSO/E address space, the TSO/E services are not available to the REXX program. For example, Batch Job 1 could be executing a REXX program outside the TSO/E address space.

Because not all services are available in all address spaces, REXX programs must use only services available in address spaces in which they will execute. For example, if a REXX program is to execute both in MVS/ESA batch and in the TSO/E address space, it could use only the MVS/ESA services, it could use the services available in all address spaces, or it could dynamically determine the address space, and use TSO/E services if available.

The remainder of this chapter refers to REXX operation in **TSO/E address spaces** and in **non-TSO/E address spaces**. This distinction is necessary because if REXX executes in the TSO/E address space, it is fully integrated with other parts of TSO/E. Outside TSO/E, TSO/E-specific services are not available. The interaction with other parts of TSO/E in the TSO/E address space greatly enhances the functions supported by REXX. In general, the function in TSO/E is a proper superset of the function in non-TSO/E.

Many products which can be installed on MVS/ESA require command languages; in some cases, they already support their own command languages. Because of REXX language extendibility, it can be adopted by many products as a command language, without those products needing add any special support other than handling their own commands.

REXX as a general-purpose language

REXX is an effective language for general applications. Figure 9 shows the relationship of CLIST and REXX in TSO/E and MVS.

Some REXX services, such as terminal, recovery, and tasking support, depend on the host address space. In TSO/E, standard input and output are provided via TSO/E terminal support. Outside TSO/E, equivalent services must be provided, via I/O to datasets or perhaps by user-supplied routines. User-supplied routines allow customization, discussed in the section "Managing the REXX Environment".

REXX in the TSO/E address space

A TSO/E command language alternative

As described earlier, CLIST originated with TSO in the early 1970s. It remained the only command language available, first in TSO and later in TSO/E, until REXX was introduced in TSO/E Version 2, Release 1, announced April 19, 1988 and shipped in December of the same year.

From the beginning of the REXX design, the intent was to provide an alternative command language, not to replace CLIST. Therefore, every effort was made to make REXX programs as similar to CLISTs as possible, in terms of how the two fit into the system (i.e., not syntactically). CLISTs are stored in partitioned datasets (PDSs) or sequential datasets, can have fixed- or variable-length record format, and can be numbered or unnumbered. REXX supports the same datasets, the same record formats, and the same numbering conventions. Therefore, there is no external difference between the two. This is very important when converting programs from CLIST to REXX (see the chapter "REXX for CLIST Programmers").

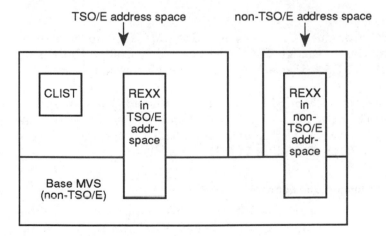

Figure 9. REXX in both TSO/E and non-TSO/E

To facilitate conversion it was important that REXX be not only externally equivalent but also functionally at least equivalent to CLISTs. This was achieved in the first REXX release, and has been improved in subsequent releases.

CMS compatibility

Many installations support both TSO/E and VM/CMS in the same computer complex, and many users and system programmers use or support both TSO/E and CMS in their daily work. Both TSO/E and CMS are Systems Application Architecture (SAA) environments, so compatibility between them is guaranteed for SAA functions. REXX is the SAA Procedures Language (see the chapter "Procedures Language in SAA"), so the language syntax must be compatible across implementations. However, CMS REXX programs almost always contain CMS commands. These commands are not defined by SAA, and therefore are not common to CMS and TSO/E.

CMS stack control commands are frequently used in CMS REXX programs, because the CMS stack is the central function around which the system is built. For TSO/E and CMS REXX to be compatible, the stack concept and associated commands had to be introduced to TSO/E.

Another common CMS command is **EXECIO**, which performs disk I/O from REXX programs. **EXECIO** was also ported to TSO/E.

In addition to the stack and I/O commands, some TSO/E programming interfaces were added or modified for CMS compatibility, even when this meant providing duplicate interfaces in TSO/E—one TSO/E-like, the other CMS-like. These new interfaces reduce the effort required to convert programs supporting REXX applications for both TSO/E and CMS.

ISPF compatibility

ISPF is a TSO/E product which was moved to CMS; the two ISPF command sets are thus the same. ISPF is not as widely used in CMS as in TSO/E, but CMS REXX programs containing ISPF commands are fully compatible.

A word of caution: CMS ISPF translates commands from lowercase to uppercase; TSO/E ISPF does not. ISPF requires commands to be in uppercase, so lowercase ISPF commands in REXX programs will execute correctly in CMS and fail in TSO/E.

The REXX environment: the concept

From the above, it is clear that different address spaces in MVS/ESA present different environments within which REXX must operate. In order to normalize this environment, the concept of a REXX environment must be created. This concept may be safely ignored by programmers who remain entirely within REXX, but it affects some REXX functions—in particular, stack control.

An environment is associated with a **task** and cannot be shared among tasks, but one task can be associated with many environments. Environments are chained in the order of creation, and inherit properties of the parent. This association with a task is forced by the system to allow accounting for resources, such as storage and datasets, used by REXX programs. When a REXX program calls another REXX program, both operate in the same REXX environment.

Environments are created and deleted by programs which call REXX programs, and may define data stacks and limits of authority for REXX programs executing in the environment. If a REXX program is to be executed without an environment having been established, the system creates a default environment before the REXX program is executed and deletes it after the REXX program terminates.

As stated above, environment details are rarely important to REXX programmers, but they should be aware of the concept. The section later in this chapter which discusses REXX environments is applicable only to programmers who use routines which manage environments.

FUNCTIONS SUPPORTING REXX

The REXX language is only part of the REXX package in TSO/E and MVS/ESA. In order to use the REXX language and have any degree of compatibility with other REXX platforms, supporting functions are implemented. They are:

- One or more data stacks, for temporarily holding data
- **EXECIO**, **EXECUTIL**, Immediate commands, and **SUBCOM**
- Some REXX functions: **LISTDSI**, **MSG**, **OUTTRAP**, **PROMPT**, **STORAGE**, **SYSDSN**, and **SYSVAR**

These constructs are discussed below.

Stack design

Stack as seen by REXX program
This section discusses the TSO/E implementation of the data stack. To the REXX program, it appears identical to the CMS stack.

Many REXX programs use the data stack only to store temporary data; as this section shows, the stack is more powerful. A good understanding of the data stack is also necessary to avoid **misplacing** data when multitasking. Data can be placed on the wrong stack and seemingly "disappear", or be deleted accidentally with a stack.

The data stack is available in any address space when a REXX program is executing. Except for the section "Stacks and multitasking", which describes managing stacks with the NEWSTACK and DELSTACK commands, this section is intended primarily for users coding applications which exploit REXX multi-processing. In such environments, data stacks can be used to communicate among REXX programs asynchronously executing different tasks.

This section also describes the converse: precautions to prevent multiple simultaneously executing REXX programs from interfering with stacks belonging to other applications executing on multiple MVS/ESA tasks.

The data stack
This section discusses several different and unrelated kinds of stacks:

- The existing stack in TSO/E is referred to as the **TSO/E input stack**.
- The existing CMS stack is referred to as the **CMS stack**.
- The stack created for TSO/E REXX is called the **data stack** or simply the **stack**.

The REXX language defines several instructions which manipulate a construct computer scientists call a **stack** or **queue**. The PULL instruction removes the top element from the stack and returns it to the caller. The PUSH instruction adds a new stack element above the top; the caller specifies a stack element to PUSH, and this element becomes the new top. The caller also supplies a stack element to the QUEUE instruction, which adds that element *below* the old bottom element. The built-in QUEUED function returns the number of elements on the stack.

This construct has a **top**, a **bottom**, and an arbitrary number of elements between those extremes. It has a length, it is read from the top to the bottom, and when an element is read (PULLed), that element is removed from the stack. This is the standard model of the CMS stack.

Neither MVS/ESA nor TSO/E supported such a stack function prior to the implementation of REXX, although TSO/E uses a construct called the TSO/E **input stack**. This is very different from the data stack required by REXX, which required a new stacking function.

As stated earlier, REXX can execute in both TSO/E and non-TSO/E address spaces, so this new stacking function must be available in all address spaces. Any stack model could have been used—for example, that used by OS/2—but for compatibility with existing CMS REXX usage, the CMS model was chosen. While not required by SAA, this increases compatibility between mainframe REXX versions, simplifying conversion of programs between operating systems.

The CMS data stack

The CMS stack is part of CMS, not REXX. It holds data placed on it by programs. Programs may also place markers on the stack, allowing removal of all elements above and including the marker. These markers define parts of the stack called **buffers**:

In the CMS stack shown in figure 10, m - 1 elements exist on the stack, followed by a **marker** and additional elements. Each element is a character string of arbitrary length, up to an implementation limit; in TSO/E this is almost 16MB. A null string—a string with zero length—is a valid element. If the stack is in the state shown and a REXX program PUSHes an element, it is placed above the top data element (element n). If a REXX program QUEUEs an element, it is placed just above the marker closest to the top, between element m and **Marker** 1. In other words, assuming a **Marker** 0 on the bottom of the stack, defining **Buffer** 0, QUEUE adds the element above the marker closest to the top.

Elements between markers and above the top marker are referred to as **buffers**. The MAKEBUF and DROPBUF commands add and remove markers. PULL instructions return the top data element on the stack, removing any markers present between the top of the stack and the top data element.

In terms of buffers, **PUSH** adds an element to the top of the top buffer, **QUEUE** adds an element to the bottom of the top buffer, and

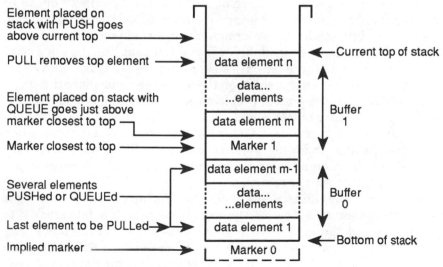

Figure 10. Example of CMS stack

PULL removes and discards any markers above the top element, removes the top element, and returns the element.

The built-in QUEUED function returns the number of elements (n in the figure). QUEUED does not count stack markers.

In CMS the stack also participates in reading terminal input. A REXX program may request input from the terminal directly, but the terminal can also be thought of as an extension of the stack. If a REXX program tries to PULL from an empty stack, data is read from the terminal. Thus PULL always returns an element (although it may be null).

The TSO/E data stack

The basic TSO/E data stack is identical to the CMS stack. This satisfies REXX language needs for a stack. Several extensions were implemented to satisfy MVS/ESA and TSO/E requirements; these extensions are not visible to casual REXX users.

The extensions have no CMS parallels:

- TSO/E data stacks can be shared among different REXX language environments.

- New stacks can be created to assure privacy in multiprocessing environments.

These extensions are discussed below.

As discussed elsewhere in this chapter, multiple independent REXX language environments can be created in a single address space, or multiple environments may be related in a hierarchy called a **chain of environments**. One of the resources associated with such an environment is the data stack. Two environments in a chain may share a stack. If they do, the dependent (daughter) environment may be allowed to share the stack with the parent—never the inverse. If two REXX language environments are created on the same task and share the stack, there are no synchronization problems of simultaneously updating the data stack, because by MVS/ESA tasking rules, only one program per task can execute at a time. REXX programs on a task are related in a call chain as any other programs are. Therefore REXX programs lower on the call chain on a task must complete first; higher programs are dormant until lower ones finish.

No general rule can be made about the sharing of stacks. Sharing is desirable for some applications, but not for others. If a data stack is to be shared and the lower environment does not contain a stack, any stack-oriented instructions or commands issued by a REXX program executing on the lower environment are directed to the data stack associated with the higher-level environment. For this discussion, environments can be thought of as being related in a call chain similar to

programs. The left side of figure 11 shows how three environments—
Env 0, its dependent Env 1, and Env 1's dependent Env 2—share one
data stack. All environments share the stack and execute under one
task, Task 0.

The term **primary data stack** implies **secondary data stacks**.
These secondary stacks are discussed later in this section.

If the stack is not to be shared, a new stack is initialized when the
lower REXX language environment is built. This isolates the stack
associated with the higher REXX language environment from programs executing in the lower environment (see the right side of the previous figure).

The sharing of the data stack between a REXX language environment and its parent is established when the dependent environment is
created. A REXX language environment can only share its data stack
with that of the immediate parent; only if that parent REXX language
environment shares a stack with *its* parent environment will all three
environments share a stack.

Stacks and multitasking

The CMS-like data stack is sufficient for non-TSO/E address spaces
when no multitasking is present. However, REXX programs can execute concurrently on multiple tasks, and need to share the data stack.
It was shown earlier that the environment blocks and associated REXX
language environments contain task-related data, such as anchors to
storage, open datasets, and the like. Thus if REXX programs are to be
interpreted on different tasks, they need to be interpreted in different
environments, one per task.

If two REXX programs execute in different environments on the
same task, they never execute at the same time: execution is

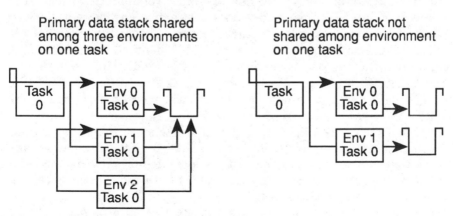

Figure 11. Sharing primary data stack under one task

synchronous. However, if different REXX language environments sharing one data stack are associated with **different** tasks, the stack becomes a resource shared among the programs, and execution may be **asynchronous**.

Sharing the stack among asynchronously executing REXX programs has several implications. The first is that REXX programs executing on different tasks may access the shared data stack at the same instant. Sharing the data stack allows REXX programs to communicate via the stack by PUSHing and PULLing stack elements. On the other hand, data stack sharing implies a lack of privacy or control. REXX programs PUSHing entries on the stack have no guarantee that another REXX program will not PUSH entries at the same time, causing mixed and unpredictable results. When the original entries are PULLed, unwanted and possibly unrecognized entries will be returned from the stack.

For example, if a REXX program stacks entries via **EXECIO** and does not process all entries, and another REXX program either places entries on the stack or PULLs some off, the results will not be what the first program expects.

Sharing a stack in a multitasking environment implies a stack **locking** mechanism. As stacks can only be shared within a chain, and the time for stack operations is very short, an internal lock, one per chain, is used to synchronize access to stacks. This minimizes both path length for locking services and interference among locks.

The privacy issue is more difficult to address, particularly because a given program may wish to share its stack at some times and not at others. Thus REXX programs themselves need to control stack sharing. This is accomplished by allowing stack creation by the program.

A new stack is created by the new **NEWSTACK** command, which creates a new stack and deactivates but does not change any currently active stack. This new "secondary" stack becomes the active stack for all REXX programs in that environment, and is identical in structure and capabilities to the deactivated stack, but is empty. It is not shared among REXX language environments, but is shared among all REXX programs in the environment in which it was created. For example, if a REXX program calls another REXX program, or calls a command which calls another REXX program, the new stack is used. Multiple secondary stacks can be created in the same way the first secondary stack was created, but only the last stack created is active and accessible to a program. The primary stack and all secondary stacks can be thought of as a **stack of stacks**.

A secondary stack has the same properties as a primary stack: entries can be PUSHed and PULLed, and when the stack is empty, input is read from the input file or terminal. Markers have the same meaning on secondary stacks as they do on primary stacks.

Another command, DELSTACK, deletes the last secondary stack and reactivates the previous stack. If a DELSTACK is issued when the primary stack is active, it is ignored, because the primary stack may be shared with REXX programs executing in other REXX language environments, and deleting a shared stack may cause failure of REXX programs associated with another REXX language environment.

The command QSTACK returns the number of existing stacks as a return code, allowing REXX programs to examine the stack structure.

Figure 12 shows a chain of three REXX language environments. Env 1, associated with Task 1, owns stack P1. This is the only stack for Env 1, and is thus both a primary stack and the active stack for Env 1. When Env 2 was created, no new primary stack was created, but the environment was to share the primary stack with Env 1. However, some program created a private or secondary stack, S2, which is the currently active stack for Env 2. After S2 is deleted, P1 will become the active stack for Env 2. Env 3 has its own primary stack, P3. Env 3 could create a secondary stack, but regardless of any actions in any environment, Env 3 can never share a stack with either of the other two environments.

REXX file I/O: EXECIO

REXX file I/O is performed by EXECIO, which is modeled on the CMS EXECIO command. EXECIO is available both within and outside the TSO/E address space, and appears to the REXX programmer as a command, although it is not a true command and therefore cannot be used in a CLIST or from the command line.

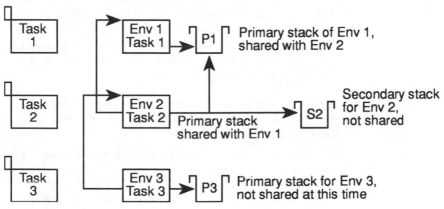

Figure 12. Sharing data stacks among different tasks

EXECIO syntax is:

EXECIO *lines|* function ddname* [*linenum*] [([*options*] [)]]

Operands are:

lines or *   **lines** is an integer defining the number of records to be read or written. An asterisk (*) defines an arbitrary number; the operation terminates when a null record (record of zero length) or the end of the dataset is reached. Zero is a valid value, and the command may still have an effect—for example, if **FINIS** is specified, the dataset is closed.

function   Three types of operation are allowed. The first operation against a closed dataset opens it, and it remains open until either it is explicitly closed by **FINIS** or the task under which it was opened terminates. When a series of REXX programs run in **READY** mode, they all execute under the same task. When the last REXX program returns to the **READY** mode, the task terminates, and all datasets are closed.

function must be one of:

DISKW   Write records at the end of the dataset. If this is the first operation against a closed dataset, open the dataset for write.

DISKR   Read record(s) from the file defined by **ddname**. If this is the first operation against a closed dataset, open the dataset for read.

DISKRU   Read record(s) for later update from the file defined by **ddname**. If this is the first operation against a closed dataset, open the dataset for update. After reading a dataset opened with this option, the last record read can be rewritten using **DISKW**. The record written should have the same length as the record read; if not, it will be padded or truncated.

ddname   The DD to operate on. A sequential dataset or a concatenation of datasets (for read only) must be allocated for that DD before **EXECIO** can be used.

linenum   If specified, indicates the record number where the operation starts. This operand implies closing the dataset, reopening it, and reading from the start. **EXECIO** I/O is QSAM-based, not BDAM-based; therefore its performance is poor, and the open type is reset by this operation. This operand is valid only on **DISKR** and **DISKRU** operations.

options are:

LIFO	Take data from or transfer data to the data stack in LIFO (last-in, first-out) order.
FIFO	Take data from or transfer data to the data stack in FIFO (first-in, first-out) order.
SKIP	Read and ignore records. Specifying an asterisk reads to end-of-file for later write.
STEM	Read/write data from/to REXX variables. Variable names are formed by concatenating the token following the **STEM** keyword and an integer. For example, ...**DISKR**...**(STEM DATA** stores the first record read into variable **DATA1**, and ...**DISKW**...**(STEM TEXT.** fetches the text for the first record written from variable **TEST.1**. After a read, variable **stem0** contains the number of variables set. **LIFO**, **FIFO**, **SKIP**, and **STEM** are mutually exclusive.
FINIS	Close the dataset after the operation completes. If *lines* is 0 and **FINIS** is specified, the dataset is simply closed.
Source and target of data	Data can be transferred between the stack and datasets, or between variables and datasets.

EXECIO example:

```
'ALLOCATE DA(WORK.EXEC(SAMP1)) F(MYDD) OLD'
'EXECIO * DISKR MYDD (FINIS FIFO'
```

EXECIO uses MVS/ESA Queued Sequential Access Method (QSAM), which is a buffered access method, and performance can be improved by increasing the number of records requested at one time. A useful technique is minimizing I/O by reading an entire dataset either into STEM variables or onto the stack. Stack use lends itself to highly structured applications, because if records are processed by different routines, one routine can read records, and leave or replace unprocessed records on the stack for another routine.

EXECUTIL Command

EXECUTIL is a true multi-function utility command, and can be issued from the **READY** mode or a CLIST, but only in the TSO/E address space.
EXECUTIL has four formats:

```
EXECUTIL EXECDD(OPEN|CLOSE|NOCLOSE)
or
EXECUTIL Immediate command
or
EXECUTIL RENAME NAME(fname) [SYSNAME(sname)] [DD(dd)]
or
EXECUTIL SEARCHDD(NO|YES)
```

Operands are:

EXECDD

Defines system action on the **SYSEXEC** DD. If **OPEN** is specified, the dataset(s) is opened the first time used, and remains open until **CLOSE** is specified or the task terminates.

SYSEXEC is the DD for datasets containing only REXX programs; it is the REXX equivalent of **SYSPROC** for CLISTs. In TSO/E, **SYSPROC** may also contain REXX programs, but is closed each time it is used. **EXECDD NOCLOSE** aids performance when most REXX programs run are in those datasets. If **CLOSE** is specified, the DD is opened for each search. This option is intended primarily for development environments where users may share, edit, and change programs within a dataset.

Immediate command

Immediate commands **TS**, **TE**, **HT**, **RT**, and **HI** may be executed via **EXECUTIL**. This implementation was chosen because many customers already have commands or CLISTs by these names, so the new commands could interfere with existing applications.

RENAME

External functions implemented as programs are grouped into function packages, which are load modules. Each such load module contains a directory listing each function in the package and the addresses of entry points within the load module. During function development, a function may be created which already exists in a loaded function package. **RENAME** deactivates the already-loaded function, avoiding the conflict. *fname* is the external function to be renamed; *sname* is the external entry point of the new function; *dd* is the DD of the new function. The **RENAME** is temporary, affecting only the current REXX environment.

SEARCHDD

SEARCHDD is used to improve performance. If **NO** is specified (the default), only DD **SYSPROC** is searched for REXX programs; **SYSEXEC** is not searched. This assures that the performance of a system which uses only CLISTs is not affected by REXX's presence. Specifying **YES**, particularly with **EXECDD(OPEN)**, offers significant performance improvement for applications entirely or mostly implemented as REXX programs.

This facility was implemented to allow applications to control searching, since installations and users cannot always predict which option assures better performance.

REXX programs may be stored along with CLISTs in partitioned datasets allocated to the **SYSPROC** DD. To distinguish members of those datasets written in CLIST from those written in REXX, the first line of a REXX program must contain a comment and the word **REXX** in upper-, lower-, or mixed case.

Immediate commands

TSO/E REXX provides Immediate commands similar to CMS Immediate commands: **HI, HT, RT, TS**. These can be issued as stand-alone commands outside TSO/E, or within TSO/E either as parameters on the TSO/E **EXECUTIL** command or after execution of a REXX program is interrupted by a **system interrupt** such as the Interrupt or PA1 keys.

- HI (Halt Interpretation) terminates interpretation of all REXX programs in the current environment; if a REXX program contains an active **SIGNAL ON HALT**, that label gains control.

- HT (Halt Typing) terminates display of output from the REXX **SAY** instruction; error and CLIST output are not halted.

- RT (Resume Typing) reverses the effects of an **HT** command.

- TS (Trace Start) starts tracing each statement executed in any REXX program in the current REXX environment.

- TE (Trace End) resets tracing to the condition prior to the **TS** command.

Subcommand environments

Part of the CMS subcommand environment concept has also been implemented in TSO/E REXX. The **SUBCOM** command takes a single argument, an environment name, and indicates via return code whether that subcommand environment is available (**0** means available, **1** means not available).

In MVS/ESA, environments **MVS, LINK**, and **ATTACH** are valid. **MVS** is the default, and supports the **SUBCOM, EXECIO**, and Immediate commands. The **LINK** and **ATTACH** environments are used to link or attach modules.

In TSO/E, the address environment **TSO** is added and is the default. If a REXX program is called while ISPF is active, two additional address environments are available, **ISPEXEC** and **ISREDIT**. **ISREDIT** may only be used from within the ISPF editor.

Special functions

Several special external functions are included in TSO/E REXX. Of these, only **STORAGE** is available outside the TSO/E address space. The reason for this limitation is that these functions are primarily intended for easing conversion of CLISTs to REXX programs. Some also rely on services available only in the TSO/E address space.

The functions are:

LISTDSI   Determines information about datasets.

MSG   Controls display of messages.

OUTTRAP   Permits trapping most screen output in REXX variables.

PROMPT   Controls prompting; used primarily by CLISTs called from
             REXX programs.

STORAGE   Reads and writes data to and from allocated main storage.

SYSDN   Returns message about a dataset.

SYSVAR   Returns values of special CLIST variables.

With the exception of **STORAGE**, described below, these functions are described in detail in the chapter "REXX for CLIST programmers".

STORAGE

The **STORAGE** function reads and writes storage. It is similar to the CMS REXX **STORAGE** function. In addition, it is the only special built-in function usable outside the TSO/E address space.

The function accepts one required and two optional parameters; unlike the CMS function, **STORAGE** with no operands to return the user's virtual storage size is not allowed.

The first, mandatory parameter is the main storage address to read or write. This address must be within allocated storage, and fetch protection and storage keys must allow access.

If a fetch or protection exception occurs during the operation, a null string is returned.

The second, optional parameter is the number of bytes of storage to return; if omitted, it defaults to 1.

The third, optional parameter is the data to store at the specified location.

LISTDSI function

The **LISTDSI** function returns information about a dataset or DD in REXX variables. Syntax is:

```
LISTDSI {dsname [loc]}|{ddname FILE} [options]
```

Operands are:

dsname   The name of the dataset about which to retrieve information.

loc   The dataset location (**VOLUME(volid)** or **PREALLOC** for an
             allocated dataset). If omitted, the system catalog is searched.

ddname   The name of a DD.

FILE   Indicates that the first token is a DD rather than a **dsname**.

options are:

DIRECTORY / *NODIRECTORY*	Specifies whether directory information is also to be returned. **NODIRECTORY** is the default, and is faster. These options apply to partitioned datasets only.
RECALL / *NORECALL*	Specifies whether the dataset is to be recalled or not.

Return codes:

0	Command successful, all information valid
4	File information valid, directory information invalid
16	Severe error

MSG and PROMPT functions

MSG and **PROMPT** control display of informational messages. Only messages issued by **PUTLINE** are affected. Messaging and prompting can be turned **ON** or **OFF**, and remain in that state until changed by the corresponding REXX functions or TSO/E commands.

OUTTRAP function

OUTTRAP is one of the most useful functions, because it stores terminal output in REXX variables.
    Syntax is:

```
OUTTRAP(OFF|stem, [max], [CONCAT|NOCONCAT]])
```

Operands are:

OFF	Stop output trapping.
stem	Start (or continue) trapping output, storing it in the named variable stem. Trapped output is placed in indexed compound variables using the specified stem (**stem**1, **stem**2, etc.).
max	Defines the maximum number of lines to be trapped; when this maximum is reached, trapping stops, and output is displayed as usual.
CONCAT / *NOCONCAT*	Controls whether the variable index is reset for each command trapped or continues to increase.

MANAGING THE REXX ENVIRONMENT

It is important to understand the REXX environment if an application is distributed over several tasks or is to personalize internal functions such as the managing of storage, terminal I/O, and recovery services.

In general, the REXX environment was designed such that a user could customize and/or replace any system service the interpreter uses. This gives the environment creator great flexibility, but also assumes that the environment is created properly. This section describes the environment, rather than the detail of each parameter, to allow the author of the application to understand how it operates and how it might be applied in specific cases.

A general requirement for products executing in MVS/ESA is the ability to customize the execution environment; this is also true for REXX. This customizing is needed because many address spaces in MVS/ESA have special conventions for obtaining and freeing storage, reading and writing to the terminal, and other system-related services. The REXX design had to support the convention of these address spaces. There had to be a focal point for such customization; this need led to the concept of the **REXX Language Processor Environment**, abbreviated as the **REXX environment**.

Need for a REXX environment

This chapter has shown that the REXX interpreter can be called in different address spaces, and that system services available in these address spaces differ greatly. To accommodate these differences, either the interpreter must be sensitive to differences, or the interpreter must run within a newly created **environment** which hides them. The REXX environment concept is that the interpreter remains address-space-independent. Whenever it requires a service which is not provided by the base MVS/ESA system, a routine is called which can, if need be, be replaced. This approach allows any application in any address space to define its own service routines. Even system services that are handled differently in different address spaces, such as storage management, can be substituted.

The interpreter can only interpret a REXX program within an environment. That environment established for the interpreter is address-space-independent, and shields the interpreter from the need for sensitivity to differences in the underlying system. It allows the execution environment to be customized to handle all differences between services provided in different address spaces. For example, in TSO/E, user input is expected to be from the terminal, and user output is also sent to the terminal. Outside TSO/E, this I/O may need to be read from or written to a file, or may be handled by another product's terminal handling routine. The REXX environment handles routing to and from the different places, and presents the interpreter with a consistent interface in all cases.

In MVS/ESA the **task** is the unit which "owns" resources and creates environments. For recovery and other reasons, the environment also "owns" resources, such as open files, storage, data stacks (discussed earlier), routines loaded into memory, locks for multi-processing, and others. Therefore it was natural to associate the MVS/ESA task and the REXX environment. Other language-related information is also associated with the REXX environment.

Associating REXX environments with tasks ensures new REXX environments on attached tasks. This is very important, for example, when entering ISPF. Assume that a user is in TSO/E READY mode. In this state, the initial TSO/E REXX environment has been established. If the user then enters ISPF, ISPF is a new task, so a new REXX environment is created, which is required because a new stack is needed. Whenever the user runs under the ISPF task, the ISPF environment and the ISPF related stack are used; when the user exits ISPF, the task and associated environment are no longer active, and the user is back in the REXX environment associated with TSO/E READY mode. This is discussed in detail later in the chapter.

The REXX environment

The REXX environment must be present when a REXX program is interpreted. If no environment has been established and a REXX program is to be interpreted, the system builds a REXX environment with the default characteristics, and deletes it before returning to the caller. Neither the REXX program nor its author are aware of that environment, its existence, when it was set up, or by whom—and that is the intent. The REXX environment can be thought of as being on a lower level; it equalizes all address spaces to a common environment within which the REXX program can be interpreted. For example, if the REXX SAY instruction is executed, the REXX interpreter cannot (and should not) determine directly if the output goes to a terminal as in TSO/E or if it is written into a file.

The discussion in this section applies both to programs calling REXX programs and programs called by REXX programs—that is, commands, service routines, or environmental routines named in the current REXX environment.

A REXX environment can be explicitly created and deleted by services IRXINIT and IRXTERM. A parameter when creating an environment is the name of the **parameter module**, which contains characteristics of the environment to be built. If none is specified, default parameter module IRXPARMS is used.

Three such parameter modules are shipped with the product, containing different parameters: IRXPARMS is for use outside TSO/E; IRXTSPRMS is used to initialize the REXX environment when TSO/E is initialized; and IRXISPPRM is used when ISPF is initialized. A user, installation, or product can create a module and use it just as the system does.

The IRXINIT routine returns the address of the control block representing the newly created REXX environment. This pointer to the ENVB control block (environment block) identifies the environment, and it is therefore possible to distinguish many environments—or one can maintain many different environments at the same time. These environments need not be related. For example, NetView uses three environments for each user. Each part of a split-screen session is one environment, allowing REXX programs to execute independently on each part of the split screen without interfering with each other. A third session is used for the HELP function; it too can execute independently, and again, will not interfere with the primary screens.

The REXX package provides many callable entry points such as the interface to manipulate REXX variables. All routines called by the REXX interpreter are passed the address of the current REXX environment block.

If no pointer is used to identify the REXX environment, it is referred to as the **non-reentrant environment**. It is located by the system as the last environment created on the current task. If no non-reentrant environment was created on the current task, the system will look on the parent task until one is found. If none is found on any parent, no non-reentrant environment exists. Environments on sister tasks are not considered.

Reentrant REXX environments must be explicitly created as such, and are more complex. They are not related to any task, and cannot be related to non-reentrant environments. In the search for a default environment, they cannot be found, because they cannot be located by the system.

REXX environment makeup

The TSO/E REXX environment holds parameters which customize and personalize it, as well as pointers to environment-unique resources. In many ways, the REXX environment establishes the execution environment, similar to the way in which the CMS operating system does so under CP.

Among parameters found in the environment are:

- Data stack anchor
- Pointers to storage control blocks
- I/O-related control blocks (for example, data control blocks, or DCBs)
- Names of routines used to customize this environment

The REXX environment is also the focal point for operating system-related constructs such as loaded modules. An environment is represented by an environment block, and contains REXX-related information such as pointers to preloaded REXX programs and the **user token**, which may be used by an application program for anything, but is most appropriately used for values related to the REXX environment. For example, an application program may pass to REXX a user token which it shares with another part of the application. A common usage is to point to an application work area, which is available to programs called as external functions from within all REXX programs in an application.

The user token along with the other values read from the parameter module make up the **ENVB**. When the environment has been established, an **ENVB** control block has been built and represents the REXX environment.

Because the REXX environment is the key to connecting REXX and the system, it is available to every program called by the interpreter. Through the environment block, these programs can examine all parameters passed in the parameter module. However, the programs *may not* change these parameters. The system retains backup copies, and if the backup copy and the values in the environment block do not agree, results are unpredictable. Also stored in the environment block, and therefore accessible to these programs, are parameters passed to the interpreter when interpretation of the current REXX program starts. A sampling of parameters available in the **ENVB** are:

- Parameter originally passed when environment was created

  - Names of replaceable routines (e.g., terminal I/O, storage management)
  - Names of command environments and routines to be called for each
  - Names of packages and functions contained with each
  - User field passed when environment was created (user token)

- Parameter relating to currently executing REXX program

  - Name of REXX program
  - Arguments passed to REXX program
  - User field passed on call to interpret REXX program (user token)

Although the REXX environment is important to the design and must always be present, REXX programmers need not be aware of its existence. To REXX programmers, REXX programs execute in an environment, and they need not be sensitive to how the environment was established or how it can be changed.

Chains of REXX environments

The previous section shows that many system-related properties are tied to a REXX environment. At times, some of these properties must be replaced or changed. As stated earlier, the environment may not be changed; therefore the only alternative is to create a new environment. It would have been more efficient to change existing environments, but that would be very error-prone, so changing such parameters is not done often. New environments can be created at any time. At the time the creation service is called, none, some, or all parameters may be passed. Environments are related hierarchically in what is known as a **chain of REXX environments**. In creating the new environment, each parameter is evaluated using the algorithm described below.

If a value for a given parameter is passed in the call to IRXINIT, that value is used. If no value is passed, the value of the parent environment is used. If the environment does not have a parent—as, for example, if it is the first one in a batch address space—the values which would have been retrieved from the parent are taken from the default parameter module, the name of which is a parameter to IRXINIT.

If more than one dependent environment is created from a given environment, the resulting structure is, strictly speaking, a hierarchy. However, the structure is referred to as a **chain**, because in most cases the structure of related REXX environments is linear—a chain—not a hierarchy.

In the previous discussion, new environments were created to possibly change values, but a more common reason for different REXX environments is the MVS/ESA tasking structure. Storage, open datasets, and other MVS/ESA resources are tracked on an MVS/ESA task level. If REXX programs operate on different MVS/ESA tasks, they must operate in different REXX environments. The dependent environment may have the same characteristics as the parent, but the new environment is associated with a different task. REXX environments of dependent tasks are chained, unless explicitly specified otherwise at creation time. The only exception to an environment on every task is in TSO/E, where a REXX program may attach a command which calls a second REXX program. The second REXX program operates on a lower-level task than the original exec, but because of this exception and the sharing of virtual storage Subpool 78 in TSO/E, both REXX programs can operate in one REXX environment. Such special cases made the implementation in the TSO/E address space different from that in other address spaces, and significantly improved performance. However, none of these differences are visible to REXX programmers or interface users.

Different chains of environments are completely independent from one another. Figure 13 shows one chain. Env 1 was the original envi-

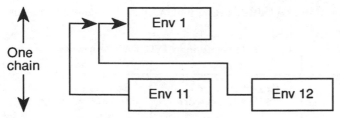

Figure 13. Chains of REXX environments

ronment, then two additional environments—**Env 11** and **Env 12**—
were created under it. This structure is present for ISPF, for example,
where the top environment represents the TSO/E **READY** mode and the
dependent environments correspond to the two applications executing
in split-screen mode. In the **READY** mode, only one environment is present, such as **Env 1**, which would represent a degenerate case of a
chain.

Typically only one chain exists in one address space at one time.
However, an arbitrary number of independent chains may be created
in an address space. (It is even possible, using a special technique
called **reentrant REXX environments**, to support an arbitrary number of independent chains of environments associated with a single
task.) In the figure, chains are identified by pointers from each REXX
environment to its parent.

Non-TSO environments in the TSO address space

In many ways the REXX environment in the TSO address space is spe-
cial. The indication that an environment is to be integrated into the
TSO/E address space is a bit which is set in the word of flags passed to
IRXINIT when an environment is created.

A call to IRXINIT outside the TSO/E environment with that flag set
is an error condition. However, a call to IRXINIT in the TSO/E address
space *in* the TSO/E address space is not an error, but a very useful feature. In this case the environment is not integrated into TSO/E, can be
modified in the same way as any environment outside a TSO/E address
space, and in effect runs in a batch address space. (Environments inter-
grated into TSO/E cannot be modified.)

Executing a REXX program in a TSO/E address space in an environment not integrated into TSO/E allows easy testing of REXX programs
targeted to execute in other address spaces. It allows testing in a
friendly environment where it is possible to dynamically set up alloca-
tions using TSO/E commands, and call with different parameters,
instead of having to create a test environment in some other address

space. This is case 2 in the table below, as compared to case 4, the normal TSO/E case.

| | | Execution in TSO/E address space | |
		no	yes
TSO/E Flag on call to IXINIT is set	no	1. Executing outside TSO/E address space	2. Executing as non-TSO/E in TSO/E address space
	yes	3. Error condition: No REXX environment is created	4. Normal condition: Case for creating integrated environment in TSO/E address space

REXX in any address space

In general address spaces, either TSO/E or non-TSO/E—cases 1, 2, and 4 in the table above—the three basic types of calls supporting the REXX functions (initialization and termination of REXX environment, interpretation of a program, and REXX-related services) are illustrated in figure 14.

The **initialization** routine (**IRXINIT**) establishes a new REXX environment by creating several control blocks, among them the **environment block (ENVB)**. This newly created environment establishes the environment in which REXX programs are to be interpreted. As stated earlier, the environment determines the routines to handle system services and commands. These service routines replace default system service routines and are therefore called **replaceable routines** (see the section "Replaceable routines or exit routines"). The names of these routines are saved in the environment block. The **termination** routine (**IRXTERM**) reverses the action of the initialization routine by deleting the current REXX environment.

Two different services support **interpretation** of a program. They differ primarily in the format of the parameters on the call. **IRXEXEC** is a general routine which allows the caller to specify virtually anything about a program, including the address of a preloaded exec, the environment within which the REXX program is to execute, or the area into which the result of a function (value on the RETURN statement in the REXX program) is to be returned. Because it is very general, it is primarily intended for advanced users and application writers. The other routine used to call for the execution of a REXX program from a program is **IRXJCL**. It has one parameter: a string containing the name of the REXX program to be executed and parameters to be passed to that program. As the name implies, this routine

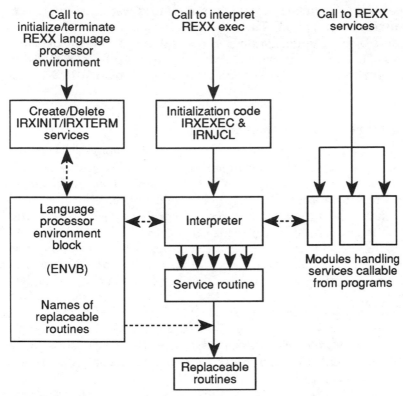

Figure 14. Main components of REXX

can be called from a JCL (job control language) **EXEC** statement. An example is:

```
//   EXEC PGM=IRXJCL,PARM='MYEXEC this is a parm'
```

In this example, the REXX program **MYEXEC** will be executed, with parameters **this is a parm**. Although **IRXJCL** is intended to be called from JCL, it can be used in any address space at any time.

When either interpretation service is called, some minor initialization steps are performed. For example, the current REXX environment is located, and if none exists a default environment is created; or if the REXX program has not already been loaded, it is loaded. (This condition exists when the interpreter is called from the JCL **EXEC** statement.) After initialization, the **interpreter** is called. This interpreter is the heart of the product. It is the code which interprets each instruction of the language, maintains variables, and issues the language-related error messages. This interpreter code is the same code used by CMS, thereby assuring compatibility between TSO/E and CMS REXX implementations.

Whenever this common code requires operating system services, **service routines** are called. These service routines are different for TSO/E and CMS. The design defines several REXX service routines. Examples of such services are fetching or setting variables, requesting stack services, performing I/O from programs, or loading REXX programs.

Replaceable routines and exit routines

It was shown earlier in this chapter that a design emphasis was the ability to tailor the REXX environment to the host address space. This is accomplished by allowing every system service to be funneled through a routine appropriate for the host address space.

The replaceable routine is a very general approach because it assures that all parameters needed to provide the service are passed to the routine; that the routine may check, change, or ignore both input parameters and results; that the routine may either provide the full service or provide partial service with calls to other service routines to complete the service; pretest to determine if the service is to be rendered, and then call the routine provided by the system which would be the default service routine for that service; or even refuse the service completely. In one application, for example, no stack operations were allowed. In that application, only the stack routine was replaced, and if a stack service was requested, it was denied.

Another example is use of these routines by NetView. NetView supports its own terminal and storage handling routines, and could not cooperate with other parts of the address space if address space-unique routines were not used. So when it creates an environment, these routines are replaced, and NetView routines are used.

This approach was taken rather than exit routines, because the routines supplied by the system were considered only a special-case routine, not the general solution, and system routines should not have any special status, as compared with routines provided by an application or a user.

The types of services handled by replaceable routines are loading of REXX programs, generalized I/O, storage management, and the data stack. The name of each replaceable routine is stored in each REXX environment when that environment is created, and, once specified, may not be changed. When any part of the TSO/E REXX component requires one of these services, the appropriate routine is called; when control returns to the caller, the service has been performed. For each of these services the system supplies at least one routine. At times, two routines are supplied: one applies to the TSO/E address space, the other outside the TSO/E address space. Routines in TSO/E are internal and not available to the user; also, if an environment is integrated into TSO/E, replaceable routines may not be specified.

Products or subsystems frequently implement an independent layer of service routines for their own internal use. A unique feature of the REXX implementation is that this independent layer is externalized, which is usually not done.

Replaceable routines are used only for those services mentioned above. Exit routines are available in other parts of the product. For example, exit routines were used in pre-initialization, in post-initialization, and during termination of a REXX environment.

Performance considerations

Performance is always a major consideration. As shown earlier, the concept of a REXX language environment was created in part to improve performance on the critical path of interpreting a program. Several functions were added to allow **tuning** performance, but in each case, defaults were chosen for the most common cases. This allows typical users to ignore tuning.

A basic trade-off in any design is choosing between code size and performance. In this product, performance was chosen, at the cost of larger code size (number of bytes required by the code).

In addition to externally available functions, code was written to optimize internal performance. For example, storage management code was included, which is called by all internal routines, and which can handle allocation and freeing of storage in arbitrary sizes from arbitrary numbers of MVS/ESA subpools, either above or below 16MB. This storage was associated with a REXX language environment. This storage management code was needed because storage management is one of the replaceable routines, and if that replaceable module were called for each individual storage request, performance would suffer. This internal storage management code acquires storage in multiple pages and doles it out to internal requests, frequently eight and twelve bytes at a time. The path length for internal main storage allocation and deallocation is very short.

External functions supporting performance

Applications can optimize performance by managing loading and freeing of frequently used functions and subroutines. Applications have three options. They can load a REXX program and pass the address of that loaded REXX program to the interpreter; they can call the replaceable routine for loading REXX programs directly, requesting that the program be loaded, and call later for its interpretation, passing its address; or they can neither preload nor call any other service, but simply call for the execution of the REXX program.

In the first case, the interpreter performs no input or output operations. The caller is responsible for creating an image of the REXX program in storage and passing it to the interpreter. The caller is also responsible for freeing the storage the REXX program resides in. From the interpreter's point of view, this is the best-performing option because the load process is totally omitted.

In the second case, the interpreter is instructed to load the REXX program and retain it for later use. Whenever that REXX program is to be interpreted, the interpreter scans the list of loaded REXX programs and, if it is found, interprets it without reloading it. The program that called for loading the REXX program may call a service to unload the program. Loaded REXX programs are associated with the REXX language environment, and when the environment is deleted, REXX programs associated with the environment are automatically freed.

In the third case, the interpreter again scans the list of LOADed REXX programs and, if the program is found, uses it without reloading it. If the REXX program cannot be found, it is loaded and internally retained as in the previous case. The REXX programs are freed when the REXX language environment is deleted or the dataset from which they are fetched is closed.

Performance of interpretation in a TSO/E address space

The design of the REXX interpreter is distinctly different from that of the CLIST interpreter. This was done partly to improve the performance of the REXX interpreter, and partly because the REXX interpreter cannot suspend operations when it encounters a command, as the CLIST interpreter does. When the TMP executes a CLIST, it executes it in two passes though the TMP code. The first step is to execute the command, calling for the interpretation of the CLIST (for example, the TSO/E EXEC command). This command loads the CLIST into storage, places a CLIST entry on the TSO/E **input stack**, and returns to the TMP. This pass is called **phase 1**. After phase 1 completes, the second pass, **phase 2**, executes the CLIST. Executing a REXX program is a one-phase process, reducing the overhead associated with calling the interpreter. Once the REXX interpreter is called, it does not return until the program terminates.

REXX programs can be stored in datasets allocated to either SYS-EXEC or SYSPROC. SYSEXEC is searched first, followed by SYSPROC. Searching an additional file degrades performance, but is necessary to distinguish between some REXX programs and CLISTs. To improve performance, searching of SYSEXEC is optional, allowing the user to bypass searching that file. Bypassing the search of SYSEXEC is also the most efficient method of using the **Virtual Lookaside Facility**, a method of retaining CLISTs or REXX programs in storage. It assures the shortest path by avoiding the input operation needed for loading.

Function packages

Function packages are an additional method of improving performance of REXX applications. They are not part of the REXX language, although they are also implemented in CMS (see the chapter "Extending CMS REXX with Function Packages" for details). As in CMS, they are typically implemented in assembler language, and allow one or more functions or subroutines commonly called by REXX programs to be **packaged** and made quickly accessible, offering improved performance. The performance gain is achieved by preloading the entire package once and retaining it in storage, thereby preventing the need for both multiple loads, one per function, and repeated loads, one per invocation. Additional performance is gained because these packages are searched first in the search sequence for functions or subroutines. Usually service routines are placed into packages, but the package capability is sufficiently general to allow any program called as a function or subroutine to be placed in a package. (REXX programs cannot be placed into packages.) The design of packages and the interfaces to the package are generalizations of the CMS implementation, providing again a great deal of compatibility between the two systems.

A package is associated with a REXX language environment, and is inherited from the parent REXX language environment. The design allows for three types, or levels, of packages; each level can hold multiple packages. Each package may contain multiple functions or subroutines. It is expected that products providing special REXX functions or subroutines will create their own packages. Based on this assumption, it is necessary to allow users to run with those packages supporting the products they plan to use.

Packages can be placed on one of three levels: the **user** level, the **local** level, or the **system** level. As the name implies, the first level is intended for private packages written by the user. Functions in these packages are searched before either of the other levels are searched. If a function or subroutine is found on this level, the search is terminated, and that function or subroutine from that package is used over functions or subroutines in packages on other levels. The second level is for packages supporting local applications; again, functions and subroutines on this level have precedence over those on the system level. The system level is for packages supporting products. There is no mechanism to enforce the placement of packages on any given level; it is only a convention.

CONCLUSION

The implementation of REXX on TSO/E is a powerful application language for TSO/E, a performance-oriented alternative to CLIST, and provides a high degree of compatibility with REXX applications written for CMS.

This implementation has been tailored to the TSO/E address space, and wherever possible shares code with the CLIST interpreter, thereby assuring equivalent functionality and compatibility. The REXX interpreter is therefore an integral part of TSO/E when executing in that address space. However, REXX programs can be interpreted in any address space. If executing outside TSO/E, the REXX interpreter does not have the benefit of the TSO/E service routines and those REXX extensions which depend on them, but the full language can be interpreted in any MVS/ESA address space.

Unlike other implementations, REXX on TSO/E executes in an environment which can be explicitly created or deleted. An application, or for that matter the user or installation, can tailor this environment, specifying how system services are to be handled, limiting REXX program access to system resources, or extending services available through external functions.

REXX for TSO/E is compatible with REXX for CMS not only because it uses the same language definition, but because it supports several of the most useful CMS commands for REXX programmers, such as **EXE-CIO**, Immediate commands, and stack manipulation commands. This commonality of commands simplifies writing REXX programs which execute on both CMS and TSO/E, and eases porting REXX programs between these two platforms.

REXX for Unix

By John Cifonelli

The Unix operating system is not one system but many. Originally developed at AT&T for the DEC PDP-7, Unix now runs on literally hundreds of hardware platforms. Unix implementations span the computing spectrum: Intel x86-based microcomputers, RISC-based workstations, proprietary minicomputers, IBM mainframes, and Cray supercomputers.

Likewise, Unix operating system software has many variants. While AT&T promotes its version (now called **System V**), many vendors market systems based on a modified Unix developed at Berkeley, known as **BSD**. **uni-REXX**, from The Workstation Group, is a REXX implementation designed to be portable to any Unix environment. Written in C and using standard Unix library facilities, uni-REXX has been ported to over 20 Unix hardware/software environments.

The language implemented by uni-REXX matches Cowlishaw's formal specification as closely as possible, rather than conforming to the CMS or TSO/E implementations from IBM. In addition, uni-REXX complies with the SAA CPI Procedures Language Level 1 definition.

Why is REXX needed for Unix?

To quote a recent Unix newsgroup communication:

> When you could use Bourne shell, or csh, or ksh, or tsh (or *sh), and all
> the Unix commands **expr**, **awk**, **sed**, why use REXX?

Precisely! The long history of Unix development has led to a multiplicity of partially redundant tools, each with idiosyncratic features and usage. In particular, the Unix PIPES and I/O redirection facilities have produced compact utilities (filters) that address specific tasks. These utilities often have diverging syntaxes, and are usually oriented toward users with programming backgrounds. The result has been a steep learning curve for non-technical users, which has been a factor in the slow marketplace acceptance of Unix.

REXX will help change this situation. Unlike a special-purpose filter or limited shell language, REXX provides the functionality required for the most demanding system control applications, yet is well suited as a development language for low-volume applications. In spite of its power, REXX's simplicity and compactness provide a very low learning curve. Further, many business-oriented data processing professionals are already familiar with the language, which will ease their transition to Unix-based platforms.

REXX can serve as a unifying influence over the many Unix variants, serving as a common command language to eliminate confusion over the many existing Unix shell languages. Applications which in the past required familiarity with one or more shell languages, as well as one or more filters (such as **awk, nawk,** or **perl**), can be implemented entirely in REXX; and with its ease of learning and use, REXX can hasten marketplace acceptance of Unix as a tool for end-users.

Invoking REXX programs

In the CMS environment, the presence of a comment clause as the first line of the program allows the operating system to recognize a REXX program. Most Unix systems have a similar (but more general) mechanism for associating a program with a language processor. This allows REXX programs to be executed by typing their filename at a shell command prompt, similar to CMS. **Implicit execution** is enabled by including a line identifying the fully qualified filename of the REXX interpreter as the first source line of the program. For example, with the REXX interpreter located in **/usr/local/bin/rxx**, the identifier would be:

```
#!/usr/local/bin/rxx
```

In addition, the program must be marked **executable** by the Unix **chmod** command.

For Unix systems which do not support implicit execution, an **explicit execution** facility is provided. The REXX interpreter is simply invoked directly, with the program name as an argument. For example:

```
rxx somename
```

would interpret and execute the REXX program **somename**. Of course, installation managers who wish to provide end-user functions via REXX programs without requiring the above syntax could easily write a trivial shell script to issue the **rxx** command.

The execution of a uni-REXX program running at a terminal may be halted by the user pressing **CTRL-C** or **DEL**. This sends a Unix **QUIT** signal to the program, causing it to terminate or to raise the **HALT** condition (if **SIGNAL** or **CALL ON HALT** is in effect).

Issuing Unix commands

As in CMS, a major use of REXX programs under Unix is to build and execute host subcommands. Unix commands can be issued from uni-REXX programs in several ways:

- By embedding a command clause in a uni-REXX program. Any clause which is not an instruction, label, or assignment is passed to Unix for execution. In CMS, many commands support a **STACK** option which directs command output to the stack, where it can be accessed by the REXX program. Since Unix commands do not support such operands, other means must be used to capture command output.

- By specifying the Unix command as the argument of an **ADDRESS UNIX** instruction. This has the same result as using a command clause.

- By using the **POPEN** built-in function (a uni-REXX language extension). The Unix command string is given as the function argument. Command output sent to **STDOUT** is redirected to the uni-REXX external data queue (program stack). This provides similar functionality to **STACK** operands on various CMS commands, but is more general and avoids the need to explicitly redirect command output to a file for further REXX processing.

Language contents

uni-REXX includes all instructions and built-in functions defined in IBM's SAA Procedures Language specification. In addition, extensions have been added to this base. These features are present in other versions of REXX, and are present in uni-REXX for compatibility:

UPPER	Instruction to convert variables to uppercase.
FIND()	Search a string of words.
INDEX()	Search a string.
JUSTIFY()	Pad a string of words.
USERID()	Return the logon userid.

To improve the REXX-Unix interface, a number of built-in functions were added, which implement common C library calls:

CHDIR()   Change current working directory.

CUSERID()   Return logon userid.

GETCWD()   Obtain current working directory.

GETENV()   Obtain value of environment variables.

LOWER()   Convert a string to lowercase. Useful to convert subcommands, because Unix command names are case-sensitive.

POPEN()   Execute a Unix command and redirect its output to the external data queue.

PUTENV()   Set value of environment variables.

External functions

External function calls are supported by uni-REXX. The function routines themselves are REXX programs residing in appropriately named disk files (i.e., `function.rex`). uni-REXX searches for the function on disk according to an order defined by the setting of Unix shell **environment variables**. The search order is:

1. Current working directory
2. Path specified by the **REXXPATH** environment variable
3. Path specified by the **PATH** variable

uni-REXX input and output

The most implementation-specific area of any language is input and output. The REXX implementation for Unix was no exception. Because of the character orientation of the Unix file system and I/O library calls, the record-oriented I/O of CMS REXX was discarded in favor of the character-oriented functions defined in Cowlishaw's book.

Unix system shell programs normally maintain default character input and output stream files, known as **stdin** and **stdout**. The uni-REXX I/O functions are set up by default to process these standard files. These functions also support the Unix **pipe** mechanism. A pipe is a means of transferring character input and/or output from one program to another program directly, without using intermediate disk files.

The uni-REXX I/O functions are:

CHARIN()   Read characters from an input stream.

CHAROUT()   Write characters to an output stream.

CHARS()   Return the number of characters remaining unread in an input stream.

LINEIN()	Read a line from an input stream.
LINEOUT()	Write a line to an output stream.
LINES()	Return the number of complete unread lines in an input stream.

The external data queue (the program stack, in CMS) is not a part of the Unix environment. This facility is implemented within uni-REXX, and accessed by the following REXX language elements:

PARSE PULL	Instruction obtains a single line from the external data queue. If the queue is empty, it obtains a line from the default character input stream.
PULL	Instruction obtains a line from the external data queue or default input stream, translating it to uppercase.
PUSH	Instruction adds a line to the top of the external data queue.
QUEUE	Instruction adds a line to the end of the external data queue.
POPEN()	Uni-REXX implementation-specific function provides an interface between Unix host commands and the external data queue.
QUEUED()	Function returns the number of unread lines on the external data queue.

Programming interfaces

uni-REXX provides programming language interface entry points to allow embedding REXX into application systems for macro processing. These interfaces were patterned after those in IBM's TSO/E REXX.

IRXJCL	Interface module to execute a uni-REXX program from within a C program
IRXSUBCM	Interface module to establish a subcommand environment to process commands issued from a uni-REXX program
IRXSTK	Interface module to manipulate entries on the external data queue from within a C program
IRXEXCOM	Interface module for sharing variables between uni-REXX and C language programs

Interpreter implementation

uni-REXX was written in the C language, to ensure portability. Use of Unix system library calls within the program code was refined through experience. In the course of porting to over 20 Unix implementations, the commonalities in Unix libraries were derived empirically! When required, Unix library functions were rewritten to provide consistency across platforms.

The language processor is implemented as a **pseudo-compiler**. Thus, while uni-REXX appears to the user as an interpreter, in reality program execution is a two-step process. First, the entire program source is processed into internal code, and errors are trapped. Then the semi-compiled code is executed. This allows uni-REXX programs to gain processing efficiencies, while retaining the single-step execution and debugging advantages of the interpretive programming style. For example, statements contained within loops are parsed once, rather than each time executed. Further, the structure of the internal code that is being interpreted each time through the loop has been optimized to improve execution speed. For typical application development use, this technology can easily improve the efficiency of the language by a factor of three or more.

Another example of improved efficiency in execution time that this technology yields is in handling of numeric data values. Numbers are stored in the internal code as floating-point or integer data types rather than character. Results are retained as numeric values until they are actually needed in character form. At execution time, these mechanisms (combined with those mentioned above) yield an order of magnitude improvement in execution speed.

Another benefit of this two-pass design is the ability to save the semi-compiled form. uni-REXX programs can be distributed in non-modifiable and secure form, to prevent users from tampering with sensitive applications.

Planned enhancements

Plans for uni-REXX product enhancements include:

External function packages	To allow external functions to be written in C.
Additional programming interfaces	To provide additional compatibility with those provided in other operating environments.
REXX Language Level 4.00 features	The **STREAM** function, the **NOTREADY** condition, the **CALL ON** condition trap, and binary string handling.
Additional Unix specific built-in functions	Particularly in the area of interprocess communications (**SOCKETS, STREAMS**) and function packages for terminal communications.
Arbitrary-precision arithmetic	In a manner consistent with the SAA standard, while retaining the existing processing efficiencies where possible. The high-speed mathematics (which is limited to nine-digit accuracy) will continue to be available as an option.

Any additional features and language definitions resulting from ANSI standards for the REXX language will also be added.

28

REXX for the VAX

By Anthony S. Johnson

INTRODUCTION

The family of VAX computers built by Digital Equipment Corporation includes many different models, ranging from small personal workstations up to the newest (30 MIPS) VAX 9000 mainframes. All VAX computers can run the VMS operating system, which provides the same environment on all models, including both a command line interface (Digital Command Language, or DCL) and a graphical user interface (DECwindows), as well as a comprehensive set of system libraries and many utility programs. Application programs developed under VMS run identically on any VAX processor.

Within the university/research environment and elsewhere, VAX computers are extremely common, being used for applications ranging from real-time data acquisition to large CPU-intensive analysis tasks.

REXX was ported to the VAX as a research project to provide a simple method of developing user interfaces for physics analysis programs being written at the Stanford Linear Accelerator Center (SLAC). With REXX used as an intermediary between users and application programs, it was only necessary for applications to understand simple, low-level commands. REXX was used to translate high-level user commands into commands understood by the application, allowing a flexible, user-friendly interface to be built. Using REXX also allowed the user interface to be uniform across several platforms, and provided a mechanism for users to customize the interface by writing REXX macros.

The REXX interpreter used was written by Charles Daney for the IBM PC (described in the chapter "REXX for PC-DOS and MS-DOS"). The C program which comprises the REXX interpreter was ported, by its author, to run under the VMS operating system on the VAX.

The successful application of REXX to the task of simplifying user interfaces for VAX applications naturally led to interest in applying the power of REXX to other areas, in particular using REXX as an alternative to the native VAX DCL command file interpreter. This chapter describes in detail a VMS-REXX interface designed to satisfy this interest. The interface again uses the C REXX interpreter mentioned above.

While DCL is well suited to writing fairly short command files, its lack of any but the most rudimentary structured language constructs and parsing tools often makes it unwieldy for more complex tasks. VMS users are thus normally forced to use high-level, compiled languages for these tasks, with their inherent longer program development times.

REXX, with its rich structured language syntax, wide range of parsing tools, and ease of program development, provides a useful complement to DCL command files. Its use can greatly speed development of programs which are too complex to be conveniently written directly in DCL, but which do not require the run-time efficiency of compiled programs.

INVOKING THE VMS-REXX INTERFACE

Once REXX is installed, a REXX program can be invoked from the VMS command prompt, using the **REXX** command. The syntax for the **REXX** command is:

```
$ REXX filespec arguments
```

where **filespec** specifies the file containing the REXX program and **arguments** are arguments to be passed to the program. The default file extension for the REXX program file is **REX**.

For example, to invoke a REXX program stored in file **MESSAGE.REX**, the command:

```
$ REXX MESSAGE "Hello from VMS"
```

can be used. In the REXX program, command line arguments are available using **PARSE ARG** in the normal way. The first occurrence of a space or slash (/) separates the file specification from the argument string; thus, unlike DCL command files, it is possible to specify VMS-type command qualifiers when invoking REXX programs. For example:

```
$ REXX MESSAGE/UPPERCASE "Hello from VMS"
```

It is, of course, also possible to use VMS command aliasing to remove the need for application end-users to know that the program is written in REXX.

```
$ MESSAGE :== REXX MESSAGE
$ MESSAGE/UPPERCASE "Hello from VMS"
```

From within a REXX program, control can be returned to VMS using the REXX **EXIT** statement:

```
EXIT
```

or:

```
EXIT returncode
```

The return code, if specified, is returned to VMS, and is thus interpreted by the operating system as a VMS completion code. If no return code is specified, then **SYSTEM-S-NORMAL** is returned to VMS.

A trivial example of a REXX program for VMS, illustrating many of the above points, follows:

```
/* MESSAGE.REX */
   case = 0                          /* Default if no option specified */
   parse arg arguments
   do while substr(arguments, 1, 1) = '/'      /* Extract options */
      parse var arguments '/'options arguments
      do until options = ' '
         parse upper var options option'/'options
         select
            when abbrev('MIXEDCASE', option, 1) then case = 0
            when abbrev('UPPERCASE', option, 1) then case = 1
            otherwise
            say 'Unrecognized option'
            exit 4
         end
      end
   end
   if case = 1 then upper arguments
   say arguments
   exit
```

ADDRESSING COMMANDS TO VMS FROM REXX PROGRAMS

From within a REXX program, any VMS command can be issued by using the REXX **ADDRESS** mechanism:

```
address vms "TYPE" message
```

At the start of the program, VMS will be the default addressing environment, so unless this is explicitly changed, VMS commands can be issued without the explicit addressing mechanism:

```
"TYPE" message
```

After completion of each command sent to VMS, three REXX variables are assigned values that depend on the completion status of the VMS command. These are:

RC   Return code

>   *-3*   Unrecognized VMS command
>   *0*   Success
>   *16*   Failure

$Status   Complete VMS completion code

$Severity VMS severity code

>   *0*   Error
>   *1*   Success
>   *2*   Warning
>   *3*   Information
>   *4*   Fatal

These variables provide some redundancy, but the RC variable will be familiar to programmers used to REXX under other operating systems, while the $STATUS and $SEVERITY variables will be familiar to DCL programmers. Thus the last two lines of the example program given in the preceding section could be rewritten as:

```
address vms "WRITE SYS$OUTPUT" arguments
exit $status
```

ACCESSING THE REXX STACK FROM VMS

To enable useful programs to be written, a method to transfer data between VMS and REXX is clearly required. The natural method from the perspective of the REXX programmer is to use the REXX stack. Almost all VMS commands allow output to be directed to an arbitrary file using some qualifier (usually /OUTPUT). The VMS-REXX interface reconciles these two interfaces by providing logical names LIFO and FIFO, which allow output from VMS commands to be written directly to the REXX stack. Output sent to LIFO is placed on the top of the stack, while output sent to FIFO is placed on the bottom of the stack.

The following commands illustrate the use of the stack from VMS:

```
address vms "TYPE/OUTPUT=FIFO" filespec
address vms "DIRECTORY/OUTPUT=LIFO/NOHEAD/NOTRAIL"
```

Similarly, VMS commands can read directly from the top or bottom of the stack, using the logical names READFIFO and READLIFO:

```
address vms "LINK PROGRAM+READFIFO/OPT"
```

When there is no more input left on the stack, reading from READFIFO or READLIFO will result in an end-of-file being read. Care should be taken only to write to LIFO and FIFO and only to read from READLIFO and READFIFO. No VMS command should be issued that would attempt to read and write the stack simultaneously, as unpredictable results will ensue.

ACCESS TO VMS ENVIRONMENT INFORMATION FROM REXX

An ideal implementation of REXX for VMS would make available a large number of REXX-callable functions for accessing information about the environment. In the current implementation a slightly less elegant (but much easier to implement) methodology was adopted.

Similar to the method used to stack output from VMS commands, the VMS WRITE command can be used to place information from VMS symbols or from VMS lexical functions onto the stack. Channels LIFO and FIFO are opened by the VMS-REXX interface for this purpose. Two examples follow:

```
address vms 'WRITE LIFO MY_SYMBOL'
address vms 'WRITE FIFO F$MODE()'
```

AN EXAMPLE REXX PROGRAM FOR VMS

This section shows a complete example of a REXX program for VMS. This program traverses the directory structure below the current directory, producing a map of the directory structure together with optional information on the disk space used in each directory. Most mechanisms for interacting with VMS are illustrated.

```
/* TREE.REX */
/*
    TREE is a REXX program for VMS to show the directory structure below
    a certain point.

    REXX TREE[/qualifiers] [root-directory]
```

```
     If the root directory is not specified, then the directories below
     the current directory are given.

Qualifiers:

     /SIZE    Include the size and number of files in each directory
     /HELP    Print this message
*/
/* Defaults if no qualifiers specified */
   help = 0                                        /* Don't give help */
   size = 0                                /* Don't give size of files */
   parse arg arguments
   do while substr(arguments, 1, 1) = '/'       /* Extract options */
      parse var arguments '/'options arguments
      do until options = ' '
         parse upper var options option'/'options
         select
            when abbrev('HELP', option, 1) then help = 1
            when abbrev('SIZE', option, 1) then size = 1
            otherwise
            say 'Unrecognized option' option
            exit 4
         end
      end
   end
   if help then do i = 1 to 1000
      line = sourceline(i)
      say line
      if line = '*/' then exit
   end
   if arguments <> '' then do
      'WRITE LIFO F$ENVIRONMENT("DEFAULT")'
      pull original_directory
      'SET DEFAULT' arguments
      if rc <> 0 then exit $status
   end
   'SET MESS/NOTEXT/NOID/NOSEV/NOFAC' /* Turn off VMS error messages */
   call SEARCH(1)                          /* Scan directory tree */
   'SET MESS/TEXT/ID/SEV/FAC'   /* Turn back on VMS error messages */
   if arguments <> '' then 'SET DEFAULT' original_directory
   exit
SEARCH: procedure expose size
   arg nest offset
   next = ''
   do until next = ''
      actdir = next
      'WRITE LIFO F$SEARCH("*.DIR", 'Nest')' /* Next subdirectory */
      pull . ']' next '.DIR'
      if actdir = '' then iterate
      'SET DEFAULT [.'Actdir']'          /* Go to next sub-directory */
      if size then do
         'DIRECTORY/TOTAL/NOHEAD/SIZE=ALL/OUTPUT=LIFO'
         if rc = 0 then parse pull result
         else result = 'Contains no files'
         actdir = actdir '('result')'
      end
```

```
    say offset'|'
    if next = '' then do
       say offset'\->'actdir
       call search(nest+1 offset'    ')
    end
    else do
       say offset'+->'actdir
       call search(nest+1 offset'|    ')
    end
    'SET DEFAULT [-]'
end
return
```

IMPLEMENTATION DETAILS

The information provided in the preceeding sections is sufficient for successful use of REXX under VMS. This section offers additional information regarding the implementation of the VMS-REXX interface.

A difficulty in implementing the interface is that execution of VMS commands often involves running images which would normally run in the same area as the REXX image itself; in such cases, VMS commands and REXX cannot trivially coexist in the same process.

Perhaps the most obvious way to overcome this restriction would be to have the REXX image (invoked by the REXX command) spawn a sub-process in which to execute VMS commands. This would, however, suffer from the serious drawback that any commands which change the VMS environment would act *only* in the subprocess, and would have no effect on the process from which REXX was invoked. It would, for example, be impossible to write a REXX program to change the default directory.

Instead, a slightly different method was adopted, in which the REXX command spawns a sub-process in which a REXX server is run. The REXX server then executes the specified REXX program and returns VMS commands to the originating process for execution. Communication between the originating process and the REXX server is via mailboxes, allowing interchange of commands and completion codes, as well as stacked data. The relationship between the two processes is illustrated in figure 15.

When the REXX program exits, control returns to the user in the originating process, and the REXX server hibernates. If a subsequent REXX command is invoked from the same process, the REXX server is woken up and instructed to execute the new REXX program. This avoids the overhead of spawning a sub-process each time the REXX command is executed. The server is automatically terminated when the user logs out or after it has been inactive for a certain period of time.

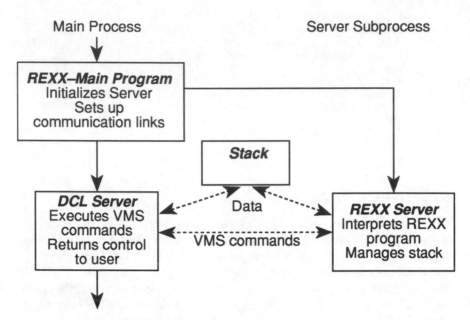

Figure 15. VMS-REXX Interfaces

The advantage of this interface is that it is almost transparent to the user, to whom it appears that the REXX program and the VMS commands invoked from it are being executed directly from the process.

Since the REXX program is being interpreted by a program written in C, the execution speed is considerably less than for the same program written in a compiled language. However, experience has shown that typical REXX applications do not run dramatically slower than the same application written as a DCL command file.

CONCLUSION

This implementation is not a formal product. However, it has validated the concept of REXX for the VAX, and shown that implementation problems are not insurmountable.

The ease of use of REXX, and the speed with which applications can be developed, make it suitable for a wide range of VMS applications.

29

The IBM Procedures Language 2/REXX Interpreter

By Rick McGuire

INTRODUCTION

The IBM Procedures Language 2/REXX Interpreter is IBM's Systems Application Architecture (SAA) Procedures Language offering for the OS/2 operating system. The implementation conforms to the SAA Procedures Language Level 2 definition.

This definition features:

- Native REXX input and output functions

- Support for Double Byte Character Set (DBCS) languages

- Full REXX language level 4.0 support

The REXX language level, however, represents only the end-user's view of using REXX. A REXX implementation usually includes programming interfaces that represent the application programmer's view of REXX. These interfaces allow programmers to use REXX as an application extension language or macro language.

This chapter focuses primarily on using these programming interfaces to add REXX support to a hypothetical OS/2 application. This is not an exhaustive treatment of the topic, but rather introduces basic concepts.

USING REXX CMD FILES

Implicit command invocation

REXX may be used as a replacement for CMD files invoked from an OS/2 command line. Create a REXX CMD file using your favorite text editor. The program must begin with a REXX comment on line one, starting in the first column. Invoke the program by typing the name of the program on the OS/2 command line. The OS/2 command shell, CMD.EXE, recognizes that the comment on the first line identifies a REXX command procedure and passes the program to the REXX interpreter. It's as simple as that.

Running under Presentation Manager

A REXX command procedure that uses SAY and PULL is inherently a linemode-oriented program. These are typically run in an OS/2 full-screen or windowed command session. However, it is possible to run a REXX command procedure as a Presentation Manager (PM) session as well.

To run REXX program under the Presentation Manager, use the PMREXX command. For example, if you wrote a simple program called FRED.CMD which you invoked as:

```
fred test.fil
```

You would use:

```
pmrexx fred test.fil
```

to run this under the Presentation Manager. The PMREXX shell provides a scrollable output area and an input area for interacting with the program. It also has menus to control execution of your REXX program.

Saving the tokenized image

The first time you run a REXX program, program source is scanned and reduced to a tokenized image. The interpreter directly executes this tokenized image. For better performance, the interpreter saves the tokenized image in the source file extended attributes. The next time you run this program, the saved image is retrieved and executed immediately. Whenever you change the program, the interpreter discards the existing image and creates a new one. Except for a possible delay the first time you run the program, this process is transparent.

USING REXX AS A MACRO LANGUAGE

Using REXX as a replacement for CMD files is fine, but REXX's real power comes from using it to extend other applications. Used this way, the interpreter is invoked by the application to execute an **application macro**. An application macro uses a command interface to communicate with the application and pass data back and forth. The OS/2 REXX interpreter provides programming interfaces that allow REXX to appear as an embedded part of an application.

Invoking REXX from an application

An application invokes the REXX interpreter by calling the **REXXSAA** dynalink library routine. When calling REXX, specify the name of the REXX program and the argument strings passed to the program. The call looks like this:

```
rc = REXXSAA(argc, argv,
        "MACRO.CMD",
        NULL, NULL,
        RXCOMMAND, NULL,
        &return, &retstr);
```

This example invokes REXX to run a program called **MACRO.CMD**. This example uses a file extension of CMD, but the extension may be anything. Choose an extension specific to your application. For example, an editor might use an extension of **ED** for editor macros.

If the program terminates with a REXX error, **REXXSAA** returns the REXX error code as a negative number. Values returned by the program with the REXX **RETURN** or **EXIT** instructions are available in the **retstr** parameter.

RXSTRINGS

Arguments passed to the REXX program and the result returned from a REXX program are in a special format called an **RXSTRING**. An RXSTRING is a REXX specific character string that eliminates two difficulties with ASCII-Z strings:

1. ASCII-Z strings are terminated by a null character. REXX character strings are not sensitive to data content, and as a result may contain the null character (X'00'). An RXSTRING uses a length field for the size of a character string. This allows programming interfaces to process any character strings that a REXX program can produce.

2. ASCII-Z strings are limited by the hardware architecture to 64
   kilobytes. The OS/2 REXX interpreter can process character
   strings up to 4 gigabytes long. RXSTRINGs can also contain
   strings longer than 64 kilobytes.

The RXSTRING data type has two parts: a string length and a pointer to the string data. Together, the length and pointer define the character string. The RXSTRING structure has the following definition:

```
typedef struct {
  ULONG strlength;                        /* Length of string */
  PCH   strptr;                           /* Far pointer to string */
} RXSTRING;
```

If the length field is greater than 64 kilobytes, **strptr** points to an area
that has been allocated via **DosAllocHuge**.

Many programs can use RXSTRINGs without knowing the actual
structure of the RXSTRING. The OS/2 Toolkit provides a series of
macros that simplifies the setting and retrieving of the string attributes.

Improving performance

When the REXXSAA routine is called, it searches for the REXX program on disk. The disk search can be avoided by loading the disk image
of the program into storage. This disk image may be passed directly to
the REXX interpreter. The **instore** parameter of the **REXXSAA** interface is used to pass the disk image.

```
rc = REXXSAA(argc, argv,
             "MACRO.CMD",
             instore, NULL,
             RXCOMMAND, NULL,
             &return, &retstr);
```

The *instore* parameter is an array of two RXSTRING structures. The
first RXSTRING is the disk image. This RXSTRING must be the image
of the disk file, including carriage return and end-of-file characters.
The second RXSTRING is the tokenized image of the program. If you
do not provide the tokenized image, the interpreter returns the image
to you when the REXX program completes. To avoid retokenization,
pass this image back to REXX on subsequent calls.

Subcommand handlers

Many applications, such as editors, support a macro processor. In these
applications, a macro language surrounds a set of application subcommands with program logic. The application processes the commands

from the macro as if the user had entered them directly. OS/2 CMD files are an example of this. The application is CMD.EXE, and the macro language is REXX.

Any application can use REXX as a macro processor. To use REXX, the application must tell the REXX interpreter how macro commands are to be processed.

When a REXX program processes a command, it passes the command to a subcommand handler as a character string. The subcommand handler interprets the command and sends a return code back to REXX. In a CMD file, the subcommand handler is the command shell program CMD.EXE. The return code sent back is the error code from the command or program.

Declaring subcommand handlers

Any application can process commands from REXX. The application must first create a named subcommand handler with the RxSubcomRegister programming interface.

A subcommand handler is a program entry point that REXX will call to process commands from a REXX macro. The subcommand handler is given a name, which is an **addressable environment**. The REXX programmer may direct commands to this named handler using the REXX ADDRESS instruction. A RxSubcomRegister call might look like this:

```
handler.scbname   = "EDITOR";            /* Name of the handler */
handler.scbdll_name = "";                /* Name of dynalink library */
handler.scbdll_proc = "";                /* Name of dynalink routine */
                                         /* Handler entry point */
handler.scbaddr = (PFN) EditorHandler;  /* Register the processor */
rc = RxSubcomRegister(&handler);
```

The application specifies the subcommand handler name, **Editor**, and the entry point that REXX will call to process commands, **(PFN) EditorHandler**. The two fields that begin with **scbdll** are used for another form of subcommand handler, which is discussed later.

The default address environment

If this hypothetical editor invokes a REXX macro, the macro must issue the REXX instruction:

```
address editor
```

Once the program issues this ADDRESS instruction, all program commands are passed to the EDITOR subcommand handler. The default target environment for commands is CMD, which passes the commands to the OS/2 command processor. Without the ADDRESS EDITOR, commands would still be passed to CMD.EXE. However, an application can

specify a different default subcommand handler with the **EnvName**
parameter of the REXXSAA interface.

```
rc = REXXSAA(argc, argv,
             "MACRO.CMD",
             NULL, "Editor",
             RXCOMMAND, NULL,
             &return, &retstr);
```

This parameter tells the interpreter to use the environment named
Editor as the default handler for subcommands. You need not issue
additional **ADDRESS** instructions.

Processing subcommands

When the REXX macro is executed, it can issue commands to the current **ADDRESS** environment. For example, if the macro contains the line:

```
'LOCATE /Fred/'
```

REXX calls the registered subcommand handler, passing the following
parameters:

```
SHORT APIENTRY EditorHandler(
       RXSTRING cmd, PUSHORT errorflag,
       PRXSTRING ReturnCode);
```

where **cmd** is an RXSTRING containing the command, **errorflag** is a
flag that controls how REXX raises **ERROR** or **FAILURE** conditions, and
ReturnCode is a character string return code. The **ReturnCode** is
assigned to REXX variable **RC**.

Returning RXSTRINGS

With many REXX programming interfaces, REXX calls a routine and
expects the routine to return an RXSTRING value. For example, the
ReturnCode string is assigned to the variable **RC**. There are two ways
to return an RXSTRING:

1. When the REXX interpreter calls the routine, it creates a default
   256-byte RXSTRING buffer. This is passed in the variable used to
   return the result. If the result length is 256 bytes or less, then you
   can copy the result into the buffer. The RXSTRING length must be
   set to the number of bytes returned.

   ```
   strcpy(RXSTRPTR(ReturnCode),"1"); /* Pass back return code of 1 */
   RXSTRLEN(ReturnCode) = strlen("1");        /* Set return length */
   ```

2. If it is necessary to return more than 256 bytes of data, a dynamically allocated RXSTRING may be returned. This string must be
   allocated with either **DosAllocSeg** or **DosAllocHuge**.

```
DosAllocSeg( retsize, (PSEL)&selTmp,0 );   /* Allocate a segment */
                                        /* Set the RXSTRING pointer */
RXSTRPTR(ReturnCode) = (PCH)MAKEP(selTmp,0);
                                        /* Copy over the data */
memcpy(RXSTRPTR(ReturnCode),return_value,retsize);
RXSTRLEN(ReturnCode) = retsize;            /* Set return length */
```

When a dynamically allocated string is returned, the REXX interpreter assumes responsibility for the storage. REXX issues a **DosFreeSeg** call to return the segment to OS/2.

Note that the return code value from a subcommand handler is a character string. It need not be a number, but if your application returns a numeric return code, you must format the number as a character string.

Errors and failures

In addition to the return code string, the subcommand processor can set an error or failure flag. These flags indicate whether the command was an **ERROR** or **FAILURE**. The **ERROR** indicator means that an error occurred in processing an individual command. This might mean that an invalid option was specified or that a file wasn't found. A **FAILURE** means that the command could not be processed. Unknown subcommands usually cause a **FAILURE** condition.

Setting the error flag to either **RXSUBCOM_ERROR** or **RXSUBCOM_FAIL-URE** can be used to trigger a **SIGNAL ERROR** or a **SIGNAL ON FAILURE** condition. These may also cause the instruction to be traced if either **TRACE ERRORS** or **TRACE FAILURE** has been turned on.

Subcommand handlers

Not all applications that accept subcommands fit the **host application with subcommand call back** model described above. Occasionally a REXX program may wish to send commands to an application that has not called REXX as a macro processor. An excellent example of this is the OS/2 Dialog Manager.

In the editor example, the **Editor** subcommand handler is an entry point within an already active program. When REXX has a subcommand to be processed, it passes control back to the original program. With the Dialog Manager, however, there is no existing program that can take control from REXX.

The Dialog Manager can still process subcommands. It creates a subcommand handler as a routine within a dynalink library file. You can declare a dynalink library resident subcommand handler with the **RxSubcomRegister** parameters not described earlier.

```
handler.scbname  = "Editor";            /* Name of the handler */
                                        /* Name of dynalink library */
```

```
handler.scbdll_name = "EDITOR";                    /* ..."EDITOR.DLL" */
                                       /* Name of dynalink routine */
handler.scbdll_proc = "EditorSubcommands";
                                       /* Handler entry point */
handler.scbaddr = (PFN)NULL;           /* No entry point for DLL */
                                       /* Register the processor */
rc = RxSubcomRegister(&handler);
```

This time you have declared that commands addressed to the **Editor** subcommand handler should go to the **EditorSubcommands** routine in dynalink library file **EDITOR.DLL**.

However, this example still requires the subcommand handler to be declared from a C program before a REXX program can use this subcommand handler.

Fortunately, a REXX programmer may use the **rxsubcom** OS/2 command to directly register a subcommand handler from REXX.

```
'rxsubcom register editor editor EditorSubcommands'
address editor
```

The command form closely follows the programming interface call shown above.

External functions

A subcommand handler is just one way of providing services to the REXX programmer. Subcommand processors, however, are best reserved for implementing entire subsystems that interact with REXX. If it is only desired to create a service that can be called from REXX, a better choice may be writing an external function or subroutine.

A programmer can create extensions to the REXX language with external functions. These external functions may be written in REXX or in a compiled language such as C. If they are written in REXX, the routines must exist in the current **PATH**. Just use the program name as if it were a built-in function. The external routine will be located automatically. Functions written in another language require a form of linkage.

Declaring functions

Before an external function written in C can be called, you must register it with the REXX interpreter. An application may register a function, or the REXX programmer may do it directly.

From an application:

Registering an external function is similar to registering subcommand handlers. You may create functions embedded within an **EXE** file or functions that are dynalink library calls. To create an embedded function, use the following **RxFunctionRegister** call:

```
return_code = RxFunctionRegister("Change",        /* Function name */
                  (PSZ)NULL,
                                  /* Function location */
                  (PSZ)change_function,
                                  /* Embedded routine */
                  RX_CALLENTRY);
```

This call declares a function named **Change** as an entry point within the current **EXE** file. The application writer may choose to extend the functions of an application with this type of embedded routine.

External functions may also be created as dynalink library routines. The same **RxFunctionRegister** routine is used to register these routines.

```
return_code = RxFunctionRegister("Change",        /* Function name */
                                  /* Dynalink name */
                  (PSZ)"EDITOR",
                                  /* Dynalink routine */
                  (PSZ)"EditorChange",
                                  /* Embedded routine */
                  RX_DYNALINK);
```

From REXX:

Dynalink library resident routines are usually declared from REXX programs. This is done using the **RxFuncAdd** REXX function. To register the external function shown above, the REXX programmer would code:

```
call RxFuncAdd "Change","Editor","EditorChange"
```

The **RxFuncAdd** parameters have the same meaning as the **RxFunctionRegister** interface parameters.

Functions that have been registered as dynalink library routines are available from all OS/2 sessions. You may wish to perform initial function registration during **STARTUP.CMD** processing. This is true for registered subcommand handlers too.

Processing parameters

When REXX calls external functions, it passes function arguments as an array of RXSTRINGs:

```
SHORT APIENTRY EditorChange(
        char * name,                /* Name of the function */
        short argc,                 /* Argument count */
        RXSTRING far * argv[],       /* Argument array */
```

```
        char far * queue,                        /* Current queue */
        RXSTRING far * retstr);                  /* Returned value */
```

The REXX language allows function arguments to be omitted. For example, you might call the **Change** function as:

```
x = change(input,output,,times)
```

You can test for an omitted argument with the **RXNULLSTRING** macro.

```
if (RXNULLSTRING(argv[2])) {                     /* Any third argument? */
   .
   .
   .
}
```

The **RXZEROLENSTRING** macro can test for a zero-length string (a REXX "").

```
if (RXZEROLENSTRING(argv[2])) {                  /* A null string? */
   .
   .
   .
}
```

Returning results

The function result is returned in the **retstr** RXSTRING. Like the subcommand return code, REXX provides a 256-byte buffer for returning a value. If this is not large enough for the result, a larger area can be allocated with **DosAllocSeg** or **DosAllocHuge**. If no result is returned, you must zero the **retstr** RXSTRING.

```
RXSTRPTR(retstr) = NULL;                         /* No return result */
```

If your function detects a processing error, it can pass the error back to REXX. REXX will raise error 40, **invalid call to routine**, if it receives a non-zero return code. Note that if an error is raised, you cannot return a result string.

AND MORE

You have now created an OS/2 application that uses REXX as a macro processor. This application can process subcommands from REXX and also provides some functions that make writing the macros easier.

In addition to the subcommand and function interfaces, there are other interfaces with which applications can interact with REXX. For example, exits are available for applications to control how REXX uses resources such as I/O. An interface, **RxVar**, can examine and manipulate REXX variables. Discussion of these interfaces is beyond the scope of this chapter, but sample programs which use these interfaces are available in the OS/2 Programmer's Toolkit.

30

IBM Procedures Language 400/REXX

By Rick McGuire

INTRODUCTION

The IBM Procedures Language 400/REXX Interpreter is IBM's Systems Application Architecture (SAA) Procedures Language offering for the OS/400 operating system. The implementation conforms to the SAA Procedures Language Level 2 definition, except for the native REXX input and output functions. This definition features:

- Support for Double Byte Character Set (DBCS) languages
- Full REXX language level 4.0 support

The REXX interpreter provides a powerful string processing language that is an alternative to the existing AS/400 CL (Control Language). The interpreter includes a set of programming interfaces that allow applications to use REXX as an extension or macro language.

This chapter introduces REXX on the AS/400. It is not a REXX language tutorial. It focuses on the basic facilities for using and exploiting AS/400 REXX.

INVOKING REXX

An AS/400 REXX program is created by entering source into a file object member. You may use any text editor, including the **Source Entry Utility (SEU)**. Give the created file member a source type of REXX to identify the member as a REXX program.

There are two ways to execute REXX programs:

1. With the STRREXPRC command
2. With a **Command Definition Object** (CDO) for the program

Using STRREXPRC

The STRREXPRC command executes a named REXX procedure. To use STRREXPRC, specify the name and location of the REXX program:

```
STRREXPRC SRCMBR(FRED) SRCFILE(MYLIB/QREXSRC)
```

The REXX interpreter will read source member FRED from file QREXS-RC in library MYLIB and run it as a REXX program.

An argument string can be passed to a REXX program with the STRREXPRC command PARM option:

```
STRREXPRC SRCMBR(FRED) SRCFILE(MYLIB/QREXSRC) PARM('PRINT')
```

The STRREXPRC command will pass the character string PRINT to the REXX program FRED. A program can access the PARM string with the REXX ARG instruction:

```
arg input              /* Assign the parm string to variable input */
```

Creating REXX Command Definition Objects

All commands on the AS/400 system have a **Command Definition Object** (CDO). The CDO identifies allowed parameters, parameter defaults, and the **Command Processing Program** (CPP) of the command. The Command Processing Program may be either a compiled language program or a REXX program.

A CDO is created for a REXX procedure with the CRTCMD command. When the CDO is created, *REXX is identified as the CPP. Multiple keyword parameters can be defined for REXX CPPs just as for other CL commands.

When you invoke a REXX program as a CL command, the command analyzer will process the parameters you specify. The analyzer passes a single argument string to the REXX CPP. This argument string is a combination of the specified parameters and the command default parameters.

For example, consider a command called **TRYREXX**, which accepts two parameters:

PGM   A fully qualified library name

PARM   A list of additional parameters to the program

TRYREXX can be invoked as:

```
TRYREXX FILE(TESTLIB/QREXSRC) PARM(HELLO 'GOOD MORNING' 123)
```

The CDO for **TRYREXX** would look like:

```
            CMD        PROMPT('Try REXX Command Objects')

            PARM       KWD(FILE) TYPE(QUAL1) MIN(1) +
                         PROMPT('File Name')

            PARM       KWD(PARM) TYPE(*CHAR) MIN(1) MAX(50) +
                         PROMPT('Parameters       (32 or less)')

QUAL1:      QUAL       TYPE(*NAME) LEN(10) EXPR(*YES)
            QUAL       TYPE(*NAME) LEN(10) DFT(*LIBL) SPCVAL(*LIBL) +
                         EXPR(*YES) PROMPT('Library name')
```

When you invoke **TRYREXX**:

```
TRYREXX FILE(QREXSRC) PARM(HELLO 'GOOD MORNING' 123)
```

Command parameters are examined and merged with any default parameters. The command analyzer passes the following character string to the REXX CPP:

```
FILE(*LIBL/QREXSRC) PARM(HELLO 'GOOD MORNING' 123)
```

Each parameter can be retrieved with the REXX **ARG** instruction:

```
arg 'FILE(' lib '/' file ')'
arg 'PARM(' parmlist ')'
```

Saving the tokenized image

The AS/400 interpreter, like the OS/2 REXX interpreter, tokenizes the REXX program the first time it is executed. The interpreter saves the tokenized image in the associated space of the database member. This image will be reused the next time the program is called. The tokenized image will be saved only when the member has a source type of **REXX**.

Calling **REXX** from an application

The REXX interpreter may also be called directly from an application. The **QREXX** program in the **QSYS** library is the program interface to the REXX interpreter. To run a REXX program with **QREXX**, you must specify the name of the program and the file and library where the program will be found.

```
QREXX ("FRED       ",                    /* Run REXX program FRED */
       "QREXSRC  MYLIB   ",              /* From my personal library */
  NULL, NULL, NULL, 0, NULL);
```

The name is specified as a 10-character field with the name left-justified. The filename and library name field is a 20-character field, with the file and library left-justified in each half (two 10-character sections).

An argument string may be passed to the REXX program. This argument string is a PL/I-style varying-length character string. A PL/I-style character string must have a two-byte length followed by the string data. This argument string is the third parameter of the QREXX routine.

```
/* Structure to pass varying-length string */
typedef struct name1 {
        short length;                    /* Length of string */
        char  string[256];               /* Actual string */
        } PARM;

PARM parm_str;                           /* Argument to QREXX */

  strcpy(parm_str.string,"PRINT");       /* Copy string data */
  parm_str.length = strlen("PRINT");     /* Move in the length */

  QREXX ("FRED       ",                  /* Run REXX program FRED */
         "QREXSRC  MYLIB   ",            /* from my personal library */
         &parm_str,                      /* with an argument string */
    NULL, NULL, 0, NULL);
```

ISSUING AS/400 COMMANDS

An AS/400 CL program consists of a series of AS/400 commands. These AS/400 commands may have constant values for parameters or may refer to CL program variables. The following command uses all constant values:

```
STRREXPRC SRCMBR(FRED) SRCFILE(*LIBL/QREXSRC)
```

The next example uses the contents of CL variable MEMBER for the SRCMBR parameter.

```
STRREXPRC SRCMBR(&MEMBER) SRCFILE(QREXSRC/*LIBL)
```

The & identifies the parameter value as a variable.

You can use variables in a REXX program by concatenating strings together:

```
'STRREXPRC SRCMBR(' member ') SRCFILE(*LIBL/QREXSRC)'
```

Concatenating variables has disadvantages:

1. The program can be more difficult to write: CL commands can have many keyword parameters.
2. REXX uses many punctuation characters as operators; you must therefore code any special characters such as (and * as literal strings.
3. Some parameters of CL commands are **RTNVAL(*YES)** parameters. A called command can pass data back to the calling CL program with **RTNVAL(*YES)** parameters. In the following example, the **RTVJOBA** command retrieves the USER job attribute and places it in the CL variable **USERID**:

   ```
   RTVJOBA USER(&USERID)
   ```

Returning a value is not possible with a concatenated string.

Pseudo-CL variables

Fortunately, the REXX interpreter on the AS/400 has special support for CL commands. You can use also variable values with CL commands from REXX:

```
'STRREXPRC SRCMBR(&MEMBER) SRCFILE(*LIBL/QREXSRC)'
```

When you issue the **STRREXPRC** command, the value of the REXX variable **MEMBER** is used for the **SRCMBR** parameter.

RTNVAL(*YES) parameters may also be used. You can use the **RTVJOBA** command to query information about your current job:

```
'RTVJOBA USER(&USERID)'
```

The RTVJOBA command places the current **USER** job attribute in the REXX variable **USERID**. The **&** identifies a variable parameter. With many CL commands, you can move the command to a REXX program by placing quotes around the command.

Return codes

CL commands do not have return codes like commands on other systems. If a CL command detects an error, it issues an escape message to the calling program. The calling program must monitor for escape messages if it wishes to process errors.

When REXX issues a CL command, it monitors for all escape messages. If the command completes without an error, REXX variable **RC** is set to 0. If REXX receives an escape message, variable **RC** is set to the escape message ID. For example, the following command ends with return code CPF2CF2 if the REXX program FRED does not exist:

```
'STRREXPRC SRCMBR(FRED) SRCFILE(*LIBL/QREXSRC)'
```

CREATING COMMAND ENVIRONMENTS

Commands placed within a REXX program are processed by the OS/400 operating system. The OS/400 operating system is a named command environment called COMMAND. You may create your own named command environments to which REXX can send commands. The REXX ADDRESS instruction may be used to direct commands to your new command environment.

Creating a command environment

A named command environment is a program object that REXX invokes when it has a command to process. The command environment is identified using the REXX ADDRESS instruction. The following example makes program object EDITOR the current target for commands:

```
address '*LIBL/EDITOR'
```

Once you issue this ADDRESS instruction, a command such as:

```
'LOCATE /123/'
```

in a REXX program will be passed to the EDITOR program object.

Processing subcommands

When REXX calls a command environment, it passes the following information:

1. The command to be processed. The command is a character string in **SHORT_VARSTRING** format. A SHORT_VARSTRING is a PL/I-style varying-length character string.

2. The return code string. The return code string will be assigned to the REXX variable RC. The return code is a buffer in SHORT_VARSTRING format. REXX allocates 500 bytes for the return code buffer and sets it to an initial value of 0. Your command environment program can place a different return code in this buffer and set the buffer length to the return code length. If the command completes without error, the 0 is already set up. The return code value is a character string, so numeric return codes must be formatted as character strings.

3. A two-byte integer error flag. The error flag is a trigger for either a

FAILURE or **ERROR** condition. The following error codes may be returned:

0   The command completed successfully. No action is taken by REXX.

1   A command **ERROR** occurred. This code should be returned for invalid command inputs. REXX will raise the **ERROR** condition if a **SIGNAL ON ERROR** or **CALL ON ERROR** instruction has been issued.

2   A command **FAILURE** occurred. This code should be returned for unknown commands or other global command failures. REXX will raise the **FAILURE** condition if **SIGNAL ON FAILURE** or **CALL ON FAILURE** has been issued.

EXTERNAL FUNCTIONS

You can also extend the REXX language by creating external functions and subroutines. These external functions and subroutines may be called from your REXX program as if they were built-in functions. These external routines may be written in REXX or in a compiled language such as C.

Creating an external function

An external routine written in C is a program object in the current library list. You invoke the routine by using the program name as a function:

```
a = myfunc('ABC')
```

You may also invoke it with the REXX call instruction:

```
call myfunc 'ABC'
```

Processing function parameters

When you call an external function, REXX passes it a list of string arguments. Up to 20 argument strings may be passed on a single call. The following example processes the parameters passed to an external routine written in C:

```
typedef struct {                       /* RXSTRING descriptor */
   char             *rxstrptr;          /* Pointer to string */
   unsigned long    rxstrlen            /* Length of the string */
} RXSTRING;

void main(argc, argv)
int argc;                               /* Number of parameters, should */
```

```
                                              /* be five (5) */
   char *argv[];                              /* Parameter array */

   {
      /* Local variables */
      RXSTRING *args;                         /* The argument array */
      short int numargs;                /* Number of string arguments */
      short int func_sub;               /* Function/subroutine flag */
      short int *errflag;                     /* Success/failure flag */

      /* Some executable code to get parameters into local variables */

      args = (RXSTRING *) argv[1];            /* Args is 1st parm, */
                                        /* referenced as an array of */
                                        /* RXSTRINGs.  An individual */
                                              /* argument is args[i]. */
      numargs = (int) *argv[2];         /* Number of arguments is */
                                              /* second parameter */
      func_sub = (int) *argv[3];        /* Function/Error flag is */
                                              /* third parameter */
      errflag = (int *) argv[4];        /* Error flag is fourth */
                                        /* parameter, referenced in */
                                        /* the program by *errflag */
```

The parameters follow:

args   is a pointer to an array of RXSTRINGs. An RXSTRING is a
             structure which describes a REXX character string. The
             RXSTRING structure has a pointer to a character string followed
             by a 4-byte binary value representing the string length. A sample
             RXSTRING structure declaration appears at the beginning of the
             example.

             Three types of argument string may be passed in this structure:

             ▪ If the pointer **rxstrptr** is non-null and the length **rxstrlen** is
               also non-zero, the RXSTRING is an actual character string
               rxstrlen characters long.

             ▪ If **rxstrptr** is non-null and **rxstrlen** is zero, this argument is
               a REXX null string. For example:

                   x = myfunc(1,'',3) /* Pass a null string for second arg */

             ▪ If **rxstrptr** is null, this is an **omitted** parameter. A parameter
               is omitted by coding an extra comma to skip over the argument.
               For example, the second parameter in the following function
               call has been omitted:

                   x = myfunc(1,,3)   /* Use default for second arg */

numargs   is a two-byte integer count of the RXSTRINGs in the **args** array.

func_sub   is a two-byte integer flag. **func_sub** identifies how the routine
             was invoked. If **func_sub** is **1**, the routine was invoked using the
             REXX **CALL** instruction:

                   call myfunc 'abc'

The routine does not need to return a result if you invoke it with the **CALL** instruction.

If **func_sub** is 2, the routine was invoked as a function call:

```
x = myfunc('abc')
```

The routine must return a result if it is invoked as a function.

errflag   is a two-byte integer return code. **errflag** indicates the success or failure of the routine. If **0** is returned in **errflag**, the routine has completed successfully and a value may have been returned. If a non-zero return code is returned, REXX will raise error 40, **Incorrect call to routine** for the routine. A return string cannot be returned if an error is raised.

Returning function results

A character string result may be returned to REXX from the external routine. The **QREXVAR** program in the **QSYS** library is used to return the result.

```
#define SHVEXTFN 9
typedef struct shvnode            /* QREXVAR interface block */
  {
    struct shvnode *shvnext;    /* Pointer to next request block */
    RXSTRING       shvname;       /* Pointer to variable name */
    RXSTRING       shvvalue;      /* Pointer to value buffer */
    unsigned char  shvcode;       /* Individual function code */
    unsigned char  shvret;     /* Individual return code flags */
  } SHVBLOCK;
  :

SHVBLOCK retstr;                  /* Return block for the result */
  :

  retstr.shvnode = NULL;                    /* Only one request */
                                 /* Point to the return value */
  retstr.shvvalue.rxstrptr = "return string";
                                 /* and set the correct length */
  retstr.shvvalue.rxstrptr = sizeof("return string");
  retstr.shvcode = SHVEXTFN;     /* Set external function result */

  /* Now use QREXVAR to pass back the actual return value */

  QREXVAR(retstr,&return_code);
  :
```

The value returned with **QREXVAR** is available inline if the routine was called as a function. If it was invoked with the REXX **CALL** instruction, the value is available in the REXX variable **RESULT**.

AND YET MORE

This chapter has described some interfaces to the REXX interpreter which are available on the AS/400. You have seen how an application can process subcommands from REXX and also provide some functions that make writing REXX programs easier.

Other interfaces allow applications to interface with REXX more fully. For example:

- Exits for the application to control how REXX uses resources such as I/O

- The QREXVAR routine to examine and manipulate REXX variables

Discussion of these interfaces is beyond the scope of this chapter. Sample programs are provided in the *Application System / 400 Procedures Language 400 / REXX Programmer's Guide*.

Add-On Products

Numerous products use REXX as a macro language, combining specific application power with REXX programming capabilities. Other products enhance REXX by providing interfaces to functions such as graphics, database, and interrupt handling. This section describes a few REXX-exploiting or REXX-enhancing products.

The following products are available from IBM:

- GDDM-REXX
- CMS Pipelines
- RXSQL
- REXXIUCV

DB/REXX is available from

VM Systems Group
1604 Spring Hill Road
Vienna, VA 22182
(703) 506-0500

REXXTERM is available from

Quercus Systems
19567 Dorchester Drive
Saratoga, CA 95070
(408) 257-3697

GDDM-REXX: Full-Screen Text, Image, and Graphics from REXX

By Gerald R. Hogsett

WHAT IS GDDM-REXX?

GDDM-REXX, IBM product number 5664-336, provides an interface between REXX programs and the IBM programs which provide presentation services, namely **GDDM**, the **Graphical Data Display Manager**. GDDM-REXX provides the linkage that makes all application programming interface calls provided by GDDM for compiled high-level languages also available to REXX programs.

The example below illustrates use of GDDM from within a simple REXX program. The program draws a picture of the phase of the moon on the day it is run. Sample output is shown in the next figure. The program demonstrates how easy it is to use GDDM from within REXX. GDDM calls are coded using REXX variables or literals as parameters. A CMS subcommand environment must be established to receive calls; the GDDMREXX INIT and ADDRESS GDDM statements accomplish this. To reference a variable within a GDDM call, the name of the variable is preceded by a period. This tells GDDM-REXX that the value to be used is to be found in, or returned to, a variable of the indicated name. Certain length information can be deduced by GDDM-REXX. In the GSCHAR call, for example, the third parameter (which specifies the length of the string) can be determined by inspection of the REXX variable itself. Thus, the length parameter is coded as a period (a placeholder).

```
/* REXX EXEC to draw phases of the moon */
address command 'GDDMREXX INIT'              /* Initialize GDDM-REXX */
address gddm                      /* Tell REXX to pass calls to GDDM */
period = 29.5306
quarter = period/4
day = date('C')-31421
tdate = date()
phase = day//period
rightrad = 20
leftrad = 20
inc = leftrad/(period/4)
select
   when phase<quarter then do
      leftrad=-(leftrad-(phase*inc))
      text='first quarter'
   end
   when phase<quarter*2 then do
      leftrad=((phase-quarter)*inc)
      text='second quarter'
   end
   when phase<quarter*3 then do
      rightrad=rightrad-((phase-quarter*2)*inc)
      text='third quarter'
   end
   otherwise
   rightrad=-((phase-quarter*3)*inc)
   text='fourth quarter'
end
'GSUWIN 0 100 0 100'       /* Define user coordinates for screen */
'GSCOL 7'                     /* Set color to white for the MOON */
'GSMOVE 50 30'                /* Move to middle x and 30 up on y */
'GSAREA 1'                    /* Begin a filled area (solid fill) */
'GSELPS 20 .rightrad 90 50 70'              /* Draw two ellipses */
'GSELPS 20 .leftrad 90 50 30'                  /* (second ellipse) */
'GSENDA'                             /* Close the fill area */
'GSCOL 5'                            /* Color to turquoise */
'GSCHAR 35 15 . .text'      /* Write out the phase description */
'GSCHAR 40 10 . .tdate'                       /* ..and the date */
'GSLSS 2 ADMUWKSF 194'       /* Load a font (symbol set) ... */
'GSCS 194'                         /* ..and start using it. */
'GSCB 13 8'                        /* Set character box size */
'GSCM 3'                           /* Character mode to vectors */
'GSCHAR 15 80 . "Moon Phase"'                /* title of picture */
'ASREAD . . .'              /* Write picture, and wait for user */
address command 'GDDMREXX TERM'/* Remove GDDMREXX-REXX connection */
exit
```

Although this example does not use arrays of values, they can be used as follows. GDDM requires one- or two-dimensional arrays of values for certain calls. In compiled language usages of GDDM (e.g.,

Moon Phase

first quarter
23 Aug 1990

Figure 16. Output from the Moon Phase program example

FORTRAN), these arrays are indexed by numbers beginning at 1. REXX has no formal notion of arrays; however, GDDM-REXX uses the common convention of using REXX stemmed variables, with all elements of the compound name beyond the stem being numeric. For example, to define a set of alphanumeric fields on a screen, GDDM provides the ASDFMT (define format) call. The first two parameters establish the number of fields to be defined and the number of attributes to be specified for each. The third parameter is a two-dimensional array with each field as a row and the attributes as the columns.

```
/* Use of arrays with GDDM-REXX */
nf = 3                           /* Number of fields to be defined */
na = 6                           /* Number of attributes per field */
flds. = 0                 /* Default all array elements to zero */

do i = 1 to 3
   flds.i.1 = i                              /* Field numbers 1..3 */
   flds.i.2 = 2*i                  /* Fields at screen rows 2, 4, 6 */
   flds.i.3 = 10                         /* All at column 10 */
   flds.i.4 = 1                    /* All fields are 1 row high */
   flds.i.5 = 30           /* All fields are 30 characters wide */
   end

'ASDFMT .nf .na .flds.'            /* Name the field array stem */
```

An alternative method of supplying literal arrays (i.e., when GDDM will not attempt to return data to REXX):

```
'ASDFMT 3 6 ((1 2 10 1 30 0)(2 4 10 1 30 0)(3 6 10 1 30 0))'
```

Since the shape of the array can be deduced by inspection of the parenthesis pattern, the dimensions can be implied:

```
'ASDFMT . . ((1 2 10 1 30 0)(2 4 10 1 30 0)(3 6 10 1 30 0))'
```

SAMPLE PROGRAMS PROVIDED WITH GDDM-REXX

GDDM-REXX provides sample programs. These are fully commented, and illustrate many techniques that may be useful when developing applications.

ERXMODEL is an EXEC intended to be a sample shell for users to expand for their own use. As supplied, it uses simple alphanumeric and graphic calls.

ERXMENU uses GDDM base graphics calls and procedural alphanumeric calls to build a restaurant menu.

ERXCHART illustrates how to call the **Interactive Chart Utility** (part of the GDDM **Presentation Graphics Facility**) from within an application.

ERXOPWIN illustrates use of GDDM windows.

ERXORDER illustrates use of mapped alphanumerics.

It is helpful for users to study and run these samples, which can then be altered to explore the special features of GDDM and GDDM-REXX.

In addition to the sample programs, GDDM-REXX provides two utilities that have proved extremely useful for beginning GDDM users.

The first utility is **ERXPROTO**. Given the name of a GDDM call, it describes the parameters in GDDM-REXX format.

This program may be invoked in CMS as a command, or in XEDIT (where it will add the call to the file being edited), or in **ERXTRY** (see below).

The second utility is **ERXTRY**. This allows users to interactively execute GDDM and/or REXX calls and see what they do. Calls are interpreted, and results are displayed on the user's screen. A logging facility writes lines to a file as they are interpreted. The resulting file can be run as a complete GDDM-REXX EXEC.

SUMMARY

GDDM-REXX provides the REXX programmer with a full set of text, image, and graphics capabilities. Additional features, not mentioned above, include:

- Double-byte character set (DBCS) support for Kanji and Hangeul
- Support for the Graphical Kernel System (GKS) feature of GDDM
- Trace facilities

These features are described in the *GDDM-REXX Guide* (SC33-0478) or in one of the several GDDM documents (for example, the *GDDM Guide for Users*, SC33-0327).

REXXIUCV

By Rainer F. Hauser

INTRODUCTION

The ability to communicate between programs adds a dimension to sequential programming languages such as REXX: the dimension of **concurrency** or **parallelism**. Concurrency opens a rich world of possibilities, but also a wide range of possible mistakes not known in traditional sequential programming.

Concurrency allows implementation of applications distributed among several processes. Such applications, implemented as sets of concurrent programs, must synchronize to share or exchange data. In other words, they need a **communications facility**.

IUCV, the Inter-User Communications Vehicle, as defined in IBM's VM operating system, is such a facility. It allows message exchange between programs, which may be running in one or more virtual machines in a VM system. Services within the VM Control Program (CP) also use IUCV to communicate with users.

REXXIUCV makes IUCV services under the VM Conversational Monitoring System (CMS) accessible to REXX programmers. It allows applications which involve multiple virtual machines to be implemented in REXX. All of REXX's advantages can be exploited for prototyping, implementing, and testing applications without requiring the use of low-level programming for accessing IUCV.

The next section introduces IUCV. It is followed by three sections on the history, design, and use of REXXIUCV. Two further sections provide more insight into programming with REXXIUCV by means of a small but complete example and a description of possible applications. A short summary closes the chapter.

IUCV AS A COMMUNICATIONS FACILITY

IUCV is a communications medium available to virtual machines for message exchange among themselves and with certain CP facilities. Communication offered by IUCV can be modeled as a set of message queues through which virtual machines exchange data.

IUCV, being a **connection-oriented** service, requires that two virtual machines first establish a connection, called an IUCV **path**, before they can communicate. They will eventually close the connection after completion of the data exchange. Accordingly, an IUCV conversation consists of a connection establishment phase, a data phase, and a termination phase.

During connection establishment, a pair of message queues between the two communication partners is created and parameters for the path are negotiated, such as maximal number of outstanding messages allowed. During the data phase, sending a message adds it to the corresponding queue, and receiving a message removes it. Both communication partners can send simultaneously and independently of each other as soon as the path is established. During the termination phase, pending messages remaining in queues are discarded and queues are released.

The IUCV service is available through interaction across the service interface which is part of the CP programming interface. This interaction, seen from a virtual machine, is described in VM manuals in terms of the **IUCV machine instruction** (X'B2F0') with its parameter list and the **IUCV interrupt** (X'4000') with its interrupt buffer describing the event. Seen as service primitives, these interactions include commands to initialize and terminate IUCV use (DCLBFR, RTRVBFR), to establish and close IUCV paths (CONNECT, ACCEPT, SEVER), and to exchange message data (SEND, RECEIVE, REPLY).

Initially, IUCV was available for only one application per virtual machine at a given moment. This application therefore monopolized the use of IUCV. The CMSIUCV interface removed this limitation by introducing a layer between the interface to IUCV provided by CP (native IUCV) and the application. This layer processes all IUCV interrupts and forwards interrupt buffers to the correct application. The CMSIUCV interface is described in *VM/SP System Facilities for Programming* (SC24-5288) and *VM/XA SP CMS Application Program Development Reference* (SC23-0402).

IUCV communication is intended for virtual machines running on the same VM system. PVM, the VM/Pass-Through Facility, Version 1, Release 4, supports cross-system IUCV communication. Applications may access PVM via IUCV protocols to communicate with virtual machines on other VM systems within the same PVM network. Cross-system IUCV using PVM is henceforth called **PVMIUCV**. PVMIUCV must be installed on both VM systems if two VM/Pass-Through virtual machines are to exploit PVMIUCV; intermediate PVM nodes in the network need not have this support. PVMIUCV is described in *Managing and Using PVM* (SC24-5374).

Unfortunately, CMSIUCV and PVMIUCV are incompatible because they use the same 8 bytes in the CONNECT function of IUCV for different purposes. CMSIUCV uses the 8 bytes in the so-called user-data field to forward the incoming connection request to an application. PVMIUCV stores the name of the PVM node requesting the connection there. REXXIUCV resolves this incompatibility and allows CMSIUCV and PVMIUCV to be used simultaneously.

MOTIVATION, HISTORY, AND STATUS

REXXIUCV was designed and implemented in early 1984 as part of a research project to develop a prototype OSI transport service allowing communication between virtual machines and LAN-attached workstations. The VM side of the service used IUCV between the virtual machine providing the transport service and the users' virtual machines. The first design of REXXIUCV was intended as a powerful test tool for IUCV-based access. It soon became clear that the best and most flexible test tool for IUCV programming was a general-purpose REXX interface to the complete IUCV facility.

In May 1984, the first version of REXXIUCV providing access to native IUCV on VM/SP was complete. A rapidly growing user community developed through its distribution over VNET, IBM's internal electronic network, and, later, the TOOLS computer conferencing system. User feedback suggested support for CMSIUCV and PVMIUCV, as well as adaptation to VM/XA SP in both 370 and XA mode. The heavy use by many users ensured that REXXIUCV has been very thoroughly tested, and this improved it significantly.

REXXIUCV became an IBM licensed program in March 1989. It is available within the Europe/Middle East/Africa marketing area as IBM program number 5785-LAT, *VM REXX Programming Support for IUCV*. It consists of one module, called **RXIUCVFN MODULE**, with an on-line HELP file, sample REXX programs, and the *REXXIUCV Program Description and Operations Manual* (SB11-8433).

DESIGN ISSUES AND DESIGN CRITERIA

Before the use of REXXIUCV is presented, some design considerations will illustrate how IUCV functions are presented to REXX programs.

There are two fundamental differences between System/370 assembler language and REXX. First, assembler language represents data as the address and length of a piece of memory, while REXX uses the notion of variables and values for the same purpose. Second, events in an assembler program are handled by an asynchronous interrupt handler, while REXX knows only synchronous function calls. To overcome these differences, REXXIUCV includes a **WAIT** function and a **QUERY** function. The **WAIT** function allows it to wait for interrupts. The **QUERY** function interrogates asynchronous events and provides status information to the REXX program.

Besides these two differences and the initial purpose of REXXIUCV as a test tool, its design and implementation were guided by the following principles:

1. The status of REXXIUCV, with all established paths, pending messages, and interrupt buffers, should not be destroyed when the REXX program terminates without cleaning up properly. This is very useful for testing because if one program terminates, another can determine the status and continue where the former program stopped.

2. REXXIUCV should provide access to the full IUCV facility, not to only a subset. The price is that there are many parameters to support all the different functions. Reasonable default values ease the use of the interface.

3. There should be one-to-one mapping between REXXIUCV function keywords and IUCV functions. Combined higher-order functions such as for a complete connection establishment phase can easily be written in REXX if needed.

4. Information contained in the interrupt buffer describing an IUCV event should be available to the REXX program, but using a representation appropriate for REXX parsing. Relevant information is extracted from the interrupt buffer and presented as a REXX-parsable character string.

5. REXXIUCV should allow high scheduling flexibility in processing pending events. For example, a REXX program may only process events from one path, leaving interrupts from other paths unserviced for some time.

6. Since the IUCV return code carries important information, it should be available to REXX programs. These return codes plus

REXXIUCV-specific return codes are passed to the program in the REXX variable **RC**.

7. Limits such as the maximum number of IUCV paths supported by REXXIUCV are necessary, but should be easy to change. (REXXI-UCV initially allowed at most four IUCV paths in parallel. Currently, this value is 2000.)

REXXIUCV FUNCTIONS

REXXIUCV must be loaded with the command **RXIUCVFN LOAD** before the **IUCV** function can be used from REXX programs. This step installs the **IUCV** function as a nucleus extension, enabling faster execution than loading it from disk for each invocation, as well as allowing it to keep necessary status information from one call to the next.

When the module **RXIUCVFN** is loaded, the **IUCV** function can ⸱ ⸱ e issued through the REXX function call:

```
var = iucv(function, arg1, . . ., argn)
```

where *function* is a function keyword (service primitive) such as **CONNECT** or **SEND**, and *arg1* through *argn* are function-dependent arguments.

Two functions manipulate the IUCV environment. **INIT** activates IUCV, either with **DCLBFR** or through the CMSIUCV interface, depending on the other arguments. **TERM** deactivates IUCV after termination of all IUCV paths created with REXXIUCV. The **CONNECT**, **ACCEPT**, **SEVER**, **QUIESCE**, and **RESUME** functions manipulate IUCV paths, and correspond to the IUCV functions of the same name. Similarly, the **SEND**, **PURGE**, **RECEIVE**, **REJECT**, and **REPLY** functions handle IUCV messages. In addition, the **QUERY** and **WAIT** functions allow the user to determine status or wait for events (interrupts).

For the **INIT** function, the first argument specifies an upper limit for the number of paths allowed. The second argument specifies the installation method: **NATIVE**, **CMS**, or **APPLICATION**. If **NATIVE** is specified, the original IUCV interface to CP is used. In order to trap IUCV and timer interrupts, the external new PSW is replaced. If **CMS** is specified, REXXIUCV takes control of the CMSIUCV interface, also by replacing the external new PSW.

In current VM versions, replacing the external new PSW is not necessary, and is undesirable because it can lead to conflicts between applications. The third installation method, **APPLICATION**, uses the CMSIUCV interface without changing the external new PSW. It is strongly recommended that **APPLICATION** be used whenever possible.

The third argument allows specification of a CMSIUCV application name. This name is used by CMSIUCV to forward connection-request IUCV interrupts to the correct application.

The fourth argument, if specified, indicates the userid of a virtual machine (such as PVM), and has been introduced to resolve the incompatibility of CMSIUCV and PVMIUCV. All connection-request IUCV interrupts from this virtual machine are directed to REXXIUCV, independent of the actual value in the user-data field.

For the QUERY function, a subfunction in arg1 specifies the information requested.

CONNECT and ACCEPT functions are used as a two-way handshake to establish a path. The QUIESCE and RESUME functions allow all message exchange on a path to be temporarily suspended and resumed. The SEND and RECEIVE functions do what their names indicate. The sender can also purge a message not yet received by the communication partner (PURGE), and the receiver can reject a message (REJECT). IUCV also supports so-called two-way communication, in which the sender sends a message and specifies the length of the expected reply. The receiver receives it and is supposed to send a reply using the REPLY function.

The SEVER function purges and rejects all pending messages on the path and terminates it. IUCV architecture requires both sides to call the SEVER function to fully terminate a path. The TERM function severs all pending and established paths and deactivates IUCV handling. REXXIUCV as a nucleus extension can be canceled with NUCXDROP RXIUCVFN. If IUCV was not yet terminated, this call issues the TERM function implicitly.

REXXIUCV maintains a queue of interrupt buffers which persist until they are processed completely. Some interrupt buffers, such as the message-complete interrupt for a one-way SEND, are deleted once they are presented to the REXX program as the result of a call to the NEXT subfunction of QUERY. Other interrupt buffers are removed from the queue by calls to specific functions. ACCEPT and SEVER functions, for example, eliminate any pending-connection interrupt for a path.

When the IUCV function is not called to process an interrupt buffer, it stays in the queue until the corresponding path is SEVERed.

The QUERY function and its subfunctions allow the user to determine all established paths, the next pending interrupt buffer (given some selection criteria), and other status information. Replies, as the result of two-way communication, must also be obtained with the QUERY function because of the intrinsic difference between REXX and assembler language. The WAIT function and the NEXT subfunction of the QUERY function, which returns the next pending interrupt buffer, are the primary means to process events. The example in the next section demonstrates their use.

EXAMPLES—RCVSAMPL AND SNDSAMPL

Two sample REXX programs, **RCVSAMPL EXEC** and **SNDSAMPL EXEC**, demonstrate the use of REXXIUCV. They are to be executed in two different virtual machines on the same VM system. **RCVSAMPL** must be started first and reacts passively to connection requests from **SND-SAMPL**. In order to keep the programs as small as possible, the (admittedly not very interesting) service provided is very simple, and both programs lack the code normally used for various checks and corresponding error messages. In other words, they are neither useful, robust, nor user-friendly without modification, but they show the basic communication structure.

The RCVSAMPL program

After initialization, server program **RCVSAMPL** waits for and processes IUCV interrupts. It accepts connection requests from other virtual machines and counts messages received on each path. When the path is **SEVER**ed, it displays the number of messages received on the path.

```
/* RCVSAMPL -- REXXIUCV receiver example */
parse arg .
address command 'CP SET TIMER REAL'              /* Enable waiting */
address command 'RXIUCVFN LOAD'              /* Initialize REXXIUCV */
if rc <> 0 then exit rc
cmsname = 'EXAMPLE '
call iucv 'INIT', 2000, 'APPLICATION', cmsname
if rc <> 0 then exit rc + 100
do forever                                 /* Process IUCV interrupts */
    call iucv 'WAIT', 900, 'NOWAIT'
    intbuf = iucv('QUERY', 'NEXT')
    parse var intbuf pending type pathid . trgcls .
    select
        when type = 1 then do                 /* Pending connection */
            call iucv 'ACCEPT', pathid, 255, 'NOPRIO', left('OK', 16)
            if rc = 0 then count.pathid = 0
            else call iucv 'SEVER', pathid, left('PROBLEMS', 16)
        end
        when type = 3 then do                         /* Path severed */
            call iucv 'SEVER', pathid, left('END', 16)
            say count.pathid 'messages received on path' pathid
        end
        when type = 9 then do                        /* Pending message */
            message = iucv('RECEIVE', pathid, trgcls)
            if rc=0 then count.pathid = count.pathid + 1
        end
        otherwise nop
    end
end
address command 'NUCXDROP RXIUCVFN'              /* Terminate REXXIUCV */
```

The SNDSAMPL program

After initialization, the client program **SNDSAMPL** connects to the virtual machine running **RCVSAMPL** EXEC. When the IUCV path is successfully established, it sends the same message as many times as requested.

```
/* SNDSAMPL -- REXXIUCV Sender Part of the Example */
parse arg vmid count message
address command 'CP SET TIMER REAL'              /* Enable waiting */
address command 'RXIUCVFN LOAD'              /* Initialize REXXIUCV */
if rc <> 0 then exit rc
cmsname = 'TEMP' || right(random(0, 9999), 4, '0')
numpath = iucv('INIT', 1, 'APPLICATION', cmsname)
if rc <> 0 then exit rc + 100
/* Connect to server */
connectdata = iucv('CONNECT', vmid, 255, 'NOPRIO', 'EXAMPLE ')
error = (rc <> 0)
parse var connectdata . msglim .
do while error = 0                        /* Process IUCV interrupts */
   call iucv 'WAIT', 900, 'NOWAIT'
   intbuf = iucv('QUERY', 'NEXT')
   parse var intbuf pending type pathid .
   select
      when type = 2 then do               /* Connection complete */
         sent = 0
         received = 0
         rc = SENDIT(pathid, message)
      end
      when type = 3 then do                   /* Path severed */
         call iucv 'SEVER', pathid, left('END', 16)
         error = 1
      end
      when type = 7 then do               /* Message complete */
         received = received + 1
         rc = SENDIT(pathid, message)
      end
      otherwise nop
   end
   if sent = count & sent = received then do
      call iucv 'SEVER', pathid, left('END', 16)
      leave
   end
end
address command 'NUCXDROP RXIUCVFN'          /* Terminate REXXIUCV */
exit error
/* Send procedure */
SENDIT: procedure expose msglim count sent received error
pathid = arg(1)
message = arg(2)
do while error = 0 & sent - received < msglim & sent < count
   call iucv 'SEND', pathid, message, 0, 0, 'NO', 'NO', 'NO'
   if rc = 0 then sent = sent + 1
   else error = 1
end
return rc
```

Sample program operation

Arguments passed to the program

Both use **PARSE ARG** to parse the input parameters. **RCVSAMPL** ignores any arguments; **SNDSAMPL** requires:

vmid   The userid of the virtual machine providing the service, in uppercase

count   The number of messages to send

message   The message text to send

Initialize REXXIUCV

The command **CP SET TIMER REAL** is needed for the **WAIT** function to work properly under VM/SP. Otherwise, no timer interrupts are generated, and the program will wait forever. This command is neither valid nor needed in an XA-mode virtual machine. It is poor programming to change virtual machine settings as the examples do; production programs should save and restore the **TIMER** setting before terminating.

RXIUCVFN LOAD loads REXXIUCV as a nucleus extension. Both REXX programs could test first whether REXXIUCV is already loaded, in which case it need not be loaded again.

Both programs call the INIT function. **RCVSAMPL** requests 2000 paths and uses the name **EXAMPLE⌀** for CMSIUCV because it expects connection requests from other virtual machines. **SNDSAMPL** needs only one path and builds a random name for CMSIUCV because other virtual machines should not be able to request a connection to it.

Connect to Server

SNDSAMPL requests a path to **RCVSAMPL**. As a client of the service provided by **RCVSAMPL**, **SNDSAMPL** first initiates a connection. The virtual machine running **RCVSAMPL** is specified as **vmid**. The argument **255** specifies how many pending messages are allowed by CP at any one time. (In the following, the REXX variable **MSGLIM** contains the value really used on the path as returned by IUCV.) The last argument of the **CONNECT** function must contain the CMSIUCV name as specified by the **RCVSAMPL** program in the **INIT** function.

Process IUCV Interrupts

Both programs loop until some exit conditions are met. Actually, **RCVSAMPL** never ends and has to be terminated by other means.

Both programs first call the **WAIT** function and the **QUERY** function with the subfunction **NEXT** for the next pending interrupt buffer. These two functions are the means in REXXIUCV to wait for and react to IUCV events.

The subfunction **NEXT** of the **QUERY** function returns a string. The first part of this string is always the number of pending interrupt buffers. If at least one IUCV interrupt buffer is pending, the next part of the string is a number indicating the interrupt type, followed by the name of the path on which the interrupt occurred. Other type-dependent information follows. This is explained below in the section on "Robustness".

Both programs respond to IUCV interrupts, depending on the interrupt type. They react only to the interrupt types they expect. This helps keep the programs small, but does *not* make them robust.

When the virtual machine running **RCVSAMPL** receives a pending-connection interrupt (**type=1**), it tries to accept it. If this function completes successfully, it initializes the compound variable **COUNT**.*pathid*. This allows **RCVSAMPL** to have more than one path established concurrently. Otherwise, it severs the pending path.

SNDSAMPL receives a connection-complete interrupt (**type=2**) and starts sending messages. **RCVSAMPL** receives a pending-message interrupt (**type=9**) for each message sent, and receives and counts these messages without looking at their content. A received message produces a message-complete interrupt (**type=7**) for **SNDSAMPL**, which continues sending further messages.

When one of the programs severs the path, the other program receives a path-severed interrupt (**type=3**) and also severs the path. **RCVSAMPL** also writes the number of messages received on the path to the screen.

At the end of the loop, **SNDSAMPL** tests whether it has sent as many messages as were requested by the user, and whether all messages sent have been received by the server.

Terminate REXXIUCV
In the termination phase, both programs terminate IUCV use.

NUCXDROP RXIUCVFN cancels the REXXIUCV nucleus extension (and thus the REXX **iucv** function). A call to the **TERM** function is not needed because it is called implicitly.

Send Procedure
SNDSAMPL calls the **SENDIT** subroutine whenever it is allowed to send a message.

Whether **SNDSAMPL** is allowed to send messages is determined by the difference between the number of messages already sent and the number of messages received by the server. If this number does not exceed the maximum value of outstanding messages (**MSGLIM**), the procedure can send further messages. A non-zero return code also terminates the program. Note that each call of the **IUCV** function sets REXX variable **RC**.

Robustness

As mentioned above, **RCVSAMPL** and **SNDSAMPL** are not robust. For example, when **SNDSAMPL** receives a pending-connection interrupt (**type=1**), it loops forever because it sees the interrupt buffer, enters **OTHERWISE NOP**, and sees the same (not yet processed) interrupt buffer again. The same happens in **RCVSAMPL** if **SNDSAMPL** sends a two-way message instead of a one-way message as expected, because **RCVSAMPL** will never send the reply in order to process the interrupt buffer. Such behavior is not acceptable for a server intended to provide services to many clients and to run unattended.

In order to make the server (**RCVSAMPL**) more robust, the interrupt-type information in the REXX variable **OTHERS** must be parsed and used when needed. Further, all interrupt types must be explicitly coded in the **SELECT** instruction. Finally, pending-message and message-complete interrupts must be processed differently, depending on the presence or absence of the keyword **REPLY** in the interrupt buffer data. The same would be necessary for priority messages. After these improvements, the loop would look like:

```
   :
do forever
   call iucv 'WAIT', 900, 'NOWAIT'
   intbuf = iucv('QUERY', 'NEXT')
   parse var intbuf pending type pathid others
   select
      when type = 1 then do                  /* Pending connection */
         parse var others msglim vmid prio '<' userdata '>'
         call iucv 'ACCEPT', pathid, 255, 'NOPRIO', left('OK', 16)
         if rc = 0 then count.pathid = 0
         else call iucv 'SEVER', pathid, left('PROBLEMS', 16)
      end
      when type = 2 then do                  /* Connection complete */
         parse var others msglim '<' userdata '>'
         call iucv 'SEVER', pathid, left('IMPOSSIBLE', 16)
      end
      when type = 3 then do                    /* Path severed */
         parse var others '<' userdata '>'
         call iucv 'SEVER', pathid, left('END', 16)
         say count.pathid 'messages received on path' pathid
      end
      when type = 4 then do                    /* Path quiesced */
         parse var others '<' userdata '>'
         call iucv 'SEVER', pathid, left('NOT ALLOWED', 16)
      end
      when type = 5 then do                    /* Path resumed */
         parse var others '<' userdata '>'
```

```
                    call iucv 'SEVER', pathid, left('NOT ALLOWED', 16)
                end
                when type = 6 then do              /* Priority msg complete */
                    parse var others msgidsrccls rpl rpllength
                    call iucv 'SEVER', pathid, left('IMPOSSIBLE', 16)
                end
                when type = 7 then do                  /* Message complete */
                    parse var others msgid srccls rpl rpllength
                    if rpl = '' then nop
                    else reply = iucv('QUERY', 'REPLY', pathid, srccls)
                end
                when type = 8 then do          /* Pending priority message */
                    parse var others msgid trgcls msglength rpl rpllength
                    call iucv 'SEVER', pathid, left('IMPOSSIBLE', 16)
                end
                when type = 9 then do                   /* Pending message */
                    parse var others msgid trgcls msglength rpl rpllength
                    if rpl = '' then do
                        message = iucv('RECEIVE', pathid, trgcls)
                        if rc = 0 then count.pathid = count.pathid + 1
                    end
                    else call iucv 'REPLY', pathid, '', trgcls, 'NO', 'NO'
                end
                otherwise nop
            end
    end
    :
```

Severing a path whenever something unexpected happens is not polite, but the above code does provide hints such as **NOT ALLOWED** in the user-data field, and it definitely makes the server more robust. If the client, for example, uses a two-way send, an empty reply will come back. The program even handles events which will never occur, such as message-complete interrupts or priority messages. (It accepts connection requests with the option **NOPRIO**.)

Not only is robustness important for servers, but so is economical resource use. Termination of an IUCV path in the virtual machine running the **RCVSAMPL** program is under control of the **SNDSAMPL** program. Release of IUCV paths as the critical resource of a server should be controlled directly by the server. The **RCVSAMPL** program can be extended to sever all paths for which no interrupt occurs within a certain time:

```
:
parse var intbuf pending type pathid others
now = time('S')
maxidle = 10
if pathid<>'' then lastused.pathid = now
pathlist = iucv('QUERY', 'PATH')
do while pathlist<>''
    parse var pathlist nextpath pathlist
    if lastused.nextpath > now then                    /* Midnight */
    lastused.nextpath = 0                              /* So reset */
```

```
    if lastused.nextpath + maxidle<now then do
       call iucv 'SEVER', nextpath, left('TIME OUT', 16)
    end
 end
 :
```

Current time is measured using the REXX TIME('S') function. Only ten seconds of inactivity (MAXIDLE) is allowed on a path in this example. If the above piece of code is revived because of an IUCV event, the LASTUSED.*pathid* variable is updated. Independent of the interrupt type, a list of established paths is obtained using the PATH subfunction of the QUERY function. The program goes through this list and for each path checks whether the inactive period has been exceeded. A path may stay established much longer than ten seconds of inactivity, but it is severed as soon as the server needs a free path for another client.

APPLICATIONS

Instead of describing what REXXIUCV could be used for, its actual use in the project for which it was developed will be described. As mentioned above, REXXIUCV was designed, built, and used to support implementation of an OSI transport service for VM systems and workstations. The service allowed communication between virtual machines and LAN-attached workstations. The VM side of it was accessible from the users' virtual machines via IUCV.

Testing and experimenting

Initially, REXXIUCV was designed as a testing tool for the IUCV-based access to the OSI transport service. The power of REXX allowed any character string to be built and sent to the service under test. Protocol test cases were systematically generated, and the behavior of the service was observed. Unexpected use of IUCV functions or options as well as invalid data formats were tested. This simple and thorough testing made the service very robust. The performance of REXX and REXXIUCV even allowed stress testing.

Later in the project, we started using an experimental IUCV RSCS line driver. Owing to lack of documentation, we started exploring its behavior experimentally. In addition to learning its essential details, we found several errors.

Rapid prototyping

In a very natural way, we derived complete client programs for the OSI transport service from the programs we used for testing. More and more phases of the protocol were completely tested, and the test programs worked through these phases the same way a client program would.

We intended to replace the early REXX prototype of the client programs with a compiled version in another programming language, but we never started this work since there was no real need for it. The difference in speed between a compiled and an interpreted language did not cause any serious degradation of service because the time-consuming part was in the server program, which was already implemented in a compiled language, rather than in the REXX client part.

Final applications

As one set of final applications, we used REXXIUCV to connect to the CP service *MSG in order to gain access to RSCS messages, messages from batch machines or other similar service machines. Since they are simple and small, such programs can be written even by casual programmers without many difficulties. (There are a few questions needing more thorough consideration because of the concurrency involved, even for such simple programs: the program has to know when it received the last relevant message, and the program should not lose messages from other virtual machines accidentally arriving during its execution.)

We also implemented very large REXX programs using REXXIUCV. Connecting to the above-mentioned IUCV line driver in RSCS, we built a complete, full-function RSCS node which provided access to the RSCS network from LAN-attached workstations. Except for a few assembler language routines to invoke certain CMS features, this RSCS node was written in REXX. (This program was part of the setup to demonstrate an X.400 mail service at the TELECOM'87 exhibition in Geneva, Switzerland, October 20-27, 1987, in connection with the IBM X.400 PROFS Connection.) This program sent and received files as well as messages using the IUCV line driver. Files were temporarily stored in the spool of the virtual machine running this program. This virtual machine communicated with the users on the LAN via a protocol developed especially for this purpose as a protocol layer on top of the OSI transport service.

Other programmers have used REXXIUCV to implement many other servers. Access to a central phone directory from several VM systems via IUCV and PVMIUCV is one example. Another programmer team built an application which allows users to view schedules and to sign up for education center courses.

Since REXX as an interpreted language already allowed programmers to develop large applications mainly or completely in REXX, availability of the REXX compiler encouraged even more development of large applications directly in REXX. Needless to say, programs using REXXIUCV can be compiled the same way as other REXX programs.

SUMMARY AND CONCLUSIONS

REXXIUCV is a REXX extension which allows inter-VM communication. The extension is system-dependent because it runs only on CMS under VM/SP or VM/XA SP. It adds the function IUCV to the rich set of built-in REXX functions.

REXXIUCV provides high-level language access to the complete IUCV facility, including support for CMSIUCV and PVMIUCV. It allows multiple communication paths in parallel and offers flexible handling of events, including IUCV and timer interrupts.

For users, it is an easy-to-use interface to IUCV and a flexible tool for IUCV programming. This does not make it trivial to write user-friendly and robust communication programs such as a server based on IUCV; it only simplifies access to IUCV. REXXIUCV helps provide experience in implementing concurrent systems, and allows testing designs prototyped or implemented in REXX or any other programming language.

33

CMS Pipelines

By John P. Hartmann

This chapter describes CMS Pipelines (IBM product number 5785-RAC) in terms that are familiar to a REXX programmer.

- REXX programs can call on CMS Pipelines to perform operations on REXX variables and stemmed arrays.
- CMS Pipelines can invoke REXX programs to process data flowing through a pipeline.

As the name implies, CMS Pipelines is designed for VM. It also works with MVS and REXX/TSO, although it is not officially supported in these environments. The examples in this chapter are CMS-based.

OVERVIEW

CMS Pipelines pumps data through programs. A program is to a pipeline what a built-in function is to a REXX expression: a building block that is combined with others (and data) to form an expression. Programs running in a pipeline read and write device-independent streams, without concern for other programs in the pipeline. An output stream from any program can be connected to an input stream of any program.

The pipeline style is to decompose a complex task into a suite of simpler ones. A few simple operations, combined in a particular order, can perform a non-trivial task. Often, a new problem can be solved with CMS Pipelines built-in programs and other programs that have already been written. Sometimes, however, a problem is not solved entirely with existing programs. In those cases:

- Apply **pipethink** to chip off bits and pieces to be done with existing programs. What remains is often an order of magnitude simpler than the original problem.

- Try to split the problem into two problems of equal complexity. The complexity of each sub-problem is often less than a quarter the complexity of the original problem.

Just as the ability to use built-in functions is one of the hallmarks of a good REXX programmer, knowing the built-in pipeline utilities saves a pipelines programmer much time and leads to faster programs. Built-in programs supplied with CMS Pipelines perform transformations and other operations on data passing through them. Using built-in programs significantly enhances the productivity of programmers and users.

CMS Pipelines is different from other pipeline styles:

- Device driver programs interface device-dependent host interfaces to pipeline streams.

- A pipeline specification can define a network of interconnected pipelines.

- Records are passed between programs without buffering. This makes the order of arrival in a multistream pipeline predictable.

- A pipeline is run only when all its stages (particular invocations of programs) are specified correctly; the syntax of built-in filters is checked before the pipeline is started.

- Programs can coordinate their progress via commit levels and can stop when one program encounters an error.

If you are a REXX programmer, the examples that follow show things that you might feel you can easily do yourself. CMS Pipelines is not a spoilsport that wants to take the fun away from REXX programming. CMS Pipelines takes the *drudgery* out of programming so that you can concentrate on the creative sides of your problem rather than, for instance, on reading or writing disk files. Once you have taken an hour or two to master a few simple concepts, you will be able to apply **pipethink** to problem solving, and you will wonder how you ever got along without it.

AN EXAMPLE

The command **PIPE** runs a pipeline. The argument to the **PIPE** command is a pipeline specification, which is a list of programs and arguments separated by stage separators. The solid vertical bar (|) is usually used as the separator character between stages. Think of the complete **PIPE** command as a diagram showing the flow of data from program to program (left to right) through stage separators.

The following example pipeline can be included in a REXX program to remove all occurrences of the string **abc** from the REXX variable **WHATNOT**:

```
/* Remove 'abc' from a REXX variable */
address command 'PIPE var whatnot | change /abc// | var whatnot'
```

The command **PIPE** obtains the variable **WHATNOT** via **EXECCOMM**, changes all the occurrences of the string **abc** to the null string, and replaces the value of **WHATNOT** with the resulting string.

In this example, the program **VAR** is invoked twice; the program **CHANGE** is used once. These are **built-in programs**; they reside within CMS Pipelines.

Many device driver programs sense their position in the pipeline. When invoked first in a pipeline, they read from a host interface into the pipeline; when they are not first, they copy input records to the interface and to the output. Thus, the first **VAR** stage reads the REXX variable, and the second one puts it back.

This example processes only one record through the pipeline because it deals with the contents of a single variable. The built-in program **STEM** (similar to **VAR**) operates on all variables in a stemmed array. Other programs read and write disk files, the program stack, files in the XEDIT ring, and many other host interfaces.

WHAT IS CMS PIPELINES?

CMS Pipelines has three parts:

Command parser

The parser (often called the scanner) scans the **PIPE** command argument string to build a control block structure describing the pipeline to run. It ensures that the pipeline specification is well formed, that all programs exist, and that the syntax is correct for those programs that make a syntax description available to the parser.

Library of built-in programs

CMS Pipelines built-in programs access host interfaces (device drivers), transform data (filters), select lines, and perform many other utility functions. Filter packages can be attached dynamically to the main pipeline module on CMS. Once installed in virtual storage, the contents of a filter package are an extension to the contents of the main pipeline module; filters in the package are invoked just like built-in programs.

Dispatcher

The pipeline dispatcher starts programs and passes control between programs to maintain an orderly flow of data through the pipeline. Programs call the pipeline dispatcher to read from and write to the pipeline. The dispatcher runs programs as **co-routines**: control passes from one program to another only when a program calls the dispatcher.

USING CMS PIPELINES FROM THE TERMINAL

The **PIPE** command in the example below displays a list of all accessed mode letters (minidisks and Shared File System directories):

```
pipe cms query disk | drop 1 | spec 12-13 1-1 left | join * | console

ABCDFHIJKQSUVWY
Ready;
```

This five-stage pipeline processes the output that the CMS **QUERY DISK** command would normally write to the terminal. Data passes from one program to the next as shown in figure 17.

Five built-in programs are selected to perform the task at hand:

CMS	Issues the command and writes the CMS response to the pipeline rather than to the terminal.
DROP	Discards the heading line from the query response.
SPEC	Puts the first non-blank character from columns 12 and 13 of the input record into column 1 of the output record. This selects the mode letter from column 12 or 13. (Some VM systems put the mode letter in column 12; others put it in column 13 with a blank in column 12.)

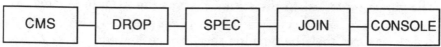

Figure 17. Pipeline to list accessed minidisk mode letters

JOIN   Concatenates all input lines; writes one output line.

CONSOLE   Writes the result to the terminal.

The SPEC utility program was inspired by the processing done by the SPECS option of the CMS COPYFILE command; hence its name and the syntax of the argument string. At first, it had no extensions to the CMS command. Conversion and alignment were added later.

USING CMS PIPELINES IN COMMAND PROCEDURES

The previous section shows how to type pipelines directly at the terminal. This is convenient for simple operations with few programs, but not for long pipelines or complex tasks.

A typical command procedure issues a mixture of host commands and pipelines to perform the task at hand. Input is usually from a disk file; output is often to a disk file or to the terminal.

To demonstrate a command procedure with a pipeline, the following example shows a program to print a file with Print Services Facility (PSF) and determine what External Attribute Buffer (XAB) PSF has set up with page and form definitions:

```
/* Run PSF and store External Attribute Buffer */
address command
arg file
'CP SPOOL 00E RSCS COPY 1 NOHOLD CLASS A DEST PSFSITE'
'CP TAG DEV 00E CPHMVS1 SYSTEM 0 (SENT=YES)'
'PSF' file
'PIPE xab | > 00e xab a'
exit rc
```

The XAB associated with device 00E is obtained with the built-in program XAB. The built-in program > writes a file containing the XAB to the A-disk. Though the program name (>) is inspired by the UNIX redirection facility, it is important to understand that with CMS Pipelines it is a program that runs as a separate stage; there must be a blank after the program name.

USING CMS PIPELINES IN REXX PROGRAMS

Many REXX programs have significantly more computation and control than host commands.

REXX and CMS Pipelines dovetail: REXX provides the programming language; CMS Pipelines accesses host interfaces and variables in the program's variable pool.

Use the **PIPE** command to run a pipeline in any REXX program, just as in EXECs. The next example is a variation on the one to generate the list of accessed mode letters. The result is stored in the variable **MODES**. The pipeline is written in **portrait format** to allow for a comment on each line.

```
/* Return highest free mode letter or null */
GETMODE: procedure
address command 'PIPE',
     '  cms query disk',                    /* Issue CMS command */
     '| drop 1',                            /* Remove heading */
     '| spec 12-13 1-1 left',               /* Get mode letter */
     '| join *',                            /* Make single line */
     '| var modes'                          /* Set result in variable */
if rc <> 0 then exit rc        /* There is something really wrong */
letters = reverse('ABCDEFGHIJKLMNOPQRSTUVWXYZ')
unused = verify(letters, modes)
if unused > 0 then return substr(letters, unused, 1)
return ''                               /* All modes in use, return null */
```

The example pipeline above is formatted with stage separators lining up to the left of the lines that the pipeline specification is written on. (This is displayed as an unbroken line when the file is edited on many terminals.) REXX computes the multiline expression to generate the argument string that CMS Pipelines sees. As far as CMS Pipelines is concerned, the pipeline specification is a string of characters.

When using GDDM/REXX (discussed in the chapter "GDDM-REXX: Full-screen Text, Image, and Graphics from REXX"), it is convenient to refer to 3270 attributes by name; for instance, **RED** instead of **2**. Setting the variable **RED** to **2** allows you to reference the variable whenever you want the constant. However, it would be cumbersome to set many variables with assignment statements in every GDDM/REXX program you write. Instead, use the built-in program **VARLOAD** to set a variable for each line in a file. Each line contains the name of a variable to set and the data to load into the variable. Because compound symbols can have any character, including blank, input lines to **VARLOAD** have the variable name in a delimited string before the value; for instance, **/RED/2**. The variable name is not substituted further; a simple variable and a stem must be in uppercase. This example loads the variables from the CMS file GDDM VARS:

```
/* Set up constants */
address command 'PIPE < gddm vars | varload'
```

The built-in program < reads a CMS file. The file must exist; it can be **EXECLOAD**ed to improve performance. The built-in program **QSAM** reads an MVS file. On MVS, use the pipeline below to read the member **VARS** from the partitioned dataset allocated to DDNAME **GDDM**:

```
address link 'PIPE qsam gddm vars | varload'
```

Pipe it when there is no built-in function

Look to the pipeline when you cannot think of a simple way to perform a task.

Sort it

REXX programmers often must sort data in REXX variables. The next example shows how to sort from stemmed array **UNSORTED** to stemmed array **SORTED**.

```
address command 'PIPE stem unsorted. | sort | stem sorted.'
```

To sort the contents of a variable containing a list of words, split each word into a separate line and rejoin them all (with a blank) after the sort:

```
address command 'PIPE var list | split | sort | join * / / | var list'
```

Discover variables with a particular stem

CMS Pipelines can read all exposed variables and the first 512 bytes of their data from the REXX environment.

The built-in program **REXXVARS** writes a line with the source string followed by a pair of lines for each exposed variable. The first position of the output line defines the type of line: **s** for the source string, **N** for the name of a variable, and **v** for the contents (value) of the variable. The second position is blank.

Filter the output from **REXXVARS** to load derived names of variables with a particular stem:

```
'PIPE rexxvars | find n STEM.| spec 3-* 1 | buffer | stem gotcha.'
```

The built-in program **FIND** is similar to the XEDIT **FIND** subcommand. It selects lines where the contents match the corresponding non-blank characters in the argument string. Blanks indicate columns that are not inspected, but must be present; leading and trailing blanks are significant in the **FIND** argument string. Thus, the stage separator must be abutted to the period to select the variable with a null index. The interface used by **REXXVARS** does not divulge the default value of a stem.

The built-in program **BUFFER** reads all its input lines into a storage buffer and writes them out when it reaches end-of-file. This ensures that all variables are read from the REXX environment before setting the result.

Who calls?

You may wish to determine the name of the calling program. Often an EXEC is superseded by some other and more efficient means, but no one dares erase the EXEC because it might be called from some obscure place. The next example, **PIPERUN**, tells you who called it before it issues the **PIPE** command to run the pipeline.

```
/* Run a pipeline */
address command
trace off    /* very quiet, messages are already issued galore... */
'PIPE rexxvars 1 | take 1 | var where'    /* Get caller's SOURCE */
parse var where . . . fn ft fm .              /* Get the fileid */
say 'PIPERUN called from' fn ft fm    /* Say where called from */
'PIPE' arg(1)                    /* Issue pipeline to bootstrap */
exit rc
```

The pipeline on the fourth line processes the caller's source string because the argument 1 tells **REXXVARS** to go back to the caller's environment rather than process the current one. The built-in program **TAKE** copies records from the beginning (or from the end) of the file to the output stream. As written here, it selects the first record, the one with the source string.

Operate on data

Use a suite of pipeline filters to operate on a stemmed array rather than writing REXX code to iterate through the array processing each instance. In this way it is particularly easy to obtain an array that contains a subset of the contents of some other array.

This example selects those entries from a stemmed array that contain a particular string:

```
address command 'PIPE stem array. | locate /abc/ | stem nuone.'
```

WRITING REXX PROGRAMS TO ACCESS THE PIPELINE

So far, this chapter has shown how to use CMS Pipelines from the terminal and in subroutines in REXX programs. This section describes how to run REXX programs as filters in the pipeline.

The mechanics are that the program has filetype **REXX** (rather than **EXEC** or **XEDIT**). To run a REXX program as a filter, mention the filename of the program in a pipeline specification as if it were a built-in program, or put **REXX** in front of the name. In a REXX pipeline program, the default subcommand environment executes **pipeline commands** rather than host commands.

The next example shows a program to reverse the contents of lines. It performs a REXX built-in function on data in the pipeline. (This is a case where REXX has something CMS Pipelines has not; they clearly complement each other.)

```
/* Reverse the contents of lines in the pipeline */
signal on error
do forever                          /* Loop through all lines */
   'readto data'                    /* Read a line into 'DATA' */
   'output' reverse(data)                /* Write the reverse */
end
error: exit rc*(rc <> 12)
```

The loop iterates until a non-zero return code forces a branch to the error label. The pipeline command **READTO** reads a line from the input stream into the specified variable and sets the return code to zero. When **READTO** reaches end-of-file, it sets return code **12** and drops the specified variable. The **OUTPUT** pipeline command writes its argument string to the output stream.

The example below shows how to use the REXX pipeline program above. The built-in program **LITERAL** writes its argument string (including trailing blanks) into the pipeline; it is handy to generate a test case for a filter program.

```
pipe literal Hi there! | reverse | console

 !ereht iH
Ready;

pipe literal Hi there! | reverse | reverse | console

Hi there!
Ready;
```

Note the simplicity of the interface between a REXX program and the pipeline:

- No files to open or close. Streams are always **open**.
- No files to read and write. The origin of input lines and the disposition of output lines are determined by the stage's position in the pipeline.

SUBROUTINE PIPELINES

Instead of writing long pipelines in EXECs and REXX programs, it is often simpler to write a subroutine pipeline for the part of a problem that does not deal with host interfaces. A subroutine pipeline is a special case of the programs described in the section "Writing REXX programs to access the pipeline"; the pipeline command **CALLPIPE** processes a subroutine pipeline. Once you have tested the subroutine pipeline, it can be used in other programs simply by writing its filename as the name of a program to run. You soon adopt a **program and forget** attitude toward subroutine pipelines. This means that once you have written the subroutine pipeline you no longer need to remember how it accomplishes its task; all you have to know is what it does. Another advantage of using subroutine pipelines rather than copying stages into REXX programs is that a change to a subroutine pipeline takes effect whenever it is called.

For example, the two pipelines to generate lists of mode letters are identical except for the disposition of the output line. Put the common portion into file **ACCESSED REXX** as a subroutine pipeline that can be referenced from other pipelines:

```
/* Mode letters of accessed minidisks and directories. */
signal on novalue
arg disktype
'callpipe',
   'command QUERY DISK' disktype '|',              /* Ask CMS */
   'drop 1 |',                              /* Remove heading */
   'spec 12-13 1-1 left |',               /* Get mode letter */
   'join * |',                                 /* Combine all */
   '*:'                            /* Pass on to caller's output */
exit rc
```

The argument to **ACCESSED** is passed to the CMS **QUERY** command. The pipeline command **CALLPIPE** runs the subroutine pipeline. The subroutine pipeline looks much like the pipeline to generate a list of mode letters, except that it ends with * : instead of a program to write to the console or to set a variable. * : is a **connector**. It tells CALLPIPE to connect the output stream from **JOIN** to the input stream of the program to the right of the program that called the subroutine pipeline (**ACCESSED**). The command to generate a list of mode letters is much simplified by use of the subroutine pipeline:

```
pipe accessed | console

ABCDFHIJKQSUVWY
Ready;
```

USING CMS PIPELINES IN XEDIT MACROS

The built-in program **XEDIT** reads from and writes to files in the XEDIT ring. The built-in program **SUBCOM** issues XEDIT commands when the argument is **XEDIT**. The built-in program **XMSG** issues lines it reads as XEDIT messages. Thus, you can run a pipeline and display the result without clearing the XEDIT screen.

XEDIT reads and writes complete lines; XEDIT does not process them in any way (zone, image, truncation, translation, and so on, are all ignored).

The following example shows a command that counts blank-delimited words in the file being edited; it displays the result as an XEDIT message.

```
:0 pipe xedit | count words | xmsg
```

MULTISTREAM PIPELINES

CMS Pipelines supports any number of streams for a program. Streams are defined in pairs, an input stream and an output stream. The input stream to the first stage in a pipeline is not connected, nor is the output stream of the last stage of a pipeline. The solid vertical bar between two stages connects an output stream to an input stream.

Figure 18 shows the **UPDATE** built-in program, which uses two input and two output streams: one to read and write the master file, and one to read the update file and write the update log. The master file is read and written on the **primary** stream; the update and log are on the **secondary** stream.

CMS Pipelines models a multidimensional structure as a set of pipelines. An invocation of a program that uses more than the primary streams is identified with a **label**.

The next example shows how a single update is applied to an assembler source file. The parentheses after the **PIPE** command define **global options** that apply to the complete pipeline specification. The global option in this example defines the backslant as the **end character**. The end character separates pipelines just as the stage separator separates stages.

```
/* Update it */
'PIPE (end \)',
'          < pipsmp assemble',              /* Read file */
'| updt:  update',                          /* Apply update */
'|        > $pipsmp assemble a fixed',      /* Write temporary */
'\',                                        /* End of first pipeline */
```

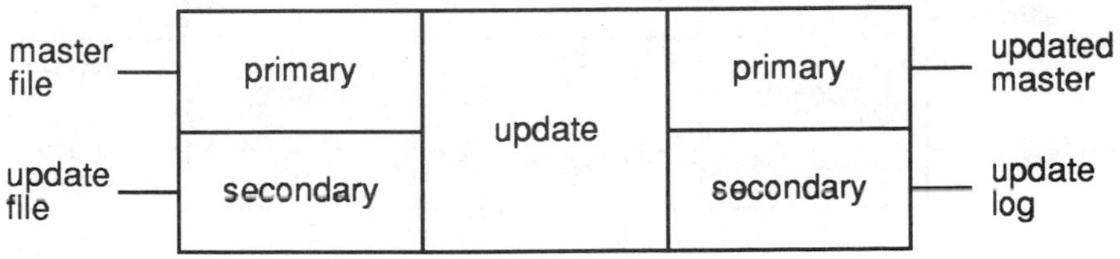

Figure 18. Updating files with multi-stream pipelines

```
'          < pipsmp update1',              /* Read update file */
'| updt:',                                 /* Into secondary stream */
'|          > pipsmp updlog a'   /* Write log from secondary */
if rc <> 0 then exit rc
```

This example has two pipelines. They intersect in the update stage
with the label `updt:`.

The primary streams (both input and output) are defined whenever
a program is requested in a pipeline. Programs that use more than one
input stream or one output stream must have a label in front of the
program name. This **defines** a label. A label is **referenced** when it is
used subsequently in the pipeline specification. The second occurrence
of the label (the first reference) defines the **secondary** input and output stream for the particular invocation defined by the label. In this
example, the primary output from the stage that reads the update file
is connected to the secondary input to the update program. The secondary output stream of the update program is connected to the primary input stream of the program that writes the update log to disk.
Note that a label defines both an input and an output stream; whether
they are connected is another matter.

The scope of a label is the pipeline specification. That is, a label
uniquely defines the invocation of a program in a pipeline specification.

The next example shows the topology of a multi-level update with
two invocations of the **UPDATE** built-in program. The primary output
stream from the first **UPDATE** is connected to the primary input stream
of the second invocation of **UPDATE**. The first invocation has label
`upd1:`; the second invocation has label `upd2:`.

The primary pipeline with a cascade of two invocations of the **UPDATE**
program processing the assembler program **PIPSMP** is shown below. It
specifies the upper pipeline in figure 19.

```
< pipsmp assemble | upd1: update | upd2: update | > $pipsmp assemble a fixed
```

The complete pipeline is shown below. The second global option (**NAME**)
declares a name to identify this particular pipeline in error messages.

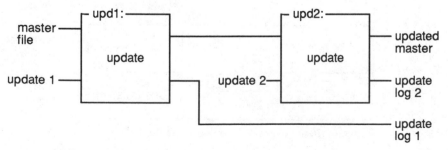

Figure 19. Multiple update pipeline processing

```
'PIPE   (endchar ? name updater)',
   '            < pipsmp assemble',
   '| upd1:  update',
   '| upd2:  update',
   '|        > $pipsmp assemble a fixed',
'?',                            /* Beginning of the second pipeline */
   '            < pipsmp update1',
   '|upd1:',
   '|        > update1 log a'
'?',                            /* Beginning of the third pipeline */
   '            < pipsmp update2',
   '|upd2:',
   '|        > update2 log a'
```

Two update logs are written in parallel as the master file passes
through the update programs. To write a single update log, the second
one is buffered and appended to the first one, as illustrated in figure 20.

   The pipeline specification to accomplish this:

```
'PIPE   (endchar ? name updater)',
   '            < pipsmp assemble',
   '| upd1:  update',
   '| upd2:  update',
   '|        > $pipsmp assemble a fixed',
'?',                            /* Beginning of the second pipeline */
   '            < pipsmp update1',
   '| upd1:',
   '| in:    fanin',
   '|        > update log a',
'?',                            /* Beginning of the third pipeline */
   '            < pipsmp update2',
   '| upd2:',
   '|        buffer',
   '| in:'
```

The built-in program **FANIN** copies all input from the primary input
stream to the primary output stream. It switches to the secondary

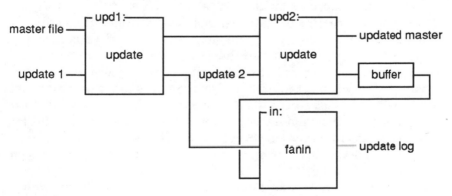

Figure 20. FANIN processing

input stream when it reaches end-of-file on the primary input stream, and so on through all defined streams.

The next example compares the file attributes of files on two minidisks (or Shared File System directories) to find files that are not on both disks and to find files that have the same name and type but have different sizes or time-stamps. The subroutine pipeline does the hard work; the program that calls it can send the result to a file or to the terminal.

```
/* Checks that two minidisks are in sync */
signal on novalue
arg m1 m2 .
if m2 = ''
   Then exit 999
'callpipe (end ? listerr)',
   '            literal LISTFILE * *' m2 '(DATE NOH',    /* CMS cmd */
   '|          command LISTFILE * *' m1 '(DATE NOH', /* Another 1 */
   '|          sort',        /* Pair files that are on both disks */
   '| both:   unique mult 1-17',    /* Select files on both disks */
   '|          unique (1-17 22-*) single', /* Take different ones */
   '|          change //<> /',                        /* Mark them */
   '| merge:  faninany',               /* Merge with uniques */
   '|          sort 4-*',                         /* Reorder */
   '| *:',                            /* Write to output */
'?',
   '  both:',                                      /* Singles */
   '|          change //+- /',              /* Mark differently */
   '| merge:'                                  /* Merge */
exit rc
```

This example issues two **LISTFILE** commands with built-in program **COMMAND**. **COMMAND** is similar to **CMS** except that it uses the same command resolution as **ADDRESS COMMAND**. Having issued the argument string as a command, CMS Pipelines command interfaces read additional commands to issue from the primary input stream. Here, a second command is specified with **LITERAL**.

The built-in program **UNIQUE** inspects fields of adjacent records. The first time **UNIQUE** is used (with the label **BOTH:**), it writes pairs of lines that have the same contents in their first 17 columns to the primary output stream; other records are written to the secondary output stream. (All selection stages write discarded lines to the secondary output stream if it is connected.) The second invocation of **UNIQUE** discards pairs of lines for files that have the same size and timestamp on the two minidisks, retaining lines for files that are different.

Lines for files that occur once are written to the secondary output stream where the label both: is referenced. The label is after an end character. This means that the secondary input stream is not connected. (Selection stages do not read from the secondary input stream, so there is no point in connecting it to anything.) The secondary output stream from the first **UNIQUE** stage is connected to **CHANGE** to insert a marker in columns 1 and 2. The output from **CHANGE** is connected to the secondary input stream of the built-in program **FANINANY**. It reads records from all input streams in whatever order they arrive.

REXX program to process multiple streams

To access more than one input or output stream, a REXX program issues pipeline command **SELECT** to select the stream on which subsequent **READTO**, **PEEKTO**, and **OUTPUT** commands are to transport data.

The following example shows a REXX program that reads and discards records from streams 0 and 1 as long as each pair of records has the same contents. The program ends with return code 0 when all pairs of records are equal and both input streams come to end-of-file at the same time. When the two input streams are not identical, the program writes the number of records discarded and exits with return code 1.

```
/* Remove matching lines from the input streams. */
signal on novalue
call PRIME 0, 0                          /* Prime stream 0 */
call PRIME 1, 0                          /* Prime stream 1 */
copy = 0                        /* Number of records the same */
do while ¬ eof.0 & ¬eof.1          .      /* Loop while records on both */
   if in.0 ¬== in.1 then leave /* Stop if they are not identical */
      copy = copy + 1                      /* Count a pair */
      call PRIME 0, 1                    /* Prime with next */
      call PRIME 1, 1
end
if eof.0 & eof.1 then exit 0             /* Files identical? */
'output' copy                        /* Write line with count */
exit 1
PRIME: procedure expose eof. in.          /* Read a record */
parse arg stream, drop
'select input' stream                 /* Read from this stream */
if drop then 'readto'      /* Drop previous record if appropriate */
'peekto in.stream'                     /* Get preview of record */
eof.stream = rc <> 0                   /* Was the record there? */
return
```

A SAMPLE APPLICATION

Melinda collects pictures. Unlike you and me, she digitizes them and keeps them on-line in the form of PostScript files. The images have 8 bits of grey scale per pixel. Here is the beginning and end of an image file:

```
%!PS-Adobe-1.0
%%Creator: sim2ps, VM/CMS Version, ICGL
```

```
 :
% **** Build Image ****
/onerow 204 string def
165.59994507 214.30580139 scale
204 264 8
204 0 0 -264 0 264
{currentfile onerow readhexstring pop} image
2f27272b2b2b2f2b272b2f2f2b2b2f2333272f2b2b272f3333332b2f272b3b1536273
327332b2f2f2b2f332b2f332b2b2f272f2b2b2b2f2f232f272f1d2b2733272b2f2b2f
2b2b27272b362f1539331d33152b2b2b232f2327152f1d2f1d2f232b2327232327232
 :
e3e333e2b3333332f363b362b3947633b3633393636406095bc45495ba9ebffffd655
33363b36363636272b27272f272b23271d2b232723272b232f151d2b0a2f2b232b232
3231d1d23231d272327232323232723271d23232723232727231d231d1d2327272723
showpage
%%Trailer
```

Melinda is not satisfied with the contrast in some of her images that do not use the entire range of the grey scale. A simple enhancement algorithm expands the grey scale based on the distribution of the pixels. A small percentage of the pixels are discarded at each end of the scale (that is, they are mapped to 0 and 255, respectively). Values between the lower and upper thresholds are expanded linearly. If the variable FIRST is the pixel value that should map to 0, and LAST is at the other end of the scale, then the new value for a pixel is:

```
pix <= first        0
first < pix < last  (pix - first) * 255%(last - first)
pix >= last         255
```

This is a trivial program for any REXX programmer. The challenge is to do it quickly and without running out of storage when the image is large.

The first part of the solution is a multistream pipeline to determine the dimensions of the picture and the distribution of pixel values.

This pipeline splits the file into two parts: the line with the picture dimensions and the picture data:

```
parse value arg(1) 'jphshi' with fn .
'PIPE (end #)',                             /* # ends pipelines */
    '<' fn 'PS |',                          /* Read input file */
    'frlab /onerow |',                      /* Discard to macro */
    'drop 2 |',                             /* Drop two lines */
    't:take 1 |',                           /* Take dimensions */
    'split |',                              /* Make one word/line */
    'stem dimensions.',                     /* Load array */
'#',
    't: |',                                 /* Lines after dimensions */
    'frlab {currentfile |',                 /* Line before image data */
    'drop 1 |',                             /* Discard it */
    'tolab |',                              /* Blank line ends image */
    'spec 1-* x2c 1 |',                     /* Pack to characters */
    'fblock 1 |',                           /* Get a character per line */
```

```
'sort count |',                     /* Find distribution */
'stem counts.'                      /* Set variables */
```

The dimensions are two lines down from the line beginning /onerow
(204 by 264). The built-in program FRLABEL copies lines from the first
occurrence of the label specified as its argument. (This label is a leading string on input lines, not the labels that define pipeline topology.)
As used here, the built-in program TAKE copies the first record it reads
to the primary output stream; the remainder of the file is copied to the
secondary output stream. The three words on the line with the dimensions are split into separate lines and loaded into the stemmed array
DIMENSIONS.

The picture is in printable hexadecimal with 4 bits per character. It
is somewhat cumbersome to process in that form, so SPEC converts it to
a packed form with one pixel per character. To get the distribution, the
built-in program FBLOCK writes a line for each character in its input
stream. Sorting and counting unique occurrences of one-character lines
gives a count of character distributions. The result is stored in the
stemmed array COUNTS. The output stream from SORT with the COUNT
option is such that columns 1 to 10 of each line in array COUNTS contain
the count of occurrences of a character; the last position is the character itself. There can be from 1 to 256 entries in this stemmed array,
depending on the distribution of the values in the input file.

The next part of the program computes the low and high 3 percent
fractile of the distribution, as well as the index of the corresponding
entries in the array of character distributions.

```
/* Determine size of picture and 3 percent cutoff points. */
points = dimensions.1 * dimensions.2          /* Compute size */
three_percent = (points * 3) % 100
/* Determine pixel value for which 3 percent are darker */
net = 0
do i = 1 to counts.0 until net > three_percent
  parse var counts.i num + 10 first
  net = net+num
  ix1 = i
end
/* Determine pixel value for which 3 percent are lighter */
net = 0
do i = counts.0 by -1 to 1 until net > three_percent
  parse var counts.i num + 10 last
  net = net + num
  ix2 = i
end
```

Rather than computing the transformation for each pixel, the transformation for each possible input value is computed (there are at most 256)
and transliteration, which is very fast, is performed on the image data.

```
/* Build arguments for an XLATE stage to perform the expansion */
/* as a transliteration.  First the values compressed to black */
/* and white. */
xlatetab = '00-'c2x(first) '00' c2x(last)'-ff ff'
first =  c2d(first)
last  =  c2d(last)
spread  =  last - first     /* Number of pixel values in original */
/* For each grey pixel, compute the new value for that pixel */
/* and add a pair of translations to the string being built. */
do i = ix1+1 to ix2-1              /* Loop through the grey pixels */
   num = substr(counts.i, 11)
   xlatetab = xlatetab c2x(num) d2x((c2d(num)-first)*256%spread, 2)
end
```

Finally, the file is read again. Though only the image data is being changed this time, the garnish must be retained. Thus, the secondary output streams of the selection stages are connected to a **FANIN** stage that reconstructs the file in its original order with the transliterated image in the right place.

```
'PIPE (end #)',
   '<' fn 'PS |',                        /* Read input again */
   'a: tolab {currentfile |',                /* Before image */
   'f: fanin |',                         /* Gather streams */
   '>' fn 'NEWPS A',                     /* Write output file */
'#',
   'a: |',                              /* From {currentfile */
   'b: take 1 |',                       /* Take {currentfile */
   'f:',
'#',
   'b: |',                              /* After {currentfile */
   'c: tolab |',                           /* End of image */
   'spec 1-* x2c|',                /* Make image 8-bit bytes */
   'xlate *-*' xlatetab '|',                  /* Map them */
   'spec 1-* c2x 1 |',              /* Back to unpacked hex */
   'xlate *-* A-F a-f |',       /* Make lowercase for compare */
   'f:',                           /* Append to picture header */
'#',
   'c: |',                              /* The trailers */
   'f:'                            /* Append to picture */
```

The built-in program **XLATE** is used twice in this pipeline specification. The first time, it performs the transformation of pixel values; the second use translates the unpacked hex data to lowercase. Running an already enhanced picture through the program should produce an output file that is identical to the input file.

Performance

The first implementation of the sample program developed in this section used a REXX stage to perform the calculation on pairs of unpacked characters (that is, without **SPEC** and **XLATE**). It took 26 seconds on an

IBM 3090 to process the benchmark picture. The final version shown here runs in less than 2 seconds.

IMPLEMENTATION OF THE REXX INTERFACE ON CMS

If you know CMS, you may be wondering how all of this can possibly work. The reason is that once a pipeline is started with the PIPE command, everything else happens without further CMS command calls. The pipeline dispatcher maintains a list of runnable threads, one for each stage in the pipeline. A stage calls the pipeline dispatcher to request a service, for instance to read a record. The dispatcher returns when the record is ready for the stage. In principle, the dispatcher needs only to load registers to dispatch a new thread; the dispatcher pathlength is about 50 instructions.

Non-SVC subcommand invocation

REXX filter programs are called using a direct branch to DMSEXI, which then calls the interpreter or the compiler run-time routine. The file block defines the default command environment to be a PSW. Thus, commands are processed by direct branch.

Managing SUBCOM environments

One snag remains, though. REXX sets up a subcommand environment (EXECCOMM) to give a command access to the variable pool. CMS maintains a push-down stack of environments with a particular name; when REXX deletes the EXECCOMM environment upon exit, CMS removes the one at the top of the stack.

CMS Pipelines must solve two related problems arising from this:

1. The topmost EXECCOMM environment must represent the particular REXX program running at any time. CMS Pipelines determines the particular environment when the program makes the first call to the command environment. Before resuming a REXX program, CMS Pipelines ensures that the corresponding environment is in front of other EXECCOMM environments.

2. Built-in programs, such as STEM, refer to variables in the environment that issues the PIPE command or one of its ancestors. The relative position changes as REXX programs start and complete. To cope, CMS Pipelines resolves the environment before the pipeline is started; variables are accessed by direct branch to the environment rather than via the CMS SUBCOM function.

CONCLUSION

CMS Pipelines moves CMS beyond the single-task single-program model. CMS Pipelines is attractive because:

- It makes the system more efficient and responsive. Passing data (in storage) between programs saves I/O operations. Running co-routines saves processor time relative to calling subroutines.

- It makes programmers more efficient. Users and programmers can often plug functional building blocks together without having to worry about procedural code. A solution is often expressed as a subroutine pipeline that can be called from other programs. Filters are easily added to tailor existing solutions.

- It makes programs more robust. A filter is tested out of context and often exhaustively. It is easy to perform a regression test.

- It supports REXX as a programming language to write both EXECs that use pipelines for processing and programs processing data in the pipeline.

- It provides multistream pipelines. Selection filters can split a file into streams that are processed in different ways. Programs using multiple streams can be cascaded.

- It supplies a library of more than 100 built-in programs to access host interfaces and operate on data.

PUBLICATIONS

- *How CMS Got Its Plumbing Fixed*. Proceedings SHARE Europe Spring Meeting 1990, pp. 175. Published by SHARE European Headquarters; 17, Rue Pierres-du-Niton; CH-1207 Geneva; Switzerland. ISSN 0255-6464.

- *CMS Pipelines Tutorial*, IBM form GG66-3158.

- *Virtual Machine CMS Pipelines User's Guide and Filter Reference*, IBM form SL26-0018.

REXX and DB/REXX

By James R. Bergsten

INTRODUCTION

This chapter describes how you can access Structured Query Language/Data System (SQL/DS) databases using the VM Systems Group program product **DB/REXX** (formerly **SQL/EXEC**).

It does not teach SQL or REXX programming, but should give a good feeling for how to quickly and easily work with SQL/DS databases using REXX.

WHY USE DB/REXX?

DB/REXX allows you to interface with IBM's SQL/DS relational database management system using the EXEC 2 or REXX system interpreter languages.

Accessing SQL/DS with a REXX application has distinct advantages:

1. It is usually much faster to develop an EXEC than a high-level language or assembler application. For one thing, REXX syntax is easier to deal with than that of most other programming languages. For another, no compile is necessary.

2. Since REXX programming is faster, EXECs coupled with DB/REXX provide a quick and easy way to retrieve, update, delete, and insert SQL/DS data.

DB/REXX is ideal for:

- "Quick and dirty" applications
- One-time, single-use applications
- Application prototyping

DB/REXX has other uses. It can issue non-query SQL/DS statements from the CMS command line—for example, to issue an INSERT statement to insert a new row into an SQL/DS table, or to allow a quick GRANT by a database administrator to let a new user access the database.

DB/REXX can also issue SQL/DS Operator commands and return command responses in a REXX variable array.

DB/REXX provides rapid access to SQL/DS. Using DB/REXX to quickly access SQL/DS is much easier than invoking ISQL, entering a number of statements, then exiting ISQL.

Besides supporting all standard SQL statements, including dynamic and extended dynamic forms, DB/REXX includes statements to simplify SQL/DS programming with REXX. For example, DB/REXX allows you to implicitly CONNECT to an SQL/DS userid other than your VM userid, or to automatically substitute a character string when an SQL/DS NULL variable is transferred to your EXEC.

DB/REXX can measure the resources used by SQL/DS or DB/REXX statements. This makes it easy to measure resources needed for any statement or statements in an application. This includes reporting on virtual CPU time (VTIME), total CPU time (TTIME), and wall-clock time, as totals and as amounts used by DB/REXX and SQL/DS individually.

DB/REXX provides an EXEC containing messages describing SQL/DS- and DB/REXX-generated error codes. This saves the time of looking up error codes during EXEC or SQL/DS application debugging. You can request that DB/REXX provide these messages automatically when errors occur.

Current releases of DB/REXX add full RXSQL (SQL/DS Procedures Language Interface) compatibility. You can run existing REXX applications that call RXSQL without change. You can even create new RXSQL applications using either the pre- or post-SQL/DS 3.1 RXSQL syntax. DB/REXX SET commands can restrict application use of either RXSQL compatibility or DB/REXX statements.

DB/REXX also supports CMS Work Units in CMS Release 6 and later, which allow simultaneous logical units of work. This means that DB/REXX applications can call each other without worrying about ending each other's LUWs.

INTRODUCING SQL AND SQL/DS

SQL/DS is an IBM relational database for VM. A **database** can be thought of as a specialized file system that has extensive knowledge about the type of data stored in it. A **relational** database allows you to dynamically define relationships among different data when your application runs.

SQL/DS imposes a two-dimensional **tabular model** of data: that is, data records are represented as **rows**, and fields within data records are represented as **columns**. Each set of data, or **table**, has a symbolic name. Each column within a table also has a name. You refer to your data by these names, which can be from one to thirty characters long. SQL/DS also supports **views**, which are subsets of SQL/DS tables. For example, you might wish to prevent certain users from accessing some of a table's data, such as employee salaries; you achieve this by defining a view encompassing only the columns you wish to be accessible, and authorizing the users to use that view.

Data in tables can be represented in several formats or **data types**, including fixed- or varying-length character strings, integers, decimal numbers, dates, or times.

A small number of primitive operations manipulate this data:

Delete   operations remove data (rows) from a table.

Immediate   operations perform administrative functions for your data, such as creating and deleting tables, authorizing other users to access your data, connecting you to a specific database, and so on.

Insert   operations add data (rows) to a table. The relational model does not define the order in which rows are placed in a table: adding new rows does not necessarily place them at the end of your table.

Query   operations retrieve data from one or more tables. To be selective in your retrieval, you **select** data to be queried. Database queries can be very simple or quite extensive. Since SQL/DS is a relational database, relationships among various tables are defined as part of your query. You can sort data returned by your query, and you can define extensive conditions to limit the data returned. You can request that SQL/DS return summaries of selected data, such as sum or average of values in columns, or number of rows selected. You can even make one selection the search criterion for another, or combine the results of a number of selections.

Update   operations change data in a table. These updates can be done using a set of selection criteria, so that you could, for example, add an amount to all records matching your selections.

Most SQL/DS statements perform one function, such as adding a single row to a table. These statements are usually referred to as **non-query** statements. Others require a set of statements to accomplish a des d result. Query and insert operations fall into this category. Here, you are dealing with multiple rows of data input or output. Thus you need to use a set of statements to define your work, **open** a **cursor** to access rows of data, retrieve data by **fetching** from the opened cursor, present data by **putting** data to the opened cursor, then **closing** the cursor.

Multiple SQL/DS activities may be in process at once, and you may not want to have any of them take effect until all are successfully completed. This is why SQL/DS has the concepts of **logical units of work**, **committing** work, and **rolling back** work. When you start any SQL/DS activity, you implicitly begin a **logical unit of work**, or **LUW**. When you are ready to make all of your changes to the database permanent, you commit your LUW. If the program encounters an error, or you have a change of heart, you **rollback** your LUW, undoing changes made during the LUW.

You access relational data by using **Structured Query Language** statements, or **SQL**—hence the product name **SQL/DS**. The SQL language is defined by the American National Standards Institute (ANSI), so there are many products that support the same SQL syntax. SQL statements are English-like, and are thus usually understandable, even if you are not intimately familiar with the language. Luckily, even though there are some anomalies in the syntax, it is difficult to inadvertently create a syntactically correct but dangerously wrong statement.

To illustrate SQL/DS data and usage, suppose you want to set up a database of employee data. You need to represent each employee's name, employee number, department, position, date of hire, salary, and so on. In SQL, part of this **EMPLOYEES** table might look like this:

Name	Number	Dept	Job	Hire	Salary
Collins, Phillip	104234	412	Programmer	01/12/1985	42,000.
Banks, Anthony	143537	414	Director	04/25/1987	56,200.
Nielsen, Gilbert	152417	414	Sales Mgr.	01/12/1990	36,200.
Jones, Howard	195937	214	Mktg. Research	10/17/1989	52,100.

You might also want a table that defines departments. This table would contain department numbers, names, managers, and so on. Here's a sample **DEPARTMENTS** table:

Name	Dept	Manager	Dept
Marketing Research	214	Emerson, Keith	200
VM Systems Programming	412	Hackett, Steven	400
Sales	414	Rutherford, Michael	400

Using these two tables, you could generate many important applications. Here are a few examples of SQL/DS statements to manipulate the tables above in likely ways:

- Display all employees in department 412 in hire date order:

```
SELECT * FROM EMPLOYEES WHERE DEPT = '412' ORDER BY HIRE
```

- Display each employee with his or her department name:

```
SELECT NAME, DNAME FROM EMPLOYEES X, DEPARTMENTS
       WHERE X.DEPT = DEPARTMENTS.DEPT
```

- Display each department manager and department employees:

```
SELECT MANAGER, NAME FROM DEPARTMENTS X, EMPLOYEES
       WHERE X.DEPT = DEPARTMENTS.DEPT
```

- Increase all programmer's salaries by 30 percent:

```
UPDATE EMPLOYEES SET SALARY = SALARY * 1.3 WHERE JOB = 'Programmer'
```

Several of these queries require access to both tables at once. For example, to print Gil Nielsen's department name, you must relate his department number to the same number in the department table.

To illustrate how easy it is to write an SQL/DS query with REXX and DB/REXX, the following REXX program implements the second example above:

```
/* Show employees and department names */
string = 'SELECT NAME, DNAME FROM EMPLOYEES X, DEPARTMENTS',
         'WHERE X.DEPT = DEPARTMENTS.DEPT'
'SQLEXEC PREPARE S1 FROM' string
if rc <> 0 then exit rc
'SQLEXEC DECLARE C1 CURSOR FOR S1'
if rc <> 0 then exit rc
'SQLEXEC OPEN C1'
if rc <> 0 then exit rc
do forever
   'SQLEXEC FETCH C1 INTO A, B'
   if rc = 100 then leave
```

```
    if rc <> 0 then exit rc
    say substr(a, 1, 20) b
end
'SQLEXEC CLOSE C1'
exit rc
```

Note the use of **SUBSTR** to make columns line up.

There are many more advanced SQL concepts, such as **relational integrity**, **normalization**, and so on; and SQL experts love to use terms from set theory. Don't panic—you need not be intimately familiar with every SQL detail to use DB/REXX effectively.

SQL/DS APPLICATION INTERFACES

Before discussing differences between an SQL/DS application written in REXX and one in a high-level language, it is useful to know how SQL/DS interfaces with applications.

When an SQL/DS application is **preprocessed** (by a program supplied with SQL/DS), all SQL statements are replaced by high-level language code and application data areas. This process creates:

1. A call to SQL/DS for each executable statement, together with an interface control block (called an RDIIN) describing the operation to be performed. When an application is preprocessed, much of the information and work needed to perform the operation is placed in an SQL/DS **access module** which resides in the SQL/DS database. Thus, within your application code, the interface control block usually only identifies which operation (stored in the access module) is to be performed.

2. An interface data area to describe the location and nature (data type and length) of your application's data area(s), sometimes referred to as **host variables**, that are involved with the SQL/DS work. This interface area is called an **SQL Descriptor Area** or SQLDA.

3. An interface area in a standard format used to return results of each SQL/DS operation. These results include error condition(s) detected, if any, the **cost estimate** (expected overhead) of the operation, and so on. This area is called an **SQL Communication Area** or SQLCA.

4. Application code is generated to handle any **WHENEVER** conditions you define, that is, actions to take if an SQL/DS statement ends in an other than a normal condition. For example, **WHENEVER SQL-ERROR GO TO X** might generate a check for a negative return code from SQL/DS, followed by a branch to program label **X**.

5. An internal table describing the nature (data type and length) of each declared host variable.

If you remember that for all practical purposes this is all any SQL/DS language precompiler does (although in practice this can be a very complicated process), you will better understand how a DB/REXX implementation differs from other host application SQL/DS interfaces.

DB/REXX

DB/REXX allows you to access SQL/DS data from REXX (and EXEC 2). It was developed with several usability goals in mind:

1. DB/REXX syntax should be as close as possible to "native" SQL— that is, you should be able to use the same statements and syntax that you would use in a high-level language application program.

2. DB/REXX should make the unavoidable differences between an interpretive language (such as REXX) and a high-level language (such as PL/I) as easy to understand and deal with as possible.

3. Input to and results from DB/REXX should match those in a high-level language application.

DB/REXX statements

DB/REXX syntax is almost identical to ANSI standard SQL. If you code the following in PL/I:

```
EXEC SQL LABEL ON TABLE MYTABLE IS 'My private table';
```

You would code the following in REXX:

```
"SQLEXEC LABEL ON TABLE MYTABLE IS 'My private table'";
```

The only difference in the formats is at the beginning of the statement. In the first case, **EXEC SQL** signals the high-level language preprocessor that this is an SQL/DS statement. In the second, **SQLEXEC** is the name of the DB/REXX program that executes this SQL/DS statement.

In most cases, if you are familiar with SQL/DS statements, it is simple to implement a DB/REXX application.

SQL/DS vs. REXX data

While SQL/DS has identifiable data types, such as integers, character strings, and so on, REXX effectively only deals with character strings.

In REXX, you can have:

```
a = 2
b = a + 5
```

and REXX will treat variables **A** and **B** as numbers. **Internally, however, they are kept as character strings**.

Consequently, DB/REXX must make conversions between SQL/DS data and REXX data transparent to your REXX application. This is done in several ways:

1. DB/REXX does implicit conversions whenever it moves data between your EXEC and SQL/DS. When passing SQL/DS data to REXX, the conversion is based on the data types defined by SQL/DS. When passing data from REXX to SQL/DS, the conversion is based on SQL/DS data types if they are available. Otherwise, the conversion is based on the first occurrence of the REXX data (i.e., an educated guess).

2. DB/REXX allows you to generate **SQL Data Areas** (SQLDAs) and manipulate them as you might in an application program. DB/REXX can create SQLDAs implicitly and explicitly, return the names and nature of columns, and allow you to modify data types "on the fly".

Data is passed between REXX and SQL/DS in three ways:

1. As REXX substitutions into DB/REXX statements as they are invoked

2. Implicitly, by moving data directly to and from REXX variables

3. Explicitly, by DB/REXX statements requesting or presenting data

Symbol substitution

In high-level languages, dynamic data passed as part of an SQL/DS statement is contained in application data areas. For example, in the statement:

```
EXEC SQL CONNECT :user IDENTIFIED BY :password
```

USER and **PASSWORD** are application host variables (SQL/DS identifies host variables by a leading colon).

To minimize DB/REXX overhead, **it is the responsibility of EXEC 2 or REXX to substitute data into an SQL/DS statement.** This means that for this example, if the REXX statements:

```
user = 'SQLUSER'
password = 'SQLPASS'
"SQLEXEC CONNECT" user "IDENTIFIED BY" password
```

are coded, REXX substitutes USER and PASSWORD before DB/REXX is called. Thus DB/REXX is passed:

```
CONNECT SQLUSER IDENTIFIED BY SQLPASS
```

Variable substitution is performed by REXX, avoiding the overhead of unnecessary variable fetching.

DB/REXX expects that EXEC 2 or REXX substitute data into SQL/DS statements before DB/REXX is called. Therefore, no preceding colons are needed or allowed.

Data passed by variable contents

In an application program, you define data areas that are used to transmit or receive SQL/DS data. These data are contained in **host variables**. You can also define **indicator variables**. These data are used to define the state of a column's data, that is, how it exists. REXX and SQL/DS both have tri-state variables: nonexistent, defined but empty, and defined with data. SQL/DS calls undefined variables **NULL** variables.

You use the same syntax you would use in high-level language SQL/DS statements to define the names of REXX host and indicator variables. For example, in PL/I:

```
EXEC SQL SELECT NUMBER INTO :NUMB FROM EMPLOYEES WHERE NAME = 'Jones, Howard';
```

sets variable NUMB to the employee number of Howard Jones. Using DB/REXX and REXX you would enter:

```
"SQLEXEC SELECT NUMBER INTO :NUMB FROM EMPLOYEES WHERE NAME = 'Jones, Howard'";
```

This sets variable NUMB to the employee number.

There are certain SQL/DS constructs where direct access to REXX **host variables** is required. These are cases where the variables could contain embedded blanks, which would make the resulting statement syntax incorrect or ambiguous.

For this reason, column names, labels, and column data are always passed via REXX variables.

These DB/REXX statements automatically fetch and/or store REXX variables:

EXECUTE USING

FETCH INTO

OPEN USING

PUT FROM

QUERY

READ

SET

WRITE

When you use these statements, DB/REXX automatically moves data between SQL/DS and your REXX application. This is done via the CMS **EXECCOMM** subcommand environment, which allows DB/REXX to directly create, drop, read, and modify REXX variables.

You can use the DB/REXX statement **SET LITERAL ON** to allow undefined variables to be treated as literals. This obviates the need for code like:

```
name = 'NAME'
hire = 'HIRE'
```

With **SET LITERAL ON**, variables **NAME** and **HIRE** would be interpreted as the strings **NAME** and **HIRE** even if they were undefined.

Explicit data requests

DB/REXX provides statements to retrieve and set SQL/DS environmental data, such as contents of the SQLCA, names and labels of data columns, data types of columns, etc. These calls alter REXX variables automatically.

DB/REXX also allows you to issue SQL/DS Operator commands and retrieve responses in REXX variables.

Explicit data requests usually name the REXX variable or variable array name, and the request fills in appropriate information. For example:

```
"SQLEXEC QUERY SQLCA ERRCODE"
```

sets **ERRCODE** to the current SQL/DS error code value.

```
"SQLEXEC QUERY LABELS MYSQLDA LABEL"
```

sets **LABEL.0** to the number of label names returned, and **LABEL.1** through **LABEL.n** to the label names for the SQLDA named **MYSQLDA**.

WORKING WITH SQL/DS STATEMENTS

Here are some SQL/DS functions you can perform with REXX and DB/REXX.

Connecting to the database

Each application must connect to SQL/DS. This may happen implicitly (in which case the VM userid is the SQL/DS userid), or explicitly, perhaps using a different SQL/DS userid. Explicit connections use the DB/REXX **CONNECT** statement. Userids and passwords should not be placed in EXECs: instead, the application should either prompt for them or require the user (or calling program) to issue a DB/REXX **SET IMPCONN** statement to have DB/REXX connect to SQL/DS automatically.

Here are some examples of **CONNECT** statements:

```
"SQLEXEC CONNECT JRB IDENTIFIED BY PASSWORD"
```

connects to the default database as userid **JRB**.

```
"SQLEXEC CONNECT TO DATA2"
```

connects to the SQL/DS database named **DATA2**.

Ending a logical unit of work

Each DB/REXX application should end its logical unit of work. This is performed by either a **COMMIT** or a **ROLLBACK**, depending on whether you want to keep your database changes.

Before returning to CMS, the last logical unit of work should be ended using the additional keyword **RELEASE**. This severs the communications link with the database.

Here are some examples:

```
"SQLEXEC COMMIT WORK RELEASE"
```

makes changes in this LUW permanent and disconnects from the database.

```
"SQLEXEC ROLLBACK WORK"
```

removes changes made in this LUW and leaves the connection to the database.

Non-query operations

Most non-query statements such as **GRANT** or **ALTER TABLE** can be issued without using any variables:

```
"SQLEXEC UPDATE STATISTICS FOR TABLE MYTABLE"
```

However, it is preferable to code these statements like this:

```
stmt = "UPDATE STATISTICS FOR TABLE MYTABLE"
"SQLEXEC" stmt
```

This is beneficial in two ways:

1. REXX does not permit statements longer than 500 characters. Using shorter strings that are concatenated when the statement is executed avoids this limitation.

2. If you use a consistently named variable to hold the SQL/DS statement currently executing, then if an error occurs, a single error-handling routine can display the contents of the variable to show which statement failed.

Since non-query statements return no data, they may also be issued directly from the CMS command line. In this case, each command will be implicitly committed (if no errors occur) upon return to the CMS **Ready;** prompt.

You could type the following without creating an EXEC to allow user **SETTLE** to access the **RESTAURANTS** table:

```
SQLEXEC GRANT SELECT ON RESTAURANTS TO SETTLE
```

Query and update operations

Since queries and updates manipulate data, they are more complicated than single-statement non-queries.

Queries can be as simple as:

```
"SELECT PHONE FROM PHONELIST INTO :PHONE WHERE NAME = 'Joel Anderson'"
```

or can be much more complicated.

It is beyond the scope of this chapter to describe all possible SQL/DS selection criteria and statement sequences. The following typical queries show some common ones used; more concrete examples follow later.

A typical simple query

```
"SQLEXEC DECLARE C1 CURSOR FOR SELECT. . ."
"SQLEXEC OPEN C1"
do forever
   "SQLEXEC FETCH C1 INTO . . .variable names. . ."
   if rc = 100 then leave
end
"SQLEXEC CLOSE C1"
```

A typical query using an SQLDA

```
"SQLEXEC PREPARE S1 FROM SELECT. . ."
"SQLEXEC DECLARE C1 CURSOR FOR S1"
"SQLEXEC DESCRIBE S1 INTO MYSQLDA"
"SQLEXEC OPEN C1"
do forever
   "SQLEXEC FETCH C1 USING DESCRIPTOR MYSQLDA"
   if rc = 100 then leave
end
"SQLEXEC CLOSE C1"
```

A typical multi-row insert

```
"SQLEXEC DECLARE C1 CURSOR FOR INSERT INTO . . . VALUES(:a:ai,:b,:c)"
"SQLEXEC OPEN C1"
do i = 1 to count
   a = a.i                              /* Set data variable */
   ai = -(symbol(a.i) = 'LIT')   /* Set indicator variable */
   b = b.i                              /* Set data variable */
   c = c.i                              /* Set data variable */
   "SQLEXEC PUT C1"
   if rc = 100 then leave
end
"SQLEXEC CLOSE C1"
```

Parameterized operations

Parameterized operations consist of **preparing** an SQL/DS statement that is incomplete. This statement is filled in when executed or opened. Parameters to be filled in are specified by question marks (?); for example:

```
"SELECT * FROM table WHERE column = ?"
```

Parameterized queries select rows on an ad hoc basis once the basic selection is defined. The query shown reads records that match a key. However, in this scenario, the key defining the rows to be selected is specified at run-time—not when the EXEC is written.

Parameterized queries can save computer resources since the subject statement is only prepared once (however, a prepared statement cannot be used across logical units of work).

Here's an example that illustrates use of a parameterized statement:

```
stmt = "SELECT * FROM PRODUCTS WHERE PRICE = ?"
"SQLEXEC PREPARE S1 FROM" stmt
"SQLEXEC DECLARE C1 CURSOR FOR S1"
do forever
   say "Enter price:"
   parse upper pull price .
   if price = '' then leave
```

```
"SQLEXEC OPEN C1 USING :price"
do while rc <> 100
   "SQLEXEC FETCH C1 INTO. . ."
end
"SQLEXEC CLOSE C1"
end
```

This EXEC retrieves information for all products that are a specified price, until the user exits the application by entering a null line.

Using SQL/DS Operator commands

DB/REXX lets you issue the SQL/DS SHOW and COUNTER statements and have the response returned into a variable array.

Here's an example of displaying the response from an Operator command:

```
arg argstring
"SQLEXEC OPERCMD" argstring
do i = 1 to opr.0
   say opr.i
end
exit rc
```

Displaying SQL/DS and DB/REXX error codes

DB/REXX provides the QUERY SQLCA and QUERY WARNING statements to provide data about the execution of the last DB/REXX or SQL/DS statement. SQLERROR EXEC displays formatted contents of the SQLCA, including any messages which correspond to the SQL/DS or DB/REXX error code.

Timing DB/REXX statements

DB/REXX provides QUERY TIMER and SET TIMER statements to measure the resources used to execute a DB/REXX or SQL/DS statement. SQLTIME EXEC displays the resources used by the last statement: virtual CPU time (VTIME), total CPU time (TTIME), and wall clock time used by DB/REXX, SQL/DS, and as a total.

WHENEVER implementation

Because a DB/REXX application is not preprocessed, DB/REXX cannot handle WHENEVER directly; DB/REXX therefore does not support the the SQL/DS WHENEVER statement.

However, it is easy to implement the equivalent function:

SQL/DS WHENEVER	REXX equivalent
WHENEVER NOT FOUND GOTO x	if rc = 100 then signal X
WHENEVER SQLERROR STOP	if rc < 0 then exit rc
WHENEVER SQLWARNING STOP	"SQLEXEC QUERY WARNING A B C D E"
	if e.1 = 'W' then exit rc
WHENEVER NOT FOUND CONTINUE	if rc = 100 then nop

In the last function, the WHENEVER is unnecessary.

You can also use the DB/REXX SET HIONERR statement to terminate execution of the EXEC when a negative return code is returned, as if an HI (Halt Interpreter) command had been entered. This terminates the EXEC after the offending DB/REXX statement.

Extended dynamic statements

DB/REXX supports SQL/DS **extended dynamic** statements. Extended dynamic statements preprocess as much information as possible about SQL/DS requests in advance, for maximum possible run-time performance.

For certain static, high-performance applications, where a query is well defined, it is worth taking the time to manually preprocess an EXEC. Elapsed run-time can sometimes be improved by a factor of 4.

While it isn't possible to automatically preprocess REXX EXECs, you may wish to manually do so for commonly used applications. When an SQL/DS statement is preprocessed, some of the work to execute the statement is performed at preprocess time, and is stored in an access module; thus this work does not need to be performed each time the application runs.

To preprocess an EXEC yourself:

1. Create an EXEC containing extended dynamic PREPARE statements for each executable statement in the run-time EXEC. These statements may include non-queries, SELECT, etc., but may not include OPEN, FETCH, DECLARE, EXECUTE, COMMIT, CONNECT, or any DB/REXX-specific statements.

2. Add a CREATE PROGRAM (or CREATE PACKAGE, in SQL/DS Release 3.1 or later) and a COMMIT to the "preprocessor" EXEC. The CREATE PROGRAM defines the name of the access module.

3. Run the EXEC to preprocess the statements. Each extended dynamic PREPARE will return a numeric value. This value is used in the run-time EXEC to associate the prepared statement with the run-time execution of the statement.

4. Create the run-time EXEC, replacing each preprocessed statement with:

```
"EXECUTE stmtid IN userid.progname [USING DESCRIPTOR sqlda]"
```

for non-queries, or:

```
"DECLARE cname CURSOR FOR stmtid IN userid.progname"
```

for queries, where stmtid is the specific statement number from the preprocessor EXEC; userid.progname is the userid and program name specified in the CREATE PROGRAM in the preprocessor EXEC, sqlda is the name of an SQLDA, and cname is the name of a cursor.

This process can be tedious. It is recommended that you make sure that the original REXX application works before converting it to this form—and retain the original EXEC and the preprocessor EXEC (you may need to preprocess it again if your SQL/DS version changes).

Sample extended dynamic REXX applications are shown in the section "Using Extended Dynamic Statements".

SAMPLE DB/REXX CODE

This section shows skeleton code for performing common SQL/DS functions. You can start with these segments and build larger DB/REXX applications.

These examples are stripped down to show only statements relevant to the task being performed, and include little error recovery and no CONNECT, COMMIT, or ROLLBACK statements. Each DB/REXX statement in a standard application should have its return code checked and appropriate action taken. You should always issue an explicit COMMIT or ROLLBACK when necessary.

Error recovery

This example shows a simple error exit. Error recovery is very application-dependent; thus this should be taken as a very basic example. It does show some things you might wish to do, especially when developing and debugging your application.

DB/REXX's SET EMSG ON obviates the need to call SQLERROR EXEC.

```
/* Error recovery example; offending statement is in variable 'STMT' */
ERROR:
say "Error" rc "occurred processing" stmt    /* Show the statement */
"EXEC SQLERROR"                              /* Display the error condition */
"SQLEXEC ROLLBACK WORK RELEASE" /* Rollback work, release connection */
"SQLEXEC QUERY SQLCA CODE"              /* Exit with the SQL/DS error */
exit code
```

Inserting data into a table

This INSERT example shows rows being added to the EMPLOYEES table. The SQL INSERT statements are built from variables STMT1 and STMT2. The INSERT statements are executed by DB/REXX calls after REXX performs variable substitution on the DB/REXX statements.

```
stmt1 = 'INSERT INTO EMPLOYEES (NAME,NUMBER,DEPT,JOB,HIRE,SALARY) VALUES ('
stmt2 = "'Collins, Phillip',104234,412,'Programmer','01/12/1985',42000.)"
'SQLEXEC' stmt1 stmt2
stmt2 = "'Banks, Anthony',143537,414,'Director','04/25/1987',56200.)"
'SQLEXEC' stmt1 stmt2
stmt2 = "'Nielsen, Gilbert',152417,414,'Sales Mgr.','01/12/1990',36200.)"
'SQLEXEC' stmt1 stmt2
stmt2 = "'Jones, Howard',195937,214,'Mktg. Research','10/17/1989',52100.)"
'SQLEXEC' stmt1 stmt2
```

Changing data in a table

This example updates a single company's address in a mailing list table. The SQL/DS UPDATE statement is assigned to variable STMT. When DB/REXX is called, REXX substitutes the contents of STMT into the DB/REXX statement.

```
stmt = "UPDATE MAILLIST",
       "SET ADDR1 = '1604 Spring Hill Road'",
       "CITY = 'Vienna, VA'",
       "ZIP = '22182'",
       "WHERE COMPANY = 'VM Systems Group'"
"SQLEXEC" stmt
```

Deleting data from a table

This example deletes a row from an SQL/DS table. The SQL/DS DELETE statement is assigned to variable STMT. When DB/REXX is called, REXX substitutes the contents of STMT into the DB/REXX statement.

```
stmt = "DELETE FROM MAILLIST",
       "WHERE COMPANY = 'Kolinar'"
"SQLEXEC" stmt
```

Retrieving a single row of SQL/DS data

These examples retrieve a single row from a table. If the data is found, it is placed into the variable names passed. If no data is found, DB/REXX sets return code 100. If some other error occurs, a negative return code is returned. The first example returns the highest ZIP code in a mailing list:

```
stmt = 'SELECT MAX(ZIP) INTO MAX FROM MAILLIST'
"SQLEXEC" stmt
```

The second example returns information about a person in the mailing list, and illustrates the use of indicator variable **IEXT** for the **EXT** field. A number will be returned in this variable; if the number is negative, the person's phone number does not have an extension.

```
stmt = 'SELECT PERSON,COMPANY,PHONE,EXT ',
       'INTO PERSON,COMPANY,PHONE,EXT:IEXT',
       'FROM MAILLIST ',
       'WHERE PERSON = 'Jim McMaster'
"SQLEXEC" stmt
```

Retrieving multiple rows of data from a table

This example retrieves multiple rows of data from a table using a cursor. As in previous examples, the SQL **SELECT** statement is assigned to a variable. The **INTO** clause is not specified in the **SELECT** statement; **FETCH** is used to reference variables instead.

Each row of data is placed into the named variables, and return code **0** is returned. When no more matching rows of data exist, return code **100** is returned. If some other error occurs, a negative return code is returned.

```
stmt = 'SELECT * FROM MAILLIST'
"SQLEXEC DECLARE C1 CURSOR FOR" stmt
"SQLEXEC OPEN C1"
do forever
   "SQLEXEC FETCH C1 INTO PER,CO,A1,A2,A3,STATE,ZIP,PHONE,EXT"
   if rc = 100 then leave
   if rc < 0 then signal ERROR
   :
   /* Process the data here */
end
"SQLEXEC CLOSE C1"
```

Updating using the cursor

This example changes records with one ZIP code to another. It uses the cursor to update records one by one. This method of updating is similar to the previous **SELECT** examples; however, the **SELECT** statement is slightly different. The **FOR UPDATE OF** clause is appended to indicate to SQL/DS that you may update specified columns in the table. It does not mean that the fields must be updated, nor is it necessary to select all fields you mean to update.

This form of update is most useful when used with a parameterized query to select rows based on a search predicate.

```
stmt = 'SELECT ZIP FROM MAILLIST FOR UPDATE OF ZIP'
```

```
"SQLEXEC DECLARE C1 CURSOR FOR" stmt
"SQLEXEC OPEN C1"
ustmt = "UPDATE MAILLIST",
        "SET ZIP = 22182",
        "WHERE CURRENT OF C1"
do forever
   "SQLEXEC FETCH C1 INTO ZIP"
   if rc = 100 then leave
   if rc < 0 then signal ERROR
   If zip = '22024' then "SQLEXEC" ustmt
end
"SQLEXEC CLOSE C1"
```

This example could be replaced by:

```
"SQLEXEC UPDATE MAILLIST SET ZIP = '22084' WHERE ZIP = '22024'"
```

However, the cursor form always updates one and only one row; the simpler form might update more than you really want updated.

Deleting using the cursor

This example deletes all mailing list records having a ZIP code of 99999. It uses the cursor to delete records.

This form of deletion is most useful when processing a table that contains duplicate rows.

```
stmt = 'SELECT ZIP FROM MAILLIST'
"SQLEXEC DECLARE C1 CURSOR FOR" stmt
"SQLEXEC OPEN C1"
dstmt = "DELETE FROM MAILLIST WHERE CURRENT OF C1"
do forever
   "SQLEXEC FETCH C1 INTO ZIP"
   if rc = 100 then leave
   if rc < 0 then signal ERROR
   if zip = '99999' then "SQLEXEC" dstmt
end
"SQLEXEC CLOSE C1"
```

This example could also be replaced by a single statement:

```
"SQLEXEC DELETE FROM MAILLIST WHERE ZIP = '99999'"
```

This format is not as flexible as the cursor format.

Retrieving column names and data types
from a table

This example retrieves column names and data types for columns returned by the SELECT statement into variables NAME.i and TYPE.i.

```
stmt = 'SELECT * FROM MAILLIST'
"SQLEXEC PREPARE STMTID FROM" stmt
"SQLEXEC DESCRIBE STMTID INTO MYSQLDA"
"SQLEXEC QUERY NAMES MYSQLDA NAMES"
do i = 1 to names.0
   "SQLEXEC QUERY DATATYPE MYSQLDA NAMES".i "TYPE."i
end
```

Retrieving column labels from a table

This example retrieves the column labels for each column to be returned by the **SELECT** statement. This example could be merged with the preceding one to retrieve the table's column names, labels, and data types.

```
stmt = 'SELECT * FROM MAILLIST'
"SQLEXEC PREPARE STMTID FROM" stmt
"SQLEXEC DESCRIBE STMTID INTO MYSQLDA USING BOTH"
"SQLEXEC QUERY LABELS MYSQLDA LABELS"
```

Dynamic non-query processing

This example lets a user interactively delete employees by entering their employee numbers. It shows how to use dynamic parameterized non-query statements.

The **SELECT** and **DESCRIBE** retrieve the SQL/DS data type of the number column of the **EMPLOYEES** table. This isn't really needed for this delete example, but would be needed if you wanted to inform DB/REXX of a data type before data is transferred from REXX to SQL/DS.

```
stmt = "DELETE FROM EMPLOYEES WHERE NUMBER = ?"
"SQLEXEC PREPARE S1 FROM" stmt
selstmt = "SELECT NUMBER FROM EMPLOYEES"
"SQLEXEC PREPARE S2 FROM" selstmt
"SQLEXEC DESCRIBE S2 INTO SQLDA"
"SQLEXEC SET LITERAL ON"
do forever
   say "Enter employee number to be deleted;"
   say "Press ENTER to exit."
   parse pull empval
   if empval = "" then leave
   "SQLEXEC WRITE SQLDA NUMBER EMPVAL"
   "SQLEXEC EXECUTE S1 USING DESCRIPTOR SQLDA"
end
```

Using the PUT statement to insert data

This example shows one way to interactively add data to a table. It prompts the user for columns of data to be inserted.

The **PUT** statement does the work of inserting data into a table. A generic **SELECT** is prepared for the entire table so that the number, names, data types, and lengths of the table's columns are returned to an SQLDA when the statement is described. The information in the SQLDA is then retrieved, and each data type code is changed so that it cannot contain null values (this is not essential; it just keeps DB/REXX from accepting null entries).

A cursor is declared and opened to make it possible to issue the PUT. An outer loop is established to process rows of data, and an inner loop is formed to process successive columns of data. The data column values are read from the terminal and written to SQL/DS. DB/REXX translates the incoming character string values into the formats equivalent to the data type codes set in the SQLDA by the DESCRIBE statement.

The PUT is executed by passing data pointed to by the SQLDA named SQLDA.

```
stmt = "SELECT * FROM EMPLOYEES"
"SQLEXEC PREPARE S1 FROM" stmt
"SQLEXEC DESCRIBE" S1 "INTO SQLDA"
"SQLEXEC QUERY NAMES SQLDA names"
string = '('strip(copies("?, ", names.0), 'T', ', ')')'
istmt = "INSERT INTO EMPLOYEES VALUES" string
"SQLEXEC PREPARE S2 FROM" istmt
do i = 1 to names.0
   "SQLEXEC QUERY DATATYPE SQLDA names."i" type."i
   parse var type.i type.i 'NOT NULL'
   type.i = type.i 'NOT NULL'
   "SQLEXEC SET DATATYPE SQLDA names."i" type."i
end
"SQLEXEC DECLARE C1 CURSOR FOR" S2
"SQLEXEC OPEN C1"
do forever
   do i = 1 to names.0
      say "Enter value for" names.i "("type.i")"
      parse pull value
      if value = "" then leave
      "SQLEXEC WRITE SQLDA names."i" value"
   end
   "SQLEXEC PUT C1 USING DESCRIPTOR SQLDA1"
end
"SQLEXEC CLOSE C1"
```

Associating a cursor with an SQLDA

This example illustrates associating an SQLDA with a cursor using the DB/REXX USE statement. Variable A contains 4441, which looks like an integer but must be handled as a character string. Variable D looks like a character string, but must be passed as a date. This example shows how to predefine ambiguously typed data so that it can be correctly entered into a table.

Data can be inserted into tables from REXX variables by specifying the list of variable names in the **INSERT** or **PUT** statement. DB/REXX makes a "best guess" at the data type of the column variable by scanning the variable. This guess can be incorrect when the variable contains numerics and the destination column is character, or the variable contains a character string and the destination column is a date, time or timestamp. This can cause SQL errors or the wrong type of data being inserted into the column. Guesswork can be eliminated by associating an SQLDA with the **INSERT** or **PUT**, either by explicitly referencing an SQLDA as a **DESCRIPTOR** or by making the association with the **USE** statement:

```
"SQLEXEC DECLARE C1 CURSOR FOR",
        "INSERT INTO A",
        "(A,D,I)",
        "VALUES (?,?,?)"
"SQLEXEC SET DATE USE"
"SQLEXEC SET LITERAL ON"
"SQLEXEC CREATE SQLDA ISQLDA A CHAR(4) NOT NULL,",
                      "D DATE      NOT NULL,",
                      "I INTEGER NOT NULL"
"SQLEXEC USE SQLDA ISQLDA FOR CURSOR C1"
"SQLEXEC OPEN C1"
a = '4441'
d = '02/04/1988'
i = 1234
"SQLEXEC PUT C1 FROM :A,:D,:I"
"SQLEXEC CLOSE C1"
"SQLEXEC COMMIT WORK"
exit rc
```

Updating statistics

This example shows updating the database statistics for a DBSPACE.

Processing **UPDATE STATISTICS** can take a noticeable amount of time, and is best done during periods of low database activity. This statement could be invoked from a REXX EXEC scheduled by a disconnected virtual machine.

```
stmt = "UPDATE STATISTICS FOR DBSPACE PUBLIC"
"SQLEXEC" stmt
```

Using extended dynamic statements

DB/REXX allows preprocessing SQL/DS statements to be used by subsequent run-time applications.

The next example shows simple data selection using "conventional" DB/REXX techniques:

```
/* Select using dynamic statements */
sel = 'SELECT TNAME FROM SYSTEM.SYSCATALOG',
      "WHERE CREATOR='SQLDBA'"
cur = 'TST'
'SQLEXEC SET EMSG ON'
'SQLEXEC DECLARE' cur 'CURSOR FOR' sel
if rc <> 0 then exit
'SQLEXEC OPEN' cur
if rc <> 0 then exit
'SQLEXEC FETCH' cur 'INTO :nam'
do while rc = 0
   say 'nam = 'nam
   'SQLEXEC FETCH' cur 'INTO :nam'
end
'SQLEXEC COMMIT WORK RELEASE'
```

The next example preprocesses the **SELECT** for the same query:

```
/* Preprocess Select using extended dynamic statements */
x = 'SELECT TNAME FROM SYSTEM.SYSCATALOG',
     "WHERE CREATOR = 'SQLDBA'"
pgm = userid()'.TMP'
'SQLEXEC DROP PROGRAM' pgm
'SQLEXEC CREATE PROGRAM' pgm 'USING OPTION DESCRIBE'
'SQLEXEC PREPARE FROM :X SETTING :S IN' pgm
'SQLEXEC COMMIT WORK RELEASE'
say 'Statement' s 'in' pgm 'created.'
```

This program is run only once. The next program is run to execute the query. Note that the value returned by the last EXEC is hard-coded into this EXEC. A better practice would be to save the value, perhaps by using GLOBALV lasting variables.

```
/* Run preprocessed SELECT using extended dynamic statements */
s = 1                    /* This value returned by preprocessing step */
pgm = userid()'.TMP'
cur = 'TST'
des = 'TSTDA'
'SQLEXEC SET LITERAL ON'
'SQLEXEC DECLARE' cur 'CURSOR FOR' s 'IN' pgm
if rc <> 0 then exit
'SQLEXEC DESCRIBE' s 'IN' pgm 'INTO MYSQLDA'
if rc <> 0 then exit
'SQLEXEC OPEN' cur
if rc <> 0 then exit
stmt = 'FETCH' cur 'USING DESCRIPTOR MYSQLDA'
do forever
   'SQLEXEC' stmt
   if rc <> 0 then leave
   'SQLEXEC READ MYSQLDA TNAME NAM'
   say 'nam='nam'.'
end
'SQLEXEC CLOSE' cur
'SQLEXEC COMMIT WORK RELEASE'
```

COMMON DB/REXX AND REXX CODING MISTAKES

Here's a list of some common user errors. Some apply to any REXX program:

- Failing to use SQL/DS indexes. Without them, SQL/DS queries run slow, slow, slow, slow.
- Placing REXX variable names within quotes, making them literals.
- Placing character constants outside of quotes, causing REXX to substitute their values before being passed as a command.
- Incorrectly mixing SQL/DS-required and REXX-required quotes, or incorrectly mixing single and double quotes.
- Omitting the comma from statements that span several REXX source file lines.
- Not initializing appropriate DB/REXX SET parameters.
- Not initializing REXX variables containing SQL/DS column names.
- Not checking SQL/DS or DB/REXX error return codes.
- Calling **ROLLBACK** or **COMMIT** in the wrong place (for example, in the middle of a **FETCH** or **PUT** loop).
- Using a constant where a host variable is required (such as column names passed to **CREATE SQLDA**).
- Leaving words out of statements, such as **DESCRIPTOR** in **USING DESCRIPTOR**.
- Passing data to **PUT USING** without an explicit SQLDA, resulting in incorrect data type conversions.
- Connecting to the wrong database or userid.
- Passing an SQLDA to a parameterized statement which has more or fewer data columns than question marks in the statement, or contains incorrect data types.
- Not ending the logical unit of work before issuing an SQL/DS Operator command, causing return code **128**.

DB/REXX-SQL/DS APPLICATION CODING DIFFERENCES

- DB/REXX and SQL/DS statements can be issued in mixed case. Except for text within single or double quotes, DB/REXX converts all statement text to uppercase.

- You can have a maximum of 60 simultaneous, distinct query statements in each logical unit of work. If you reuse statement names, there is no logical limit. There is also no limit on the number of non-query statements.

- Prepared statements cannot be used across logical units of work. Extended dynamic prepared statements can be used across LUWs, but can only be used in a specific database unless the statements are prepared in multiple databases and return identical statement number values.

- The userid and password in a CONNECT statement are substituted by REXX variable substitution; leading colons are not permitted.

- The leading colons for host variables are optional. The colon separating a host variable from an indicator variable is required (you can also use the ANSI syntax INDICATOR keyword).

- BEGIN DECLARE SECTION and END DECALRE SECTION are neither supported nor necessary in REXX applications.

- INCLUDE is not supported.

- WHENEVER is not supported. You can implement equivalent function by checking DB/REXX return codes.

WHERE TO GO FOR MORE INFORMATION

The following lists SQL/DS and DB/REXX reference documentation you may find useful when developing DB/REXX applications.

- *DB / REXX User's Guide and Reference*, available from VM Systems Group, Vienna, VA

- *SQL / DS Messages and Codes for IBM VM Systems*, available from IBM

- *SQL / DS Application Programming for IBM VM Systems*, available from IBM

- *SQL / DS SQL Reference for IBM VM Systems and VSE*, available from IBM

   Manuals for your SQL/DS version may have different names or order numbers.

ACKNOWLEDGMENTS

Thanks go to Adrian Blakey, who in 1983 began and championed SQL/DS product development at Kolinar Corporation. Adrian was instrumental in getting the first version of DB/REXX developed. He was also active in the SQL/DS groups at SHARE and GUIDE, and was Kolinar's primary SQL/DS customer support specialist.

Thanks also go to Charles Reinking, who, with Adrian, developed the initial version of DB/REXX.

Finally, kudos for Jean Lockwood, who spent a majority of her time at Kolinar improving as much product documentation as she could get her hands on.

35

RXSQL

By Heather Dawson

INTRODUCTION

The SQL/DS Procedures Language Interface (RXSQL) provides REXX access to IBM's Structured Query Language/Data System (SQL/DS) product. Data can be entered in and retrieved from a database managed by the SQL/DS database management system using RXSQL interactively or in a REXX program.

SQL/DS program product users will find RXSQL beneficial. The interactive SQL/DS user can use RXSQL to:

- Issue queries from the CMS command line
- Manipulate data stored in SQL/DS tables
- Simplify database operation and administration tasks
- Retrieve information about error conditions

Application programmers can use RXSQL to:

- Transfer data between a database and REXX variables
- Prototype application programs
- Write SQL/DS applications that need not be preprocessed or compiled

- Test SQL statements before putting them in an application program
- Use dynamic and extended dynamic SQL

This chapter provides information for both types of users. The section "Using RXSQL Interactively" is for users familiar with the relational data model who can manipulate data stored in SQL/DS databases. These users may not know how to write applications that access databases.

The next section, "Programming with RXSQL", is for users who need to write application programs which access SQL/DS databases. It assumes that programmers are familiar with the functions provided by the Structured Query Language. Programmers may also benefit from functions described in the section "Using RXSQL Interactively".

RXSQL commands and statements are explained using Structured Query Language terminology because the RXSQL functions mirror those of SQL.

As you read this chapter, you may want more detailed information about the Structured Query Language.

USING RXSQL INTERACTIVELY

To use SQL/DS interactively, use RXSQL's general-purpose EXECs. These can be called by your EXECs or invoked interactively from the command line. They are used to execute SQL statements, display HELP information, query a database, or issue operator commands. Output is stored in a temporary CMS file giving you the ability to create a report quickly.

The general-purpose EXECs are discussed here.

RXSQLEX

RXSQLEX executes SQL statements. SQL statements include INSERT, UPDATE, DELETE, ACQUIRE, CREATE, ALTER, COMMENT, LABEL, DROP, GRANT, REVOKE, and EXPLAIN. This EXEC is equivalent to the SQL EXECUTE IMMEDIATE statement.

Programmers can test the validity of SQL statements using this EXEC. The final program may be written in COBOL, for example, but all SQL statements can be tested using RXSQL. Without this tool, programmers must preprocess and compile programs to find out if SQL statements are correct.

RXSQLHLP

If you encounter RXSQL or SQL/DS errors in your EXEC, you can get more information by using RXSQLHLP.

RXSELECT

Another use for the general-purpose EXECs is to create reports. RXSELECT retrieves data from a table and displays it using XEDIT. This file can be saved or can be incorporated into reports.

RXSQLOP

Operator commands SHOW and COUNTER can be executed from any command line using RXSQLOP, making it easy for an operator to monitor performance while working at other tasks.

Examples

RXSQL provides sample EXECs that create tables, load data into them, and then select data from them. The EXECs can be run by users with access to RXSQL and authority to create SQL/DS tables.

Sample EXECs are explained in more detail later in this chapter.

To use RXSELECT to select data stored in the RXEMP table, type:

```
rxselect * from rxemp
```

If the table has been created and data has been loaded into it using the EMPCRE sample EXEC, the following will be displayed:

```
SELECT * FROM RXEMP
EMPNO   FIRSTNME MIDINIT LASTNAME WORKDEPT PHONENO   HIREDATE   JOB        EDLEVEL
------  -------- ------- -------- -------- -------   ----------  --------   -------
002130 GARY     M       SAMS     B12      5643      1969-10-01 MANAGER     17
002300 JANET    L       HEDGLEY  B09      2345      1972-12-15 ANALYST     16
001010 RON      A       LOWRY    D14      2313      1978-01-15 ANALYST     20
000990 RANDY    M       SCHENKER A07      1430      1983-03-22 OPERATOR    15
002020 TERRY    A       RAINEY   D11      3243      1989-09-05 DESIGNER    20
001840 PAUL     P       CORDON   B09      7070      1985-07-21 FILEREP     18
002330 LES      H       FABER    A10      2119      1977-03-18 CLERK       14
ELO2121I ************* End-of-Data ****************
```

If you have not run EMPCRE, and the table therefore does not exist, you will encounter an error. The type of error will be indicated by the number returned in **SQLCODE**. In this case SQLCODE will be **-204**.

To get more information about SQLCODE **-204**, enter:

```
rxsqlhlp -204
```

The following will be displayed:

```
===============================================================
3QL/DS HELP '-204'
===============================================================
TOPIC NAME:  -204

-204     owner.object-name was not found in the system catalog.
```

If you have database operator privileges, you can execute SQL/DS operator commands using **RXSQLOP**. If you type the following:

```
rxsqlop show lock user
```

The following will be displayed:

```
=====================================================================
SQLOP SHOW LOCK USER
=====================================================================
               DBSPACE   LOCK                                            NUMBER
AGENT   USER   NUMBER    TYPE   SIX   IS   IX    S    U    X   WAITERS
  2     JHEDGLY          DB      0     0    1    0    0    0     0
ARI0065I SQL/DS OPERATOR COMMAND PROCESSING COMPLETE
```

PROGRAMMING WITH RXSQL

Using RXSQL, you can write REXX programs that use SQL/DS services. Your REXX programs need not be compiled or preprocessed by an SQL/DS preprocessor. If you are using dynamic SQL you need not create or maintain packages, but you can create your own package if you use extended dynamic SQL. Assembler is the only other programming language that allows programmers to use extended dynamic SQL.

To use dynamic SQL in your REXX program, you must **PREPARE** your SQL statement for later execution, then **OPEN** or **CALL** your SQL statement. After you have opened the statement, or cursor, you can **FETCH** data from the database or **PUT** data into the database. You would then **CLOSE** your cursor and issue a **COMMIT** or **ROLLBACK** statement. RXSQL statements are described in more detail in the section "RXSQL Commands and Statements". An example of dynamic SQL appears in the "Sample EXECs" section.

RXSQL also supports the use of extended dynamic SQL. Reasons for using extended dynamic SQL include the following:

- With dynamic SQL, the user directs RXSQL to prepare the SQL statement each time the user invokes the EXEC; with extended dynamic SQL, RXSQL prepares the statement only once. Extended dynamic functions provide a distinct performance advantage over dynamic functions.

- Preparing a statement requires shared locks on catalog tables Using extended dynamic SQL reduces concurrency problems caused by locking, because the prepare is done only once.

- A dynamically prepared **SELECT** statement must have **SELECT** authority to the table, regardless of who is using the program. If the table contains sensitive data, the owner may not want to grant this authority. With extended dynamic SQL, the owner can create queries that give access to only the necessary data for a particular user. The table owner can then grant RUN authority to particular users for queries that are combined into packages.

- Dynamic RXSQL allows 40 simultaneously active prepared statements. There is no limit in extended dynamic RXSQL.

Programs using extended dynamic SQL require more maintenance than those using dynamic SQL.

When the **extended prepare** (XPREP) statement is processed, SQL returns a statement number identifying the position in the package that the prepared statement occupies. The same statement number, returned by the XPREP, is used when the statement is **declared**.

Since XPREP need be done only once and DECLARE must be done every time you wish to use the prepared statement, two EXECs are typically used. One contains the XPREP statement, and the other, a run-time EXEC, contains the DECLARE statement.

Typically one EXEC:

- CREATEs a package
- PREPAREs SQL statements

The second EXEC then allows general users to access the prepared statements.

Prepared statements are then OPENed and CLOSEd as described for dynamic SQL.

Refer to section "RXSQL Commands and Statements" for more information about RXSQL. The section titled "Extended Dynamic RXSQL" illustrates use of extended dynamic SQL in EXECs.

Debugging

The RXSQL HELP facility provides:

- Details on error conditions
- CMS HELP for RXSQL

RXSQL returns the status of a RXSQL statement or command in the return code. Three types of return codes exist: CMS-related, SQL/DS-related, and RXSQL-related. The number returned indicates the type of error. The following settings can occur:

0	Normal return
4	SQL warning

8	SQL error
1nn	RXSQL error
-3, 28, 41	CMS error

RXSQLHLP provides more information about error conditions. The user types:

```
rxsqlhlp nnn
```

where **nnn** is either the RXSQL return code or the SQLCODE.

The CMS HELP that comes with RXSQL contains information on the following topics:

- Syntax of all RXSQL commands and statements
- Information for invoking the RXSQL general-purpose EXECs
- Information about which RXSQL statements can be used for each SQL statement

RXSQL COMMANDS AND STATEMENTS

This brief discussion introduces the syntax and functions provided by RXSQL. RXSQL commands and statements are used in REXX EXECs to access a database.

A RXSQL command is a request for the performance of a task. These commands do not have equivalents in the Structured Query Language. RXSQL statements are instructions that represent steps in a sequence, and do have SQL equivalents. The "Sample EXECs" section illustrates the use of these commands and statements in EXECs.

RXSQL Commands

NAMES	Returns existing SQL statement names in the REXX variable **RXSQLNAMES**. The **STATE** and **STMT** commands can be used to receive additional information.
OP	Issues an SQL/DS operator command and returns the results in REXX variables.
PURGE	Purges and reuses statement names.
SQLDATE	Specifies output format for date columns. You can view dates as **dd.mm.yyyy**, **yyyy-mm-dd**, or **mm/dd/yyyy**.
SQLISL	Specifies isolation level. This controls how long SQL/DS holds locks it places on data. The two different levels are **Repeatable Read (RR)** and **Cursor Stability (CS)**.
SQLTIME	Specifies output format for time columns. You can specify **hh.mm<.ss>** or **hh.mm xM** (where **xM** is **AM** or **PM**).

STATE	Returns the type and state of a specified SQL statement. Possible types are **dynamic** and **extended dynamic**; states are **undeclared, unprepared, declared, prepared**, and **opened**.
STMT	Returns the SQL statement associated with a given name. The REXX variable **RXSQLSTMT** contains the string value of the SQL statement.
TRACE	Sets the trace level for specified RXSQL modules.

RXSQL Statements

CALL	Invokes a prepared or declared SQL statement. If you specified REXX variables in the SQL statement or gave a variable list as an argument to **CALL**, the variable values are passed to the SQL/DS machine.
CLOSE	Closes an open cursor.
COMMIT	Commits database changes made after the last **COMMIT** statement, **ROLLBACK** statement, or since the beginning of the session.
CONNECT	Passes a new authorization ID and password to the SQL/DS machine. You can use it to switch databases between logical units of work or to query the current authorization ID and database.
CREATE	Creates a package. The **XPREP** statement adds prepared SQL statements to a package, and the **DROPSTMT** statement deletes them from a package. The package is stored in the database by a **COMMIT** statement.
DECLARE	Declares the statement name for a particular SQL statement in an existing package.
DESCRIBE	Provides column names, labels, and data types for prepared **SELECT** statements, and puts results directly into a predefined set of REXX variables.
DROPSTMT	Selectively deletes a statement from a package.
EXEC	Executes an SQL statement that has no REXX variables.
FETCH	Reads a row of a result table into REXX variables. It is valid only for a **SELECT** statement already processed by an **OPEN** statement. The parameter list specifies variable names that will receive result field values.
OPEN	Invokes a prepared SQL **SELECT** statement. If REXX variables were specified in the SQL **PREP** statement or a list of variable names is given as an argument to **OPEN**, the values of the variables are passed to SQL/DS. The **OPEN** statement defines a result table. You can then retrieve rows with subsequent **FETCH** statements.

PREP	Prepares an SQL statement for later execution. The **PREP** statement can prepare a **SELECT** statement for a subsequent **OPEN** statement, a block **INSERT** statement for a subsequent **OPEN** statement, and all other SQL statements for a subsequent **CALL** statement.
	Parameter markers (the **?** character) may be used in positions where a REXX variable will occur when the SQL statement is **OPEN**ed. The variable values must be provided on subsequent **CALL**, **OPEN**, or **PUT** statements.
PUT	Inserts a row into a table. This statement is valid only for a block input statement that has been processed by an **OPEN** statement. The parameter list specifies variable names to be used as input values.
ROLLBACK	Backs out database changes since the last **COMMIT** statement or **ROLLBACK** statement, or since the beginning of the session. If the **RELEASE** option is specified, SQL/DS releases the database connection.
XCALL	Invokes a prepared SQL statement processed by a previous **XPREP** statement.
XPREP	Prepares an SQL statement and stores it in a package for later execution. The SQL statement cannot contain REXX variables, but can have parameter markers (the **?** character) in positions where variable values will be provided on subsequent **CALL**, **OPEN**, or **PUT** statements.

SAMPLE EXECS

Sample EXECs illustrate the use of RXSQL statements in EXECs. They can be used for modelling. Two sets of sample EXECs come with RXSQL. The first set of sample EXECs, **EMPCRE** and **EMPSEL**, illustrate dynamic SQL. The second set, **EMPPRP**, **EMPDCL**, and **EMPSELX**, illustrate extended dynamic SQL.

In the examples shown here, the input file and some of the REXX instructions, like error handling, have been removed to illustrate RXSQL more clearly.

Dynamic RXSQL

The **EMPCRE EXEC** creates a table and inserts data into it. **EMPSEL** retrieves data from this table.

Create Table

In the following example, **EMPCRE** creates table **RXEMP**:

```
    creat_emp = 'CREATE TABLE RXEMP (',
                    'EMPNO      CHAR(6) NOT NULL,',
                    'FIRSTNME   VARCHAR(12) NOT NULL,',
                    'MIDINIT    CHAR(1),',
                    'LASTNAME   VARCHAR(15) NOT NULL,',
                    'WORKDEPT   CHAR(3),',
                    'PHONENO    CHAR(4),',
                    'HIREDATE   DATE,',
                    'JOB        CHAR(8),',
                    'EDLEVEL    SMALLINT NOT NULL,',
                    'SEX        CHAR(1),',
                    'BIRTHDATE  DATE,',
                    'SALARY     DECIMAL(9,2),',
                    'BONUS      DECIMAL(9,2),',
                    'COMM       DECIMAL(9,2) )'
    'RXSQL EXEC' creat_emp                          /* Create the table */
```

Load Data

Variables are prefaced by colons because the SQL **INSERT** statement is
prepared using the RXSQL **PREP** command. The RXSQL **CALL** command
passes variable values to SQL/DS. The following example illustrates this:

```
ins_emp = 'INSERT INTO RXEMP VALUES (:emp,:fname,',
  ':mid,:lname,:wdpt,:ph,:hire,:job,',
  ':ed,:sex,:birth,:sal,:bon,:comm)'

'RXSQL PREP IEMP' ins_emp        /* Prepare the INSERT statement */

do forever                            /* Input data to the table */
    'EXECIO 1 DISKR EMPLOYEE INPUT * (LIFO'      /* Read from file */
    if rc <> 0 then leave
/* Get the data into REXX variables */
    parse upper pull emp fname mid lname wdpt ph hire job,
                    ed sex birth sal bon comm .

    'RXSQL CALL IEMP'        /* Call the prepared INSERT statement */
end
```

Finishing

The RXSQL **COMMIT** command ensures that data is inserted into the
table, unless there is an error, in which case the error routine in the
EXEC issues the RXSQL **ROLLBACK** command. The last command in
the EXEC is the RXSQL **PURGE**, which removes the prepared SQL
statement from RXSQL so that the number of prepared statements
does not exceed the limit of 40. Purging allows the SQL statement
name to be reused.

```
'RXSQL COMMIT'                     /* Commit the inserted data */
'RXSQL PURGE IEMP'                 /* Purge prepared statement */
```

Prepare

EMPSEL retrieves data from the database after the user passes arguments JOB and SALARY. Again, the REXX variables are prefaced with a colon because the SQL SELECT statement must be prepared. In this example the RXSQL statement name is SELEMP, which is also the cursor name.

The following fragment illustrates this:

```
/* Define the select statement to retrieve data from table EMPVIEW */
sel_emp = 'SELECT * FROM EMPVIEW WHERE SALARY ',
'< :salary AND JOB = :job'

'RXSQL PREP SELEMP' sel_emp        /* Prepare the SELECT statement */
if rc <> 0 then signal ERROR
```

OPEN and FETCH

The RXSQL OPEN statement opens cursor SELEMP using values of input variables JOB and SALARY. One row of data is read each time the RXSQL FETCH statement is executed, and data is placed in the REXX variables.

```
'RXSQL OPEN SELEMP'                /* Open the SELECT statement */
if rc <> 0 then signal ERROR

If rc = 0 then do forever/* If no errors, get data from the table */

/* Get the data into REXX variables from the SQL/DS machine */
   'RXSQL FETCH SELEMP :emp :fname :mid',
   ':lname :job :ed :sal'
   :
```

This EXEC will finish with RXSQL COMMIT and RXSQL PURGE, or RXSQL ROLLBACK.

Extended Dynamic RXSQL

An XPREP request can accomplish the same results as the PREP used in EMPSEL, described earlier.

Two EXECs are needed in place of EMPSEL when using the XPREP request. One creates and prepares a package, while the other allows users to access the data.

Creating a Package

The EMPPRP EXEC contains the XPREP statement and generates the intermediate EMPDCL EXEC. EMPSELX is a run-time EXEC that invokes EMPD-CL to declare statement names for the appropriate SQL statements.

Even though this example generates a package with only one statement, many statements can be put into a single package.

```
/* EMPPRP */

/* EXEC to create and prepare SQL statements available to the users */

/* Define the select statement to retrieve data from table EMPVIEW */
/* Note:  Use parameter markers, not variable names */

/* Values substituted on OPEN */
sel_emp = 'SELECT * FROM EMPVIEW WHERE SALARY < ? AND JOB = ?'

/*****************************************************************/
/*** The following technique is used to pass STMTNUM returned by ***/
/*** XPREP on to the interactive EXEC (EMPDCL called by EMPSELX) ***/
/*****************************************************************/

/* Prepare to add DECLAREs to a generated EXEC called EMPDCL */
'ERASE EMPDCL EXEC'
/* Put in comment so EXEC will be a REXX EXEC */
'EXECIO 1 DISKW EMPDCL EXEC A (STRING /* EMPDCL */'

/*****************************************************************/
/***   End of technique.                                     ***/
/*****************************************************************/

/* Create package */
'RXSQL CREATE PACKAGE' myid'.EMPPROG USING BLOCK'

/* Prepare the SELECT statement */
'RXSQL XPREP' myid'.EMPPROG' sel_emp

/*****************************************************************/
/*** The following technique is used to pass STMTNUM returned by ***/
/*** XPREP on to the interactive EXEC (EMPDCL called by EMPSELX) ***/
/*****************************************************************/

/* Generate DECLARE with result of XPREP for EMPSELX to use */
decl = "'RXSQL DECLARE SELEMP CURSOR FOR" sqlstmtn "IN" myid".EMPPROG'"
'EXECIO 1 DISKW EMPDCL EXEC A (STRING' decl

/*****************************************************************/
/***   End of technique.                                     ***/
/*****************************************************************/

'RXSQL COMMIT WORK'                  /* Commit the transaction */
'RXSQL EXEC GRANT RUN ON EMPPROG TO PUBLIC'
'RXSQL COMMIT WORK'                  /* Commit the transaction */
exit
```

The generated EMPDCL EXEC follows:

```
/* EMPDCL */
'RXSQL DECLARE SELEMP CURSOR FOR 1 IN ownerid.EMPPROG'
```

EMPSELX is a slight modification of EMPSEL, described previously. Instead of a PREP request, it has a DECLARE request that defines a statement name for a prepared statement in a package.

```
/* EMPSELX version using extended dynamic SQL */
/* An EXEC to display employees with a salary less than some amount */
/* Defaults:  ANALYSTs with a salary less than $38,000 */
parse upper arg job salary .
if job = '' then job = 'ANALYST'
if salary = '' then salary = 38000
/* Declare name for SELECT statement prepared in EMPPRP */
'EXEC EMPDCL'                           /* EXEC generated by EMPPRP */
/* Open the SELECT statement and give the input parms */
'RXSQL OPEN SELEMP salary job'
if rc = 0 then do                       /* If no errors occurred then */
   do forever                           /* Get data from the table */
   /* Get the data into REXX variables from the SQL/DS machine */
      'RXSQL FETCH SELEMP emp fname mid lname job ed sal'
      if (rc = 4 & sqlcode = 100) then leave        /* If no more */
   /* Type the data on the user's terminal */
      say 'Employee: 'emp '      ' fname mid lname
      say 'Job:'job'    Education:'ed'    Salary:'sal
      say ''                            /* Space down one line */
   end
   'RXSQL CLOSE SELEMP'                 /* Close the SELECT statement */
end
'RXSQL COMMIT'                          /* Commit the transaction */
'RXSQL PURGE SELEMP'                    /* Purge declared name */
```

More information

A complete description of the RXSQL product is contained in the *SQL/Data System Procedures Language Interface* (SH09-8103). RXSQL is available as a priced feature of SQL/DS Version 3 Release 1 (and later releases), program number 5688-103.

36

REXXTERM

By Charles Daney

OVERVIEW

REXXTERM is an asynchronous communication package for MS-DOS/PC-DOS and OS/2 that supports communication scripts written in REXX. A **communication script**, also known as a **procedure** or **macro**, is simply a REXX program that utilizes commands and functions provided by REXXTERM to automate some procedure, usually involving another computer connected through the PC serial port. Procedures may be as simple as a **logon script** invoked to initiate a remote session by waiting for prompts from the remote computer and sending information like a user name and password; they may be as complex as a system of programs which retrieves information from remote sources, processes it through one or more local applications, and eventually communicates the results to other locations.

The REXX language is ideal for writing communication scripts for many reasons: it has a rich collection of control structures (**IF**, **DO**, **SELECT**, **CALL**), variables, arithmetic, string manipulation, subroutines, I/O routines, debugging facilities, and many useful built-in functions. Another big advantage is that if one already knows and uses REXX for another purpose, say for writing system command procedures, much of what is already known is applicable to writing communication scripts. REXX capabilities, in conjunction with commands and functions added by REXXTERM, provide one of today's most powerful packages for communication script writing.

To the casual user, REXXTERM is a fairly standard communication program with customary facilities such as terminal emulation, file transfer, a dialing directory, and so forth. To the REXX programmer, REXXTERM is a collection of powerful commands and functions that may be orchestrated, together with other facilities in REXX or separate programs, to build complex composite applications.

REXXTERM does not implement any form of REXX internally. Instead, it communicates with any of several implementations of REXX through standard, published programming interfaces. Supported REXX versions are Mansfield Software's Personal REXX under DOS, and either Personal REXX or IBM's SAA REXX under OS/2.

Although most REXXTERM features are available in both the DOS and OS/2 versions, it is in the OS/2 environment that opportunities for application building are the greatest. This is because of OS/2's multitasking ability, its freedom from memory limitations, and its superior functionality in interprocess communication, networking, and database management—and REXX is the "glue" that ties these disparate elements together.

REXXTERM FEATURES

In the REXXTERM release current at the time of writing (version 2.3), the most noteworthy features are:

- Supported terminal emulations are ASCII, VT102, VT52, and CompuServe VIDTEX.
- Supported file transfer protocols are Xmodem, Xmodem-1K, Ymodem, Ymodem-G, Zmodem, Kermit, and CompuServe B+.
- Multiple dialing directories are supported for storing phone numbers and communication parameters for connecting with other computers.
- A built-in text editor facilitates simple editing tasks such as browsing text files, writing short messages, or maintaining communication scripts.
- The screen height and width may be changed at any time, within the range of values supported by the underlying PC hardware and operating system.
- Advanced, high-speed modems are supported through availability of hardware flow-control, parameter settings in the dialing directory, and (under OS/2) support for the Hayes ESP hardware, at speeds up to 57.6KBPS.

- A built-in file manager allows listing directories and selecting files for transfer or editing. Executable files, including REXX scripts, can also be run directly from the file manager.

- A **host mode** capability implemented in REXX provides for password-protected remote logins, file transfers, and remote execution of linemode commands. Because it is written in REXX, it is easily tailored and extended.

- Incoming data may be captured on disk or in a scrollback buffer that is limited in size only by available memory. The buffer may be reviewed in the built-in editor just as if it were a file, strings may be searched for, and any portions may be copied to other files, to disk, or to a printer.

- There is a **learn** feature which monitors user behavior and can write a REXX script to automate repetitive sequences, such as logins.

THE REXXTERM USER INTERFACE

At least three styles of user interface exist for controlling a text-oriented application like REXXTERM. Each appeals to certain types of users more than others, or to the same user at different stages of the learning process. In the first style, actions and options are selected from menus. This is a good way to get started, with minimal learning requirements, but it is slow for experienced users. In the second, frequently used commands are assigned to function keys or alphanumeric keys in combination with the **Alt** key. Supplementary parameters, if any are required, are prompted for. This is very efficient for users who have learned key assignments, but is not adequate for representing all options of a large number of complex commands. The third interface style, the oldest and requiring the most effort to learn, involves commands with parameters entered on a command line. Although hard to learn, this offers the most power and flexibility.

Since no single style of interface satisfies all needs very well, REXXTERM offers all three styles. All major program functions are accessible through each type of interface. Only the command interface, however, offers complete control over program operation. Any function or configuration setting that can be selected with menus or keystrokes can also be invoked by command. Indeed, internally REXXTERM is completely command driven. Both menu selections and keyboard actions translate into commands. Not only is this a logical, efficient way of structuring the program, but it is also really required in order to make all program capabilities easily accessible from REXX scripts.

Another aspect of the REXXTERM user interface merits discussion. As a communication and terminal emulation program, REXXTERM's main function is to connect with other computer systems. Given the current state of the art in telecommunications, it is not feasible to use a modern graphical user interface with remote computers over serial connections that usually operate at a speed of 19.2KBPS or less. Most remote systems, whether bulletin board, large information service, or corporate mainframe, still use what is essentially a command line interface (with some mixture of text menus). Although this is not at all "modern", a number of good ideas have been introduced over the years to make such interfaces more tolerable. Unfortunately, most individual systems implement only one or two of these improvements, at best— and never in a manner consistent with other systems.

REXXTERM attempts to help this situation by implementing—at the local workstation—as many of these command line assists as possible. Some of these improvements are available with no special effort on the user's part. Others require simple REXX programming, but with a potentially large gain in ease of use.

A feature always popular for enhancing command-driven systems is a command history facility. That is, previously issued commands can be easily recalled, edited, and reused with minimal keystrokes, instead of requiring complete reentry. REXXTERM does this automatically. The last 20 commands (or lines of data) sent are available for editing and reuse.

Most remote computer systems offer little, if any, help with editing new commands as they are entered. If a mistake is made, it is necessary to abandon the command and start over. REXXTERM provides an optional terminal mode in which commands can be edited locally before being sent to the remote system.

Another feature frequently found in conjunction with command history and editing capabilities is a command synonym or alias facility. This allows one command word to substitute for another (presumably longer or more obscure). Generally, a whole series of commands may be associated with one synonym, and parameters may be substituted into the series of invoked commands. This is a true macro facility, and, of course, it is exactly what REXX makes possible. While REXXTERM doesn't offer a synonym capability per se, use of REXX scripts offers something even better: not only can a complex series of remote commands be issued from a REXX script, with parameter substitution, but execution can be made conditional on intermediate results. Because the script can (for instance) check for error conditions or use results of earlier commands, it is possible to build entirely new commands for specialized processing. It can be almost as good as if one were creating REXX programs to run on any system, even if no REXX interpreter is available on that system.

The next feature one encounters as an enhancement to a command line interface is the ability to **redefine** keys, that is, to bind new meanings to them. In the DOS world there are many different keyboard macro packages available that do this, and the ability is so useful that most serious applications now have this feature built in. In REXXTERM, accordingly, it is possible to redefine all function keys and many other key combinations involving the editing keys (cursor keys, `Insert`, `Delete`, etc.) and various `Ctrl-`, `Alt-`, and `Shift-` combinations.

Because REXXTERM is a communication program, there are two possible meanings that a key assignment can have. It can be either a command for REXXTERM itself, or it can be a command (or arbitrary string of characters) to send to a remote computer. The two kinds of assignment are treated equally. While REXXTERM provides built-in assignments for most keys, they can all be changed. This is the basis for support of different terminal emulations, where different data sequences need to be assigned to the cursor and editing keys. Function keys can be changed as well, which is particularly important for being able to work smoothly with protocol converters on IBM mainframes. Since entire REXX scripts can be attached to any key, REXXTERM can allow quite complex operations to be initiated with a single keystroke.

While this addresses the needs of users who prefer a single-key interface for application control, REXXTERM also addresses the needs of those who prefer menus by providing a menu-building system. Menu builders are another class of utility frequently found among the favorite enhancements to DOS. The REXXTERM menu-builder provides for multi-page, multi-level menus. Menus can contains a mixture of text and menu choices. Choices are made from menus by selection with a light bar or by number. Pop-up HELP text can be provided for each menu choice. Each choice causes execution of one or several REXXTERM commands, including REXX scripts. Since REXX variables can be set, a whole series of menu-prompted choices can be provided and acted upon later in a REXX program. Menus can be defined and redefined on the fly, making it possible to build menus dynamically, reflecting data received during a session. One could, for instance, retrieve a list of files from a remote computer, present the names in a series of menus, then cause all files selected by the user to be downloaded.

If more elaborate menu facilities are required, one may use the `RXWINDOW` function package supplied with Personal REXX for DOS and OS/2. This gives much more control over menu and window layouts. Almost any style of text menu, such as the Lotus-style menu bar and drop-down menus, can be programmed. In addition, windows may contain multiple input fields and use the keyboard much more flexibly.

(See the chapter "REXX for PC-DOS and MS-DOS" for more details on RXWINDOW.)

Another useful feature, not strictly related to command handling yet still found in many systems, is **session management**. This is often called **scrollback**. It refers to the ability to capture all data that appears on the screen in a buffer for later review. Many packages can capture only a few screens of data; REXXTERM can capture as much as available memory will hold. Under OS/2 or DOS with EMS (expanded memory), this can be megabytes of data—tens of thousands of lines. The interface which is used to review this data is REXXTERM's built-in editor, the same one used for editing disk files. This allows data to be searched for and portions to be copied to other files or the printer.

One interesting feature of this capture buffer is that it is programmatically accessible from REXX. Scripts can use a REXXTERM function to read lines from the buffer so that they can be scanned or processed by the script. One way this might be used is to take some list of files, messages, options, etc., that have appeared anywhere in the session and can be positively identified, and place them in dynamically constructed menus that in turn lead to appropriate processing choices.

COMMANDS AND FUNCTIONS USED IN REXX SCRIPTS

From the REXX script-writer's point of view, the REXXTERM user interface is secondary, and what really matters is that, to the programmer, REXXTERM appears to be a rich library of commands and functions that can be used in developing communication applications. This section describes these basic building blocks.

Commands and functions are largely equivalent ways of utilizing the same program features. From the REXX programmer's point of view, a command is addressed to a specific environment for handling. In communication scripts, the default environment is REXXTERM, although the system command environment can also be addressed when necessary. A function, on the other hand, appears to be an integral part of the language, although the communication functions provided by REXXTERM are supported outside of the language interpreter itself by means of the external function API.

REXXTERM implements many capabilities as both commands and functions, in which case the two can be used interchangeably. Function syntax tends to be somewhat more convenient for passing multiple parameters and returning result strings, but command syntax is more traditional in script writing.

One general point that might be noted about using these commands and functions in REXX scripts is that powerful native REXX capabilities for string manipulation, such as the **PARSE** instruction and string-handling functions, come in very handy. Script programming consists largely of dealing with character strings, and native REXX primitives complement REXXTERM's commands and functions very nicely.

Output can be sent to the serial port with the **SEND** command. Its only parameter is the string to be sent. Very often data sent to another computer must be followed by a carriage return to signify line end. This can easily be done by concatenating the REXX string `'OD'x`. REXXTERM also has a convention of certain escape sequences whereby certain frequently used control characters can be represented easily in combination with a backslash (\) as an escape symbol. So, in particular, a carriage return can also be represented symbolically in a string as `\r`.

An alternative to the **SEND** command for output is the **SEND** built-in function. It has an additional parameter which controls whether or not escape sequences as described above will be recognized and converted. It is useful not to do anything with escape sequences when transmitting arbitrary data, such as might be read directly from a file.

In general, input in a communication script is much more complex than output. This is because, in asynchronous communications, there is no concept of a record and no clear indication when all expected data has been received. In the simplest case, one simply looks for a predictable sequence of characters which is, or serves as, a prompt from the remote system signifying that a response may be sent. This is, of course, typical of situations where one is automating a terminal-oriented sort of interaction.

REXXTERM provides the **MATCH** command for the simplest form of waiting for such a prompt string. The only command parameter is the string which is to be matched. The command terminates when the string is seen in the input or when it is interrupted by the REXXTERM user. A return code indicates what terminated the command. Since line noise or unexpected circumstances may intervene to prevent the expected character sequence from being seen, reliable automated operation also requires some provision for the command to terminate after a certain timeout period. This is under the script-writer's control. In fact, there are two types of timeouts supported, corresponding to different error situations. In one scenario, the expected prompt isn't forthcoming and the remote system simply stops and waits. This kind of timeout expires when no input is received for a specified length of time. In an alternative scenario, the remote computer enters a state where it is sending a continuous stream of unexpected data. To handle this, a second kind of timeout can expire if the desired string is not matched at all after a certain period of time. This "no match" timeout is perhaps the more generally useful, since it largely subsumes the "no data" timeout. However, the latter is applicable when a large quantity of unpredictable data is expected before an eventual prompt sequence is received.

Very often no one particular string can reliably be expected as a prompt. If the remote computer encounters an error situation, or if it is capable of generating different prompts depending on unpredictable circumstances, any of several prompts may reasonably be expected. REXXTERM provides for this quite simply with the **MATCHX** command, which terminates when any one of several strings is seen in the input. Timeouts that work the same way as with **MATCH** are also provided. The actual string that caused the match is indicated by the return code. A REXX **SELECT** instruction can then be used to take alternative courses of action.

Again, there are function analogs of string-matching commands—the **READSTR** and **READSTRX** built-in functions. Because of their function syntax, it is possible to control certain options when calling them. **MATCH** and **MATCHX** scan specified match strings for escape sequences (beginning with \) as described above. If this is not desirable, an option of the built-in functions can disable it. Another feature sometimes nice in automated procedures is suppressing screen output during a match process. This too can be requested with an option. As a final extra provided by built-in functions, up to 1024 characters preceding (and including) the matched string are returned as the function value. This may be used for further control of the script.

Two other built-in functions sometimes provide useful alternative ways of reading data. **READNEXT** reads a specific number of characters, if the amount of data to read is known in advance. There is also a **READLAST** function, which in effect rereads a certain number of characters already received. This may be useful after a **MATCH** operation if further clarification of the context is required.

Many additional REXXTERM commands and built-in functions may be used in scripts, but those discussed above are the principal ones used for reading and writing serial data, and hence the ones most commonly used. It might be noted that, by means of service routine exits supported in both DOS and OS/2 versions of the REXX API, it is possible to use REXX **SAY** and **PULL** instructions to communicate with the user at the keyboard in a way that interfaces smoothly with REXXTERM. In particular, **SAY** displays output on the screen just as if it came from the serial port. This allows taking advantage of terminal emulation control sequences to control screen formatting. It also means that **SAY** output gets added to the capture buffer, and does not interfere with or overwrite received data.

EXAMPLE APPLICATIONS

This section describes in very general terms some applications that have been created with REXXTERM and REXX. In each case, commercial or shareware packages exist that perform similar functions. However, the hallmark of these applications is function customization. The basic strength of REXX is end-user programming, the ability to implement computer services in a way that serves real users' needs instead of what someone else thought those needs might be. A major purpose of both REXXTERM and REXX is empowering users to do things like the following in ways that suit them best.

Electronic mail management system

Users of electronic mail have experienced a proliferation of mail services. It is not unusual for one person to have mailboxes on many and varied systems, such as MCI Mail, CompuServe, bulletin boards, BIT-NET, the Internet, and the company mainframe. Although there is a trend towards interconnecting many of these systems, it will be a long time before this is really convenient. Further, users such as consultants often have no alternative to using a variety of private mail systems operated by their clients.

The problem with so many mail systems is the variety of interfaces they present for sending and receiving mail, as well as the simple inconvenience of checking in many places for new mail. It would be nice if it were possible to automatically access all mailboxes periodically, download any new mail, and save it in a single queue on your own computer. Further, you would want to be able to answer, forward, or file each message in a uniform way. Replies, of course, should be delivered automatically. Mail filed for future reference should be accessible by various paths, such as name of recipient(s), date, or subject.

REXXTERM with appropriate scripts provides most of the tools to build such a system. The window and menu handling facilities in REXX implementations like Mansfield's Personal REXX even make it possible to provide a reasonably decent user interface. Presumably, your favorite text editor or word processor would be used for creating messages. The only additional tool which might be required is a database system for storing mail, although quite a bit can be done with ordinary flat files.

Mail gateways

REXXTERM could also directly address the problem of interconnecting mail systems. Much as in the preceding example, REXXTERM could be programmed to connect to designated services to pick up mail for anyone in a group defined by a routing table. The table could specify rules such as "If mail for Casey Jones arrives on MCI Mail, forward it to her secretary's mailbox on the PROFS system". In an operating environment like OS/2, such a process could run in the background without any manual intervention.

Uniform front-ends to information services

Along with the proliferation of electronic mail systems, there is a burgeoning of on-line information services. In additional to traditional services like Dialog, BRS, Medline, and Lexis, which have been around for a long time, there are now many special-purpose systems, which are often very inexpensive or even free (except for the phone call). Many of these are operated by federal or state governments. The problem of a bewildering array of incompatible interfaces remains, to say nothing of the comparatively simple problem of keeping track of the phone numbers and passwords.

No completely automated front-end could hope to keep up with this welter of systems, but a shell could be built using REXXTERM and REXX that would offer various tools to save time and money. To justify investing time necessary for its development, it is assumed that there is a community of individuals with similar needs who will be using the same services. The shell could provide hierarchical menus leading to the specific services for which assistance is provided. One kind of facility that would be included is simply a database of HELP information covering each service. Such information should be available on the local computer in a relatively uniform format so it could be reviewed easily off-line. Another kind of support that could be included is a form-driven dialog for composing queries, with automatic conversion into whatever query language is actually provided on the system.

Customized bulletin board systems

Many commercial BBS packages are now available, but they tend to present a very high learning and administrative burden. A user in a small office may want a system with a relatively limited range of functions, such as electronic mail, a place for clients or colleagues to send or receive files, or a menu-driven facility that allows prospective customers to request information or place orders. Most BBS packages are loaded with general-purpose capabilities but offer few tools for building special-purpose applications.

REXXTERM includes a host mode that functions as a very basic BBS, in that it validates callers in a password file and then offers a limited menu of functions like file transfer. This host mode is implemented as a REXX script for which the source is provided, so it is very easy to extend. Many features one might want to implement can be done directly in REXX. Or, as is typical in the building-block approach which REXX facilitates, complex subsystems can be implemented in other languages and simply made available through the host mode shell.

Not only is it possible to implement custom functionality like this easily on a "host" with REXXTERM, but application-specific front ends can also be built. For example, perhaps a number of field personnel need to submit reports in a certain format on a periodic basis. An application could be prepared that would allow easy entry of the required data, formatting it in some appropriate way, and automatic transmission of the report to the central site. The whole process could be initiated by a single command on the portable computer of the user in the field, and it would not be necessary to instruct such users in the intricacies of modems and data communications.

CONCLUSION

REXXTERM has demonstrated the power and versatility of REXX as a **universal macro language** by providing a solid base of asynchronous communications capabilities that can be controlled through REXX in support of many communications applications. REXX is well suited for this task because of its character-string handling features and its ability to integrate with other system services. The future direction that REXXTERM takes will very probably involve a variety of general-purpose and semi-custom communications applications such as those suggested by the examples above.

In Depth

This section presents information on REXX implementations, describes REXX language facilities in terms of EXEC 2 and CLIST, identifies issues and resources in REXX education, and concludes with a large bibliography of REXX reading material.

37

SAA Portability

By Stephen G. Price

INTRODUCTION

Many REXX programs are written to handle tasks that only pertain to a specific system. For those programs, portability is not a concern. In other cases, programs originally written on one system will be moved to another system. IBM has tried to make REXX implementations consistent between systems to ease portability and help users adjust rapidly to writing REXX programs on different systems. This chapter describes differences between IBM's various REXX language processors (the interpreters for CMS, TSO/E, OS/2, and OS/400, and the CMS compiler), as well as some differences between systems that often affect REXX programs.

OVERVIEW

Some principles of the original REXX design affect the system independence of REXX programs—the **portability**.

Commands in REXX programs usually present the biggest portability problem, and almost all REXX programs use commands for an important part of their function.

The second major area to consider is differences between language implementations. This is primarily a matter of one implementation being ahead of another in introducing new features of REXX, but it also includes system-specific functions and instructions.

Besides differences in commands and in the REXX language itself, there are certain system interfaces that REXX depends on which vary between systems and can affect the results of REXX programs.

SYSTEM INDEPENDENCE

REXX was designed to run on VM systems, but one of its design principles was to be a general-purpose language not tied to that one system. This principle led to several features of the language which have, in fact, made REXX suitable for many different systems.

Numbers and arithmetic

REXX's method of storing and handling numbers is the most significant aspect that shows its system independence. The definition of numbers and arithmetic operators is in terms of their representations as character strings—the way people see them. The REXX language definition does not insist that numbers actually be stored internally as character strings, but it does insist that they behave as if they were. This frees REXX from being tied to any machine's architecture and ensures that programs performing numeric computations produce the same results on different machines.

REXX includes one deviation from this character-only principle, in the definition of the exponential or power operator. System independence is preserved, however, because the definition is expressed in terms of the way people can perform binary operations, not how machines do it. No register size or machine operation is required, so any machine can implement the REXX power operator correctly.

Other aspects

Cowlishaw emphasizes that REXX was designed for the convenience of people, not computers. This principle is clearly seen in many ways and is the foundation of REXX's system independence. People are the same regardless of which computer they are using, and REXX must be the same, too.

Another part of the language definition that ensures consistency between implementations is the specification of limits on such items as clause length and string length to be handled by certain data conversion functions.

System-dependent areas

There are a few places in the language definition where REXX explicitly allows implementations to include system-specific features and variations in function. The most significant of these is **REXX stream I/O**. This reflects the fact that many systems have widely differing file system structures and underlying I/O operations. It also takes into account the desire for good performance of the language implementation. For instance, REXX allows positioning within a file to be done in terms of line numbers (using **LINEIN** and **LINEOUT**) or byte numbers (using **CHARIN** and **CHAROUT**). The language definition does allow implementers to limit some of these operations. Implementers, therefore, can drop some features that would be difficult to implement and very slow in execution.

For instance, PC-DOS/MS-DOS and OS/2 have a byte-oriented file system. The end of each line is indicated by the presence of a line-end character within the stream of characters that make up the file. Byte positioning on this system is easy, but line positioning is not; it would require examining the file character by character. Some PC implementations—such as IBM's OS/2 REXX and Mansfield Software's Personal REXX—do not support line positioning (although positioning to line 1 is supported).

In general, when system-dependent features are required, REXX compartmentalizes them. This keeps their effects well defined and helps the programmer become aware of treading on system-dependent ground. The best example of this is the **STREAM** function, which retrieves information about the status of I/O operations and allows system- and stream-dependent operations to be performed on available streams.

Other areas where system-dependent effects are permitted include the **CONDITION** function (where arbitrary character strings may be returned to provide information about the most recent exception condition raised) and command return codes (REXX does not specify a length for return codes, and does not even require them to be numbers). This last decision was particularly good, as some operating systems do not include the concept of command return codes, e.g., OS/400.

COMMAND PORTABILITY

Almost all REXX programs include embedded system commands. Command names, options, and syntax are system-specific, so commands for one system will fail or produce unexpected results when run on a different system. This is usually the biggest barrier to REXX program portability. For some commands, there are direct equivalents available on other systems, so conversion is easy. In other cases, a similar function is not provided, so major changes are required.

In the case where a REXX program issues commands to an application program which has been implemented on more than one system, commands are usually not a great problem because applications are usually kept compatible when they are ported.

Although changing commands requires work in porting a program, it is usually easy to identify the places in the program where commands must be changed. A more subtle aspect of issuing commands is that not all systems treat commands the same way. The REXX language defines the mechanism for passing commands to the system and receiving the return codes, but the system's handling of the command and return codes is not governed by REXX at all. Several problems can arise:

- Return code conventions vary between systems. For instance, FILE NOT FOUND yields 28 on CMS, and 1 on OS/2. OS/2 also uses 1 for many other common errors. On OS/400, return codes are not numbers (except for 0); they are seven-character message identifiers. The one return code convention that all systems observe is that 0 means success.

- Error and failure definitions are not consistent. On CMS and TSO, issuing an unknown command produces return code -3 and raises the REXX FAILURE condition. On OS/2, it produces return code 1 and raises the ERROR condition. On OS/400, it will cause escape message CPF0001, set a return code of CPF0001, and raise the FAILURE condition.

- Some systems use the value specified on EXIT and RETURN instructions for setting a return code when REXX procedures are run as commands. CMS and TSO require the value to map directly to 32-bit integers and use the value as the return code. CMS, however, displays only the last five digits in its Ready message. OS/2 sets the errorlevel (which is similar to a return code) to 1 if the REXX interpreter itself fails and sets it to zero otherwise. On OS/400, a REXX command that ends with a non-zero return code causes message CPF7CFF, REXX procedure name ended; return code n, which sets a return code of CPF7CFF, not n.

REXX programs as commands

All of the SAA systems have a system command that takes the name of a REXX program as an argument, and runs that program. CMS and TSO both name the command EXEC, but the command format and operands are different. On OS/2, the command is CALL. On OS/400, the command is Start REXX Procedure (STRREXPRC).

CMS and OS/2 automatically support REXX programs as system commands, i.e., the standard command search order includes a search for system command procedures (EXEC files on VM, CMD files on OS/2), which may be written in REXX. TSO supports use of REXX programs as system commands by allocating data sets containing REXX programs to system files SYSPROC and SYSEXEC. OS/400 does not check for REXX programs automatically during its command search, but it does allow REXX programs to run as commands. It does this by allowing REXX programs to be the **Command Processing Program** (CPP) for commands when they are created with CRTCMD (create command).

Most systems allow execution of REXX programs from within REXX programs by issuing the name of the REXX program as a command. On CMS, this is allowed using ADDRESS CMS (or by specifying EXEC *exec-name*). On TSO, it is bound by the same setup process, involving allocation of SYSEXEC and SYSPROC, as commands entered at the command prompt. OS/2 does not allow issuing names of REXX programs as commands in REXX programs; the OS/2 CALL command (which is distinct from the REXX CALL instruction) accomplishes this. On OS/400, most commands provided by IBM are of type *IREXX (valid in REXX programs in an interactive job) and *BREXX (valid in REXX programs in batch job). New commands may also be created with the *IREXX and *BREXX attributes, including commands that have REXX programs as their CPPs.

Programs will be more portable if they invoke other REXX programs with subroutine or function calls, instead of as commands.

LANGUAGE DIFFERENCES

Built-in functions

Each REXX implementation includes several system-specific functions that are not part of the SAA Procedures Language definition. These functions are listed in Table 3. Note that if you have an external function and that function's name is used for a built-in function on a certain system, you will not be able to port your function to that system under the same name because the REXX function search order puts built-in functions ahead of externals.

Table 3. System-Specific Functions

Function	CMS	TSO	OS/2	OS/400
BEEP			X	
CMSFLAG	X			
CSL	X			
DIAG	X			
DIAGRC	X			
DIRECTORY			X	
ENDLOCAL			X	
EXTERNALS	X	X		
FILESPEC			X	
FIND	X	X		
INDEX	X	X		
JUSTIFY	X	X		
LINESIZE	X	X		
LISTDSI		X		
MSG		X		
OUTTRAP		X		
PROMPT		X		
RXFUNCADD			X	
RXFUNCDROP			X	
RXFUNCQUERY			X	
RXQUEUE			X	
SETLOCAL			X	
SETMSGRC				X
STORAGE	X	X		
SYSDSN		X		
SYSVAR		X		
USERID	X	X		

A few other functions vary somewhat between systems.

DATATYPE   All implementations have included **C** and **DBCS** options on this function as part of their DBCS support.

DATE   The **Century** and **Julian** options are supported only on 370 systems. The **Language** option is supported only on OS/2.

The 370 interpreters allow a null string as a parameter and treat it the same as no parameter. This is a bug and should be fixed in the future. For successful execution on all systems, use no parameter at all —**DATE()**—when you want the default. The **Normal** option on **DATE** (introduced in language level 3.45) also returns the default format.

ERRORTEXT   Wordings (but not meanings) of some REXX error messages vary between systems. The SAA definition covers most error messages, but there are some system-unique messages. For instance, on OS/2, error 1 means **File table full**; on OS/400, it means **Pseudo-CL variable name not valid**; CMS and TSO do not use error 1.

RANDOM

The language definition allows for implementation-specific variations for **RANDOM**. However, all implementations use the same algorithm, so results will be consistent between systems.

Stream I/O functions (LINEIN, LINEOUT, LINES, CHARIN, CHAROUT, CHARS, STREAM)

The stream I/O functions (which provide file input and output as part of the language) have been implemented (by IBM) only on OS/2 at this time. REXX stream I/O will work the same way on all systems unless you use the parts that are defined to be system-dependent, such as the "stream commands" option of the **STREAM** function, and system-specific error codes. Also, because OS/2 has a byte-oriented file system, the OS/2 implementation supports character positioning within a file but not line positioning.

TIME

As with the DATE function, the 370 systems allow null strings as parameters, but OS/2 and OS/400 do not. The 370 systems should be fixed in the future.

The 370 systems report time results for elapsed time and **TIME('L')** to six decimal places. OS/400 reports the time to three decimal places, padded with three zeros. OS/2 reports results to two decimal places, padded on the right with four zeros.

Operators

There are a few variations to be concerned with regarding operators on the 370 systems:

Logical not operator

On early CMS systems, only the ¬ character is supported as a logical not. More recent systems support both ¬ and the backslash (\).

Also, the not symbol is not an invariant character across different code pages (i.e., in some code pages, you must enter a different character to produce the code that REXX recognizes as a not symbol).

Slant bar in not equal operator

The 370 systems support the forward slant (/) for use in "not equal" operations (**if a /= b then. . .**). This is a non-SAA extension and is not supported on non-370 systems.

Vertical bar (OR, Concatenate)

There is only one vertical bar supported by REXX as an operator. Confusion arises because some systems have multiple vertical bars in their code pages, which look similar on some displays and keyboards. Also, as with the not symbol, the vertical bar is not an invariant character across different code pages.

Instructions

In a few cases, there are system-specific extensions or variations to the SAA definitions of REXX instructions:

Assignment   The 370 interpreters and CMS compiler accept an assignment instruction with no expression (which is not permitted according to the language definition). OS/2 and OS/400 reject it.

ADDRESS   The default command environment name is different on the different systems. The valid formats and possible values vary between systems.

INTERPRET   All implementations allow and ignore labels appearing within the expression being interpreted. The SAA definition does not allow labels at all in the expression.

OS/2 and OS/400 limit the length of the expression being interpreted to 64,000 characters. The 370 systems are limited only by available memory.

The CMS compiler does not support the **INTERPRET** instruction.

OPTIONS   The 370 interpreters and CMS compiler accept an **OPTION** instruction with no operand (which is not permitted according to the language definition). OS/2 and OS/400 reject it.

PARSE EXTERNAL   CMS and TSO support **EXTERNAL** as a sub-keyword on the **PARSE** instruction.

PARSE NUMERIC   CMS and TSO support **NUMERIC** as a sub-keyword on the **PARSE** instruction.

PARSE SOURCE   The first token is either CMS, TSO, OS/400, or OS/2. The second token is either **COMMAND**, **SUBROUTINE**, or **FUNCTION**, depending on how the REXX procedure was called. The implementations provide a consistent definition of how this is set.

The remaining tokens are defined as follows.

CMS Compiler   The following items are included, separated by blanks:

filename (or synonym if the program is running as a compiled **MODULE**)

filetype (* if the program is running as a **MODULE**)

filemode (* if the program is running as a **MODULE**)

Name the program was invoked by (possibly a synonym or ?)

Default address environment

CMS Interpreter	The following items are included, separated by blanks:
	filename filetype (possibly *****) filemode (possibly *****) Name the program was invoked by (possibly a synonym or **?**) Default address environment
TSO	The following items are included, separated by blanks:
	Name of the program in uppercase or **?** Name of the DD for the program or **?** Name of the data set for the program or **?** Name of the program as it was invoked or **?** Default address environment in uppercase Name of the address space in uppercase Eight-character user token
OS/2	Fully qualified filename of the REXX procedure. Note that this may include blanks because the OS/2 file system allows blanks in filenames.
OS/400	Library, file, and member of the REXX procedure, separated by blanks.
PARSE VERSION	The first token is either **REXX370** (CMS and TSO interpreters), **REXXC370** (CMS compiler), or **REXXSAA** (OS/2 and OS/400 interpreters). The second token is the language level number as listed below.
PROCEDURE	The REXX language definition requires that the **PROCEDURE** instruction, if used, must be the very first instruction in an internal routine. Until Release 6, CMS also allowed other instructions to precede the **PROCEDURE** instruction in an internal routine. This made it possible for **PROCEDURE** to be an instruction in an **INTERPRET** expression, so that the list of variables to be exposed could be constructed dynamically and could be longer than the 500-byte limit for CMS REXX instructions. This irregularity was exploited by some people running on earlier releases, so the removal caused some migration problems.
	REXX Language Level 4.00 adds a **variable reference** feature to **PROCEDURE EXPOSE** which provides a level of function similar to using **INTERPRET** on a **PROCEDURE** instruction, but level 4.00 is not yet available on CMS or TSO.
SIGNAL	The 370 interpreters will perform a case-insensitive search for labels.

TRACE	The CMS compiler does not support the **TRACE** instruction.
TRACE Scan	CMS and TSO support **TRACE Scan**, but OS/2 and OS/400 do not.
TRACE !	CMS and TSO support the exclamation point prefix on alphabetic trace options; OS/2 and OS/400 do not.
UPPER	CMS and TSO have an **UPPER** instruction.

Language levels

The REXX definition has been extended several times. The extensions have generally been upwardly compatible. With each extension, the language version number has been increased, and new features have been added.

- The first edition of the *SAA CPI Procedures Language Reference* (SC26-4358-0) describes language level 3.40. More recent editions (-1, -2, and -3) describe language level 3.46.

- The *SAA CPI Procedures Language Level 2 Reference* (SC24-5549) describes language level 4.00.

The following lists show highlights of each level and the release number of the products that implement it, and also the system-specific new features that have been provided:

3.20 (CMS Release 3)

The original externally distributed REXX implementation.

3.40 (CMS Release 4)

The **OPTIONS** instruction added, with **ETMODE** and **NOETMODE** the only defined options; DBCS literals supported.
CMS-specific addition:

- The **8C** option added to the **DIAG** and **DIAGRC** functions.

3.40 (CMS Release 5 and 5.5)

This is the original SAA Level 1 definition.

The **Basedate** option of the **DATE** function added.
CMS-specific addition:

- The **C8** and **CC** options of the **DIAG** and **DIAGRC** functions added to support CP language repositories.

3.45 (CMS Release 6 and TSO/E Version 2 Release 1)

Strict comparison operators added.

OPTIONS EXMODE and OPTIONS NOEXMODE added.

DBCS functions added.

DIGITS, FUZZ, and FORM functions added.

Normal option added to DATE and TIME functions.

Civil option added to TIME function.

Nomatch (default) option added to VERIFY function.

WORDPOS function added.

TRACE instruction and TRACE function added the FAILURE option.

Value option added to NUMERIC FORM instruction.

FAILURE option added to SIGNAL instruction.

Backslash added as additional not operator.

System-specific additions:

- DBCS and C options added to DATATYPE function (CMS and TSO).
- CSL function added (CMS).
- DIAG function option 64 added subfunction code N (CMS).

3.46 (CMS Release 6 with SPE, TSO/E Version 2 Release 1 with APAR change, and CMS compiler)

This is the updated SAA Level 1 language definition.

CALL ON/CALL OFF added.

NAME sub-keyword added to SIGNAL ON instruction.

CONDITION function added.

Limit on number of parameters on function and subroutine calls raised to 20 (from 10).

Power operator provides higher accuracy (not implemented in 370 interpreters yet).

Integer division and remainder definitions require whole number results (not implemented in 370 interpreters yet).

Century option of DATE function deleted (the 370 interpreters and the CMS compiler still support it).

The currency 2 character (¢ in United States) deleted as a valid character in a symbol (370 interpreters and the CMS compiler still support it).

The exclamation point added as a valid character in a symbol (the 370 interpreters and the CMS compiler have supported it all along).

3.48 (OS/400 Release Version 1 Release 3)

This is the level in the first release of REXX for OS/400; it indicates level 4.00 without the stream I/O.

3.50

This was never implemented in an IBM product. It is the language level defined by Cowlishaw in the first edition of his book, *The REXX Language*. REXX 3.50 is approximately equivalent to REXX 3.45 plus stream I/O and minus DBCS support.

4.00 (OS/2 EE 1.2 and later, OS/2 SE 1.3 and later)

This is the SAA Level 2 language definition, and the level defined by Cowlishaw in the second edition of his book, *The REXX Language*. The SAA definition includes DBCS support and the variable pool and REXX exit interfaces; these items are not included in Cowlishaw's language definition.

Stream I/O functions (**LINEIN**, **LINEOUT**, **LINES**, **CHARIN**, **CHAROUT**, **CHARS**) added, along with the **NOTREADY** condition and **STREAM** function.

Scan option of the **TRACE** instruction removed.

Binary literals added.

X2B and **B2X** functions added.

Subsidiary lists added to **DROP** and **PROCEDURE EXPOSE** instructions.

VALUE function extended to allow setting REXX variables and variables in other environments.

Variable patterns added to **PARSE** instruction.

Certain built-in functions have numeric parameters rounded according to the current numeric digits setting before the function value is calculated:

```
ABS
DATATYPE
FORMAT
MAX
MIN
SIGN
TRUNC
```

Minor incompatibilities in REXX/SAA PL levels

As features have been added to the language, a few incompatibilities have been introduced.

- SAA Level 2 (REXX 4.00)

  - Binary literals have changed the meaning of direct abuttal between a literal and the symbol **B**. This can introduce a syntax error or an incorrect result. For instance, the following code will work only at REXX levels lower than 4.00:

```
b ='Apis Mellifera (honeybee)'
say 'My favorite insect is 'b 'because I love honey.'
```

This feature is implemented in OS/2 and OS/400.

A simple program that will help identify binary literals in REXX programs appears at the end of this chapter.

- Rounding of function parameters.

This change has been implemented in all the language processors since they were released, so there should be no portability problems.

- Updated SAA Level 1 (3.46)

  - **CALL ON** and **CALL OFF** prevent the use of the symbols **ON** and **OFF** as subroutine names (except as condition handling routines: **CALL ON HALT NAME ON** works just fine).

    This change is implemented in the 370 interpreters and compiler and the OS/2 and OS/400 interpreters.

  - The power operator now provides higher accuracy, and hence different answers for some data. The effect is most pronounced for higher powers. Programs using the power operator will generally not need to be changed.

    This change is implemented in the CMS compiler and the OS/2 and OS/400 interpreters but not in the 370 interpreters.

  - Integer division and remainder operators raise the syntax condition when the result cannot be represented as a whole number.

    This change is implemented in the CMS compiler and the OS/2 and OS/400 interpreters but not in the 370 interpreters.

  - The **Century** option of the **DATE** function is deleted. The 370 interpreters and CMS compiler continue to support **DATE('C')** but OS/2 and OS/400 do not.

  - The currency 2 character (¢ in the United States) is deleted as a valid character in a symbol. Again, the 370 interpreters and CMS compiler continue to support it but OS/2 and OS/400 do not.

Other language differences

Definition of symbols
All implementations support English uppercase and lowercase alphabetic characters, numeric characters, the underscore, the period, the exclamation point, and the question mark as characters in symbols. CMS and TSO also support the at sign (@), the number sign (#), the currency 1 character ($ in the United States), and the currency 2 character (¢ in the United States). The currency 2 character was included in the original SAA definition but has been removed because of national language support concerns.

Trace output   There are some differences in trace output between the systems. The main differences appear on OS/2 and OS/400, where trace output is constructed from the tokenized image of the program rather than being copied verbatim from the source. The result is that an instruction such as:

```
say             "Hello" /* Greet the user */
```

is traced as

```
say 'Hello';
```

Here are some details:

Comments   CMS and TSO trace comments; OS/2 and OS/400 do not.

Continuation characters   CMS and TSO trace commas used as continuation characters; OS/2 and OS/400 do not.

Traceback after error   CMS and TSO trace back through all active function calls and interpret instructions when a syntax error terminates a program; OS/2 and OS/400 do not.

Literals   CMS and TSO allow literals to span lines; OS/2 and OS/400 do not. On TSO, a blank is inserted between the different pieces of the literal; CMS does not insert the blank.

Limits   Many limits on such items as clause length and symbol length are listed in the SAA Reference and not repeated here. One type of limit not listed is the limit on function call nesting, which is similar but not identical to the control structure nesting that is documented.

Table 4. Nesting Levels

Construct	CMS interpreter	CMS compiler	TSO interpreter	OS/2 interpreter	OS/400 interpreter
Internal Function	125	Memory	125	100	100
External Function	200	100	Memory	100	100
DOEND pairs	250	Memory	250	100	100

Another limit is the length of the name of the command environment.

Table 5. Environment name length

CMS interpreter	CMS compiler	TSO interpreter	OS/2 interpreter	OS/400 interpreter
8	8	8	250	21

Compiler differences

The CMS REXX compiler imitates the CMS interpreter very closely, with the following exceptions:

INTERPRET	instruction not supported.
TRACE instruction	treated as a **NOP** instruction, and the compiler issues a warning message.
TRACE function	returns **O** and does not change the trace setting.
OPTIONS ETMODE	must be the first instruction in the program, and **ETMODE** must be specified as a literal.
Number range	limited from **1E-999999999** to **9E999999999**. This is a very slight restriction from what the interpreters allow. The size of the exponent is the same.
SIGNAL	The compiler performs a case-sensitive search for the label. This is in accordance with the language definition but different from the CMS interpreter. This will be visible only when the label name is coded as a literal, not a symbol.
SOURCELINE	This function returns the source line from the program only if the program was compiled with the **SLINE** compiler option.
Syntax error detection	Certain syntax errors will be caught at compile time (preventing the program from being run at all), while the interpreter detects those errors only upon executing the faulty instruction. These errors include:

SIGNAL ON a condition that does not exist.
SIGNAL to a label that does not exist.
Mismatched parentheses.
Invalid sub-keywords on instructions.

CHARACTER ENCODINGS

The 370 and AS/400 systems use EBCDIC character encoding, and OS/2 uses ASCII. Because of this difference, some character translation functions (e.g., **D2C**) and DBCS functions return different results. Besides problems caused by individual characters that have different encodings, some programs may have problems because of assumptions about relative positions of characters. For instance:

- Numbers come before letters in ASCII and after letters in EBCDIC.

- Uppercase letters come **X'20'** before lowercase letters in ASCII, and **X'40'** after lowercase letters in EBCDIC.

IBM's REXX implementations use the NOT sign (¬) for the same operations on both ASCII and EBCDIC systems. This is consistent for all REXX programs, but may still cause some confusion because some other languages (notably C) and other REXX implementations use the caret (^) on ASCII systems as a not operator. This is a problem if you move your REXX source between EBCDIC and ASCII systems, and you use a conversion program which automatically changes the not sign to a caret. To avoid this problem, and since ASCII keyboards normally do not have the not sign on them, use the backslash (which is interchangeable with the not sign). However, some national keyboards do not have the backslash.

Another solution is to avoid the unary not operator altogether; instead of coding ¬a, code (0 = a). This looks awkward, but ports well.

Another operator character that causes some confusion is the vertical bar used as the logical OR operator and in pairs as the concatenate-without-a-blank operator. The problem is that there are several different vertical bars that look quite similar. On EBCDIC systems, the X'4F' character is the "right" vertical bar for REXX. On ASCII systems, the X'7C' character is "right". In both cases, most common U.S. keyboards and displays represent this character as a split vertical bar (|), but that is not universal. This character will not be a common problem because most EBCDIC-ASCII translation programs handle this correctly. It can be vexing, though, because it may be hard to tell which vertical bar you are looking at.

SYSTEM DIFFERENCES

Several factors outside the REXX language affect execution of REXX programs.

Queue implementation

The implementation of the queue that is used by REXX is system-specific. Limitations exist in the length of individual items that can be put on the queue, the total amount of storage that is available for holding queued data, and the number of queue entries that may exist at once.

Table 5. Queue implementation maxima

Sytem	CMS	TSO	OS/2	OS/400
Element length	255 bytes	16M-1 bytes	64K-64 bytes	32,767
Number of elements	Memory	Memory	Available selectors (usually thousands)	Memory
Total quantity of data	Memory	Memory	Memory	15.5 MB

External trace controls

Different means are provided for telling REXX to start interactive trace when a REXX program is started, without adding a TRACE instruction to the program source:

CMS   SET EXECTRAC ON and TS

TSO   EXECUTIL TS and TS

OS/2   SET RXTRACE=ON

OS/400   Trace REXX (TRCREX)

CMS and TSO also provide HI (Halt Interpretation), TS (Trace Start), and TE (Trace End) Immediate commands. The HI command affects compiled programs only if the program is compiled with the TESTHALT option. These commands do not have equivalents on OS/2 or OS/400.

OS/2 has a Presentation Manager host program called PMREXX for running REXX procedures, which has pull-down controls for turning tracing on and off and raising the HALT condition. <Cntrl>-BREAK will halt a REXX procedure running in a linemode (full-screen or windowed) OS/2 session.

OS/400 has no means of signaling a halt condition or starting tracing while a program is running.

Initial comment

Some systems require a REXX comment on the first line of a REXX program to determine that the program is REXX. OS/2 requires it to begin in column 1; CMS allows it to start anywhere before column 255. In some cases, TSO requires the string REXX to appear in the initial comment. OS/400 never requires the comment.

When there is no need to distinguish REXX programs from programs in other languages (e.g., when a call is made directly to a REXX interpreter), the initial comment is usually not required.

Application programming interfaces (APIs)

All implementations provide APIs for interaction between REXX and programs written in other languages.

Availability in other languages

Some of the REXX interfaces are available only to programs written in certain languages. This is due to the linkage conventions used by the system and the data structures and parameter lists used by REXX. For instance, the only CMS language that can use **all** the APIs is assembler. This availability varies between systems.

API descriptions

The APIs provide the following functions:

Invoke REXX Programs in other languages can execute REXX procedures by calling the interpreter and providing the name of the procedure and a parameter list. The mechanism for this varies between systems:

TSO

- Call **IRXJCL** (in batch or any address space).
- Call **IRXEXEC** (in any address space); more flexible than **IRXJCL**.
- Call **IRXEX** (an entry point in **IRXEXEC** for FORTRAN programs).
- Use TSO service facility to invoke the **EXEC** command (for high-level languages).

CMS Interpreter

- Use CMSCALL assembler macro, specify **EXEC**; tokenized, extended, and six-word extended PLISTs are supported.
- Call CSL routine **DMSCCE** from high-level languages.

CMS Compiler

- Compiled EXECs: same as for CMS interpreter.
- Object files: link object file with your program; an SVC parameter list must be provided.
- MODULE files: as any module.

OS/2

Call the function **REXXSAA**, contained within **REXX.DLL**.

OS/400

Call program **QREXX**.

External functions (not in REXX) REXX programs can call programs written in other languages as external functions, passing a variable number of parameters and returning a result value, which may be a string.

All implementations offer this capability.

Subcommand handlers Programs in other languages can act as subcommand processors for REXX programs, receiving text of commands issued in REXX programs.

All implementations offer this capability.

Variable pool Programs in other languages can read, set, and create variables in the variable pool of the REXX procedure which invoked them. System data, such as the parameters passed to the REXX procedure and the REXX version information, are also available.

All implementations offer this capability. This interface has been defined in the SAA Procedures Language Reference. One minor variation in the variable pool interface is documented on CMS and TSO: the delete function does not indicate whether or not variables were affected by the delete.

REXX Exits   Programs in other languages can be used as exit handlers for specific events that may occur in a REXX procedure. The exit programs are called when events occur and may extend or replace normal REXX event handling. These events are:

- Initialization
- Queue access (**PUSH, QUEUE, PULL,** or **QUEUED( )**)
- Session I/O (**SAY, PULL, TRACE** output, and interactive debug pauses)
- External function call
- Subcommand
- External halt indicator
- External trace indicator
- Termination

REXX exit APIs are provided in CMS Release 6 via an SPE, and in OS/2 and OS/400. TSO provides the initialization and termination exits, and allows for the use of **replaceable routines** to achieve desired results for other classes of exits. This interface has been defined in the SAA Procedures Language Level 2 Reference.

Within the main groups listed above, certain subfunctions may not be available on all systems. For instance, CMS has a **LINESIZE** function and provides an exit for servicing this request as part of the session I/O exit. OS/2 and OS/400 do not have this exit because they do not have a **LINESIZE** function.

Semantics of the REXX APIs are generally similar in all implementations. The syntax of the interfaces, however, is unique to each system. This is due to differences between register number, size, and usage; memory structure; calling conventions; and so on, between systems. If you have programs in other languages that interface with REXX and need to port them to another system, plan on altering code that talks to REXX. You may find that the interface you are using is not available in your language on another system.

For details, refer to the REXX language reference manual for the system in which you are interested.

SUMMARY

This chapter has covered many differences programmers may encounter when using REXX on various SAA systems. Fortunately, language differences have been minimized. When new language implementations have been introduced, the language level provided has usually been at least as high as in other existing implementations. This allows easy migration of REXX instructions and functions.

Commands and system services, however, often require significant rework when you port a program from one system to another. This problem is outside the scope of the REXX language. Using data provided by the **PARSE SOURCE** and **PARSE VERSION** instructions, however, you can write multiple-path procedures that issue commands correctly on any system.

Rules for safe REXX

My summary of rules for safe REXX follow:

General recommendations

- Isolate system-specific code in subroutines.
- Use SAA Procedures Language features where possible.
- Use the SAA Procedures Language Reference books as primary references.

Command recommendations

- Don't make assumptions about command structure, format of file-names, etc.
- Treat return code and **ERROR** and **FAILURE** condition handling as system-dependent.
- Call REXX programs as REXX routines, not commands.

REXX programming recommendations

- Start programs with comment in column 1 containing the word **REXX**.
- When using **ETMODE**, code **OPTIONS 'ETMODE'** (with the quotation marks) as the first instruction of your program.
- Avoid **INTERPRET**.
- Don't use **B** as a variable name.
- Remember what instructions and functions are non-SAA.

- Keep stack usage simple—use only PUSH, QUEUE, and PULL.
- Use only SAA-defined symbol characters.
- Use positive seeds for RANDOM.
- Don't use forward slash in not equals.
- Don't use null assignment or OPTIONS.
- Don't pass null parameter to DATE or TIME.
- Don't use Century, Julian, or Language options on DATE.

PROGRAM TO FIND BINARY LITERALS

```
/* *REXX* This program will scan a given input file and report anything
** that looks like a binary literal.  It does, however, produce false
** alarms where a lone B is the first thing inside of a literal.

** This program works on CMS, TSO, OS/2, and OS/400, and may be
compiled.
*/
arg infile
if infile = '' | infile = '?' then signal HELP
say 'Searching for possible binary literals in' infile
call READFILE
if result <> 0 then exit
do ii = 1 to pgm.0
   call FINDTHESE pgm.ii, "'B", ii
   call FINDTHESE pgm.ii, '"B', ii
end
say 'That''s all for' infile'.'
exit
/* This routine reads the input file into a stemmed variable.
** It issues a message in case of error, and returns to its caller
with
** RC = 0 for success, RC <> 0 for failure.
*/
READFILE: procedure expose pgm. infile
parse source sys .
select
   when sys = 'CMS' then do
      'EXECIO * DISKR' infile '(FINIS STEM PGM.'
      if rc <> 0 then say 'Error on EXECIO command.  RC='rc
      return rc
   end /* CMS */
   when sys = 'TSO' then do
      'ALLOC DA('infile') F(INDD) OLD'
      'EXECIO * DISKR INDD (FINIS STEM PGM.'
      if rc <> 0 then say 'Error on EXECIO command.  RC='rc
      return rc
   end /* TSO */
   when sys = 'OS/2' then do
      do ii = 1 while lines(infile) > 0
         pgm.ii = linein(infile)
```

```
      end ii
      pgm.0 = ii - 1
      if (stream(infile,'S') = 'READY') then
         return 0
      else do
         say 'I/O Error.  Error indicator is' stream(infile,'D')
         return 1
      end /* I/O Error */
   end /* OS/2 */
   when sys = 'OS/400' then do
      /* The program must be in a source physical file, with */
      /* sequence numbers (or blanks) in columns 1 through 12. */
      parse var infile library file member
      'OVRDBF FILE(STDIN) TOFILE('library'/'file') MBR('member')'
      do ii = 1 until line = ''
         parse linein . +12 filearea 1 line
         pgm.ii = strip(filearea, 'Trailing')
      end ii
      pgm.0 = ii - 1
      return 0
   end /* OS/400 */
   otherwise say 'Sorry, This program does not support system' sys
   return -1
end /* Select */
/* This routine will check one line for all possible binary
** literals, and show where they are found, if any.

** input:    line      line to check
**           target    string to search for:  'B or "B
**           linenum   line number
** returns:  nothing
*/
FINDTHESE: procedure
arg line, target, linenum
here = 1
do while pos(target, line,here) <> 0
   here = pos(target, line,here)
   if symbol(substr(line, here+1,2)) = 'BAD' then do
      say format(linenum, 8) line
      say copies(' ', here+8)||'|'
      say ' '
   end
   here = here + 1
end
return
HELP:
say 'This program will scan for binary literals in a REXX program.'
say 'It will show the line, the line number, and a column pointer'
say 'for each one it finds.'
say ''
say 'It does, however, produce some false alarms.  For instance,'
say 'the following instruction will be flagged:'
say '    say date("B")'
return
```

38

Exploiting Compiled REXX and the REXX Compiler

By Mark Cathcart

Before considering how to exploit compiled REXX, it's worth looking at why you might want to compile REXX and what compiled REXX is.

WHY COMPILE REXX?

The *CMS REXX Compiler General Information* (GH19-8118) and *CMS REXX Compiler User's Guide and Reference* (SH19-8120) list several reasons for compiling REXX, but in many cases it is done solely for the increased performance of compiled REXX compared to interpreted REXX.

In at least one case, the source REXX program is no longer provided to protect design and techniques used in the code. However, this program was first compiled for performance reasons. Having achieved that, the developers added significant function, which they decided to protect by no longer providing REXX source.

What performance gains can be made by compiling REXX? Gains can be significant, but vary greatly with program type. If a REXX program contains more system commands than REXX instructions, the performance gain will be negligible; in some instances, compiling even incurs additional overhead. Consider a program that spends 50 percent of its time executing system commands: it can never be improved by a factor of 2, as this would require the REXX program time to be reduced to zero. The REXX compiler can do nothing to improve the performance of system commands.

Most people, when first given access to the compiler, will compile their PROFILE EXECs, hoping to reduce the time it takes to logon, but are disappointed when they find little, if any, performance improvement. This is because the typical PROFILE EXEC contains mostly system commands to set up the session.

Of installations worked with during early availability of the REXX compiler, the performance gain was almost always expressed as CPU savings—on average, 40 to 45 percent. (CPU savings were defined as the percentage reduction of CPU used by the same program when run interpreted. For example, a 25 percent saving means that the compiled program used only 75 percent of the CPU used by the interpreted version.)

There were many cases where CPU savings were 60 to 68 percent, and some REXX-intensive programs recorded 90 percent+ savings, but these were rare. In all cases, though, the compiler cost was offset by the CPU savings. At my installation, savings were significant. We were often running the CPU 100 percent busy; compiling all REXX programs achieved a total CPU reduction of a factor of 3 to 4. Overall CPU utilization fell from an average of 90 percent to 65 percent, delaying a CPU upgrade.

WHAT TO COMPILE?

On our system, after some experimentation, our system programmer compiled all REXX programs on public disks, and set up a REXX program (compiled, of course) to submit the compilations to CMSBATCH. When a program was compiled successfully, the interpreted program was automatically replaced with the compiled one.

However, some installations took a more restrained and measured approach. One large PROFS-intensive system measured their compilations and reported the following numbers:

	Total	Average
Lines of source code compiled	153,177	145
Source program file size (blocks)	2,179	2.07
Compiled EXEC size (blocks)	4,597	4.36
Compiler listing size (blocks)	6,249	5.92
CPU consumed during compilation (seconds)	3,952	3.74

A quick review of these numbers shows that the disk space needed for a compiled REXX program is about double the space required by its source. With the compiler defaults of SOURCE and NOXREF, listing files require nearly three times the space of the source. Finally, although the compiler development group has asserted that "compilation performance is not a critical item, so we decided to implement the compiler in C", compilations are very fast!

COMPILER OUTPUT

The compiler can produce two types of compiled REXX: **CEXEC** (compiled EXEC format, filetype CEXEC) and **TEXT** (object format, filetype TEXT). Before considering how to exploit compiled REXX, one must understand what these are and how to use them.

The two types of compiled REXX are identical, they are just packaged differently. Compiled REXX consists of three sections:

1. 240 bytes of run-time setup code.

2. R/O code; length is in a fullword at offset 240 in the compiled code.

3. R/W code; length is in a fullword at offset 244 in the compiled code.

Compiled REXX runs with storage protect key 0, as does interpreted REXX.

CEXEC

This is the most common and default form of compiled REXX. It consists of fixed-length 1024-byte records. CEXEC code can be:

- Used to replace filetype EXEC, XEDIT, or other REXX programs that can be processed by the CMS interpreter

- EXECLOADed into virtual storage

- Loaded into the installation segment (INSTSEG) via DCSSGEN

- Loaded into application (logical saved) segments using SEGGEN (in VM/SP Release 6 and VM/ESA)

Using CEXEC format, compiler output should replace the original, interpreted program in the CMS search order, with the same filename, filetype, and filemode as the original. CEXEC files, having logical record length 1024, cannot be processed by any of the CMS EXEC processors. When a CEXEC file is executed, CMS reads the first record, which indicates that the CEXEC file is to be handled by an Alternate Format EXEC processor named EAGRTPRC, and invokes EAGRTPRC accordingly to process the file.

The following shows a dump of the first 255 bytes of compiled REXX in CEXEC format. The name of the Alternate Format EXEC processor can be seen 12 bytes into the dump. EAGRTPRC is the run-time module or library for compiled REXX. After initial setup and storage management, it returns control to the CEXEC.

```
* A partial dump of a compiled REXX program
0000   47FF0068   C5E7C5C3   D7D9D6C3   C5C1C7D9   *....EXECPROCEAGR*
0010   E3D7D9C3   40C39694   97899385   8440D9C5   *TPRC Compiled RE*
0020   E7E740F1   4BF14BF0   40404040   F840C1A4   *XX 1.1.0      8 Au*
0030   8740F1F9   F8F940F0   F97AF5F4   7AF4F540   *g 1989 09:54:45 *
0040   C3D4E240   D9C5E7E7   C3F3F7F0   40F34BF4   *CMS REXXC370 3.4*
0050   F640F3F0   40D1A495   40F1F9F8   F9404000   *6 30 Jun 1989  .*
0060   000000F0   FFFFFFFD   900FD020   185F58B0   *...0...........*
0070   50601AB5   9101B008   471050A8   1B004110   *&-..j.....&y....*
0080   500C9180   05EA4710   50940ACA   00000001   *&.j.....&m......*
0090   47F0509E   41F00001   89F0000F   0ACC12CF   *.0&..0..i0......*
00A0   58F05064   47D050E6   1B669180   05EA4780   *.0&...&W..j.....*
00B0   50CC4120   50C24130   00018930   001F1623   *&...&B....i.....*
00C0   0B628860   001F4120   00031762   58F0C018   *..h-.........0..*
00D0   45E0F018   05504120   00031962   47705010   *..0..&........&.*
00E0   41205010   0B02980E   D02007FE   00000000   *..&...q.........*
00F0   00000468   00000758   01000000   00000190   *...............*
```

TEXT

It has already been stated that both CEXEC and TEXT format compiled REXX have the same contents. TEXT format code differs from CEXEC in that it consists of fixed-length 80-byte records that follow the IBM System/370 object file format. This allows TEXT format code to be:

- Executed via LOAD and START commands
- Built into a module via GENMOD
- Loaded into user virtual storage via NUCXLOAD (having been previously built into a module)
- Loaded into a discontiguous saved segment
- Combined with object files produced by other compilers and assemblers to form an application
- Combined with other object files to form a REXX function library

Execution of TEXT format compiled REXX starts at offset 0 in the compiled code. The first instructions branch around the Alternate Format EXEC processor constants required in CEXEC code. Following this, a CMS supervisor call (SVC) instruction invokes run-time module EAGRTPRC. The SVC uses the same constant (at offset 12) to identify the run-time module that is used to invoke the Alternate Format EXEC processor for CEXEC. Once the run-time module is executing, subsequent execution of the compiled REXX is the same as with CEXEC.

This design allows for two external storage formats which meet different requirements, yet provide a single compiled REXX format and execution.

The compiler listing

The compiler listing is an extremely valuable tool for REXX programmers. Several REXX programs exist which format and print REXX programs, but none produced the type of information now available via the compiler listing. The listing can contain the following sections:

- Options summary
- Optional source listing, suppressed with **NOSOURCE** option
- Optional cross reference, enabled with the **XREF** option
- Optional message summary, controlled by **FLAG/NOFLAG** options

The compiler listing can be suppressed entirely with the **NOPRINT** option.

Of these, obviously the messages are important, but the source and **XREF** sections are extremely useful both as program documentation and for debugging purposes. The source section contains three separate counters for **IF**, **DO**, and **SELECT** nesting, and shows where these change. The **XREF** section shows both item attributes, such as **SIMPle VARiable**, **LITeral STRing**, etc., and also shows where variables are set and referenced, by line number. The next example shows a sample compiler listing, edited for inclusion:

```
CMS REXX COMPILER 1.1.0                 TIME: 12:07:15          1
COMPILER OPTIONS

        SOURCE
        XREF
        NOTERMINAL
        NOSLINE
        NOTESTHALT
        NOSAA
        NODUMP
        NOCOMPILE
        FLAG      (I)
        PRINT     (SAMPLE    LISTING  A1)
        CEXEC     (SAMPLE    CEXEC    A1)
        NOOBJECT
        LINECOUNT (55)

IF  DO SEL  LINE C ----+----1----+----2----+----3----+----4----+----5
            1   /* Contains an error ! */
            2   parse upper arg name 'AT'   node
            3   'SMSG RSCS CMD' node 'CPQ USER' name
            4   /* ask RSCS
                |
```

```
+++EAGPAR0654S Unmatched "/*"
                              |
+++EAGPAR0651S End of program found before end of clause

ITEM                          ATTRIBUTE LINE REFERENCES


----- CONSTANTS -----

'AT'                          LIT STR   2
'CPQ USER'                    LIT STR   3
'SMSG RSCS CMD'               LIT STR   3

----- SIMPLE VARIABLES -----

NAME                          SIMP VAR  2(s) 3
NODE                          SIMP VAR  2(s) 3
```

WHEN AND HOW TO COMPILE

With interpreted REXX, it commonly takes two or three attempts to run a large new program to conclusion just to find syntax errors. Having done that, the next task is to devise test cases to make sure that all the code paths are tested. The interpreter will not find coding mistakes in code segments which have not been executed.

In a single compilation, the compiler does a static syntax check of all code paths and reports any errors found.

It is a good idea to compile newly written or changed programs with the **XREF** and **NOCOMPILE** options. This provides a detailed listing but does not produce executable code. After fixing errors indicated by compiler messages, examine the **XREF** section. Make sure you understand and can explain everything you find there.

Why not produce executable code? The compiler does not support either interactive or non-interactive tracing. The **TRACE** instruction, when found in a compiled program, generates a **NOP** instruction, and the **TRACE** function always returns **O** (**OFF**).

This means that until a program is fully debugged and tested, it is best to use the interpreted source code version. Once a program is ready to be put into production or submitted for final testing, it can be compiled. Compiling at this stage will not introduce new or unknown errors. Some installations even insist that a full compiler listing with **XREF** be available during formal program review.

Sometimes it is worthwhile uploading complex OS/2 **CMD** and MS-DOS/PC-DOS Personal REXX applications, and using the CMS REXX compiler to syntax-check them.

The compiler is supplied with sample **compiler shells** for line-mode and full-screen usage. Both shells provide all necessary setup and logic to fully integrate the compiler with CMS.

These shells are "samples" because the developers assumed that users will modify them. Both are provided as source code interpreted programs, which can, of course, be compiled! The developers made modification as simple as possible by providing several variables, assigned at the beginning of the program, for this purpose. For example, a variable called **INSTOPTS** sets compiler defaults.

Another possible modification can enhance the full-screen dialog to detect compilation errors, then XEDIT source program and automatically position at the first line in error; subsequently a PF key could locate the next line, and so on. The shells could also be interfaced with **EXECUPDT**.

Both line-mode and full-screen dialogs are invoked by typing their name with the filename of the program to be compiled. Both shells search all accessed disks for a source code program with this filename and a supported filetype. Supported filetypes are also set in a variable for easy modification. The example below shows a sample compiler command to syntax-check the **NOTEBOOK EXEC**, producing an **XREF** listing and no object code:

```
rexxc notebook (xref nocompile
```

Compiler manuals illustrate usage of the line-mode and full-screen shells, as well as invoking the compiler without them.

COMPILATION ERRORS

As already stated, the compiler does not support the **TRACE** instruction or function. There are other differences between the compiler and the interpreter that can cause compilation errors.

The most common is the use of the **INTERPRET** instruction. **INTERPRET** is not supported by the compiler, and causes an error when found. To compile a program, any use of **INTERPRET** must be eliminated. There are several ways to achieve this, depending on why **INTERPRET** was used. The following example shows program fragments which demonstrate various methods.

The CMS REXX compiler also includes source code for an assembler language program called **RXSETVAR**. This can also replace **INTERPRET**. It is documented in compiler reference manuals, along with other differences between the CMS interpreter and the CMS REXX compiler.

```
/* Four ways to avoid using INTERPRET */

/* #1 -- Computed SIGNAL */
a = 'EXMP1'                          /* A label name */
interpret signal a                   /* Don't use this!! */
```

```
a = 'exmpl'                              /* Use this instead!! */
signal value a      /* Can be simply coded as a computed SIGNAL */

/* #2 -- Variable assignment */
name = 'Mark'
pointer = 'name'
interpret 'a = 'pointer                  /* Don't use this!! */

a = value(pointer)                       /* Use this instead!! */

/* #3 -- Dynamic calculation */
c = '28.4 * 9 / 1.8'                     /* Some calculation */
interpret say c                          /* Don't use this!! */

/* Build external function instead!! */
c = '28.4 * 9 / 1.8'                     /* Some calculation */
'EXECIO 1 DISKW DOIT EXEC A3 (FINIS STRING '/* */ return' c
say doit()               /* Mode 3 means 'erase after reading' */

/* #4 -- Assignment to dynamic variable */
do i = 1 to 2
   interpret 'a'i '= somestem.'i         /* Don't use this!! */
end

/* Use internal function and GLOBALV instead!! */
do i = 1 to 2
   call ASSIGN 'A'i, 'SOMESTEM.'i
end
  :
ASSIGN:
name = arg(1)
data = translate(arg(2))
address command 'GLOBALV SELECT $$TMP$$ SETL' name data
address command 'GLOBALV SELECT $$TMP$$ GET' name data
address command 'GLOBALV SELECT $$TMP$$ PURGE'
return
```

USING CEXEC

It is necessary to decide on a naming convention before attempting to exploit the CEXEC format of compiled REXX. CMS requires EXECs to have filetype **EXEC**, XEDIT requires **XEDIT**, and so on. CEXEC must have the same filetype for the compiled version that you would use for the interpreted one. Also, if you are using **EXECUPDT** and the XEDIT update facility, your source program will have its filetype prefixed with a currency 1 character ($ in the United States), and so you might have:

TEST $EXEC A—Source file for input to **EXECUPDT**.

TEST EXEC A—Output from **EXECUPDT** and input to compiler. Used for testing via interpreter, or if **EXECUPDT** is not used, this will be the source.

TEST CEXEC A—Output from compiler. You can use the **CEXEC** compiler option to output a file with a filetype other than CEXEC; the compiler will not overwrite the input file.

This means that before using the CEXEC you must either change the filetype to one supported by CMS, or **EXECLOAD** the CEXEC with that filetype. The next example shows a program which, by means of CMS global variables, dynamically selects either the compiled or interpreted version of the program to run, and uses **EXECLOAD** to give it the correct filetype.

```
/* Generic program which can be renamed to the name of any    */
/* other program and used to automatically run either the     */
/* compiled or interpreted version of that program.  Use the  */
/* following commands to externally control the choice:        */
/*                                                             */
/*  Compiled version:    GLOBALV SELECT REXXCOMP SET RUN ON    */
/*  Interpreted version: GLOBALV SELECT REXXCOMP SET RUN OFF   */
/*                                                             */
/* This program based on one by Steve Johnson of IBM Raleigh.  */
trace off
address command
parse arg args
parse upper source . . thisprogram .
'GLOBALV SELECT REXXCOMP GET RUN'                /* Run compiled? */
exprogram = strip(left('$'thisprogram, 8))
'ESTATE' exprogram 'CEXEC *'
if (rc = 0) & (run = 'ON') then do
   parse value diag(8, 'QUERY SET') with . 'EMSG' emsg ',' .
   call diag 8, 'SET EMSG OFF'
   'EAGRTPRC'                                    /* Check for run-time */
   if rc <> -3 then                              /* Run compiled */
   'EXECLOAD' exprogram 'CEXEC *' exprogram 'EXEC (PUSH'
   if emsg <> 'OFF' then call diag 8, 'SET EMSG' emsg
end
else 'EXECLOAD' exprogram 'IEXEC * (PUSH'   /* Run interpreted */
'EXEC' exprogram args; erc = rc            /* Run the real one! */
'EXECDROP' exprogram 'EXEC'
exit erc
```

For programs put into production, copy the program above as *filename EXEC*; the interpreted version as *$filename IEXEC*; and the compiled version as *$filename CEXEC* (in CEXEC format). When invoked, the program does several things: it tests to see if it should run interpreted or compiled; it checks for existence of compiler run-time support; it then loads either the interpreted or the compiled version of the "real" program into storage; and finally it executes it, passing the argument string that it was passed.

The following shows the naming convention used by the above program:

Source REXX   If used in conjunction with **EXECUPDT**, source REXX programs have a filetype prefixed with a currency 1 character ($ in the United States). Programs for which source is not kept in this form are not usually compiled.

Interpreted REXX   Output from **EXECUPDT**. The filename is prefixed with **$**, and the filetype is prefixed with **I**.

Compiled REXX   The filename is prefixed with **$**, and the filetype is prefixed with **C**.

This may not be the simplest way to do it, but it works, and, using the program above, users can easily switch from compiled to interpreted program versions for debugging. The full-screen shell supplied with the REXX compiler can also help with this. It contains a menu item to rename/switch between compiled and interpreted REXX versions.

In CEXEC format, compiled REXX can replace the original, interpreted REXX on the same disk; no other action is needed.

Files in CEXEC format can also be loaded into saved segments in two ways:

1. Using the installation program segment, **CMSINST**. This name is coded in the CMS Nucleus Generation Profile (**DMSNGP**) and is defined by the system programmer. **CMSINST** can contain only EXEC 2 and REXX programs. There can only be one **CMSINST** segment.

2. Using application segments (logical saved segments) built by the **SEGGEN** command. This command is available on VM/SP Release 6, VM/SP HPO Release 6, and VM/ESA systems. Because application saved segments can contain any number of objects, such as modules, EXEC, CEXEC, NLS files, etc., this is a much better way to share compiled REXX programs. System code can either continue to exist in the **CMSINST** segment or be put in common "tool" segments created with SEGGEN.

USING TEXT

Most CMS REXX compiler users do not make extensive use of TEXT format compiled REXX. One installation used it for REXX PROFS extensions. These programs are run by many users, and some of the programs are quite large. This made them ideal candidates for the **CMSINST** segment, where they could be loaded by all users into shared virtual storage. However, by the time the segment was built for the compiled REXX and the IBM PROFS programs, it was too large to fit comfortably within the system layout—that is, in most cases it would prevent another segment from being loaded for a required product or application.

Since this was a VM/XA system, another alternative was available: compile the code in TEXT format, and load the TEXT format programs into an ordinary saved segment above the 16MB line.

In VM/SP and VM/SP HPO, all programs must reside and execute within a 16MB address space. In VM/XA, EXECs must reside and execute within 16MB addressability, but programs may reside and execute beyond that address. VM/ESA allows both EXECs and programs to reside and execute beyond 16MB addressability. VM/XA allows use of TEXT format compiled REXX to create REXX programs that can reside and be executed from beyond 16MB, thus freeing up valuable virtual storage below it.

This worked for most programs, although it was not as powerful as the application segments available in VM/ESA. Once VM/ESA was available, the programs were recompiled into CEXEC format and used in these segments instead.

Another use for TEXT format compiled REXX programs is as **ENDCMD** nucleus extensions: programs which have been **NUCXLOAD**ed with the **ENDCMD** attribute. Prior to the CMS REXX compiler, this precluded using REXX, and it still precludes the use of CEXEC format compiled REXX. The example below shows a program and the process for using it as an **ENDCMD** nucleus extension.

```
Ready;
type endit sexec

/* */
say substr(time(), 1, 5) "Do you know where your compiled REXX
programs are?"
address command "QUERY DISK A (LIFO"
parse pull . cuu . . . . . . used .
parse pull .
parse var used .'-'used
say '       ' cuu "is currently your A-disk, it is" used"% used."
exit
Ready;

rexxc endit sexec (obj nocexec
Ready;

load endit (rldsave
Ready;

genmod endit (map system
Ready;

nucxload endit (endcmd
14:33 Do you know where your compiled REXX programs are?
       191 is currently your A-disk, it is 94% used.
Ready;
```

As shown above, the **ENDCMD** is invoked before CMS issues the **Ready;** message.

COMPILED REXX CODING CONSIDERATIONS

There are differences between the compiler and the CMS interpreter. Some, such as **INTERPRET** and **TRACE**, have already been discussed. This section discusses others.

First, there are no restrictions on mutual invocation of compiled and interpreted REXX. The compiler complies with REXX language level 3.46. This is the same as the REXX interpreter in VM/SP Release 6. The maximum size of a single variable is about 16MB.

TRACE

Compiled REXX cannot be traced. If the **TRACE** instruction is found in a program, it is replaced with a **NOP** instruction. If the **TRACE** function is executed in a compiled REXX program, it returns O (**TRACE OFF**); this differs from the interpreter, which defaults to **TRACE NORMAL**. CMS Immediate commands **TS** and **TE** cannot be used to turn tracing on or off.

Halt Interpretation

The CMS **HI** Immediate command is supported only if the program is compiled with the **TESTHALT** option. This adds additional code to the program and requires extra processing, thus reducing the benefit of compiled REXX.

SOURCELINE function

In compiled programs, the **SOURCELINE** function does not normally return a program line as in an interpreted program. The developers realized this, and added the **SLINE** option. If this is specified when the program is compiled, the compiler appends a copy of the source program to the compiled REXX output. This increases the size of compiled REXX (from about twice the size of the source program to three times the size). Also, it is simple to strip in-line source from compiled REXX; if a purpose of compilation was preventing users from understanding or modifying the program, **SLINE** will allow them to do so anyway. The compiler default is **NOSLINE**.

%PAGE compiler directive

The **%PAGE** compiler directive forces a new page in the compiler listing. In large REXX programs, it may be useful to force a page break before every major code section. The directive is included in the source program as a REXX comment.

```
  ⋮
exit rc                                 /* end of mainline */

/*%page*/
/**********************************************************/
/*** Subroutines start here                          ***/
/**********************************************************/
  ⋮
```

INTERPRET

See the section "Compilation errors" for a discussion of **INTERPRET** support, and suggested alternatives.

PARSE VERSION

The **PARSE VERSION** instruction allows REXX programs to find out if they are running compiled or interpreted:

```
parse version how .
if how = 'REXXC370' then say 'REXX running compiled.'
if how = 'REXX370'  then say 'REXX running interpreted.'
```

Coding for compiled performance

Compiler manuals list several topics for consideration when writing compiled REXX. Of these, two seem good coding guidelines for any REXX program: code all constants as literal strings (in quotes), and avoid labels in loops. Two recommendations are made for arithmetic operations: do not set **NUMERIC DIGITS** less than **9**, and do not code numbers with a decimal point unless necessary.

This leaves two recommendations:

Compound variables   Use compound variables only where required for arrays and lists.

Exposing variables   Where **PROCEDURE EXPOSE** is used with compound variables, it is more efficient to **EXPOSE** the entire stem, rather than individual compound variables.

For example, a REXX program written to analyze a 3.5MB file and optionally compare it with another 3.5MB file was coded carefully, using many REXX/CMS coding tricks and techniques. The performance interpreted was reasonable, and compiling it achieved a 20 percent CPU saving.

The program was then recoded according to these two recommendations.

In several instances, the program set the tail of a compound variable to a count, and referenced these variables by their common stem and count. However, since the count was never specified as a variable, it could be changed as follows:

```
/* code this */
a1 = 'your data goes here'
a2 = 'and here...            '

/* instead of */
a.1 = 'your data goes here'
a.2 = 'and here...           '
```

In other cases, the entire stem was EXPOSEd, rather than specific compound variables:

```
CODE_THIS: procedure expose all.

INSTEAD_OF: procedure expose all.single all.other
```

When the program was recoded according to these recommendations, the compiled REXX version achieved an additional 10 percent CPU saving.

Run-time support

It is sometimes useful to establish the PTF level of the run-time library, especially if code being developed will be distributed to multiple installations.

The compiler does not provide this information. The following program can be run as a command or called as a function.

```
/* Find information about REXX run-time segment.   */
/*                                                 */
/* This program is based on one by Steve Swift, IBM */
/* UK Technical Support Staff Systems Programmer.   */
address command
parse source . how .
entry = 'EAGRTPRC'
entry
'MAKEBUF'
old = queued()
'NUCXMAP (LIFO'
do queued()-old until name = entry
   pull name addr .
end
'DROPBUF'
if name <> entry then exit 100
'EXECIO * CP (STEM L. STRING DISPLAY' strip(addr, 'L', '0')'.100'
string = ''
do i = 1 to l.0
   interim = space(subword(l.i, 2), 0)
   cut = length(interim)//8   /* XA adds storage key to display */
   string = string 33 left(interim,length(interim)-cut)
end
```

```
'QUERY CMSLEVEL (STACK'
parse pull  . . rel ','
If rel = 5 then parse var string 17 11 21 string
            else parse var string  9 11 13 string
level = left(x2c(string), x2d(11))
if how = 'FUNCTION' then return level
else say level
exit
```

An example of running the above program, named **RXCLVL**:

```
Ready;

rxclvl
 EAGRTLIB 1.1.0 PTF UL65035 Generated 12/14/89 15.25
Ready;
```

The IBM System/370 REXX
Interpreter

By Rick McGuire

Five distinct IBM REXX implementations are available, created from
two base REXX interpreters. The interpreters for CMS, TSO/E, and
GCS use a base interpreter kernel written in System/370 assembler
language. This chapter examines the System/370 REXX interpreter in
detail. The interpreters for OS/2 and OS/400 use a base interpreter
written in C, and are discussed in a later chapter.

INTERPRETER PORTABILITY

The REXX implementations for CMS, TSO/E, and GCS are essentially
the same interpreter. These versions share a system-independent kernel of code that is the main part of the REXX interpreter. The kernel is
maintained and enhanced jointly so that all three versions remain at
the same language level.

Portable code

REXX interpreters for CMS, TSO/E, and GCS are built from two sets
of code. The first set is independent of the underlying operating system.
It can also use either 24- or 31-bit addressing. The second code set pro-

vides system services required by the system-independent kernel. There is different system-dependent code for each system that supports this interpreter.

The system-dependent code has two parts:

1. The interpreter front-end. The front-end allocates interpreter work areas and locates the program to be interpreted. The front-end prepares the program for execution and calls the main entry point of the system-independent kernel. The kernel interprets the prepared REXX program and issues error messages.

2. System service processors provide operating system services to the interpreter. These services are very specific to the underlying operating systems and include:
   - Managing storage
   - Processing host commands
   - Terminal input and output

The system-independent kernel accesses operating system services with assembler macros. There is a different macro for each service required. For example, when the interpreter issues an operating system command, it evaluates an expression and passes the resulting character string to a macro called SYSHOST. SYSHOST hides the processing and logic necessary to issue the command from the system-independent kernel code. On CMS, SYSHOST builds a CMS command parameter list and uses the CMSCALL macro to invoke the command.

SYSHOST returns a character string to the kernel. The system-independent kernel assigns variable RC to this return code string. SYSHOST also returns an ERROR or FAILURE indicator used for condition trapping.

Porting the interpreter to another System/370 operating system is simple. The kernel provides all REXX language processing and control, so only the front-end and system service macros must be rewritten. Building a new interpreter is as easy as reassembly with the correct macro library.

TOKENIZING

The program in storage

When the interpreter is invoked, the system-dependent front end prepares the source file for interpretation. This may require reading the file from a disk or other source. The program is then placed into **in-storage descriptor** format.

The in-storage descriptor list has an entry for each REXX program line. A line descriptor points to the line and the line length. Figure 21 shows a typical descriptor list. Consecutive file lines need not appear in contiguous storage. They may be in scattered locations because each line is uniquely described.

The tokenized form

Once the descriptor list has been created, the front-end calls the interpreter main execution loop. The loop tokenizes each instruction and manages the control flow within the program. The tokenizer reduces REXX instructions to an intermediate form. The main loop passes this intermediate form to a clause executor, where most REXX instructions are processed. **IF**, **THEN**, and **ELSE** instructions are processed in the main execution loop.

The intermediate form contains instruction tokens reduced to an easily interpreted form. Consider a simple example:

```
say   a +   1  /* Print out the answer */
```

This shows a **SAY** instruction with a simple expression, **a + 1**. A comment and some extra blanks have also been included. The tokenizer recognizes and saves the following instruction elements:

- Keyword **SAY**. This is stored as a 1-byte instruction code.
- A single blank between the keyword and the start of the expression. The blank is translated to a special internal code.

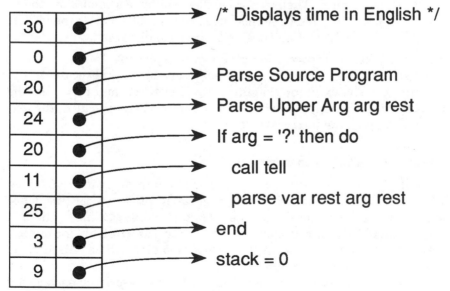

30	●
0	●
20	●
24	●
20	●
11	●
25	●
3	●
9	●

```
/* Displays time in English */

Parse Source Program
Parse Upper Arg arg rest
If arg = '?' then do
    call tell
    parse var rest arg rest
end
stack = 0
```

Figure 21. An in-storage REXX program

- Symbol A, which will be used as a variable. Symbols are stored as a three-part token:

  1. A 1-byte code that tags the token as a **symbol**.
  2. A 1-byte length (this is possible since a symbol cannot be longer than 250 bytes).
  3. The symbol value. This is stored as A. The tokenizer converts all lowercase characters to uppercase.
     A tokenized symbol has a maximum length of 252 bytes. This allows manipulation of the entire token with MVC and CLC instructions.
     A literal string such as **Hello world** is stored in a similar format. However, the 1-byte code identifies the token as a **string** rather than a **symbol**.

- Operator +. This is also converted to a special internal code.

  Note that all blanks between the end of a and the start of the + have been discarded.

- Symbol 1. The 1-byte code for this token is still **symbol**. The tokenization process does not distinguish between symbols that are valid variables and symbols that are valid numbers. As syntactic elements, they are both considered **symbols**.

  All blanks between the + and the 1 have been discarded.

- Trailing semicolon. The instruction does not have a semicolon; therefore the tokenizer adds a semicolon as the last instruction token. The trailing comment and all trailing blanks are discarded.

The fully tokenized instruction is shown in figure 22.

The tokenized instruction is now passed to the main executor of the interpreter. The executor examines the first token and processes the indicated instruction. When the instruction has been executed, the tokenizer prepares the next instruction.

The instruction lookaside buffer

Initially, the main execution loop tokenizes each program instruction when it is first executed. However, several events can alter this. Once the interpreter encounters a label, IF, DO, or SELECT instruction, it begins saving tokenized instructions in the **instruction lookaside buffer**. Instructions saved in the lookaside buffer will be reused if the instruction is executed again.

The lookaside buffer is a linked list of blocks describing each saved instruction. The blocks are saved in top-down execution order. In addi-

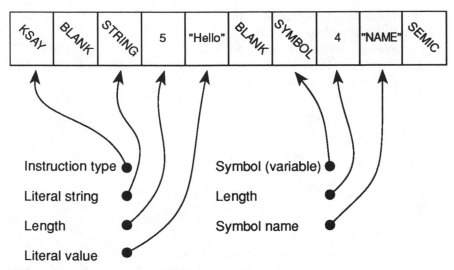

Figure 22. A tokenized instruction

tion to the tokenized instruction, each block contains links to the next and previous instructions. It also contains pointers to the beginning and end of the instruction in the in-storage source file. Source pointers are maintained as line number/offset pairs because there may be multiple instructions per line or instructions may span lines. The trace facility uses these pointers to map executed instructions back to the original program source.

The label lookaside table

The REXX interpreter remembers the positions of all labels in the REXX program in a **label lookaside table**. When a SIGNAL instruction, CALL instruction, or function call references a label, the label lookaside buffer is searched. If a match is not found, the tokenizer searches the remainder of the program for a label with the required name. Instructions passed over are saved in the instruction lookaside buffer. All labels are saved in the label lookaside table.

If a subroutine or function is called and the label is not found in the program, the interpreter searches for a built-in function or external function with the same name. If a built-in function is found, an entry is added to the label lookaside table. This entry has a flag that identifies the label entry as a built-in function. The address of the built-in function routine is placed in the lookaside entry. The next time the REXX program calls this built-in function, it will be immediately located in the label lookaside table and a direct call can be made to the built-in function. It is not necessary to search the table of built-in functions.

External subroutines are also entered in the lookaside table.

skip directly to the external function handler. It is not necessary to first search the built-in function table.

Whenever an entry is located in the table, that entry is moved to the front of the chain. Over time, frequently invoked routines move to the front, providing slightly faster access.

To quote or not to quote?

REXX experts are frequently asked: "Does quoting built-in function calls improve performance?" That is, does coding:

```
x = 'SUBSTR'(a, 1, 3)
```

perform better than:

```
x = substr(a, 1, 3)
```

Answering this requires understanding what happens in the two cases. A call to SUBSTR without quotes goes through the following steps:

1. Search the label lookaside buffer for entry SUBSTR. Assuming that this is the first call to function SUBSTR, it is not found.
2. The remainder of the source file is scanned for a label because the routine was not found in the label lookaside table. Each instruction tokenized during the scan is saved in the instruction lookaside buffer. A call occurring near the beginning of a large program may have a noticeable delay on this first call. This search also fails because SUBSTR is a built-in function. However, the entire REXX program has now been tokenized and added to the instruction lookaside buffer.
3. The table of built-in functions is searched, and this search is successful. An entry is added to the label lookaside table for the SUBSTR built-in function.

According to the REXX language definition, a call to a subroutine using a quoted string for the name must bypass internal labels. Therefore, a search for 'SUBSTR' uses an abbreviated search process:

1. The label lookaside table search is bypassed because the name is a quoted string.
2. The tokenizer does not scan the remainder of the program because this cannot be an internal routine.
3. The built-in function table is immediately searched and the function is located. An entry for this function is *not* added to the label lookaside table.

At first glance, it would appear that quoting the call is faster; but is it really? It is certainly faster on the first call, since the search through the remainder of the program is bypassed. On the second call, however, the unquoted call will be located in the label lookaside table *immediately*. Because the lookaside entry contains the address of the built-in function routine, the function handler immediately passes control to the built-in function.

The quoted call must search the built-in function table **each** time the function is called. In general, when multiple calls to a function are used, the unquoted call will be faster than the quoted call.

EXPRESSION HANDLING

Once the tokenizer passes an instruction to the clause executor, processing is simple. The clause executor contains a routine for each REXX instruction. These routines use utility routines to execute instructions. For an instruction such as:

```
a = b + 1
```

the executor calls the interpreter expression handler to evaluate the right side of the assignment. The expression handler uses the variable manager and the arithmetic routines to evaluate many of the terms and operators.

Variable management

The REXX interpreter dynamically creates and destroys variables, as required. Variables are stored in a balanced binary tree that has some interesting features.

A simple tree

When variable **A** is assigned a value, the variable manager processes the assignment. The variable manager searches the variable tree. If the variable is not found, the variable manager inserts a new tree entry. This entry contains the variable name and the variable value in a single control block. It also contains left child, right child, and parent pointers. The variable tree is sorted first by variable size and then by variable name. The variable manager uses this to avoid many string comparisons during tree searches. Figure 23 shows a typical variable tree.

When a block is inserted, a balancing routine ensures that the tree has not grown too far down one branch.

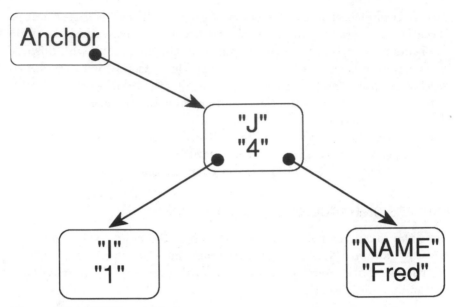

Figure 23. A REXX variable tree

Compound variables

REXX can perform several operations on entire collections of compound variables that share a common stem. The following operations can be performed on compound variable collections:

- Assignment
- Dropping
- Exposing

Operations work on a compound variable collection when the stem name is specified as a variable name.

Compound variable manipulations add complexity to the variable tree structure. Compound variables are stored in a second level of tree in the variable pool. For example, consider the assignment:

```
a.1 = 1
```

where **A.1** is the first assignment of a variable using stem **A.**. Assignment of **A.1** uses the following steps:

1. The variable tree is searched for the variable **A.**; this search fails.
2. Because the variable was not found, the variable manager inserts an entry for **A.** in the variable tree. This entry is the anchor point for a second-level tree.

3. The variable manager searches for the tail portion of the variable (that is, 1) in the second-level tree. This search also fails.

4. A new entry is added to the tree for the tail (1) because the variable did not exist. This new entry has the same structure as top-level entries. Figure 24 shows a variable tree with compound variables.

If you assign a value to a stem:

```
a. = 1
```

the stem entry assumes a second role. The assignment above releases every node of the **A.** subtree. Each compound variable on **A.** is reset to an uninitialized state. An **initial value block** is added to the **A.** anchor entry. New assignments to compound variables on **A.** proceed as before. However, if a compound variable that does not currently exist on **A.** is referenced, the value in the **A.** initial value block is returned. Figure 25 shows a compound variable with an initial value assigned.

Dropping variables

The DROP instruction returns a variable to its uninitialized state. The uninitialized state of a variable is defined as `symbol(var) == 'LIT'`. It is not a statement about storage utilization. Accordingly, dropping an individual variable does not release the storage for that variable. DROP locates the variable in the tree and flags the variable entry as a dropped variable. Subsequent references to this variable will treat it as

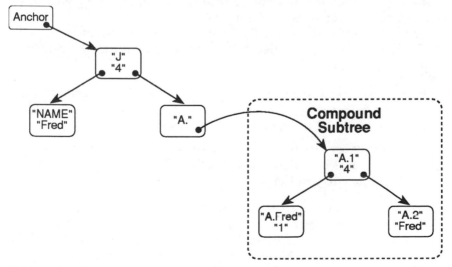

Figure 24. Variable tree with compound variables

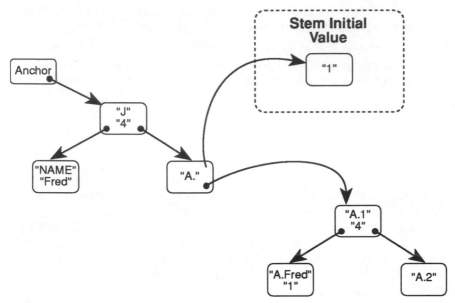

Figure 25. Stem with an initial value

a non-existent variable. In some cases, such as dropping stems, it is safe to release the variable entry storage.

Exposing variables

When a subroutine begins with a PROCEDURE instruction, the interpreter **pushes down** the existing variable pool and creates an empty variable set. When the subroutine returns, the interpreter releases all tree entries and restores the prior level.

When a variable is exposed, REXX must access both the new variable level and the old variable level. The interpreter takes the following steps to expose a variable:

1. It locates the exposed variable in the old level. If the variable did not exist prior to this, the interpreter inserts an entry in the old variable level and marks it as a dummy block.

2. The interpreter inserts an entry in the new variable level. This new entry does not contain a value field. The new entry points to the variable entry in the previous generation.

Figure 26 shows an exposed variable.

When PROCEDURE EXPOSE instructions are nested to multiple levels, there is a chain of exposed variable blocks pointing to the original level. When an exposed variable is referenced, the interpreter locates the variable in the current level. The variable manager traverses the chain

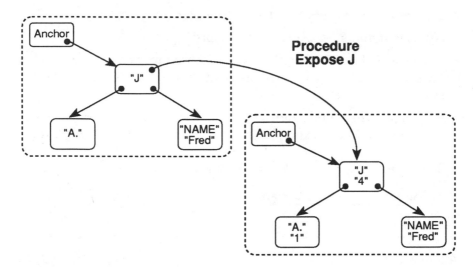

Figure 26. An exposed variable

of exposed variables to the root level. The root level block contains the variable value. The process is the same for exposed simple variables, compound variables, or stems.

Big arithmetic

A major part of expression evaluation is arithmetic operations. REXX arithmetic operations allow arbitrary-precision arithmetic. The REXX interpreter performs arithmetic in base 10, using numbers in character string form. The same arithmetic algorithms are used with NUMERIC DIGITS 9 and NUMERIC DIGITS 1000. Therefore, REXX returns consistent arithmetic results for all arithmetic precisions.

Normalized numbers

When REXX performs arithmetic, the interpreter reduces numbers to **normalized** form. It then performs operations directly on the normalized numbers.

When a number is normalized, the interpreter first verifies that the string is a proper REXX number. The validated number is copied into a math work area. This work area is large enough to process all the arithmetic operations for the current NUMERIC DIGITS setting. When NUMERIC DIGITS is changed, the work area is reallocated to the new size.

When REXX normalizes the number -123.456, it breaks the number down into several fundamental pieces:

- Sign, expressed as either 1, -1, or 0. The example above has a sign of -1.
- Number of digits. -123.456 has 6 digits.
- Exponent value. The length of the number plus the exponent value gives the location of the decimal point. For -123.456, the exponent is -3.
- Raw digits. All leading zeros, the minus sign, and the decimal point are removed. In this example, the buffer contains characters 123456.

The normalized number looks like this:

Number	Sign	Exponent	Length	Digits
-123.456	-1	-3	6	123456

Addition

REXX addition is simple. Consider adding 123.456 and 1.1. The normalized forms of these two numbers are:

Number	Sign	Exponent	Length	Digits
123.456	1	-3	6	123456
1.1	1	-1	2	11

The numbers are first adjusted so that they have the same exponent value. The adjustment is done by adding zeros to one of the operands. In the example, the temporary exponent values of the numbers are reduced to zero, and the number 1.1 has two zeros added on the end.

Number	Sign	Exponent	Length	Digits
123.456	1	0	6	123456
1.1	1	0	4	11

After the adjustment, addition proceeds. Starting from the right end of the numbers, pairs of digits are added together. If the sum of two digits is greater than 10, a carry is propagated to the next digit. The addition is performed so that the result overlays the longer operand. The value of the first number becomes 124556. Once the digits have been added together, the exponents are readjusted and the result is formatted to yield 124.556.

Subtraction is similar to addition. Instead of propagating a carry, subtraction propagates a borrow digit.

Multiplication

Multiplication uses rules similar to those taught in elementary school. As in addition, the numbers are normalized. The multiplication process is repeated additions to an accumulator. For example, to multiply 123 by 45, 5*123 is added to an accumulator of zero. To this result is added 4*1230. The multiplication occurs at the time of the addition. One of the digits is increased by a multiplication factor before adding. In the example, 5*3 would be added to 0 to process the first digit. The new digit is 5, with a carry of 1 added to the next digit.

The division operation is similar to multiplication, but considerably more complicated.

LOOKING BACK

The design of the System/370 REXX interpreter has not changed much since it was first released in 1983. Between the first REXX version in 1979 and 1983, the REXX language and the interpreter evolved through many different levels. When new features were added to the language, the existing interpreter was also enhanced. This process resulted in interpreter design choices that would not be made with a new implementation. The tokenization-on-demand process used by the main execution loop is one of these design choices.

Tokenization-on-demand was created in the early days of the REXX interpreter, when only external functions could be called from a REXX program. Because there were no internal labels or built-in functions, it was never necessary to search through the file for a label. Tokenization-on-demand was used so that only the instructions that were actually executed got tokenized.

As additional features were added to the REXX language, tokenization became more complicated. For most REXX programs today, every instruction in the program is tokenized, even instructions that are not executed. If the System/370 interpreter were to be totally reimplemented from the current REXX language definition, it would probably tokenize the entire program before beginning execution. This new interpreter already exists on OS/2 and OS/400.

40

The IBM OS/2 and OS/400 REXX Interpreter

By Rick McGuire

The IBM REXX interpreters for OS/2 and OS/400 use a common base REXX interpreter written in C. Similarities between the C REXX interpreter and the System/370 interpreter occur primarily in the variable manager and the arithmetic processor. However, this chapter focuses on *differences* between the C and System/370 REXX interpreters.

SYSTEM INDEPENDENCE

The C REXX interpreter provides the same division of responsibility as the System/370 interpreter. The interpreter is split between a system-independent code kernel and a system-dependent code set. There is a different system-dependent code set for each supported system.

The C system-independent kernel was more difficult to write than the System/370 kernel because it needed to hide more underlying system features. In addition to shielding differences in the underlying operating system, it was necessary to account for differences in the underlying hardware architecture and differences between EBCDIC and ASCII encodings. OS/2 is an ASCII-based system, while the AS/400 is an EBCDIC-based system.

The system-dependent code set contains a front-end processor to handle interpreter initialization and system service routines used by kernel code. Additionally, some system and machine architecture differences are shielded by C macros, #define constants, and typedefs. A new interpreter is built by compiling the source with a merged set of system-dependent and system-independent #include files.

Double Byte Character Set (DBCS) support

ASCII and EBCDIC encoding differences are most apparent with the Double Byte Character Set (DBCS) support. On EBCDIC-based systems, DBCS fields within a string begin with a **shiftout** character and end with a **shiftin** character. Between the shiftout and shiftin, the characters are 2 bytes long, and each byte must be within the range X'41' to X'FE', inclusive. The special DBCS blank character, X'4040', is also allowed.

On ASCII systems, a country-specific set of code points is reserved for use as DBCS first bytes. When one of these first bytes appears in a character string, the next byte in the string completes a single DBCS character. No control characters are used to delimit DBCS fields.

Consequently, the REXX code for processing DBCS character strings requires two distinct sets of code. DBCS processing is isolated in two sets of DBCS routines. One set handles the EBCDIC shiftout/shiftin encoding scheme; the second set handles the ASCII reserved first byte encodings. A new system implementation is built by linking in the appropriate DBCS routines.

System-dependent built-in functions

The system-independent kernel allows creation of system-dependent built-in functions. These system-dependent functions appear in the function search order after the built-in functions, but before all external functions.

To add these functions, two system-dependent routines must be written. The first routine resolves the built-in function name at tokenization time. See section "Label resolution" for details on function resolution. The second routine is a function dispatcher that calls the built-in function handler when passed the function identifier token provided by the name resolver. System built-in functions have access to all utility and service routines in the kernel code. Therefore, a system-dependent built-in function can be faster than an equivalent external function.

TOKENIZING

The System/370 interpreter uses a **tokenize-on-demand** method of processing, where each instruction is tokenized when required and the tokenization reduces the instruction to a simple canonical form.

The C REXX interpreter uses a **parsing** method, in which the entire source file is processed before execution. The C REXX tokenization process does more than a simple reduction to canonical form. Items which are resolved at execution time by the System/370 interpreter are resolved at tokenization time by the C REXX interpreter.

Tokenization is more costly in the C REXX interpreter, though better performance can be obtained by reusing the tokenized image on subsequent program executions. With the OS/2 interpreter, the tokenized image is saved in the file system extended attributes. With the AS/400 interpreter, the tokenized image is saved in the database member associated space.

The pcode buffer

The tokenization process creates several pieces that form the program **meta data**. The first piece is the **pcode buffer**. The pcode buffer holds a sequence of fixed-size structures that describe the individual instruction tokens. Each structure contains a token identifier and a data field. The meaning of the data field changes with each type of token.

The first token of every clause is an **instruction token**. An instruction token identifies the REXX instruction being executed. Instruction tokens are at a finer level than the instruction name. For example, the instruction token may be the NUMERIC_DIGITS instruction rather than the NUMERIC instruction. The instruction token data field contains the program line number that contains the instruction. Line number information is used for tracing and error reporting.

Instruction operands are verified at tokenization time. If an error is detected in an instruction, the tokenizer adds an error message token to the pcode buffer. The error message token contains the REXX error number of the problem detected. When the incorrect instruction is executed, the error message token raises the SYNTAX condition. The interpreter issues an error message or branches to a trap created with the SIGNAL ON SYNTAX instruction.

An instruction that uses variables or literal strings contains a special form of pcode token. Unlike the System/370 interpreter, these pcode tokens identify strings and symbols by their particular subclasses. For example, a literal string may be a STRING, a HEX_STRING, or a BIN_STRING. Similarly, a symbol may be a NAME, a COMPOUND_NAME, a STEM, a NUMBER, a LITERAL, or a LITERAL_DOT.

String and symbol tokens are the same size as instruction tokens. The data field of a string or symbol token contains a reference to the string or symbol value. The reference is an offset into a second data structure called the **literals buffer**.

The literals buffer

The **literals buffer** contains the values of the literal strings and symbols used in the REXX program. Only one copy of each literal string or symbol exists within a program, regardless of how many times the string or symbol is used. Values are stored as three fields:

1. The **cache index**. The cache index is used to optimize variable accesses. This cache index is explained in more detail in the section "The variable cache".

2. The length of the string or symbol value.

3. The variable name or the literal string value.

All references to symbols or strings use indirect references into the literals buffer.

Tracing

The System/370 interpreter holds the entire interpreted source file in memory during execution. When an instruction is traced, it is displayed from the source file.

The C REXX interpreter holds only the tokenized image in memory. When a program instruction is traced, the instruction is reconstructed from the tokenized image. The reconstruction of the instruction causes several differences in the instruction trace:

- Comments are not available for tracing.

- Spacing of operators is not maintained.

- Instruction keywords may appear with different uppercasing.

- A semicolon is added to each traced instruction.

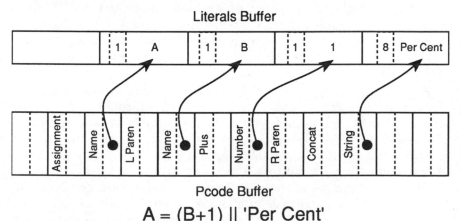

Figure 27. The pcode buffer and literals buffer.

The variable cache

The **cache index** associated with each variable name is an index into a **variable cache buffer**. Each unique variable name used in the program is assigned a slot in the variable cache buffer. The variable cache saves references to variables so that subsequent references can access the variables directly.

The variable tree

The C REXX interpreter uses a two-level balanced binary tree similar to the one used by the System/370 interpreter. References, insertions, drops, and exposes are handled the same way, except that variable values are not stored in variable tree entries. This separation of the data from the name allows constant and literal data to be shared, rather than duplicated for each occurrence of the value.

Blocks on the tree contain additional fields:

- Variable creation level. The creation level identifies the PROCEDURE nesting level where the variable was created.
- Pointer to a cache index entry.
- Save area for cache pointers from prior variable levels.

These are the pieces necessary to step through a variable access sequence. Assume a program has the following instructions:

```
a = b * 2
say a
```

The first instruction assigns variable **A**. When the variable is looked up, the following steps are taken:

1. The cache slot for this variable is checked. Because this is the first reference to the variable **A**, the cache slot contains a null pointer.
2. Because the cache entry is null, the variable tree is searched. The variable **A** is not found, so it is added to the current variable tree.

The variable manager then takes the following actions:

1. The creation-level tag in the variable entry is set to the current PROCEDURE nesting level.
2. The existing value of the variable's cache slot is saved in the variable block.
3. The cache slot is set to a pointer to the variable entry in the tree.
4. The cache pointer in the variable block is set to point at the cache slot for this variable.

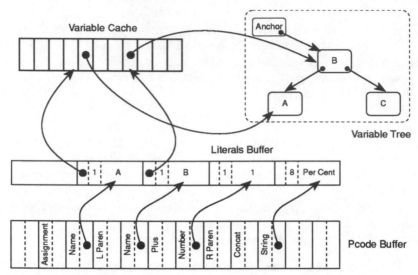

Figure 28. Variable cache references.

The first instruction is now complete. When variable **A** is referenced in the **SAY** instruction of the example, the interpreter can take a short-cut to access the variable. Accessing **A** uses the following steps:

1. The cache slot for **A** is examined. This time, the cache slot contains a non-null pointer. Quick access to the variable *may* be possible if the pointer passes a validation check.

2. The pointer in the cache slot points directly at an entry in the variable tree for variable **A**. The creation-level field in the variable entry is compared with the current **PROCEDURE** nesting level. If the two numbers are equal, the cache slot contains a pointer to the current value of variable **A**.

3. The value is retrieved immediately from the variable tree and used in the **SAY** instruction.

When the new variable was created, the existing cache value was saved in the variable block. This may appear to be unnecessary, because the old value was null. The following program illustrates why the old value must be saved:

```
do i = 1 to 10
   x = x + fred(i)
end
exit
:
fred: procedure
arg value
```

```
x = 0
do i = 1 to value
   x = x + i
end
return
```

In the example above, the subroutine uses a local variable, I, with the same name as a variable in the calling routine. When variable I is referenced for the first time in the subroutine, the following process is used:

1. A non-null cache pointer is found in the slot for variable I.

2. The creation level for variable I is compared with the current procedure level. This time the two fields do not match because a PROCEDURE instruction was issued at the start of the subroutine.

3. A new entry for variable I is added in the current variable tree.

4. The current cache slot value for I is saved in the new entry.

5. The cache slot pointer in the new entry is set to the address of the cache slot for I.

The next reference to variable I in the subroutine can use the cache pointer to access the variable.

When the subroutine returns, the cache slot pointer in the entry for I is used to restore the original cache pointer. The next reference to the variable I in the calling routine will have a valid cache pointer for the variable.

Label resolution

The C REXX interpreter takes advantage of the complete program preprocessing by resolving references to function and subroutine calls. When the program is tokenized, the interpreter builds a list of the labels in the program. It also maintains a list of all function calls, CALL instructions, and SIGNAL instructions. With this information, the interpreter changes each function call, CALL instruction, and SIGNAL instruction to point to the final instruction target. References to a label or routine have a special **reference** token inserted in the pcode buffer. Each reference token is updated with the proper reference target. There are four types of references:

Label	The token data field is set to the program location of the label.
Built-in Function	The data field is set to the function table index of the built-in function.

System Built-in Function	The data field is set to a table index for the built-in function. System-specific built-in functions are managed by system-specific handlers.
External Routine	The data field is set to zero.

All calls go directly to the target location without a run-time search because this resolution has been performed. Unlike in the System/370 interpreter, there is no performance difference in the C REXX interpreter when quoted strings are used for function names.

MANAGING CHARACTER STRINGS

The REXX interpreter creates and destroys many character strings when REXX programs are executed. These character strings may be variable values or intermediate expression results. The System/370 interpreter optimizes its use of temporary character strings to avoid creating unnecessary temporary values. The C REXX interpreter further optimizes character string creation.

The C REXX character string

The C REXX interpreter's internal representation of a character string includes a header block and a data block. The character string data block contains the string value. The character string header block contains information about the string. For example, the header block has a field containing the length of the string.

The character string header contains a field that the C REXX interpreter uses to optimize character string creation. This header field is the character string **reference tag**. The reference tag has two uses:

1. It identifies the source of the character string.

2. It allows multiple variables to share a character string.

Constant character strings

A REXX character string may be either a constant string or a dynamically created string. A constant character string would be created by the following assignment:

```
a = 'Hello World'
```

The literal string **Hello World** is created during program tokenization. When variable **A** is assigned the string **Hello World**, the variable tree entry points to the constant string. The variable manager does not make a new copy of this string.

When the tokenizer creates the character string `Hello World`, it places -1 in the string reference tag. This tags the string as a constant string. Routines which modify character strings directly recognize the -1 tag as a special string, and replace the constant string with a dynamically created string. The interpreter routine used to release a character string will not destroy a string containing a -1 tag.

Constant strings are created by different operations:

- Literal strings, including hexadecimal and binary literals.

- Literal numbers—for example:

```
x = 1
```

creates a constant string for the number 1.

- Operation results—for example, the 1 or 0 result from a comparison operation uses a constant string.

- Built-in function results. Built-in functions which return constant results use constant strings. For example, the SYMBOL built-in function can return the tokens VAR, LIT, or BAD. These strings are all constant strings.

Constant strings may be referenced in multiple places. For example, the following program creates only one copy of the constant string `Hello World`.

```
do i = 1 to 1000
   a.i = 'Hello World'
end
```

The variable entries for each compound variable point to the same copy of the `Hello World` constant.

Dynamic character strings

Not all REXX expressions can create constant-value character strings. Operations like concatenation and addition create new strings that did not exist at tokenization time. When REXX creates a dynamic string, it places a 0 in the reference tag. The 0 identifies the string as a **safe** character string. A safe character string may be returned to the storage manager or updated directly.

REXX arithmetic operations create dynamic strings. In the following example, the + operator will create a dynamic string with the value 5.

```
say 3 + 2
```

In the example above, these steps are used:

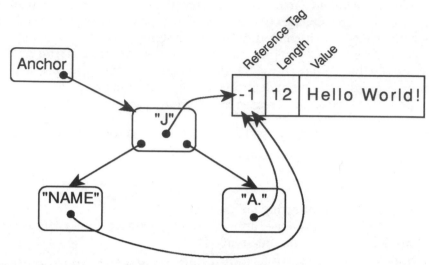

Figure 29. Multiple references to a constant string.

1. The **SAY** instruction calls the expression handler to evaluate the expression.
2. The expression handler returns a dynamically created string as the expression result.
3. The **SAY** instruction displays the result.
4. The **SAY** calls the string handler to release the result.
5. The string handler recovers the character string storage because the reference tag is zero.

   Consider a slightly different example:

```
x = 3 + 2
say x
```

The assignment instruction assigns the expression result to the variable **x**. When the expression result is assigned to variable **x**, the variable manager increments the reference tag of the string. A positive reference tag means that the string is no longer **safe** because the variable manager holds a reference to the string. Like a constant string, a referenced string cannot be updated directly or returned to the system.

   The **SAY** instruction has a different result now:

1. The **SAY** instruction calls the expression handler to evaluate the expression.
2. The expression handler returns a pointer to the value of variable **x**.

3. The **SAY** instruction displays the result.

4. The **SAY** calls the string handler to release the result.

5. The string handler does not recover the character string storage because the reference tag is not zero. The variable handler has placed a **lock** on the string that prevents it from being destroyed.

A dynamic character string may be referenced by more than one object. For example, the following program creates a dynamic character string with 1001 references:

```
x = 3 + 5                    /* Create the dynamic string */
do i = 1 to 1000     /* Point 1000 variables at the string */
    a.i = x                           /* One by one */
end
```

When a variable is assigned a new value, the variable manager decrements the reference tag for the old variable value, and releases the old value only if its reference tag becomes zero. The character string is preserved for other references if the reference tag is non-zero.

THE C REXX INTERPRETER VERSUS SYSTEM/370

The C REXX interpreter borrows many design features of the System/370 interpreter. However, the C REXX interpreter is more than a translation of the original System/370 assembler into C. This

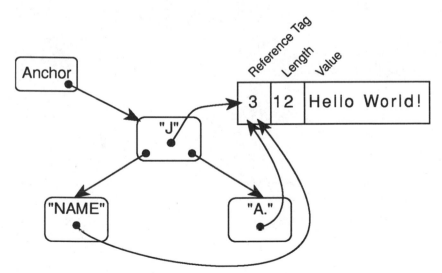

Figure 30. Multiple references to a dynamic string.

interpreter has many features that extend the design of the System/370 interpreter. These features include:

- Enhanced program tokenization
- Cached variable references
- No run-time label searches
- Enhanced string management

Over time, these features will be incorporated into the System/370 interpreter.

41

REXX for EXEC 2 Programmers

By Jeff Karpinski

OF REXX, EXEC 2, AND BABY DUCKS

"Duckling Thinks Cocker Spaniel Is Its Mother!"

We smile at the headline in the newspaper and read about the baby duck who latched onto a dog as its parent. It doesn't matter to the duckling that the dog isn't very good at nesting, and is really terrible when it comes to quacking or laying eggs. No one can convince the poor animal that it really should associate with other ducks—it's happy the way it is. It knows the spaniel; it's comfortable with it.

Perhaps part of our amusement at this behavior results from laughing at ourselves. Think of that well-worn pair of shoes we know we ought to discard . . . maybe we can't wear them to the office, but they're so comfortable, and they still keep our feet dry. Or what about that reliable old portable typewriter? Even though it doesn't have many fancy features, it's still good for typing letters, and besides, we know which keys stick, and it has a satisfying click-click about it.

This "baby duck syndrome" even extends to computer languages. We're comfortable with certain languages, and tend to use them exclusively. Thus we write our mortgage calculator in COBOL because we don't want to brush up on our FORTRAN, we write a string processor in FORTRAN because it's a pain to switch to PL/I or C, and (you see this coming, don't you?) we continue to write our control programs and macros in EXEC 2. Three people down the hall have been pestering us about the use of REXX, but why should we bother? EXEC 2 gets the job done, we know the language, and we're comfortable with it.

Indeed, why *should* we learn REXX when we already can accomplish our tasks in EXEC 2? Quite simply put, all those tasks can be accomplished more quickly and easily in REXX; moreover, many of the programs we never even would have attempted in EXEC 2 can be written readily in REXX. Finally we decide to walk down the hall and talk to the guru who always seems to have a REXX manual sitting out on the desk. Of course, says the guru, you have much to look forward to:

- The language has a natural "feel" to it. Programs can be written in top-down fashion, using approaches common to other programming languages. They can be read and maintained easily, even by people who are not REXX experts.

- REXX supports powerful parsing and string manipulation, allowing construction of sophisticated user interfaces with minimal effort.

- REXX has a rich library of intrinsics, so it's not necessary to do a lot of wheel reinvention.

- It has a large set of control and data structures, allowing complicated logic to be handled in a straightforward manner.

- It's easy to learn and write, and it's just plain fun to use!

As we delve deeper into the new world of REXX, we start to see more details of the differences between the two languages.

First, the "feel" of the language is what we have come to expect from a modern programming language. Coding is free-format and in mixed case. Variable names may be up to 250 characters long, and may contain special characters such as _ and #. Clauses, verbs, and quoted strings give an English-like flow to the syntax. For example:

```
if first_name <> '' then say 'Hi there' first_name
```

EXEC 2 uses **operator** notation to express functions; REXX function notation follows rules we are used to from algebra, with arguments enclosed in parentheses following function names. For example, EXEC 2 would use a statement like:

```
&NAMELEN = &LENGTH OF FIRSTNAME
```

to determine the length of a variable, while REXX would use:

```
name_len = length(first_name)
```

Comments are delimited by /*. . .*/ pairs as in PL/I and C, instead of leading asterisks. (In fact, the first line of a REXX program *must* be a comment so that the CMS EXEC processor will recognize the file as REXX and not EXEC 2 or EXEC.)

Next, REXX provides parsing and string handling capabilities which allow sophisticated operations to be performed with a minimum of effort. Various parsing instructions can be used to decompose strings into constituent tokens in much the same way we do when we read text from a page. For instance, **pattern** parsing is possible, allowing programs to scan tokens exactly as we would with our eyes:

```
parse var todays_date yr . '/' mon . '/' day .
```

This statement tells REXX to scan the contents of variable **TODAYS_DATE**, assigning text up to but not including the first slash to a variable called **YR**, text up to the next slash to **MON**, and the remainder to **DAY**. This statement will provide reasonable results no matter how the date is formatted: **85/7/4, 85/07/04**, and **85b/b7b/b4** are all handled similarly. (Periods in the **PARSE** statement are a REXX subtlety. In this particular example they act as placeholders, resulting in suppression of blanks when tokens are parsed.)

Arguments passed to REXX programs are also readily handled using **PARSE** instructions. While EXEC 2 programs use predefined arguments **&1, &2**, and so forth, REXX provides **PARSE ARG** (and the related **ARG**), allowing direct assignment of arguments to variables following specified parsing rules. A program requiring as arguments a CMS filename, filetype, and filemode might assign these values to variables in EXEC 2 via:

```
&FN = &1
&FT = &2
&FM = &3
```

while a REXX program would only need the statement:

```
arg fn ft fm .
```

Pattern parsing, too, could be incorporated into the **ARG** statement. The date in the previous example could be provided as an argument using the same pattern:

```
arg yr . '/' mon . '/' day .
```

In this way one statement scans input and assigns variables regardless of their format.

Other interesting variations on the **PARSE** and **ARG** statements result when the number of variables to be set does not match the number of tokens to be parsed. If there are fewer tokens than variables, variables are matched with all available tokens and extra variables are set to nulls, making it easy to check for missing or defaulted arguments. For example:

```
fileid = 'MY FILE'
parse var fileid fn ft fm .
```

would set **FN** to **MY**, **FT** to **FILE**, and **FM** to a null string.

On the other hand, if the number of tokens exceeds the number of variables, REXX provides an interesting twist: the last variable in the instruction receives *all* extra tokens as literals, including embedded or trailing blanks:

```
xampl = 'THIS IS A  PARSING   EXAMPLE '
parse var xampl w1 w2
```

would assign **THIS** to **W1** while **W2** would receive the entire remainder of the string, including blanks; i.e., **W2** would contain **ISℵAℵℵPARSINGℵℵℵEXAMPLEℵ**. The principle here is analogous to that of the **&READ STRING** instruction in EXEC 2, but it is much more flexible because it can be used to set arguments or to parse strings as well as to read from the program stack. For example, to pass an arbitrary message string to a REXX program, you could use a fragment such as:

```
parse arg msg
say msg
```

to assign the entire message text to variable **MSG** and display it at the terminal. By contrast, an EXEC 2 program would require a list of arguments as long as the maximum possible number of words in the message—if that could be determined!

(The function of the . in some of the previous parsing examples should now be clearer: by creating a dummy position in the list of variables to be created, the period absorbs any extraneous tokens or blanks, ensuring that all named variables are set to appropriate blank-delimited values.)

The converse operation of reassembling tokens into strings is also straightforward in REXX: two variables written next to each other are joined with an intervening blank, while abutting concatenation requires only the concatenation symbol. If **X** contains **blue**, and **Z** contains **bird**, the value of the REXX expression **X Z** would be **blueℵbird**, while **X||Z** would create **bluebird**. This example illustrates yet another nicety of REXX: literal strings are expressed as you would expect, as text enclosed by single or double quotation marks.

Intrinsic functions and operations are the hammers and screwdrivers of any language—they're the tools which help us to build our application programs. To this end, REXX provides a rich set of intrinsics. Generally, these intrinsics assume a compact, functionlike form, as opposed to the operator notation used in EXEC 2. Simply multiplying two numbers in EXEC 2 requires the &MULT OF operator:

```
&Z = &MULT OF &X &Y
```

while in REXX the expression takes on the algebraic form we would expect:

```
z = x * y
```

Many REXX intrinsics provide more powerful capabilities than do their EXEC 2 counterparts, and still more provide functionality not present at all in EXEC 2. For instance, EXEC 2's &TRIM OF instruction will only remove trailing blanks from a string, but REXX's STRIP function has optional arguments which specify removal of leading blanks, trailing blanks, or both—or even characters other than blanks! REXX's TIME and DATE intrinsics provide options such as elapsed time and day of week, rather than just current time and date. Other functions such as FORMAT, which formats numbers for output, SUBWORD, which selects a substring of words from within another string, and ABBREV, which checks for abbreviations of words, have no parallels in EXEC 2.

Arithmetic and logical operations are also much more extensive in REXX. Rather than being limited to integers, REXX supports the four basic operations on real numbers, along with modulo and integer division and integer exponentiation. Because REXX operates on numbers as character strings, operations can be carried out to arbitrary levels of precision by setting the NUMERIC DIGITS option to the desired level. Logical operators are also more extensive, including parentheses, AND, OR, XOR (exclusive or), and exactly equal (blanks and zeros are respected).

Compare REXX to EXEC 2 for a task as simple as averaging two numbers:

```
&X = 2
&Y = 7
&SUM = &X + &Y
&AVG = &DIV OF &SUM 2
&TYPE &AVG
```

Note that we have to create one intermediate variable, &SUM, to hold the sum of the numbers before we can apply &DIV, and a second, &AVG, before we can display the answer. No great problem, but examine the result if only one of &X or &Y is even—because EXEC 2 handles only integer arithmetic, we find that the average of 2 and 7 is 4! In REXX, all we need is:

```
x = 2
y = 7
say (x + y) / 2
```

and we're told that the average of 2 and 7 is 4.5. (Note that the REXX verb SAY is the equivalent of &TYPE—that is, evaluate and display the expression.)

If we had to set a third variable based on our little X and Y, that too provides an interesting contrast: using the | operator (OR) in REXX, we could write something like:

```
if (x = 3) | (y = 4) then z = 12
```

while EXEC 2 would require that the test be split into two separate statements:

```
&IF &X EQ 3 &Z = 12
&IF &Y EQ 4 &Z = 12
```

The control structures found in REXX are those expected of a modern computer language. The richness of the structures allows easy programming of logical constructs which can become awkward or confusing in EXEC 2. Because EXEC 2 does not support IF/THEN/ELSE structures, something as simple as testing alternative conditions produces redundant code:

```
&IF &LEN EQ 0 &ERRMSG = &STRING OF No text supplied
&IF &LEN NE 0 &ERRMSG = &BLANK
```

This requires &LEN to be examined twice even though the conditions are mutually exclusive. In REXX, this statement becomes:

```
if len = 0 then errmsg = 'No text supplied'
else errmsg = ''
```

which has the added benefits of being easier to read and maintain.

REXX also provides several varieties of DO structures, including simple blocks, FORTRAN-style DO loops, and WHILE and UNTIL blocks. The simple DO block alone provides much greater flexibility in design. To execute a group of statements conditionally in EXEC 2, you have three alternatives:

1. Test the opposite condition and use &GOTO to transfer processing to a label following the group.
2. Test the condition prior to each statement in the group.
3. Use the &SKIP instruction to skip around the group. The first alternative is probably the best but can quickly lead to "spaghetti code" remi-

niscent of old-style FORTRAN. The second is inefficient, and anyone using the third method should hope that they never have to maintain the code! Consider how much easier it is to read and maintain:

```
if name = '' then do
   msg = 'No name supplied'
   name = default_name
end
```

versus:

```
&IF /&NAME NE / &GOTO -HAVENAME
&MSG = &STRING OF No name supplied
&NAME = &DFLTNAME
-HAVENAME
```

If you have to add an alternative block to the REXX fragment, all you need do is tack an **ELSE** to the other side of the DO block, while EXEC 2 requires more labels and &GOTOs.

Beyond the simple DO block, REXX provides full loop structures controlled either by loop increments (similar to FORTRAN loops), **WHILE** or **UNTIL** tests, or combinations of these. Within loops, the **ITERATE** instruction can step to the next pass of the loop, and **LEAVE** can transfer out of the loop prior to its normal end. Since loops are delimited by DO/END pairs, labels and transfer (i.e., &GOTO) instructions are not required in REXX as they would be in EXEC 2.

To illustrate the differences, consider the following EXEC 2 loop structure:

```
* Add the integers till the sum of their squares is > 1000
&INT = 1
&SUM = 0
&LOOP -ENDSUM UNTIL &SUM GE 1000
&SUM = &SUM + &MULT OF &INT &INT
&INT = &INT + 1
-ENDLOOP
&TYPE The sum is &SUM
```

The same fragment can be written in REXX as:

```
/* Add the integers till the sum of their squares is > 1000 */
sum = 0
do int = 1 until sum >= 1000
   sum = sum + int * int
end
say 'The sum is' sum
```

This loop can be written more compactly in REXX because INT is used as the loop control variable. Its initialization and incrementing are thus handled implicitly.

The use of **LEAVE** and **ITERATE** also simplify loop design. Consider the following fragment:

```
* Request names, ignoring anyone named 'REX'
&LOOP -ENDLOOP *
&TYPE Enter a name:
&READ ARGS
&IF /&1 = /REX &TYPE I'm ignoring you
&IF /&1 = /REX &GOTO -ENDLOOP
&IF /&1 = /QUIT &GOTO -XIT
&TYPE Hi there &1
-ENDLOOP
-XIT
```

One way to rewrite this in REXX would be:

```
/* Request names, ignoring anyone named 'REX'   */
   do forever
      say 'Enter a name:'
      pull name
      if name = 'REX' then do
         say 'I''m ignoring you'
         iterate
      end
      if name = 'QUIT' then leave
      say 'Hi there'
   end
```

Here the **ITERATE** instruction parallels the **&GOTO -ENDLOOP** transfer in the EXEC 2 example; that is, all lines between the **ITERATE** and loop **END** statements are skipped, and the next cycle of the loop is processed. **LEAVE**, on the other hand, tells REXX to branch out of the loop and begin processing at the first statement following the terminating **END**. Of course, there are other ways to achieve the same results in REXX, by use of **IF/THEN/ELSE** constructs and multiple exits.

The **SELECT** statement is another powerful REXX control structure. **SELECT** is identical to the **CASE** statement in languages such as ALGOL, and is analogous (though not identical) to the **SWITCH** statement in C. **SELECT** statements test a series of conditions until a value of "true" is determined; the object of the **WHEN** is then executed, after which control is transferred to the first line following the end of the **SELECT**. None of the conditions following the true one will be evaluated. If the most commonly true condition is placed first in the list of alternatives, the other tests will most likely be skipped, resulting in increased execution efficiency. To produce a parallel structure in EXEC 2 requires a series of **&IF** tests and **&GOTO**s. Consider the following:

```
* Check for return codes 0, 10, 20, or other
&IF &RETCODE NE 0 &GOTO -NOT0
&TYPE Result OK
```

```
&GOTO -NEXT
-NOT0
&IF &RETCODE NE 10 &GOTO -NOT10
&TYPE Module had warnings
EXEC SENDFILE WARNINGS FILE TO &USER
&GOTO -NEXT
-NOT10
&IF &RETCODE NE 20 &GOTO -NOT20
&TYPE Module had errors
EXEC SENDFILE ERRORS FILE TO &USER
&GOTO -NEXT
-NOT20
&TYPE Unknown problem -- return code was &RETCODE
-NEXT
```

In REXX, how much more direct and compact this becomes!

```
select              /* Check for return codes 0, 10, 20, or other */
   when retcode = 0 then say 'result OK'
   when retcode = 10 then do
      say 'Module had warnings'
      'EXEC SENDFILE WARNINGS FILE TO' user
   end
   when retcode = 20 then do
      say 'Module had errors'
      'EXEC SENDFILE ERRORS FILE TO' user
   end
   otherwise
   say 'Unknown problem -- return code was' retcode
end /* End of SELECT block */
```

If our module completes successfully (which we hope happens more often than the other cases), only that condition is checked. The others are ignored, and interpretation continues following the last END. The worst-case condition—that of an unknown error code—is pushed off to the OTHERWISE part of the block. This branch can be reached only if all other conditions are false. The EXEC 2 version achieves exactly the same result, but all those labels and &GOTOs get to be a bit much, so we tend instead to use redundant &IF tests or a lot of &SKIPs, with much teeth-gnashing when we have to modify the code later.

While REXX and EXEC 2 both support the concept of a subroutine, those in REXX are once again more flexible and powerful. External subroutines in both languages are identical in concept—they're merely other EXECs on disk invoked by the currently running program. Variables can only be communicated between the two programs via arguments, the console stack, GLOBALV, or temporary files; thus variables in the two programs are isolated from one another. On the other hand, internal subroutines in REXX programs have the possibility of being **open** to the rest of the program (all variables are available to both the caller and the callee), **closed** (analogous to external), or a combination of the two, with some variables shared and others isolated. Further, the **RETURN** statement allows arbitrary strings to be passed back to the caller, thus creating new variables on the fly in the caller.

This small EXEC 2 program uses a subroutine to sum and multiply two numbers:

```
* Create PROD and SUM
&CALL -SUMPROD &1 &2
&TYPE The sum is &SUM and the product is &PROD
&EXIT
-SUMPROD
&SUM = &1 + &2
&PROD = &MULT OF &1 &2
&RETURN
```

Note that the variables &SUM and &PROD are created within the -SUMPROD subroutine and must be referred to by those names in the caller. Arguments &1 and &2 of the main program are temporarily unavailable while the -SUMPROD code is being interpreted. A direct translation of this routine into REXX might be:

```
/* Create PROD and SUM */
    arg x y .
    call SUMPROD x y
    say 'The sum is' sum 'and the product is' prod
    exit
SUMPROD:
    arg num1 num2 .
    sum = num1 + num2
    prod = num1 * num2
    return
```

In this translation, variables **NUM1** and **NUM2** are created via the **ARG** instruction and are distinct from **X** and **Y**. This is an **open** subroutine, so the variables **SUM** and **PROD** (as well as **NUM1** and **NUM2** if we want them) are available to the caller. If we know that the subroutine will *always* use the two values stored in **X** and **Y**, we can exploit the fact that these values are available to both routines and simplify the example as:

```
/* Create PROD and SUM */
    arg x y .
    call SUMPROD
    say 'The sum is' sum 'and the product is' prod
    exit
SUMPROD:
    sum = x + y
    prod = x * y
    return
```

The **SUMPROD** routine is now just a kind of internal fragment which can be referenced at any point in the main program, so long as we use only the variable names mentioned. But wait! Suppose we can't guarantee that our program will always be careful about its variable names? We'd like to keep **SUM** and **PROD** as reserved names, but maybe **X**, **Y**, **NUM1**, or **NUM2** will be reused. REXX provides yet another variation: by declaring **SUMPROD** to be a procedure, we can isolate its variables from those of the caller. Those which we need to share can be made available via the **EXPOSE** instruction:

```
/* Create PROD and SUM  */
    arg x y .
    call SUMPROD x y
    say 'The sum is' sum 'and the product is' prod
    exit
SUMPROD: procedure expose prod sum
    arg y x .
    sum = x + y
    prod = x * y
    return
```

Now variables **X** and **Y** in **SUMPROD** are distinct from those in the main program (note that they're even in reverse order). That is, changes made to **X** or **Y** in the subroutine do not affect variables with the same names which are part of the calling program. The instruction **EXPOSE PROD SUM** tells REXX to share those particular values with the main program; they do not have to be passed in or returned back.

Yet another variation uses REXX's ability to return strings from subroutines and parse those strings into new variables. The example can be further compacted into:

```
/* Create PROD and SUM  */
    arg x y .
    call SUMPROD x y
    parse var result prod sum .
    say 'The sum is' sum 'and the product is' prod
    exit
SUMPROD: procedure
    arg y x .
    return x*y x+y
```

Here the special variable **RESULT** contains values of **X*Y** and **X+Y**; **PARSE VAR** decomposes that string into its two components and assigns their values to the local variables **PROD** and **SUM**. There is no need to create extra variables in the subroutine, nor to share them with the caller. Even this example can be further simplified somewhat by using **PARSE VALUE** to evaluate the **SUMPROD** call as if it were a function and set the variables in one statement:

```
/* Create PROD and SUM  */
    arg x y .
```

```
  parse value SUMPROD(x y) with prod sum .
  say 'The sum is' sum 'and the product is' prod
  exit
SUMPROD: procedure
  arg y x .
  return x*y x+y
```

Finally, compound variables in REXX provide an analog of EXEC 2's compound variable names, though again with greater flexibility. Compound variable names in EXEC 2 are formed by abutting names of two or more variables; for example, &ADDRESS&CITY and &ADDRESS&STATE. The parallel concept in REXX uses a period to separate the primary name (the **stem**) from each of its compound modifiers; e.g., ADDRESS.CITY and ADDRESS.STATE would be the corresponding variables. Compound variables thus become a sort of "super-array", where the index variable may be anything, not necessarily an integer as we are used to in FORTRAN or C. Moreover, REXX provides still more power in that it is possible to assign a default value to a compound variable—unless otherwise set, REXX will assign that value to *any* variable beginning with the specified stem. For example, a calendar program could assign the number of days in each month by the following:

```
days. = 31
days.apr = 30
days.jun = 30
⋮
```

The first statement instructs REXX to use **31** as the default value for any compound variable beginning with the stem **DAYS.**; thus **DAYS.JAN** and **DAYS.MAR** are both **31** even though not set explicitly. The other statements override the default value for the particular cases of **DAYS.APR, DAYS.JUN**, and so on. (For this example we'll ignore how many days hath February.)

Well, you say to the local guru, all this power and flexibility is great, but if I'm going to write all these sophisticated REXX programs, how do I debug them? Even when things go sour, REXX comes to the rescue with powerful internal helpers. Probably the most useful of these is the TRACE instruction. Like EXEC 2's &TRACE, REXX's TRACE can do things like echoing interpreted lines at the terminal or identifying nonzero return codes, but it goes much further: various modifiers allow displaying the results of evaluating clauses, or even of the intermediate steps the interpreter takes to produce the final result. If you wish, you can further modify the trace to wait for input after each traced clause, so that you can make changes to the program while it runs.

Using the product-sum example from before and changing the &TRACE to &TRACE ALL &PRINT, EXEC 2 displays at the terminal:

```
3. &CALL -SUMPROD 5 10
6. -SUMPROD
7. &SUM = 5 + 10
8. &PROD = &MULT OF 5 10
9. &RETURN
4. &TYPE The sum is 15 and the product is 50
The sum is 15 and the product is 50
5. &EXIT
```

This certainly tells us where we are, but compare it to the output from one of the REXX examples using the **TRACE R** (trace results) instruction:

```
 3 *-* arg x y .
   >>>   "5"
   >>>   "10"
   >.>   ""
 4 *-* call SUMPROD x y
   >>>   "5 10"
 7 *-* SUMPROD:
 8 *-* arg num1 num2 .
   >>>   "5"
   >>>   "10"
   >.>   ""
 9 *-* sum = num1 + num2
   >>>   "15"
10 *-* prod = num1 * num2
   >>>   "50"
11 *-* return
 5 *-* say "The sum is" sum "and the product is" prod
   >>>   "The sum is 15 and the product is 50"
 6 *-* exit
```

Here not only is each line echoed but the results of interpreting that line are also displayed. At line 8, the two **>>** symbols indicate the values assigned, in order, to arguments **NUM1** and **NUM2**, while the **>.>** symbol indicates the text, if any, scanned into the period placeholder. Lines 9 and 10 show the results of the indicated operations: 5 + 10 = 15 and 5 * 10 = 50.

If we wanted to alter the behavior of the program while it was executing, we could change **TRACE R** to **TRACE ?R**. The interpreter then would pause after each statement and wait for input. Entering **X = 6** would override the input value of **5** and produce results of **6** and **16**, without changing the program or its invocation. Instead of grinding through the program manually inserting intermediate clauses and **&TYPE** statements to find a classic off-by-one bug, we can let **TRACE** do most of the work for us!

What else does the future hold? First, our guru says, you'll be writing functional REXX within a few hours. It may take a while to reach some of the more sophisticated concepts in the language, and to become familiar with the many functions and structures, but basic, workman-like REXX should come tumbling out of your terminal after less than a day's practice. As you progress, you'll find that the natural feel to the language and its top-down flow allow you to produce large amounts of code rapidly. Because REXX's structure is similar to that of other procedural languages, you may want to use it for prototyping applications—you can first write that nasty algorithm in REXX and debug it using TRACE, then translate it into the application language. You may even find that you're writing application programs directly in REXX because of its superior user and CMS interfaces.

Okay, you've convinced me, you tell the guru. You'll stop following the spaniel around and begin quacking in REXX!

AFTERWORD

To help speed the transition process, here is a brief summary of some major EXEC 2 constructs and their REXX counterparts. Where REXX functions are referenced, they are indicated by empty parentheses following their names. Usage formats are detailed in the REXX reference manual. In addition, there are many more REXX functions and constructs not listed here.

Transferring data:

```
In EXEC 2              In REXX

&READ ARGS | VARS      PULL  <list of variables>
&PRINT | &TYPE         SAY  <expression>
&1, &2, &3, ...        ARG  <list of variables>
   (&CASE U in effect)
&1, &2, &3, ...        PARSE ARG  <list of variables>
   (&CASE M in effect)
&STACK FIFO            QUEUE  <expression>
&STACK LIFO            PUSH  <expression>
&BEGTYPE               invoke SAY multiple times
&BEGSTACK              invoke QUEUE or PUSH multiple times
```

Controlling program flow:

```
&SKIP                  appropriate DO/END block
&LOOP n                DO <n>;  DO <expression>
&LOOP WHILE | UNTIL    DO WHILE | DO UNTIL
&LOOP *                DO FOREVER
&IF                    IF/THEN; IF/THEN/ELSE;
                       SELECT
&CALL                  CALL; function invocation
&GOTO                  not usually paralleled -- use appropriate
                       DO/END blocks to group statements;
                       use CALL to transfer control;
                       LEAVE or ITERATE to alter loop flow;
```

SIGNAL instruction is available but is
best used for handling extraordinary
events such as fatal program errors or
extensive recursion

String manipulation:

```
&CONCAT                    abuttal; || (concatenation operator)
&LENGTH                    LENGTH()
&LEFT                      LEFT()
&RIGHT                     RIGHT()
&STRING | &LITERAL         literal string enclosed in quotes
&DATATYPE                  DATATYPE()
&PIECE                     SUBSTR()
&TRIM                      STRIP()
&LOCATION                  POS() or INDEX()
&POSITION                  FIND() or WORDPOS()
&TRANSLATION               TRANSLATE()
&WORD                      WORD()
&UPPER                     UPPER or TRANSLATE()
(No EXEC 2 counterparts, but often useful):
                           COPIES():  replicates a string
                           COMPARE(): compares strings
                           INSERT():  inserts a string in another
                           OVERLAY(): overlays a string on another
                           CENTER():  centers a string
                           DELSTR():  deletes a string
                           JUSTIFY(): justifies a string
                           VERIFY():  compares character sets
                           SUBWORD(): wordwise substring
                           DELWORD(): deletes a word string
                           WORDS():   number of words in a string
```

Arithmetic operations:

```
&MULT OF                   *
&DIV OF                    /  (real division)
                           %  (integer division)
                           // (modulo division)
and other goodies not available in EXEC 2:
                           **:        integer exponentiation
                           FORMAT():  formats a number
                           TRUNC():   take integer part of real
                           NUMERIC DIGITS: set arithmetic precision
```

Execution environment:

```
&FILENAME | TYPE | MODE  PARSE SOURCE
&PRESUME                 ADDRESS <environment>
&ERROR                   SIGNAL ON ERROR
```

42

REXX for CLIST Programmers

By Gerhard E. Hoernes

INTRODUCTION

This chapter describes considerations for translating CLISTs to REXX programs. It discusses CLIST constructs, shows REXX equivalents, and describes problems in the translation process. It describes only CLIST-to-REXX translation, not the reverse.

WHAT ARE THE PROBLEMS IN TRANSLATION?

The REXX and CLIST languages are similar in many ways. Both have variables and variable indexing; both support testing the truth of an expression using the **IF/THEN/ELSE** construct; both allow selectively executing one section of code out of a list (**SELECT/WHEN/OTHERWISE**); both have the same concept of untyped variables. However, for several reasons, translating CLISTs to REXX is more **reprogramming** than **transliteration**. Basic differences include:

- CLIST can repeatedly scan a statement, substituting variables on each scan; REXX scans once.
- CLIST has a **GOTO** statement; REXX does not.
- CLIST intermixes CLIST statements and data; REXX does not.

This does not mean that CLISTs using these functions cannot be translated into REXX; it means these functions must be expressed differently.

Another difficulty is that CLIST is not always predictable. This does not mean that a CLIST will generate different results on repeated execution or on different releases of TSO/E; it means that reading CLIST code may not allow intuitive understanding of execution results. This problem is mainly due to the history of CLIST, and does not imply that CLIST is a bad language. CLIST has served thousands of users for many years; it has evolved from a simple command language introduced in the late 1960s to the rich procedures language it is today. When introduced, CLIST allowed execution of commands with minimal decision making; looping and other constructs normally found in higher-level languages were not available. Today CLIST supports most statements found in higher-level languages. These constructs were fitted into the existing language and retrofitted to assure backward compatibility, which limited designers' ability to define some constructs in the most general or most natural way. This led to special cases.

If translating means reprogramming in some cases, why would one want to translate at all? That question must be asked before starting translation. In most cases, the reasons for translation are:

- REXX is easier to read and maintain. Since program maintenance is often more costly than initial coding, this is important. Even when a routine already exists in CLIST, rewriting it (or translating it) often saves money in the long run. The problem is deciding when to take the leap and invest in translation, rather maintaining the existing CLIST.

- In some installations with both MVS/ESA and VM, the same programmers maintain MVS/ESA and VM. Programmers trained in REXX from CMS can apply that knowledge immediately on MVS.

- REXX applications written for TSO/E can be ported easily to other address spaces or platforms; although TSO/E commands must be changed, most code will not need rewriting.

- Applications written for MVS/ESA may be needed on CMS. This is not as common as translating CMS applications to run on MVS, but it does occur.

- REXX will continue to be enhanced; CLIST will not.

Translation technique

Because of special cases in CLIST, and the lack of direct translation of some CLIST constructs into REXX, the translation process must be done in stages.

1. Translation—essentially, transliteration—of CLIST statements to analogous REXX statements. Examples: SET, IF, DO.

2. Translation of CLIST statements which cannot be translated directly, but for which **one-to-one equivalents** exist. Example: multiple scan.

3. Reprogramming constructs which cannot be translated. Examples: GOTO.

Only the first two steps can be generalized; the last cannot. The remainder of this chapter discusses the first two steps in detail, concentrating primarily on techniques.

Performance can be a consideration. Translating CLIST code may result in code which is not "natural"—that is, it may differ greatly from the way the same function might have been coded had the application initially been coded in REXX. In such cases, translated REXX programs may perform poorly. In one case, a 10-line CLIST was translated to REXX by a junior programmer, resulting in a 30-line REXX program. The REXX program required over three times the resources of the original CLIST! The function was recoded in REXX; the resulting 24-line program outperformed the original CLIST.

Expected performance gains should not be a reason for translating CLISTs to REXX. In general, REXX will not outperform CLIST, although well-written REXX will perform similarly. That may change in future releases.

Scope of translation

Most complex TSO/E CLIST applications consist of several CLISTs. Some may also include other components, such as specially written TSO/E commands, or include ISPF dialogs which are made up of panels, messages, tables, and the like.

The best time to translate such applications from CLIST to REXX is when one or more component CLISTs must be updated or maintained. At that time, affected CLISTs can be translated; unaffected CLISTs may be left for another opportunity. These other CLISTs require translation only if the interface with those translated into REXX changes. One reason for the interface to change is the lack of a CLIST-type PRO-CEDURE statement in REXX. If a CLIST PROCEDURE statement is changed to a more REXX-like interface in translation, calling CLISTs must be changed. If a REXX program transmits data using the stack, CLISTs may also need to be translated, because CLISTs cannot manipulate the stack.

As with any programming project, the order in which CLISTs will be translated must be considered before starting.

Translation of CLISTs using TEST

REXX does not support the TSO/E **TEST** command. **TEST** assumes that control returns to the TMP (the TSO/E Terminal Monitor Program) between commands. As **TEST** is a program "between" the TMP and the program being tested, it can trap and execute **TEST** subcommands. For example, **AT** is passed to the TMP by CLIST; **TEST** recognizes it and sets a breakpoint.

On the other hand, when REXX encounters commands, it passes them to a new copy of the TMP. This means that **TEST** cannot filter commands between the original TMP and the REXX interpreter, and will thus never see or execute the **AT** command.

A CLIST containing **TEST** commands or called from other CLISTs while **TEST** is active cannot be translated.

If such programs *must* be translated, the only technique available is to **QUEUE** the **TEST** subcommands and the command to invoke the other program, and exit. The TMP which called the program will read the data stack, interpret the commands correctly, and call the next program. This technique can be used only in the **READY** mode, and requires care and knowledge of operation and tasking of the TMP.

Therefore it is best not to use REXX with TSO/E **TEST**.

GENERAL SYNTACTICAL TRANSLATIONS

This section compares syntax rules of the languages.

Important note about examples

- In the examples below, literal values are used for simplicity. In either language, all literal values can be replaced by variables. In CLIST, multiple scanning may be performed, which means that multiple ampersands may be processed during different scans. If a variable contains only one ampersand, it will be processed only by the first scan.

- Variable **VAR** represents any valid variable name.

- Frequently it is possible to code functions in several ways. Some examples show different ways of implementing the same function in different parts of the example. This is deliberate, although it may appear inconsistent.

Capitalization	All text read by the CLIST processor—both keywords and variable names—must be in uppercase.
	REXX is not case-sensitive: it folds key words and variable names to uppercase before using them.

Continuation

In CLIST the plus sign (+) or minus sign (−) at the end of a line indicates continuation. The difference is that the minus sign means that leading blanks on the continued line are included in the interpreted statement.

The REXX continuation character is the comma (,); leading blanks on continuation lines are not included in the interpreted statement.

The CLIST continuation symbol must be the last symbol on the line.

The REXX continuation symbol may be followed by a comment.

Comments

CLIST comments are terminated either by */ or by end of line, and comments cannot be nested. If a CLIST comment does not fit on a single line, and the continuation line does not start with /*, the initial line must be continued.

REXX comments *must* be terminated by */, and may be nested. REXX comments may span lines without additional /*s or continuation symbols.

```
/* A /* B */ C */ D

CLIST:
    A is a comment
    B is a comment
    C is executed
    D is in error, because of the unexpected */
REXX:
    A is a comment
    B is a comment
    C is a comment
    D is executed
```

Length of Statement

CLIST statements can be 32,756 characters long.

REXX statements are limited to 250 characters.

To create longer strings in REXX, portions less than 250 characters long can be concatenated to form a longer statement: the limit applies only to the source program. REXX variables can hold strings up to about 16MB (provided storage is available).

Blank Lines and Indentation

Both CLIST and REXX allow blank lines at any point; neither is sensitive to leading or embedded blanks on lines, with the exception of continuation of CLIST lines with the minus sign (−), as discussed above.

TRANSLATING BASIC STATEMENT COMPONENTS

This section shows how basic statement components—variables, system variables, strings, and commands—are translated.

Variable Names   CLIST variables are defined as a token preceded by an ampersand (&), so variable **PAY** is written **&PAY**. CLIST variable names may be used in REXX by removing the ampersand.

CLIST strings are commonly combined to form variable names, for example, for indexed variable references. These variables are usually translatable into REXX compound variables:

```
/* I is the control variable in a loop */
/* PART is an array to be indexed with I */

CLIST:
    &PART&I

REXX:
    part.i
```

Variables to be stored in ISPF variable pools cannot use this technique, since REXX compound variables are not supported. Use **INTERPRET** to build non-stemmed variables in such cases:

```
interpret 'PART'i '= "this is the value"'
                /* Build PARTn for ISPF */
```

CLIST variable names can be terminated by a special character or a blank. Periods encountered in names terminate the variable name, allowing a following literal string to be used in building the variable name. The next example uses variable **&VAR1** and literal string **2** to build the name of another variable, **&STARTTOM2**:

```
SET &VAR1 = TOM
SET &START&VAR1.2 = 27   /* Set &STARTTOM2 to 27 */
```

Note that the period is only a delimiter, to terminate **&VAR1**.

Such an example might be translated to REXX:

```
var1 = 'TOM'
start.var1.2 = 27  /* Set START.TOM.2 */
```

Variable values   Unlike most languages, neither CLIST nor REXX defines variable "types" such as **BINARY**, **FLOAT**, **STRING**, etc., although functions are provided to determine variable data types. This greatly simplifies programming in either language—and translation between them!

An important difference, however, is how the two languages define initial variable values. In CLIST, the initial value of a variable is null; in REXX it is the **name** of the variable.

The REXX **SIGNAL ON NOVALUE** statement detects references to uninitialized variables. Many REXX programmers consider this statement valuable for debugging. It is particularly useful in translating CLISTs, to avoid references to uninitialized variables, since this is harmless in CLIST, but in REXX can alter statements.

Variable names in text

Variable names in text strings are a common translation problem.

CLIST variables can be embedded in strings by simply naming them; in REXX, the literal string must be terminated before the variable. For example, if CLIST variables **&STREET** and **&CITY** (or REXX variables **STREET** and **CITY**) are to be embedded in a string:

```
CLIST:
When entering &CITY., &STREET is the first street.

REXX:
'When entering' city','  street 'is the first street.'
```

Note that in CLIST, variable **&CITY** is terminated to avoid a blank between it and the comma, while in REXX, the comma is concatenated to the value of **CITY** by abuttal.

Parameters within strings

When calling built-in CLIST functions, parameters may be required. Parameter values may be built and passed in variables; for example, variable **&ARG1** might contain arguments for a substring (**&SUBSTR**) function call:

```
SET VARX = 1234567890abcdefg  /* Value to parse */
SET ARG1 = &STR(3:9,)    /* Set &ARG1 to "3:9," */
SET PART = &SUBSTR(&ARG1&VARX) /* Get the substring */
```

The built-in function sees **3:9,This is some value** and returns **3456789**

Translating such expressions can be challenging because this code must be totally rewritten. However, although permitted, such techniques are only rarely used in CLISTs.

Labels

Labels need not be changed. CLIST labels must be associated with an executable statement; REXX labels need not be. Thus the only change required is that if a CLIST continuation sign follows the label, it should be deleted—or, to be consistent, replaced by the REXX continuation sign (a comma):

```
CLIST:
    ALABEL: +
    SET &SOMEVAR = . . .
REXX:
    ALABEL: ,
    SOMEVAR = . . .
```

Return codes

The CLIST special variable **&LASTCC** receives return codes, and is exactly equivalent to REXX variable **RC**:

```
CLIST:
    :
    SYSCALL SUB    /* Call some routine */
    WRITE &LASTCC  /* Write &LASTCC */
    :
    SUB: +
    :
    RETURN CODE(5)

REXX:
    :
    call SUB    /* Call some routine */
    say rc      /* Write RC */
    :
    SUB: ,
    :
    return 5
```

Variable **&LASTCC** is set when a routine returns, but is otherwise ordinary; the same is true of **RC** in REXX.

When translating, CLIST variable **&LASTCC** should always be translated to **RC**.

TSO commands

CLIST and REXX treat TSO commands the same way: as strings which the language cannot itself handle. In CLIST, the string is always passed to the TSO/E environment (the TMP) for execution. In REXX, the string will be passed to the current **ADDRESS** environment, which may be **TSO** when executing in the TSO/E address space.

The TMP assumes that statements in a CLIST not recognized as CLIST statements are commands. (See the chapter "REXX in TSO/E and Other MVS/ESA Address Spaces" for details about TMP operation.)

In REXX, commands are (or should be) enclosed in quotes, and may be preceded by **ADDRESS TSO**. Since

CLIST can execute only TSO commands, translated CLISTs will not use any other **ADDRESS** environments. In the TSO/E address space, **ADDRESS TSO** is the default. An example:

```
CLIST:
ALLOCATE F(MYDD) DA('HOERNES.WORK.EXEC') SHR

REXX:
"ALLOCATE F(MYDD) DA('HOERNES.WORK.EXEC') SHR"
/* Or: */
address tso "ALLOCATE F(MYDD) DA('HOERNES.WORK.EXEC') SHR"
```

To change commands from CLIST to REXX, add quotes and (optionally) **ADDRESS TSO.**

TRANSLATING CLIST SYSTEM VARIABLES TO REXX

Several CLIST system variables with prefix **SYS** contain information about the operating environment. REXX has no system variables; external functions are used instead.

Some CLIST system variables have REXX equivalents; others do not. Some equivalent REXX built-in functions are unique to the TSO implementation of REXX—that is, they are not defined by the formal REXX or SAA Procedures Language specifications.

CLIST system variables can be translated as follows:

Date and time

REXX **DATE** and **TIME** functions provide equivalents to date- and time-related CLIST system variables:

```
CLIST statement: SET VAR = &SYSDATE          VAR is set to: 07/26/91
REXX equivalent: var = date('U')

CLIST statement: SET VAR = &SYSJDATE         VAR is set to: 91.207
REXX equivalent: var = date('J')

CLIST statement: SET VAR = &SYSSDATE         VAR is set to: 91/07/26
REXX equivalent: var = date('O')

CLIST statement: SET VAR = &SYSTIME          VAR is set to: 12:28
REXX equivalent: var = substr(time(), 1, 5)

CLIST statement: SET VAR = &SYSSTIME         VAR is set to: 12:28:02
REXX equivalent: var = time()
```

DATE and **TIME** are defined by the formal REXX language specifications.

Terminal-related information

Two terminal-related system CLIST variables return the screen size.
REXX function **SYSVAR** was created to supply equivalent values:

```
CLIST statement: SET VAR = &SYSLTERM        VAR is set to: 24
REXX equivalent: var = sysvar('SYSLTERM')

CLIST statement: SET VAR = &SYSWTERM        VAR is set to: 80
REXX equivalent: var = sysvar('SYSWTERM')
```

SYSVAR is an external function.

System-related information

Several CLIST system variables determine system information about
the execution environment. REXX **SYSVAR** function operands return
equivalent information:

```
CLIST statement: SET VAR = &SYSCPU          VAR is set to: 31.02
REXX equivalent: var = sysvar('SYSCPU')

CLIST statement: SET VAR = &SYSHSM          VAR is set to: 2040
REXX equivalent: var = sysvar('SYSHSM')

CLIST statement: SET VAR = &SYSSRV          VAR is set to: 577778
REXX equivalent: var = sysvar('SYSSRV')

CLIST statement: SET VAR = &SYSISPF         VAR is set to: ACTIVE
REXX equivalent: var = sysvar('SYSISPF')

CLIST statement: SET VAR = &SYSRACF         VAR is set to: AVAILABLE
REXX equivalent: var = sysvar('SYSRACF')

CLIST statement: SET VAR = &SYSLRACF        VAR is set to: 1090
REXX equivalent: var = sysvar('SYSLRACF')

CLIST statement: SET VAR = &SYSTSO          VAR is set to null
REXX equivalent: var = sysvar('SYSTSO')
```

SYSVAR is an external function.

Command- and environment-related information

All command- and environment-related CLIST system variables have
SYSVAR equivalents:

```
CLIST statement: SET VAR = &SYSENV          VAR is set to: FORE
REXX equivalent: var = sysvar('SYSENV')
```

```
CLIST statement: SET VAR = &SYSICMD        VAR is set to: XLATE2
REXX equivalent: var = sysvar('SYSICMD')

CLIST statement: SET VAR = &SYSPCMD        VAR is set to: EXEC
REXX equivalent: var = sysvar('SYSPCMD')

CLIST statement: SET VAR = &SYSSCMD        VAR is set to null
REXX equivalent: var = sysvar('SYSSCMD')

CLIST statement: SET VAR = &SYSNEST        VAR is set to: NO
REXX equivalent: var = sysvar('SYSNEST')
```

SYSVAR is an external function.

Prompting

CLIST special variable **SYSPROMPT** sets a prompting string. The REXX **PROMPT** function is equivalent:

```
CLIST statement: SET VAR = &SYSPROMPT      VAR is set to: OFF
REXX equivalent: var = prompt()

SET SYSPROMPT = ON               /* Set the system variable to ON */
var = prompt('ON')        /* Set prompt to value passed as argument */
```

PROMPT is an external function.

CLIST-related variables

Several CLIST system variables are directly related to CLIST and its interpretation. These cannot be translated because they have no meaning in REXX. Variables which cannot be translated are:

```
CLIST statement         Sample value   Explanation:ehp1.
SET VAR = &SYSSCAN          16         Number of statement rescans;
                                       REXX has no rescan concept.
SET VAR = &SYSASIS          ON         Control uppercasing of CLIST text;
                                       REXX never folds literals.
SET VAR = &MAXCC            0          Maximum CC encountered;
                                       no REXX equivalent, must be
                                       programmed.
SET VAR = &SYSFLUSH         OFF        Controls removal of CLISTs from
                                       the TSO stack if errors occur;
                                       REXX does not use the TSO stack.


Examples of variable use
SET SYSSCAN = 5                  /* Sets maximum number of scans */
SET &SYSASIS = ON                      /* From now on do not fold */
SET &SYSFLUSH = OFF                    /* From now on do not flush */
SET &MAXCC = 20/* Maximum CC is 20; just another variable in REXX */
```

Variables controlling tracing during execution

These variables cannot be directly translated to REXX equivalents. However, they are only used in debugging and do not control data or execution, so this is not a problem. Native REXX debugging facilities are in any case superior to CLIST's.

These variables can be examined or set:

```
SET VAR = &SYSSYMLIST
SET &SYSSYMLIST = ON
SET VAR = &SYSCONLIT
SET &SYSCONLIT = ON
SET VAR = &SYSLIST
SET &SYSLIST = ON
SET VAR = &SYSMSG
SET &SYSMSG = ON
```

Trapping output

CLIST system variables **SYSOUTTRAP** and **SYSOUTLINEnn** control terminal output trapping. Equivalent function is provided in REXX:

```
CLIST:
    SET &PREVVAL = &SYSOUTTRAP               /* Save OUTTRAP status
    SET &SYSOUTTRAP = 10     /* Trap next 10 lines in SYSOUTLINEm
    LISTD WORK.EXEC MEMBERS                  /* List dataset WORK.EXEC +
                            and its members; first 10 lines are +
                            trapped -- any others are displayed +
    SET &CNT = &SYSOUTLINE          /* Get number of lines trapped
    DO &LOOPCNT = 1 TO &CNT          /* Process all trapped lines
       WRITE &&SYSOUTLINE&LOOPCNT          /* Write trapped data (in +
                        variables SYSOUTLINE0, SYSOUTLINE1, ...)
    END                             /* Terminate loop

REXX:
/*
   Set variable stem for trapped data, and set limit of 10 lines.
   SYSOUTLINE is not a special variable name; it is used only to
   correspond to CLIST.  Any variable stem could be used.
*/
    prevval = outrap('SYSOUTLINE', 10)  /* Save & set output trap */
    'LISTD WORK.EXEC MEMBERS'               /* No change from CLIST */
    cnt = sysoutline.0              /* Get number of lines trapped */
    do loopcnt = 1 to cnt                   /* No change from CLIST */
        say sysoutline.loopcnt    /* Note difference in indexing */
    end                                     /* No change */
```

Aside from the change in indexing of the **SYSOUTLINE** variables, this translation is straightforward.

REXX features for which no CLIST equivalent exists are described in the chapter "REXX in TSO/E and Other MVS/ESA Address Spaces." It may be useful to review the information on **OUTTRAP** to understand the example fully.

Parsing

CLIST system variables **SYSDVAL** and **SYSDLM** have no REXX equivalents. These are discussed in detail in the section "The READDVAL statement".

TRANSLATING CLIST FUNCTIONS

Many built-in CLIST functions translate directly to built-in or external REXX functions.

Translating CLIST functions to equivalent REXX code results in a valid translation. However, after translation, the code should be inspected, because in many cases REXX functions that produce the desired result can be recoded as fewer REXX statements or even a single REXX function. Such reworking is usually quick and easy, and simplifies code, improving size, readability, and performance.

The reminder of this section provides translations for CLIST built-in functions to REXX equivalents; it does not address recoding CLIST constructs.

DATATYPE

The CLIST **DATATYPE** built-in function determines the data type of a variable value:

```
CLIST:
    SET VAR = &DATATYPE(Abcde)          /* VAR is set to: CHAR
    SET VAR = &DATATYPE(12345)          /* VAR is set to: NUM

REXX:
    var = datatype('Abcde')             /* VAR is set to: CHAR */
    var = datatype(12345)               /* VAR is set to: NUM */
```

These functions are completely equivalent. The REXX **DATATYPE** function also provides other functions to test data types more extensively.

EVAL

The CLIST **EVAL** built-in function evaluates the argument passed it.

This adds an extra level of interpretation, and is often used to force evaluation of an expression which would otherwise be interpreted as a literal string. In REXX, literal strings are enclosed in quotation marks and expressions are not; thus in many cases it is not necessary to translate this function at all.

If a similar function is really needed, the REXX **INTERPRET** statement can be used:

```
CLIST:
   SET VAR = &EVAL(3+5)                        /* VAR is set to: 8

   SET &ST = &STR(1+3+&VAR)                     /* Set ST to: "1+2+8"
   SET &VAR2 = &EVAL(&ST)                       /* VAR2 is set to: 11

REXX:
   interpret 'var = 3+5'

   st = '1+3+var'                               /* Build the string */
   interpret 'var2 = ' st /* Build and interpret: var2 = 1+3+var */
```

A REXX subroutine may be used to provide an exact equivalent:

```
EVAL: procedure              /* Argument is string to be evaluated */
   interpret 'RC =' arg(1)              /* Evaluate the string */
   return rc                            /* Return the result */
```

Because there is no exact equivalent, care must be taken in translating this function.

LENGTH

The CLIST and REXX **LENGTH** functions both return the length of the argument string, and are identical:

```
CLIST:
   SET VAR = &LENGTH(abcdef g)                 /* VAR is set to: 8
   SET &ST = 123
   SET VAR = &LENGTH(&ST)                      /* VAR is set to: 3

REXX:
   var = length('abcdef g')                    /* VAR is set to: 8 */
   st = '123'
   var = length(st)                            /* VAR is set to: 3 */
```

NRSTR

The CLIST **NRSTR** built-in function prevents evaluation of a string, and is used when a literal string must contain an ampersand. REXX does not identify variables with any special characters, so this function is not needed and has no equivalent.

Note that if a CLIST variable name contains ampersands, CLIST will repeatedly scan and replace variable values on each scan. For more details, see the section "Variable names" above.

STR:

The CLIST function **STR** assigns a string. In CLIST each variable is replaced by its value within the string using multiple scans.

Converting this to REXX requires breaking the string into multiple quoted parts, to ensure appropriate variable substitution. If only one scan were required to evaluate all variables and the string were only capital letters, this function would be equivalent to the REXX assignment instructions shown below:

```
CLIST:
    SET &DAY = MONDAY
    SET &WEATHER = RAIN
    SET &VAR = &STR(ON &DAY IT WILL &WEATHER)
    /* VAR is set to: ON MONDAY IT WILL RAIN

REXX:
  day = 'MONDAY'
  weather = 'RAIN'
  var = on day it will weather
  /* Undefined variables are replaced by their names in capitals */
  /* So VAR is set to: ON MONDAY IT WILL RAIN */
```

This example demonstrates the simplest translation of the CLIST **STR** function into REXX. In a better translation, **STR** function arguments are broken into individual strings, which are combined with variables:

```
CLIST:
    SET &DAY = Mon                    /* Assume ASIS is in effect
    SET &WEATHER = rain
    SET &VAR = &STR(On &DAY.day it will &WEATHER)
    /* VAR is set to: On Monday it will rain

REXX:
    day = 'Mon'
    weather = 'rain'
    var = 'On' day'day it will 'weather
    /* VAR is set to: On Monday it will rain */
```

In the REXX fragment there is no space between the quote after the variable **DAY** and the literal string **day**; this avoids a blank between **Mon** and **day**. The same effect is achieved in CLIST using the period delimiter. Note that the word **day** is used as both a variable and a literal value in both languages.

SUBSTR

Both CLIST and REXX have similar **SUBSTR** built-in functions, although with minor syntax differences:

```
CLIST:
    SET &ST = Whatever
    SET VAR = &SUBSTR(3:4,&ST)                /* VAR is set to: at

REXX:
    st = 'Whatever'
    var = substr(st, 3, 2)
    /* 2 is derived from (4-3)+1; the third argument is a length, */
    /* not a column position, so the +1 is required. */
```

Alternatively, a REXX subroutine could be used to handle the CLIST SUBSTR syntax. All CLIST-style SUBSTR references could be changed to a different function name, for example, C_SUBSTR:

```
/* C_SUBSTR -- Handle CLIST-style SUBSTR calls */
/*             Arguments: start:end, string */
C_SUBSTR: procedure
if arg(2, 'O') then arg s ':' e ',' string
else arg s ':' e, string
return substr(string, s, e-s+1)
```

SYSCAPS

The CLIST SYSCAPS function translates a string to uppercase. The REXX TRANSLATE function can provide equivalent function:

```
CLIST:
    SET &ST = A mIxEd StRiNg
    SET VAR = &SYSCAPS(&ST)        /* VAR is set to: A MIXED STRING

REXX:
    st = "A mIxEd StRiNg"
    var = translate(st)
```

Alternatively, a simple REXX subroutine can provide an exact equivalent:

```
SYSCAPS: return translate(arg(1))
```

SYSDSN

The CLIST SYSDSN function determines whether a dataset exists. An external REXX function with the same name provides the same function:

```
CLIST:
    SET VAR = &SYSDSN('HOERNES.WORK.EXEC')  /* If dataset exists,
                                    /* VAR is set to: OK
    SET VAR = &SYSDSN('BAD.DSN')    /* If dataset does not exist, +
                                VAR is set to: DATASET NOT FOUND

REXX:
    var = sysdsn("'HOERNES.WORK.EXEC'")      /* VAR is set to: OK */
    var = sysdsn('BAD.DSN')                  /* Same result as in CLIST */
```

In the REXX example, a fully qualified dataset name (HOERNES.WORK.EXEC) was specified. To assure that TSO interprets this token as a fully qualified name, it is passed to TSO surrounded by single quotes. The double quotes define the string; the single quotes are passed to TSO.

In the second example, the dataset name is *not* fully qualified; the single quotes define the string and are not passed to TSO.

Omitting one or both sets of quotes on a fully qualified dataset name is a very common error in this and other functions using dataset names as arguments.

SYSINDEX

The CLIST SYSINDEX function is very similar to the REXX INDEX function. They differ only in the order of the arguments. An exact translation can be made:

```
CLIST:
    SET &ST = A string value                /* This is any string
    SET VAR = &SYSINDEX(v,&ST,4)/* Search variable ST for value v
    /* VAR is set to: 7
REXX:
    st = 'A string value'
    if length(st) < 4 then var = 0      /* If start past end, set 0 */
    var = index(st, 'v', 4)
    /* VAR is set to: 7 */
```

Again, a simple REXX subroutine can provide an exact equivalent:

```
/* SYSINDEX -- Simulate TSO &SYSINDEX function */
/* Arguments: needle, haystack<, start> */
SYSINDEX: procedure
    if arg(3) = '' then start = 1; else start = arg(3)
    return index(arg(2) arg(1), start)
```

SYSLC

The CLIST SYSLC function translates a string to lowercase. In REXX, this function must use the TRANSLATE function:

```
CLIST:
    SET VAR = &SYSLC(ThIs Is A sTrInG aLsO)
    /* VAR is set to: this is a string also

REXX:
var = translate("ThIs Is A sTrInG aLsO", ,
     'abcdefghijklmnopqrstuvwxyz', 'ABCDEFGHIJKLMNOPQRSTUVWXYZ')
```

A REXX subroutine to provide equivalent function:

```
SYSLC:
return translate(arg(1), ,
 'abcdefghijklmnopqrstuvwxyz','ABCDEFGHIJKLMNOPQRSTUVWXYZ')
```

SYSNSUB

The CLIST SYSNSUB function cannot be directly translated because it specifies the number of substitutions. The concept of multiple substitutions does not exist in REXX.

This function is rarely used and can be very difficult to translate, because it is often very difficult to determine how many ampersands precede a variable name if that variable was set in some other part of a larger CLIST. If SYSNSUB is used heavily, the CLIST may not be a good candidate for translation.

TRANSLATING SPECIAL STATEMENTS

PROC statement

The CLIST PROC statement is a difficult translation challenge. There are two techniques:

1. Invoke the translated routine identically

   This is necessary if the translated routine is part of a larger application and is called from one or more CLISTs which will not be translated.

   In this case, the REXX program must accept parameters and set variables as the original CLIST would have. This is discussed in detail in the next section.

2. Recode invocation of the translated routine

   This is possible only if the translated routine is called from a routine which will be translated, or is called from the command line and end-users can be trained to invoke it differently.

   This allows redesign of the input interface, but this is not always possible, and is not the point of most translation. In fact, it represents not a translation but a redesign. Although not discussed here, it should not be ignored. It can be easier than a "simple" translation, and result in much better REXX code.

Description of the CLIST PROC statement

This section discusses translation of the CLIST PROC statement into REXX. The goal is to set variables in the called REXX program which would have been set in the original CLIST.

The CLIST PROC statement has two distinct parts: **positional** parameters and **keyword** parameters. The general form of the CLIST PROC statement is:

```
PROC n pp1 pp2 . . . ppn                    +
            kw1 (kv1)                    +
            kw2 (kv2) . . .                    +
            kwm(kvm)
```

where:

n	is the number of positional parameters
ppn	are positional parameters
kwm	are (optional) keywords or CLIST variable names
kvm	are (optional) values for variables named

In CLIST the format of the positional parameter string is not checked. Thus if a CLIST expects three positional and three keyword parameters, and only two positional parameters and two keyword parameters are passed, the CLIST processor will take the first three tokens as positional and interpret the last parameter as a keyword parameter.

If insufficient parameters are passed, the action depends on the prompting setting. If prompting is ON, values for parameters not passed are solicited from the user at execution time; if OFF, omitted parameters cause an error.

Keyword parameters specified on a PROC statement are optional on calls to that CLIST. These keywords are the only keywords which may be passed to that CLIST. Values specified on the PROC statement define default values if not otherwise specified; if no value is specified on the PROC statement or on invocation, the variable is null. The number following the word PROC is the number of positional parameters.

Here are some examples:

```
PROC 2 ARG1 ARG2      /* ARG1 and ARG2 are positional, no keywords

PROC 0 ARG1 ARG2      /* ARG1 and ARG2 are keywords with no default +
                         values; if not specified on invocation, +
                         &ARG1 and &ARG2 will be null.

PROC 1 ARG1 ARG2  /* &ARG1 is positional, &ARG2 is a keyword with +
                         no default value

PROC 1 ARG1 ARG2(woof)/* &ARG1 is positional, &ARG2 is a keyword; +
                         if a value is passed for ARG2, variable +
                         &ARG2 will contain that value.  If omitted, +
                         variable &ARG2 will contain "woof".
```

Replacing the PROC statement

The CLIST PROC statement contains information for parsing input parameters. That information needs to be translated into REXX code. A general yet simple method is to place the CLIST PROC format in a variable and place the code to set the actual variables in a subroutine.

That subroutine must be internal to the program so that it can set variables in the mainline; however, it could be externalized. The program would call the external routine and INTERPRET the result to set the variables in the mainline. A single entry could set all variables, but is limited to a total length of slightly under 16MB.

For example, assume that the following PROC appeared in CLIST PROCTEST:

```
PROC 2 A B KEY1 KEY2(value2)
```

PROCTEST would be invoked:

```
PROCTEST 111 222 KEY2(other)
```

An equivalent REXX program fragment:

```
result = PROCXLAT arg(1)              /* Call external REXX routine */
interpret result                      /* Interpret the data from PROCXLAT */
```

This assumes the string returned would be something like:

```
a = '111'; b = '222'; key1 = 'KEY1'; key2 = 'other'
```

The above is a very simple and specific example. A more general solution would pass the pattern to be parsed, allowing a generalized external subroutine:

```
pattern = '2 A B KEY1 KEY2(value2)'      /* Define the pattern */
result = PROCEXT(arg(1), pattern) /* Returns INTERPRETable string */
if result = '' then signal ERROR                /* Handle errors */
interpret result                            /* Set the results */
```

The only non-general line in this last example is the line assigning a value to variable **PATTERN**. That value is unique to the program, and comes directly from the CLIST. It is known at the time of translation.

The external routine is a modification of the routine below.

Moving code into external subroutines reduces the size of the original program, because the external routines need be loaded only once and are not part of every program using them; however, this degrades performance, because each call to a translated program with a CLIST **PROC** statement to be handled requires a call to another program. This **PROC**-equivalent program could be shared among many programs. This approach lends itself particularly well for prototyping, applications which are executed infrequently, or routines outside mainline paths.

A full **PROC** replacement routine is possible, but would be quite large and expensive to execute. It is better to convert the call to a more REXX-like syntax, or to handle the CLIST-type operand syntax in the called program.

Translating I/O statements

It is relatively straightforward to translate the basic I/O statements from CLIST to REXX because there is a one-to-one relationship between the two languages. However, subtle differences can cause problems.

CLIST supports **OPENFILE**, **CLOSEFILE**, **GETFILE**, and **PUTFILE**. REXX supports all these functions with the **EXECIO** command.

The EXECIO command

Although it is used from REXX as though it were a true TSO/E command, **EXECIO** is not; it is part of REXX itself. This means that **EXECIO** may be used only from REXX programs. Its syntax is similar to the **EXECIO** command in CMS, with modifications to handle MVS/ESA datasets. The main differences between the two versions is that the CMS `filename filetype filemode` is replaced by a single token—the `DD`.

For a detailed discussion of the syntax, see the chapter "REXX in TSO/E and Other MVS/ESA Address Spaces" or appropriate product manuals. The basic `EXECIO` syntax in TSO/E is:

```
EXECIO lines type filename (options
```

where:

lines is a number or * (for all) representing the number of records to be read or written.

type is the type of operation: **DISKR, DISKW,** or **DISKU** (the last record read may be overrewritten; the record to be written must be the same length as the record it replaces).

filename is the DD from which to read or to which to write.

options are:

  STEM is a variable stem to/from which records are to be read/written. See note on stem variables below.

  FIFO (DISKR or DISKU only) Place records on the data stack. After the operation, the first record read is at the top of the stack.

  LIFO (DISKR or DISKU only) Place records on the data stack. After the operation, the last record read is at the top of the stack.

  FINIS After the operation, close the dataset.

Examples of **EXECIO** are shown later in the chapter.

An important note on **STEM**: if this option is used, records are placed into variables starting with the stem. Normally in REXX a stem includes a period; here it does *not*! Thus, if stem **ABC** is specified, the first record is stored in **ABC1**. If stem **ABC.** is specified (that is, a period is included after the name of the stem), the first record is stored into **ABC.1**. This appears to be inconsistent with the definition of REXX, but has two justifications:

1. CMS has the same definition; the inconsistency was maintained for compatibility.

2. If the variables are to be used with ISPF, they must not include the period.

It should be noted that **EXECIO** does not support an **OPEN**-type function. Datasets are automatically opened when first read or written. The type of open depends on the **type** specified when the dataset is first used. For example, if the type is DISKR, the dataset is opened for input; DISKW opens the dataset for output, and DISKU for update. Once the dataset is open, successive actions must be compatible with the first, or an error occurs.

Translating CLIST file I/O statements

The CLIST OPENFILE statement is not translated, because REXX opens datasets automatically, but in order to assure the proper open, the proper type must be used on the first command executed against a given filename.

The CLIST GETFILE statement can be translated into the DISKR form of EXECIO. In REXX an additional instruction is required: EXECIO reads the record, and REXX PULL places it in the same variable as CLIST would.

```
CLIST:
    GETFILE datavar

REXX:
    'EXECIO 1 DISKR ddname (FIFO'
    pull datavar
```

The CLIST PUTFILE statement can be translated into the DISKW form of EXECIO. Here again, two steps are required: the first to place the record on the data stack and the second to write it into the dataset.

```
CLIST:
    PUTFILE datavar

REXX:
    push datavar
    'EXECIO 1 DISKW ddname (FIFO'
```

The CLIST CLOSEFILE statement directly translates into an EXECIO command which reads no records and uses the FINIS option:

```
CLIST:
    CLOSEFILE datavar

REXX:
    'EXECIO 0 DISKW ddname (FINIS'
```

Translating end-of-file

End-of-file processing in CLIST and REXX are different. CLIST treats EOF as an error and transfers control, while REXX simply sets a return code.

In most CLIST programs program execution at EOF is as follows (this example represents execution sequence, not code):

```
Sequence   CLIST statement
1          GETFILE . . .
2          EOF detected by CLIST processor transfer to ERROR unit
3          in ERROR unit
4          IF &LASTCC 400 THEN DO
5              other code, e.g.: CLOSEFILE, set EOF switch
6              RETURN to caller (instruction following the GETFILE)
7          continue processing last record in original code
```

If the CLIST code does not return (line 6 in the example) to the statement after the **GETFILE** in the original code, the translation into REXX requires recoding. However, most CLISTs do contain such a **RETURN**.

The translated REXX code in essence follows the same flow, although it appears different. The basic difference is that the REXX interpreter does not transfer into an error block. In the example below, the line numbers refer to those in the CLIST example:

```
Sequence   REXX statement
1          'EXECIO 1 DISKR filename . . .
4          if rc = 2 then do                        /* RC = 2 is EOF */
5              other code, e.g.: close file, set EOF switch
           end                                      /* if rc = 2 */
7          continue processing last record in original code
```

In some cases, particularly for very large CLISTs, it is difficult to rearrange the code as shown in the example above because the error unit may be very complex. In such cases, a more literal translation may be easier. In that case the CLIST error unit can be translated into a REXX error subroutine, and the transfer into the error unit by the CLIST **GETFILE** can be simulated as shown below. Again, the line numbers are those found in the CLIST example:

```
Sequence   REXX statement
1          'EXECIO 1 DISKR filename . . .'
2          if rc = 2 then call ERROR
3          /* in ERROR subroutine */
4          if rc = 2 then do
5              other code, e.g.: close file, set EOF switch
6              return to caller (instruction following the EXECIO)
7          continue processing last record in original code
```

There are, however, other subtle differences between **EXECIO** and CLIST I/O. For example, if the number of records to be read by **EXECIO** is "*", then the return code is not set because it is understood that the remainder of the dataset is read. In most cases it is best to experiment with **EXECIO** and the corresponding CLIST to understand the differences.

Translating terminal I/O

CLIST provides a number of mechanisms to communicate with the end-user on the terminal, if the CLIST runs in the foreground, or to obtain data for TSO commands, if the CLIST runs in the background.

WRITE and **WRITENR** write on the screen or the output file in batch mode. **WRITE** translates directly into the REXX **SAY** instruction. **WRITENR** performs the same function as **WRITE**, except that the cursor remains on the line following the last character written out. REXX does not have such a function; REXX programs do not have control of the cursor. In CLIST, output case is controlled by the **CONTROL** setting, one of **ASIS**, **CAPS**, or **NOCAPS**. REXX code must translate output appropriately before **SAY** is issued.

```
CLIST:
    WRITE string
REXX:
    say string
```

The CLIST **READ** statement reads tokens from the terminal; the tokens are separated by commas. CLIST has two forms, one with variables specified on the **READ** instruction and the other without. The REXX equivalent of **READ** is shown in the next example. The input case follows the same rules as described for **WRITE** above:

```
CLIST:
    READ var1,var2,var3
REXX:
    parse pull var1 ',' var2 ',' var3 ','
```

The other form of the CLIST **READ** statement is not followed by variables. The CLIST processor saves the input string in system variable **SYSDVAL**. This is a normal CLIST variable and can be used on either side of a CLIST **SET** statement. A very common way of processing this variable is with the **READDVAL** statement.

The READDVAL statement

This statement is similar to, but not nearly as powerful as, the REXX **PARSE** instruction. It parses the content of variable **SYSDVAL** and places tokens into variables using the same rule **READ** uses for tokens in the record read:

```
CLIST:
    READDVAL var1,var2,var3
REXX:
    parse var SYSDVAL var1 ',' var2 ',' var3 ','
```

Translating the TERMIN statement

After the **TERMIN** statement is executed, the user can invoke any TSO/E command or call any program. To the user this is equivalent to the TSO/E **READY** mode. Part of the **TERMIN** statement is the condition or conditions for termination:

```
CLIST:
1       TERMIN                     termination by null line only
2       TERMIN A,B                 termination by typing A or B
3       TERMIN ,OUT,EXIT,QUIT      termination by typing null line or
                                   one of the words OUT, EXIT, or QUIT
REXX:
1       sysdlm = termin('')
2       sysdlm = termin('A,B')
3       sysdlm = termin(',OUT,EXIT,QUIT')

/* Function: REXX equivalent of TERMIN */
if sysvar('SYSISPF') = 'ACTIVE' then exit   /* Cannot use in ISPF */
arg term_c               /* Build array of terminating conditions */
term. = ''                              /* Default values to null */
term.0 = 1                   /* Default count = 1 for null string */
do term.0 = 1 while length(term_c) > 0
   parse var term_c term.i ',' term_c
end
do forever       /* First check, than process USER_INPUT from user */
   say 'Enter a command or one of the following to terminate TER-
MIN:',
     arg(1)
   pull user_input                     /* Get next input from user */
   do i = 1 to term.0                  /* Check for termination loop */
      if term.i = user_input then return i
   end
   address tso user_input
   say 'Return code from "'user_input'" was:' rc
end
```

This REXX program appears to present significant performance degradation, but if it is an internal subroutine, the added path length is insignificant compared to the path length involved in even attaching one TSO/E command. If this routine is made an external routine, the performance is slightly worse, but is still only a fraction of the cost of invoking one command.

The DATA/ENDDATA statements

The text between the **DATA** and **ENDDATA** statements is not part of a CLIST, and may be either commands to TSO/E or subcommands. The translation for these two cases is different.

If the text between these statements represents commands which could be issued in the **READY** state, the **READY** state must be simulated.

One technique to simulate the **READY** state is to place the text between these statements on the stack, place a null entry on the stack to be read after the stack is exhausted, and call the routine described above for the **TERMIN** statement. Here is an example:

```
CLIST:
        . . . some CLIST statements . . .
        DATA
            n TSO/E commands
        ENDDATA
        . . . remaining CLIST statements . . .
REXX:
        . . . some REXX statements . . .
        'NEWSTACK'                              /* Create new stack */
        queue . . . 1st TSO command . . .
        queue . . . 2nd TSO command . . .
        . . .
        queue . . . nth TSO command . . .
        queue '' /* This is the null which terminates the operation */
        sysdlm = termin("")            /* The routine described above */
        'DELSTACK'                                    /* Delete stack */
```

The second use for **DATA** and **ENDDATA** is to provide input for a subcommand. In that case the code above can be used, but instead of calling **TERMIN**, the command is called for which the data represents subcommands or input data.

In both cases, the strategy is to first place the data on the stack and then issue the command which uses the data.

A new stack is used in this case because if the command is not well behaved and overruns the input data, data could be pulled off the stack and cause errors in other parts of the program or other programs. By using a new stack, potential problems of failing commands can be isolated.

The CONTROL statement

The CLIST **CONTROL** statement has numerous options. Many of them correspond to functions supported in REXX, but often translation is not direct. Corresponding functions are:

PROMPT/NOPROMPT

This corresponds directly to REXX function **PROMPT**.

```
CLIST                   REXX
CONTROL PROMPT          var = prompt('ON')
CONTROL NOPROMPT        var = prompt('OFF')
```

SYMLIST/NOSYMLIST LIST/NOLIST CONLIST/NOCONLIST

These options print CLIST statements as they are executed. The REXX **TRACE** instruction supports similar functions:

```
CLIST                                        REXX
CONTROL   SYMLIST   LIST   CONLIST           trace r
CONTROL NOSYMLIST NOLIST NOCONLIST           trace off
```

CAPS/NOCAPS/ASIS

These options control case translation. REXX does not support forced translation. If input is to be translated to uppercase or lowercase, REXX functions must be used. REXX always assumes the equivalent of ASIS, except for PARSE UPPER ARG and PARSE UPPER PULL and their shorthand forms ARG and PULL, which translate to uppercase.

MSG/NOMSG

The REXX MSG function provides equivalent function:

```
CLIST                    REXX
CONTROL MSG              var = msg('ON')
CONTROL NOMSG            var = msg('OFF')
```

FLUSH/NOFLUSH/MAIN

These CONTROL options manage TSO/E's input stack when errors occur. When errors occur, CLISTs with FLUSH active are flushed from the input stack until a CLIST with MAIN or NOFLUSH is encountered. (Flushing a CLIST means terminating its execution and removing it from the call chain.) REXX does not use the TSO/E input stack, so these options have no meaning for a REXX program. This means that if a REXX program terminates, it must handle its own recovery, while CLISTs can depend on others to recover the errors. In translation, this must be reviewed from a global point of view; there is no easy way to replace one piece of code with another. It must be considered for the entire application.

REXX operates as though CONTROL NOFLUSH were in effect.

END

This option is needed in CLIST because the language syntax does not distinguish between keywords and data. In REXX this is not a problem because string data is enclosed in quotes, and thus distinct from keywords. This option has no meaning in REXX.

Error conditions

The CLIST ERROR condition is very similar to the REXX SIGNAL ON ERROR statement: both check for non-zero return codes from commands. Caution must be taken when translating such a unit, because the return codes of CLIST commands may be different from those in REXX. An example is the CLIST end-of-file condition, which returns 400, whereas the return code from the REXX EXECIO command is 2.

```
CLIST:
    ERROR DO                                  /* Start of ERROR block
        . . . code handling error conditions . . .
    END                                       /* End of ERROR block
        . . . other CLIST code . . .
REXX:
    SIGNAL ON ERROR
        . . . other REXX code . . .
    ERROR:                                    /* Start of ERROR subroutine */
        . . . code handling error conditions . . .
    return                                    /* From ERROR subroutine */
```

There is a difference in placement of the code. The CLIST **error** block is at the beginning of the routine, where it is skipped during execution; in REXX only the **SIGNAL ON ERROR** instruction is at the beginning of the routine, and the actual **ERROR** routine is usually near the end of the routine, often among subroutines.

Disabling error trapping is one executable statement in both languages:

```
CLIST:
    ERROR OFF
REXX:
    SIGNAL OFF ERROR
```

LISTDSI command

The CLIST **LISTDSI** command is directly translatable into the external REXX function of the same name. It has been included in REXX to allow fully compatible conversion.

```
CLIST:
    LISTDSI dsname . . .
    LISTDSI filename . . .
REXX:
    code = LISTDSI(dsname . . .)
    code = LISTDSI(filename . . .)
```

CLIST sets a number of variables to values pertaining to the dataset or file being examined; in REXX the same variables are set.

Here is an example in both CLIST and REXX. An important note is quoting: if a fully qualified dataset is defined, it must be enclosed in quotes. Since REXX also needs quotation marks to define a string, both double and single quotation signs are needed:

```
CLIST:
    LISTDSI 'HOERNES.WORK.REXX'
    IF &SYSREASON = 0 THEN DO
        WRITE Logical record size is:  &SYSLRECL
        WRITE Record format is:        &SYSREECFM
        WRITE Block size is:           &SYSLRECL
        END
```

```
REXX:
    code = listdsi("'HOERNES.WORK.REXX'")
    if sysreason = 0 then do
        say 'Logical record size is:' &SYSLRECL
        say 'Record format is:' &SYSREECFM
        say 'Block size is:' &SYSLRECL
    end
```

EXIT statement

The CLIST **EXIT** statement is equivalent to the REXX **EXIT** statement.
The only difference is that REXX does not support the **QUIT** option.
This option is associated with the TSO input stack, which is not used
by REXX. This little-used option must be translated by forcing termi-
nation of programs which would be flushed if the corresponding
CLISTs were flushed.

Examples of **EXIT**:

```
CLIST:
    EXIT CODE(number)
REXX:
    exit number
```

GLOBAL statement

The CLIST **GLOBAL** statement allows referencing the same storage
location representing a variable from different CLISTs. One major
problem with this function is that only the position of the name in the
GLOBAL statement defines the variable. This technique can introduce
errors because variable names may but need not match in different
CLISTs. Because of this problem, this statement is not heavily used.
REXX does not support any similar function.

If a CLIST which uses **GLOBAL** variables must be translated, there
are several options, all requiring some additional programming:

Use ISPF variables   If the application being translated executes under ISPF,
                            VPUT and **VGET** can store and retrieve ISPF shared
                            variable pool variables. These variable names are
                            limited by ISPF rules, but this represents a simple
                            name mapping. Also, the names of variables, rather
                            than position in the **GLOBAL** statement, are significant.
                            The best approach is to make a global change in each
                            program, from the old name to the new name, and to
                            assure that each time the variable is set, a **VPUT**
                            statement is inserted to store the new value. The
                            GLOBAL statement is replaced by a **VGET** to fetch the
                            variable values. In the highest-level routine, values may
                            not be necessary, or if they are, the values will be set to
                            null, the uninitialized value for ISPF.

Passing the values	If variables are read but not set in lower-level routines, it is often possible to pass values as additional arguments. This is possible only if all routines in an application are translated, because the values must be passed through *all* routines to reach the lowest ones in the calling sequence.
Stack the values	If the stack is not used and all routines using values are translated, one approach is to stack the values on the data stack, PULL them in the lower-level routines, PUSH new values on the stack, and have the higher-level routine PULL the new values.
Creating a dataset	This is a last resort because it carries a performance penalty. However, it is not difficult to write a small set of subroutines to write variable names and associated values into a file, and read that file when required.

All these approaches are inadequate in one form or another, but if the GLOBAL statement must be translated, they will usually suffice.

SUMMARY

Translating CLISTs into REXX programs greatly depends on the CLISTs to be translated. Most CLISTs can be translated relatively easily, and the resulting REXX programs are of relatively good quality. However, in some cases, translation is definitely not recommended, or cannot be done without total recoding. After translating a few CLISTs, one learns what can be translated easily and what is better left untranslated. Some CLISTs, particularly those extensively using TSO/E TEST or GLOBAL variables, simply cannot be translated. Translating and knowing what to translate is art, not science.

From a performance point of view, the larger size of a resulting REXX program may not cause problems because of the internal design of the REXX interpreter compared to that of the CLIST interpreter.

A final note: mechanical languages are not unlike natural languages. A true translation is, if not impossible, at least nearly impossible; nevertheless, in many cases we are forced to translate. So it is with translating from CLIST to REXX. As long as resulting REXX programs execute correctly within the real-world environment of data and environmental variables encountered, the translation is considered a success. The benefits of translation include the advantages of the REXX language over the CLIST language, REXX's predictability, and the fact that REXX programs are easier to change than CLISTs. The disadvantages of translation are real but minor. First, there is a learning curve with REXX as there is with any other language. Second, if pushed to the limit, boundary and error condition handling within a translated REXX program will almost always differ from those of the original routine.

43

REXX Education

By Gary R. McClain

INTRODUCTION

Education in the MIS department often receives about as much respect as it does in society as a whole: for many, it is an afterthought, slapped into place "just in case" it is needed, while the bulk of attention goes toward "real" concerns, like schedule milestones, productivity, and debugging. Yet, when effectively managed, education provides a solid foundation that can more than compensate for both time and money spent.

The key to gaining payoffs from education is careful planning, before the fact. Planning means determining what the training audience already knows and what they need to know, as well as the constraints, such as time and budget. This is essentially "first base". From here, alternatives, such as classroom or computer-based options, can be considered, with the best solution chosen from a position of strength.

REXX introduces unique considerations into the planning process. Because of its very structure, it is a language that can be used powerfully by application programmers, system programmers, and technically oriented users. Thus, the audience level and the desired results of the training must be carefully understood, with the goal of choosing the best alternative for the majority of students.

ESTABLISHING THE FOUNDATION

Before alternatives can be adequately considered, the foundation must be established. This foundation involves answering three questions:

1. Who is the audience?
2. What needs to be taught?
3. What are the constraints?

The audience

As implied, educational approaches are often based on the needs of the majority, with the hope that those at the center of the normal curve can somehow be reached. This is a matter of time and money. In REXX education, the normal curve is an approximation of the technical backgrounds of the audience, ranging from end-user to experienced programmer.

Because of the flexibility of the REXX language, this can get tricky. For example, system programmers, application programmers, systems analysts, and higher-level end-users can all use REXX with equally impressive results. However, mixing experienced VM system programmers with inexperienced end-users is never a great idea, regardless of the subject being discussed. The normal curve might lie somewhere in the middle of the two extremes, but the training would have to be geared such that neither group would be reached. To really get the most from technical education, participants must feel comfortable with each other as well as with the course level. If diverse groups must be reached, it is best to educate the groups separately. This saves frustration and, in the long run, the prospect of retraining.

One means of answering this concern is through designing a modular course, taught classroom style, such that, initially, it is attended by individuals at all levels of technical expertise. This arrangement has often been used in teaching fourth-generation languages as well as more advanced languages such as REXX. By sequencing modules, from more basic to advanced, everyone's needs can be accommodated. For example, initial modules can focus on basic commands and their use in accomplishing specific functions, while more advanced modules would focus on developing and writing REXX programs. All would attend the initial modules. An individual whose training needs are met could essentially drop out of the course, with each person continuing until the needed level of expertise has been gained. The instructor of a course designed to allow students to gradually drop out has the responsibility of talking to the lowest common denominator of the students in the module. With careful design, so that each module is relatively self-contained, this can be accomplished to the benefit of all, or at least most, of those attending. Specific objectives for each course module, so that students know exactly what to expect, are needed. Objectives are discussed in the next section.

Unfortunately, participants in an educational experience also bring their past baggage to the class. Attendees who have received poor teaching learn to expect it in the future, while, in turn, those who have had good experiences expect them to continue. Participants in computer-based or multimedia approaches also have certain expectations. It is impossible to control likes and dislikes. Taking time in the planning process to assess expectations, in terms of what participants want to learn and how they want to learn it, can make a large difference in subsequent receptiveness.

What is the desired result?

There is much more to approaching REXX education than simply trudging through a list of commands. In fact, planning a REXX course should begin with a detailed list of desired results. Should participants be able to design detailed REXX-based application programs? Or will they be maintaining existing programs? Should they be able to build user exits to use with system software packages? Do they only need to know when to use a few commands?

Clearly, the results—the **goal**—must be understood and carefully defined in task-oriented terms. Equally important, all involved must agree on the goal. From this agreement, approaches and timetables can be chosen with confidence.

These desired results are the objectives of the training. They should be presented as specific, measurable functions that participants will be able to perform as a result of the training.

In developing objectives for REXX education, consider:

1. Specific REXX functions that attendees should be able to perform after the course (or this module of the course), and the circumstances (e.g., development, maintenance) in which the attendee will perform them.
2. Specific REXX language components (commands, syntax) that support these functions.

The more specific and functional the approach, in terms of what is covered, the greater the likelihood that students will be able to subsequently transfer what was learned to the real world on the job.

Objective is a widely used term in education, and the importance of taking time to formulate the training objectives cannot be overestimated. How do you know if the training was worthwhile if you never decided exactly what it should accomplish, in functional terms? As simplistic as this sounds, it is surprising how often students are thrown into a course on a subject like REXX that consists of five days of everything the instructor can think of, with the hope that students will figure out enough about the language to subsequently use it.

What are the constraints?

Rarely is a blank slate handed to individuals charged with establishing a training program. More likely, there is a long list of constraints, beginning with a seemingly inadequate budget. Other constraints to remember are time and location. Can trainees get away from work for a week, or even a few days, or must training take place during shorter periods of time? Is a room dedicated to training, with comfortable seating, individual terminals for practice sessions, and an absence of interruption?

The ideal scenario is conducting training during large blocks of time, preferably for one or more days, during working hours when participant and instructor energy is highest. This should take place in a comfortable, well-equipped classroom. Again, this is the ideal, but not unique, scenario. Most important is to understand the available resources clearly and plan accordingly.

CHOOSING THE ALTERNATIVES

The major alternatives for technical education can be divided into **standard classroom** and **media-based** training. These are described in more detail below.

Classroom training

Because adults equate education and training with a classroom led by a teacher who is an expert in the subject being taught, this is often the approach taken in technical education. If the instructor is both technically qualified and an adequate teacher, this can be best. However, the importance of having the class led by a teacher who knows how to teach cannot be overestimated.

In-house trainers should be the first resource considered for REXX training. This is cost-effective, because they are already on-site and most likely know how to teach. They must be knowledgeable in REXX, to a level beyond that of the students in the class, preferably with experience in using the REXX language, and supplemented by well-designed training materials (purchased or developed in-house) and lab exercises. Throwing a training manual at a system programmer and making a path to the door of the classroom is not the same as using an in-house trainer, unless this individual is both people-oriented and trained to run a classroom. Good teaching is the result of instinct and training, and the skilled technical person may have extensive knowledge about the subject but be unable to communicate it to someone else. Placing this person in a teaching role, without preparation, will be a waste of time.

Outside consultants and/or technical instructors can be adequate, and even excellent, teachers. Generally, they are polished speakers and are experienced enough to provide a positive experience. It is important, however, to work closely with outside trainers to make sure that they know exactly what is to be taught, and are willing and able to do it. Often courses are "canned," with the instructor specifically trained by the vendor company to teach the course materials. Can the instructor modify the course to match the diversity of the students, as well as tailor certain materials to the customer's needs? If so, at what cost? Students pushed through a canned course can end up knowing a little about many things, but still not know how to put a decent REXX program together. Does the outside consultant guarantee success? It's worth finding out!

Off-site training is an option, given the level of specialized training required and the available funds. Sending a few individuals with specialized needs, such as senior system programmers, can have multiple benefits. It adds skills not currently available in the organization. It places attendees in a concentrated situation, with few day-to-day interruptions, and it gives them a breather, and even an ego boost. Off-site training is particularly good for those needing high-level training. It can also be a means of preparing in-house instructors by sending a few people for training and having them come back to teach others. Off-site training can also allow evaluating courses that might later be taught on-site. But again, the courses are "canned," and the teaching aimed at the middle of the class. Thus, the syllabus and course materials should be examined before the fact, to assure that the course will be of value.

Media-based training

Media-based training consists of courses taught interactively with computer software or delivered through videotape, or a combination of the two.

Computer-based training has progressed a long way since the early days of mainframe courses that essentially engaged the student in hours of electronic page turning through materials that were little more than a rehash of documentation. With the aid of the personal computer, computer-based training now incorporates answer checking with personalized messages to the student, extensive color, and even audio and video messages. Multimedia courses can (almost) successfully compete with the best video games.

However, as a medium for training technical people, media-based education has its limitations. Regardless of the flash involved, the trainer is still a machine. It corrects answers and offers assistance, but these are programmed responses and, as such, can quickly become predictable and even boring. For a repetitive skill, like memorizing facts or commands, or doing a quick review, the computer can be a fine teacher. For example, computer-based training can be a great way to learn and review commands. Depending on how well the course itself is programmed, it can also be useful for syntax. Answer checking must be highly sensitive to nuances of syntax, and be able to effectively check for possible errors and combinations of errors. There is nothing more frustrating than to repeatedly enter a string of code only to receive the message, `Try again`. Student responses must provide guidance in making correct answers. Computer-based training can also be used in a laboratory situation to supplement the instructor. It's a matter of drill and practice. However, when complex reasoning is involved, with multiple approaches to be considered, the computer often begins to look and act like a machine. When this happens, technical people often try to prove this by attempting to break the program.

For less technical users, who need to learn and try a few basic commands in a simulated situation and then review them from time to time, computer-based training can serve the purpose well. The course is readily available whenever students have time, is as accessible as their computers, and quietly goes away when more urgent tasks arise.

Before submitting students to a computer-based training course, bring it for a trial. Send untrained users through it to see if they learn anything. Send system programmers through it to see if it is technically accurate, up-to-date, and easily breakable. Before purchasing the course, make sure that the vendor will provide maintenance and updates.

The role of supplemental experience

Regardless of the instructor, it is critical that classroom and media-based training be supplemented by extensive laboratory experience. REXX is a "living" language, best learned through practice. Lectures should be interspersed with terminal time to reinforce what has been discussed. Multimedia programs must also include extensive practice sessions.

There is no substitute for sitting at a terminal and, through trial and error, figuring out how something works. Exercises must be based on real-life situations, so that students can build commands, try them out, and discover the error messages and actions that result.

When evaluating any type of course, examine the amount and relevance of exercises. Whenever possible, tailor them to the kinds of REXX applications that students will be involved with after the training.

REXX EDUCATION RESOURCES

Below are a few examples of REXX education offerings. This list is by no means exhaustive, but it is a good place to begin. Resource descriptions are based on vendor materials.

The Adesse Corporation
36 Mill Plain Road
Suite 307
Danbury, CT 056811
(203) 790-9473

The Adesse Corporation has a strong reputation in the VM marketplace. The company offers classroom courses at locations around the country. Course titles include *REXX Programming*, *VM/SP Performance and Tuning*, and *CMS for System Programmers*.

Amdahl Corporation
Education Headquarters
1250 East Arques Ave., M/S 306
P.O. Box 3470
Sunnyvale, CA 94088-3470
(800) 233-9521

Amdahl offers courses at their own training centers as well as at customer sites. Course offerings include *VM/CMS Workshop* and *REXX/XEDIT Workshop*.

CRWTH Computer Courseware
2850 Ocean Park Boulevard
Santa Monica, CA 90405
(800) 445-5940

CRWTH was one of the first companies dedicated to providing computer-based training courses, and offers the CRWTH Programmer Curriculum with courses that include *TSO REXX Application Programming*, *VM/SP REXX Application Programming*, and a variety of related courses.

DELTAK Training Corporation
East-West Technological Center
1751 West Diehl Road
Naperville, IL 60540-9075
(312) 369-3000

DELTAK offers an extensive list of computer-based, interactive videodisc, multimedia, videotape and instructor-led training. The company offers *The VM/SP CMS Series* of multimedia courses which include an *Introduction to REXX and the System Product Interpreter*, a computer-based training course, *VM/SP Facilities and REXX*, and many related courses.

G.F. Gargiulo and Associates
Box 936
27 Glendale Road
Manchester, CT 06040
(203) 646-9531

This company offers classroom training for REXX in both the VM and TSO environments.

Hitachi Data Systems
Education Services
4621-C Boston Way
Lanham, MD 20706-4393
(800) 543-2979

Hitachi Data Systems, formerly National Advanced Systems, has a long list of classroom courses that can be delivered on-site and customized. Course offerings include *REXX/EDIT Workshop* and *Basis MVS/REXX Workshop*.

Centre for Advanced Technology Education
Ryerson Polytechnical Institute
350 Victoria Street
Toronto, Ontario
Canada M58 2K3
(416) 979-5106

Seminars are offered in REXX and other technical topics.

Science Research Associates (SRA)
155 North Wacker Drive
Chicago, IL 60606
(800) SRA-1277

SRA has a long tradition of offering technical training. Offerings include a computer-based training course, *Using the CMS System Product Interpreter*, which includes instruction in writing REXX procedures.

Michael Teitelbaum Associates, Inc.
175 West 79th Street
New York, NY 10024-6450
(212) 799-2200

Michael Teitelbaum Associates is a full-service consulting and education company specializing in SQL/DS. Among their classes are *REXX Programming for VM* and *Using IBM's REXX-SQL / DS Interface (RXSQL)*. RXSQL is described elsewhere in this book.

VM Assist
Two Roundhouse Plaza
10 Lombard Street, Suite 450
San Francisco, CA 94111
(415) 362-3310

VM Assist offers classroom training nationwide. Courses include *Introduction to REXX* and *Intermediate / Advanced REXX*.

QED Information Sciences, Inc.
170 Linden Street
Wellesley, MA 02181
(617) 237-5656 (within Massachusetts)
(800) 343-4848 (outside Massachusetts)

QED offers classroom training in REXX and a variety of other technical and leadership topics at locations around the country and at client sites.

Additionally, the *IBM Education Catalog* includes an extensive list of REXX-related courses.

Evaluating options

As implied, the best way to evaluate training is to begin by asking as many questions as possible. These questions include:

1. What are the technical qualifications and past experience of individuals delivering the training? This is important regardless of whether the course is classroom or media-delivered.

2. How educationally sound is the course? Training must be delivered by people who know the principles of adult education, and who understand how to deliver the material and guide learning. Additionally, direct applicability in the real world is the ultimate test of the value of a technical training course. How should attendees' knowledge of REXX increase as a result of the training?

3. Is the training based on the most recent product release? IBM enhances its products periodically, and educational materials must be based on the latest developments.

4. At what level is the material presented, and is it relevant to highly technical people, such as system programmers, or end-users? "Aimed somewhere in the middle" is not an acceptable answer.

Unfortunately, much of the educational decision-making process is intuitive. Even after the questions are satisfied, there still must be a basic chemistry between the medium and the students. Sending a few key people off-site to evaluate a classroom course or bringing a media-based course in-house on a trial basis can help establish the presence of this chemistry before the actual financial commitment is made. It is helpful, from a political standpoint, to involve management in this evaluation process as much as possible. If they endorse the decision, chances are greater that this enthusiasm will trickle down to the attendees.

CONCLUSIONS

Optimal education in REXX is a result of balancing technical and people elements, and success is the result of a careful mix of course content, method of delivery, and psychological chemistry. Beginning with solid educational objectives, addressing these issues will result in a valuable, and measurable, outcome.

44

Language Evolution and Standards Activities

By Brian Marks

Spoken languages have a natural way of evolving—words that people find useful get used, and less useful words fall into disuse. Anybody can invent a new word and hope that it becomes established. A programming language does not have the same freedom to evolve: implementations of language compilers and interpreters determine the practical usefulness of language features. Some mechanism is needed to foster the relationship between what is most useful and what gets implemented.

In the earliest years of REXX there was just one implementation, by Mike Cowlishaw himself. As Mike explains in his book *The REXX Language*, the IBM VNET electronic mail system allowed a wide range of opinions to influence REXX. These were analyzed by Mike and used to guide the implementation. When that implementation was made available to IBM's customers on the VM system, a further group of implementors and users had views to express. Their opinions flowed through user groups, and review mechanisms were established within IBM.

In 1987, it was decided that REXX would play a central role in IBM's Systems Application Architecture (SAA). As explained in the chapter "Procedures Language in SAA", this implied that there would be implementations of REXX on several systems. The decision was made to strengthen the IBM review mechanisms, and integrate them with the mechanisms that were evolving SAA. The rest of this chapter describes the aims of the new mechanism, the Architecture Review Board that was put in place, the strategic directions considered by the Review Board, and what may eventually diminish the significance of the Board.

THE AIMS FOR THE NEW MECHANISM

The new mechanism needed to be directed towards maintaining the **fundamental language concepts** and **design principles** of REXX, as stated in *The REXX Language*. In particular, it would encourage the **user-driven** spirit of REXX. As Mike Cowlishaw says in his book, "The language user is usually right". There was no shortage of creative suggestions for extending REXX; the new Board's role was to evaluate them and to develop versions of suggestions that fitted together well.

The new mechanism needed to recognize considerations that might lead to contention between operating systems. REXX carries system independence further than most languages, but there are inevitable system influences. Some influences are subtle—you might wonder whether REXX would have a PUSH instruction if the operating system it was first implemented on had not had stacks as a system feature. Some influences are blunt—for example, the input/output model for REXX is incompatible with the basic input/output model for some operating systems.

The new mechanism needed to consider features that were not strictly part of REXX, but were to be part of SAA Procedures Language, and which would be so closely associated with REXX that users would not make a distinction; for example, the **variable pool** feature.

The new mechanism needed to be distinct from the mechanism for developing products. Individual products are optimized to particular subsets of REXX users, and sometimes suffer emergencies in their development schedules. It would not be appropriate to bias the outcome for REXX as a whole according to these optimizations and emergencies.

THE RESULTING MECHANISM

No single person has adequate knowledge of all the forces bearing on REXX evolution, so a committee was necessary—the Procedures Language Architecture Review Board (ARB). The absence of **REXX** from the title is deliberate, so that the scope of the Board can extend beyond language into, for example, uniform limits on the maximum NUMERIC DIGITS supported across SAA implementations. (For other examples, compare the *SAA CPI Procedures Language Reference* to *The REXX language*.)

The use of **Architecture** in the title emphasizes two points: wide range of planning in topics and time, and need for detailed specification of the results of the Board's deliberations.

The Board includes representatives from each SAA system, and from any non-SAA systems that IBM may be considering as candidates for REXX support. There are also representatives from development groups for each implementation—these are not one-to-one with the systems, since a development group may be supporting two systems (by writing common code for them), or a single system may have more than one implementation (such as compiler and interpreter).

Some members, including Mike Cowlishaw (the most influential member!), are concerned principally with the language rather than the implementations.

Decisions are not made by voting, but by the chairman's assessment of the prevailing opinion. In principle there is a procedure for appealing this assessment, but it has never been used.

Inputs to the Architecture Review Process are many and varied. One crucial input comes from SAA, directing the role of Procedures Language in SAA. This input comes via the Procedures Language Interface Owner, as explained in the chapter "Procedures Language in SAA". Where user groups like SHARE have their own mechanisms for defining REXX requirements, these requirements come to the Board via the same person.

Within IBM, there are two tiers of REXX discussion by electronic conferencing. One level is open to all IBM employees and covers beginners' questions, programming styles, etc., as well as suggestions for improvements. About 1000 lines are appended to these discussions each week. The second level provides conferencing for the ARB and about 50 REXX experts, specifically for proposals about language improvements. Some ARB work is done on this conference, and some is done by face-to-face meetings held twice a year. The Board members also follow some REXX forums outside IBM, on Internet and other networks.

The Board's output consists of definitions for **language levels**. Language levels increase—each increment adds a collection of extensions that add up to a major change in the language. So far SAA Procedures Language Levels 1.0 and 2.0 have been defined. (The notion of REXX language levels predates SAA. The REXX levels, with values returned by **PARSE VERSION**, are retained and kept synchronized with SAA levels. For instance, SAA PL Level 2.0 is REXX level 4.00.)

This packaging of smaller language changes into levels serves more than one purpose. It ensures that IBM products do not exhibit large numbers of small variations, since each product implements a particular level. It helps separate architecture work from product development—the bulk of development work does not occur until after a level has been defined. Similarly, user manuals for a product are written using the level definition as a source of information.

This mechanism has met the aims laid down for it in 1987, during the creation of SAA Procedures Language Levels 1.0 and 2.0. It remains in place to consider whether a Level 3.0 is called for, and what it might contain.

STRATEGIC LANGUAGE DIRECTIONS

When considering proposals for change to the language, certain recurrent themes and conflicts can be detected.

How much language do we want?

One all-encompassing concern is the risk of an overweight language. As with an overweight person, separate individual decisions may seem justified at the time, even though the total effect is regrettable. For example, the ARB considers many proposals for particular new built-in functions to be added to the language. Any new built-in function is likely to be valuable to the people who can use it in their problem solving, since they are saved the effort of writing an equivalent function themselves. The people who don't have a use for it will not find that their programs are affected by the addition of the new built-in function. So at first glance, the addition is a clear winner; however, a more strategic view takes into account the cumulative effect of more functions. A larger manual is intimidating to new users, and for experienced users it delays the day when they can feel they have mastered all the language. IBM feels it is desirable that REXX should be a part of the base operating system, so that applications can rely on it being available; a larger language increases the risk of implementation size being an impediment to packaging REXX with the operating system. Thus some potential built-in functions must be judged as lacking enough utility to justify the increment in language bulk. Of course there is room for a few more. The C programming language has about 140 functions in its Standard Library, which no doubt contributes to its reputation for complexity. REXX language level 4.0 has 66 built-in functions; how many more can be added before the REXX reputation as a small language is threatened?

The boundary between REXX and the operating system

The boundary between REXX and the operating system is an important strategic concern. Most users "glue together" calls to the system with their REXX applications. Directly porting such programs to a dissimilar operating system will not work, since the calls to one system will not work on another. It would be ideal if everything else in a program could be ported without change. At first sight this would appear to give the maximum advantage to the REXX programmer operating on an unfamiliar operating system, or on a mixture of operating systems. However, this uniformity would be a theoretical victory and a practical defeat if the uniformity was achieved by the **least common denominator** approach—throwing out of REXX any facility that could not easily be implemented on all systems. So there is an area of debate about which facilities have a usefulness that outweighs the disadvantage of system dependence.

Communication using stacks

One obvious "ragged edge" between REXX and the system is in communication between REXX and commands. It is reasonable to expect the operating system to accept the command in the form of a character string—most systems have a "shell" which parses commands like this. This gives a common way of passing information into the command, as arguments on the command. It is also common for the system to give an indication of how successfully it completed, an indication that REXX maps into the RC variable and the ERROR and FAILURE conditions. For some commands, this mechanism alone may be sufficient, e.g., "clear the screen", but other commands may be queries. Difficulties arise with returning results from such commands. REXX was originally implemented on the Conversational Monitor System (CMS), in which stacks play a key role. It was therefore natural to expect commands to return results by placing them on the stack, known to REXX as the external data queue. This approach is integral to REXX, so implementors of REXX on other systems have usually felt obliged to provide a stacking mechanism as an extension to the system when the base system did not provide suitable stacking. The REXX interface to stacking (i.e., EXTERNALS(), QUEUED(), PULL, PUSH, QUEUE), is an interface to only a subset of the system function. The system function may allow named stacks, stacks of stacks, and other features controllable through commands. So the external data queue is an example of where the line has been drawn and held—some stacking function is regarded as valuable enough to define in REXX, despite system implications, while other stacking function is available (at best) in a system-dependent way, despite difficulties that may cause for programmers working on different systems.

Communication using REXX variables

There is another form of communication where the boundary is not so clear-cut. Data put on the external data queue needs to be read into variables by some variant of PULL before it can be processed further. This consideration has led to design of other interfaces where the names of REXX variables are made available to the system services. One example is the EXECIO command. The following CMS example reads lines from a file directly into variables ABC1, ABC2, . . ., ABC*n*:

```
EXECIO * DISKR X Y (STEM ABC
```

Similarly, in IBM MVS TSO/E REXX, the OUTTRAP(ABC) function traps the output of subsequent commands into variables ABC1, ABC2, ABC3, . . ., ABC*n*.

The strategic questions are how far such examples should be regarded as part of REXX, since they are meaningless without the notion of REXX variables, and how far they should be regarded as part of the operating system. Can the REXX programmer rely on them being in an implementation of REXX, or are they as specialized as any other system command?

In practice, one or two implementations have chosen to add EXECIO to systems that lacked it, but it is clear that the peculiarly CMS syntax is an inelegant graft onto other systems. CMS users regard EXECIO as part of their system, but other users of EXECIO find it described in their REXX manuals. The EXECIO example and many others demonstrate that there is a difficult boundary to be established, and the judgments must encompass operating system trends and performance implications, as well as functional and architectural elegance concerns.

The Procedures Language role

IBM's SAA approach does not offer a complete solution to these problems, but it offers a framework for the solution. The approach makes a division into the REXX language as described in Cowlishaw's book, the Procedures Language superset described in the SAA reference manuals, and the supersets of Procedures Language described in the various product manuals. The core language, highly system-independent, is a target for all implementations, on SAA systems and others. The product manuals gather information optimally for the user who is concerned with only one system. The Procedures Language tackles a middle level of commonality.

The Procedures Language does not specify how programs should communicate with services by using REXX variables, as in examples like EXECIO and OUTTRAP, but it does specify the mechanism by which such communication is made possible. It specifies the interface from non-REXX code to the pool of REXX variables which an SAA implementation must provide. In contrast to the features of REXX itself, this interface is difficult to learn—a knowledge of a suitable systems programming language is a prerequisite. The systems programmer can use the interface to provide a wealth of system services. Commands in the style of **EXECIO** can be programmed. Collections of commands can be tailored to address some subcomponent of the operating system, such as communications or database. These commands need not simply take a command string as input and return a string result; they can parse the command string to find REXX variable names, and can then read or write the variables directly.

User Exits

User exits specified by Procedures Language are another example of specifying some underlying commonality in a situation where a full rigid specification would be unattainable or undesirable. The problem is far removed from the everyday problems of REXX programmers, but is often faced by systems programmers and REXX implementors when they try to fit a REXX product onto an operating system that is slightly different from the one it was designed for. If there were no exits, the only way to do this would be by altering the original implementation. The exits allow a tailored version to be made with less risk, and without the need to have the original source of the implementation.

Exchange of control between REXX and the system

Just as the communication of values between REXX and the operating system raises strategic issues, so does the question of the **exchange of control** between REXX and the system. The REXX model for this is that a string which is a command is passed to the environment and eventually the command returns. However, this is not the only approach. As users, we may know that the **DATE()** and **TIME()** functions are supported by the operating system, but we choose to access them through function calls, not by issuing commands. There is a trend in operating systems to make more and more services available by calling them. Perhaps it would be a good strategy to strengthen REXX in the area of directly calling services.

As usual in the operating systems arena, there is little prospect of agreeing about the names, arguments, and functions involved. (Each REXX implementation offers some system function via callable routines that are not built-in functions, making roughly 50 routines in total, but there is little commonality among them.) The commonality can only be in the way the routines are called and arguments passed to them. There is potential for a section of Procedures Language which fosters this commonality. It is noteworthy that the challenge of calling system services is not very different from calling non-REXX application code from REXX. The glueing together of an application by various calls to code written in different languages has become a trend in these days when more programmers have acquaintance with a variety of languages, and when the operating system often provides a common library for the languages to use.

If we look beyond this trend, there is reason to expect that object-oriented messaging will be used to integrate pieces of the application that are themselves collections of calls. The reason is that an object orientation has advantages, when remote calls and multiprocessing are considered. This approach has a very different terminology than REXX has now, but REXX could adapt without brutal changes to its existing form.

In summary, the IBM strategic direction can be viewed as:

- Restricting expansion of core REXX to features with a high ratio of usefulness to language bulk
- Providing in Procedures Language mechanisms which give a common underpinning to the wide variety of services and applications that the user can create
- Allowing individual REXX products to provide desired services that are special to particular operating systems

SAMPLE TACTICAL CONSIDERATIONS

Strategy is worked out in practice, through a series of tactical decisions which can be thought-provoking in themselves. An example is:

Where in REXX are expressions allowed, and where only symbols?

Beginning REXX programmers with experience in other programming languages are often surprised that they cannot write:

```
alpha.(j+1) = 2
```

with the same effect as:

```
t = j+1; alpha.t = 2
```

At first glance it might appear that extending REXX to allow the first form would be a simple choice. In fact, some of the related issues are simple, such as checking that performance and implementation costs are not high enough to deter the extension; other issues are much more complex. The mooted extension modifies concepts that are at the heart of REXX interpretation, changing how a symbol is interpreted to give the period character some flavor of an operator, rather than just a character in a symbol. Does the extra complexity at the heart of REXX outweigh the benefit of what is, after all, only a shorthand?

The "breakage" also has to be considered. Breakage occurs when existing programs change their semantics because the language has been extended. This is not a new problem for REXX—every new built-in function damages existing programs that already have a routine with the same name as the new built-in function. The breakage with **BETA.(J+1)** occurs because in existing programs **BETA.** could be a function invoked with **J+1** as an argument. This is not particularly likely, perhaps, but that is a more difficult question to assess than questions of performance or implementation cost.

A simple decision on the extension would ignore other parts of REXX which might have analogous shorthands. Some other places where current REXX allows symbols but not expressions are immediately following **ADDRESS**, **CALL**, **NUMERIC FORM**, **PARSE**, **SIGNAL**, and **TRACE**. Perhaps the most effective approach, in terms of utility gained against new concepts introduced, would be to introduce the idea that bracketed expressions can be used in all these contexts. Many people would find it attractive to be able to write **CALL (DELTA) (J+1)** as a call to one of many routines, according to the content of **DELTA**.

Again, breakage must be considered; breakage caused by interpreting **(GAMMA) (J)** as a function call selected by the content of **GAMMA**, rather than the concatenation of **GAMMA** and **J**, would be intolerable. However, this breakage would not happen if a different syntax was chosen—for example, square brackets around the selector **GAMMA**. This would be a bigger conceptual change than using round brackets, since round brackets are already used to mean "evaluate the expression within and use the result". It would also bring into play other considerations about character sets for REXX.

Character sets for REXX have always been a source of difficulty. User requirements have often been several steps ahead of operating system facilities. The result has been a number of ad hoc solutions about substitute characters like the backslash, and about Double Byte Character Set handling.

IBM has now, in 1990, formulated its **Character Data Representation Architecture**. Perhaps now is the time to exploit such advances, allowing REXX users to program in the character set of their choice and to use extra characters like square brackets, curly brackets, and the tilde. However, if the REXX character set were extended, there would be a new form of breakage—existing programs would be unbroken, but existing terminals might not be able to enter all new programs. This opens up the question of trends in terminals, and so on.

The thread of deliberation above illustrates how an apparently simple, isolated choice regarding an extension can, on analysis, prove to be related to many other potential language changes. To a degree, this lessens the benefit of user group input to the language modification process, when that input consists only of requests for individual changes.

THE FUTURE

The appearance of REXX on more systems and the trend for applications to be built from many heterogenous parts will lead to increased REXX use. This will foster a continued language development effort by the REXX community to maintain and enhance REXX's suitability for the job. The mechanisms for that process have been extended by a project to create an American National Standard for REXX. (Although IBM remains the major supplier, there are as many implementations of REXX outside IBM as there are IBM implementations.)

Since there will always be a big gap between what can be programmed solely in REXX and what can be constructed using REXX as glue, we should expect enhancement in the Procedures Language features that aid in that construction, as well as enhancement of the core language.

The background provided by this chapter should encourage REXX experts to be actively involved in the network of activities that drive the REXX language.

45

Suggested Reading List and Bibliography

By Linda Suskind Green

This chapter contains a suggested reading list and brief description of selected REXX materials, categorized by operating system or use. Also included is a list of all the books, articles, and presentations on REXX or SAA Procedures Language. Full availability information for references in the reading list is in this latter section.

This chapter only includes items available as separately orderable items as of November 1990. Items listed add new or different information on the subject, and were selected based on what the author found to be available.

If something should be listed in a future edition of this book, please use the Reader Comment Form to bring it to the editors' attention.

SUGGESTIONS FOR FURTHER READING

Generic books and manuals

- *The REXX Language*, Michael F. Cowlishaw

  This is the original REXX book written by the creator of the language. It is not implementation-specific, but lists basic language features. In addition to the language definition, it covers the history of the language, including design principles and fundamental language concepts. The second edition adds a glossary, plus new language features added by IBM's SAA Procedures Language definition. Several non-IBM implementations use this book as their reference manual.

- *The Design of the REXX Language*, Michael F. Cowlishaw

  This *IBM Systems Journal* article by the language originator introduces REXX, describing general concepts and some language features. It describes the fundamental language concepts and language design concepts used.

- *SAA CPI Procedures Language Level 2 Reference*

  This IBM manual documents the SAA Procedures Language (PL) architecture definition. It explains language elements that must be present in an SAA implementation. For the four SAA IBM system implementations, deviations from the architecture are indicated in green ink. This is the book to use to code portable programs. Descriptions include language use and syntax, as well as explanations of how the language processor interprets the language as programs execute. It details the three pieces of PL: REXX, extensions to REXX, and environmental interfaces. This book documents Level 2 of the architecture, which is a superset of Level 1. A separate book called *IBM SAA CPI Procedures Language Reference* documents the Level 1 definition.

- *Modern Programming Using REXX*, Bob O'Hara and Dave Gomberg

  This book teaches programming, using REXX as the programming language. It is also useful for experienced programmers who do not know REXX. It includes numerous, detailed program examples, often starting as exercises for the reader, with a solution detailed later. Each chapter has a summary and series of questions at the end, so it can be used as a classroom text. In addition to discussing some REXX syntax, it has chapters on communicating with the system.

- *Proceedings of the REXX Symposium for Developers and Users: June 11, 1990*

  This publication from the Stanford Linear Accelerator Center documents the first annual REXX symposium. As keynote speaker, Mike Cowlishaw presented the new features in REXX language level 4.0, after reviewing the language history. The book also includes materials from other presentations:

  - *IBM REXX Compiler* (Walter Pachl)
  - *The Astonishment Factor* (Kevin Kearney and Charles Daney)

- *I/O and Environment Challenges* (Keith Watts)
- *IBM SAA REXX for OS/2* (Rick McGuire)
- *REXX for UNIX* (Neil Milsted)
- *Object Oriented REXX* (Brian Marks)
- *Why REXX Died (A Retrospective)* (Bob O'Hara)
- *SLAC Use of REXX on VM and MVS* (Tony Johnson)
- *Developing Full-Screen REXX Applications* (Larry Oppenheim)
- *CMS Pipelines* (Bebo White)
- *REXX in Three Different Environments: VM/MVS/OS/2* (Mason Kelsey)

The book ends with a list of 1990 attendees and an announcement of the 1991 Symposium.

- *REXX: Understanding a Puzzle*.

This article in the *The SAA Spectrum* discusses availability of SAA REXX implementations, and REXX uses, roles, and shortcomings.

VM-specific

- *Virtual Machine/Enterprise Systems Architecture Procedures Language VM/REXX Reference*

This IBM manual describes the REXX language as implemented on VM, listing the SAA definition and system-specific extensions for VM. It includes the language grammar (syntax), and chapters on system interfaces, and invoking communication and resource recovery routines. Appendices cover REXX in the GCS environment and interpreter error messages.

There are similar manuals for pre-ESA versions of VM.

- *Virtual Machine/Enterprise Systems Architecture Procedures Language VM/REXX User's Guide*

This IBM manual teaches programming by explaining the REXX language as implemented on VM. It also explains how the VM REXX interpreter processes the language. It can be considered a cookbook for VM REXX recipes and ideas.

The book consists of a series of reading lessons, followed by questions and answers. It assumes VM knowledge but not programming knowledge.

There are similar manuals for pre-ESA versions of VM.

- *CMS REXX Compiler User's Guide and Reference*

This IBM manual describes how to write programs that use the CMS REXX compiler. Topics include how to compile and run REXX programs, a description of compiler options, differences between the compiler and the interpreter, compiler installation and customization, and an explanation of compilation and run-time error messages.

- *VM/IS Writing Simple Programs with REXX*

  This IBM manual provides an introduction to REXX for VM/IS users, assuming no programming experience. Sections cover getting to know REXX, writing programs, and improving skills.

- *The System Product Interpreter (REXX) Examples and Techniques*, Gary Brodock

  This IBM manual acquaints readers with techniques for writing EXECs and XEDIT macros in REXX on VM. The book discusses examples that demonstrate the main features of the language, as well as ways to improve the readability of REXX EXECs. One example is an EXEC for interactively executing REXX statements entered by the user.

- *A Unified Approach to REXX EXECs and Macros*, Dave Fraatz

  This *Mainframe Journal* article describes differences between EXECs and macros. It uses a CMS XEDIT example to show how to write a single REXX program to serve both purposes.

TSO/E-specific

- *REXX in the TSO Environment*, Gabriel Gargiulo

  This book describes how REXX works on IBM's MVS operating system in the TSO programming system. The first part of the book explains REXX in the TSO world. It briefly compares CLIST and REXX in terms of function and how they work, and how REXX EXECs work in sequential and partitioned datasets. The second part of the book introduces the reader to the major parts of the REXX language and how they work on TSO. It also has chapters about interfaces to TSO-specific topics, including:

  - Dialoguing with the terminal
  - Using the TSO stack
  - EXECIO: reading and writing files
  - Edit macros
  - Converting from CLISTs

  Each chapter concludes with questions and/or problems, with answers and solutions in an appendix. Another appendix discusses using REXX instead of JCL.

- *TSO Extensions Version 2 Procedures Language MVS / REXX Reference*

  This IBM manual describes the language as implemented on TSO, listing the SAA definition and system-specific extensions for TSO, and the grammar (syntax) of the language. The book includes chapters on TSO/E REXX programming and customizing services, and explains interpreter error messages.

- *TSO Extensions Version 2 Procedures Language MVS / REXX User's Guide*

  This IBM manual describes how to use REXX in TSO/E. The book has two parts: *Learning the REXX Language* and *Using TSO/E REXX*. The first part teaches the REXX language, and includes exercises and solutions. The second part contains chapters on:

  - Issuing commands from an EXEC
  - Diagnosing problems within an EXEC
  - Using TSO/E external functions
  - Storing information in the data stack
  - Processing data and input/output processing
  - Using REXX in TSO/E and other MVS address spaces

  One of the appendices compares CLIST and REXX.

  Part one of the book is geared to inexperienced programmers who are somewhat familiar with TSO/E commands and have used Interactive System Productivity Facility/Program Development Facility (ISPF/PDF). The second part assumes knowledge of REXX and experience with TSO/E.

- *REXX on TSO / E*, Gerry Hoernes

  This *IBM Systems Journal* article describes the REXX implementation on TSO/E, including a brief definition of the REXX language elements and the MVS/ESA operating system. REXX requirements on TSO/E are discussed, including CMS and SAA compatibility, along with several design alternatives that illustrate how REXX was integrated with the existing operating system. TSO REXX language processor environments, replaceable routines, data stacks, and performance considerations are discussed.

OS/2- and DOS-specific

- *Portable / REXX Examples*

  This manual presents approximately 70 examples designed for Kilowatt Software's Portable/REXX implementation for MS-DOS and PC-DOS. Generally, these examples can be ported exactly as written or adapted to other REXX implementations. The first section of the book includes detailed descriptions of the examples. The second section includes the actual REXX code for the programs. Examples include programs for computing the future value of an annuity, showing the time for a specified city, state, or country, and pasting two files side by side to default output.

- *IBM Operating System / 2 Procedures Language 2 / REXX*

  This IBM manual describes the language as implemented on OS/2, listing the SAA definition and system-specific extensions for OS/2, and the grammar (syntax) of the language. It includes chapters on the OS/2 Application Programming Interface, useful OS/2 commands, and an explanation of interpreter error messages.

- *IBM Operating System / 2 Procedures Language 2 / REXX User's Guide*

  This IBM manual describes how to write programs using REXX. Since it assumes only basic OS/2 knowledge, it can be used to learn programming. Each chapter is broken up into basics and advanced topics, to allow people with varied amounts of programming experience to use the book. Topics range from descriptions of features of REXX to programming style.

- *Personal REXX User's Guide*

  This manual describes how to use Mansfield Software Group's Personal REXX, including chapters on installing and running the product. Chapters cover REXX language compatibility, as well as the essential elements of REXX for new REXX programmers. Numerous examples illustrate the language. Implementation-specific functions and commands are also described. Several appendices include a description of the Personal REXX Application Interfaces, and error messages and return codes.

- *The REXX Language on the PC*, Andrew Chalk

  This *Programmer's Journal* article describes the REXX language and provides several examples. It also describes Mansfield's Personal REXX product (which at the time of the article ran only on MS-DOS/PC-DOS). REXX uses, including code for a utility to create and maintain a computer usage log, are discussed.

- *Procedures Language 2 / REXX*, Marvin Boswell, Mike Cowlishaw, Rick McGuire, and Steve Price

  This *IBM Personal Systems Developer* article describes major language features and Application Programming Interfaces that allow OS/2 programmers to extend applications with REXX. Topics include using the REXX APIs, extending REXX via subcommands and functions, and macrospace.

- *REXX in Charge*, Charles Daney

   Subtitled *You're not really multitasking in OS/2 unless you're using REXX*, this *Byte* article describes how REXX can control and coordinate all aspects of the OS/2 environment. It contains a brief history of and design goals for the language, outlines language features that differentiate REXX from other languages, and discusses the four important parts of the REXX interface definition in OS/2.

AS/400-specific

- *IBM Application System/400 Programming: Procedures Language 400/REXX Reference*

   This IBM manual describes the language as implemented on OS/400, listing both the SAA definition and system-specific extensions for OS/400, and the grammar (syntax) of the language. It includes a chapter on the OS/400 system interfaces.

- *IBM Application System/400 Programming: Procedures Language 400/REXX Programmer's Guide*

   This IBM manual provides programming information and examples to new REXX coders on OS/400. Basic language features are described, along with examples illustrating their use. Appendices include descriptions of communication between REXX and other languages.

- *REXX—Portrait of a New Procedures Language*, Paul Conte

   This *NEWS/34-38* article provides a review of the REXX language with many illustrative examples, including comparisons of REXX with the System/38 CL and the System/34/36 OCL.

Amiga-specific

- *SLAC Takes Up the Amiga*, Michael Bloom

   This article in *Bay Area Computer Currents* describes how Stanford Linear Accelerator Center (SLAC) came to use the Amiga and the ARexx implementation for it. The article describes ARexx and some of its uses, such as communications between programs.

- *ARexx at Work*, Steve Gilmor

   This *Byte* article analyzes the inclusion of ARexx in version 2.0 of the AmigaDOS operating system. It includes many examples of hypermedia products that depend on ARexx as an integral part of the product.

UNIX/AIX-specific

- *uniREXX Reference Manual*

  This manual describes the uniREXX language and implementation. General language structure is explained, as well as specific instructions and functions. Chapters cover uniREXX operation in the UNIX environment, programming interfaces, and sample programs, and appendices discuss error messages and common pitfalls.

REXX usage

- *NetView Release 3: REXX Presentation Guide*, W. K. Gibbons and P. J. Quigley

  This IBM technical bulletin consists of foils and presentation text on the use of REXX in NetView Command Lists. It assumes prior knowledge of NetView Command Lists, but little or no REXX experience. Many examples are given of NetView REXX CLISTs, as well as REXX functions. It explains REXX commands unique to the NetView implementation, and discusses a CLIST-to-REXX conversion tool. There is also a section on managing NetView CLISTs.

- *CUA Application Coding Techniques in VM REXX—an Educational Tool Kit with Samples and Examples*, Charles Naul

  This IBM publication describes a tool that assists VM application builders in building application development aids. It contains an introduction to the tool, programming ideas and techniques, and detailed interfaces, with explanations of how to use the tools to build EXECs. MS-DOS/PC-DOS and OS/2 diskettes are provided.

- *IBM Virtual Machine/System Product Interpreter: SQL/Data System Interface: Program Description/Operations Manual*

  This IBM manual describes the programming interface between VM REXX and SQL/DS. This allows REXX programs to use the SQL language via RXSQL commands. The manual assumes familiarity with both REXX and SQL, and covers installing the product, completion codes and messages produced by RXSQL, and syntax of RXSQL commands, with illustrative examples.

- *GDDM-REXX Guide*

  This IBM manual describes an IBM program product that allows GDDM to be used from CMS REXX programs. It presents the tool and learning sessions, followed by information about installation and diagnosis, and reference material on commands and subcommands provided. Many examples illustrate points being made throughout the book.

- *CMS Pipelines Tutorial*, J. P. Hartmann, L. S. Kraines, and J. C. Lynn

  Describes the CMS Pipelines program offering to new users, including chapters devoted to writing REXX filters, using Pipelines in EXECs and XEDIT macros, and examples with suggested solutions.

- *Communications Program for DOS and OS/2 Uses REXX for Script Development*, S. P. Ricciardi

  This *PC Magazine* article reviews the REXXTERM communications product, which uses Personal REXX as its script language.

ALPHABETICAL BIBLIOGRAPHY

This is a list of all books, manuals, and user presentations that are generally available.

- Abacus, A., *REXX: A Beginner's Alternative*, Computer Language, Volume 3, no. 6 (June 1986)

- Bloom, M., *SLAC Takes Up the Amiga*, Bay Area Computer Currents (May 2-May 15, 1989)

- Boswell, M.; Cowlishaw, M. F.; McGuire, R. K.; Price, S. G., *Procedures Language 2/REXX*, IBM Personal Systems Developer (Fall 1989), IBM order no. G362-0001-03

- Brodock, G., *The System Product Interpreter (REXX) Examples and Techniques*, IBM reference manual, order no. GG22-9361

- Campbell, J., *REXX for Application Programmers*, Proceedings of SHARE 75, Volume 2, New Orleans, LA (August 1990)

- Campbell, J., *REXX for CLIST Programmers (part 1)*, Proceedings of SHARE 74, Volume 2, Anaheim, CA (March 1990)

- Campbell, J., *REXX for CLIST Programmers (part 2)*, Proceedings of SHARE 74, Volume 2, Anaheim, CA (March 1990)

- Campbell, J., *REXX in MVS*, Proceedings of SHARE 72, Volume 2, Los Angeles, CA (February 1989)

- Cathcart, M., *REXX: The Systems Application Architecture Connection*, PC User, no. 63 (August 1987)

- Chalk, A. J., *The REXX Language on the PC*, Programmer's Journal, Volume 6, no. 5 (September/October 1988)

- Coffee, P.; Schmidt, D., *Lotus Makes a Case for REXX to Foil Microsoft's BASIC Plan*, PC Week, Volume 7, no. 24 (June 18, 1990)

- Cohen, M., *Extending a Presentation Manager Application with REXX*, Proceedings of SHARE 75, Volume 1, New Orleans, LA (August 1990)

- Conte, P., *REXX—Portrait of a New Procedures Language*, NEWS/34-38 (June 1988)

- Cormier, P., *Power of RXSQL*, Proceedings of GUIDE 77, Chicago, IL (July 1990)

- Cowlishaw, M. F., *REXX 4.0*, Proceedings of SHARE 74, Volume 1, Anaheim, CA (March 1990)

- Cowlishaw, M. F., *REXX—the SAA Procedures Language*, Proceedings of SHARE 72, Volume 1, Los Angeles, CA (February 1989)

- Cowlishaw, M. F., *The Design of the REXX Language*, SIGPLAN, Volume 22, no. 2 (February 1987)

- Cowlishaw, M. F., *The REXX Language, a Practical Approach to Programming*, Prentice-Hall (1985, 1990) ISBN 0-13-708651-5 in English for the second edition

- Cowlishaw, M. F., *The Design of the REXX Language*, IBM Systems Journal, Volume 23, no. 4 (1984), Reprint order no. G321-5228

- Cowlishaw, M. F.; McGuire, R. K.; Price, S. G., *Overview of the Procedures Language 2/REXX*, IBM Personal Systems Developer (Summer 1989), IBM order no. G362-0001-02

- Daney, C., *REXX in Charge*, Byte, Volume 15, no. 8 (August 1990)

- Daney, C., *REXX in the Age of Presentation Manager*, Proceedings of SHARE 74, Volume 1, Anaheim, CA (March 1990)

- Duntemann, J., *Structured Programming*, Dr. Dobb's Journal, Volume 14, no. 9 (September 1989)

- Dyck, L., *TSO/E Mail—An ISPF Dialog in REXX*, Proceedings of SHARE 75, Volume 2, New Orleans, LA (August 1990)

- Edborg, D., *REXX as a CMS Application Development Language*, Proceedings of SHARE 74, Volume 2, Anaheim, CA (March 1990)

- Fisher, J. W., *Database Manager Programming with Procedures Language 2/REXX*, IBM Personal Systems Technical Solutions, Issue 2 (1990), IBM order no. G325-5006

- Flannagan, T., *REXX the Wonder Language*, SAA Age, Volume 2, no. 2 (1989)

- Fraatz, D., *A Unified Approach to REXX EXECs and Macros*, Mainframe Journal, Volume V, no. 6 (June 1990)

- Gargiulo, G. F., *REXX in the TSO Environment* (1990), QED Information Sciences, Inc., ISBN 0-89435-354-3

- Gibbons, W. K.; Quigley, P. J., *IBM NetView Release 3: REXX Presentation Guide*, IBM reference manual, order no. GG66-3144

- Gilmor, S., *ARexx at Work*, Byte, Volume 15, no. 8 (August 1990)

- Good, M., *SQL/DS: RXSQL*, Proceedings of SHARE 75, Volume 2, New Orleans, LA (August 1990)

- Green, L. S., *Procedures Language (REXX) Structure in SAA*, Proceedings of SHARE 74, Volume 2, Anaheim, CA (March 1990)

- Green, L. S., *REXX: The SAA Procedures Language: An Overview*, Proceedings of SHARE 73, Volume 2, Orlando, FL (August 1989)

- Green, L. S., *REXX: The SAA Procedures Language: A Tutorial*, Proceedings of SHARE 72, Volume 2, Los Angeles, CA (February 1989)

- Green, L. S., *SAA Procedures Language/REXX Trends and Directions*, Proceedings of SHARE 75, Volume 2, New Orleans, LA (August 1990)

- Greenberg, R., *Utilize the Power of REXX/CP/CMS*, Mainframe Journal (February 1990)

- Hartmann, J. P., Kraines, L. S.; Lynn, J. C., *IBM CMS Pipelines Tutorial*, IBM reference manual, order no. GG66-3158

- Hauser, R., *REXX/IUCV Package*, Proceedings of SHARE 75, Volume 2, New Orleans, LA (August 1990)

- Hayden, P., *Introduction to REXX Programming*, Computing (February 16, 1989)

- Heavener, Z., *TSO/E REXX An Overview*, Mainframe Journal (October 1989)

- Hoernes, Dr. G. E., *A REXX Tutorial for the TSO/E Environment*, Proceedings of SHARE 71, Volume 2, New York, NY (August 1988)

- Hoernes, Dr. G. E., *MVS/E REXX Overview*, Proceedings of SHARE 71, Volume 2, New York, NY (August 1988)

- Hoernes, Dr. G. E., *REXX on TSO/E*, IBM Systems Journal, Volume 28, no. 2 (1989), reprint order no. G321-5359

- IBM, *All Hail REXX*, The SAA Spectrum, Volume 2, report 2 (May 1988)

- IBM, *Application System/400 Programming: Procedures Language 400/REXX Programmer's Guide*, IBM reference manual, order no. SC24-5513

- IBM, *Application System/400 Programming: Procedures Language 400/REXX Reference*, IBM reference manual, order no. SC24-5512

- IBM, *CMS REXX Compiler Diagnosis Guide*, IBM reference manual, order no. LY19-6262

- IBM, *CMS REXX Compiler General Information*, IBM reference manual, order no. GH19-8118

- IBM, *CMS REXX Compiler User's Guide and Reference*, IBM reference manual, order no. SH19-8120

- IBM, *GDDM-REXX Guide*, IBM reference manual, order no. SC33-0478

- IBM, *Operating System/2 Procedures Language 2/REXX*, IBM reference manual, order no. S01F-0284

- IBM, *Operating System/2 Procedures Language 2/REXX User's Guide*, IBM reference manual, order no. S01F-0283

- IBM, *REXX/EXEC Migration to VM/XA SP*, IBM reference manual, order no. GG24-3401

- IBM, *SAA CPI Procedures Language Reference*, IBM reference manual, order no. SC26-4358

- IBM, *SAA CPI Procedures Language Level 2 Reference*, IBM reference manual, order no. SC24-5549

- IBM, *TSO Extensions Version 2 Procedures Language MVS/REXX Reference*, IBM reference manual, order no. SC28-1883

- IBM, *TSO Extensions Version 2 Procedures Language MVS/REXX Users Guide*, IBM reference manual, order no. SC28-1882

- IBM, *Using REXX in Practice: EXEC 2 to REXX Conversion Experiences*, IBM reference manual, order no. GG24-1615

- IBM, *Virtual Machine/Enterprise Systems Architecture: Procedures Language VM/REXX Reference*, IBM reference manual, order no. SC24-5466

- IBM, *Virtual Machine/Enterprise Systems Architecture: Procedures Language VM/REXX Reference Summary*, IBM reference material, order no. SX24-5251

- IBM, *Virtual Machine/Enterprise Systems Architecture: Procedures Language VM/REXX User's Guide*, IBM reference manual, order no. SC24-5465

- IBM, *Virtual Machine/Extended Architecture System Product: System Product Interpreter Reference*, IBM reference manual, order no. SC23-0374

- IBM, *Virtual Machine / Extended Architecture System Product: System Product Interpreter Reference Summary*, IBM reference material, order no. SX23-0391

- IBM, *Virtual Machine / Extended Architecture System Product: System Product Interpreter User's Guide*, IBM reference manual, order no. SC23-0375

- IBM, *Virtual Machine / Integrated System: Writing Simple Programs with REXX*, IBM reference manual, order no. SC24-5357

- IBM, *Virtual Machine / System Product Interpreter: SQL / Data System Interface: Program Description / Operations Manual*, IBM reference manual, order no. SH20-7051

- IBM, *Virtual Machine / System Product Program Update Information: Restructured Extended Executor Language Enhancements: VM / SP Release 6 APARS VM36993, VM36994, VM36988*, IBM reference manual, order no. GC24-5406

- IBM, *Virtual Machine / System Product: System Product Interpreter Reference*, IBM reference manual, order no. SC24-5239

- IBM, *Virtual Machine / System Product: System Product Interpreter Reference Summary*, IBM reference material, order no. SX24-5126

- IBM, *Virtual Machine / System Product: System Product Interpreter User's Guide*, IBM reference manual, order no. SC24-5238

- IBM, *REXX: Understanding a Puzzle*, The SAA Spectrum (November 1989)

- IBM, *REXX: What Is It?*, The SAA Spectrum, Volume 2, report 2. (May 1988)

- IBM, *SRA VM Using the CMS System Product Interpreter*, IBM reference manual, order no. SR21-0864

- Jeffries, R., *Hello, REXX—Goodbye, .BAT*, PC Magazine (February 25, 1986)

- Karpinski, J., *Tips, Techniques, and Coding Standards—Confessions of a REXX Addict*, Proceedings of SHARE 72, Volume 1, Los Angeles, CA (February 1989)

- Kawakami, C., *The REXXPERT: Conquering the XEDIT Macro*, VM Read, Volume 1, no. 3 (third quarter 1988), RD Labs Inc., 3825 Atherton Road, Rocklin, CA 95677

- Kearney, K.; Daney, C., *Unifying the VM and PC Environments: Kedit and Personal REXX*, Proceedings of SEAS Spring Meeting 1986, Volume 2, Published by SHARE European Association Inc., Netherlands (April 1986)

- Kiesel, P., *IBM Suggestions for REXX Coding Guidelines*, Proceedings of SHARE 73, Volume 2, Orlando, FL (August 1989)

- KiloWatt Software, *Learning to Program with Portable / REXX*, 1945 Washington St., #410, San Francisco, CA 94109

- KiloWatt Software, *Portable / REXX Examples*, 1945 Washington St., #410, San Francisco, CA 94109

- KiloWatt Software, *Portable / REXX Guide*, 1945 Washington St., #410, San Francisco, CA 94109

- KiloWatt Software, *Portable / REXX Reference Manual*, 1945 Washington St., #410, San Francisco, CA 94109

- KiloWatt Software, *Portable / REXX Reference Summary*, 1945 Washington St., #410, San Francisco, CA 94109

- Land, B., *True Blue Batch Language*, OS/2 and Windows Magazine, Volume 1, no. 3 (November 1990)

- Lewis, D. J., *Full-Featured Batch Language for PCs*, IEEE Software, Volume 13, no. 1 (November 1988)

- Loebenberg, E. M., *CMS REXX Compiler Evaluation at Bell Canada*, Proceedings of SHARE 74, Volume 2, Anaheim, CA (March 1990)

- Loebenberg, E. M., *More REXX Programming Hints and Tips*, Proceedings of SHARE 75, Volume 2, New Orleans, LA (August 1990)

- Loebenberg, E. M., *REXX Programming Standards, Hints and Tips*, Proceedings of SHARE 74, Volume 1, Anaheim, CA (March 1990)

- Lovelace, *REXX Techniques*, Proceedings of SEAS Spring Meeting 1986, Volume 2, Published by SHARE European Association Inc., Netherlands (April 1986)

- Mansfield Software Group, *Personal REXX User's Guide*, Mansfield Software Group, P.O. Box 532, Storrs, CT 06268

- McGuire, R. K., *CMS REXX Interpreter Internals*, Proceedings of SHARE 74, Volume 2, Anaheim, CA (March 1990)

- Moser, Dr. E. J., *CMS Compiler*, Proceedings of SEAS Spring Meeting 1989, Volume 1, Published by SHARE European Association Inc., Netherlands

- Moser, Dr. E. J., *CMS REXX Compiler*, Proceedings of SHARE 72, Volume 2, Los Angeles, CA (February 1989)

- Nash, S., *Object Orientated REXX*, Proceedings of SHARE 74, Volume 1, Anaheim, CA (March 1990)

- Naul, C., *CUA Application Coding Techniques in VM REXX—an Educational Tool Kit with Samples and Examples*, IBM reference material, order no. GR23-6961

- Oakley, H., *AREXX (The Integrative Language)*, AMIGA User International (August 1990).

- O'Hara, R. P.; Gomberg, D. G., *Modern Programming Using REXX*, Prentice-Hall (1985 and 1988) ISBN 0-13-579329-5 for the second edition

- Pedersen, E. H., *VM Neural Network in REXX*, Out of the Blue, Blueline Software Inc. (Summer 1989)

- Powell, D. G., *REXX — A Multifaceted Tool*, Shareware Magazine, Volume 5, no. 1 (January-February 1990)

- Pournelle, J., *A User's View: Dirt-Infested Killer WORMs Blown to Bits by Force of Dry Air*, Infoworld (September 11, 1989)

- Price, S. G., *REXX Portability*, Proceedings of SHARE 75, Volume 1, New Orleans, LA (August 1990)

- Price, S. G.; Green, L. S., *Procedures Language Program Portability*, Proceedings of SHARE 74, Volume 1, Anaheim, CA (March 1990)

- Stanford Linear Accelerator Center, *Proceedings of the REXX Symposium for Developers and Users: June 11, 1990*, SLAC Report-368, National Technical Information Service, U.S. Department of Commerce, 5285 Port Royal Road, Springfield, VA 22161 (June 1990)

- Quigley, P. J., *NetView REXX Hints and Tips*, Proceedings of SHARE 75, Volume 2, New Orleans, LA (August 1990)

- Quigley, P. J.; Taylor, H. A., *NETVIEW R3 REXX Support & CLIST Performance Improvements*, Proceedings of SHARE 72, Volume 2, Los Angeles, CA (February 1989)

- RD Labs Inc., *RDUTIL: The RD/COMM REXX Sample Application*, VM Read, Volume 1, no. 3 (third quarter 1988), RD Labs Inc., 3825 Atherton Road, Rocklin, CA 95677

- RD Labs Inc., *REXX: A User's Dream in a System Programmer's World*, VM Read, Volume 1, no. 3 (third quarter 1988), RD Labs Inc., 3825 Atherton Road, Rocklin, CA 95677

- Ricciardi, S. P., *Communications Program for DOS and OS/2 Uses REXX for Script Development*, PC Magazine (March 13, 1990)

- Robin, D., *Why Is REXX so Popular?*, Technical Support (August 1989)

- Rudd, Anthony S., *Practical Usage of REXX*, Prentice-Hall (1990), ISBN 0-13-682790-X

- Rutherford, J., *Utility Programming with REXX*, Online Review, Volume 11, no. 6 (December 1987)

- Sacksteder, C., *REXX Programmer Tools*, Proceedings of SHARE 73, Volume 1, Orlando, FL (August 1989)

- Seadle, M., *VM in the Development Center*, Mainframe Journal (June 1989)

- Shammas, N. C., *Personal REXX*, Byte, Volume 13, no. 1 (January 1988)

- Silcock, J. R., *Introduction to REXX Programming*, Proceedings of SEAS Anniversary Meeting 1986, Volume 1, Published by SHARE European Association Inc., Netherlands

- Silcock, J. R., *REXX on the Host and PC*, Proceedings of SEAS Anniversary Meeting 1986, Volume 2, Published by SHARE European Association Inc., Netherlands

- Software Professionals Inc., *T-REXX Reference Summary*, 999 Baker Way #390, San Mateo, CA 94404

- Software Professionals Inc., *T-REXX User Manual*, 999 Baker Way #390, San Mateo, CA 94404

- Swiniarski, R., *Automatic Generation of Simulation Software. REXX Language Application*, Advances in Modeling and Simulation, Volume 16, no. 3 (1989)

- The Workstation Group, *uniREXX Reference Manual*, The Workstation Group, 6300 North River Road, Rosemont, IL 60018

- Vandewater, B. J., *An Introduction to REXX for ISPF*, Proceedings of GUIDE 74, Toronto, Canada (July 1989)

- Vandewater, B. J., *Extending REXX for Your Business*, Proceedings of GUIDE 75, Los Angeles, CA (November 1989)

Biographies

Jim Bergsten has been involved with VM and the VM community for over fifteen years. He founded Kolinar Corporation, and was its President and CEO. Kolinar merged with VM Systems Group in 1988.

Jim wrote **XMENU**, an interactive full-screen product for VM/CMS, **XMENU/CUA**, **XMENU/DTL**, **DB/REXX**, and **SQL/MENU**. Products that he has either developed or designed have earned over fourteen million dollars to date.

Jim is presently engaged in mainframe and microcomputer hardware and software consulting and product development. Having threatened for years to "just go off and start a rock group", he indulges himself with music composition, recording, and production.

Jim Bergsten, 11404 Georgetown Pike, Great Falls, VA 22066-1316, Phone: (703) 450-8895.

Gary K. Brodock joined IBM in June of 1969 after receiving a B.Sc. in Mathematics from the Rochester Institute of Technology, Rochester, NY. His first few years were spent working on an automated warehouse in Endicott, NY, and subsequent automated warehousing projects.

In March of 1981, Gary transferred to the CMS Development organization at the Glendale Laboratory in Endicott and began working on getting REXX included in CMS. He is currently in the SAA REXX Development Area at Glendale working on future enhancements.

Gary K. Brodock, G09/21A1, IBM Corporation, PO Box 8009, Endicott, New York 13760, Phone: (607) 752-3069.

Mark Cathcart, a senior system engineer in IBM UK Technical Support, has technical "ownership" of large systems VM software and the REXX language for IBM UK.

He has worked in the computer industry since 1974; prior to that he was a photographic journalist. He has spent most of his career working on IBM VM systems software. In 1983, whilst working for a bank in New York, he installed an early version of VM/SP Release 3, with the first commercially available version of REXX.

In 1985 he assisted in the development of the IBM/SRA self study course on REXX, *Using the System Product Interpreter*. Mark spoke numerous times at SHARE and at local New York user groups before returning to the UK in 1986 and joining IBM UK in 1987.

He accepted his current position in 1990 and also became the IBM representative to the SHARE Europe VM Project. Mark has written several articles for the UK Computer press, and teaches and presents REXX for VM, OS/2, and TSO.

Mark Cathcart, IBM UK Technical Support, PO Box 118, Normandy House, Alencon Link, Basingstoke, Hampshire RG21 1EJ, United Kingdom, Phone: 44 25 65 61 44.

After twenty years experience as an MVS and VM system programmer, **John Cifonelli** is attempting to make the transition to programming on UNIX-based workstations. He believes that cyberspace will soon be a reality.

The Workstation Group will be an active participant in the ANSI committee on REXX standards.

John Cifonelli, Software Manager, The Workstation Group, 6300 N. River Road, Rosemont, IL 60018, Phone: (708) 696-4800, Email: uunet!wrkgrp!jac.

Mike Cowlishaw joined IBM's UK Laboratory at Hursley in 1974, with a B.Sc. in Electronic Engineering from the University of Birmingham. Until 1980, he worked on the design of the hardware and software of display test equipment. Any spare time was spent exploring the human-machine interface, including implementation of the STET Structured Editing Tool (an editor which gives a tree-like structure to programs or documentation), several compilers and assemblers, and the REXX programming language.

In 1980 Mike was assigned to the IBM T.J. Watson Research Center in Yorktown Heights, NY, to work on a text display with real-time formatting. In 1982 he moved to the IBM UK Scientific Centre in Winchester, England, to work on color perception and the modelling of brain mechanisms. In 1985 he was seconded to the Oxford University Press to write an editor (LEXX) for the New Oxford English Dictionary project. This is now a product for VM/CMS in the UK and the USA, and has also been implemented for OS/2 and AIX. From 1986 to 1990 he worked in the IBM UK Laboratories Systems Technology Group on electronic publishing and REXX.

Mike was appointed to the IBM Academy of Technology in 1989, and has received a number of IBM awards, including two Outstanding Technical Achievement awards, and, in 1988, a Corporate Award for Outstanding Technical Innovation for his creation and development of REXX.

Mike was named an IBM Fellow in 1990. His current technical interests (in addition, of course, to REXX) include user interfaces, lightweight computers, and Neural Networks.

Mike Cowlishaw, IBM United Kingdom Laboratories Limited, Hursley Park, Winchester, Hampshire SO21 2JN, United Kingdom, Phone: 44 96 28 44 43 3.

Chip Coy joined IBM in 1983 as a VM programmer in the T.J. Watson Research Center in Yorktown Heights, NY. In 1987 he moved to Endicott, NY, where his work in VM planning led to a position of focal point for VM/SAA System Planning. In 1990 Chip moved to a technical position in the VM and Programmable Workstation (PWS) Synergy area, concentrating on platforms and products to enable VM and programmable workstations to work together to solve today's business needs. Currently Chip is the technical lead for the VM/PWS Synergy area and is responsible for the technical structure of the VM/PWS Synergy products.

Chip Coy, Advisory Programmer, IBM Data Systems Division, Endicott Programming Laboratory, PO Box 6, Endicott, NY 13760, Phone: (607) 752-1567.

Charles Daney is president of Quercus Systems, a software development company that specializes in REXX-related products, and applications involving communications, electronic mail and conferencing, textual databases, and augmentation of knowledge work. He is a developer of Personal REXX for MS-DOS and OS/2, and of the REXXTERM communication package for MS-DOS and OS/2. Formerly he worked for a number of years as developer and administrator of the VMSHARE computer conferencing facility. Charles has written for *PC Magazine* and *Byte*, is a sysop of the IBM PC conference on the WELL, and is now writing a book on REXX for McGraw-Hill. He has a B.Sc. degree in Mathematics from MIT and an M.A. in Political Science from Yale.

Charles Daney, Quercus Systems, 19567 Dorchester Drive, Saratoga, CA 95070, Phone: (408) 257-3697.

Heather Dawson is an Information Developer at the IBM Canada Laboratory in Toronto. She has been responsible for the last two releases of the Procedures Language Interface manual. Having been an RXSQL user before joining the writing team, she enjoyed shedding light on its more complicated concepts. She currently works on developing customer partnerships that will help her and other writers improve IBM's documentation.

Prior to working full-time at IBM, she attended the University of Toronto from which she graduated with a B.Sc. in Statistics.

The IBM Canada Laboratory is known within the IBM Corporation as a young and progressive site. It develops the Structured Query Language/Data System (SQL/DS) database management system, and the SQL/DS Procedures Language Interface (RXSQL).

Heather Dawson, IBM Canada Laboratory, Department 830 Computing Systems, 895 Don Mills Road, Don Mills, Ontario, Canada M3C 1H9, Phone: (416) 448-2512.

Sir John Fairclough managed the IBM laboratory in which Mike Cowlishaw developed REXX. He later served as Scientific Advisor to the British Prime Minister's cabinet.

Carl Forde graduated from the University of Victoria in 1987 with a combined degree in Mathematics and Computer Science. He has been employed by BC Systems since graduation in the VM Database and Development Support Centre. Off-hours, Carl can be found hiking on the trails around Victoria.

As a Crown Corporation of the provincial government, BC Systems provides a variety of computer-related services for government ministries and agencies in British Columbia. BC Systems is a central store of government information for computer users across the province. This is done through shared computer processing, telecommunications, professional consulting, and information access services.

Carl Forde, Technical Analyst, VM Database and Development Support Centre, British Columbia Systems Corporation, 4000 Seymour Place, Victoria, British Columbia, Canada V8X 4S8, Phone: (604) 389-3101, Email: cforde@bcsc02.bitnet.

Gabriel Goldberg is a consultant specializing in VM and IBM-based computing. He worked for VM Systems Group (VMSG) in Vienna, VA, for six years, most recently as Vice President of Technology, responsible for product planning and evolution. He previously managed VMSG product development, documentation, and customer support. His nearly twenty years of VM experience and in-depth user group activities provide strong VM technical and market insights, and strengthened VMSG's product direction with additions such as the V/SEG product family. He writes and edits *V/Update*, the technical VMSG newsletter received every two months by more than 20,000 VM system programmers and users around the world. VMSG develops and markets data center and end-user software for VM installations.

Before joining VMSG, he was senior staff at The MITRE Corporation, where his involvement with VM began in 1972, by coordinating conversion from MVT to Release 1 of VM/370; he has been a VM enthusiast ever since. Prior to MITRE, he worked in IBM's OS System Design Department in Poughkeepsie, NY. Gabe has consulted for a variety of clients, including The World Bank, The University of California, and the Association for Computing Machinery. He obtained a B.Sc. in Mathematics from The Polytechnic Institute of Brooklyn.

Gabe is active in many national and local IBM user groups; he is a founding member and former Director of MVMUA (Metropolitan New York VM Users Association, the oldest and largest local VM user group), a member of the Hillgang (Washington, DC, area VM user group) steering committee, and has held several offices in SHARE, most recently serving as CMS Project Manager. He has given hundreds of presentations to these and other groups, and frequently contributes to trade publications.

Gabe Goldberg, PO Box 3882, McLean, VA 22103, Phone: (703) 378-5895.

Dave Gomberg is a computer consultant in San Francisco. He has been a programmer and analyst for over 30 years, beginning as a FORTRAN programmer for the Navy. Since then, Dave has been deeply interested in PL/I and CMS. Most recently he has concentrated on Personal REXX.

Dave has worked for several research projects, as well as CMS vendors. He has done substantial work for the University of California, in Berkeley and San Francisco. There, he did application tuning and CMS system support and modification. He has also taught CMS courses for vendors.

As an Early Support Customer for VM/SP Release 3, Dave had an early opportunity to sample REXX. He became more familiar with the language and tried using it in unconventional ways (not just as a procedures language). Based on his experiences, he wrote the first non-IBM REXX book, *Modern Programming using REXX*, with Robert O'Hara.

Now, Dave offers consulting services on VM problems and systems analysis from his San Francisco office. His focus is on practical considerations in application delivery, especially with reference to REXX as a tool. He also publishes a restaurant guide for San Francisco's many visitors.

Dave Gomberg, 7 Gateview Court, San Francisco, CA 94116-1941, Phone: (415) 731-7793.

Linda Suskind Green graduated from New York University with a double degree in Computer Science and Mathematics. She joined IBM Federal Systems Division in 1973 doing application programming. She later went on to develop compilers and data reduction programs for government contracts. In 1981, she received her M.Sc. in Computer Science from State University of New York at Binghamton. She was the lead programmer on the Host Displaywriter Data Interchange (HDDI) program. She has held a variety of jobs in the VM Design area specializing in usability. Her current position as the SAA Procedures Language Interface Owner requires her to oversee and direct all IBM activities relating to Procedures Language (REXX).

Linda Suskind Green, IBM Endicott Programming Lab, PO Box 6, Endicott, NY 13760, Phone: (607) 752-1172.

John Hartmann, the author of the CMS Pipelines product, is a systems engineer in the IBM Field Systems Centre in Copenhagen, Denmark.

John's two main hobbies are sewing and writing operating systems. He wrote his first operating system in 1972 for an experimental computer at the Technical University of Denmark. His second operating system ("the toy") was written in 1979-1981; it runs in symbiosis with CMS. In the '80s, John's main interests were concurrent programming and pipelines.

John began working for IBM in Denmark in 1965 while still a student. His IBM career has included a stint at the IBM Canada Toronto Data Centre in 1967 and an assignment at the IBM UK Installation Support Centre in Greenford from 1979 to 1983.

John holds an M.Sc. degree in Computer Science from the Technical University of Denmark. He is a member of the Association of Computing Machinery, and a Knight of VM.

John P. Hartmann, IBM FSC, Nymollevej 85, DK-2800 Lyngby, Denmark, Phone: 45 45 93 45 45.

Rainer Hauser received his diploma in Mathematics and a Ph.D. in Computer Science from the Swiss Federal Institute of Technology (ETH), Zürich in 1977 and 1984, respectively.

He has worked for IBM since 1978, initially as a temporary employee. Since 1984 he has been a Research Staff Member in programming projects in the area of image processing and communications at the IBM Zürich Research Laboratory in Rüschlikon.

Rainer F. Hauser, IBM Research Division, IBM Zürich Research Laboratory, Säumerstrasse 4, CH-8803 Rüschlikon, Switzerland, Phone: 41 17 24 83 43, Email: rfh@zurlvm1.bitnet, or rfh@ibm.com.

Graeme Hewson has 17 years experience with IBM mainframe systems. For most of this time, he has worked with VM. He currently works for VMSolutions of Stanmore, Middlesex, UK, specializing in CP and CMS products. VMSolutions supply system software and consultancy for IBM mainframes. He makes frequent use of CIX, Europe's premier electronic conferencing system.

Graeme Hewson, VM Solutions Ltd., Stanmore Hall, Wood Lane, Middlesex HA7 4ST, United Kingdom, Phone: 44 81 95 48 51 9, Email: ghewson@cix.compulink.co.uk.

Gerhard E. Hoernes, a Senior Programmer at IBM, designed REXX in TSO/E. Before that he was lead designer for the ISPF dialog manager. He has held assignments in RMF design, MVS/ESA and MVS/SP performance, micro programming, database, and logic design.

He has published papers on logic design, micro programming, and data base; he has written several IBM internal books and a McGraw-Hill book on logic design. He is also a contributor to the first edition of the *Handbook of Electronics*, published by McGraw-Hill.

He holds several patents and has been awarded by IBM for patent activity and his outstanding contributions, including the REXX TSO/E design. He has also taught extensively both in and outside of IBM, including in the Computer Science department of Vassar College and the IBM System Research Institute.

Gerry holds a Ph.D. in Computer Science from Syracuse University, which he received while on a residency study program from IBM. He also hold Master's and Bachelor's degrees in Electrical Engineering from Rensselaer Polytechnic Institute.

In his spare time, he operates a travel agency with his wife.

Dr. Gerhard E. Hoernes, Data Systems Division, PO Box 950, Poughkeepsie, NY 12603, Phone: (914) 296-5492.

Gerald R. Hogsett received his B.Sc. in Electrical Engineering from Stanford University, Stanford, CA, in 1962. He was a Project Engineer at the NASA/CalTech Jet Propulsion Laboratory, Pasadena, CA, from 1962 to 1963.

Mr. Hogsett joined IBM in 1963. His work has included involvement with the IBM Electronic Circuit Analysis Program; a joint effort with Lockheed Aircraft Corporation in the development of CADAM; and the IBM Electronic Circuit Analysis Program II.

In 1974, Mr. Hogsett joined the IBM Scientific Center in Palo Alto, and participated in a large database development project. In 1985, he accepted a temporary assignment to the IBM Development Laboratory in Hursley, England, where he developed the GDDM-REXX Program Product.

Mr. Hogsett's emphasis and expertise lie on both sides of application programs (interfaces to systems and interfaces to the user) and in system integration. He has concentrated his efforts in extending the availability of graphics and graphics display support systems.

Gerald R. Hogsett, Member of Technical Staff, IBM Scientific Center, 1530 Page Mill Road, Palo Alto, CA 94304, Phone: (415) 855-4207.

Ken Holt is a Software Developer/Analyst at LEGENT Corporation in Pittsburgh, PA. He has migrated two major VTAM-based products from MVS to VM, and has assisted in the migration of a third one. Ken is currently a member of a "tools" group, developing internal applications. He has given numerous presentations to promote the understanding and exploitation of the GCS component of VM at SHARE, SEAS (now SHARE Europe), and at various local VM user group meetings. He began working on GCS-based applications in February, 1986.

LEGENT Corporation is a leading international supplier of systems software and services for the management and operation of IS enterprises. The company's solutions are designed for IS organizations supporting heterogeneous networks managed by IBM mainframes. LEGENT has been a leader in the use of GCS to provide common application services for VM and MVS environments.

Ken Holt, LEGENT Corporation, Two Allegheny Center, Pittsburgh, PA 15212, Phone: (412) 323-2600.

Pete Hunsberger works as an Advisor for the Systems Technology Department of Bell Canada. His work includes the development of processing strategies for VM and MVS platforms and services within Bell, including work on cooperative processing with Programmable Workstations.

Prior to joining Bell seven years ago, Pete worked for the University of Waterloo as a VM system programmer. Pete is also active in SHARE, where he has served as CMS Project Manager. More recently he has been working with the SHARE VM Technical Steering Committee.

Pete Hunsberger, Bell Canada, F12N, 483 Bay St., Toronto, Ontario, Canada M5G 2E1, Phone: (416) 581-5853.

Anthony Johnson, employed by the Boston University Physics Department, works as part of the SLD experiment at the Stanford Linear Accelerator Center, studying properties of the newly discovered Z particle. He has a Ph.D. in Nuclear Physics from Oxford University, England. He spends much of his time developing software tools for physics analysis, an activity in which REXX has played a large role.

Anthony S. Johnson (Boston University), c/o, Bin 71, Stanford Linear Accelerator Center, PO Box 4349, Stanford, CA 94309.

Ted Johnston started in data processing in 1960 as an IBM Systems Engineer. In the 1960s, while with an insurance company, he wrote a time-sharing monitor for on-line updating of insurance databases. In 1969 he joined the Stanford Linear Accelerator Center (SLAC) as a programmer, and was later promoted to Manager of Systems Programming.

In 1969, SLAC ran HASP (the predecessor to JES2) on a System/360 Model 91. In 1974, SLAC installed two System/370 Model 168 computers and converted to ASP and SVS. In 1981, SLAC installed the first customer 3081 and brought up VM production on it.

Eighteen months later, SLAC removed the 360/91 and the 370/168s and became a VM-only installation. In 1990 SLAC converted to VM/XA SP.

Ted Johnston, Stanford Linear Accelerator, PO Box 4349 (Bin 97), Stanford, CA 94309, Phone: (415) 926-2689.

Jeff Karpinski is a lead systems analyst for Towers Perrin, a multinational consulting firm specializing in actuarial, management and employee benefits services.

He holds a Bachelor's degree in Mathematics from Ursinus College, and a Master's degree from Lehigh University. Prior to joining Towers Perrin, he was a senior systems analyst for Burroughs Corporation and taught for several years at the college level.

Jeff Karpinski, Towers Perrin, 1500 Market Street, Philadelphia, PA 19102, Phone: (215) 246-6003.

Brian L. Marks has worked at IBM's UK Laboratories since 1963, mainly in the field of languages and compilers. He was a major contributor to the language PL/I, and project manager for the PL/I Checkout Compiler. He is currently chairman of IBM's Procedures Language Architecture Review Board.

Dr. Brian L. Marks, IBM United Kingdom Laboratories Limited, Hursley Park, Winchester, Hampshire S021 2JN, United Kingdom, Phone: 44 96 28 41 12 2.

Gary R. McClain, Ph.D. is a Vice President at Techvantage, Inc. in New York City. He has held a variety of training and marketing positions at Martin Marietta Data Systems; Infodata, Inc.; Systems Center, Inc. (formerly VM Software); and Information Builders. Techvantage is an independent market research firm, serving technology companies.

Gary McClain, Techvantage, Inc., Suite 933, 342 Madison Avenue, New York, NY 10017, Phone: (212) 986-9000.

Richard K. McGuire is an Advisory Programmer for the IBM Corporation in Endicott, NY. Mr. McGuire earned a B.Sc. degree from Ohio State University, and joined IBM in 1981, where he has worked in various areas relating to the VM/SP operating system. He is a former chairman of the IBM Procedures Language Architecture Review Board, and currently has the lead design and development responsibility for REXX on all IBM SAA systems. He has been active in the design and development of REXX since 1982. He is co-author, with M.F. Cowlishaw, of two articles on Procedures Language 2/REXX in the Summer and Fall 1989 issues of the *IBM Personal Systems Developer*.

Rick McGuire, REXX Developer, G09/21, IBM Corporation, PO Box 9008, Endicott, NY 13760, Phone: (607) 752-1865.

Simon Nash graduated from Oxford University in 1974 with a B.A. in Mathematics. He has worked at IBM United Kingdom Laboratories since 1974 on a wide variety of software development projects. From 1983 to 1985 he was assigned to IBM Corporation, Raleigh, NC, where he designed and implemented the programming language FAPL (Format and Protocol Language). Since 1988 he has been responsible for the design of object-oriented REXX.

Simon Nash, IBM United Kingdom Laboratories Limited, Sheridan House, Hursley Park, Winchester, Hampshire SO23 8RY, United Kingdom, Phone: 44 96 28 41 12 2.

Laurence Oppenheim has been a VM system programmer for over ten years. He has been a REXX instructor since 1987, having taught his own REXX class for University of California Extension in Berkeley, CA and since 1989 for VM Assist, Inc. in San Francisco, CA. Other classes he has taught include XMENU (a menu generator available from VM Systems Group, Vienna, VA); VM/CMS fundamentals; Pascal; C; and IBM PC assembler.

Laurence Oppenheim, Penguin Computing, Suite 347, 236 West Portal Avenue, San Francisco, CA 94127, Phone: (415) 585-1009.

Willi Ploechl studied Mechanical Engineering and "Moderne Rechentechnik" (precursor of Informatics) at the Technical University of Vienna, Austria; graduated 1960. He joined IBM 1960 and worked in Western Germany, Eastern Germany, USA, and Austria. Main activities: Design and implementation of various compilers and operating systems; working as a System Engineer at customer's sites. His current activity is supervising work on the REXX Compiler proper.

Willi Ploechl, IBM, Vienna Software Development Laboratory, Cobdengasse 2, A-1010, Vienna, Austria, Phone: 43 22 25 14 40 x4477.

Steve Price is a Staff Programmer in the SAA REXX Development group. His responsibilities include testing, developing, and documenting IBM's REXX interpreters for OS/2 and OS/400.

Mr. Price has a B.Sc. degree in Computer and Communication Sciences from the University of Michigan, and a M.Sc. degree in Computer and Information Science from Syracuse University. He joined IBM in Endicott, NY, in 1982, where he first worked in VM/SP System Test. He joined the SAA REXX Development department in 1988.

Steve Price, IBM Corporation, G09/21A-F3, PO Box 6, Endicott, NY 13760, Phone: (607) 752-1866.

Perry Ruiter graduated from the University of Victoria in 1985 with a degree in Computer Science. Since graduation he has been employed as a VM system programmer at BC Systems. Outside of work Perry can be found restoring and riding antique motorcycles.

As a Crown Corporation of the provincial government, BC Systems provides a variety of computer-related services for government ministries and agencies in British Columbia. BC Systems is a central store of government information for computer users across the province. This is done through shared computer processing, telecommunications, professional consulting, and information access services.

Perry Ruiter, Senior Technical Analyst, Operating Systems Support, British Columbia Systems Corporation, 4000 Seymour Place, Victoria, British Columbia, Canada V8X 4S8, Phone: (604) 389-3101, Email: pruiter@bcsc02.bitnet.

Jeffrey Savit is Manager of VM Technical Services at Merrill Lynch in New York, and is responsible for system support of a large CMS-intensive VM/ESA environment. He has also been an independent consultant, with clients in the financial, petrochemical, and software industries.

Mr. Savit is President of the Metropolitan VM Users Association (MVMUA), the world's largest and oldest VM user group. Jeff has presented talks on VM performance, new versions of VM, and VM applications at MVMUA, VM Workshops, and SHARE.

Mr. Savit is author of *VM and CMS: Performance and Fine Tuning*, and was a contributing author of the *VM Applications Handbook*, both published by McGraw-Hill. He has also been published in *SIGPLAN Notices*, a journal of the Association for Computing Machinery. Jeff has an M.Sc. in Computer Science from Cornell University, and a B.Sc. in Computer Science from the Polytechnic Institute of NY.

Jeffrey Savit, Merrill Lynch & Co., Inc., 570 Washington Street, OSSD, 3rd floor, New York, NY 10080-6803, Phone: (212) 807-2084.

Richard Schafer is the Manager of Networking and Systems Support in the Office of Networking and Computer Systems at Rice University. He has been involved with VM for over 7 years, and is the author of a popular CMS electronic mail package written in REXX. Schafer has a B.A. in Mathematical Sciences and a Master's of Applied Mathematical Sciences from Rice University.

Richard Schafer, Rice University, Networking and Computing Systems, PO Box 1892, Houston, TX 77251, Phone: (713) 527-4984.

Philip H. Smith III is Manager of Product Development at VM Systems Group, in Vienna, Virginia. He has developed and enhanced successful CP and CMS products, and is now responsible for managing VMSG's systems software products.

He has worked with VM since 1979, starting at Bell-Northern Research in Ottawa as a student, and continuing at the University of Waterloo in Ontario, Canada, long the home of extensive VM knowledge and enhancements. While at the University, he participated in support and enhancement of their heavily-modified VM running VM/CMS Unlimited's Single-System Image product to link two IBM 4381s and two IBM 4341s. An XEDIT expert, he has also authored and distributed several extensive and popular XEDIT modifications.

Phil is a member of the Hillgang steering committee and contributes regularly to various trade journals. He is a frequent speaker at SHARE and local user groups, a Knight of VM, and an avid participant on VMSHARE, the VM electronic conference, where he signs himself and is known as . . .**phsiii**.

Philip H. Smith III, VM Systems Group, 1604 Spring Hill Road, Vienna, VA 22182, Phone: (703) 506-0500.

Keith Watts is the founder and sole employee of Kilowatt Software. He developed and distributes Portable/REXX for the IBM PC MS-DOS/PC-DOS environment. He cooperated with Software Professionals Inc. of San Mateo, CA, in transforming this product to become T-REXX.

He has worked as a developer and R&D manager of software vendors for IBM systems. He recently aided Ingres in their migration of Open SQL to co-reside with Tandem's NonStop SQL DBMS offering.

In the more distant past, Mr. Watts has worked for major West Coast financial institutions and IBM. He obtained a B.Sc. in Physics at Pennsylvania State University in 1970.

Keith Watts, Kilowatt Software, 1945 Washington Street, #410, San Francisco, CA 94109, Phone: (415) 775-8360.

Marvin Weinstein is a theoretical physicist at the Stanford Linear Accelerator Center (SLAC). His main research interest lies in developing non-perturbative calculational tools for problems in quantum field theory. As a side-line he is also interested in problems in condensed matter physics; e.g., high temperature superconductors and the fractional quantum Hall effect.

Weinstein's involvement with the Amiga began several years ago when SLAC began seeking a good, cost-effective TEX workstation. The Amiga's unique graphics capabilities and multitasking operating system, coupled with its low price, made it a natural candidate for the position. The goal was eventually creating an inexpensive, scientific, almost WYSIWYG, interface to TEX which worked in symbiosis with the SLAC IBM mainframe, as well as with the assorted distributed VAXes. Finding a terrific implementation of TEX for the Amiga proved no problem, but it wasn't until ARexx appeared that the rest of the pieces began coming together. At this time all the original goals for the Amiga project have been met and exceeded. The only remaining problem is that the continual flood of ARexx-capable applications which Weinstein receives present so many opportunities for creating new working tools that the process of getting his Amiga set up just the way he wants it seems to be unending.

Marvin Weinstein, Stanford Linear Accelerator, PO Box 4349 (Bin 81), Stanford, CA 94309, Phone: (415) 926-2214.

Bebo White is a member of the technical staff of the Stanford Linear Accelerator Center (SLAC), a major VM/CMS installation. A REXX Beta-test site, SLAC had the opportunity to develop thousands of lines of REXX programs even before it was an IBM product. Bebo has developed and taught classes on VM/CMS and REXX for various academic and private institutions in the United States and Europe. He has also presented papers and seminars on REXX at varied industry conferences and trade shows including the first REXX Symposium last year at SLAC.

Bebo wrote the chapter on REXX in the *VM Applications Handbook*, McGraw-Hill, 1989. He also wrote three additional books, (*Programming BASIC*, Cushen-White Publications, 1983; *Programming REXX*, Adesse Corporation, 1986; and *Programming Techniques for Software Development*, Van-Nostrand Reinhold, 1989) and numerous articles on programming languages and techniques.

Stanford Linear Accelerator Center, PO Box 4349 (Bin 97), Stanford, CA 94309, Phone: (415) 926-2907, Email: bebo @slacvm.slac.stanford.edu, or bebo @scsw3.slac.stanford.edu.

Appendix—REXX Language Levels

By Michael F. Cowlishaw

The REXX language has gone through many versions and releases since its first specification ("language level 0.0") in March 1979. The fixed points in the series are the two editions of *The REXX Language*, which define language levels 3.50 and 4.00, respectively. IBM implementations that do not implement the full language as defined in one of these two books use language level numbers that are smaller than 3.50 or 4.00, as appropriate.

The language level of any implementation can be found by using the REXX instruction **PARSE VERSION**. This instruction also returns an identifier for the language processor, and its date.

1.00 First IBM internal release (November 1979).

2.00 1980—Added decimal arithmetic, internal subroutines, etc.

2.50 1981—Internal functions, **ARGS** changed to **ARG**, etc.

3.00 1982—**EXPOSE**, improved variables and performance.

3.20 1983—First commercial implementation, in IBM's VM/SP Release 3—minor enhancements to 3.00.

3.40 1984–1988—IBM VM/SP Releases 4, 5, and 5.5—DBCS support and improved performance.

3.45 1988–1989—IBM VM/SP Release 6 and TSO/E Version 2, Release 1—additional strict comparison operators, etc.

3.46   1987–1989—IBM VM/SP Release 6 with SPE, TSO/E Version 2, Release 1 with APAR, VM/SP CMS REXX compiler, first *SAA CPI Procedures Language Reference*—full SAA Level 1 compliance, SAA flagging in the compiler, etc.

3.48   1990—IBM OS/400 Release 1.3—REXX 4.00, except lacks stream input/output.

3.50   1985—*The REXX Language* (first edition)—3.20 with addition of stream input/output and minor enhancements.

4.00   1990—*The REXX Language* (second edition), OS/2 EE Releases 1.2 and 1.3, OS/2 SE Release 1.3, *SAA CPI Procedures Language Level 2 Reference*—3.50 plus enhanced error handling, stream input/output, and numerous small functional enhancements.

Index

Reader's Comment Form

Twelve years after initial development and eight years after first commercial implementation, REXX availability and usage are accelerating. This book presents information on diverse REXX techniques, computing platforms, enhancements, exploitations, and literature. We will appreciate your answers to the following few questions, using a copy of this page or additional sheets, if necessary. Please send them to: J. Ranade Series, Attention: REXX Handbook, POB 338, New York, NY 10163.

To help focus future editions, tell us:

1. Which sections and chapters of the book were most interesting and/or useful? Why?
2. Which sections and chapters of the book were least interesting and/or useful? Why?
3. Are the code examples useful? Should there be more or fewer of them?
4. Is the REXX tutorial (Chapters 3 and 4, *Fundamental Concepts* and *I/O Model*) the right level and length?

How did you use this book?

☐ As an introduction   ☐ For reference

☐ As a student   ☐ As an instructor

☐ Other (please describe) _____

To help make future editions as inclusive as possible, please provide REXX news on:

1. New REXX platforms
2. New products which exploit REXX
3. New REXX enhancements
4. New REXX literature

What is your occupation? _____

How did you hear about *The REXX Handbook*? _____

Where did you buy *The REXX Handbook*? _____

We would appreciate your identifying yourself:

Name _____ Phone/FAX _____/_____

Title _____

Company_____

Address _____